P9-BYG-610

Fundamentals of Counseling

Fundamentals of Counseling
Third Edition

Bruce Shertzer / Shelley C. Stone *Purdue University*

Houghton Mifflin Company   Boston

Dallas   Geneva, Illinois   Hopewell, New Jersey   Palo Alto   London

To C. Gilbert Wrenn, whose words and deeds have exemplified professional counseling

Printed in the U.S.A.

Library of Congress Catalog Card Number: 79-88448

ISBN: 0-395-28580-1

Contents

Preface

The production of a counseling textbook and its revision is a rich, varied, and protracted experience. It entails frustration, pleasure (perhaps of a masochistic nature), grim persistence, dissonance, insight, but above all, a feeling that closure is lacking. In such undertakings, decision after decision has to be made—decisions concerning level, style, length, inclusion, exclusion, sequence, organization, approach, terminology—even punctuation! We hope some of these decisions were made logically, based on experience in counseling and a sense of educational strategy.

The third edition of *Fundamentals of Counseling* incorporates several changes. A new chapter on the counselor's work in special settings and with special clientele subgroups has been added in Part Four. Part Three—Counseling Approaches—has been expanded by the inclusion of two more theories bringing the total presented to eleven. In addition to these major changes, modifications have been made in each chapter in the book. These changes consist of some deletions and additions that update, expand, and clarify the material presented.

Fundamentals of Counseling is designed for use as a textbook in counselor education courses often entitled "Introduction to Counseling," "Techniques of Counseling," "Principles of School Counseling," "Theories of Counseling," "School Counseling Practices," and the like. Such a course is usually taken by students with a major area of concentration in counseling and guidance, by student development trainees, and by clinical and counseling psychology students (as part of either their major or minor areas of concentration). Other school personnel—teachers, administrators, and social workers—are sometimes "found" in these courses, too. The content has been selected with this broad audience in mind. It should be noted that the book emphasizes counseling rather than the broader range of guidance services and student development work, and presupposes some prior preparation in and familiarity with the aforementioned services. We believe there are six objectives common to the type of course in which this book will be used:

1. to develop an awareness of how one's self-structure, skills, and competences interact to influence the formation and development of a professional counselor's role
2. to provide students with a framework that will develop into a perception of what counseling has been, what it is now, and what it may become in the future
3. to introduce students to representative counseling approaches so that counselee and counselor behavior may be better understood
4. to promote an understanding of counseling practices, their strengths and their limitations
5. to provide an orientation to counseling as a profession and to facilitate the individual's development of an identity as a counselor
6. to help students understand the problems, issues, and concerns confronting counseling practitioners

This text does not offer a new theory of counseling or introduce any major innovative ideas or practices. Why then has it been written?

First, many existing textbooks present the author's own counseling theory. Often they present counseling "theories" without treating practices, or they discuss techniques without regard to theory. This work incorporates both theory and practice in one volume and takes up a wider range of topics than is usually found in other books.

Second, the book is flexible in organization and comprehensive in treatment so that it can serve the needs of many counselor education institutions offering individualistically oriented introductory counseling courses.

Third, in the fast-growing field of counseling, a great many new developments have occurred during the past five years. These warrant examination by the beginning counselor. Moreover, knowledge of counselor and counselee behavior has expanded. Our intent has been to consolidate these recent findings meaningfully within the boundaries of existing knowledge.

Fourth, we have attempted to present detailed material of both a factual and interpretive nature, in a style that is easily read and understood and has relevance for students.

We believe that the authors of a counseling textbook should explain and clarify and not urge a particular point of view. For this reason we have attempted to give students basic facts that will help them draw their own conclusions. Our objective is to develop a coherent framework that includes a good deal of detail and encourages investigation of gaps exposed. By means of this perspective, it is hoped, more workable decisions in the practice of counseling can be made.

The nineteen chapters in this book contain an in-depth examination of the major findings of those who have studied and presented counseling theory, practices, and processes. We have tried through this revision to keep the material up to date, but perhaps the desire to do so vastly exceeds the accomplishment.

Before the critics who justly complain of incompleteness we bow our heads; but prepotent over the response of *mea culpa* is the one of "Let them try!" We can be certain of two factors. First, we have been conscientious in attempting to be fair and sympathetic to the various theorists and researchers whose views and findings we have dealt with. Second, the coverage and its extensive bibliography can serve the student as a bridge to the vast primary literature.

A book of this length is never error free despite great effort to make it so. Publicly we acknowledge responsibility for any such error, although privately each blames the other, our typists, and that mysterious, elusive, and concealed individual, the copyeditor.

Naturally, the assistance of many people in this endeavor deserves acknowledgment. We are indebted to the authors (and their publishers) who have permitted us to draw on their work. While footnotes acknowledge permission from Professors Norman Kagan (Michigan State University) and Jane S. O'Hern (Boston University), both have extended the right to use certain experimental materials which they developed. We are grateful for this professional courtesy. A special debt of gratitude is due Professor S. Samuel Shermis of Purdue University's Department of Education for his excellent chapter entitled "Counseling and the Social Sciences." Much is owed to Barbara Krause and Linda Layton, our typists . . . and friends. . . . Appreciation is expressed to those reviewers who read prepublication manuscripts and who offered helpful suggestions that improved this work. They include Joseph Hollis, Ball State University; Allen Ivey, University of Massachusetts, Amherst; Dorothy Johnson, Purdue-Calumet Campus; Douglas Mickelson, University of Wisconsin; Elizabeth Van Dalsem, San Francisco State University; and Stephen G. Weinrach, Villanova University.

Finally, two guilty husbands and fathers acknowledge the support and encouragement of two temporarily (25 years!) abandoned families who give meaning to work and life.

B.E.S.
S.C.S.

Fundamentals of Counseling

Part one
Counseling: past and present status

The six chapters that constitute Part One have a specific purpose, namely, to provide a systematic orientation to the theory and practice of counseling. We believe that this orientation will be helpful for an understanding of what follows. Essentially, it calls for examination of the helping relationship, the historical development of counseling, the characteristics and concerns of counselees, the expectancies and goals of counseling, counselor characteristics, and role and function.

Analysis of the six chapters reveals that our direction is from the general (helping relationship) to the more specific (expectancies and goals). This direction seems logically and psychologically sound.

Because counseling is a helping relationship, it seems fitting that Chapter 1 interpret the helping relationship. Its nature and characteristics are defined and described. Professionals who practice a helping relationship are identified. Similarities and differences between the various helping professions are presented. The chapter returns to counseling per se and terminates with a discussion of definitions of counseling.

The entire development of organized counseling services extends over only seven decades. However, its history encompasses the efforts of hundreds of persons, whose activities subdivide into a dozen occupations. Chapter 2 traces the origin and development of counseling. Emphasis is placed on analysis and interpretation of the events, persons, and forces instrumental in advancing it to its present state. There is no claim that the chapter gives a comprehensive history of counseling, which would be quite beyond the scope of this book. The intent here is to present as clear a treatment as possible, especially of recent developments in the field. These changes are evident in the direction and focus of counseling, its professional organizations and journals, its practitioners, and its critics.

Chapter 3 focuses on the counselee, particularly of school or college age. It examines pertinent views of the developmental characteristics of counselees, some frequently encountered counselee concerns, and selected problems that confront contemporary youth. Such treatment will not, of course, satisfy everyone, and considerable risk attends any generalizing about counselees. Nevertheless, the authors have found the content valuable for encouraging discussion and exploration into why individuals seek counseling.

Chapter 4 identifies the expectancies for counseling held by counselees, teachers, parents, administrators, and others. Counseling goals are stated. Finally, counseling expectancies and goals are contrasted.

Chapter 5 is based on an extensive literature on the subject of the characteristics of counselors. There are many reasons why this scholarly literature exists and why it continues to expand. Personal experience and contact with many counselors indicate that most of them engage in self-examination to try to ascertain why they entered or continued in the field and why they were successful with one person or in one situation but not with others in different situations. But identifying the characteristics of counselors and counselees is difficult, and understanding the effects and interaction of personal and other factors in the counseling process is an extremely complex endeavor. More, of course, is known than was the case a decade ago. Much remains to be done.

In Chapter 6 attention is given to the meanings of role, function, and role conflict. Role theory and the role of the counselor are treated. Some of the forces and factors that cause role variability are identified and discussed. Finally, descriptions of current counselor role behavior are presented.

1   The helping relationship

The words *helping relationship* are used often by counselors, social workers, psychotherapists, and physicians to characterize the services they provide. No doubt the words are meaningful to their users, but are they to others? The phrase *a helping relationship* is deceptively straightforward; most people understand that *helping* means assisting or aiding and *relationship* means some personal connecting bond or reference.

Helping relationship defined

Presumably, when counselors, social workers, and others use the term *helping relationship*, they mean the endeavor, by interaction with others, to contribute in a facilitating, positive way to their improvement. Helping professionals engage in activities designed to enable others to understand, to modify, or to enrich their behavior so that positive change takes place. They are interested in the behavior of people—living, feeling, knowing people—and in their attitudes, motives, ideas, responses, and needs.

Rogers has defined the helping relationship thus:

> My interest in psychotherapy has brought about in me an interest in every kind of helping relationship. By this term I mean a relationship in which at least one of the parties has the intent of promoting the growth, development, maturity, improved functioning, improved coping with life of the other. The other, in this sense, may be one individual or a group. To put it in another way, a helping relationship might be defined as one in which one of the participants intends that there should come about, in one or both parties, more appreciation of, more expression of, more functional use of the latent inner resources of the individual.[1]

[1] Carl R. Rogers, *On Becoming a Person* (Boston: Houghton Mifflin Company, 1961), pp. 39–40, and "The Characteristic of a Helping Relationship," *Personnel and Guidance Journal*, 37 (1958), 6–16. Copyright 1958 American Personnel and Guidance Association. Reprinted with permission.

Benjamin defined *helping* as enabling acts, so that those who are helped recognize, feel, know, decide, and choose whether to change. In providing a helping relationship, professionals give of their time, their capacity to understand and listen, their skill, knowledge, and interest. In short, those who conduct helping relationships draw on themselves in ways that facilitate and enable others to live more harmoniously and insightfully.[2]

These and other definitions of a helping relationship are sufficiently broad to include many nurturing and uplifting contacts among people. Presumably, bank clerks and politicians do not use the term to describe their work because their occupations, though providing services of an external nature, do not have the primary purpose of facilitating the individual's personal development. However, relationships between teacher and pupil, husband and wife, mother and child, counselor and counselee, psychotherapist and client would normally be called helping relationships.

All too often, *helping relationship* is thought to mean that one person helps one other. In most helping situations this is the case, but the term is also applied to individual-group interactions. Furthermore, some supervisory and administrative relationships are conducted to facilitate maximum growth through processes that free individual potentialities.

Need for the helping relationship

Those engaged in helping relationships seem to be markedly out of step with the beat of today's drums. A dozen different revolutions are taking place in industry, education, medicine, and government. They are profoundly affecting every field of human activity: transportation, communication, merchandising, marketing, health, weather control, the substance and structure of work and home life. We live in a

[2] Alfred Benjamin, *The Helping Interview*, 2nd ed. (Boston: Houghton Mifflin Company, 1974), p. xi–xii.

time known for its application of scientific knowledge and advanced technology. It is a time aptly characterized decades ago by W. B. Yeats: "The visible world is no longer a reality and the unseen world is no longer a dream."

A computerized age

Electronic data storage and retrieval are commonplace in the 1980s. The focus is on use of automated equipment in communication, industry, defense, government, and education and has led some to label the era "the computerized age." Certainly the constant and conscious attention to "hardware," as well as the investment of resources devoted to it, *seems* to push to the fringes those whose efforts are directed toward establishing and maintaining helping relationships. In everyday life, attention is paid to everything but people—capital requirements, technology, material resources, managerial resources, political pressures, cost controls, and markets.

The paradox

Despite technological progress, the individual's essential and perennial problems remain: Who am I? How did I become the way I am? Am I normal? What is good? What is reality? Of what value is life? How can I be more productive . . . more sensitive . . . more sensible . . . more alive? A person's dreams, drives, concerns, and very humanness can be observed in a bewildering variety of behavioral situations.

The methods used for aiding people to live together amicably on an alarmingly shrinking planet are still rudimentary. This combination of factors confronts society with a fantastic and frightening paradox: humans are able to control and improve everything except the one element that may spell their doom—human conflict. Talent and unprecedented amounts of money are being employed to enable people to live better and longer, to enjoy leisure, and to take full advantage of brilliant technological breakthroughs. But whether people survive and improve depends on the resolution of differences within and among the members of humanity.

Contemporary life

During the past few years, more and more people have become increasingly concerned about improving the quality of life in American society. Many aver that those who call for change have in mind a return to some simplistic, bygone notion of an individual's relationship to people and to the environment. Others hope that behind the catchwords lies a movement toward establishing meaningful, nonexploitative relationships among people and with the environment. Ever larger numbers of people appear willing to share the burdens of coping with an advanced industrial society and problems of living peacefully and fully within it. The challenge to do so is essentially constructive, particularly if a better society is to emerge.

Perhaps because of society's increasing focus on nonhuman concerns, loneliness seems to be the fate of many and even the aspiration of depressingly large numbers of Americans. More and more people have claimed to attain happiness from the solitude of private, personal burrows. One wonders whether Americans are becoming a people who are simply afraid of others or whether they are finding such joy in self-love that it can only be spoiled by contact with other humans.

Some among contemporary youth are reluctant to marry. When they do, they are reluctant to produce children, and all too often quick to divorce. When men and women live together, in wedlock or out, the arrangement often is formalized as a "relationship." Sometimes this is defined in a legal contract, as though it were a deal for an exchange of services between parties who distrust each other. The "relationships" or contracts commonly are designed to provide escape clauses for the parties to be invoked when long-term human involvement inevitably develops its interpersonal friction and complications. A distaste for the inherent messiness in extended human relationships is not new, of course. It has always been a characteristic of one of the stock comic figures of American society, the crotchety bachelor who avoids an entangling alliance because he cannot stand babies' diapers and women's stockings drying over his bathtub. What made the bachelor comic was his willful refusal to undertake life's interesting complications, the sterility of life he chose deliberately because he was too timid to try the water. Nowadays, however, the bachelor is no longer the source of comic literature and film, but a figure of admiration whose example is celebrated as a happy adjustment to the exigencies of a mean-spirited society. In a parallel fashion, some within the women's movement have sought to lionize the female bachelor. Newspapers, books, and magazines recite rosy tales of women, who, having successfully skirted the perils of husbands and nest building, have found contented anchorage in private harbors alone with their television sets, their books, their wines, their pictures, their telephones, and their self-fulfillment.

Nowadays Americans come to large cities to be alone, and the drift is toward loneliness. To seek out loneliness and isolation is a long step from the day when settlers traveled heavy miles a few times a year to escape the loneliness and boredom of prairie solitude in quilting bees, barn raisings, and harvest feasts. The term *anomie*, "a state of being without organization or system in which individuals lose contact with their community," has often been applied to contemporary social reality. During periods of rapid social change, disorganization occurs with a lack of social norms to anchor and direct behavior. Contemporary social scientists and philosophers often cite anomie as a contributing factor that leads people to be preoccupied with human relationships because they feel lonely and isolated in a normless, confusing mass society. An alternative to preoccupation with human relations is withdrawal from human contact such as has been described. For those who work toward providing helping relationships, neither alternative is attractive, productive, psychologically healthy, or beneficial to society. As idealistic, or, as some would say, as presumptive as their goals may be, those providing professional helping relationships address their energies to assisting others to cope with and resolve the social and human paradoxes of the times.

Coping with life's situations

Life may be reduced, from a gross biological point of view, to a simple continuum: birth, maturity, reproduction, death. But even the biologist acknowledges that many other significant events occur along the way. Individuals embroider upon the fundamental biological pattern. In fulfilling one's destiny, every individual experiences these four biological stages. They are often seen as critical periods and approached with varying degrees of apprehension. Some

people, acting in response to their culture, habitually treat them in a matter-of-fact manner. Others exhibit much anxiety and uncertainty because their very fate hangs in the balance. Consequently, individuals are not disposed to leave the outcome supinely to chance. They seek assistance in coping with these crises and the feelings and emotions associated with them.

Significant multiple forces, both external and internal, operate to inhibit as well as facilitate one's definition and perception of one's world and oneself. Because individuals often feel distressed, ineffective, bewildered, anxious, disturbed, or uninformed about themselves and their world, they turn to others for aid in simplifying reality so that they can effectively cope with it. They seek help in understanding their and others' behavior, their relationships with others, their decisions, their choices, their situations, their goals—their very beings. They seek help in preventing or remedying stressful situations involving the unpredictability and inconsistency of existence. In the past, humans feared realistically the catastrophes of nature, such as plague, drought, famine. Today persons fear, perhaps equally realistically, enervation through mechanical equipment. Many have speculated that the complexities and perplexities of the modern world nurture feelings of gnawing uncertainty and powerlessness. A by-product of these feelings is alienation and disaffection. In previous ages, setback, privation, or disease were more readily attributed to divine punishment. With this type of deified rationale it seemed reasonably clear when the individual was to act and when to submit. But in contemporary times few simplistic or clear answers are available.

When things went wrong in American society in the past, political and moral reformers offered solutions. Today, confidence in the old approaches is lacking, and people are searching for help that is more personal and more individual.

The objects of people's apprehensions have changed, but the basic theme remains the same. Adversity and its attendant fear and anxiety have to be managed and mastered. Individuals therefore look for help to overcome unfavorable situations, to establish unity in life, and to achieve integration of self. They do so because they are capable of learning how to increase their chances for satisfaction and survival.

When individuals need help, they turn to other people. Even in those contexts where the nature of the help provided is direct and physical (for example, the administration of medication), the relationship between two people adds much to the experience.

Finally, it should be noted that not all people regard providing help to others as a constructive, positive function. They view the helping relationship with alarm, contending that it weakens character and is a sign of overindulgence and protectiveness. In this view, the individual who struggles unaided with the inexorable imperatives of life is better equipped for the stresses and strains of survival.

To be aware of the importance of personal relationships and to make society less impersonal are the helping person's responsibility, opportunity, and challenge.

Characteristics of the helping relationship

The helping relationship is complex and therefore difficult to reduce to its component parts without destroying its meaning. Written descriptions must fractionate its internal, logically consistent pattern. With this limitation noted, ten characteristics summarizing the nature of the helping relationship will be treated briefly. These elements will, it is hoped, reveal not only that which is essential or typical in the relationship but that which distinguishes it from other relationships. Much research exists to support these descriptive statements. Because the remaining chapters describe and deal with it, we have chosen not to cite the large number of references from which the characteristics are derived. It should be noted that these descriptions present a general overview of the helping relationship rather than specific qualities established and maintained by a particular professional helping person, such as a school counselor or a psychiatrist. Whitehead's advice should be remembered.

Should we not distrust that jaunty assurance with which every age prides itself that it at last has hit upon the ultimate concepts in which all that happens can be formulated? The aim of science is to seek the simplest explanations of complex facts. We are apt to fall into the error of thinking that the facts are simple because simplicity is the goal of our quest. The guiding motto in the life of every natural philosopher should be "seek simplicity and distrust it."[3]

[3] Alfred North Whitehead, *The Concept of Nature* (London: Cambridge University Press, 1930), p. 163.

1. *The helping relationship is meaningful.* It is valued by the participants, and it is meaningful because it is personal and intimate, because it is relevant, because it is both anxiety evoking and anxiety reducing, and because it involves mutual self-commitment.

2. *Affect is evident in a helping relationship.* Affect is present because those in the relationship are self-revealing, self-absorbed, and sensitive to each other. Disclosure of frequently unique and always private perceptions, information, or attitudes produces tension and ambiguity. Although both cognitive and affective factors are operative, the emphasis tends to be on the affective.

3. *Integrity of person is present in the helping relationship.* The participants intend to be intellectually and emotionally honest with each other. Respect is accorded each individual because each is a person of worth. There is a restorative quality to the relationship that excludes sham, pretension, and deceit. The participants relate to each other as authentic, reliable individuals.

4. *The helping relationship takes place by the mutual consent of the individuals involved.* Consent is given either explicitly or implicitly because of choice, tradition, deference, or need. Even in child-parent or teacher-pupil relationships, agreement and/or acquiescence by the participants is needed if the relationship is to be helpful. Whereas individuals can be coerced into certain relationships, the absence of pressure is the hallmark of a helping relationship. The point seems abundantly clear: one cannot be compelled to be helpful or to receive help because the very use of force precludes helpfulness. Duress tears at the fabric of understanding and creates mistrust rather than bringing about improvement.

5. *The relationship takes place because the individual to be helped needs information, instruction, advice, assistance, understanding, and/or treatment from the other.* Persons who seek help do so because they lack knowledge or competence, feel distressed, inept, anxious, or ineffective. Persons who extend help do so because of greater maturity, the possession of special knowledge or competence, and/or the trust others place in them. The helper exhibits enough personal power, charm, authority, skill, energy, or perceptiveness to induce and sustain trust so that the individuals to be helped believe that they will be prepared, that they will endure, or that somehow they will be better than they were before. The confidence reposed in the helper is a crucial characteristic of the relationship. Although helping per-

sons often are viewed as mind readers who have some peculiar capacity for knowing what is going on, in reality they have no completely reliable device for penetrating the thoughts of others. But their experience and training enable them to make more accurate inferences than those who are untutored, and their theories of human behavior permit them to observe more accurately, to infer more precisely, and to organize better the meaning of various kinds of behavior.

6. *The helping relationship is conducted through communication and interaction.* Each participant is affected by the other's verbal and nonverbal communication. The helper and the person helped observe and involve each other's interest and attention. Each talks, reacts, responds to the other verbally as well as nonverbally, and both kinds of behavior have current and residual import. Nonverbal behavior—facial expressions, gestures, body motions—may relate directly to verbal content or to affective experience.

Both parties convey, exchange, transfer, or impart knowledge, information, and/or feelings. Axiomatically, the more lucid and articulate the communication between them, the more meaningful the relationship. The communication and interaction will be both cognitive and affective and will contain both positive and negative experiences—that is, the individual to be helped not only develops new behaviors but may eliminate competing or discordant responses.

7. *Structure is evident in the helping relationship.* The working arrangement for conducting the relationship begins when the helper and the person to be helped come together. Invariably, the latter initially conceives the former as an authority or expert who is to take the lead, while his or her own role is usually preconceived as that of an assistant. Both participants introduce their total life experiences into the relationship. Their attitudes stem from these experiences and determine how they relate to each other. The helper is expected to and often does give explanation or definition (sometimes tentatively and ambiguously) as to what may happen in the relationship, and either or both are instrumental in establishing expected outcomes. The clues and cues each receives from the other determine ways of working together. Although varying amounts of freedom are given to the persons who are to be helped, they must have an opportunity to respond and be expansive. Structure varies, depending on the type of helping relationship, but its essential features—patterns of stimuli and response—are always present. Structure enables the relationship to even-

tuate in growth and productivity. In reality, responsibility for the structure is reciprocal. Both the helper and the person to be helped have needs—to achieve, to be recognized, to be adequate—that determine structure and set in motion responses that the helping person must be prepared to meet if he or she is to build a helping relationship.

8. *Collaborative effort marks the helping relationship.* The participants work together toward an acceptable goal. They search for contributions and resources useful in attaining the goal. The one to be helped feels free to reject skills, suggestions, or contributions that seem inappropriate or to accept without resistance those that are appropriate. The helper puts his or her repertoire of skills and information at the disposal of the other while simultaneously working toward freeing and supporting the individual's selective powers of initiative. The helper accords dignity to the person to be helped whether the latter accepts or rejects the help. This collaborative effort intensifies the relationship and validates its effectiveness. The helping person's task is to function in such a manner that the other can achieve the emotional strength and security to express his or her viewpoint, problem, or situation.

9. *The helping person is approachable and secure as a person.* Helpers are accessible in the sense that others feel free to draw close to them. They are accepting of others, their ideas, actions, suggestions. They are free from undue fear, doubt, anxiety. They exhibit steadiness and stability in the relationship.

10. *Change is the object of the helping relationship.* The participants learn from each other, and the experience results in change. The individual to be helped is different from what he or she was before the relationship. The helpee no longer suffers as much, is not as disabled, becomes more self-aware, achieves more satisfying ways of behaving, becomes more of a person. Internal and external change occurs in attitudes, actions, and perceptions of self, others, and the world.

Examination of these ten characteristics reveals that they are to some degree interrelated. For example, the first one (meaningfulness) is certainly either a function or a product of affect (the second one).

Among the searching questions used by Rogers to identify qualities of those who extend helping relationships were the following:

Can I *be* in some way that will be perceived by the other person as trustworthy, as dependable or consistent in some deep sense?

Can I be expressive enough as a person that what I am will be communicated unambiguously?

Can I let myself experience positive attitudes toward this other person—attitudes of warmth, caring, liking, interest, respect?

Can I be strong enough as a person to be separate from the other?[4]

The helping professions

Rogers has noted that the helping person is approachable and secure as a person. Rogers' questions give further insight into the kind of person who can conduct helping relationships. The qualities possessed by counselors will be dealt with at some length in Chapter 5. Treatment here is given to the professions that exist to create and conduct helping relationships. McCully, citing the absence of an authoritative definition of the term *helping professions*, had this to say:

A helping profession is defined as one which, based upon its specialized knowledge, applies an intellectual technique to the existential affairs of others toward the end of enabling them to cope more effectively with the dilemma and paradoxes that characterize the human condition.[5]

McCully further asserted that the definition did not limit the helping professions to those that practice psychotherapy, that existential problems are those that imply the need for choice or decision, that valuing is central in the relationship, and finally, that under this definition counseling psychology and social work would be included as well as two aspiring professions: school psychology and school counseling and, in certain settings, clinical psychology and psychiatry. McCully did not specify which settings ruled out clinical psychology and psychiatry as helping professions.

He did identify two characteristics that distinguish helping from other professions:

The first is that in the application of his intellectual technique to the existential affairs of others, the practitioner cannot do so completely as a scientist. [There are no sure external guides to the resolution of existential problems.]

The second inference is that in the case of the helping professions the obligation to benefit and not to injure is a much heavier obligation than it is in other professions.[6]

The following view of the helping professions is presented to show (1) the range of professionals engaged in them and (2) the commonalities and differences among them.

Social work

Social work has frequently been called the "conscience of the community." This description seems to suggest the humanistic philosophical foundation of social work and the community's control over its practice. Improvement of the basic organization of society is a commonly stated purpose of social work. The United Nations characterizes social work as being an "organized activity that aims at helping to achieve a mutual adjustment of individuals and their social environment."[7] Social work has been defined by the Model Statute Social Workers' Licensing Act as "helping individuals, groups, or communities enhance or restore their capacity for social functioning and creating societal conditions favorable to this goal."[8] Initially, correctional work and poverty (administration of poor relief funds) were the major focus of social work. But it now covers a wide spectrum of social phenomena. More specifically, Kadushin points out that psychiatric social work agencies are concerned with the social antecedents and consequences of emotional disabilities; medical social workers consider the social ante-

[4] Rogers, *On Becoming a Person*, condensed from pp. 50–55.

[5] C. Harold McCully, "Conceptions of Man and the Helping Professions," in *Challenge for Change in Counselor Education*, comp. Lyle L. Miller (Minneapolis: Burgess Publishing Company, 1969), p. 132.

[6] Ibid.

[7] United Nations, Department of Economic and Social Affairs, *Report on the World Social Situation* (New York: United Nations, 1963), p. 185.

[8] National Association of Social Workers, "Model Statute Social Workers' Licensing Act," NASW *News*, 1967, p. 12.

cedents and consequences of physical illness; family- and child-welfare agencies focus on the social aspects of marital disruption and parent-child relationship difficulties; the correctional social worker deals with the social aspects of a disordered relationship with legal institutions of society; the income maintenance agencies are concerned with the social aspects of a disordered relationship with the economic institutions of society.[9]

SOCIAL WORK APPROACHES While three basic techniques (casework, group work, and community- or social-welfare organization) are usually cited as social work approaches, casework represents the core of the professional helping relationship. Casework objectives include remediation of personality defects and maintaining and improving social and personal functioning. Kadushin states that "the general purpose of most social work interviews can be described as informational (to make a social study), diagnostic (to arrive at an appraisal), and therapeutic (to effect change)."[10]

Caseworkers may arrange financial assistance, facilitate family or institutional care, or plan for health services. Through counseling they seek to modify feelings, attitudes, and behavior detrimental to individual and family development.

Group work, designed to help people benefit from group activities and achieve common goals by working with others, is often employed in youth-serving agencies, settlements, and correctional institutions. Community- or social-welfare organization is used in planning, organizing, and managing health, welfare, and recreational activities. Organization workers often coordinate community social services and help with fund raising.

SETTING In the early 1900s social work was practiced chiefly in correctional institutions and welfare agencies. Since that time there has been a proliferation of practice settings into the medical, school, public assistance, child adoption, legal aid, and other facilities. Its clientele is no longer limited to the economically deprived. Family-service and child-welfare workers are often employed by govern-

ment and voluntary agencies; school social workers or visiting teachers by school systems; medical social workers by hospitals, health agencies, and public welfare agencies; psychiatric social workers by mental hospitals and community mental health clinics; and rehabilitation social workers by hospitals and governmental agencies.

Psychiatric social workers may be differentiated from other social workers because they deal primarily with emotionally disturbed persons and their families. Their work in mental health clinics and hospitals includes diagnosing psychological, cultural, social, and economic factors that influence the patient's history, health, and general outlook. By counseling, they also help patients to deal with emotional and environmental problems. They assist the members of the patient's family in understanding emotional illness and in determining how they can help. Some psychiatric social workers specialize in children's treatment.

NUMBERS AND NEED The *Occupational Outlook Handbook* reports that about 330,000 social workers were employed in 1976.[11] Some 66 percent were in state, county, and city governmental agencies; about 1 percent in federal governmental agencies; and the remainder in voluntary or private agencies. Many hold positions in mental health establishments.

Traditionally, women have predominated in the field of social work, but there has been a consistent increase of men. During the 1980s many new social workers will be needed annually to meet expansion and replacement demands. The supply from graduate schools of social work is not expected to keep pace with the demand through the mid-1980s.

PREPARATION AND PROFESSIONAL ORGANIZATIONS Some eighty-six graduate schools of social work, accredited by the Council of Social Work Education, offered training in 1976. Full professional status requires two years of graduate study. Estimates are that only a fifth of current social workers meet this graduate education criterion. Those who have completed accredited two-year graduate programs of social work are eligible for membership in the National Association of Social Workers.

[9] Alfred Kadushin, *The Social Work Interview* (New York: Columbia University Press, 1972), p. 12.
[10] Kadushin, p. 15.
[11] Department of Labor, *Occupational Outlook Handbook* (Washington: Superintendent of Documents, 1978–1979), p. 564.

Psychiatry

Psychiatry (*psyche*, "the mind," plus *iatreia*, "healing") is a branch of medicine concerned with the study and treatment of disorders of the mind. A *psychiatrist* is a physician who seeks to prevent, diagnose, and treat mental illness and emotional disorders. Historically, psychiatry dealt with the medical care of the mentally ill, but as its science and art progressed, much of its treatment became nonmedical, for many patients were not ill (in the strict sense of the word), either somatically or mentally. Consequently, the practice of psychiatry is often indistinguishable from other helping specialties.

A *psychoanalyst* is also a physician and a psychiatrist—there are some exceptions—who treats milder forms of emotional disorders (the term *neuroses* is no longer used in psychiatric classification systems) primarily through the use of an approach developed by Sigmund Freud with modifications by others. Psychoanalysis is based on concepts of unconscious motivation, conflict, and symbolism. Its boundaries are not sharply defined, but traditionally, it has been asserted that the nature of psychoanalytical influence differed qualitatively and quantitatively from that of psychotherapy. However, Strupp's analysis of a case history reported by a psychoanalyst led him to conclude that this thesis was untenable. He suggested that psychoanalysis was "education for optimal personal freedom in the context of social living."[12]

PSYCHIATRIC APPROACHES   Treatments used by psychiatrists include chemotherapy (administration of antidepressants and sedatives); shock therapy (inducing shock, with or without convulsions, in a patient by means of insulin or of electric current through the brain); individual psychotherapy (including hypnosis, suggestion, supportive therapy, re-education, desensitization, and other forms of consultation); group psychotherapy, family therapy, and psychoanalysis.

SETTING   A psychiatrist may concentrate practice on child, adult, or community psychiatry; mental deficiency; alco-

holism; geriatrics; military, legal, or industrial psychiatry. As of May 1979, the American Psychiatric Association reported that some 27,000 psychiatrists were in practice in mainland United States. Of these, 21,000 were members of the American Psychiatric Association. Some 54 percent were in private practice, but only 40 percent were engaged full time in private practice. About 38 percent served in outpatient clinics, 35 percent in mental hospitals, 21 percent in institutions of higher education, 20 percent in general hospitals, 11 percent in government administrative agencies, 7 percent in retardation centers, and others (3 percent) in schools, foundations, and nonhealth settings. Some 40 percent were reported to be in general psychiatry, 25 percent in adult psychiatry, 9 percent in psychoanalysis, and 9 percent in child psychiatry. Although the private office remains the predominant work setting for psychiatrists, Knesper reports that recently trained graduates were entering public work in increasing numbers.[13]

NUMBERS AND NEED   Knesper asserts that a considerable shortage of psychiatrists exists and that they are maldistributed geographically. The shortage is particularly acute in state mental hospitals where thirty-two states averaged but two psychiatrists or less per hundred state hospital inpatients. Psychiatry, according to Knesper, has a high proportion of foreign medical graduates compared to other medical specialties. Some 88 percent of psychiatrists are men; their median age is 43 (women, 46). Approximately 48 percent of them have been certified by the American Board of Psychiatry and Neurology.[14]

PREPARATION AND PROFESSIONAL ORGANIZATIONS   Psychiatric practice requires lengthy training. Four years, after college, are spent in medical school followed by one year of hospital internship and three years of residency in an approved hospital or agency concerned with the diagnosis and treatment of mental and emotional disorders. Two additional years of experience are required before examination for certification by the American Board of Psychiatry and Neurology. The American Psychiatric Association includes

[12] Hans H. Strupp, "Psychoanalysis, 'Focal Psychotherapy,' and the Nature of the Therapeutic Influence," *Archives of Psychiatry*, 32 (January 1975), 127–135.

[13] David J. Knesper, "Psychiatric Manpower for State Mental Hospitals," *Archives of General Psychiatry*, 35 (January 1978), 19–24.
[14] Henry Mason, "Manpower Needs by Specialty," *Journal of The American Medical Association*, 219 (1972), 1621–1626.

two major membership types—associate and general. Associate members are physicians who have had one year or more of full-time training or experience in psychiatry. A general member is a physician who has been an associate member for at least one year or has had three years' experience in psychiatry.

Psychology

The helping relationship typifies the major activity of clinical, counseling, and school psychologists.

Clinical psychologists (about 38,000 nationally) employ psychological knowledge and practice to help individuals cope with behavioral disorders and secure better adjustment and self-expression. Like their counterparts in psychiatry, clinical psychologists perform diagnoses, treatment, and prevention of emotional problems, but they cannot prescribe chemotherapy, shock therapy, or other medical methods. Historically, the classification and treatment of mental illness were responsibilities of psychiatrists. The need for psychologists arose when it was found that intelligence tests might be helpful in estimating what could be accomplished in psychiatric treatment. With the advent of personality testing, more and more reliance was placed on clinical psychologists for assistance in personality diagnosis. Major functions of the clinical psychologist have evolved from evaluation of behavioral problems to performing psychotherapy, conducting psychological consultation, and carrying on research in treatment procedures and other behavioral concerns.

Shakow, reviewing the history of clinical psychology, suggested that "psychologists work from the normal end of the distribution toward the middle and psychiatrists work from the pathological end toward the middle. There is bound to be a very considerable area of overlap where definition *is* not, and *cannot* be, clear."[15]

Counseling psychologists (about 7,500 nationally) are among the more recent psychological specialists. Counseling psychologists are equipped to deal with personal problems not classified as mental illness though they may be sequels or corollaries of either mental or physical illness.

The boundary between clinical and counseling psychology is not precise and has led Kagan to construct this humorous incident about the beginning of counseling psychology:

I see one counselor saying to the other, "you know your professional parentage?" "Nope." "Me neither, let's write some bylaws and apply for divisional status in APA. We'll call ourselves counseling psychologists; whenever we're with counselors we'll talk psychology; whenever we're with psychologists we'll talk counseling. If ever we're with a group of counselors and psychologists we'll talk about the weather."[16]

Super suggests that the difference between clinical and counseling psychology is that "clinical psychologists tend to look for what is wrong and how to treat it, while counseling psychologists tend to look for what is right and how to help use it. Oversimplification? Of course, but one that magnifies and clarifies without distorting or obscuring the truth."[17] Counseling psychologists usually concentrate on educational-vocational problems and transient situational personal problems and neuroses. Their training internship is spent in settings other than mental hospitals.

School psychologists (about 4,000 nationally) study school situations to improve learning conditions. In the past, they devoted much time to intellectual evaluation, but their role and function are being redefined. The modern-day school psychologist may conduct individual and group psychotherapy with pupils and consult with teachers, parents, counselors, and administrators.

PSYCHOLOGICAL APPROACHES Considerable difference exists in theoretical approaches to the helping relationship among psychotherapists. Approaches range from environmental manipulation, supportive therapy, insight therapy, re-education, persuasion, and attention to intellectual cognitive processes to providing a warm, permissive relationship with a focus on the affective, emotional processes. Commonalities lie in the establishment of a personal relationship between the participants. Some time ago, Snyder and

[15] David Shakow, "Clinical Psychology Seen Some 50 Years Later," *American Psychologist*, 33 (February 1978), 156.

[16] Norman Kagan, "Presidential Address, Division 17," *The Counseling Psychologist*, 7, No. 2 (1977), 4.
[17] Donald E. Super, "The Identity Crises of Counseling Psychologists," *The Counseling Psychologist*, 7, No. 2 (1977), 14.

Snyder cited five differences in approaches to psychotherapy that still seem appropriate today.

> . . . (1) the degree of ambiguity or consistency of therapeutic role, (2) the amount of therapist warmth or coolness, (3) the emphasis upon recall of the past versus dealing with present problems, (4) the degree of activity or passivity of the therapist, and (5) the emphasis on client affect versus cognition.[18]

SETTING   Clinical and counseling psychologists work in mental and general hospitals, mental health clinics, family-service and marriage clinics, Veterans' Administration and rehabilitation centers, centers for the aged, courts and prisons, and college and university student counseling centers and psychological clinics. Some psychologists serve both elementary and secondary schools.

NUMBERS AND NEED   Estimates are that in 1978 there were some 90,000 psychologists in this country. There were approximately three male psychologists for every two female psychologists. During the 1960s there were more vacancies for psychologists than qualified applicants to fill them. Shortages were severe in state mental hospitals, federal government agencies, and educational institutions (some 56 percent of psychologists are employed in educational institutions). But the 1970s closed this gap and it was reported that unemployment among psychologists during 1971–1972 was 1.5 percent (experimental psychologists experienced greatest difficulty in finding academic positions). While the 1978–1979 *Occupational Outlook Handbook* reports employment to be "generally favorable through the mid–1980s," many involved in the preparation of psychologists believe the annual increase in numbers means that the sup ply will exceed the demand, especially for those trained at less than the doctoral level.

PREPARATION AND PROFESSIONAL ORGANIZATIONS   A doctorate is needed for most positions in clinical, counseling, and school psychology. In all instances, approved preparation includes one year of internship or supervised experience in a setting appropriate to the population the individual will ul-

timately serve. The American Psychological Association (APA) has three types of membership and contains thirty divisions that recognize the specialized interests of its members. Divisional membership frequently requires special qualifications.

The APA was founded in 1892 and incorporated in 1925. By 1978, the APA had grown to over 44,000 members. Its purpose is to advance psychology as a science, a profession, and a way of promoting human welfare. It works toward this goal by holding annual meetings, publishing many psychological journals, and working toward improved training and service. In addition to its three types of membership, the APA also examines and approves members for diplomate status in those specialties covered by boards of examiners in professional psychology and in psychological hypnosis.

Counseling

This book is about counseling; therefore, the treatment here of functions, approaches, and setting will be brief. The title *counselor* is used by many individuals to describe what they do. This rather indiscriminate use of the title has been detrimental to attempts at specifying clearly defined functions for those on whom the title has been conferred (indeed, sometimes self-conferred). The lack of definition by function stems from the fact that counseling (in its modern sense) is relatively new, and confusion and uncertainty are inevitable in any emerging profession. Professional maturation will undoubtedly reduce excessive variation and bring consolidation in function.

Not unusually, the title *counselor* is preceded by another word or words used to describe either the setting, the function, or the behavior primarily dealt with by that counselor. For example, school counselors are those who practice in schools. We, the authors, have long fought against the use of the term *guidance counselor* for such professionals, but in listening to graduate students, teachers, parents, and counselors themselves during recent years, we appear to be losing that battle (we intend to keep trying). Other examples are *career counselor, drug counselor, marriage and family counselor, college counselor, financial planning counselor, psychological counselor, community counselor, employment counselor, rehabilitation counselor, vocational counselor, career planning and placement counselor, agency counselor, sex counselor, public offender counselor, mental*

[18] William U. Snyder and B. June Snyder, *The Psychotherapy Relationship* (New York: Macmillan, 1961), p. 10.

health counselor, geriatrics counselor, to cite but a few. Three observations are in order here. First, the prefixes to the word *counselor* cited here represent a bewildering mixture of function, setting, or targeted behaviors for intervention. Second, this text focuses primarily on the term *counselor* in its generic sense but this does not mean to deny the usefulness of some prefixes attached to the word *counselor.* Third, the generic concept of *counselor* conveys a professional who possesses knowledge of human behavior, demonstrable personal intervention skills, and attitudes and values consonant with a code of ethics.

Regardless of setting, counselors (in the generic sense) perform certain functions. Treatment of these functions is given in Chapter 6. It may be noted here that Wrenn has summed up the counselor's functions, regardless of setting, in a very useful way. He states that it is a function of the counselor

a) to provide a *relationship* between counselor and counselee, the most prominent quality of which is that of mutual trust of each in the other; b) to provide *alternatives* in self-understanding and in the courses of action open to the client; c) to provide for *some degree of intervention* with the situation in which the client finds himself and with "important others" in the client's immediate life; d) to provide leadership in developing *a healthy psychological environment* for his clients; and, finally, e) to provide for *improvement of the counseling process* through constant individual self-criticism and (for some counselors) extensive attention to improvement of process through research.[19]

COUNSELING APPROACHES Many methods are used to create a relationship to assist counselees in self-understanding, select courses of action, intervene in interpersonal situations, and exercise leadership in developing healthy psychological environments. The approaches cited for psychologists—counseling relationships or interviews, use of test and nontest appraisal devices, and consultative endeavors—apply equally well to counselors.

[19] C. Gilbert Wrenn, "Crisis in Counseling: A Commentary and a Contribution," in *Counselor Development in American Society,* ed. John F. McGowan (Washington: U.S. Department of Labor, 1965), p. 237.

SETTING Estimates are that during 1978 some 88,000 counselors (recognized as such by competent authority) were employed in various settings in the United States. The settings in which they worked illustrate in some measure the degree of public support for such services in our society. The predominant setting is the school. While historically the secondary school level has been the major locus, today counselors in substantial numbers work in elementary schools, junior colleges, technical institutes, colleges, and universities. The United States Employment Service, rehabilitation centers, churches, Veterans' Administration installations, the Peace Corps, city welfare agencies, correctional institutions, Economic Opportunity Act programs, community action programs, private practice—all these make use of counselors.

NUMBERS AND NEED The number of individuals who bear the title *counselor* is extremely difficult to secure, but, as already mentioned, it is estimated (by state certification, by being employed and assigned the title, and so on) at 88,000. Some work part time. Approximately 66,000 are employed in educational institutions. Based on desirable counselor-client ratios, strong arguments can be made for increases in the number of counselors.

Given declining enrollments in educational institutions, the employment of counselors is expected to grow more slowly during the early 1980s than was true of the 1970s. Employment of counselors in community agencies, employment services, and other areas appears to be promising, but expansion of positions will not be rapid or dramatic. Best estimates are that replacement demands due to deaths, retirements, and job changes amount to approximately 10 percent each year. The need for counselors is always contingent on the degree to which society values their services and is willing to support them financially.

PREPARATION AND PROFESSIONAL ORGANIZATIONS Most states require counselors employed in public schools to be certified by state departments of education. Educational requirements for work in rehabilitation, employment, and the like vary. A master's degree in counseling is being accepted more and more as the *minimal* preparation. Counselor education programs at the graduate level are available in approximately 453 colleges and universities, most frequently in the departments of education and/or psychology.[20]

Two professional organizations claim the loyalty of most professional counselors: the American Personnel and Guidance Association and, to a somewhat lesser degree, the American Psychological Association. A discussion of these organizations is presented in Chapter 2.

The helping professionals: commonalities and differences

The demand for a helping relationship in American society has resulted in the establishment of several types of professionals. The boundaries, focus, goals, and significance of their service are transitory, uncertain, and often the subject of dispute.

Commonalities

More qualities are shared by than separate the helping professions. Of the many qualities held in common, five will be commented on here.

1. The concept that behavior is caused and can be modified is shared by all helping professions. It is agreed that every act is an attempt to satisfy some need, that a behavioral pattern is the result of many causes, and that any single cause may lead to many different sorts of adaptation. Although the latitude for change may vary considerably among individuals, it is widely assumed that almost all have the potentiality for changing behavioral liabilities and deficits. For some, the psychological barriers to change are immense, and modification is extremely difficult to achieve.

2. The ultimate goal of all helping professions is to help individuals become more fully functioning persons and achieve integration, personal identity, and self-actualization.

3. The primary means of extending assistance is through a helping relationship, the major characteristics of which have already been presented. It is through a personal, interacting relationship that helping skills and attitudes are

[20] Joseph W. Hollis and Richard A. Wantz, *Counselor Education Directory: Personnel and Programs*, 3rd ed. (Muncie, Indiana: Accelerated Development, Inc., 1977), p. 25.

productively released to enable clients needing assistance to cope with their difficulties and concerns.

4. All helping professions emphasize prevention. Each one knows that care and treatment are not enough, that causes must be uncovered. Individual treatment alone is inadequate because of the magnitude of mental problems among the public. Substantial attention has to be given to prophylaxis. While preventive efforts have been slow and often uncertain, education of the public about interpersonal behavior has been a long-term crusade for the National Association for Mental Health. Preventive efforts have been designed to inform the public on (a) the care provided patients in state hospitals and community centers, (b) the magnitude and nature of mental disorder, (c) the characteristics of good mental health, (d) misconceptions about mental disorders and interpersonal relationships, and (e) ways to enable individuals, particularly teachers and parents, to make discriminations and judgments concerning behavior and personal development.

Helping specialists give a preventive focus to their work when they foster a client's interest in improving his or her relationship with others. When clients become aware that their needs are reflected in how they relate to others, their flexibility may increase—and hence their acceptance of others' behavior. Certainly, achieving insight into one's values, expectations, and goals often brings realization and modification of the demands one makes on others.

5. Practitioners in all helping professions undergo a period of preparation and training. The length of preparation varies, but the goal is understanding behavior and creating helping relationships.

Differences

Attempts to differentiate social work, psychiatry, psychotherapy, and counseling have not had much success. Many helping specialists believe that differences are artificial, contrived, and theoretical rather than qualitative and practical. Others insist that the distinctions are there and should be known if for no other reason than the fact that the specialties exist.

1. Professional preparation and training varies. As just noted, the length of professional preparation differs substan-

tially. Two years of graduate work is the established standard in social work; psychiatry is a specialty attained in a two- to four-year program after receiving the medical degree, and psychoanalysis as a specialty requires an additional two to four years of preparation. Counseling and clinical psychology call for a doctorate. Two years of graduate study is now the established standard for school counseling personnel at professional certification levels.

Perhaps more important than length of preparation is the stress given certain content areas. Certainly social workers, prepared in graduate schools of social work, are more intimately grounded in societal and environmental bases of behavior. Study of individual development as affected by social environment, groups as a context for human interaction, family organization, forces producing social organization and disorganization, and the influence of the presence, beliefs, actions, and symbols of other cultures on behavior provides a backdrop for a social worker's interpretation and understanding of human behavior and his or her establishing of a helping relationship.

The focus of psychiatric education is on study of the total personality. Psychoneuroses and allied conditions, functional psychoses, and psychopathic conditions, deviations, and addictions are extensively studied. Personality development, unconscious motivation, and dynamic consideration of clinical cases are emphasized. Among the trends in psychiatric education is the fact that psychiatry is taught more and more during all four years of medical education rather than as a postmedical specialty. Raskin reports training programs are moving toward an integrated theory of psychiatry in an attempt to coordinate neurobiological, physiological, and sociological data.[21]

Preparation in clinical psychology emphasizes behavioral pathology, personality evaluation—especially diagnosis of emotional disorders—and, increasingly, psychotherapeutic involvement. On the other hand, preparation in counseling psychology stresses total development of the "normal" personality. In fact, preparation programs for counseling and clinical psychologists are rather similar. The clinician's preparation does tend to include a greater emphasis on the more seriously disabling psychological disturbances. Prepa-

ration in counseling and guidance pays major attention to developmental behavior and seeks to improve the quality of the helping relationship.

2. Recipients of the helping service extended by social workers, psychiatrists, psychotherapists, and counselors differ somewhat. Psychiatrists and clinical psychologists usually treat individuals with psychological disorders ranging from transient personal problems to chronic psychoses that are disabling, incapacitating, or disintegrating. Counseling psychologists, social workers, and counselors help essentially "normal" people remove frustrations and obstacles—ranging from situational temporary concerns, educational and vocational decisions, transient moderate-to-severe personal problems to mild disorders—that impair their development. The term *patient* is more often applied to the recipient of psychiatric and psychotherapeutic services; *counselee* and *client* are generally preferred by counseling psychologists, social workers, and counselors.

3. Depth of involvement and length of treatment may vary. Psychiatry and psychotherapy usually entail a deeper involvement with the individual's personality because they are more often concerned with the amelioration of serious behavioral conditions. The counseling relationship is likely to be characterized by less intensity of emotional expression than is found in the psychiatric relationship. Psychotherapy usually takes a longer period of time with its focus on personality reorganization, whereas counseling is conducted in shorter, more limited contacts.

4. The typical setting in which social work, psychiatry, counseling, and clinical psychology and counseling are performed varies somewhat. The usual locale for psychiatrists and clinical psychologists is a hospital. Counseling psychologists and social workers frequently practice in community clinics. Counselors are found in educational settings. It should be noted (see pp. 10–16) that variety characterizes the setting for all helping professions.

What is counseling?

The foregoing material described counseling as a helping profession. Because this book is about counseling and those who practice it, some definition of counseling seems imperative if its boundaries are to be known.

[21] David Raskin, "Psychiatric Training in the 70's—Toward a Shift in Emphasis," *The American Journal of Psychiatry*, 128 (March 1972), 1130.

Although *counseling* is a word used by many to describe what they do, dictionary definitions stress advice and the verbal exchange of ideas. Such definitions usually identify a legal adviser at an embassy, a lawyer, and a person in charge of a group of children at a camp as *counselors*. The historical use of advice to define *counsel* still is prevalent and is the cause of much conflict and confusion when counselors in educational and noneducational settings insist that they do not parcel out advice. Nor is the situation helped when automobile salespeople and representatives from brokers' firms, loan agencies, and mortuaries distribute cards bearing such titles as "Automotive Counselor," "Investment Counselor," "Financial Counselor," and "Grief Counselor"! Perhaps there is one saving grace—they usually spell the word as counse*ll*or!

Counseling has been used to denote a wide range of procedures including advice giving, encouragement, information giving, test interpretation, and psychoanalysis. H. B. English and A. C. English define counseling as "a relationship in which one person endeavors to help another to understand and to solve his adjustment problems."[22] They point out (1) that areas of adjustment are often indicated (for example, educational counseling, vocational counseling, personal-social counseling), (2) that reference is usually to helping "normal counselees" but creeps imperceptibly into the field of psychotherapy, and (3) that although everyone occasionally undertakes counseling, the word is preferably restricted to professionally trained persons.

A few of the definitions of counseling contained in the literature are given here. They reflect some of the subtle differences that have been emphasized or have evolved over the years.

. . . a process in which the counselor assists the counselee to make interpretations of facts relating to a choice, plan, or adjustments which he needs to make.[23]

. . . a process which takes place in a one-to-one relationship between an individual troubled by problems with which he cannot cope alone, and a professional worker whose training and experience have qualified him to help

others reach solutions to various types of personal difficulties.[24]

. . . the process by which the structure of the self is relaxed in the safety of the relationship with the therapist, and previously denied experiences are perceived and then integrated into an altered self.[25]

. . . that interaction which a) occurs between two individuals called a counselor and client; b) takes place in a professional setting, and c) is initiated and maintained as a means of facilitating changes in the behavior of a client.[26]

. . . a process by which a troubled person (the client) is helped to feel and behave in a more personally satisfying manner through interaction with an uninvolved person (the counselor) who provides information and reactions which stimulate the client to develop behaviors which enable him to deal more effectively with himself and his environment.[27]

. . . helping an individual become more fully aware of himself and the ways in which he is responding to the influences in his environment. It further assists him to establish some personal meaning for this behavior and to develop and clarify a set of goals and values for future behavior.[28]

Counseling or psychotherapy is defined as the helping process in which the relationship is necessary and sufficient. It is the specific treatment for those persons whose problems inhere in or relate to the lack of or inadequacy of good human relationships.[29]

Counseling is a process of helping people with their troubles. . . . Behavioral counseling is a process of helping

[22] H. B. English and A. C. English, *A Comprehensive Dictionary of Psychological and Psychoanalytical Terms* (New York: David McKay Co., 1958), p. 127.
[23] Glenn E. Smith, *Counseling in the Secondary School* (New York: Macmillan, 1955), p. 156.
[24] Milton E. Hahn and Malcolm S. MacLean, *Counseling Psychology* (New York: McGraw-Hill Book Co., 1955), p. 6.
[25] Carl R. Rogers, " 'Client-Centered' Psychotherapy," *Scientific American*, 187 (November 1952), 70.
[26] Harold Pepinsky and Pauline Pepinsky, *Counseling Theory and Practice* (New York: Ronald Press, 1954), p. 3.
[27] Edwin C. Lewis, *The Psychology of Counseling* (New York: Holt, Rinehart and Winston, 1970), p. 10.
[28] Donald H. Blocher, *Developmental Counseling*, 2nd ed. (New York: Ronald Press, 1974), p. 7.
[29] C. H. Patterson, *Relationship Counseling and Psychotherapy* (New York: Harper & Row, 1974), p. 13.

people to learn how to solve certain interpersonal, emotional, and decision problems.[30]

These definitions, presented chronologically, are representative of several dozen that are available and can profitably be examined for changes and meanings. Some of the more obvious differences are presented here.

1. The early emphasis was on cognitive concerns ("make interpretations of facts") whereas more current definitions stress affective experiences ("establish some personal meaning for his behavior") as well as cognitive dimensions.
2. Earlier definitions identified counseling as a dyadic (one-to-one) relationship, whereas current definitions usually incorporate the possibility of one or more than one counselee.
3. The definitions vary as to the importance placed on the relationship established between counselor and client.
4. The definitions vary in their description of the participants: the counselor as a professional or as older or as more mature or as possessing special knowledge; the client as troubled, anxious, upset, or frustrated.
5. The definitions vary in specifying the expected outcomes of counseling.

Some years ago, Patterson noted that it is sometimes useful to approach a definition by exclusion, or by designating what a thing is *not*.[31] By exclusion, many of the misconceptions surrounding counseling can be identified. Among Patterson's exclusions (paraphrased here) are that counseling

1. is not the giving of information, though information may be given in counseling.
2. is not the giving of advice, suggestions, and recommendations (advice should be recognized as such and not camouflaged as counseling).
3. is not influencing attitudes, beliefs, or behavior by means of persuading, leading, or convincing, no matter how indirectly, subtly, or painlessly.
4. is not the influencing of behavior by admonishing, warning, threatening, or compelling without the use of physical force or coercion (counseling is not discipline).

5. is not the selection and assignment of individuals for various jobs or activities (counseling is not personnel work even though the same tests may be used in both).
6. is not interviewing (while interviewing is involved, it is not synonymous).

The nature of counseling, according to Patterson, is to be found in the following characteristics:

1. Counseling is concerned with influencing voluntary behavior change on the part of the client (client wants to change and seeks counselor's help to change).
2. The purpose of counseling is to provide conditions that facilitate voluntary change (conditions such as the individual's right to make choices, to be independent and autonomous).
3. As in all relationships, limits are imposed on the counselee (limits are determined by counseling goals that in turn are influenced by the counselor's values and philosophy).
4. Conditions facilitating behavioral change are provided through interviews (not all counseling is interviewing, but counseling always involves interviewing).
5. Listening is present in counseling but not all counseling is listening.
6. The counselor understands clients (the distinction between the way others understand and the way counselors understand is qualitative rather than quantitative and understanding alone does not differentiate counseling from other situations).
7. Counseling is conducted in privacy and the discussion is confidential.

A final crucial characteristic Patterson cites is that counseling involves an interview conducted in private in which the counselor listens and attempts to understand the client, and in which it is expected that there will be a change in the client's behavior in some ways that he or she chooses or decides. Finally, two other characteristics necessary for a relationship to be labeled counseling are: that the client have a psychological problem, and that the counselor be someone skilled in working with clients with psychological problems.

We have no new definition of counseling. An adaptation of Blocher's definition seems most adequate and is used throughout this book: *Counseling is an interaction process that facilitates meaningful understanding of self and envi-*

[30] John D. Krumboltz and Carl Thoresen, *Counseling Methods* (New York: Holt, Rinehart and Winston, 1976), p. 1.
[31] C. H. Patterson, *An Introduction to Counseling in the School* (New York: Harper & Row, 1971), p. 108.

ronment and results in the establishment and/or clarification of goals and values for future behavior.

Issues

Issue 1 Counseling is a profession.

True, because
1. Counseling meets the criteria commonly used to determine whether occupations are classified as professions: a code of ethics has been adopted, members possess a common body of knowledge, entry into membership requires an extensive period of specialized training, and members perform a unique and definite social service.
2. Society has delegated to qualified members exclusive authority to provide the specified social service by virtue of incorporating counseling into twenty-five to thirty federal laws.

False, because
1. Assurance that individuals who become counselors meet minimum competence cannot be given by the corporate group.
2. The unique social service performed by counselors has yet to be identified, let alone delegated by society to counselors.
3. Counselors are not autonomous in performing their work, being directed by others.

Discussion This issue has long been a source of contention, being debated at national conventions and conferences. Even today it is implicit, if not explicit, in considerations governing the credentialing of counselors.

Occupations recognized as professions in the United States (law, medicine, and so on) have certain roots and traditions that stem from European origins. The characteristics that distinguish professions from other occupations are in part indigenous to American culture. A striking phenomenon of the labor market is the prestige that professions have been able to win and maintain. This prestige and status explain in part the yearnings of many occupational groups, including, no doubt, counseling, to become professionalized. Perhaps even more important, when professionalization is achieved, individual practitioners receive advantages owing to the monopoly given them to render a particular social service that is in demand. Too, professions in America have

been characterized by an idealism and an integrity that have rebounded to the untold benefit of society. On the other hand, it should be obvious that when an occupation achieves professionalization it is purchased at a price to society. In promoting its legitimate goals and standards, any profession constantly runs the risk of becoming parochial, self-serving, and self-protective.

We believe that counseling is moving toward bona fide professional status but has yet to identify the unique social service that counselors perform or to differentiate it sufficiently from services performed by others to warrant being accorded the status of a profession. Progress is being made in this task, probably the most important feature in professionalization. The task will be completed when counselors can distinguish what they do from the amateur, from other helping occupations, from administrators, from educators. Completion of that central task would make it possible for society to delegate exclusive authority to provide the unique social service. Counselors would be credentialed by licensure or certification.

Despite the fact that we believe that counseling is but an *emerging* profession, terms such as *counseling professional* and *counseling profession* will be used throughout this book. In no way does that mean that by identifying counselors as professionals or their work as professional counseling has somehow become a profession. It takes more than verbal reiteration to make a profession!

Issue 2 The school counselor should be exempt from the student discipline process.

No, because
1. Those who misbehave are most in need of counseling to clarify their emotions and actions.
2. If counselors are not involved in disciplinary cases, their usefulness is limited to the well-behaved, conforming pupil.
3. Since the causes of misbehavior must be diagnosed and treated, it is logical that the counselor, as the knowledgeable person in school in this field, be involved.
4. Disciplinary work at its best is preventive, and the counselor's skills and attitudes are attuned to preventive work.
5. The goals of discipline—self-control, self-direction, self-growth, and self-development—match those of counseling.

Yes, because
1. Supervision and enforcement of regulations are a responsibility of the administration.

2. Counselors involved in discipline become identified as authority figures; in consequence, the accepting, nonjudgmental role required for effective counseling is threatened.
3. Adequate handling of discipline cases requires exhaustive investigation, which would allow counselors little time to use their skills with other students.
4. Counseling calls for a permissive, self-initiated relationship rather than the compelled relationship that characterizes discipline.
5. Discipline—enforcing conformity—is a public process; counseling is private and confidential.

Discussion This is the oldest unresolved issue in the field, although the contemporary tendency seems to be toward little or no *direct* involvement of counselors in the disciplining of students. The more appropriate view appears to be that, although counselors retain some responsibility in the disciplinary process, they do not serve as disciplinarians. Most regard the counselor's role in the discipline process as working with students who have done something requiring disciplinary action in an effort to help them modify the kind of behavior that brought about punishment or as working with students to help them understand the disciplinary action taken against them and their reactions to it.

There are still large numbers of people who equate discipline and counseling. They overestimate the effect of their "counsel" and, perhaps even more detrimentally, view the counselor's task as persuading, cajoling, and subtly maneuvering students into conforming to institutional rules and requirements.

No one expects counselors to abrogate their adult responsibilities when confronted with a serious breach of school rules. Like other adults, they cannot ignore or walk away from serious behavior infractions. However, this is a different order of events from being deliberately placed in a position that constantly requires the exercise of disciplinary authority.

Issue 3 Is vocational counseling a distinct specialty within the field of counseling?

Yes, because
1. The increasing complexity of vocational decisions demands expert specialized assistance.

2. Despite its seeming narrow specificity, this type of helping relationship is highly complex.
3. Choice of a vocation is the fundamental factor in achieving happiness and satisfaction in life and therefore merits special treatment.

No, because
1. Choice of a vocation cannot be separated meaningfully from the totality of the individual's life choices.
2. Decision making based on self-examination and awareness is a basic outcome of all counseling and should be applied to all areas of life, not just the vocational.
3. Vocational pursuits are no more fundamental to a happy and successful life than many others.

Discussion In the history of counseling an early and almost exclusive preoccupation with vocational choice was followed by a swing toward viewing vocational decisions as only a part of the broader problem of existence. The current literature on career education indicates a resurgence of interest in vocational counseling, stemming in part from an increasing concern for the relatively large proportion of young people who enter the labor market directly after completion of high school. Critics claim that this group—conservatively estimated at over half the school population nationally—receive little assistance in career choice. Counselors give preference to students who continue their education and consequently are not immediately pressed to make binding vocational choices.

One of the original reasons for abandoning a narrow vocational emphasis in counseling was a growing awareness of the complexity of vocational choices. What appears on the surface to be a simple decision involves such factors as the assessment of job requirements and worker characteristics, a highly fluid labor market, and the entire complex of the individual's psychological makeup. Many would argue that despite the tremendous advancements of the past fifty years counselors are not much better able to cope with vocational choice than they were decades ago. Additional knowledge has served to contribute to the intricacy of the problem rather than to its solution.

The only reasonable solution seems to be to provide assistance to individuals that will permit them to make the best available decision in all life situations, whether vocational, educational, social, or personal.

Annotated references

Benjamin, Alfred. *The Helping Interview*. 2nd ed. Boston: Houghton Mifflin Company, 1974. 167 pp.

Benjamin describes the conditions influencing helping interviews, the philosophy behind them, and communications within them. His book amply illustrates helping relationships.

Blocher, Donald H. *Developmental Counseling*. 2nd ed. New York: Ronald Press, 1974. 318 pp.

Chapter 1 (pp. 3–27) presents a human effectiveness model, new models for professional practice, and an ecological approach to helping relationships. The author defines counseling and other processes.

Brammer, Lawrence M. *The Helping Relationship*. 2nd ed. Englewood Cliffs, N.J.: Prentice-Hall, 1979. 184 pp.

Sets forth the meaning of helping and the characteristics of helpers. The helping process is explained and fundamental skills for helping are presented.

Gilmore, Susan K. *The Counselor-in-Training*. New York: Meredith Corporation, 1973. 314 pp.

Section 1 (pp. 3–37) describes the content of counseling. The author suggests that work, relationship, and aloneness are the major life tasks for which clients come to counselors for assistance.

Holleb, Gordon P., and Walter H. Abrams. *Alternatives in Community Mental Health*. Boston: Beacon Press, 1975. 166 pp.

This small, well-written book describes the alternative counseling center movement from its beginnings in the early 1960s to the mid 1970s by focusing on why it began, how it developed, and what lies in the future. The philosophy, evolution, trials, and tribulations of alternative counseling services are fully and sensitively treated.

Further references

Banks, William. "Group Consciousness and the Helping Professions." *Personnel and Guidance Journal*, 55 (February 1977), 319–330.

Boy, Angelo V., and Pine, Gerald J. "Needed: A Rededication to the Counselor's Primary Commitment." *Personnel and Guidance Journal*, 57 (June 1979), 527–528.

Brammer, Lawrence B. "Who Can Be a Helper?" *Personnel and Guidance Journal*, 55 (February 1977), 303–308.

Carter, Jean A. "Impressions of Counselors as a Function of Counselor Physical Attractiveness." *Journal of Counseling Psychology*, 25 (January 1978), 28–34.

Dimond, Richard E., Ronald A. Havens, and Arthur C. Jones. "A Conceptual Framework for the Practice of Prescriptive Eclecticism in Psychotherapy." *American Psychologist*, 33 (March 1978), 239–248.

Fridman, Myron S., and Shelley C. Stone. "Effect of Training, Stimulus Context, and Mode of Stimulus Presentation on Empathy Ratings." *Journal of Counseling Psychology*, 25 (March 1978), 131–136.

Heller, Kenneth. "Facilitative Conditions for Consultation with Community Agencies." *Personnel and Guidance Journal*, 56 (March 1978), 419–423.

Highlen, Pamela S., and Nancy L. Voight. "Effects of Social Modeling, Cognitive Structuring, and Self-Management Strategies on Affective Self-Disclosure." *Journal of Counseling Psychology*, 25 (January 1978), 21–27.

Johnson, Richard H. "Toward a Unified Consciousness Theory." *Counselor Education and Supervision*, 16 (June 1977), 246–256.

Kurpius, DeWayne. "Consultation Theory and Process: An Integrated Model." *Personnel and Guidance Journal*, 56 (February 1978), 335–338.

McCarthy, Patricia R., Steven J. Danish, and Anthony R. D'Augelli. "A Follow-Up Evaluation of Helping Skills Training." *Counselor Education and Supervision*, 17 (September 1977), 29–35.

Menacker, Julius. "Toward a Theory of Activist Guidance." *Personnel and Guidance Journal*, 54 (February 1976), 318–321.

Nowicki, Stephen, Jr., and Marshall P. Duke. "Examination of Counseling Variables Within a Social Learning Framework." *Journal of Counseling Psychology*, 25 (January 1978), 1–7.

Warnath, Charles F. "Relationship and Growth Theories and Agency Counseling." *Counselor Education and Supervision*, 17 (December 1977), 84–91.

2 Counseling: origin and development

Remembering past events is often a favored activity of those who are bored or driven to despair by the world about them. Perhaps their contemplation of times gone by brings relief from current anxieties and difficult decisions. But it has another meaning to those who not only observe but also participate in the challenge of today and help create the promise of tomorrow. Careful examination of the past illuminates the present and suggests the pattern of the future. That which *is now* was shaped by the experiences of a *then* that extends back in an unbroken sequence.

This chapter is designed to show where counseling has been and how it arrived at its present state. Reflection will suggest, however, that the past is in reality intelligible only across spans of time much longer than that in which we have had organized counseling services. The chapter deals with five major subjects: the historical development of counseling, its current status, its professional organizations and journals, counselor supply and demand, and the criticisms leveled at it and its practitioners.

Historical development

The history of counseling reflects, as do all histories, continuous change and progressive development. This does not mean that there have not been crises or that development has necessarily been smooth or uniform. Counseling has been and continues to be a dynamic movement. It is important for every counselor to be acquainted with the broad dimensions of its evolutionary process, because, as Santayana has said, "Those who cannot remember the past are condemned to repeat it."

Landmarks or "firsts" in the history of counseling, such as who the first counselor was, are hard to establish with any degree of certainty. Resolving the issue of "first" depends on how counseling is defined. If its traditional definition—"giving of advice"—is accepted, then the point at which one person first sought and received verbal aid or instruction from another marked the advent of counseling.

Some would point out that certain counseling concepts can be traced back to the Greek philosophers, to parts of the Old Testament, or to other early sources. In this sense, the social philosophers of ancient Greece, for example, Plato (427?–347 B.C.) and Aristotle (384–322 B.C.); the hedonists; the philosophers of the British associationist school, such as John Locke (1632–1704), George Berkeley (1685–1753), David Hume (1711–1776), and James Mill (1773–1836), and others were influential because they sought to define the nature of humankind, the nature of society, and the relationship between the individual and society.

An American product

Counseling emerged and developed as an American product. In no other country has it flowered as it has here. Why it emerged in America has never been satisfactorily explained. Some claim that the American social environment, strongly influenced by the belief in the importance of the individual, was especially congenial to its development.

The pervasive concept of individualism, the lack of rigid class lines, the incentive to exercise one's talents to the best of one's ability may have provided a philosophical base, or perhaps counseling originated in America because its economic system was affluent enough to afford it. It may have appeared here because American society has long been child centered (some say child ridden). Undoubtedly all these factors were instrumental in the emergence of counseling in America.

Historical events

Restricted to its modern and technical definition, counseling has a much more contemporary history and therefore a much shorter one. Some of its highly significant events as well as those individuals influential in the events have been capsuled and are presented chronologically in Table 2.1.

TABLE 2.1 **Milestones: a chronology of counseling historical events**

Date	Individual	Event
1878	Wilhelm Wundt	Established first psychological laboratory in Leipzig, Germany
1883	G. Stanley Hall	Initiated child study movement and child guidance clinic
1890	James McKeen Cattell	The term *mental tests* first used in psychological literature (*Mind*)
1896	Lightner Witmer	First psychological clinic established at University of Pennsylvania
1898	Jessie B. Davis	Began 10 years of service as a counselor at Central High School, Detroit
1905	Alfred Binet	First individual intelligence scale
1906	Eli W. Weaver	Principal at Boy's School, Brooklyn, published *Choosing a Career*
1908	Frank Parsons	Established Vocational Bureau of Boston and described guidance procedures used with some 80 clients
1909	Frank Parsons	Published *Choosing a Vocation*
1909	Sigmund Freud	Lectures at Clark University marked recognition of psychoanalytic theories
1909	Clifford Beers	Published *A Mind That Found Itself* and was impetus for formation of the National Committee for Mental Hygiene, forerunner of National Association for Mental Health
1910		First national conference on vocational guidance held at Boston
1911	Frederick J. Allen	*Vocational Guidance News-Letter* published, the forerunner of *Personnel and Guidance Journal*
1911	Meyer Bloomfield	Taught first university-level course in vocational guidance, Harvard University
1912		Grand Rapids, Michigan, established citywide department for vocational guidance within school system
1913	Frank M. Leavitt	Founding of the National Vocational Guidance Association, forerunner of the American Personnel and Guidance Association (APGA)
1917	Arthur S. Otis	Use of *Army Alpha*, forerunner of group tests of mental ability
1918		Vocational Rehabilitation Act
1920		National Vocational Guidance Association (NVGA) reorganized as a federation of local and regional branches
1921		Veterans' Bureau established
1924		Organization of National Association of Appointment Secretaries, a forerunner of the American College Personnel Association
1925	Harry D. Kitson	Publication of *The Psychology of Vocational Adjustment*
1927	E. K. Strong, Jr.	First edition of *Strong Vocational Interest Blank*
1927	Elton Mayo	Launched precedent-setting series of studies on industrial behavior at Hawthorne (Chicago) plant of Western Electric Company revealing importance of human relations and worker morale to productivity
1927	Clark Hull	Published pioneering work, *Aptitude Testing*, in which vocational testing was conceived as a predictor of occupational success
1930	Robert Hoppock	Appointed field secretary of NVGA
1933		Passage of Wagner-Peyser Act brought the United States Employment Service (USES) into existence
1934	Harry D. Kitson	First president of a loose federation called the American Council of Guidance and Personnel Associations
1935	Robert Hoppock	Classic work, *Job Satisfaction*, published
1936		Passage of George-Deen Act, extending federal aid to public schools for vocational education
1937	Walter V. Bingham	Published *Aptitudes and Aptitude Testing*, a standard reference work for many years

TABLE 2.1 **Milestones** *(cont.)*

Date	Individual	Event
1938	L. L. and T. G. Thurstone	Publication of *Tests of Primary Mental Abilities*
1938	Harry A. Jaeger	Headed the first Occupational Information and Guidance Service established with U.S. Office of Education
1938		The B'nai B'rith Vocational Service Bureau started in Washington, D.C.
1939	E. G. Williamson	Published *How to Counsel Students*, a standard text used for many years
1939		First edition of *Dictionary of Occupational Titles* published by USES; titled, coded, and described some 18,000 occupations
1940		Occupational Outlook Service established in U.S. Department of Labor to compile and publish reports on trends, etc.
1942	John M. Brewer	*History of Vocational Guidance* published
1942	Carl R. Rogers	Published *Counseling and Psychotherapy*
1943		Enactment of PL 16 provided counseling and training for disabled veterans
1944		Enactment of PL 346 (G.I. Bill) extended training and counseling to veterans
1945	Ira Scott	Publication of *Manual of Advisement and Guidance* detailing Veterans' Administration counseling
1945		Introduction of USES *General Aptitude Test Battery*
1946	American Psychological Association	Establishment of the American Board of Examiners in Professional Psychology
1949	John W. M. Rothney	Published *Counseling the Individual Student*, long a standard reference in counseling
1950	Erik H. Erikson	First edition of *Childhood and Society* describing stages of development
1951		Founding of the American Personnel and Guidance Association
1951	Carl R. Rogers	Published *Client-Centered Therapy*
1951	Fritz Perls	*Gestalt Therapy* published, starting movement
1951	Donald Super	Launched Career Pattern Study
1952		American School Counselor Association was formed as a division of APGA
1953	Leona F. Tyler	Publication of *The Work of the Counselor*, a standard text for many years, now in its third edition
1953	Robert J. Havighurst	Published *Human Development and Education*, with developmental tasks
1954	C. Gilbert Wrenn	One of the founders and first editor of the *Journal of Counseling Psychology*
1956	USES	Publication of *Estimates of Worker Trait Requirements for 4,000 Jobs*
1957	Robert Hoppock	Publication of first edition of *Occupational Information*, now in its fourth edition
1957	APGA	Forerunner of the International Association of Counseling Services created to approve counseling agencies
1958	Albert Bandura	Published *Principles of Behavior Modification*, emphasizing social learning
1958	U.S. Congress	Passed the National Defense Education Act, providing funds for programs and training counselors
1959	James B. Conant	Published *The American High School Today*, recommending employment of counselors
1959	Robert Stripling	5-year grassroots study of counselor education started
1960	Harold McCully and Ralph Bedell	Directed NDEA institute programs for U.S. Office of Education and required supervised counseling practice
1962	C. Gilbert Wrenn	Published *The Counselor in a Changing World* reported current and future prospects of counseling
1962	Albert Ellis	Published *Reason and Emotion in Psychotherapy*, start of rational emotive therapy

TABLE 2.1 **Milestones** *(cont.)*

Date	Individual	Event
1962	U.S. Congress	Enactment of Manpower Development and Training Act, instituting on-the-job training and research in labor power
1964	John Krumboltz	Publication of behavioral counseling theory and practice
1964	U.S. Congress	NDEA amended to include preparation of elementary school counselors
1964	Robert Stripling	Standards for preparing secondary school counselors were approved by APGA
1965	C. B. Truax and Robert Carkhuff	Measures of empathy and other facilitative conditions
1965	Norman Kagan	Started video taping of interviews that led to *The Interpersonal Process Recall* studies
1966	Jane Loevinger	Publication of ego development sequence
1968	Merle Ohlsen	Standards for preparing elementary school counselors were approved by APGA
1968	Lee Isaacson	Standards for preparing college student personnel approved
1968	Joseph Kamiya	Introduction of biofeedback
1969	Lawrence Kohlberg	Publication of moral development stages and sequence
1972	Robert Stripling	The three sets of standards for preparing counselors merged into one statement and approved by APGA
1973	Normal Sprinthall	Deliberate psychological education programs started and assessed
1974	U.S. Congress	Passed PL 93-380, established federal funds for gifted and talented programs in schools
1974	Kenneth B. Hoyt	Enactment of career education (PL 93-380) established unit in Office of Education with Hoyt as head
1975	U.S. Congress	Passed PL 94-142, the Education of All Handicapped Children mandating all handicapped individuals, ages 3–21, must be educated in least restrictive environment
1975	Thomas Sweeney	Headed APGA counselor licensure commission
1976	State of Virginia	Passed first state counselor licensure law
1976	Gail Sheehy	Publication of *Passages*, adult development stages
1977	U.S. Congress	Career Education Incentive Act passed
1978	Robert Stripling	Guidelines for Doctoral Preparation in Counselor Education approved by Association for Counselor Education and Supervision
1978	Roger Gould	Publication of *Transformations*, adult developmental stages
1978	Bryan Gray	Heads the counseling and guidance unit re-established in U.S. Office of Education
1979	Edwin Herr	Publication of *Guidance and Counseling in the Nation's Schools*

Historical factors and forces

The events cited in Table 2.1 only mark the high tides of certain prevailing forces that facilitated counseling's development. The evolution of modern concepts and techniques of counseling is best seen as a movement influenced by social, economic, psychological, and environmental factors. The climate provided by the interaction of these factors enabled counseling to emerge and maintain itself.

At first glance, the factors appear to be so numerous that any attempt to analyze their cause-and-effect relationships seems hopeless. No one, in fact, has been able to suggest any acceptable single factor that gives *the* key to understanding the historical process. This does not mean, however, that the history of counseling must be confined to description or that it is impossible to show that some forces had relatively greater influence on the character of counseling than others.

THE INFLUENCE OF SOCIAL REFORM Counseling originated at a time (between 1890 and 1920) known for social reform. The growth in the nineteenth century of cities, great fortunes, and new ways of living brought economic and social inequities. From 1890 to 1920 the entire fabric of American life was subjected to careful analysis and severe criticism. Aroused by the horror of poverty, injustice, and corruption, individuals and groups sought reform.

A remedy was sought for every evil. The poverty, misery, and unemployment that came as a result of the transformation of America into an industrialized and urbanized society led to the establishment of organized charities, settlement houses, philanthropic associations, and government bureaus for corrective and custodial services. Especially notable was the early-twentieth-century concern for the welfare of children. Playgrounds and parks, more understanding treatment of children who came into conflict with the law, and correction of child labor abuses were brought about. Better conditions of living, continuous employment, and general education—reforms that strike at the causes of poverty and crime—were themes mounted and enlarged on by numerous social reformers.

A period of ascendancy for counseling occurred during the 1960s. That period also was known for its reform efforts. Stirred by the exposure of poverty, racism, sexism, remedies were applied to improve society. Educational institutions, in particular, were viewed as important places to initiate corrective and preventive efforts. The point is that the social climate, demanding the elimination of prevailing inequities, permitted if not facilitated not only the beginning but the ascendancy of counseling.

VOCATIONAL GUIDANCE Most authorities[1] identify the emergence of *vocational* guidance as the beginning of modern-day counseling. The work of Jesse B. Davis in Detroit, the publications of Eli Weaver, and the activities of Frank Parsons in Boston have been cited in Table 2.1. Parsons, often called the "father of guidance," began his work at the Vocational Bureau of Boston to improve the post-school placement of individuals. In his report to the Vocational Bureau's executive committee Parsons coined the term *vocational guidance* to describe the methods he used with young people and urged that vocational guidance become part of the public school program and that experts conduct it.

Parsons's observations of young people led him to the conclusion that they needed careful and systematic help in choosing a vocation. His idea was to match the characteristics of the individual to the requirements of the occupation. He reasoned that three major steps were necessary in selecting a vocation and that they suggested how an experienced counselor could assist the young person. These steps may be summarized as *individual analysis* (careful study of the counselee's capabilities, interests, and temperaments); *job analysis* (counselee study of occupational opportunities, requirements, and employment prospects in various lines of work); and *true reasoning* (based on the relationships between these two sets of data).

Counseling originated to help individuals choose, enter, and progress in an occupation. Given that today, strong emphasis on career counseling has emerged, it may be observed that counseling has come full circle.

THE CHILD STUDY MOVEMENT The child study movement contributed to the development of counseling. G. Stanley Hall of Clark University aroused popular interest in child study. Through his influence the child came to be looked on as an individual person, and studies were made of children's physical and mental characteristics. During the 1920s and 1930s child study centers in some states (California, Iowa, Minnesota) and scientific journals and organizations designed to promote the well-being of children came into existence. The questionnaire method of inquiry, popularized by Hall, resulted in the rapid accumulation of data relating to different phases of the mental life of all ages.

The effect of the child study movement in America was fourfold: (1) It emphasized the individual as the focal point of study; (2) it stressed the importance of the formative years as the foundation for mature personality development; (3) it pointed up the need for reliable factual knowledge about children; and (4) it led to better-controlled, more analytical and accurate methods of child study.

PSYCHOMETRICS Another factor instrumental in the development and expansion of counseling was the testing

[1] See Donald E. Super, "Transition: From Vocational Guidance to Counseling Psychology," *Journal of Counseling Psychology*, 2 (Spring 1955), 3–9.

movement (see Table 2.1). The testing movement influenced counseling in that it (1) led to the objective study of individual differences, such as sex, race, and social status differences; (2) served as a base for development of the trait-and-factor concept of personality; (3) enabled scientific investigations to be made of problems like the rate of growth of intelligence and the constancy of intelligence measures over a period of time; (4) focused attention on the diagnosis and evaluation of maladjustment; (5) facilitated prediction, classification, and placement of individuals; and (6) resulted in the formulation and publication of a code of ethics to be used as a guide for responsible testing practices.

INFLUENCE OF THE MENTAL HEALTH MOVEMENT Sparked by Clifford Beers' book *A Mind That Found Itself* (the story of his experiences, observations, and recovery during three years in mental hospitals), a group of people led by Beers organized the Connecticut Society for Mental Hygiene (1908). This marked the beginning of the organized mental health movement in America. Beers also supplied the leadership for the formation (1909) of the National Committee for Mental Hygiene (now the National Association for Mental Health). This association has been responsible for or contributed to significant innovations in legislative reform, aftercare, and free clinics for the mentally ill. Most assuredly, it has reduced public apathy and resistance to the discussion of mental illness and mental health. Beginning as a humanitarian program designed to ameliorate the living conditions of those who had succumbed to serious mental disorders, the association endeavored to insure humane treatment, adequate living quarters, and intelligent commitment laws. Later, the association focused on the study, treatment, and rehabilitation of individuals suffering from less serious mental disorders. Its work and influence have been broad in scope and far-reaching in effect. By calling attention to the need for prevention and early identification and treatment of mental illness, it has encouraged educators and parents to become more sensitive to the deep insecurities and loss of identity among youth and has thus fostered the initiation of counseling programs in schools and community clinics.

COMPULSORY EDUCATION After 1880, when the legal status of the high school as a free public institution became established, school enrollments increased substantially. As the number of students increased, the curriculum was changed to meet the needs, interests, and abilities of a heterogeneous population. The effect was reciprocal, for the enriched and broadened curriculum was not only a result of increased enrollment, but also a cause of retaining still more pupils.

Compulsory school attendance, improved child labor laws, and expanded curricula brought thousands of young people into school who sometimes had no desire to be there and few clear ideas of why they were there or what they wanted. School administrators soon saw that individual, personal attention was needed to help individuals marshall their assets to find their way through the school and the complex environment outside it.

DEPRESSION AND WAR The spectacular stock market crash of 1929 was followed by a rapid deterioration of virtually every branch of economic activity. Large-scale unemployment (resulting in deterioration of morale, loss of trade skills, and so on) led to the establishment (Wagner-Peyser Act, 1933) of the United States Employment Service to provide testing, counseling, and placement services to workers. When the United States entered the Second World War, military and civilian work-force problems became acute. Selection, training, and placement procedures were refined as a result of military and civilian research efforts. Products of these efforts were the *Army General Classification Test* (1941) and the U.S. Employment Service *General Aptitude Test Battery* (1945). Counseling centers were established in the Veterans' Administration to render service to disabled veterans and later to all veterans. The civil service position of Counseling Psychologist was established in 1952, and in 1954 the Office of Vocational Rehabilitation was created and began administrating training contracts to prepare vocational rehabilitation counselors. In short, depression and war influenced the development of counseling by highlighting the critical need for counselors and, through the urgency it generated, the need to refine and improve psychometric instruments, counseling, and placement methods.

FEDERAL GOVERNMENT SUPPORT The federal government, principally through the Department of Labor and the Department of Health, Education, and Welfare, has been influential in the development of counseling. Vocational education legislation (see Table 2.1) paved the way for establishing guidance divisions within state departments of education. In 1938 the U.S. Office of Education created the

Occupational Information and Guidance Services Bureau with Harry Jaeger as director. Its publications and research efforts consistently stressed the need for school counselors and the kinds of services they provide. Counseling, in settings ranging through rehabilitation centers, community agencies, veterans' agencies, mental health centers, schools, and colleges, has received support from federal acts.

EMPHASIS WITHIN PSYCHOLOGY Certain forces operating within the field of psychology have influenced the development of counseling. Particular schools of thought or viewpoints have emerged, dominated for periods of time, and then been replaced by others. During the early twentieth century at the time counseling originated, *structuralism* became prominent in psychology. Advocates of structuralism believed that mental images, thoughts, and feelings should be investigated if human behavior was to be understood. Concentration on structuralism ruled out attending to learning, intelligence, the environment, and so on. Stress was placed on perceiving, thinking, and imagery. Shortly thereafter, *functionalism* became fashionable in psychology. Its objective was to discover how thinking, emotion, and other mental processes were used to fulfill an individual's needs. Also, *behaviorism* was initiated at about the same time (1914) by John B. Watson, who believed that structuralism was too narrow. The main objective of psychology, he said, was to study doing and action, not consciousness.

Expose an animal or a human being to a stimulus and measure its responses; record this behavior objectively so that real scientific evidence is available. Present-day behaviorists continue to stress that doing and action behaviors are the targets of counseling interventions and urge counseling to rid itself of mentalistic terms. Wolfgang Kohler and Max Wertheimer, originators of *gestalt psychology*, maintained that experience and behavior could not be analyzed into elements of consciousness, as claimed by the structuralists. Nor could consciousness be broken down into stimulus-response units, as the behaviorists suggested. Gestaltists believed that behavior and experience are unanswerable wholes, though certain relationships between the whole and its parts can be discerned. They emphasized here-and-now behaviors, attention to physiological features of behavior, and forming a total impression of the individual. *Humanistic psychology* became prominent during the 1960s. It called for recognition of the fact that the supposedly objective point

of view was dependent on or subsequent to other matters that were clearly subjective and stressed the humanness of the individual. Each of these psychological movements have influenced counseling, particularly in theory building and practice.

SUMMARY Various social, economic, educational, and psychological forces have encouraged and facilitated the growth of counseling although the exact influence of each of these factors is not easy to determine. Certainly its present status, the expectations held for it, the criticisms made of it, its purpose, and many other characteristics may be traced back to the ideas, ideals, and patterns inherent in these forces.

Current status of counseling

The rate of counseling development has not followed a steady upward curve. Counseling at present justifies being termed emergent and is marked by both continuity and discontinuity. It spurts ahead, then settles down to a slow steady pace. New imbalances induce a new burst of growth. At this time little really is known about why development is sometimes so vigorous and dynamic and sometimes so sluggish. The following points summarize some ideas about the current status of counseling and its practitioners.

1. *Professional associations.* It should be noted that professional associations have attracted and held an unprecedented number of members. The major association for counselors—the American Personnel and Guidance Association (APGA)—has expanded its divisions, improved its governance, modified its national conventions, revised its code of ethics, and upgraded its placement services to serve its members and the public better.

2. *Professional journals and publications.* Professional journals designed for counselors are thriving. Not only has the number of journals increased but their size has expanded. Moreover, publications other than journals—monographs, digests, newsletters—have increased rapidly. Finally, other media such as films, filmstrips, audio and video tape, records, and cassettes are being utilized slowly but increasingly to transmit information about counseling and counselors to the public and to the student.

3. *Public's belief about counselors.* The evidence on the public's belief about counseling is scanty. During the early 1970s, public opinion polls queried a national sample about its attitudes toward public school counselors. Some 75 percent of those questioned reported that school counselors were worth the added cost.[2]

Parochial school parents had attitudes similar to public school parents: 79 percent reported that counselors were worth the extra cost; 12 percent believed they were not and 9 percent had no opinion. Many would interpret these poll data as suggesting that the public is highly supportive of counseling services, but more believe that slippage has occurred in the attitudes of the public toward counseling.

4. *Prestige of counselors.* The prestige attached to an occupation presumably has an impact, not only on whether individuals enter and continue in it but also on how well they function within the institution that employs them Granger's study of the prestige rankings of individuals in psychological professions placed school counselors near the bottom (among twenty specialties) of the psychologist's hierarchy.[3] Granger's questionnaire was modified by Kondrasuk[4] and given to 292 graduate students in the Department of Psychology, University of Minnesota. High school counselors were ranked above psychometrists and employment interviewers but below the other sixteen job titles including vocational rehabilitation counselor, school psychologist, social psychologist, clinical psychologist, and so on. Kondrasuk points out that research on occupational prestige of jobs is viewed as repugnant by many psychologists who believe it to be a deterrent to building a profession and especially harmful to low-ranking areas such as school counselors.

When school counselors are compared to educational professionals other than psychologists, their prestige rankings differ dramatically. Moses and Delaney, studying the hierarchy of common school occupations, reported counselors ranked sixth among eighteen relatively distinct posi-

tions.[5] They were placed below teachers, but above school psychologists. Scott and Cherlin asked students in graduate courses in guidance, school administration, and supervision of instruction to rank fourteen school occupations. High school counselors ranked eighth (below superintendents, principals, school psychologists, supervisors of instruction, directors of guidance, and departmental chairmen) among the fourteen occupations, but above teachers, social workers, librarians, nurses, and head custodians. Scott and Cherlin believe that school counselors are placed consistently near teachers in prestige because of the similarity of salaries and the fact that teaching experience has been required of counselors.[6]

These data indicate that currently the prestige or occupational status of counselors varies according to with whom they are compared and who does the ratings. Counselors rank low on the psychological hierarchy but among school personnel they fare much better. No doubt, the attractiveness of the occupation will improve as the identity of counselors is clarified and their preparation becomes more rigorous.

5. *Counselor practices.* The dyadic relationship is still the most common mode of operation among counselors. The last few years have brought increasingly to the front counselor practices that facilitate career development. During the 1970s the U.S. Office of Education sought to implement career education, promoting career exploration, planning and decision making. Counselors dusted off old practices and developed new ones to assist students in career development. The current status of counselor practices includes increasing use of group counseling and intensive group experiences to facilitate personal development. The use of behavior modification techniques has permeated counselor practices.

6. *Counselor role and function.* This perennial problem is still unresolved. More and more counselors have invested time and effort in defining their role and function. Agreement seems to be increasing that counselors function as counselors to individuals and small groups and as consul-

[2] George Gallup, "The Public's Attitude Toward the Public Schools," *Phi Delta Kappan*, 52 (October 1970), 99–112.

[3] S. G. Granger, "Psychologists' Prestige Rankings of Twenty Psychological Occupations," *Journal of Counseling Psychology*, 6 (Fall 1959), 183–188.

[4] John N. Kondrasuk, "Graduate Students' Rankings of Prestige Among Occupations in Psychology," *Journal of Counseling Psychology*, 18 (March 1971), 142–146.

[5] H. Moses and D. J. Delaney, "Status of School Personnel," *Journal of the Student Personnel Association for Teacher Education*, 9 (December 1971), 41–46.

[6] C. Winfield Scott and Mary M. Cherlin, "Occupational Status of the High School Counselor," *Vocational Guidance Quarterly*, 20 (September 1971), 31–38.

tants to others in the institution or agency in which they are employed as well as to others significant in the lives of their clientele.

7. *Numbers and need.* The force of counselors in the United States, Great Britain, and France grows ever larger. Although growth in the United States during the 1970s slowed somewhat, the number of counselors continues to increase. The need for counselors as represented in desirable counselor-client ratios continues to be urgent.

8. *Counselor preparation.* As pointed out in Chapter 1, some 453 colleges and universities are preparing counselors. Counselor preparation is changing. Today's programs give high priority to supervised counseling practice with individuals and groups, to counseling skill–building laboratories, to the use of simulated materials in classroom activities, and to more intensive treatment of a broader range of counseling theories. Problems persist in the selection of students for programs. A small decrease recently has occurred in the numbers of students who apply for admission to graduate programs in counselor education. The authors' experience is that these candidates are younger, brighter, and better prepared in the social sciences than were their predecessors of five or ten years ago.

9. *Federal government support.* Since 1967, the amount of financial support categorically earmarked for counselor preparation and employment has declined. While sizeable amounts are available from the Education Professions Development Act, Elementary and Secondary Education Act, and the Vocational Education Act and its later amendments, these funds have shrunk from those provided during the years of the National Defense Education Act of 1958 and its amendments.

10. *Public school enrollments and financial problems.* A marked decline in the birthrate and persistent financial problems continue to vex the educational system of the United States at all levels. By the late 1970s falling enrollments due to the birth of fewer children were felt forcefully in the elementary and secondary schools and inevitably will confront colleges and universities in the 1980s. While census experts indicate the birthrate decline will stop and an increase in births occur in the mid 1980s, none predict much more than a modest increase in population. Simultaneously, the educational system has been beset by rather severe financial problems. Inflation has been a chronic problem eroding the dollars available to finance education.

At the state and local levels, tax dollars are increasingly difficult to obtain not only because taxpayers also face tremendous inflationary pressures but also because it is difficult for them to believe that the financial need is great in view of the fact that school populations are declining.

The current status of counseling, then, is one of fluidity. Though the years 1970 to 1979 may be viewed in retrospect as a period when counseling reached a plateau, there is little evidence to justify pessimism about its future. The changes that have taken place do not mean that the future will be settled and inactive. Struggles for power and prestige seem ever present among counseling practitioners. Differences in opinion exist and will persist among counselors themselves as well as between counselors and other groups. It is highly probable that the process of defining these differences will permit new functions and new specialties to emerge.

The need to communicate more effectively to the public and to other professionals what the counselor is and does will require resourceful and able practitioners. Counselors with enthusiasm, confidence, and sensitivity can build on the foundation represented by this history.

Professional organizations and journals

The APGA

Several separate professional organizations (see Table 2.1) merged in 1951 to form the American Personnel and Guidance Association (APGA). Its purposes are stated in its 1978 bylaws:

> The purposes of the American Personnel and Guidance Association are to enhance individual human development by: seeking to advance the scientific discipline of guidance, counseling and personnel work; by conducting and fostering programs of education in the field of guidance, counseling and personnel; by promoting sound guidance, counseling and personnel practices in the interests of society and the individual; by stimulating, promoting and conducting programs of scientific research and of education in the field of guidance, counseling and personnel work; by publishing scientific, educational, and professional literature; by advancing high standards

of professional conduct; by conducting scientific educational and professional meetings and conferences; by informing and educating the general public about the human development profession; by establishing contacts with various organizations for scientific and educational pursuits; and by examining conditions which create barriers to individual development and working to remove them.

In 1979, some 41,000 individuals were members of the APGA. The APGA has thirteen divisions that span diverse specialties, interests, and settings:

American College Personnel Association (ACPA)
Association for Counselor Education and Supervision (ACES)
National Vocational Guidance Association (NVGA)
Association for Humanistic Education and Development (AHEAD)
American School Counselor Association (ASCA)
American Rehabilitation Counseling Association (ARCA)
Association for Measurement and Evaluation in Guidance (AMEG)
National Employment Counselors Association (NECA)
Association for Non-White Concerns in Personnel and Guidance (ANWC)
Association for Specialists in Group Work (ASGW)
Public Offender Counselor Association (POCA)
Association for Religious Value Issues in Counseling (ARVIC)
Association of Mental Health Counselors (AMHC)

ASCA contains the largest membership (13,000 to 14,000) of the APGA divisions. Analysis of the thirteen divisions reveals that some represent professional interests and others reflect functions and settings. An individual holds general membership in the APGA and may belong to one or more divisions depending on interests and qualifications. In addition to divisional membership, state branches have been chartered by APGA in fifty-two states or territories. A state branch in turn charters chapters (regional organizations) and divisions (ACPA, ACES, ASCA, and so on) within the state.

The present APGA governmental structure consists of a senate, elected from the various divisions and state branches; a board of directors, composed of divisional presidents and eight branch representatives plus the APGA president, president-elect, past president, and the executive vice president and treasurer (ex officio); and an executive committee composed of the APGA president, president-elect, past president, two members of the board of directors and the executive vice president and treasurer (ex officio). APGA government remains complex, unwieldy, and burdensome. Each division has a somewhat parallel governmental structure and the inevitable overlap between the divisions' government and the APGA's central government, coupled with a network of standing and ad hoc committees appointed to investigate basic professional issues or to accomplish specific goals, hinders the organization's functioning.

The APGA conducts a placement service at its national convention and publishes in its newsletter, *Guidepost,* positions open in the field of guidance and personnel work and APGA members' availability for employment. The International Association of Counseling Services, an affiliate of the APGA, publishes a list of counseling agencies that meet the professional standards established by the association. A directory gives the address, office hours, fees, clientele served, and professional staff of each agency.

The APGA long has been involved in securing federal legislation to provide financial support for the preparation and employment of counselors. It has actively sought to interpret counseling, guidance, and student personnel work to the public and to other professional organizations.

The APA Division of Counseling Psychology

The Division of Counseling Psychology (Division 17) of the American Psychological Association is part of another association that claims the professional loyalty of counselors. Division 17 exists to give recognition to the specialized interests of psychologists concerned with counseling. After becoming an APA member and if one meets additional specialized requirements, an individual may join the Division of Counseling Psychology, originally called the Division of Counseling and Guidance but renamed in 1953. Throughout the years, the division has issued policy studies of its specialty and conducted research on the expectations, characteristics, and attitudes of its members. It also sponsors symposia at conventions as well as local and regional

TABLE 2.2 **Journals useful to counselors**

Major counseling journals	Counseling-related journals
Personnel and Guidance Journal	*American Psychologist*
Journal of Counseling Psychology	*Journal of Consulting and Clinical Psychology*
The Counseling Psychologist	*Counselor Education and Supervision*
The School Counselor	*Journal of Specialists of Group Work*
Journal of Vocational Behavior	*Review of Educational Research*
Rehabilitation Counseling Bulletin	*The Humanist Educator*
Measurement and Evaluation in Guidance	*Journal of College Student Personnel*
Elementary School Guidance and Counseling	*National Vocational Guidance Quarterly*
	Journal of Employment Counseling
	Journal of Non-White Concerns in Personnel and Guidance

discussions. By 1979, Division 17, with over 2,500 fellows, members, and associates on its membership rolls, was one of the larger divisions of the American Psychological Association.

Journals

Today's counselor must examine a veritable outpouring of professional literature. Each APGA division publishes a journal, as does APGA itself. In addition to the journals generic to counseling, counselors must be conversant with literature from related, sometimes external, areas. A few of the journals designed specifically for counselors that students will find helpful in their years of preparation are identified in Table 2.2.

Counselors: numbers, need, and supply

Numbers

A precise census of counselors practicing in the United States is almost impossible to obtain. First, the problem of who is to be counted as a counselor again arises because the conditions under which a person is classified as a counselor have yet to be specified uniformly. Second, some individuals who serve as counselors also serve in other capacities for varying amounts of their time. Translation of the actual allotted share of counseling time into full-time equivalents produces marginal data at best. Third, no single authority exists to recognize counselors. In some settings—for example, private practice—no legal or administrative authority may exist for recognizing counselors as such. The authority to confer the title *counselor* is held by many persons, agencies, and organizations. Currently, an employer exercises this right. Undoubtedly, the employer's judgment is guided by legislative, regulatory, and policy stipulations imposed on institutional settings. But the title is often abused: people are called *counselors* who have not been prepared as such. Indeed, the title may at times be self-conferred.

Periodically, individuals, professional organizations, and federal government agencies have estimated the number of counselors working in the United States. Van Hoose, for example, has conducted three surveys of the number of counselors employed in elementary schools. He and his associate reported that during 1970–1971, some 7,982 counselors were employed in the fifty states, the District of Columbia, and the Virgin Islands. Of this number, 78 percent were employed full time.[7] Based on previous surveys of elementary school counselors, Van Hoose and Carlson concluded that counselors increased by approximately 1,000 per year in elementary schools. That projected increase has not held constant, being diminished particularly since 1975. For example, Myrick and Moni[8] reported in 1976 that some 10,770 counselors were employed in public elementary schools. They estimated a 1-to-6 ratio of counselors to elementary schools on a nationwide basis. Based on partial data, about 15 percent of counselors were working in more than one school, but Myrick and Moni believed the general norm was much higher than that.

[7] William Van Hoose and John Carlson, "Counselors in the Elementary School: 1970–1971," *Personnel and Guidance Journal,* 50 (April 1972), 679–682.
[8] Robert D. Myrick and Linda Moni, "A Status Report of Elementary School Counseling," *Elementary School Guidance and Counseling,* 10 (March 1976), 156–164.

TABLE 2.3 **Estimated number of counselors by setting, 1978**

Setting	Estimated number (full-time equivalent)
Junior and senior high schools	44,000
Elementary schools	10,000
Rehabilitation agencies	13,000
College counseling centers (mostly Ph.D.'s)	5,000
College career planning and placement centers	4,000
Junior and community colleges	1,500
Technical institutes, vocational schools	1,000
State employment agencies	6,500
Private or community agencies	2,500
Industry	300

SOURCE: Based on data reported in the 1978–1979 *Occupational Outlook Handbook* and estimates by Charles Lewis, executive vice president, American Personnel and Guidance Association.

TABLE 2.4 **Number of secondary school guidance personnel employed and counselor-counselee ratio, 1958–1978**

Year	Total full-time equivalents	Counselor-counselee ratios
1958–1959	12,000	1-960
1962–1963	27,180	1-600
1966–1967	36,200	1-490
1970–1971	41,000	1-470
1974–1975	43,000	1-460
1978–1979	44,000	1-450

SOURCE: Based on data from U.S. Office of Education, personal communications from Donald Twiford (Office of Education), and from Charles Lewis, executive vice president, American Personnel and Guidance Association.

Need

Estimates of the number of counselors needed now and in the future (1) are based on attaining some ratio of counselors to counselees deemed necessary or desirable to provide adequate counseling service, (2) normally reflect only the supply needed for traditional or existing settings, and (3) often fail to take into account attrition rates. Most projections have been based on one full-time counselor for 600 pupils in elementary schools, one full-time counselor for 300 pupils in secondary schools, and one full-time counselor for 750 or 1,000 students in junior colleges, four-year colleges, and universities.

Many counseling practitioners take issue with the ratios used in estimating the need for counselors. They question, for example, the adequacy of a ratio of one full-time counselor to 600 elementary school pupils or to 1,000 college students. Although some fixed ratio of clients to a full-time counselor may be desirable and useful, other factors, such as the characteristics of the setting, the community, and the population being served, have to be taken into account. To replace a counselor-pupil ratio, Hitchcock recommended one full-time counselor for not more than seven full-time teachers in elementary and secondary schools, junior colleges, colleges, and universities. He proposed that in non-educational settings the number of counselors be based on the population to be served. For example, to provide counseling services for the labor force he suggested (on rec-

It was observed in Chapter 1 that approximately 88,000 counselors are at work in America. The number of counselors believed employed, classified by various settings, is presented in Table 2.3. For many reasons these numbers represent only best estimates made by many people in the profession. Previously, the Guidance and Counseling Services Branch of the U.S. Office of Education was a reliable source of information about the supply of counselors, particularly school counselors, but it was discontinued from 1970 to 1978. However, Metz and his associates at the National Center for Educational Statistics, Department of Health, Education, and Welfare, reported 66,000 public school counselors employed in the spring of 1970.[9]

Secondary school counselors made dramatic gains in number during the 1960s but during the 1970s increases have diminished. Table 2.4 shows the increase in their number and the corollary decrease in counselor-pupil ratios. In Table 2.4, guidance personnel includes school counselors and directors or supervisors of guidance. Since 1970, there has been approximately a 3 percent annual increase in public secondary school counselors.

[9] Stafford Metz et al., *Counselors in Public Schools, Spring 1970* (Washington, D.C.: U.S. Government Printing Office, 1973), p. 1.

TABLE 2.5 **Estimated earned degrees in counseling**

Year	Bachelor's	Master's	Sixth year	Doctorate
1963–1964	45	4,579	75	230
1968–1969	175	9,411	115	401
1973–1974	325	17,507	375	632
1978–1979	1,161	19,000	625	900

SOURCE: Based on *Earned Degrees Conferred* (Washington, D.C.: U.S. Department of Health, Education, and Welfare, annual publication) and Joe W. Hollis and Richard A. Wantz, *Counselor Education Directory—1977* (Muncie, Indiana: Accelerated Development, Inc., 1977).

ommendation by John F. McGowan) that 50 percent of the individuals 22 years of age and younger need counseling, 10 percent of those from 22 to 44, and 25 percent of those aged 45 years and older. Dropouts and the handicapped need even more help.[10] More recently, Erpenbach, based on data provided by state educational agencies, projected that by 1980 some 21,000 more school counselors would be needed than are available in addition to the 23,000 needed to replace those now employed.[11]

An important factor to be borne in mind is that estimates of the need for counselors are based on attaining a ratio of counselors to students that is desired by the profession. Whether schools and communities, individually and collectively, agree with the profession's judgment and try to attain that ratio is seriously open to question. Actual demands (that is, actual job openings) for counselors are often markedly different from demands based on desirable ratios established by professional groups.

Supply

The supply of counselors is most dependent on graduate degree production. For the past ten years, this production has increased by about 1,000 per year. Table 2.5 presents data on

[10] Arthur A. Hitchcock, "Counselors: Supply, Demand and Need," in *Counselor Development in American Society*, ed. John F. McGowan (Washington: U.S. Department of Labor and U.S. Office of Education, June 1965), p. 87.
[11] William J. Erpenbach, "The Case for Guidance: Testimony Before Congress," *Personnel and Guidance Journal*, 51 (February 1973), 551–557.

master's and doctorate degrees awarded in counseling starting in the year 1963–1964.

Factors affecting counselor supply and demand

The fact that many variables interact to influence the supply and demand for counselors makes it difficult if not impossible to gauge the impact of each separately. These factors are identified and discussed in this section.

Counselor preparation

The supply of counselors available obviously depends on how many complete preparation. Approximately 19,000 counselors currently (1978–1979) are prepared annually at the master's degree level by some 453 institutions. We estimate that about 200 to 250 of these institutions have programs adequate to meet the minimally acceptable professional standards of content, staff, and resources.

Attrition

Loss of counselors occurs in four major ways: (1) after preparation some do not enter the field; (2) experienced counselors leave the field because they accept administrative assignments; (3) counselors leave because they become disillusioned, or burned out, and so on; (4) retirements and deaths remove some. Reliable data are not available to document the exact loss for any one of these reasons. The U.S. Office of Education reported a 5 percent attrition rate among individuals who, during the 1960s, completed academic-year NDEA Counseling and Guidance Institutes. But data from institute program participants are probably misleading because nationwide there is a higher loss of counselors who, after completing preparation, do not enter the field. Many counselors report that in their school systems there are individuals who have master's degrees with major concentration in counseling but who have no desire to leave teaching assignments or change employment settings to a counseling position.

Annual attrition among teachers exceeds 10 percent. Estimates of annual attrition among counselors vary from percent for employment service counselors to 9 percent among rehabilitation counselors. The Bureau of Labor Statistics estimates attrition among school counselors at 8–10 percent and that, during the period 1968 to 1980, some 23,000 school counselors will be needed to replace those who die, retire, or leave the field for some reason.

Salaries

The authors believe that many counselors who support families are forced out of counseling and into administrative positions by economic necessity. Some alert school administrators have attempted to remedy this situation by paying counselors increments (from $300 to $900) above teacher salary schedules. Others give extended contracts (eleven or twelve months) rather than the usual academic year contracts (nine or ten months).

Even where salary schedules exist, salaries are affected by supply and demand. When demands for counselors are high, salary is often used to attract competent counselors. Although salary is only one of many factors that bear on recruiting and retaining able people, it is an extremely important one. The prestige attached to a position is also partially a function of salary. According to the 1978–1979 *Occupational Outlook Handbook*, $15,000 was the average annual salary of school counselors in 1976.

Working conditions

In far too many situations, counselors are expected to practice in inadequate physical facilities. Moreover, most counseling staffs (equally true of other school staffs) are not given adequate secretarial and clerical assistance. Finally, counseling—the function for which counselors are presumably employed—is often usurped by quasi-administrative tasks and demands. The net effect of these poor working conditions is to discourage some competent counselors and cause them to seek employment elsewhere.

Current criticisms

This chapter has, it is hoped, enabled the reader to gain a historical and current perspective of counseling, but it is incomplete without an understanding of the persistent and pervasive criticisms leveled against counseling and its practitioners. Locating the criticisms in a particular time period is extremely difficult, simply because most of them represent issues that cannot be satisfactorily resolved or that, if laid to rest at one time, tend to re-emerge at another. Some charges have their roots in fundamental attitudes about the nature of humankind. Others appear to be related to difficulties involved in altering the status quo or introducing innovations. Still others derive from scientifically based thinking or expert judgment within the field of counseling and related disciplines.

The criticisms considered in this section are highly interrelated. They can be separated only for discussion purposes. The knowledgeable critic uses them all, directly or implicitly, in either their outright or disguised forms. The knowledgeable practitioner should be prepared to cope with these charges as well as others in a manner that honors the critic's position yet clearly defends viable alternatives.

First, it can be said that the utility of counseling cannot be demonstrated. It must be recognized at the outset that questioning the efficacy of counseling and other helping relationships is always legitimate. It is a challenge that should be raised not only by critics but equally often by counseling practitioners.

This particular criticism appears to stem from three major sources. One source is that group that is predisposed philosophically to regard the helping of others as inappropriate. Their beliefs require them to view the need for or the provision of personal help as a sign of weakness and character deficiency.

A second source is those who have tried counseling in some form and emerged disgruntled and unsatisfied. The causes of such experience-based beliefs are undoubtedly complex. Certainly contributing to this attitude would be such factors as unrealistic initial expectations, counselor incompetence, and anxiety and defensiveness found among clients who have attempted to modify their life situations and were unable to do so.

A third source, and in some ways the most damning, is the findings of practitioners themselves. In this instance, the question of the utility of counseling is posed by professionals about their own activities in a systematic attempt to evaluate their own and others' results. If the relatively large number of studies of the outcomes of counseling and psychotherapy are taken at face value, the results are discouraging to the practitioner and tend to support the critics. This criticism, the evidence supporting it, and the problems inherent in outcome research will be discussed in greater detail in Chapter 17.

A second criticism is that counseling fosters in its recipients a play-it-safe approach to life. Career counselors, particularly, are sometimes charged with encouraging their clients to enter safe, secure occupations. Often this criticism is coupled with another: that counseling leads to conformity despite its avowed concern with the uniqueness of the individual and that it tends to discourage high-risk ventures. It is sometimes true that activities that involve a gamble, whether economic or personal, may be abandoned when a person examines them carefully. A rational, studied approach often does encourage caution. In addition, the very evidence used by counselors that may dissuade the individual from risking himself or herself often rests on shaky grounds (for example, test results from instruments of doubtful utility). However, the alternative seems to be action by impulse, which may pay high dividends but which may also result in personal disaster.

The position of counseling in regard to this criticism is obvious. Decision making is required and because humankind strives to be rational, choices are best made thoughtfully and with full awareness of all factors involved. In the area of choice making in particular, counselors must realize how their personal values may influence client change. More specifically, the counselor's own needs for safety and security should not be the basis for discouraging clients' aspirations.

The third criticism, closely related to the second, is that counselors deceive themselves and others by talking about freedom of choice but actually practicing a deterministic psychology. Prior experience, early life influences by others, and available opportunities all help determine the current life of the individual. For example, it would seem obvious that a decision to enter a specific school curriculum at a relatively early age automatically limits the choices and opportunities available later on. Life itself is in many ways deterministic, each step affecting the direction of the next one. If, through counseling, individuals are better able to perceive the alternative routes ahead, at least they participate actively in the determinism. The counselor's function is to provide the information about opportunities and to assist clients to gain self-knowledge that permits them to choose

appropriately among alternatives. Obviously, counselors must accept the fact that whether they wish it or not they occupy an influential position in decisions made by those they serve.

A fourth criticism is that counseling does not represent a discipline in and of itself. This charge seems a straw man, and it is applicable to many if not all fields that attempt to assist others. Outside the rarefied atmosphere of academic life, few pure disciplines exist, especially if the term is used to indicate a specific body of knowledge. In most fields practitioners draw heavily on bits and pieces of many disciplines. The counselor's subject matter is humankind and, beyond this, humankind in relation to others and the environment they share. Hence, virtually any knowledge is of value in helping another in his or her struggle to cope with life's problems. Although some kinds of knowledge are undoubtedly more valuable than others, the intent here is to underscore the difficulty of confining counselor preparation to a narrow field that is then labeled a *discipline.* The general area of knowledge encompassed by the behavioral and life sciences represents the base for the preparation of counselors. It includes psychology, sociology, biology, anthropology, economics, and political science.

A fifth criticism, directly related to the previous one, is that counselors are inadequately prepared to perform the tasks assigned them. If, as pointed out above, the domain of counselors is humankind, preparation will always be inadequate. Certainly it must continue beyond the formal preparation period. The whole issue becomes confounded when one considers the variety of personnel and situational demands in the field. As described in Chapter 1, many of the helping professions overlap considerably and at the same time vary in the specificity of tasks from setting to setting. There is little argument about the tasks of school physicians because their activities within the school are clearly defined and limited to specific professional competences. At present the school counselor remains many things to many people and sometimes nothing to some. To level the charge of inadequate preparation without adequate agreement regarding job expectancies seems the height of presumption. If counselors are individuals who counsel (as indicated in Chapter 1), the required preparation for their task seems relatively clear. Unfortunately today's counselor, somewhat like the school's all-purpose room, has a multiplicity of functions but simultaneously is inadequate for any specific activity.

One solution to this paradox lies in a specific definition of role and function within the setting accompanied by increased specialization of personnel where the setting requires diverse kinds of activities.

A sixth criticism is that counseling is extended only to selected subpopulations rather than provided for all. Counselors have been charged with giving preferential attention to such groups as the college bound, crisis situations, and so on. In theory at least, counseling is available to all individuals; undoubtedly in practice it is available to all in only some situations. However, in certain settings it may be quite legitimate to focus attention on specific subgroups. For example, potential dropouts may become a focal point if the need is great and if the individuals responsible have the integrity to admit and defend restricted delivery of services. It should be kept in mind that restricting services to a specific group must be based on a thorough demonstration of need and should be subject to continuous review.

A seventh criticism is that counseling practitioners pamper their clients. The counselor who exhibits warmth and understanding is sometimes called soft and overindulgent. Acceptance of the individual is interpreted as sanctioning any form of behavior. This criticism usually comes from people who find it difficult to separate the individual from his or her actions. Most counselors not only are predisposed to believe, but during training are thoroughly steeped in, the credo that the individual's worth is independent of actions and behavior. To label this basic attitude toward human beings mollycoddling is to question the integrity of a group whose ultimate goal is to assist the individual to cope constructively rather than destructively with problems. Unquestionably the counselor is less concerned with a specific behavioral act than with the motivation behind it and its potentially harmful consequences to the individual and ultimately to society. No counselor need feel constrained to apologize for acceptance of the worth of an individual.

An eighth criticism is that counseling is an unwarranted invasion of privacy. The right to privacy—exemption of one's intimate affairs, characteristics, books, papers from the scrutiny of others—is fundamental. This kind of criticism assumes that individuals can have counseling imposed on them, an extremely unlikely circumstance. It is questionable that any counselor can successfully exceed the limitations set by the counselee in the relationship. Even if the counselee does not seek assistance voluntarily, in reality he or she controls the content of and places restraints on the interaction. Even in the most extreme example, where the client is very young, naïve, or psychologically highly vulnerable, built-in safeguards exist in codes of ethics and institutional checks that make it difficult for a counselor to engage in a "seduction of the innocent." All counselors have a primary obligation to respect the integrity of those with whom they work.

Finally, counseling practitioners are criticized for overreliance on professional jargon in their communications with others. The implication here is that a jingoistic double talk based on pseudopsychometric, pseudo-Freudian terminology serves as a smoke screen that counselors use to confuse and control others. To some degree every profession creates its own technical language. However, the use (or misuse) of such terminology with those who are unfamiliar with it fosters misunderstanding and negative reactions. By its very nature, technical language is intended as a shorthand permitting economical communication among those conversant with it. The very fact that it is a professional shorthand makes it unsuitable and confusing for use with outsiders. The true professional seeks to communicate in precise, understandable terms. For counselors to do otherwise creates misunderstanding, and because of misunderstanding they risk the brand *charlatan* in its clearest sense—"one who pretends to knowledge."

These criticisms frequently have a devastating effect on counselors in preparation, particularly if in discussing them one admits that they have some validity. Recognition of such problems is essential in preparing for many fields of endeavor. The idealized image of an occupation is seldom accurate. No occupation can discharge all of its obligations to the satisfaction of everyone. Without doubt, to some degree all occupational groups perform on faith tempered with the hope of resolving glaring deficiencies.

Criticism is useful in encouraging examination of what is known and what is not known in the field. Too many counselors cannot bring themselves to believe that any criticism is honestly motivated. Correction of shoddy practices and shallow thinking is an ever-present responsibility of the professional counselor. It is to be hoped that criticism, both from within and without the field, leads to an examined professional life and eventually stimulates improvement in counseling practices.

Issues

Issue 1 The term *guidance* should be abandoned.

No, because
1. The term accurately describes certain noninstructional activities that must be performed in any school.
2. The term conveys appropriately the notion that many individuals are involved in helping students.
3. The term has historic worth, and its use places in perspective the role of the counselor within the educational setting.
4. A better, more acceptable term cannot be found to replace it.

Yes, because
1. The term is meaningless, vague, and ambiguous especially when applied directly to the work of the counselor.
2. The concepts most called to mind by the term are those of direction, authoritarianism, and paternalism, which are in direct opposition to what counselors attempt to do.

Discussion As C. Gilbert Wrenn and others have suggested, *guidance* is an outmoded term meaning various things to different people and possibly never accurately describing what is done. Laymen tend to think of guidance as "steering" and "directing" students while practitioners view it broadly as an entire complex of services designed to help students become what they are capable of becoming. Perhaps the very fact that we can never reconcile the two divergent views call for abandonment of the term.

Social psychologists, in an effort to highlight the interdependence of language and environment, point out that the Eskimo vocabulary contains numerous words for snow, in all its forms, and very few words for earth. In contrast, our vocabulary has many highly descriptive words for earth in all its forms and relatively few for snow. Clearly, both in their diversity and in their specificity, vocabularies incorporate that which is important to people. As it now stands, *guidance* is most commonly used to refer to a set of services; its practitioners, by hook or crook, bear a title, *counselor*, that derives from only one of these services. We face a curious semantic dilemma in using the term *guidance*. It no longer has any logical relationship to what its practitioners do, if indeed it ever did. It is devoid of the specificity re-

quired for what counselors mean when they use it now. If its usage were restricted to the actual meaning of the word, those practicing guidance should be called guides, not counselors. They then properly could perform guidance. However, no self-respecting counselor would agree to the title *guide* because it implies activities inimical to counseling.

While educators *usually* are aware of what they mean by guidance, they have never quite been able to explain the term adequately to the public. The school's boiler tender may refer to himself or herself as an "engineer," but any parent who asks what is actually done immediately knows that the person is not a professional engineer but tends the furnace. The parent who is told by a member of the school staff that he or she is a "school counselor" and asks what this means receives an answer that can only confuse. Frequently this answer includes little, if any, reference to actual counseling with students. It is usually a listing of many activities that better describe the several services comprising the entire guidance program. Perhaps concern with this issue will dissipate when school counselors counsel and supporting guidance services are assigned to subprofessionals. But one thing is evident: we need to eliminate vague language and move to a term more clearly descriptive of what counselors do that is understandable and acceptable to laymen and professionals alike.

Issue 2 Should professional journals stress theory and research or application and practice?

Application should be stressed, because
1. Counseling practitioners do not possess the research skills to assimilate much of the technical research material that is published in professional journals.
2. Most working counselors tend to take a practical "how and what to do" approach to their work.

Theory and research should be stressed, because
1. The problem of consumer inability to assimilate published material stems from inadequate preparation and does not reflect upon the appropriateness of journal content, since advances in the field depend on competent research.
2. Application depends on soundly conceived theory and research. It is common sense that "how and what to do" must stem from a thorough understanding of why things are done.
3. Journals can publish only what is contributed. Editorial

boards have relatively little power except that inherent in the obligation to select the best from among the contributions submitted for publication.

Discussion Many practicing counselors have long claimed that the professional journals do not reflect their interests or contain what they need to improve their functioning. They complain that journals exist to serve professors who must publish or perish. Seemingly, they want articles that will provide them with specific direction in particular situations. These same people tend to overlook the lack of realism involved in prescribing general solutions for specific settings. Indeed, they appear to overlook their own obligation to draw conclusions and implications for their own setting from that which does appear in the literature. All journals clearly state their publication policy, which provides consumers with information concerning the kind of content available. They must then translate it to their own situation and needs.

Issue 3 Should school counselors be paid higher salaries than teachers with comparable preparation and experience?

Yes, because
1. Compared to teachers, the responsibility of counselors is greater and their task more complex and more difficult because they are concerned with individual personal development.
2. The counselor's day is longer because evenings are spent in counseling with students, parent conferences, research, and the like.
3. The counselor has to deal with a wide-ranging public and is more exposed to public pressures.

No, because
1. The degree of difference in responsibility is not demonstrable.
2. The teacher's day is similarly extended through grading homework and tests, the supervision of student activities, and so on.
3. There is no function in the school more important than teaching.

Discussion Some counselors are currently paid salary increments above those received by classroom teachers with equivalent training and experience in their field of speciali-

zation. However, the additional pay often results from an extension of contract time with some pre– and post–school year responsibilities. Payment of increments without extended employment is frequently due to supply and demand considerations rather than the weight of the arguments cited above.

Given equivalent preparation, for example, currently a master's degree, there seems little to support a pay difference for counselors unless an extended work period is involved. Undoubtedly, the practice of rewarding experience and extensive training will continue to prevail, as will the necessity to entice specialized personnel financially.

Annotated references

Hansen, Donald A., ed. *Explorations in Sociology and Counseling.* Boston: Houghton Mifflin Company, 1968. 456 pp.

This book presents an interesting view of counseling by professionals outside the field. A series of fifteen essays by sociologists is provided that examines counseling within its social context.

Pietrofesa, John J., Alan Hoffman, Howard H. Splete, and Diana V. Pinto. *Counseling: Theory, Research, and Practice.* Chicago: Rand McNally, 1978. 449 pp.

Chapter 1 (pp. 2–27) describes the meaning, history, and current status of counseling. Significant influences, people, and events are explained. Types of counseling are identified.

Van Hoose, William H., and John J. Pietrofesa, eds. *Counseling and Guidance in the Twentieth Century.* Boston: Houghton Mifflin Company, 1970. 346 pp.

The book provides a sampling of leaders active in the counseling field. The twenty-two individuals provide an autobiographical sketch, some ideas about counseling, its past and present, and a list of their publications.

Further references

Aubrey, Roger. "Historical Development of Guidance and Counseling and Implications for the Future," *Personnel and Guidance Journal,* 55 (February 1977), 288–295.

Dooley, David, Carol K. Whalen, and John V. Flowers. "Verbal Response Styles of Children and Adolescents in a Counseling Analog Setting: Effects of Age, Sex, and Liking," *Journal of Counseling Psychology*, 25 (March 1978), 85–95.

Frey, David H. "Science and the Single Case in Counseling Research," *Personnel and Guidance Journal*, 56 (January 1978), 263–268.

Gerler, Edwin R. "New Directions for School Counseling," *The School Counselor*, 23 (March 1976), 247–251.

Humes, Charles W., II. "School Counselors and PL 94–142," *The School Counselor*, 25 (January 1978), 192–195.

Kunze, Karl R. "Business and Industry Look Out for Their Own," *Personnel and Guidance Journal*, 52 (November 1973), 145–150.

McClelland, David C. "Managing Motivation to Expand Human Freedom," *American Psychologist*, 33 (March 1978), 201–210.

Miller, Jane W., and Ann W. Engin. "Tomorrow's Counselor: Competent or Unemployed?," *Personnel and Guidance Journal*, 54 (January 1976), 262–267.

Sinick, Daniel. "Rehabilitation Counselors on the Move," *Personnel and Guidance Journal*, 52 (November 1973), 167–170.

Walsh, William M. "Classics in Guidance and Counseling," *Personnel and Guidance Journal*, 54 (December 1975), 218–221.

Walz, Garry, and Libby Benjamin. "A Change Agent Strategy for Counselors Functioning As Consultants," *Personnel and Guidance Journal*, 56 (February 1978), 331–334.

Zultowski, Walter H., Richard D. Arvey, and H. Dudley Dewhirst. "Moderating Effects of Organizational Climate on Relationships Between Goal-Setting Attributes and Employee Satisfaction," *Journal of Vocational Behavior*, 12 (April 1978), 208–216.

3 The counselee: developmental characteristics and concerns

Counseling requires that two individuals attempt to verbalize intellectually that which for both lies at emotional and existential levels. Acceptance of this view of counseling presents a dilemma to the participants and complicates description by those who seek to write about it. As noted at the outset of this book, counselors approach the situation committed to providing a helping relationship. Counselees approach the situation, usually in a highly vulnerable state, seeking assistance. Yet they do so in a way that will permit them to salvage their own self-esteem and personal integrity.

Each participant seeks to communicate with the other. The counselor's efforts are directed primarily toward providing acceptance, understanding, and freedom in order to facilitate communication. The client, although probably not using the same labels, is looking for these conditions because they are necessary to the clarification, understanding, and solution of his or her own concerns. Clients present themselves as they perceive themselves to be or as they would like to be perceived. Although it is sometimes difficult to maintain, this is the only productive view of the situation counselors can permit themselves.

Regardless of what clients initially submit, they are trying to tell the counselor what troubles them. Often clients attempt to do this through what appear to counselors to be disconnected examples. In fact, however, they typify a recurring concern or a core problem that manifests itself in diverse, seemingly unrelated areas. In an eagerness to secure help, the client may assault the counselor with a multitude of facts and descriptions that for him or her clearly illustrate a basic concern but that often confuse and sometimes exasperate the counselor. Counselees would like to do simultaneously all the things individuals do in interpersonal situations: present themselves favorably, respond intelligently, stay in control of themselves and the situation, and so on. Yet the counselee must also say "I need help" in a way that will "purchase" assistance while maintaining self-respect.

All of this, and more, counselors must accept as part of the human condition the counselee brings to the setting.

Once having done so, they may for their own convenience apply to the counseling interaction some objective criteria in order to make sense of what is happening. It is essential that an understanding of the basic human condition precede the application of intellectual efforts to describe and understand the individual who seeks help.

Developmental characteristics of counselees

The social sciences, especially psychology and sociology, provide the counseling practitioner with a variety of ways of thinking about clients. Some, if not most, of the tools from the social sciences are descriptive rather than explanatory. Definitive answers are seldom available, but normative data and cultural expectancies can often be illustrated graphically. Some of the major conceptions of the life cycle have been presented here.

Developmental tasks

Havighurst[1] presents the sequence of human development as tasks to be mastered within a sociopsychological framework that remains particularly attractive to counselors in educational settings. Havighurst explains that developmental tasks are the learnings individuals must acquire if they are to be judged and to judge themselves reasonably happy, successful persons. He defines a *developmental task* as "a task which arises at or about a certain period in the life of the individual, successful achievement of which leads to happiness and to success with later tasks, while failure leads to unhappiness in the individual, disapproval by the society and difficulty with later tasks."[2] Essentially, Havighurst is pointing out that developmental tasks, like biological

[1] Robert J. Havighurst, *Human Development and Education* (New York: David McKay Company, 1953).
[2] Ibid., p. 2.

growth, follow a pattern and build on each other. They are partly biologically, partly culturally, and partly psychologically determined. For instance, an infant must follow the sequence of learning to creep-stand-walk, then advance to talking before progressing to reading and childhood games. Accomplishment of these tasks at appropriate ages permits and fosters movement to adolescence and subsequently to adulthood.

The age at which a specific developmental task is learned varies among cultures and among social classes within cultures. For example, cultures differ in their timing and methods of toilet training. Toilet training in American culture, compared to others, tends to be early and severe. Middle-class parents handle it differently from the way lower-class parents do. Some tasks, such as dating, are found only within certain cultures.

Havighurst points out that development is continuous and that there is no abrupt or marked change at a given period in time. Further, developmental tasks change within a culture from time to time; for example, marriage now occurs at a later age than it did two decades ago. Finally, each developmental task can be broken down into units or smaller tasks.

The developmental tasks of middle childhood (ages 6 to 11) are associated with pushing out of the home into the world of school and playmates, of pushing into a life of games and work, and of expanding into the realm of adult concepts and symbols. Elementary school counselors can view their clients as to whether they are on schedule, coping with six developmental tasks, including (1) learning physical skills necessary for ordinary games; (2) learning appropriate masculine or feminine social roles; (3) acquiring a social personality; (4) learning the 3 R's; (5) developing conscience, morality, and a scale of values; and (6) achieving personal independence. Among the ten developmental tasks set forth for adolescence (ages 12 to 18) by Havighurst were those of achieving a masculine or feminine social role, accepting one's physique and using the body effectively, and selecting and preparing for an occupation. Among the eight developmental tasks established for early adulthood (ages 19 to 30) were selecting a mate, starting a family, and getting started in an occupation. These developmental tasks, expected of its members by the culture at particular ages, have been analyzed and sorted by Havighurst according to their biological, psychological, and cultural bases. The tasks fit together in a pattern, with growth being continuous. Experience and successful accomplishment of one task pave the way for achievement of later tasks.

Cronbach has summarized in tabular form some of the major tasks of adolescence and some of the conditions affecting their development.[3] His tabular description is presented here as Table 3.1.

Examining Table 3.1 reveals that tasks are related to certain fundamental psychological and social needs and involve ways of discovering means for satisfying them. Cronbach's placement of the tasks within a need theory context is a convenient way of analyzing behavior and personality. The need theory is that of Abraham H. Maslow[4] who identified basic human needs and arranged them in a hierarchy from the most basic and biological to the most advanced and socialized (see Table 3.2).

Maslow's scale of human needs has met with wide acceptance. Maslow's point is that a person's behavior is directed first to satisfying the basic needs. As these basic needs are satisfied, then the individual can direct his or her behavior to higher order needs. As presented in Table 3.2, feelings, situations, and behavior identified with the various levels of needs grow more complex from the first to the fifth level. Upper-level needs and tasks are more likely to involve behavior that is abstract or symbolic. The point of this is simple to state but difficult to implement: counselors who can discern the physiological or psychological needs directing client behaviors can help them find appropriate ways of satisfying these needs.

Stages of identity crises

Erikson[5] has outlined a sequence of psychosocial development. While each phase is described in terms of the extremes of successful and unsuccessful solutions that can be arrived at within it, generally the outcome is a balance between these polarities.

[3] Lee J. Cronbach, *Educational Psychology*, 3rd ed. (New York: Harcourt Brace Jovanovich, 1977), pp. 180–181.

[4] Abraham H. Maslow, *Motivation and Personality*, 2nd ed. (New York: Harper & Row, 1970).

[5] Erik H. Erikson, *Identity: Youth and Crisis* (New York: W. W. Norton and Company, 1968).

TABLE 3.1 **Developmental tasks from infancy to adulthood in the United States**

Age (years)	Physical landmarks	Characterization	Need for affection
0–1½ (Infancy)	Creeps by age 1	Dependent; learns to interpret sensory impressions	Establish feeding schedule, weaning; develop confidence in adult care
2–4 (Early childhood)	Walks and talks by age 2	Energetic play; social regulation imposed with or without understanding	Accept newborn brother or sister; form secure identification with like-sex parent
5–9 (Early schooling)		Adapts to organization; develops tool skills; evaluates self comparatively	
10–11 (Middle childhood)		Stable group activities; projects extending over longer periods	
12–15 (Early adolescence)	Puberty: Girls 10–14, Boys 12–16	Reasons systematically; dating begins; increased sense of unique personality, planning for future	
16–23 (Youth)		Direct preparation for work; sexual intimacy; tension between youth culture and adult expectation	Form close comradeship with member(s) of opposite sex; attain sex adjustment
24–28 (Transition)		Establishes own home; settles into career path	Devote self to infant (women, sometimes men)

SOURCE: From *Educational Psychology*, Third Edition, by Lee J. Cronbach, copyright © 1977 by Harcourt Brace Jovanovich, Inc. Reprinted by permission of the publisher.

Erikson has elaborated on his ideas of how the healthy individual emerges from inner and outer conflicts with an increased sense of inner unity, good judgment, and capacity to do well. A fundamental premise underlying his description of growth is the *epigenetic principle.* Fundamentally, this states that "anything that grows has a *ground plan*, and that out of this ground plan the *parts* arise, each part having its *time* of special ascendancy until all parts have arisen to form a *functioning whole*."[6] Personality develops according to steps predetermined in the individual's readiness; each item of personality is systematically related to all others, and all depend on the proper development in the proper sequence.

The individual's encounter with the environment conveys particular ideas and concepts that contribute to character, efficiency, and health. Erikson describes each encounter with its resulting crisis for each stage of development. A *crisis* exists "because incipient growth and awareness in a new part function together with a shift in instinctual energy and yet also cause specific vulnerability in that part."[7] Successive steps constitute potential crises because of changes in the individual's perspective.

It should be noted that his use of the word *crisis* is not in the sense of impending catastrophe. Rather, it designates "a necessary turning point, a crucial moment, when development must move one way or another, marshaling resources of growth, recovery, and further differentiation."[8]

Erikson's concept of *mutuality* specifies that the crucial coordination is between the individual and the social environment and that this coordination is mutually determined. Care-taking persons (for example, parents) are coordinated to the developing individual by their specific responsiveness to the individual's needs and, in turn, by phase needs of their own.

[6] Ibid., p. 92.

[7] Ibid., p. 95.
[8] Ibid., p. 16.

TABLE 3.1 **Developmental tasks from infancy to adulthood in the United States** *(cont.)*

Age (years)	Need for secure relation with authority	Need for approval by peers	Need for autonomy	Need for competence and self-respect
0–1½ (Infancy)				Master objects within reach; gain eye-hand coordination
2–4 (Early childhood)	Accept rules, schedules, denial of wishes; begin to understand principles behind regulations	Develop social skills: share, take turns, inhibit aggression; learn property rights	Accept separation from parent; express own desires via requests; successfully make demands on others	Accept and meet parental performance standards; successfully make demands on environment
5–9 (Early schooling)	Accept rules and procedures; control emotions; understand rights of others; accept teacher as model and guide	Care for own appearance; win acceptance in school group; develop play skills		Succeed in schoolwork; master physical skills for games; accept own physical characteristics, aptitude for school
10–11 (Middle childhood)	Make effort toward school achievement	Learn style respected by own-sex peers; accept group code; learn to compete within the code	Carry on tasks without supervision; enjoy own industriousness; accept some conflict with authority	Develop interests; find means of earning pocket money
12–15 (Early adolescence)	Accept more impersonal direction in departmentalized school; hold self to schedule	Gain acceptance from opposite sex; acquire new sex-appropriate skills and styles	Find satisfaction in nonfamily recreations; search for own views on basic issues	Accept own body, role of own sex; accept own abilities and talents; settle on some interests that define one's individuality
16–23 (Youth)	Carry out tasks assigned in general terms		Take responsibility for car, job; take stands on political matters; make decisions despite parental opposition	Find general vocational direction and demonstrate ability; develop vocational skill; find part-time job
24–28 (Transition)	Apply standards set by authority to own work with minimal supervision		Plan with mate	Establish self securely in job

Erikson uses the concept *identity* to refer to "a persistent sameness within oneself (selfsameness) and a persistent sharing of some kind of essential character with others."[9] He further explains that identity has a number of connotations:

At one time, then, it will appear to refer to a conscious sense of *individual identity*; at another to an unconscious striving for a *continuity of personal character*; at a third, as a criterion for the silent doings of *ego synthesis*; and, finally, as a maintenance of an inner *solidarity* with a group's ideals and identity.[10]

[9] Erik H. Erikson, "Identity and the Life Cycle," *Psychological Issues*, Monograph 1, vol. 1 (1959), 102.

[10] Ibid., p. 102.

TABLE 3.2 **A system of behavior based on Abraham H. Maslow's basic needs**

Basic needs	Characteristics	Results of threat to basic needs
Self-actualization (express oneself, be creative, etc.)	Relatively complex and other centered	Anxiety
Self-esteem (prestige, status, etc.)		
Love needs (companionship, affection)		
Safety needs (housing, warmth)		
Physiological needs (hunger, thirst)	Relatively simple and individual centered	Fear and anger

A sense of identity—that this is the real me—is described by Erikson as a process "located" in the core of each person and in the core of his or her communal culture. A person's identity is formed by a

> process of simultaneous reflection and observation, a process taking place on all levels of mental functioning, by which the individual judges himself in the light of what he perceives to be the way in which others judge him in comparison to themselves and to a typology significant to them; while he judges their way of judging him in the light of how he perceives himself in comparison to them and to types that have become relevant to him. This process is, luckily, and necessarily, for the most part unconscious except where inner conditions and outer circumstances combine to aggravate a painful, or elated, "identity consciousness."[11]

Erikson identifies and describes the ego qualities that emerge during critical periods of development. These are briefly sketched here from his portrayal of the eight stages of development.[12]

BASIC TRUST VERSUS BASIC MISTRUST The first component is an attitude toward oneself and the world derived principally from the experiences of the first year of life. *Basic* means that it is not especially conscious, but a sense of it pervades the individual. *Trust* implies that one learns to rely on sameness and continuity of others and simultaneously learns to trust oneself. Parents create a sense of trust or confidence by their sensitive ministrations to their infants' needs. Trust forms the basis for a sense of identity, of feeling all right, of being oneself, of becoming what other people trust one will become.

AUTONOMY VERSUS SHAME AND DOUBT Muscular maturation sets the stage for the individual's experimentation with holding on and letting go, for example, bladder and bowel elimination. Conflict within these modalities leads to either hostile or benign expectations and attitudes. Outer controls on the infant should be firmly reassuring during this stage. The environment must be such as to encourage the child to "stand on one's own," yet protect the child from meaningless experiences of shame and early doubt. Too much shaming leads to a secret determination to try to get away from things and to doubt. The sense of autonomy is fostered from a sense of self-control without loss of self-esteem. In short, during the second and third years the healthy individual acquires a sense of his or her own individual existence and the power of decision.

INITIATIVE VERSUS GUILT The child of 4 or 5 years old is faced with the next step and next crisis: finding out what kind of person he or she is going to be. Erikson cites three strong developments that help at this stage: (1) the child learns to move around more freely and therefore establishes a wider radius of goals; (2) the child's sense of language becomes perfected to the point where he or she understands and can ask about many things; and (3) language and locomotion permit the child to expand his or her imagination over so many things that the child cannot avoid frightening himself or herself with what has been dreamed.[13] The individual emerges from this stage with a sense of initiative (or motion into the future) or a sense of guilt.

The child is now developing the prerequisites for masculine and feminine initiative, that is, the selection of social

[11] Erikson, *Identity: Youth and Crisis*, pp. 22–23.
[12] Ibid., pp. 91–141.

[13] Ibid., p. 115.

goals and perseverance in approaching them. However, secret fantasies may result in a deep sense of guilt. The child may feel guilty for mere thoughts and for deeds that no one has seen or knows about. Conscience, the governor of initiative, becomes established.

INDUSTRY VERSUS INFERIORITY Erikson has characterized this stage as "I am what I learn." The individual develops a sense of industry by adjusting to the inorganic laws of the tool world. The individual's aim is to bring a productive situation to completion. Through some form of systematic instruction the individual learns the fundamentals of technology. Danger lies in outer and inner hindrances to the use of new capacities, which leads to despair, discouragement, and feelings of inadequacy and inferiority. This is a decisive stage because industry involves doing things beside and with others. The child experiences the first sense of division of labor and of equality of opportunity.

IDENTITY VERSUS ROLE CONFUSION Puberty brings a questioning of the sameness and continuities relied on at earlier stages. Faced with a physiological revolution within themselves, youth are concerned with what they appear to be in the eyes of others as compared to what they feel they are. *Role confusion*, or the inability to fix on the kind of person one wants to be, is the danger of this stage. It may derive from previous doubt as to sexual identity or it may be based on the inability to settle on an occupational identity. Falling in love may be an attempt to arrive at a definition of identity by projecting one's diffused ego image on another and seeing it reflected and gradually clarified.

INTIMACY VERSUS ISOLATION The successful search for identity leads to a willingness to fuse with others. The individual is ready for intimacy, ready to commit to affiliations and partnerships. Close affiliations, friendships, sexual union—all call for commitments, sacrifices, and compromises. Avoidance of such experiences because of fear of ego loss may lead to a sense of isolation and self-absorption. The counterpart of intimacy, according to Erikson, is distantiation or the repudiation or isolation of forces and people believed to be inimical to oneself.

GENERATIVITY VERSUS STAGNATION The concern in this stage is in establishing and guiding the next generation.

Generativity incorporates productivity and creativity and may be applied not just to offspring but to altruistic concerns. Regression from generativity may lead to pseudointimacy with a pervading sense of stagnation and interpersonal impoverishment.

INTEGRITY VERSUS DESPAIR The final stage is characterized by belief in oneself and one's particular life cycle. Integrity is the belief in the value or goodness of one's contributions to humankind. Loss of integrity is signified by despair, by fear of death, by displeasure with particular institutions and people (allied with the individual's contempt of self).

Erikson's diagram of the life cycle is presented here as Figure 3.1. The diagonal represents the normative sequence of psychosocial gains. The squares of the diagonal signify progression through time of a differentiation of parts and indicates that each item is systematically related to all others. Each item exists in some form before its crucial time normally arrives.

Adult developmental tasks

The last few years have marked the emergence of increased attention to developmental tasks engaged in during adulthood. It should not be overlooked that the developmental sequences formulated by both Havighurst and Erikson set forth certain experiences to be coped with throughout the life cycle, not just during adolescence. Undoubtedly, however, increasing interest, at both the popular and research levels, in older Americans has produced statements about behavioral patterns beyond adolescence, the crises associated with early, middle, and later life. Sheehy's best-selling volume[14] presents some 115 case studies of adults coping with life tasks during their 20s, 30s, and 40s and illustrates the intensity of current public interest in adult growth, shifts, and changes. At another level, Levinson,[15] based on intensive, long-term data collection of the life experiences of forty selected men (ten executives, ten biologists, ten

[14] Gail Sheehy, *Passages* (New York: E. P. Dutton & Company, 1976).
[15] Daniel J. Levinson, *The Seasons of a Man's Life* (New York: Alfred A. Knopf, 1978).

FIGURE 3.1 **Erikson's stages of man**

	1.	2.	3.	4.	5.	6.	7.	8.
1. INFANCY	Trust vs. Mistrust				Mutual recognition vs. Autistic isolation			
2. EARLY CHILDHOOD		Autonomy vs. Shame, Doubt			Will to be oneself vs. Self-doubt			
3. PLAY AGE			Initiative vs. Guilt		Anticipation of roles vs. Role inhibition			
4. SCHOOL AGE				Industry vs. Inferiority	Task identification vs. Sense of futility			
5. ADOLESCENCE	Time perspective vs. Time confusion	Self-certainty vs. Self-consciousness	Role experimentation vs. Role fixation	Apprenticeship vs. Work paralysis	Identity vs. Identity confusion	Sexual polarization vs. Bisexual confusion	Leader commitment vs. Authority confusion	Ideological commitment vs. Confusion of values
6. YOUNG ADULT					Solidarity vs. Social isolation	Intimacy vs. Isolation		
7. ADULTHOOD							Generativity vs. Stagnation	
8. MATURE AGE								Integrity vs. Despair

SOURCE: Reproduced from ''Identity and the Life Cycle,'' from *Psychological Issues*, Vol. I, No. 1, with the permission of W. W. Norton & Company, Inc. Copyright © 1959 by International Universities Press.

FIGURE 3.2 **Developmental periods in early and middle adulthood**

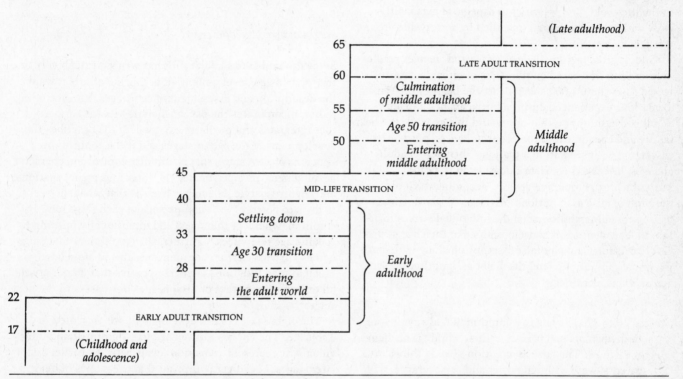

SOURCE: Reprinted from *The Seasons of a Man's Life* by Daniel J. Levinson. By permission of Alfred A. Knopf, Inc. Copyright © 1978 by Alfred A. Knopf, Inc.

factory workers, ten novelists) mapped the developmental tasks starting with early adult (ages 17 to 22) through mid-life (ages 40 to 45) to the age 50 transition (ages 50 to 55) and beyond. Each stage was described in terms of its typical danger and stress points, ambitions, dreams, successes, and failures. Figure 3.2 depicts the markings of the male life cycle by Levinson.

The male life cycle depicted in Figure 3.2 evolves through a sequence of eras, each lasting roughly twenty-five years. Each period or era overlaps another with a new one beginning as a previous one ends. The sequence is as follows: childhood and adolescence (ages 0 to 22); early adulthood (ages 17 to 45); middle adulthood (ages 40 to 65); late adulthood (age 60 and on).

Levinson has identified and described three sets of developmental tasks that must be coped with during adult-

hood.[16] The first set of tasks is to build, modify, and enhance the life structure within the periods of each era depicted in Figure 3.2. The second set of tasks is composed of forming and modifying single components of the life structure. Five such components discussed by Levinson were particularly important. These included (1) forming and modifying a dream, creating a structure in which the dream can be lived out and attaining goals to fulfill the dream; (2) forming and modifying an occupation; (3) forming love-marriage-family relationships; (4) initiating, forming, and terminating mentoring relationships; (5) forming mutual relationships (friendships are rare; amicable relationships are more likely). The third set of tasks is associated with becoming more individuated and involves reintegrating basic polarities

[16] Ibid., pp. 330–336.

of young-old, destruction-creation, masculine-feminine, attachment-separateness in ways appropriate to a new place in the life cycle. The polarities or aspects of personality exist within the self but are modified by society and are worked on over time.

Gould,[17] too, has detailed the crises and changes predictable in adult life, based on five years of research data collected from some 1,000 subjects. At the heart of the transformations experienced during adult years lies a major childhood assumption that one would live an adult life near family and friends. *Childhood consciousness*, particularly associated with separation situations, intrudes on adult changes, because it coexists alongside one's rational, adult view of reality. Protective devices, according to Gould, in the form of false assumptions are triggered to overcome feelings of vulnerability when the individual strives to attain independent adult consciousness. For each age period, Gould sets forth a major false assumption along with component assumptions. Here, the major assumption of each age period is identified:

Ages 16 to 22. The false assumption "I'll always belong to my parents and believe in their world" is challenged.
Ages 22 to 28. The false assumption "Doing things my parents' way, with willpower and perseverance, will bring results. But if I become too frustrated, confused or tired or am simply unable to cope, they will step in and show me the right way" is challenged.
Ages 28 to 34. The false assumption "Life is simple and controllable. There are no significant coexisting contradictory forces within me" is challenged.
Ages 35 to 45. The false assumption "There is no evil or death in the world. The sinister has been destroyed" is challenged.
Ages 45 on. The false assumptions fall away and a directness finally prevails; the challenge is to own oneself.

Finally, Gould points out that individual growth has an effect on and is affected by marriage, career, social change, and the women's liberation movement. The transformations experienced during adulthood occur within a changing structure of behavioral patterns and values and produce both discomfort and satisfactions.

Stages of ego development

Since the mid 1960s Loevinger[18] has written extensively on the topic of ego development, directing her efforts toward the description and assessment of ego stages. Ego, according to her, incorporates the psychoanalytic view as a process that integrates and mediates experience. She describes the development of the ego in stages and the accompanying concerns of each stage; that is, impulse control and character development, interpersonal style, conscious preoccupations, and cognitive style. Loevinger stresses that what she seeks to do is to portray ". . . what persons of each stage have in common, whatever their age" and intentionally minimizes specific age references.[19] Further, she emphasizes that stage names are derived from common speech and are related to broad human functions or characteristics that do not arise at all once within a stage or disappear as one passes to the next stage.

The eight stages of ego development are presented in Table 3.3. The entries Conscientious-Conformist and Individualistic represent transition levels between earlier and later stages. Loevinger points out that the names of her stages are meant to delineate characteristics at a maximum during that stage but nothing less than a total pattern defines a stage.[20] Some remarks about each stage drawn from Loevinger's work follow.

PRESOCIAL STAGE This stage can be viewed as one before the ego or self has come into being because at birth the child cannot be said to have an ego. The first task is to learn to differentiate self from surroundings.

SYMBIOTIC STAGE Interpersonal style is symbiotic and inextricably bound with the existence of those who care for the child. Consciousness is focused on differentiating self from the rest of reality. Only as the child emerges from this stage does he or she differentiate self from nonself and begin to consolidate the ego.

[17] Abstracted from Roger L. Gould, *Transformations* (New York: Simon & Schuster, 1978).
[18] Jane Loevinger, *Ego Development* (San Francisco: Jossey-Bass, 1976).
[19] Ibid., p. 14.
[20] Ibid., p. 15.

TABLE 3.3 **Some milestones of ego development**

Stage	Code	Impulse control, character development	Interpersonal style	Conscious preoccupations	Cognitive style
Presocial			Autistic		
Symbiotic	I-1		Symbiotic	Self vs. non-self	
Impulsive	I-2	Impulsive, fear of retaliation	Receiving, dependent, exploitative	Bodily feelings, especially sexual and aggressive	Stereotyping, conceptual confusion
Self-Protective	△	Fear of being caught, externalizing blame, opportunistic	Wary, manipulative, exploitative	Self-protection, trouble, wishes, things, advantage, control	
Conformist	I-3	Conformity to external rules, shame, guilt for breaking rules	Belonging, superficial niceness	Appearance, social acceptability, banal feelings, behavior	Conceptual simplicity, stereotypes, clichés
Conscientious-Conformist	I-3/4	Differentiation of norms, goals	Aware of self in relation to group, helping	Adjustment, problems, reasons, opportunities (vague)	Multiplicity
Conscientious	I-4	Self-evaluated standards, self-criticism, guilt for consequences, long-term goals and ideals	Intensive, responsible, mutual, concern for communication	Differentiated feelings, motives for behavior, self-respect, achievements, traits, expression	Conceptual complexity, idea of patterning
Individualistic	I-4/5	*Add:* Respect for individuality	*Add:* Dependence as an emotional problem	*Add:* Development, social problems, differentiation of inner life from outer	*Add:* Distinction of process and outcome
Autonomous	I-5	*Add:* Coping with conflicting inner needs, toleration	*Add:* Respect for autonomy, interdependence	Vividly conveyed feelings, integration of physiological and psychological, psychological causation of behavior, role conception, self-fulfillment, self in social context	Increased conceptual complexity, complex patterns, toleration for ambiguity, broad scope, objectivity
Integrated	I-6	*Add:* Reconciling inner conflicts, renunciation of unattainable	*Add:* Cherishing of individuality	*Add:* Identity	

NOTE: "Add" means in addition to the description applying to the previous level.
SOURCE: From *Ego Development* by Jane Loevinger, copyright 1976, by Jossey-Bass, Inc., Publishers, and reproduced with their permission.

IMPULSIVE STAGE Affirmation of a separate identity occurs through the child's impulses. Self-assertions, especially those of a negativistic character, are initially curbed by restraint and later through reward and punishment. Others are both viewed and prized according to what they can provide the child. The child's energies and interests tend to focus on impulses, especially sexual and aggressive impulses appropriate to the age. The sense of time is present oriented and there is little if any sense of psychological causation. Cognitive style is conceptually confused. Motive, cause, and logical justification are confounded.

SELF-PROTECTIVE STAGE The developing ego begins to take on ideas of blame and conceptions of right and wrong. Although conceptions of blame are acquired during this stage, they are conceived of as external; that is, due to other people or circumstances beyond their control or a part of themselves for which they are not responsible. Impulses are largely controlled through fear of being caught and the child's conscious preoccupation is with self-protection and gaining control and advantage through domination and competition.

CONFORMIST STAGE This stage is characterized by early internalization of moral values. Simplistic identification with parents, adults, and peers marks this widely recognized period in ego development. The stage is marked by conformity to external rules and shame and guilt feelings when rules are broken. A patina of niceness and a strong need for belonging marks interpersonal interactions that are accompanied by concerns with social acceptance and appearance. The individual's cognitive style tends to be simplistic and characterized by cliché-type reasoning that mirrors an interpretation of those emulated.

CONSCIENTIOUS STAGE This stage is characterized by an increased recognition of the person's inner states, motivations, feelings of guilt, and an awareness of distinctions between behavior and perceived experiences. It is important to note that the movement to this stage is gradual, progressing, according to Loevinger, from the conformist stage through a transitional level (labeled Conscientious-Conformist) through the conscientious stage to a second transitional level (labeled Individualistic) eventually to the autonomous stage that follows. Typical of the maturing and mature adolescent, psychological maturation and growth from the stage of conformity through conscientious to the stages of autonomy and integration are both complex and multifaceted. The process is marked by differentiation of norms and goals from those of others, the establishment of self-imposed standards and the evolution of long-range goals, values, and ideas as well as feelings of guilt for those things not accomplished or for those infractions committed. An awareness of

the self vis-à-vis the group and mutual help accorded and received blends into an interpersonal style resting on intense, responsible, concerned feelings and actions toward others and an accompanying concern for interpersonal communication. This complex stage and its accompanying transition phases are marked by a conscious preoccupation with adjustment motives, the attainment of self-respect, self-attainment, and achievement.

AUTONOMOUS STAGE A hallmark of this stage is the person's ability to recognize and cope with the inner conflict generated by competing personal needs and duties. The autonomous person views the world as complex and frequently filled with incompatible possibilities and is characterized by much tolerance for ambiguity that permits uniting and integrating alternatives. Autonomous persons are aware that others need autonomy yet also know that emotional interdependence places limitations on autonomy because they prize personal ties highly. Achievement as a goal is partly supplanted by self-fulfillment. Persons at this stage are cognizant that they fulfill different roles in life at different times and function differentially to meet various role expectations and demands.

INTEGRATED STAGE The highest stage of ego development is said to be difficult to describe except to indicate that the description provided for the Autonomous Stage applies with the added factor that the individual's sense of identity is consolidated. The comparative rarity of this stage in the population makes it difficult to describe, as does the fact that persons at the integrated stage are often at a higher level of ego functioning than those who seek to describe them. Loevinger asserts that the best description of this stage is that provided by Maslow, which Loevinger presents:

> The characteristics of self-actualization are, according to Maslow: not a fixed state but a changing process, thus, openness to development; more efficient perception of reality, that is, "lesser blindness"; availability of inner life; vivid perception of the outer world; capacity for both abstractness and concreteness; tolerance for ambiguity; capacity for guilt and sense of responsibility; capacity for spontaneity, as opposed to intensive striving; existential as opposed to hostile humor; gaiety, particularly in sexual and other love relations; transcending of contra-

dictions and polarities; acceptance of reality; greater integration, autonomy, and sense of identity; increased objectivity, detachment, and transcendence of self; democratic character structure.[21]

Moral development

Kohlberg[22] has presented moral development as progressing through an invariant sequence of stages. In his view, moral development is reasoning about what is right or just. Each stage in the sequence is characterized by various issues used by individuals in making decisions about right and wrong and just and unjust. Moreover, each stage is also associated with a different social perspective. Table 3.4 presents Kohlberg's sequence of moral development, descriptions of what is right, reasons for doing right, and the social perspective characteristic of each stage.

The evidence amassed primarily by Kohlberg,[23] Kohlberg and Turiel,[24] and Rest, Turiel, and Kohlberg[25] strongly suggests that individuals go through an invariant sequence of moral development stages, but at different rates. A given individual's movement can stop at any level. Rest[26] has constructed a method of assessing moral development, *The Defining Issues Test* (DIT). His measure presents subjects with moral dilemmas. For each of six stories, subjects evaluate a set of twelve issues and are asked to rate how important each issue is in deciding what ought to be done. Rest investigated the hierarchical nature of movement along the

sequence and reported that high school students comprehended reasoning derived from all stages below their own and that about half of the students comprehended reasoning derived from one stage above their own. An individual at stage three may induce movement in a stage two individual by dialogue, whereas the reverse does not occur. Moreover, evidence by Rest was that students preferred the highest stage reasoning they were able to comprehend. This finding was taken as support that each successive stage of development is more complete, complex, and useful.

Longitudinal findings, according to Kohlberg,[27] suggest four critical period focuses of mental health intervention during the school years. The first period occurs during ages 6 to 9, where concern is for cognitive orientation, interest, style, and attention. The second, during ages 9 to 12, is the special concern for peer relations and relations to adults. It is during this period that conventional moral character development appears to become crystallized. The third, during adolescent years, comes with discovery of the self, inner life, and abstract values. The fourth critical period occurs during late adolescence as the actual transition to adulthood takes place.

Comparison of developmental approaches

These approaches to understanding the development of individuals vary in their complexity and terminology. However, they share the characteristic of attempting to portray a continuous process of events from birth to death. Presumably the systems describe best the individual who develops in middle-class American culture. Each scheme is composed of generalizations about development that are difficult if not impossible to apply to other cultures and may fit some American subcultures quite poorly. Similarly, the three approaches are time bound to some degree in the sense that society's expectancies may shift from generation to generation. The various levels do not match because each theorist stresses the fact that development is a continuous process and they vary in regard to the degree to which they are willing to assign even general age ranges to the various levels.

[21] Ibid., p. 140.

[22] Lawrence Kohlberg, "Moral Stages and Moralization: The Cognitive-Developmental Approach," in *Moral Development and Behavior Theory, Research and Social Issues*, ed. T. Lickona (New York: Holt, Rinehart and Winston, 1976), pp. 31–53.

[23] Ibid.

[24] Lawrence Kohlberg and E. Turiel, "Moral Development and Moral Education," in *Psychology and Educational Practice*, ed. G. S. Lesser (Glenview, Illinois: Scott, Foresman, 1971), pp. 410–465.

[25] J. Rest, E. Turiel, and L. Kohlberg, "Relations Between Level of Moral Judgment and Preference and Comprehension of the Moral Judgment of Others," *Journal of Personality*, 37 (June 1969), 225–252.

[26] J. Rest, "New Approaches in the Assessment of Moral Judgment," in *Moral Development and Behavior Theory, Research and Social Issues*, ed. T. Lickona (New York: Holt, Rinehart and Winston, 1976), pp. 198–218.

[27] Lawrence Kohlberg, "Counseling and Counselor Education: A Developmental Approach," *Counselor Education and Supervision*, 14 (June 1975), 250–256.

TABLE 3.4 **Kohlberg's six moral stages**

Stage	What is right	Reasons for doing right	Social perspective of stage
Level I—Preconventional			
Stage 1—Heteronomous morality	To avoid breaking rules backed by punishment, obedience for its own sake, and avoiding physical damage to persons and property.	Avoidance of punishment and the superior power of authorities.	*Egocentric point of view.* Doesn't consider the interests of others or recognize that they differ from the actor's; doesn't relate two points of view. Actions are considered physically rather than in terms of psychological interests of others. Confusion of authority's perspective with one's own.
Stage 2—Individualism, instrumental purpose, and exchange	Following rules only when it is to someone's immediate interest; acting to meet one's own interests and needs, and letting others do the same. Right is also what's fair, what's an equal exchange, a deal, an agreement.	To serve one's own needs or interests in a world where you have to recognize that other people have their interests, too.	*Concrete individualistic perspective.* Aware that everybody has own interest to pursue and these conflict, so that right is relative (in the concrete individualistic sense).
Level II—Conventional			
Stage 3—Mutual interpersonal expectations, relationships, and interpersonal conformity	Living up to what is expected by people close to you or what people generally expect of people in your role as son, brother, friend, etc. "Being good" is important and means having good motives, showing concern about others. It also means keeping mutual relationships, such as trust, loyalty, respect, and gratitude.	The need to be a good person in your own eyes and those of others. Your caring for others. Belief in the Golden Rule. Desire to maintain rules and authority which support stereotypical good behavior.	*Perspective of the individual in relationships with other individuals.* Aware of shared feelings, agreements, and expectations which take primacy over individual interests. Relates points of view through the concrete Golden Rule, putting yourself in the other guy's shoes. Does not yet consider generalized system perspective.
Stage 4—Social system and conscience	Fulfilling the actual duties to which you have agreed. Laws are to be upheld except in extreme cases where they conflict with other fixed social duties. Right is also contributing to society, the group, or institution.	To keep the institution going as a whole, to avoid the breakdown in the system, "if everyone did it," or the imperative of conscience to meet one's defined obligations. (Easily confused with Stage 3 belief in rules and authority.)	*Differentiates societal point of view from interpersonal agreement or motives.* Takes the point of view of the system that defines roles and rules. Considers individual relations in terms of place in the system.

SOURCE: From *Moral Development and Behavior Theory, Research and Social Issues*, edited by Thomas Lickona. Copyright © 1976 by Holt, Rinehart and Winston. Reprinted by permission of Holt, Rinehart and Winston.

TABLE 3.4 **Kohlberg's six moral stages** *(cont.)*

Stage	What is right	Reasons for doing right	Social perspective of stage
		Level III—Postconventional, or principled	
Stage 5—Social contract or utility and individual rights	Being aware that people hold a variety of values and opinions, that most values and rules are relative to your group. These relative rules should usually be upheld, however, in the interest of impartiality and because they are the social contract. Some nonrelative values and rights like *life and liberty*, however, must be upheld in any society and regardless of majority opinion.	A sense of obligation to law because of one's social contract to make and abide by laws for the welfare of all and for the protection of all people's rights. A feeling of contractual commitment, freely entered upon, to family, friendship, trust, and work obligations. Concern that laws and duties be based on rational calculation of overall utility, "the greatest good for the greatest number."	*Prior-to-society perspective.* Perspective of a rational individual aware of values and rights prior to social attachments and contracts. Integrates perspectives by formal mechanisms of agreement, contract, objective impartiality, and due process. Considers moral and legal points of view; recognizes that they sometimes conflict and finds it difficult to integrate them.
Stage 6—Universal ethical principles	Following self-chosen ethical principles. Particular laws or social agreements are usually valid because they rest on such principles. When laws violate these principles one acts in accordance with the principle. Principles are universal principles of justice: the equality of human rights and respect for the dignity of human beings as individual persons.	The belief as a rational person in the validity of universal moral principles, and a sense of personal commitment to them.	*Perspective of a moral point of view from which social arrangements derive.* Perspective is that of any rational individual recognizing the nature of morality or the fact that persons are ends in themselves and must be treated as such.

Importance of developmental schemes

Considerable space has been given to the developmental sequences presented here. It is hoped that they illuminate human behavior and give a clearer view of the terrain of development. Such schemes are believed to be useful to counselors by providing a contour map, as it were, within which to examine their clients' behaviors. Hypotheses can be formulated as to whether the client's development is on, behind, or ahead of schedule. Anxiety often is generated by moving too fast, with a need to slow down to consolidate the growth experienced as well as by being too slow to transgress outdated tasks. The counselor can plan interventions that will enable the individual to catch up to schedule. Finally, it should be noted that given that development is lifelong, counseling cannot be confined to the adolescent period. Its relevance for all ages becomes ever more evident.

Concept of normality

School counselors usually distinguish themselves from clinical psychologists or psychiatrists, who work predominantly with abnormal or disturbed individuals, by asserting that their clients are normal. But how is normality to be defined?

Abnormal behavior is usually regarded as a departure from the normal, differing from it in kind. Others view it as an extension of the habitual range, distinctive only in degree. For example, Sigmund Freud pointed out that neurotic conflict is not very different in content from the normative conflicts that every individual experiences in childhood, the residues of which adults carry with them in the recesses of their personalities. He believed that humans, in order to remain psychologically alive, constantly resolve these conflicts just as their bodies unceasingly combat the encroachment of physical deterioration.

Much literature exists dealing with the characteristics of the behavioral deviant, the disturbed, and the anxious, but much less is known about the nature of psychological normality. Basically, two approaches to defining *normality* have been used. First, normality has been related to the statistical facts of *average* or *typical*. By this approach, the average individual and those near him or her (conventionally, those in a distribution obtained from any measure who are one standard deviation above and below the mean) are considered normal. Individuals above and below this central area in a distribution would be labeled abnormal. The second approach is to consider normality a relative thing. Normality means acceptance by reference to some group. Groups or cultures vary in what is considered acceptable. This approach raises the issue of whether normality is not basically conforming behavior.

Perhaps what school counselors really mean when they say that their clientele is made up of normal individuals is that their services are available to all students. Further, counseling is not restricted to a narrow segment of the population characterized by deficit. Although those with severe deficits of one kind or another are likely to be referred to more specialized personnel, it seems fairly obvious that those at the positive pole of any description (for example, the gifted) that purports to describe normality are not referred because positive behavior is rarely seen as abnormal. Clearly, the service demands on school counselors are made mainly by psychologically intact individuals confronted with the usual developmental stresses of human existence.

Several general descriptions of mentally healthy individuals have been advanced. Jahoda labels psychologically healthy an individual who actively masters his or her environment, shows a considerable unity of personality, and is able to perceive himself or herself and the world realistically.[28] Such an individual is independent and able to function effectively without making undue demands on others.

Shoben's definition goes beyond self-sufficiency.[29] He proposes that the healthy person exhibits self-control, personal responsibility, social responsibility, social interest, and ideals. Shoben believes that his tentative formulation of integrative adjustment avoids the notion that normal persons are always happy and free from conflict, or without problems, but acknowledges that such persons may fall short of their ideals because of ignorance, the limitations under which they live, or immediate pressures. Further, they may at times behave in ways that prove shortsighted or self-defeating.

Yamamoto[30] presents, in tabular form (see Table 3.5), some characteristics of the emotionally healthy person set forth by various authors. His own concept of such a person describes one who lives fully at a particular point in his or her development and is constantly "becoming" or actively changing self and environment to attain the next stage.

Many protest the use of terminology such as *mental illness* and insist that decisions regarding maladaptive behavior rest primarily on judgments involving conventionality and social norms. The concept of mental illness is not analogous to that of physical illness, in which deviation from optimal organic functioning serves as a base for decisions.

Common counselee concerns

Sociologists study the young, politicians profess to worry about them, and parents, teachers, and counselors try to understand them. Few diagnoses as to what they are really like are accurate. Too often, the complaint is that they are insolent, unkempt, and unprepossessing. But the war between the generations is nothing new. Socrates bitterly attacked youth's "bad manners, contempt for authority, disrespect for their elders. Children nowadays are tyrants." All through history, denouncing the young has been a tonic for tired blood. Conversely, defying elders is hygienic for the young. An adolescent's task is self-definition (see Havighurst, Erikson, and Loevinger) unless the individual can distinguish self from culture, though on the culture's terms, the child never quite becomes an adult. Growing up

[28] Marie Jahoda, "Toward a Social Psychology of Mental Health," in *Symposium on the Healthy Personality,* ed. M. F. E. Senn (New York: Josiah Macy, Jr., Foundation, 1950).

[29] Edward Joseph Shoben, Jr., "Toward a Concept of the Normal Personality," *The American Psychologist*, 12 (April 1957) 183–189.
[30] Kaoru Yamamoto, "The 'Healthy Person': A Review," *Personnel and Guidance Journal*, 44 (February 1966), 596–603.

TABLE 3.5 **Models of a healthy person postulated by several authors**

Shoben (1957)	Jahoda (1958)	Allport (1960)	Rogers (1962)	Combs (1962)
			Openness to experience	Openness to experience and acceptance
Self-control	Accepting attitudes toward self	Self-objectification	Trust in one's organism	Positive view of self
Personal responsibility	Growth and self-actualization	Ego-extension		
Social responsibility		Warm and deep relation to others		
Democratic social interest		Compassionate regard for all	(Trustworthiness of human nature)*	Identification with others
Values and standards	Integration	Unifying philosophy of life	Living as a process (existential living)	
	Autonomy Perception of reality	Realistic perceptions		Rich and available perceptual field
	Environmental mastery	Realistic coping skills and abilities		
			(Creativity)	(Well-informed) (Imaginative and creative)

*Characteristics in parentheses are implied or deduced corollaries of the respective models.
SOURCE: Kaoru Yamamoto, "The 'Healthy Person': A Review," *Personnel and Guidance Journal*, 44 (February 1966), 600. Copyright © 1966 American Personnel and Guidance Association. Reprinted with permission.

is a process that requires forces and people against whom one can push in order to become stronger. Growth requires limited war against worthy opponents because a child matures by testing limits set by caring adults. Study after study shows that two factors are vital to children's later independence: first, warmly firm parents who respect each other and on whom children can model themselves while breaking away; second, opportunities to prove their competence in work and love. Youth often reveal in what they say their special awareness of the faults and virtues of the adult world; they hold up a mirror to society. They expect much from this world and are ready to give much; for example, many have made sincere commitments to civil rights, the Peace Corps, Vista, and the like.

Causes of youth problems

That we live in a time of widening uncertainty and chronic stress has been observed by many chroniclers. Some time ago, Tuchman stated,

Man in the twentieth century is not a creature to be envied. Formerly he believed himself created by the divine spark. Now, bereft of that proud confidence, and contemplating his recent record and present problems, he can no longer, like the Psalmist, respect himself as "a little lower than the angels." He cannot picture himself today, as Michelangelo did on the Sistine ceiling, in the calm and noble image of Adam receiving the spark from the finger of God. Overtaken by doubt of human purpose and divine purpose, he doubts his capacity to be good or even to survive. He has lost certainty, including moral and ethical certainty, and is left with a sense of footloose purposelessness and self-disgust. . . .[31]

Numerous other statements alluding to the problems and complexity of today's world could be cited. Although their validity probably cannot be seriously questioned and although their ready acceptance frequently stems from their

[31] Barbara W. Tuchman, "The Historian's Opportunity," *Saturday Review*, February 25, 1967, p. 28.

persuasive nature, in our opinion they frequently appear to underrate the very segment of humanity with which they are concerned. The contemporary world may be more complex or more anxiety provoking, less safe and secure in the eyes of adults who were born and reared at an earlier point in time. What seems to be missing in such views is the obvious fact that humans adapt, cope with, and master that which has historically confronted them.

Children born into the atomic age may not suffer and be as incapacitated by events as their elders fear. Although the same threat is there for adults and youth, it is a fact of the latter's existence and has not been suddenly thrust upon them. For this reason it may not affect youth to the degree that adults think that it would. It could probably be demonstrated that many anxiety-producing factors either no longer exist or have diminished impact in contemporary society. Perhaps physical health is a good example. Many major diseases that constantly threatened society fifty years ago are relatively rare in modern America. Each person is a product of his or her own times. People deal with that which confronts them regardless of the dire predictions of those in an older age group.

But admittedly, something is obviously wrong among some segments of the youth culture. Quite a few young people are clearly discontented; even more disturbing, too many of them are withdrawing rather than warring. Alienation drives young people into private exile. At the heart of this anomie lie vast technological changes in Western culture that have steadily lengthened childhood and sharply diminished communication between generations.

Surveys have described the problems and concerns of the elementary-, secondary-, and college-age groups. Their chief value is in alerting counselors to areas of sensitivity among their clientele.

Concerns of elementary school children

"Wanted: Someone to care for a child outside of the home, six hours a day. Must teach child to read and write and to respond and be responsive to others." This fictitious want ad should appear every fall when millions of youngsters swarm into the nation's public and private elementary schools. Public elementary schools enrolled some 25.8 million in 1978. The nonpublic elementary sector of the educational system enrolled an additional 5.6 million in 1978.

Perhaps these numbers convey some idea of the problems confronting the schools as they attempt to provide an educationally meaningful experience for youngsters. But all too often, numbers obscure the wide range of behavior, the different bases of motivation and aspiration, the differential in experiences that exist among the millions who attend school.

Elementary school pupils are in the process of becoming—physically, socially, emotionally, and as total personalities. Their experiences in coping with normal developmental tasks vary widely. These developmental differences create adjustment problems both in the tasks of school and in social life.

No matter how exacting or ingenious an educational program may be, it cannot reach children who are beset with psychological and emotional disturbances. Recent estimates are that up to 10 percent of school children have emotional disturbances that require professional treatment.

Taken at face value, the term *emotional disorder* would appear to be almost self-defining. The simplistic view of this condition is that a disproportionate emotional reaction attends a reality situation. *Maladjustment* and *behavior disorder* frequently are used interchangeably with the term *emotional disturbance*. A useful example of a description of the emotionally disturbed student is to be found in the administrative manual of the Bureau of Educationally Handicapped and used with Title VI of the Elementary and Secondary Education Act. This source says the disturbed child is characterized by: (1) an inability to learn that cannot be explained by intellectual, sensory, or health factors; (2) an inability to establish or maintain satisfactory interpersonal relationships with peers and teachers; (3) inappropriate types of behavior or feelings under normal circumstances; (4) a generally pervasive mood of unhappiness or depression; and (5) a tendency to develop physical symptoms, pains, or fears associated with personal or school problems. It is within this type of working definition or description that most school personnel, including counselors, operate in making day-to-day judgments about the presence, degree, and effects of emotional disturbance on pupils.

Estimates of the number of school children encountered each year who exhibit some emotional, behavior, or psychosomatic problem vary widely. This variation is due to the lack of a common definition and to differences in the cutoff points used in categorizing a student as disturbed. Interwoven with these factors are the criteria employed in making judgments, which stem from definition and which affect the precision of decisions. Without detailing the literature, estimates can be found that vary from 4 to 20 percent. Even though precision in rates is not possible, if one applies either extreme of this range to the total school enrollment in the United States, one is faced with a tremendous number of elementary school children who need help.

Certain other problems regarding estimates of emotional disturbance among school children must be pointed out. Estimates do not necessarily apply in all settings because the incidence of disturbance varies, depending on the type of school setting measured, for example, inner-city or suburban school, and the student population within the setting. Estimates within two apparently similar settings may also vary according to the level of awareness of the staff and the services available within the school or community. A sensitive, child-centered, and alert staff with many special services available may identify a far larger number of children who need specialized assistance than will a less sensitive staff. In short, estimates of nationwide scope are of little value in a specific locality.

Lastly, it must be added that before PL 94-142 was enacted, the very seriously disturbed children often were not found in public schools. Such children were either institutionalized or placed in special private school settings because it was believed they could not cope with a regular school environment. Even now, most emotionally disturbed children who are in public schools would be judged as having mild, minor, or transitory problems that stem from developmental or situational causes.

A not uncommon, serious concern for some elementary school children is a feeling of panic about attending school. Traditional concepts of school phobia have been primarily psychoanalytical in nature, stressing the parent-child separation or sexual aspects of the disorder. Long states that phobic children view school as a "preaversive stimulus" in that they regard separation from a parent (usually the mother) as a loss of positive reinforcement. Excessive dependency creates fear of separation. Long suggests that counselors employ behavior modification treatment procedures, primarily desensitization, for elementary school phobia cases.[32]

Stiltner[33] administered an assessment instrument to obtain information about what elementary school pupils, their teachers, and parents considered needs of students. The questionnaire for pupils in grades three through six was composed of thirty-five statements beginning with the item "I'd like help in . . ." although only seventeen items were included in a questionnaire for kindergarten through grade two. Pupils reported they would like help in "learning about jobs," "finding out how people feel about me," and "finding out what things I can do best." Table 3.6 presents the items ranked most highly by intermediate pupils, their teachers, and parents.

Some years ago, Rice[34] examined the types of concerns at different grade levels that were referred to a central guidance agency. Those mentioned consistently by teachers in referring pupils were categorized as (1) emotional problems such as anxiety, hyperactivity, immaturity, impulsiveness, moodiness, and withdrawal; (2) intellectual disabilities, such as short attention span, low ability, defective memory, perceptual malfunctioning, poor study habits, underachieving, and inability to understand; (3) motivational inadequacies including lack of ambition, poor or negative attitudes, frustrations, lack of interests, and low levels of aspiration; (4) moral defects such as lying, obscenity, psychosocial indiscretions, stealing, and undeveloped values; (5) physical ailments including chronic illness, poor health habits, orthopedic handicaps, and psychosomatic manifestations; (6) social maladjustment including aggressive antisocial behavior, family conflicts, isolation, and uncouth behavior. Table 3.7 shows these referrals.

Rice noted that primary pupils were referred largely for intellectual problems, particularly those involving low ability. Other problem categories were mentioned, but not as repeatedly or as consistently as at higher grade levels. Intermediate pupils were also referred primarily for intellectual problems, but more perceptual difficulties complicated by underachieving were included. Teachers increasingly referred intermediate pupils because of social problems.

In the classroom the quiet youngster is often perceived by teachers as less of a problem than the aggressive youngster. Wickman, in an extensive investigation five decades ago of

[32] James D. Long, "School Phobia and the Elementary Counselor," *Elementary School Guidance and Counseling*, 5 (May 1971), 289–294.

[33] Barbara Stiltner, "Needs Assessment: A First Step," *Elementary School Guidance and Counseling*, 12 (April 1978), 239–246.

[34] Joseph P. Rice, Jr., "Types of Problems Referred to a Central Guidance Agency at Different Grade Levels," *Personnel and Guidance Journal*, 42 (September 1963), 52–55.

TABLE 3.6 **Items ranked most highly by intermediate students, teachers, and parents**

Item	Student's %*	Rank	Teacher's %**	Rank	Parent's %**	Rank
Learning about jobs I'd be happy in	50	(1)	54	(32)	78	(22)
Finding out what things I can do best	50	(2)	84	(16)	88	(6)
Finding out how people feel about me	49	(3)	77	(24)	75	(28)
Learning to solve my problems	46	(4)	95	(5)	89	(4)
Finding out what different jobs I like	45	(5)	60	(30)	80	(18)
Learning to make good choices	44	(6)	89	(10)	83	(14)
Learning how to get along with people who "bug" me	44	(7)	87	(13)	81	(17)
Finding out things I do that "bug" others	44	(8)	91	(7)	75	(27)
Knowing what to do when I am with kids who are doing things I know they shouldn't do	42	(9)	88	(12)	92	(1)
Getting along better with my brother or sister	42	(10)	53	(33)	69	(30)
Learning to resolve conflicts	—		97	(1)	—	
Learning to keep my mind on my work until I finish it	40	(11)	97	(2)	88	(7)
Learning to organize my time better	38	(12)	97	(3)	—	
Learning to listen better in school	23	(30)	96	(4)	87	(8)
Being more aware of the feelings of others	—		91	(6)	83	(13)
Being more sure of myself	31	(23)	90	(8)	88	(5)
Feeling satisfied with what I do	32	(30)	90	(8)	90	(2)
Learning how my feelings change (affect) what I do	34	(22)	90	(9)	90	(3)
Being able to accept criticism better	25	(30)	78	(23)	87	(9)
Feeling more comfortable in class discussions	27	(28)	68	(25)	86	(10)

*Students selected from the responses "yes," "maybe," and "no." The percentage reported here is the percentage of students selecting the "yes" response.

**Teachers and parents responded on a four-point scale from "of great importance" to "of no importance." The percentage reported here is the percentage selecting the two responses "of great importance" and "important."

SOURCE: Barbara Stiltner, "Needs Assessment: A First Step," *Elementary School Guidance and Counseling,* 12 (April 1978), 244. Copyright © 1978 American Personnel and Guidance Association. Reprinted with permission.

TABLE 3.7 **Types of problems referred to a central guidance agency at various grade levels by percent (N = 283)**

Problem categories	Primary (1–3) N = 70 Reason	Mention	Intermediate (4–6) N = 88 Reason	Mention	Junior high (7–9) N = 80 Reason	Mention	High (10–12) N = 45 Reason	Mention	χ^2
Emotional reactions	12.9	31.4	13.6	30.7	10.0	38.8	13.3	35.6	0.60
Intellectual disabilities	55.7	37.1	47.7	31.8	18.8	42.5	35.6	33.3	24.90[a]
Motivational inadequacy	5.7	21.4	8.0	13.6	10.0	15.0	17.8	20.0	5.37
Moral defect	2.9	11.4	3.4	15.9	22.5	47.5	13.3	40.0	22.45[a]
Physical ailments	8.6	28.6	2.3	17.0	5.0	12.5	4.4	11.1	3.43
Social maladjustment	14.3	44.3	25.0	45.4	33.8	48.8	15.6	33.3	9.59[b]

[a]Significant at the 1 percent level with three degrees of freedom.

[b]Significant at the 5 percent level with three degrees of freedom.

SOURCE: Joseph P. Rice, Jr., "Types of Problems Referred to a Central Guidance Agency at Different Grade Levels," *Personnel and Guidance Journal,* 42 (September 1963), 52–55. Copyright © 1963 American Personnel and Guidance Association. Reprinted with permission.

teachers' attitudes toward children's behavior, reported that the more extrovertive reactions, such as whispering, defiance, profanity, moving about, lack of courtesy to members of the opposite sex, destroying school property, lying, and the like, were believed by the majority of classroom teachers to be symptomatic of maladjustment. On the other hand, the types of pupil behavior often associated by clinicians with maladjustment, such as unsociability, suspicion, depression, sensitiveness, and fearfulness, were rated by teachers as harmless and even desirable forms of adjustment to school life.[35]

In the years since Wickman's study was made, greater emphasis has been placed on an understanding not only of the emotional needs of children but also of their way of defending themselves or dealing with their environment. That teachers and mental hygienists have moved closer together in their judgments of the serious problems of children than they were at the time of Wickman's report has been the conclusion reached by many investigators, too many to need citation here. However, teachers still consider politeness and obedience to be criteria of good adjustment, whereas clinicians regard them as being equivocal indexes of satisfactory mental health.

Like many institutions, the school tends to be a world unto itself. All too often the school attempts to deal with seriously disturbed pupils in educational terms, using discipline and exhortation. By the time patience is exhausted, serious damage may be done. Skillful referral by teachers to counselors, either those in school or those in community mental health agencies, should not be overlooked or delayed too long. Some prominent characteristics that frequently suggest referrals include:

1. lack of response to conventional classroom approaches
2. inadequate performance in communication skills
3. high-level tension and emotional responses
4. apathy toward others
5. indifference to responsibility
6. nonpurposeful activity
7. socially unacceptable behavior
8. physical defects and poor health habits
9. disoriented or disrupted family or home patterns

[35] E. K. Wickman, *Children's Behavior and Teachers' Attitudes* (New York: Commonwealth Fund, 1928), Chaps. 5–9.

These characteristics cause children to gain less from schooling than they might and less than they need to function as competent learners. The reinforcements and support that children need are often intangible: an acceptable self-image, an implicit sense of identification with an adult, self-confidence, and motivation to achieve. These positive factors are essential to the healthy development of children. They are the firm ground beneath the learning process.

Concerns of high school students

The concerns of high school students evolve from developmental tasks and from living within the social system represented by the school. The employment of a counselor in a school is usually based on the premise that students have certain unmet needs that necessitate a counseling relationship. Some of these needs are rooted in the modifications that have been made in some schools. Greater use is being made of educational technology, teacher aides, team teaching, and small instructional groups. Subject matter, particularly mathematics, science, and foreign languages, continues to be emphasized along with attention to the career education of students.

In some respects, change seems ever-present in the high school milieu. Today, "back to basics" has become a true sentence stopper. Many insist it means instilling a new intellectual rigor and a new qualitative excellence in education, ending permissiveness, social promotions, and violence in schools. But there are clouds on the horizon. Some have used "back to basics" as a call for a series of countermarches to make authoritarianism respectable or to justify harsh, unyielding punishments. Still others are using the slogan to back their opinions about whom, what, and how to teach. Is "back to basics" to be equated with quantity of study? Will a "heavy assignment binge" cause a tired student to become twice as smart by doing homework four nights a week rather than two?

Aside from the social aspects of schools, many of today's students express negative reactions to what happens to them. The subjects they take often seem unreal, dead, and unrelated to life or to the community. Their attitudes are caught in these comments:

We just seem to do the homework, memorize, take tests, and get the marks. It's all just to get into college. I'd like

TABLE 3.8 **Purdue opinion panel report on high school students' concerns about developmental tasks**

Developmental concerns	Very much		Some		Little or not much	
	Boys	Girls	Boys	Girls	Boys	Girls
My physique	26%	44%	29%	28%	44%	28%
Friendships	33	32	26	26	41	42
Relationship with parents/adults	25	34	26	25	48	41
Having own money	40	42	22	24	34	31
Job or occupation	37	39	27	27	32	31
Skills and abilities	20	18	28	28	50	52
My behavior	17	17	20	21	61	60
Family life in future	37	53	25	23	37	23
Values	25	33	26	25	46	41
Myself (who I am, what I can do)	29	38	25	23	42	36

SOURCE: Based on the Purdue Opinion Panel, "Counseling and Educational Needs of Adolescents," Report of Poll 93 (Lafayette, Indiana: Purdue University, Measurement and Research Center, January 1973).

some chance to think some in a course. Where is this big deal about education widening the horizons and challenging the mind about life, and all that?

Everything's all known and worked out. Even the teacher's course is all finished. There's nothing for us to do but learn the answers and agree.

I haven't had a chance in any course to really think.

The school is not supposed to influence you. It's where you do the assignment.

What many students seek and generally are unable to find are (1) the opportunity to bear genuine responsibility within the school and outside (students want more than doing assignments and keeping out of trouble); (2) purpose—striving for high marks and test scores is not enough; and (3) the challenge to think, to explore, and to come to grips with their work in each subject in some kind of personal, meaningful way.

Today, there is danger that too many individuals confuse education with the "programming" of students for information storage and retrieval as though they were machines. These are the dangers of compulsive attention to content in the absence of attention to process. Tiedeman has declared that "if the student is to become responsible and hence 'to outlive his teachings' . . . he must consider the *process* of education simultaneously with its content." [36] Heathers has

defined the process of education as (1) acquiring the power to assimilate through the framing and solving of problems; (2) exercising initiative for, and during the course of, problem solving; and (3) evaluating one's efforts at problem solving using mastery as a criterion. [37] This process stands in bold relief to information storage and retrieval. Process is something that takes place within the individual learner. Process implies motivation, action, initiative, value judgments, and responsibility on the part of the student.

Some youths report difficulty with and concern about developmental tasks. Based on some 17,600 high school pupils drawn from all sections of the United States, the Purdue Opinion Panel [38] reported that high school students worry most about (1) family life in the future (finding a suitable mate, deciding "whether I'm in love"), (2) having their own money, and (3) jobs. Little concern was expressed by these students about their behavior or their skills and abilities. Table 3.8 summarizes the proportions of responses by these students. As can be seen by examining the data reported in Table 3.8, considerable concern about developmental tasks is expressed by girls, especially about physique, friendships, family life, values, and self.

Gibson and Mitchell surveyed educators in Great Britain and the United States to compare the educational and voca-

[36] David V. Tiedeman, "Status and Prospect in Counseling Psychology," mimeographed (Cambridge, Massachusetts: Graduate School of Education, Harvard University).

[37] Glen L. Heathers, "Notes on the Strategy of Educational Reform," mimeographed (New York: Experimental Teaching Center, School of Education, New York University).

[38] The Purdue Opinion Panel, "Counseling and Educational Needs of Adolescents," Report of Poll 93 (Lafayette, Indiana: Measurement and Research Center, Purdue University, January 1973), p. 10.

TABLE 3.9 **Rankings of seriousness of 22 problems by British and American educators**

Problem	Ranking United States	British Isles
Failing to work to capacity	1	1
Home environment	2	2
Failure to acquire basic reading, writing, and reasoning skills	3	18
Behavior out of school	4	6
Lack of interest in the academic program	5	3
Lack of appropriate curriculum	6.5	7
Lack of parental cooperation	6.5	8
No post–high school vocational-technical educational opportunities	8	21
Outdated or inadequate vocational-technical facilities	9	16
Lack of public understanding and cooperation	10	15
No jobs for graduates	11.5	4
Inadequate guidance programs	11.5	17
Neighborhood environment	13	14
Lack of financial resources	14	19
Excessive employment	15	10
Outdated or inadequate physical facilities in general	16.5	20
Inability to hold science or technical faculty	16.5	11.5
Lack of interest in school activities	18	5
Dropping out of school	19	22
Behavior in school	20	9
Inability to hold a quality faculty	21	13
Failure to aspire to appropriate careers	22	11.5

SOURCE: Robert L. Gibson and Marianne H. Mitchell, "Theirs and Ours: Educational-Vocational Problems in Britain and the United States," *Vocational Guidance Quarterly*, 19 (December 1970), 110. Copyright © 1970 American Personnel and Guidance Association. Reprinted with permission.

tional problems that affect secondary school students in these two countries. These educators' ranking of the seriousness of twenty-two problems is reported in Table 3.9.

As the data in Table 3.9 reveal, the problem of pupils failing to work to capacity or achieve near capacity was viewed as most serious by the school administrators, teachers, and counseling-psychological personnel in both coun-

tries. These two researchers interviewed a small sampling of pupils in both countries. Their interviews indicated that American pupils were most concerned with, in order, (1) lack of appropriate curricular offerings, (2) lack of post–high school vocational and technical educational opportunities, and (3) inadequate guidance programs. Their British counterparts were most concerned about (1) lack of job opportunities, (2) lack of post–high school vocational and technical educational opportunities, and (3) inadequate guidance programs.[39]

Mezzano administered a questionnaire (based on the Mooney Problem Check List) to some 1,495 students enrolled in grades seven through twelve in three Wisconsin public school communities. The rankings given to certain problem areas are reported in Table 3.10. These data reveal that high among students' concerns are those that involve educational and vocational opportunities, followed by school life. Mezzano also asked these students to indicate their preference for talking to a male or female counselor, given these problem areas. Most students (both boys and girls) chose to discuss most of these concerns with male counselors.[40]

Diederich and Jackson have identified two forms of student failure in the classroom. The unsuccessful attempt to master required material is the most well known. Equally important, but less widely discussed, is the second form, the student who fails to accept as his own the goals and values of the school. Numerous surveys report that between 25 and 30 percent of all high school students are dissatisfied with school. Boys are generally more dissatisfied than girls. The two forms of failure—the academic and the attitudinal—are commonly thought to be closely related. The usual premise is that the student who does well in school likes or is satisfied with school. But the findings of many studies indicate that this premise does not hold true. Teenagers' dissatisfaction or discontent with their school experiences appears to be a reflection of their total psychological élan rather than a specific reaction to their academic progress or lack of it. Diederich and Jackson surveyed 258 high school

[39] Robert L. Gibson and Marianne H. Mitchell, "Theirs and Ours: Educational-Vocational Problems in Britain and the United States," *Vocational Guidance Quarterly*, 19 (December 1970), 108–112.
[40] Joseph Mezzano, "Concerns of Students and Preference for Male and Female Counselors," *Vocational Guidance Quarterly*, 20 (September 1971), 42–47.

TABLE 3.10 **Ranking of areas of concern by boys and girls**

Grade		7th		8th		9th		10th		11th		12th	
		Boys	Girls	Boys	Girls	Boys	Girls	Boys	Girls	Boys	Girls	Boys	Girls
Area of concern	N =	132	117	119	120	244	247	74	92	105	77	71	97
Health/physical development		4	1	4	1	3	3	6	3	7	5	6	6
School		3	2	1	3	2	1.5	2	5	2	3	2	3
Home and family		1	3	3	2	5	4	4	3	4	7	5	5
Boy-girl relationships		5	6	5	4	4	5	3	6	3	4	4	2
Future—educational/vocational		2	4	2	5	1	1.5	1	1	1	1	1	1
Moral and religious		7	7	6	6	7	7	7	7	6	6	7	7
Self-centered		6	5	7	7	6	6	5	3	5	2	3	4

SOURCE: Joseph Mezzano, "Concerns of Students and Preference for Male and Female Counselors," *Vocational Guidance Quarterly*, 20 (September 1971), 45. Copyright © 1971 American Personnel and Guidance Association. Reprinted with permission.

juniors and reported that there was no significant relationship between the students' evaluation of school experiences and their achievement, as measured by standardized tests and teachers' grades. Teachers rated satisfied students as less impulsive and more responsible than average students.[41]

Redfering and Anderson[42] investigated the extent that the perceptions of students, counselors, and counselor educators were congruent about the concerns of today's youth. Some 1,800 Florida high school students, 31 high school counselors, and 31 counselor educators were surveyed and the means and *t*-scores reporting results from a stratified sample are presented in Table 3.11. Negligible differences existed among the groups about the importance of boy-girl relationships, school, and social injustices. Areas considered by counselors and counselor educators as most important tended more toward self-concept and social adjustment, whereas students' concerns were sometimes more basic, such as personal appearance, money-job, and health. The investigators concluded that youth problems are in flux and warned counselors not to take the client's presented problem too lightly.

More high school students today are seeing counselors than in previous years. During a five-year period, the proportion of high school students who had not talked to a counselor declined from 34 to 15 percent. Table 3.12 reports students' contacts with counselors for that period.

Gallup[43] reported that as many teenagers believe their parents are not strict enough with them as believe they are too strict. Questioned about how well they got along with their parents, 52 percent responded "very well" and 45 percent "fairly well." These responses were the same for males and females. These teenagers were asked what they argued about most with their parents and Table 3.13 gives a breakdown of their responses.

During the past few years, the Purdue Opinion Panel has assessed the degree of concern students have about their vocational choices or decisions. Table 3.14 reports the most current data collected on this matter. Students who plan to attend college express "very much" concern about making vocational decisions. They report that they need information and help to choose a vocation, to understand themselves, their interests, skills, and values. The counselor and parents are viewed as the best sources of assistance with vocational planning and choice making.

[41] Richard C. Diederich and Philip W. Jackson, "Satisfied and Dissatisfied Students," *Personnel and Guidance Journal*, 47 (March 1969), 641–649.

[42] David L. Redfering and Jacquelyn Anderson, "Students' Problems as Perceived by Students, Counselors and Counselor Educators," *The School Counselor*, 22 (January 1975), 198–201.

[43] George Gallup, *Gallup Youth Survey.* (New York: The Associated Press, 1978).

TABLE 3.11 Means and *t*-scores for students, counselors, and counselor educators

Item	Means			t-values		
	Student	Counselor	Counselor educator	Students vs. counselors	Students vs. counselor educators	Counselors vs. counselor educators
My future	1.82	2.87	3.19	−3.956***	5.096***	.831
Boy-girl relationships	2.17	2.03	2.55	.505	−1.300	1.335
Personal appearance	2.24	3.36	3.29	−3.705***	−3.641***	−.160
Money-job	2.28	3.23	3.77	−3.438***	−5.424***	1.559*
Health	2.46	4.77	4.81	−7.130***	−7.102	.086
Social adjustment and responsibility	2.60	3.03	2.65	−1.508	−.159	−1.145
Home life and family relationships	2.61	2.74	3.16	−.404***	−1.636	1.087
War, world problems	2.73	4.00	3.61	−3.753***	−2.563*	−.853
Physical safety	2.75	5.32	5.19	−8.254***	−7.639***	−.335
Self-concept	2.76	2.39	2.45	1.239	1.014	.154
Religion	3.01	4.61	4.55	−4.452***	−4.191***	−.172
Social injustices	3.03	2.84	3.00	.544	.079	.421
School	3.45	3.71	3.81	−.715	−.972	.273
Drugs	4.65	2.68	2.84	4.621***	4.169***	.457
Military service	4.66	4.45	3.55	.537	2.832**	−2.422*

*$p < .02$ (2-tailed).
**$p < .01$ (2-tailed).
***$p < .001$ (2-tailed).

SOURCE: David L. Redfering and Jacquelyn Anderson, "Students' Problems as Perceived by Students, Counselors and Counselor Educators," *The School Counselor*, 22 (January 1975), 199. Copyright © 1975 American Personnel and Guidance Association. Reprinted with permission.

Concerns of college students

Houston[44] reviewed the research on the sources and effects of psychological problems of college students. As expected, the general academic area is consistently identified as most stressful for students. Other prevalent problems include dating, making and breaking friendships, becoming independent of parents, and making vocational plans. Houston reports that freshmen experience more problems than stu-

dents during the other three years of college. A greater proportion of freshmen seek psychological assistance than upperclassmen. Peak periods of help seeking occur at midterm and final examination times. Anxiety, depression, character traits, or emotional sensitivity were reported as hampering some 12 to 35 percent of students across various campuses. Concern over studies, unusual physical complaints, and difficulties with interpersonal relationships often led to successful or attempted suicide. In summary, both psychological and academic adjustment are influenced by college students' problems. Houston believes college students' anxiety states may be related in some complex, as yet unclear fashion to their current or anticipated academic performance.

[44] B. Kent Houston, "Sources, Effects and Individual Vulnerability of Psychological Problems for College Students," *Journal of Counseling Psychology*, 18 (March 1971), 157–161.

TABLE 3.12 **Students' contacts with counselors 1966–1971**

Talked to counselor last year	Poll 78 1966	Poll 85 1968	Poll 88 1970	Poll 93 1971
Never	34%	22%	21%	15%
Once or twice	40	45	41	44
Three or four times	16	22	22	23
Five times or more	9	9	15	15

SOURCE: The Purdue Opinion Panel, "Counseling and Educational Needs of Adolescents," Report of Poll 92 (Lafayette, Indiana: Measurement and Research Center, Purdue University, January 1972), p. 9.

TABLE 3.13 **Conflict sources between parents and teenagers**

	Total	Boys	Girls
Freedom/rights	25%	27%	23%
Curfew	17	17	17
Going out/ places we want to go	16	13	18
Dates/friends	10	3	17
Household chores/duties	9	10	8
Grades	7	9	5
Studies/home-work	4	5	3
Brothers/sisters	3	3	4
Dress/hygiene	2	2	3
Miscellaneous	4	4	4
Nothing/don't argue much	18	19	17
No opinion	3	3	4
	124%	122%	129%

NOTE: Totals add to more than 100% due to multiple responses.
SOURCE: George Gallup, *Gallup Youth Survey* (New York: The Associated Press, 1978). Reprinted with permission of The Associated Press.

TABLE 3.14 **Degree of student concern about making vocational decisions**

Degree of concern	Grade 10	Grade 11	Grade 12
Very much	19%	27%	39%
Quite a bit	26	28	28
Somewhat	25	23	17
A little	16	10	7
Not very much	13	12	9

SOURCE: The Purdue Opinion Panel, "Vocational Plans and Preferences of Adolescents," Report of Poll 94 (Lafayette, Indiana: Measurement and Research Center, Purdue University, May 1972), p. 5a.

counseling staff, campus climate, range of services publicized, and so forth.

Fry[45] hypothesized that a decrease would occur in negative attitudes toward authority when students left the university and shifted their identifications and affiliations to individuals and employment agencies that were detached and uninvolved in their past lives. Further, she hypothesized that the move to an occupational environment would bring an increase in submissiveness and a decrease in self-assertiveness and disliking among previous college students. Three different male college student samples, drawn from engineering, education, and social science, were assessed before and after a period of full employment for changes in attitudes toward authority. Fry reported significant differences between students who directly entered graduate school and those who became employed. Her hypotheses were supported in that negative attitudes toward authority declined and liking and submissiveness responses increased for students (all three areas) who were employed. Those students who continued a university career showed very little decline in their critical attitudes.

Fry interpreted the findings as supporting the recommendation by Kell and Burows[46] that a clearly articulated counseling approach, implemented by counselors through frequent but brief contacts with youth, was useful in countering the excessive submissiveness of youth making the

The functions frequently performed in a college counseling center are educational counseling for choice of major; vocational counseling for choice of career; and personal counseling for emotional conflicts, clarifying interpersonal relationships, and achieving self-understanding. College counseling centers vary considerably in the types of students who become clients. This variation may be due to the

[45] P. S. Fry, "Changes in Youth's Attitudes Toward Authority: The Transition from University to Employment," *Journal of Counseling Psychology*, 23 (January 1976), 66–74.
[46] B. L. Kell and J. M. Burows, *Developmental Counseling and Therapy* (Boston: Houghton Mifflin Company, 1970).

transition to the labor market. Further, Fry was in accord with Coleman[47] who suggested that college counselors arrange for ongoing seminars, group discussions, counseling interactions, and intervention programs that enable youth to explore their values, present and future goals, and related anxieties.

Matteson, who earlier had reported that students who moved from home to campus showed an increase in negative attitudes toward authority,[48] questioned whether Fry's findings that youth who moved from the university to work and became less negative toward authority could be explained or interpreted by psychoanalytic theory.[49] He suggested that the changes in attitudes of youth were best explained by a developmental model in that youth go through certain stages such as acceptance of authority, critical search among alternatives, and commitment. Fry[50] agreed with Matteson that psychoanalytic theory failed to account for change in attitudes toward authority in both transitions and suggested that the two sets of studies could be interpreted either within a cognitive developmental or a social learning context.

Special problems of youth

The decade of the 1970s was a time of expansion in human consciousness. The most fundamental liberation of all has been from the notion that the development of human potentiality is at best a distant prospect. The human mind is beginning to perceive itself as an instrument of infinite capacity. The realization is growing that the only justification for all the vaunted research laboratories and institutions of advanced learning is the ennoblement of the individual human being.

[47] James Coleman, *Youth: Transition to Adulthood* (Chicago: University of Chicago Press, 1974).
[48] David R. Matteson, "Changes in Attitudes Toward Authority Figures with the Move to College: Three Experiments," *Developmental Psychology*, 10 (May 1974), 340–347.
[49] David R. Matteson, "Two Transitions and Two Crises in Youth: A Response to P. S. Fry's 'Changes in Youth's Attitudes Toward Authority,'" *Journal of Counseling Psychology*, 24 (January 1977), 79–80.
[50] P. S. Fry, "A Reply to David R. Matteson's 'Two Transitions and Two Crises in Youth,'" *Journal of Counseling Psychology*, 24 (January 1977), 81–82.

Despite progress realized during the 1970s, numerous youth problems persisted. To treat each one carefully and fully is beyond the scope of this chapter, but six major problems will be discussed briefly. Most assuredly, they are not entirely school problems. Their origin lies in the complex social discontinuities that exist in America, and their solution lies in a multi-institutional approach.

School and college dropouts

As of 1978, most teenagers, aged 15 to 19, were in school, but most young adults, aged 20 to 24, were not. Eight out of 10 teenagers, but only 1.5 of every 100 young adults were in school. Although more young people are getting a high school education today (74 percent in 1978; 51 percent in 1930; 45 percent in 1910) than ever before and the percentage (but not the actual numbers) of college-age people actually in college is expected to grow rapidly by 1985, dropouts pose a major problem to schools and college personnel.

The point of greatest danger for high school dropouts has moved from the eighth to the tenth grade in three decades. Study after study has probed for the reasons why students leave school. These studies have, with remarkable consistency, arrived at similar conclusions. Typical reasons for dropping out of school are work, early marriage, grade failures, inability to get along with teachers, dislike of social relationships in the school, and a belief that school course work is unrelated to individual needs.

Years of research have focused on the personal characteristics of high school dropouts. Although these research findings are often in conflict, the views that most commonly emerge are that high school dropouts (1) distrust and suspect authority, (2) have unrealistic aspirations and work attitudes, (3) are hypersensitive to criticism or rejection, (4) display a facade of toughness, (5) evidence dependency needs, (6) possess impaired and confused self-concepts, and (7) reject social values. The problems they present to counselors include (1) employment, (2) family relationships, (3) health concerns, (4) school-related difficulties, (5) anxiety, and (6) responsibility for raising children.

Increasingly the college dropout is becoming the focus of widespread concern. A dropout rate of approximately 60 percent nationally over the four-year period has been reported by numerous investigators. However, it is to be noted that the rate varies greatly (from 12 to 82 percent) with the type of institution and within type. Public institutions show an average rate of 68 percent whereas private institutions show only 52 percent.

Many descriptive studies indicate that the most crucial college dropout period is the freshman year, with the chances for survival increasing to 65 percent or better by the junior year. The most commonly stated reasons for leaving college include (1) lack of finances, (2) academic difficulty, (3) dissatisfaction with program and college, (4) marriage, (5) military service, and (6) illness.

Some time ago, Williams argued persuasively that consideration of the college environment would help to resolve some of the apparent contradictions among the various characteristics attributed to the college dropout.[51] He offers the hypothesis that a student is more likely to leave college when behavior reinforced by the college environment is incompatible with behavior previously reinforced. Therefore, interpersonal relationships with peers, instructors, and significant others are conceptualized as the processes mediating reinforcement for college students. Further, parents, teachers, and others view the act of dropping out of school as a social ill to be eradicated. Consequently, this viewpoint reinforces the negative values in the self-concepts of students who leave school. Potential dropouts cannot make the changes in self-perception requisite to changes in overt behavior.

Associated with the above concept is the view that some students seem almost predestined to leave college because they are pulled in opposite directions by the reinforcement of opposing modes of behavior. Williams points out that the potential dropout may well perform some actions oriented toward achieving the goal of a college degree and engage in other actions directed away from that goal. Further, the avoidance component in such a conflict appears to be stronger than the approach component. Student personnel workers at all levels, Williams suggests, should begin to question with students and their parents the assumption that higher education is necessary for attaining the "good life." He doubts that recommending counseling and psychotherapy for all students in conflict is realistic because of lack of demonstrable gains and strain on available resources.

The future of the college dropout is not as bleak as that of the school dropout. For the latter, unemployment, marginal jobs, proneness to delinquency, anxiety, humiliation, and the inability to live life as a fully developed person are usually in store. Because contemporary America lacks adequate provisions for living in decent poverty, many dropouts rapidly retreat to hopelessness and apathy and become another generation of the community dependent, living on welfare, in the clinics, and in jail.

Pregnancies, youthful marriages, and divorce

According to a *Time* article,[52] teenage girls are greatly misinformed about the times they are most likely to become pregnant, and most teenagers do not use contraceptives. *Time* reported that Melvin Zelnik and John Kantner, two demographers who prepared a study for the President's Commission on Population Growth and the American Future, interviewed 4,611 unmarried white and black women, aged 15 to 19. While error-free statistics about sexual habits are difficult to come by, these demographers project from their sample that at age 15, 13.8 percent of unmarried girls have experienced sexual intercourse. For age 16, the figure was 21.2 percent; age 17, 26.6 percent; age 18, 37.1 percent; and age 19, 46.1 percent. Even so, Zelnik and Kantner conclude that "the picture is not one of rampant sexuality among the sexually inexperienced." Nevertheless, youth's sexual revolution is not just franker talk and greater openness; more teenagers, especially younger ones, are having at least occasional sexual intercourse.

The United States has one of the highest rates of teenage pregnancies in the world. The pregnancy rate among unmarried girls continues to spiral. The number of illegitimate births per thousand teenagers has risen from 8.3 in 1940 to 21 in 1977. Of an estimated 1.7 million abortions performed in the United States in 1977, it is believed that close to one third were performed on teenagers. Nationwide, the pregnancy rate from college to college varies from 6 to 15 percent.

The rapid rise in teenage pregnancy led Congress to approve the Health Services and Centers Amendments of 1978, including new comprehensive services to prevent

---

[51] Vernon Williams, "The College Dropout: Qualities of His Environment," *Personnel and Guidance Journal*, 45 (May 1967), 878–882.

[52] Melvin Zelnik and John Kantner, *Time*, August 21, 1972, pp. 34–40.

adolescent pregnancy and to provide help for teenage girls who become pregnant. The program authorized $50 million in fiscal 1979 for grants to the public and nonprofit agencies that can provide a wide range of health, education, and counseling services for teens in a single setting or a network of locations. Core services grantees must provide pregnancy testing, maternal counseling and referral, family planning, pre- and post-natal care, nutrition instruction, referral for screening and treatment of venereal disease, sex education, adoption counseling, and vocational planning. Funding for the program increases from $50 million in 1979 to $65 million in 1980 and to $75 million in 1981.

Though the number of teenage marriages seems to be declining, one fourth of all 18- and 19-year-olds are married. The number of teenage brides who are pregnant when they walk down the aisle is impossible to compute. However, some estimates exist that indicate that the pregnancy rate among teenage brides at the time of marriage may be as high as 33 percent. Although clearly not all teenage marriages occur because of pregnancy, it is reasonable to conclude that pregnancy is an influential factor in many youthful marriages. Otherwise, the couples would wait a few years to marry.

Currently there are 461 divorces for every 1,000 marriages. The divorce rate among teenagers is three times higher than for those who marry later. This means that a teenage marriage has no better than a 50-50 chance of survival.

An overwhelming percentage of youth who marry in high school leave school and only a few re-enter. Although estimates vary, it appears that about 40 percent of boys and 90 percent of girls who marry while in school drop out, and few return.

Many teens are suspicious of medical care and many deny that they are pregnant. Despite the availability of contraceptives, most teenagers do not have advice on how to use them. But contraceptives appear not to be the answer, because most pregnant teens are sexually active before they become pregnant and before they ask for contraceptives. Changing social attitudes encourage young people to believe that living together and having sex are not strong social taboos. Also encouraging teens toward pregnancy is the knowledge that abortions are available, that more young women are keeping their babies, and that society is willing to help these single and young parents. Although it is true that more and more unmarried teenage mothers have cho-

sen to keep their babies when they are first born, they put them up for adoption after two or three years when the care becomes too much to handle.

Although the curtailment of education is serious in itself, the personal, social, and legal aspects of early marriage are even more disturbing. Annulment and divorce rates are highest among those who marry in their teens.

Crime and delinquency

Delinquency is now recognized as a pervasive social problem, although little is known empirically about its origin. By any standard of measurement, the statistics are staggering, and their impact can be felt at every level of American life. One boy in every six will turn up in a juvenile court for a nontraffic offense before he is 18. Over one third of all persons arrested by police in 1977 were in the age group 16 to 24, easily the most lawless group in America. Delinquency cases handled by the juvenile courts increased 10 percent in 1977 over the previous year, at a time when the total child population in this age group (10 to 17) increased by only two percent. Seven out of ten delinquents are 16 or under.

Charges brought against boys are generally more serious than those against girls. More than half of the offenses committed by girls were for conduct not ordinarily considered a crime, such as runaway, truancy, curfew, and the like, but only one fifth of the boys were charged with these minor offenses. About half of the offenses committed by boys were against property—larceny, auto theft, vandalism, robbery, and burglary.

Available evidence suggests that delinquent behavior is higher in economically depressed sectors of urban areas. But delinquent behavior patterns can be found in all parts of American society. The number of concealed delinquent acts is probably also large. By some estimates, undetected delinquency is as much as triple that which is discovered. Further, undetected as well as unrecorded delinquency is more common among middle and higher income groups.

The most frequent disposition of delinquency cases is "warning" or "adjusted." Although complaints are not substantiated in about 8 percent of the cases, a delinquent act was usually identified. However, the stability of the family of the delinquent and the potential for receiving proper parental supervision bring about dispositions of "warning" or "adjusted."

Juvenile courts in the United States have long made their own rules and regulations and generally answer to no higher authority. The first juvenile court, created in 1899 in Illinois, was established not to punish children but to treat them. Presiding judges were given great latitude in disposing of cases. But, however high the motive or enlightened the practice that led to the development of the juvenile court system, inequities and impingements on individual rights developed. In May 1967, the Supreme Court *In the matter of Gault* ruled that accused juveniles are entitled to timely notice of the charges against them. They must be given the right to confront and cross-examine witnesses against them. They must be told of their right to counsel and counsel must be provided if they are indigent. They must be told of their right to remain silent. The majority opinion delivered by Justice Fortas noted that it was still acceptable for the courts to keep a juvenile's record secret to protect him or her. The juvenile can still be classified as a delinquent instead of a criminal, and a record of delinquency need not operate as a civil disability or disqualify one for civil service appointment.

Causes of delinquent behavior have been the subject of much clinical observation and considerable research. The evidence produced appears inconsistent at worst and inconclusive at best with various interpretations. Emphasis on instant need gratification is often believed to cause dissatisfaction and discontent with present conditions and positions. Discrepancies between social and economic aspirations and opportunities to achieve these aspirations by legitimate means is another reason. Traditional channels to higher positions, such as college, are restricted for large categories of people. Lack of good models, inadequate parents, poor socioeconomic conditions are other reasons. Many delinquents have been described as alienated from the social order, conventional rules, and ideologies but such characterizations of causes seem circular in that they also denote delinquency.

The cost of combating juvenile delinquency—detection, study, diagnosis, treatment—is high. But the real tragedy lies in the human suffering, misery, and waste of human lives.

Youth unemployment

The importance of work is self-evident. Gainful employment is the accepted means of attaining monetary rewards in our money-oriented culture. Since 1947, the unemployment rate for teenagers (aged 16 to 19) has been higher—sometimes three times higher—than for the total labor force. Estimates are that during the early 1980s the problems of youthful unemployment will be aggravated by the entry of 26 million new workers into the labor market (many of whom are married women), or an increase of 40 percent over the entries during the preceding decade.

Job opportunities fluctuate with the economy and vary by geographic region. Labor force participation for young people tends to be somewhat higher than the national average for those in the Midwestern, mountain, and Pacific states. The greatest single concentration of employed teenagers (aged 14 to 19) is in wholesale and retail trade, followed by manufacturing. Approximately one fourth of young workers are school dropouts. Unemployment among dropouts tends to be twice as high as that for high school graduates.

The traditional first jobs for young people that generally require little or no skill are diminishing in number. These jobs—as laborers, operatives, farm workers—that provided for about 60 percent of employed young people entering the labor force are rapidly disappearing because of mechanization and high minimum-wage rates.

The creation of new jobs and employment opportunities for young people is a responsibility shared by local, state, and national agencies. But school personnel can publicize existing opportunities and the routes to taking advantage of them. Sensitive vocational counseling can aid youth in trial work experiences, developing career plans, and clarifying what preparation is needed for careers.

Alcohol and drugs

Counselors are increasingly dealing with alcohol and drug problems among secondary school students. Riester and Zucker point out that pressures to conform to certain drinking norms exist in every society that makes use of beverage alcohol. These two investigators examined teenage drinking customs in the context of the informal social structure of the high school. Their subjects were the entire junior and senior classes (754) of a public high school in a Middle Atlantic state. Some of their principal findings were that (1) the frequency of drinking and the amount consumed are related to informal social status group membership (college-bound, "leathers," [described by the investigators as young persons not involved in school activities, who were often discipline problems, and who spent their nonschool time working or hanging around town], average or quiet students, intellectuals, true individuals or hippies, students who go steady)—identification with either the collegiate or "leather" subgroups is associated with high use of alcohol; (2) religious affiliations are not related to teenagers' use or nonuse of alcohol; (3) students' whose parents are semi-professional drink more frequently than do students whose parents are in other social positions; (4) high use of alcohol is not related to lower social class background; (5) non-whites were characterized as low users (nondrinkers and moderates) of alcohol; (6) teenagers are more likely to be high users if both parents are users of alcohol; and (7) the most frequent situation for using alcohol is a social one involving groups of people, rather than solitude or the company of one friend of the opposite sex. Riester and Zucker reported that 91 percent of the juniors and seniors had consumed alcohol.[53]

Hard data about teenage drug use are limited; estimates vary widely, ranging from as low as 5 to as high as 70 percent among some groups in some schools. Hager, Vener, and Stewart[54] investigated drug use among 4,220 white, middle-American adolescents in grades eight through twelve in three communities selected deliberately to ascertain socioeconomic influences on drug use. One community was predominantly upper-middle, lower-upper class, the second was mainly lower-middle and upper-lower class, and the third was primarily a working-class semirural area. Table 3.15 presents their report on the use of various drugs by age of students. As shown by Table 3.15, the youth of this middle-American sample were not deeply involved in drug use.

These authors reported that greater drug use was associated with higher socioeconomic communities (hard drugs excepted). Marijuana consumption, for example, increased from about 6 percent in the working-class community to a high of almost 21 percent in the professional-managerial community. Hager and his associates suggest that

. . . drug users may comprise a subculture in which the use of one drug greatly increases one's chances of using other drugs. Hard drugs do not seem to be as integral a part of this drug subculture.[55]

More than half of the high school seniors who graduated in 1975 had smoked marijuana, according to the National Institute on Drug Abuse.[56] Their sampling of 13,000 seniors revealed that 8 percent of them had used marijuana twenty times or more in the previous month, compared with 6 percent who had taken an alcoholic drink that many times. The report stated that 55 percent of the class of 1975 disapproved of the occasional use of marijuana, but this figure dropped to 48 percent in 1976.

The use of marijuana appears no longer to be an act of protest, but a behavior that for some has entered the mainstream of their lifestyles. The idea that marijuana is safe, although accepted by many young people as well as some not so young, is clearly not endorsed by most of the drug research community.

Venereal disease

Next to the common cold, syphilis and gonorrhea are the most common infectious diseases among young people, outranking hepatitis, measles, mumps, scarlet fever, strep throat, and tuberculosis combined. The incidence of syphilis is much lower than gonorrhea; however, syphilis is a much more serious disease.

In 1975 there were at least 4,150 cases of syphilis among the 26 million teenagers in the United States and 180,000 cases of gonorrhea, more than in any other country except Sweden and Denmark. From 1965 to 1975 the number of reported cases of venereal disease among girls, age 15 to 19, increased 144 percent. The percentage known does not begin to tell the story, for it is estimated that at least three out of four cases go unreported.

Penicillin and the antibiotics brought into mass production during the Second World War came close to eliminating venereal diseases in America. But since 1970 more and more people, particularly teenagers, have become infected. There

[53] Albert E. Riester and Robert A. Zucker, "Adolescent Social Structure and Drinking Behavior," *Personnel and Guidance Journal*, 47 (December 1968), 304–312.
[54] David L. Hager, Arthur M. Vener, and Cyrus S. Stewart, "Patterns of Adolescent Drug Use in Middle America," *Journal of Counseling Psychology*, 18 (July 1971), 292–297.

[55] Ibid., p. 296.
[56] National Institute on Drug Abuse, *Sixth Annual Report to Congress* (Washington, D.C.: U.S. Government Printing Office, 1977).

TABLE 3.15 **Drug use by age (in percents)**

Age	N	Never used	Once	2–4 times	5–7 times	8 or more times
13 years and younger	816					
Marijuana		95.0	2.3	1.1	.6	1.0
Hallucinogens		97.0	1.2	.9	.5	.4
Amphetamines		96.7	1.7	.6	.1	.9
Hard		97.4	1.0	1.0	.2	.4
14 years	907					
Marijuana		93.5	2.6	1.3	.6	2.0
Hallucinogens		95.0	2.3	.9	.5	1.3
Amphetamines		95.2	2.0	1.5	.3	1.0
Hard		97.2	1.5	.1	.2	1.0
15 years	823					
Marijuana		89.7	3.0	2.3	1.0	4.0
Hallucinogens		94.0	3.2	.8	1.5	.5
Amphetamines		94.2	2.0	1.6	.6	1.6
Hard		97.0	1.2	.9	.5	.4
16 years	867					
Marijuana		81.8	5.7	3.8	1.7	7.0
Hallucinogens		90.4	3.5	2.6	.7	2.8
Amphetamines		90.7	3.0	3.5	.6	2.2
Hard		97.0	1.0	.7	.5	.8
17 years and older	807					
Marijuana		77.9	4.2	5.2	2.5	10.2
Hallucinogens		90.5	2.6	2.9	2.0	2.0
Amphetamines		88.9	3.3	3.3	1.4	3.1
Hard		97.3	1.3	.4	.4	.6

SOURCE: David L. Hager, Arthur M. Vener, and Cyrus S. Stewart, "Patterns of Adolescent Drug Use in Middle America," *Journal of Counseling Psychology*, 18 (July 1971), 294. Copyright © 1971 by the American Psychological Association. Reprinted by permission.

is, in fact, a largely unnoticed epidemic of venereal disease among teenagers—an epidemic infecting youngsters from all social strata.

One of the problems involved is the sexual ignorance of teenagers. Girls with gonorrhea often do not know they have it. Boys may have a vague idea that penicillin will cure it, then take ineffective dosages to cure themselves. Because the initial symptoms normally disappear in a few weeks, they believe they are cured—usually they are not.

Boys are more readily aware of the symptoms of gonorrhea—a discharge, difficulty or strain in urinating. That the discharge goes away without treatment does not mean the disease is cured. Actually, the infection begins to go further up the urinary tract and beyond, sometimes involving other organs. For the girl, a discharge as a symptom of gonorrhea is more complicated, because some discharge is normal in females. It may go unnoticed until the Fallopian tubes become infected and pain sets in. Before the infection reaches this point, changes in color and odor of the discharge will develop as early symptoms. However, there are ten or more causes for such discharges, therefore a discharge does not always signify gonorrhea. Symptoms of syphilis are more difficult to spot than are those of gonorrhea. They include fever, rash, loss of hair, and even a sore that is not painful. Through ignorance, promiscuity, and a changing morality, this hidden epidemic spreads its gray plague.

Summary

In American society the above problem areas are natural occurrences during the developmental processes. The selection cited is not complete but does represent areas in which various age groups are frequently involved. For this reason, most if not all counselors in the school setting will come into contact with these problems at some time during their careers. Although in some instances the percentages reported are small, the absolute numbers they represent are not. They are of major concern to adults because each is potentially tremendously damaging to the individual. It is when such severe problems occur that the individual is most in need of assistance of many kinds. Among these is the helping relationship provided by the counselor in avoiding such problems, coping with them if present, or dealing with their aftereffects.

Issues

Issue 1 Developmental approaches to behavior such as those presented by Havighurst or Erikson are of little value to counselors.

True, because
1. Clients are individuals whose development, problems, and concerns must be dealt with directly and uniquely.
2. Developmental approaches are generalizations about behavior that do not account for a particular individual's specific circumstances, realities, and aspirations.
3. Developmental approaches are by nature descriptive and inferential; they do not set forth individual cause-and-effect relationships.
4. Such approaches are limited because they reflect middle-class behaviors and patterns.

False, because
1. Such approaches are like maps in that they give counselors a sense of the terrain of behavior, representing relative life positions.
2. Such approaches suggest patterns of behavior that need to be and can be explored in counseling.
3. Developmental approaches suggest timetables of behavior that enable counselors to know whether a particular individual is off schedule; furthermore, they suggest activities useful in helping an individual to catch up.

Discussion Developmental approaches present a broad overview of behavior, spanning the range from complex human social interaction to individual physical progress. A major goal of developmental approaches is the description of age changes in behavior and psychological functions and the explanation of the processes underlying these changes. Their principal purpose is to convey a sense of human functioning and what it means. Almost all aspects of human development are influenced by many interrelated factors—genetic, constitutional, social, and familial. Development in one function is likely to have repercussions in others. Thus, as clients become more self-confident, improvements are likely to be seen in other behaviors. Developmental approaches enable counselors to understand that although change is orderly and predictable, it is not always smooth and gradual; further, that experiences at one developmental stage may affect later development.

We believe that developmental descriptions of behavior are highly useful to counselors. They provide a foundation of knowledge and understanding—a framework—against which a particular individual's behavior can be viewed, explored, and studied. They provide a focus that can be used by counselors to observe conditions within as well as external to the individual that point up striking individual differences. An important feature of such approaches is that they enable counselors to conceptualize the individual's behavior, admittedly from a broad perspective, but one that sharpens and highlights its forms, sources, and functions. Such conceptualizations are counselors' tentative hypotheses or explanations of relationships among characteristics, conditions, or events that guide any coherent functioning with individuals.

Issue 2 Youth problems such as alcohol and drug abuse, venereal diseases, unmarried pregnancies are outside the domain of school counselors' functions.

True, because
1. These situations require specialized assistance.
2. These problems stem from complex emotional factors better dealt with by psychologists.
3. Treatment of these problems requires long-term therapy; schools, by nature, must limit their treatment to educational short-term matters.

False, because
1. Individuals with such problems are still students who are expected to cope with and achieve in classrooms and other school activities.
2. Youth who have such problems are the reason why counselors are employed in schools.

Discussion This issue is best viewed from two perspectives. First, it is true that students who are involved in such situations *often* require specialized remedial treatments. From that perspective, school counselors should rightfully be viewed as offering the front-line defense of knowing what specialized corrective service is needed and where and how it may be obtained. To do so effectively means that counselors must involve themselves with such youth, often occupying much of the counselor's time. The second perspective is that preventive-intervention approaches in these situations are rightfully within the domain of school counselor functions. Preventive strategies and procedures can be formulated and implemented by counselors through individual counseling, small group procedures, and curricular experiences that will do much to enable students to comprehend their behaviors, decisions, values, and life situations. No doubt the problems of alcohol or drug abuse, for example, are serious but they can be handled much better by viewing them as behavior problems essentially similar to many other problems and by clarifying the kinds of forces that surround and perpetuate them.

Annotated references

Erikson, Erik H. *Identity: Youth and Crisis.* New York: W. W. Norton and Company, 1968. 336 pp.
Chapter 3 (pp. 31–141) describes the eight stages of man and Chapter 4 (pp. 141–207) presents autobiographical material of Bernard Shaw to illustrate creative confusion associated with stages of identity. Additionally, clinical case material is used to illustrate severe identity crisis.

Havighurst, Robert J. *Human Development and Education.* New York: David McKay Co., 1953. 338 pp.
The book is organized into five parts paralleling stages of human development. The developmental tasks of each stage are identified, discussed, and illustrated. Studies of developmental tasks in middle childhood and adolescence are presented.

Hobbs, Nicholas, ed. *Issues in the Classification of Children.* Vols. I (444 pp.) and II (596 pp.). San Francisco: Jossey-Bass, 1975.
An extensive treatment of the issues involved in labeling, diagnosing, and classifying children. These two volumes exhaustively cover theory, practice, shortcomings, and problems involved in the diagnosis and provision of treatment and education of those who are "different."

Loevinger, Jane. *Ego Development.* San Francisco: Jossey-Bass, 1976. 504 pp.
Extensive treatment of ego development. Describes the stages and gives the clinical observations and research findings supporting development stages.

Sheehy, Gail. *Passages.* New York: Bantam Books, 1976. 560 pp.
Sets forth crises of adult life and illustrates these crises with 115 case histories. Cycles of change in both men and women are detailed. The book is very readable.

Further references

Abbott, Anne Haigher. "Individual Counseling with High-Risk Students: A Practical Approach." *The School Counselor,* 25 (January 1978), 206–208.

Archer, James, Jr., and Ann Lopata. "Marijuana Revisited." *Personnel and Guidance Journal,* 57 (January 1979), 244–251.

Bickel, Frank, and Maude O'Neill. "The Counselor and Student Discipline: Suggested Roles." *Personnel and Guidance Journal,* 57 (June 1979), 522–526.

Fry, P. S. "Changes in Youth's Attitudes Toward Authority: The Transition from University to Employment." *Journal of Counseling Psychology,* 23 (January 1976), 66–74.

Green, Logan. "Rural High School Students' Perceptions of the Basic Values and Educational Philosophies of Significant Secondary School Role Models." *Personnel and Guidance Journal,* 57 (April 1979), 392–397.

Hutchins, David E., and Claire Cole. "A Model for Improving Middle School Students' Interpersonal Relationships." *The School Counselor,* 25 (November 1977), 134–137.

Krumboltz, Helen B., and Johanna Shapiro. "Counseling Women in Behavioral Self-Direction." *Personnel and Guidance Journal,* 57 (April 1979), 415–418.

Miller, Gary M., and Mary Lou Reinken. "A School-Community Mental Health–Counseling Effort." *The School Counselor*, 25 (September 1977), 36–43.

Schaum, Maurie. "Delinquent Behavior Comes from Delinquent Minds." *The School Counselor*, 25 (March 1978), 276–282.

Stiltner, Barbara. "Needs Assessment: A First Step." *Elementary School Guidance and Counseling*, 12 (April 1978), 239–246.

Warnath, Charles F. "Relationship and Growth Theories and Agency Counseling." *Counselor Education and Supervision*, 17 (December 1977), 84–91.

4 Counseling: expectations and goals

The intent of Part One is to provide an orientation to counseling, therefore, it would seem imperative that consideration be given to the expectancies and goals of counseling. *Expectancies* refers to the anticipations held, or the inferences made, about counseling. *Goals* are the end results sought through counseling. This chapter presents what certain groups and individuals expect or want from counseling, as compared to the goals stated for counseling.

Expectancies for counseling

The expectancies for counseling are diverse, often contradictory, and sometimes impossible. They are derived from experience, stem from need, and are nurtured by hope among those who seek assistance and those who provide it.

Expectancies of counselees

The majority of counselees expect counseling to produce personal solutions for them. Those in stressful situations anticipate that counseling will bring relief. Those who are vacillating over a decision expect counseling to result in a choice. Those who perceive themselves as personally unpopular expect counseling to lead to their becoming popular. Those who are lonely expect solace and the discovery of ways to interact meaningfully with others. Those who want to go to college view counseling as guaranteeing them admission, scholarship, or financial aid. Those who are about to fail, either in school or in other ventures, expect failure to turn to success as a result of counseling. Those who seek employment counseling expect quick placement, job satisfaction, and easy promotion. All too often, it is presumed that counseling will be of short duration. Counselees usually expect to be tested, analyzed, and, above all, directed or told how and what to do to obtain whatever it was that led them to seek counseling.

Research on expectations held for counseling was stimulated by Levitt[1] who hypothesized an "expectation-reality discrepancy." He suggested that a negative correlation existed between counseling effectiveness and the discrepancy between what clients expect of, and the reality encountered in, counseling. The more that clients experience counseling as being contrary to their preconceptions, the less likely it is that counseling affects them favorably. Examinations of the studies now to be discussed, grouped by type of population studied, amplifies the inferences related to expectancies, such as where clients turn for help and whether they stay in counseling.

ELEMENTARY SCHOOL STUDENTS Relatively few studies have explored expectations of counseling held by elementary school students, particularly those in the first three grades. A major limitation to collecting data of this type lies in the fact that surveys usually require written responses that are difficult to obtain from young children. Bachman[2] reported that the mother was the preferred person elementary school children would go to for help with a problem. Characteristics generated by these children as being important in a helping person included understanding, trust, and the ability to give good advice.

Stiltner[3] conducted a needs assessment for establishing an elementary school counseling program. She reported that at least 50 percent of students in grades three through six of a Colorado sample reported that they would like help in "learning about jobs I'd be interested in," "finding out how people feel about me," and "finding out what things I can do best."

[1] Eugene E. Levitt, "Psychotherapy Research and the Expectation-Reality Discrepancy," *Psychotherapy: Theory, Research and Practice*, 3 (November 1966), 163–166.
[2] Randall W. Bachman, "Elementary School Children's Perception of Helpers and Their Characteristics," *Elementary School Guidance and Counseling*, 10 (December 1975), 103–109.
[3] Barbara Stiltner, "Needs Assessment: A First Step," *Elementary School Guidance and Counseling*, 12 (April 1978), 239–246.

TABLE 4.1 **Summary of where students go for help with various types of problems**

	Career indecision		Truancy		Poor work		Personal problems	
	N	%	N	%	N	%	N	%
Counselor	142	26	269	54	142	27	23	4
Dean of students	1	0	18	4	0	0	0	0
School psychologist	3	1	5	1	5	1	22	4
Principal	0	0	6	1	0	0	2	0
Homeroom teacher	47	9	14	3	221	42	0	0
Subject area teacher	47	9	14	3	221	42	0	0
Relative or friend	83	16	61	12	38	7	300	54
Parent	240	45	86	17	100	19	159	29
Other	19	4	15	3	13	3	45	8
$\Sigma N =$	536		502		523		552	

SOURCE: Harvey S. Leviton, "Consumer Feedback on a Secondary School Guidance Program," *Personnel and Guidance Journal*, 55 (January 1977), 243. Copyright © 1977 American Personnel and Guidance Association. Reprinted with permission.

HIGH SCHOOL STUDENTS Recent years have brought a reduction in the research conducted to determine the expectations of counseling and counselors held by secondary school students. The following are representative of studies conducted with that age group. The expectations of 181 secondary school students were obtained by Gladstein before and after counseling.[4] His subjects were clients who came to the University of Rochester Practicum Counseling Center from nine different schools representing various ethnic, socioeconomic, and religious backgrounds. Some seventeen different statements were used to classify what these students expected to accomplish in counseling before experiencing it. For example, they expected to do general career planning; obtain help in choosing a vocation; discover their abilities, interests, capabilities; come to understand themselves better; to pick the right college; improve their study habits, and so on. Contrary to many reports, their expectations were not restricted to educational-vocational matters, either before or after counseling.

Van Riper examined junior high school students' perceptions of the counselor's role, how helpful the assistance given by counselors was to students, and to what extent counselors were utilized by students.[5] He reported that stu-

dents expect counselors to help them with educational planning and, to a lesser extent, with other school problems. His subjects did not regard highly the assistance given by counselors, but they reported that counselors were more often helpful to them than teachers or principals but were rated as less helpful than other students.

Leviton, based on data obtained from 550 students, representing about one third of a Minnesota high school, reported that 45 percent indicated they would go first to a parent in deciding on a career, with counselors being viewed as the next likely source of help.[6] His summary of preferred helping services for various types of situations is presented here as Table 4.1. These same students ranked twelve guidance functions as to their importance in meeting student needs. High school program planning, post–high school planning, help with academic problems and with career education were, respectively, the first four functions.

COLLEGE STUDENTS Warman[7] was among the first to report perceptions of how various campus groups view counseling. A one-hundred item questionnaire was administered to 250 college students. The results were factor analyzed, yielding one general and three specific factors. The questionnaires

[4] Gerald A. Gladstein, "Client Expectations, Counseling Experience and Satisfaction," *Journal of Counseling Psychology*, 16 (November 1969), 476–481.
[5] B. W. Van Riper, "Student Perception: The Counselor Is What He Does," *The School Counselor*, 19 (September 1971), 53–56.

[6] Harvey S. Leviton, "Consumer Feedback on a Secondary School Guidance Program," *Personnel and Guidance Journal*, 55 (January 1977), 242–244.
[7] Roy E. Warman, "Differential Perceptions of Counseling Role," *Journal of Counseling Psychology*, 7 (Winter 1960), 269–274.

were then scored on the specific factors (college routine, vocational choice, and adjustment to self), and comparisons were made among the subjects. Help in vocational choice was rated as most appropriate for discussion in college counseling centers, followed by college routine problems. Adjustment to self and others was rated as least appropriate. Warman suggested that if counselors were to provide the full range of appropriate counseling services, they must better orient and educate others as to what counseling is and can do.

Wilcove and Sharp followed up Warman's investigations and surveyed parents of students, student services personnel, faculty, counselors, and the student body at the University of Wyoming to gain an understanding of how they viewed the counseling center. All groups except counselors endorsed (in order) vocational choice, college routine, and adjustment to self and others as being appropriate for discussion at the college counseling center. Counselors thought that students' adjustment problems were more appropriate for their services than did the other groups.[8] Resnick and Gelso also replicated and extended Warman's study. They reported that all groups viewed problems of adjustment to self and others as more appropriate for counseling attention now than a decade ago. However, their data did not suggest that counselors had succeeded in reducing the communications gap between themselves and such other relevant groups as faculty, students, and parents.[9]

Strong and his associates[10] compared sixty-seven female college students' views of counselors, advisors, and psychiatrists. Counselors and advisers were viewed as more warm and friendly than psychiatrists. Psychiatrists were considered appropriate sources of help for specific personal problems but students regarded counselors as likely to help them achieve personal development and gain knowledge of their strengths and weaknesses.

Bryson and Bardo[11] hypothesized that black students' experiences and attitudes toward counselors and counseling differed sufficiently from their white counterparts to warrant theoretical approaches that were different. But Cheatham's investigation of the counseling services extended by predominantly black colleges found that they were similar (79 percent overlap) to those offered at predominantly white colleges.[12] Later, Johnson[13] investigated perceptions that black students located at black universities have of counselors in relation to other available sources of help. His results were similar to those reported in previous investigations, namely, that college students were more willing to discuss educational and vocational concerns with counselors than personal-social concerns.

Dreman and Dolev[14] studied the relationship between preferences and expectations for counselors held by a nonclient population. These nonclient students preferred counselors who were more active than they expected them to be in removing symptoms and changing behaviors. Dreman[15] then compared these results to those obtained from a hundred student clients before their initial counseling session. Clients' expectations were significantly more conventional than nonclients. Clients expected counselors to explain and interpret problems, analyze emotional problems, help clients to achieve insight. Clients had significantly diminished expectations that the counselor would be activistic, by seeking to influence their moral judgments, consult with their family, and so on. Dreman concluded that both college clients and nonclients *want* more counselor activity than they *expect* to get.

[8] Gerry Wilcove and W. Harry Sharp, "Differential Perceptions of a College Counseling Center," *Journal of Counseling Psychology*, 18 (January 1971), 60–63.

[9] Harvey Resnick and Charles J. Gelso, "Differential Perceptions of Counseling Role: A Reexamination," *Journal of Counseling Psychology*, 18 (November 1971), 549–553.

[10] Stanley R. Strong, Darwin D. Handel, and Joseph C. Bratton, "College Students' Views of Campus Help-Givers: Counselors, Advisors, and Psychiatrists," *Journal of Counseling Psychology*, 18 (May 1971), 234–238.

[11] S. Bryson and H. Bardo, "Race and the Counseling Process: An Overview," *Journal of Non-White Concerns in Personnel and Guidance*, 4 (October 1975), 5–15.

[12] H. Cheatham, "Counseling in Black Colleges and Universities: A Profile," *Journal of Non-White Concerns in Personnel and Guidance*, 4 (October 1975), 16–22.

[13] Howard N. Johnson, "A Survey of Students' Attitudes Toward Counseling at a Predominantly Black University," *Journal of Counseling Psychology*, 24 (March 1977), 162–164.

[14] Solly B. Dreman and A. Dolev, "Expectations and Preferences of Nonclients for a University Student Counseling Service," *Journal of Counseling Psychology*, 23 (November 1976), 571–574.

[15] Solly B. Dreman, "Expectations and Preferences of Clients for a University Student Counseling Service," *Journal of Counseling Psychology*, 24 (September 1977), 459–462.

Webster and Fretz[16] investigated Asian American, black, and white college students' rank ordering of twelve help-givers for educational-vocational and emotional problems. Rankings did not differ significantly for the group as a whole or for any subgrouping by sex or racial classification. Students identified parents, friends, relatives, counseling centers, and either a faculty member or a physician as the five most preferred helping sources. Venzor and his associates[17] reported that both client and nonclient groups most frequently select adjectives that describe nurturant counselors, but that neither group had any preferential counselor response style.

Tinsley and Benton[18] reported that college clients differed in their conceptualizations of what counseling would be like (expectations) and what they wanted counseling to be like (preferences). College clients' preferences of seeing experienced counselors, understanding the purpose of what happens in the interview, taking tests, and doing assignments outside the counseling interview exceeded their expectations. The greatest discrepancy between expectation and preference occurred for outcome. Clients wanted counselors to help them but were doubtful that counselors would do so.

Tinsley and Harris[19] reported that undergraduate college students expected to see counselors who were experienced, expert, genuine, trustworthy, and accepting. The expectancy that counselors be understanding and directive in order to produce a beneficial outcome was expressed but valued somewhat less.

Why some students fail to make use of university counseling facilities was investigated by Snyder, Hill, and Derksen.[20] They hypothesized that stigma, seriousness of

problems, student attitudes, counseling experience, and information (or lack of it) would affect students' use of counseling services. Their findings were that students were favorable to counseling; stigma was of little concern; students generally possessed little information about counseling; and friends were the first choice of help with personal and social problems (close relatives were the second choice and faculty and psychological services the last choice). This suggests that diversity in client expectations need not interfere with the counseling relationship if counselors handle them skillfully.

ADULTS Overall and Aronson[21] surveyed the expectations of therapy among a group of lower-socioeconomic-class patients in an outpatient clinic. A questionnaire was administered prior to initial interviews to determine patients' expectations and again following initial interviews to ascertain their perceptions of the degree to which these expectations were met. Therapists were administered the same questionnaire following initial interviews to assess their views. Findings suggested that the patients and therapists generally agreed on the process that occurred in the interview. Further, those patients whose expectations were more nearly congruent with actual conditions provided by therapists were more likely to return for further treatment.

Sherman[22] investigated the effect of client expectations held about counseling theory, process, and duration on counseling effectiveness. His findings led him to alter Levitt's original hypothesis: the probability of successful counseling will be enhanced if (a) there is an initial similarity between the theoretical expectations of client and counselor *or* (b) initial discrepancies between the expectations of the client and counselor are resolved during the course of counseling in such a manner that the clients' expectations become more similar to those of the counselor.

A three-phased model to describe the way clients form impressions in counseling has been proposed by Bodden and

[16] Daniel W. Webster and Bruce R. Fretz, "Asian Americans, Black, and White College Students' Preferences for Help-Giving Sources," *Journal of Counseling Psychology,* 25 (March 1978), 124–130.
[17] Eddie Venzor, John S. Gillis, and Donald G. Beal, "Preferences for Counselor Response Styles," *Journal of Counseling Psychology,* 23 (November 1976), 538–542.
[18] Howard E. A. Tinsley and Barbara L. Benton, "Expectations and Preferences in Counseling," *College Student Personnel,* 19 (November 1978), 537–543.
[19] Howard E. A. Tinsley and Donna J. Harris, "Client Expectations for Counseling," *Journal of Counseling Psychology,* 23 (May 1976), 173–177.
[20] John F. Snyder, Clara E. Hill, and Timothy P. Derksen, "Why Some Students Do Not Use University Counseling Facilities," *Journal of Counseling Psychology,* 18 (July 1972), 263–268.

[21] Betty Overall and H. Aronson, "Expectations of Psychotherapy in Patients of Lower Socioeconomic Class," *American Journal of Orthopsychiatry,* 33 (April 1963), 421–430.
[22] Donald Sherman, "The Influence of Client-Counselor Theoretical Orientation Differences on Counseling Outcome," (Ph.D. diss., Purdue University, 1979).

Winer.[23] The model proposes that clients' initial impressions are about the physical setting for counseling and the counselor's age, promises of help, physical appearance, credentials, reputation, warmth and concern, trustworthiness, ethical and cultural background. If clients' initial impressions based on these data are not positive, they discontinue counseling within three sessions. The model by Bodden and Winer proposes that the data of phase two are the client's impressions based on counselor performance and the counselor's statements that the client is making progress. Phase two impressions are drawn from the counselor's calm and confident manner, attentiveness, advice giving, use of specific techniques, use of tests, capacity to avoid backtracking, and explanations of client progress. The model proposed that after about nine sessions, impression formation shifts from clients' impressions of the counselor's actions to concern over whether clients themselves are changing. The data of phase three are based on the client's noting personal progress, accomplishing goals, and the counselor's confidence in clients' capacity for change. In their attempt to empirically validate the model, Bodden and Winer found some, but not complete, support for the model.

Parent expectations

Some years ago, Dunlop surveyed the attitudes of counselor educators, counselors, high school administrators, parents, and high school seniors to determine their perceptions of the appropriateness of counselor performance of various defined tasks.[24] Tasks were representative of several areas commonly associated with counseling, including educational, vocational, and personal counseling and testing and diagnosis. All groups reacted favorably to counseling associated with educational and vocational planning. Dunlop comments that "the expectation by students and parents that counselors should serve as advice-givers leads to

speculation that their experiences with counselors have led to this kind of expectation."[25]

One parent, Janet Worthington, believes that counselors are extensions of parents and facilitators of learning. An important dimension in their work, according to her, is that counselors accept each student as he or she is.[26]

According to many surveys, parents expect counseling to improve student selection of high school subjects and to help students formulate plans for future education or work. They do *not* expect it to be as powerful or useful in resolving personal-emotional social problems as it is in educational-vocational situations. Thus, from the parents' point of view counseling (1) exists primarily for generating programs of study for students, (2) has a persuasive function in the individual's educational and vocational development, and (3) remedies child-rearing errors. Most counselors would regard the first expectation as outmoded and/or naive and the second and third expectations as unrealistic or ill conceived. Counseling cannot provide children with instant aspiration or persuade them to make right choices and decisions especially if right is defined as synonymous with agreement or submission to parental demands and desires.

Teacher expectations

Gibson's 1965 survey revealed that 208 secondary school teachers in eighteen schools in a four-state area recognized counseling as the primary responsibility of school counselors.[27] However, their responses to the questionnaire and to individual interviews led Gibson to conclude that they did not understand counseling and that "many seemed to feel that it was a 'telling' or 'directing' process. . . ."[28] It should be noted that these teachers were employed in high schools where guidance services had been in existence for at least four years.

Many school counselors believe that teachers have little understanding of counseling. But some research reports evi-

[23] Jack L. Bodden and Jane L. Winer, "A Model of Client Impression Formation," *Counselor Education and Supervision,* 18 (September 1978), 21–28.

[24] Richard S. Dunlop, "Professional Educators, Parents, and Students Assess the Counselor's Role," *Personnel and Guidance Journal,* 43 (June 1965), 1024–1028.

[25] Ibid., p. 1028.

[26] Janet Worthington, "A Parent's View of School Counselors," *The School Counselor,* 19 (May 1972), 339–340.

[27] Robert F. Gibson, "Teacher Opinions of High School Guidance Programs," *Personnel and Guidance Journal,* 44 (December 1965), 416–422.

[28] Ibid., p. 421.

dence to the contrary. For example, Kandor and his associates[29] reported that practicing teachers, practicing counselors, student teachers, and student counselors agreed more than they disagreed about functions counselors were to perform. These four groups differed on nine of twenty-six statements about counselor behavior. The greatest discrepancy occurred in areas of discipline, students' freedom of choice, and use of class time for counseling activities. Maser also presented a counselor function inventory to counselors, administrators, and teachers employed in a Seattle school district and reported high agreement (r = .80 and .90) among these three groups about appropriate counselor functions.[30]

While little direct evidence exists to substantiate it, the major impression is that teachers expect counseling to reduce or eliminate pupil behavior that causes classroom friction and disturbance; that is, it is intended for students who either directly disturb the teacher or disrupt the teaching of other students. In short, teachers expect counselors to engage in activities that make teaching easier and more effective.

Expectations of school administrators

School principals' views of six counselor role dimensions were compared by Hart and Prince[31] with ideal counselor roles set forth by counselor educators. The school principals (n = 164) had three or more years of administrative experience. The principals disagreed with counselor educators about counselors being involved in clerical tasks, maintaining confidentiality of client communications, providing personal-emotional counseling, and some noncounseling functions. However, those principals with some counselor training or experience were closer to counselor educators in expectations concerning discipline, confidentiality, and clerical tasks than those principals without such training or experience. But the views of all these principals contrasted markedly with the ideal counselor role defined by counselor educators. These findings led Hart and Prince to conclude that "the conflict is real; school counselors are taught many role philosophies and behaviors which are in conflict with the expectations of principals."

We have four impressions of school administrators' expectations for counseling. First, they assume that counseling will result in an efficient school organization. Filbeck's comparison of the views of high school counselors and principals reflected that the latter wanted counseling to support school policies and to reinforce student conformity and acceptance of the status quo.[32] In short, counseling ought to produce fewer organizational disruptions, reduce conflict and friction among personnel, and smooth educational production. Far too many administrators expect counselors to ferret out information on students' misbehaviors and pass it on to them so that they can take action. Counselors who attempt to meet administrators' desires in this regard face serious questions concerning the ethic of confidentiality. Also obviously forgotten or ignored is the notion that the school as an institution should also liberate individual diversity, originality, and inventiveness despite the sometimes disruptive and unconventional directions these latter pursuits take.

The second impression is that school administrators view counseling primarily as educational and vocational advising. They expect students to be told what academic subjects they should take, what colleges to enter, and what jobs they should seek.

The third impression is that school administrators expect little or nothing from counseling. Some tolerate it and its practitioners, because a group of their articulate patrons demand it, because other schools have it, or because accrediting associations require it as a criterion for membership. They do not understand counseling; they never have, and make no effort to comprehend what it has to offer. Study after study could be cited to show that counselors frequently serve as attendance clerks, quasi administrators, substitute teachers, and the like. Certainly under such conditions administrators must not expect much of counseling per se.

[29] Joseph Kandor, Charles Pulvino, and Richard R. Stevic, "Counselor-Role Perception: A Method for Determining Agreement and Disagreement," *The School Counselor*, 18 (May 1971), 373–382.

[30] Arthur L. Maser, "Counselor Functions in Secondary Schools," *The School Counselor*, 18 (May 1971), 367–372.

[31] Darrell H. Hart and Donald J. Prince, "Role Conflict for School Counselors: Training Versus Job Demands," *Personnel and Guidance Journal*, 48 (January 1970), 374–380.

[32] Robert W. Filbeck, "Perceptions of Appropriateness of Counselor Behavior: A Comparison of Counselors and Principals," *Personnel and Guidance Journal*, 43 (May 1965), 891–896.

The fourth impression is that administrators expect counseling to solve every educational difficulty and to remedy every real and imagined community ill. Some administrators, in fending off criticisms that the school has failed to cope with school dropouts or to provide for disadvantaged children, or in responding to demands that the school develop compensatory programs for these and other situations, have cited the existence of counseling in their schools as a solution. Their easy answer that counseling is the magic cure for these diverse troubles is absurd. Such social symptoms stem from pervasive sociological, economic, and psychological disharmonies in our culture. To see them as isolated problems to be solved or even ameliorated by counseling is inappropriate. Although counseling may be *one* useful agent in their prevention and alleviation, it is obviously inadequate as a cure-all. It cannot materially alter or eradicate a host of social defects.

Expectations of governmental agencies

Numerous federal laws, containing provisions for extending counseling to various clientele, demonstrate that Congress and governmental agencies expect much from counseling. But precise expectations are difficult to pin down because they shift with variations in policy across time. Two major expectations have been prominent in federal legislation. The first is that counseling will identify and nurture human talent. Indeed, Title V was included in the National Defense Education Act of 1958 for that very purpose. The launching of Sputnik in October 1957, brought about the notion that education was the nation's defense. Schools were to engage in an unprecedented search for talent. Counseling was supposed to ferret out more of our brighter youngsters and encourage them to obtain advanced education that would enable them to employ their pre-identified and labeled talents at the highest levels of production.

A recent (1975) example of government generated expectancies for counseling exists in PL 94-142, the Education for All Handicapped Children Act. This law unquestionably produces the expectancy that counselors will participate actively in providing services for the handicapped by becoming involved in individual program planning, strategies for mainstreaming, monitoring programs, and counseling handicapped students and their parents. The demands of this legislation will require altered roles and functions for school counselors in the area of nurturing and developing the most appropriate services for the handicapped. Because implementation of this law will evolve over a period of years its full impact on what may be expected of counselors is yet to be determined.

The second expectancy is that counseling is to be used to put youngsters into careers where labor shortages exist. Counseling is seen as a means of persuading or directing individuals into critical occupations. Provisions for counseling services have been written into legislation dealing with the labor force, development training programs, school dropouts, migratory workers, and the like.

The key issue here is whether counseling is to serve as a manipulative experience to satisfy needs for the nation. If so, the mental health and welfare of the individual are relegated to a lesser position.

Summary

The overwhelming lay expectation for counseling is that it direct or manage the affairs of those who seek it. Many do not know and are puzzled over what counseling is and can do. Failure to understand its true purposes has led to countless mistaken and unrealistic assumptions. Everyone would like to find specific remedies in counseling for an almost infinite array of problems. An important objective for every counselor is to enlighten potential clients and the general public as to the legitimate goals and realistic limitations of counseling.

Goals of counseling

Are the public's counseling expectancies and the practitioner's statements of counseling goals congruent, or can they become so?

Questions about counseling goals and/or expected outcomes rightfully are raised by individuals preparing to become counselors, by those who seek counseling, by other helping specialists, by public officials in various organizations and agencies, and by the public. The queries take many forms and reflect several levels of sophistication. The following questions are examples:

What do you try to do in counseling?
What is the purpose of counseling?
What is the aim of counseling?
What are the objectives of counseling?
What results are expected from counseling?

Essentially, the words *try to do, purpose, aim, objective,* are loosely used as synonyms for *goal,* which is generally preferred by professional counselors. More precisely, *purpose* refers to that which makes a goal attractive. *Goal* is defined as the end result sought or, in this case, the objective that counseling strives to accomplish.

Statements of counseling goals are often general, vague, and rife with implications. In examining them, an additional problem may be noted: to what degree is the goal dependent on the counselee or on the counselor?

Behavioral change

Almost all statements indicate that the goal of counseling is to effect change in behavior that will enable counselees to live more productive, satisfying lives as defined within society's limitations. Areas often mentioned where change may be desirable are relations with others, family situations, academic achievement, job experiences, and the like. Rogers points out that one outcome of counseling is that experiences are not as threatening, individuals have less anxiety, and their goals are more nearly in harmony with their perceived self and appear more achievable. "Thus therapy produces a change in personality organization and structure, and a change in behavior, both of which are relatively permanent,"[33] and the "essential outcome is a more broadly based structure of self, an inclusion of a greater proportion of experience as a part of self, and a more comfortable and realistic adjustment to life."[34] Change as a goal may be more simply defined as redirection of typical responses to frustrations or different attitudes toward other people or to self.

Positive mental health

Some have identified the preservation or attainment of positive mental health as the goal of counseling. If it is reached, the individual achieves integration, adjustment, and positive identification with others. The client learns to accept responsibility, to be independent, and to gain behavioral integration. Patterson has stated that "the counseling relationship is for the sole purpose of improving or restoring the mental health, adjustment, or functioning of one of the participants."[35]

Some see the goal of counseling as prevention of certain kinds of problems. Identification and treatment of persons who have a high probability of developing pathology or who show signs of developing pathology could only be labeled *prevention* in a relative way because the symptoms indicate an already existent problem. In this case, counseling is prophylactic only in the sense of preventing a small problem from becoming worse.

Kell and Mueller, in their examination of impact and change in counseling relationships, suggest that what is failure to one counselor may be success to another. They indicate that counselors may wish to help clients learn that all human beings share likenesses. To them, "promotion and development of feelings of being like, sharing with, and getting and giving interactive rewards from other human beings is a legitimate counseling objective."[36]

Problem resolution or symptom removal

The goal of counseling is sometimes thought to be the resolution of whatever problems were brought to the counseling relationship or the elimination of symptoms such as test anxiety, phobias, frigidity, impotence, enuresis, alcoholism, and the like. Most often, behavioral counselors speak of their goal as being that clients unlearn unadaptive habits and learn adaptive habits or that clients have relief from suffering or are able to function socially.

[33] Carl R. Rogers, *Client-Centered Therapy* (Boston: Houghton Mifflin Company, 1951), p. 195.
[34] Ibid.
[35] C. H. Patterson, *An Introduction to Counseling in the School* (New York: Harper & Row, 1971), p. 111.
[36] Bill L. Kell and William J. Mueller, *Impact and Change* (New York: Appleton-Century-Crofts, 1966), p. 142.

Krumboltz, in presenting the rationale and research of behavioral counseling, wrote the following:

> The central reason for the existence of counseling is based on the fact that people have problems that they are unable to resolve by themselves. They come to counselors because they have been led to believe that the counselor will be of some assistance to them in resolving their problems. The central purpose of counseling, then, is to help each client resolve those problems for which he seeks help.[37]

In an earlier statement comparing the goals of client-centered counseling with those of behavioral counseling, Krumboltz stated,

> While not relinquishing his ethical responsibility for helping the client define worthwhile goals, the behavioral counselor is primarily interested in helping the client change whichever behavior the client wishes to change. If the client wishes to overcome an overpowering fear of taking tests, then the counselor endeavors to structure a situation where his fear can become extinguished. He makes no pretense of working toward high-sounding and elaborate goals which involve a whole restructuring of the client's personality. He is only interested in helping the client make the particular change that the client himself desires. Therefore, the behavioral counselor would actually play a smaller part in determining the goals of counseling than would the client-centered counselor.[38]

In commenting on the Krumboltz article, Patterson responded,

> Do such counselors accept all the goals of all clients? I don't believe this. Are the immediate, professed goals of the client his ultimate or real goals? I doubt this. Acceptance by the counselor of such limited, immediate goals may prevent his recognizing and accepting different, more long-term goals. Clients, when given the opportunity, appear to desire and accept the goals of the client-centered counselor; indeed, many of the expressed goals of the client (*e.g.*, "All I want is to get rid of my fear of giving speeches in class") cannot be adequately achieved without, or except by working toward, broader goals of self-understanding, self-acceptance, etc.[39]

And in a further comment Patterson pointed out that

> it is thus not a matter of who selects goals, but what are the goals of counseling or psychotherapy. The counselor who "makes no pretense of working toward high-sounding and elaborate goals" is thereby not necessarily free of such goals. He is imposing ultimate goals whether he knows it or not—such goals as dependence, short-term gratification, or accomplishment or removal of symptoms.[40]

In a later analysis of behavioral goals for counseling, Krumboltz argues against putting counseling goals in terms of subjective states such as "self-understanding" and "self-acceptance."[41] He believes that goal statements such as these lack precision and are incapable of being assessed. He urges that counseling goals be couched in terms of objective behavior changes. His three criteria for judging counseling goals are as follows:

1. The goals of counseling should be capable of being stated differently for each individual client.
2. The goals of counseling for each client should be compatible with, though not necessarily identical to, the values of his counselor.
3. The degree to which the goals of counseling are attained by each client should be observable.[42]

Most recently, Krumboltz and Thoresen have said that "if counseling can be said to have a single goal, it is to help each individual take charge of his or her own life."[43] Catego-

[37] John D. Krumboltz, "Behavioral Counseling: Rationale and Research," *Personnel and Guidance Journal*, 44 (December 1965), 383–384.
[38] John D. Krumboltz, "Parable of the Good Counselor," *Personnel and Guidance Journal*, 43 (October 1964), 121.
[39] C. H. Patterson, "Comment," *Personnel and Guidance Journal*, 43 (October 1964), 125.
[40] Ibid.
[41] John D. Krumboltz, "Behavioral Goals of Counseling," *Journal of Counseling Psychology*, 13 (Summer 1966), 153–159.
[42] Ibid., pp. 154–155.
[43] John D. Krumboltz and Carl E. Thoresen, *Counseling Methods* (New York: Holt, Rinehart and Winston, 1976), p. 4.

ries often suggested to classify behavioral counseling goals include altering maladaptive behavior, learning decision-making skills, and preventing problems. Originally, behavioral counseling goals were usually confined to changes in clients' overt, observable behaviors, but Krumboltz and Thoresen suggest that changes in clients' covert and cognitive behaviors are now viewed as legitimate goals for behavioral counselors.

Personal effectiveness

Closely related to preservation of good mental health and behavioral change is the goal of improving personal effectiveness.

Two counseling goals defined in terms of personal effectiveness have been identified by Blocher.[44] First, counseling seeks to maximize the possible freedom within the limitations supplied by clients and their environments, and second, counseling seeks to maximize clients' effectiveness by giving them control over their environment and the responses within them that are evoked by the environment.

Patterson, noting that stating the ultimate counseling goal as personal effectiveness, has called attention to the fact that such questions as "effectiveness for what?" or "competence for what?" have to be answered. He then states that "it is proposed here that self-actualization is the ultimate goal of counseling or psychotherapy."[45]

Decision making

To some, the goal of counseling is to enable individuals to make decisions that are of critical importance to them. It is not the counselor's job to decide what decisions clients should make or to choose alternate courses of action for them. Decisions are the clients', and they must know why and how they made them. They learn to estimate probable consequences in terms of personal sacrifice, time, energy,

money, risk, and the like. They learn to take cognizance of the range of values and to bring their own choice of values into full consciousness in the decision making. Representative of this view of counseling is the writing of Katz, who sees the beginning and terminating of high school as two critical decision-making points.[46] Over three decades ago Williamson defined the objectives of counseling as follows: ". . . the counselor assists the student to choose goals which will yield maximum satisfaction within the limits of those compromises necessitated by uncontrolled and uncontrollable factors in the individual and in society itself."[47]

Counseling helps individuals obtain information and clarify and sort out personal characteristics and emotional concerns that may interfere with or be related to making decisions. It helps them acquire understanding, not only of abilities, interests, and opportunities but also of emotions and attitudes that can influence choice and decision.

Krumboltz and Thoresen present an eight-step model to be used by counselors with clients who have trouble making decisions. The steps include (1) formulating the problem by specifying the client's goals and values; (2) committing time and effort; (3) generating alternative solutions; (4) collecting information about alternatives; (5) examining the consequences of alternatives; (6) re-evaluating goals, alternatives, and consequences; (7) successively eliminating the least desirable alternatives until a tentative choice has been made; and (8) generalizing the decision-making process to future problems.[48]

Tyler has defined the goal of counseling primarily as decision making:

. . . The purpose of counseling is to facilitate wise choices of the sort on which the person's later development depends. Counseling should not be *just* for persons who are anxious, unhappy, or unable to cope with the circumstances of their lives.[49]

[44] Donald H. Blocher, *Developmental Counseling*, 2nd ed. (New York: Ronald Press, 1974), pp. 5–6.
[45] C. H. Patterson, *Relationship Counseling and Psychotherapy* (New York: Harper & Row, 1974), p. 18.
[46] Martin Katz, *Decisions and Values: A Rationale for Secondary School Guidance* (New York: College Entrance Examination Board, 1963).
[47] E. G. Williamson, *Counseling Adolescents* (New York: McGraw-Hill Book Co., 1950), p. 221.
[48] Krumboltz and Thoresen, *Counseling Methods*, pp. 11–13.
[49] Leona E. Tyler, *The Work of the Counselor*, 3rd ed. (New York: Appleton-Century-Crofts, 1969), p. 13.

Counseling, then, helps clients learn what is needed to choose and subsequently to make choices. In this way they become independently able to cope with future decisions.

Unacceptable goals

Arbuckle considers the following counseling goals unacceptable or questionable: (1) counselor solution of counselee's problems; (2) counselee happiness or satisfaction (Arbuckle views this as a by-product rather than a primary objective); (3) making society happy and satisfied with the counselee; (4) persuading the counselee to make decisions and choices that are "right." Further, Arbuckle believes there is consensus among counselors on the following statements: (1) objectives are affected by the humanistic belief that people are capable of self-determination; (2) counselors help counselees move toward self-acceptance and self-understanding; (3) counseling helps individuals develop a greater level of honesty, particularly honesty toward self; (4) objectives should be based on counselee need rather than counselor need.[50]

Classification of goals

Sometime ago, Byrne separated counseling goals into three categories: ultimate, intermediate, and immediate.[51] Ultimate goals take their substance from views of universal humankind and of the nature of life. They are philosophical goals. Intermediate goals relate to the reasons why individuals seek counseling. Immediate goals are the moment-by-moment intentions in counseling. "To help the individual maintain an adequate level of development," "to help the individual become and remain a constructive, well-adjusted happy, mentally healthy person," "to help the individual develop his potentialities"—all these are classified by Byrne as intermediate goals. He added that each counselor has to hold to a goal that includes values, encompasses a comprehensive psychological view of behavior, and applies to all counselees.

Dolliver classified counselor goals as expressive or instrumental.[52] The expressive goal spurs the counselee to be more expressive and is usually stated in self terms (such as Freud's "to live, to love, and to work" or personal happiness, and so forth). The instrumental goal is usually more specific; for example, it refers to a reduction in certain kinds of behavior. Dolliver believed that the expressive and instrumental approaches may be complementary at times but generally are not.

Frey subjected statements of goals and processes set forth by various counseling theorists to analysis of variance techniques to determine their similarities and differences. He employed a linear arrangement of classifying counseling theories, going from highly rational approaches at one end of the continuum to strongly affective approaches at the other. Counseling goals were classified by the action-insight dichotomy formulated by London.[53] The theorists selected include Alexander (psychoanalytic therapy), Dreikurs (Adlerian therapy), Dollard and Miller (reinforcement therapy), Ellis (rational-emotive therapy), Frankl (logo-therapy), Krumboltz (behavioral therapy), Rogers (client-centered therapy), Thorne (eclectic therapy), Williamson (trait-and-factor counseling), and Wolpe (therapy by reciprocal inhibition). Some thirty-seven counseling students rated 671 process statements and 318 goal statements. Mean ratings and standard deviations were computed across the theorists' statements on both process and goal dimensions. Figure 4.1 depicts the results.

Analysis of variance techniques, followed where appropriate by Newman-Keuls procedures for making post hoc comparisons, revealed the following similarities and differences in these theorists' goal statements:

$$\underline{WO} \ \underline{KU} \ \underline{WI} \ \underline{DM} \ \underline{DR} \ \underline{TH} \ \underline{EL} \ \underline{AL} \ \underline{RO} \ \underline{FR}$$

Wolpe and Krumboltz do not differ from each other and are more action oriented than all other theorists. At the other end of the continuum, Frankl is the most insight directed and differs from Rogers, the second most insight-oriented theorist. A mid range insight group is composed of Dreikurs,

[50] Dugald S. Arbuckle, *Counseling and Psychotherapy*, 3rd. ed. (Boston: Allyn & Bacon, 1975), pp. 181–189.
[51] Richard Hill Byrne, *The School Counselor* (Boston: Houghton Mifflin Company, 1963), pp. 6–25.

[52] Robert H. Dolliver, " 'Expressive' and 'Instrumental' Conceptualizations of Counseling," *Journal of Counseling Psychology*, 12 (Winter 1965), 414–417.
[53] Perry London, *The Modes and Morals of Psychotherapy* (New York: Holt, Rinehart and Winston, 1964), p. 34.

FIGURE 4.1 **The London-Patterson model**

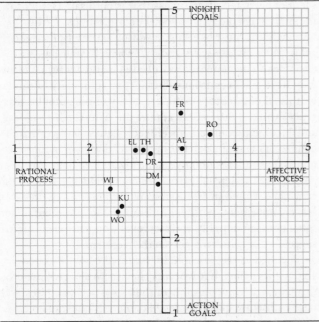

SOURCE: David H. Frey, "Conceptualizing Counseling Theories: A Content Analysis of Process and Goal Statements," *Counselor Education and Supervision*, 11 (January 1972), 245. Copyright © 1972 American Personnel and Guidance Association. Reprinted with permission.

TABLE 4.2 **Classification of goals of counseling**

Cognitive (thinking)	Affective (feeling)	Overt behavior (doing)
Increased self-awareness	Improved self-esteem	Improved grades
Choice of major	School or job satisfaction	Reduction in school or job absenteeism
Choice of career	Reduction of anxiety	More assertive behavior

apy Processes and Goals was used to measure therapeutic preferences. "Sensing-thinking" types tended to prefer rational strategies and action-oriented outcomes whereas persons with "intuitive-feeling" cognitive styles endorsed affective processes and insight-oriented goals. A surprising finding was that subjects tended to endorse rational strategies but insight-oriented goals.

Finally to be noted is that the past five years have brought efforts to conceptualize and categorize counseling goals into a three-fold classification system: cognitive, affective, and overt behavior. Table 4.2 illustrates such a classification. As can be observed by examining Table 4.2, most counseling goal statements do not fit easily into any one category because they, in fact, overlap such categories.

Clarification of goal statements

The reader who attempts to chop some way out of the semantic jungle of descriptions of counseling goals and outcomes is frequently lost. For example, Burton[56] after surveying the literature, listed forty different aims of psychotherapy. He reported it impossible to combine or integrate these goals into a generally acceptable goal. Three points bear on this condition. First, the goals expressed by these and other individuals may reflect their own needs rather than those of the clients. In this case they are indicative of their authors' professional background, experience, and philosophy.

Thorne, Ellis, and Alexander, whereas Williamson and Dollard and Miller are together near the action end of the goal axis. Frey points out that these results could be influenced by item-selection procedures and rater reliability.[54]

Baker[55] investigated the relationship between index of cognitive style (extraversion-introversion, sensing-intuition, thinking-feeling and judging-perceiving) and preferences for therapeutic processes and goals. Subjects were thirty female and twenty-one male students pursuing advanced degrees in either counseling or clinical psychology. Cognitive style was assessed by the Myers-Briggs Type Indicator and a modified version of Frey's Inventories of Counseling and Psychother-

[54] David H. Frey, "Conceptualizing Counseling Theories: A Content Analysis of Process and Goal Statements," *Counselor Education and Supervision*, 11 (June 1972), 243–250.

[55] Sherry Baker, "Cognitive Style and Preference for Therapeutic Orientation" (Ph.D. diss., Purdue University, May 1978).

[56] Arthur Burton, *Interpersonal Psychotherapy* (Englewood Cliffs, New Jersey: Prentice-Hall, 1972), pp. 10–11.

For example, Thompson and Zimmerman[57] administered a goal check list to 315 clients and their 27 counselors at several points during the counseling process. Clients were asked to check the goals they thought appropriate for themselves, and counselors were asked to check goals they considered appropriate for their clients. Correlation coefficients between counselors and clients in the same time period and between counselors with themselves and clients with themselves at different time periods were not high. These authors conclude that there is little correlation between counselor goals and client goals, regardless of time period.

Further, both sets of goals show much instability. The major problem, according to Thompson and Zimmerman, is that many clients have feelings of general confusion or discomfort that they find difficult to translate into specific goals. If they could do so, doubtless they would not need or seek counseling.

Second, perhaps there are more likenesses than differences among the statements of counseling goals. Patterson, viewing goals against a backdrop of various counseling orientations, says,

> . . . we can find some agreement among the various approaches. The behaviorists stress specific goals as direct outcomes of the treatment process. Other therapists emphasize long-term or ultimate goals, and although they express these goals in somewhat different ways, the concept of self-actualization seems to represent them.[58]

Burks and Stefflre agree that there are many common elements among the various systems of counseling:

> All seek free, informed, responsible persons who are conscious of themselves—their strengths and weaknesses, their sickness and health—and are capable of viewing the world unblinking and unafraid; capable, too, of making decisions for themselves in harmony with their unique natures and with at least minimal societal requirements.[59]

Third, the focus of all counseling goals is the achievement of personal effectiveness that is both satisfactory to the individual and within society's limitations. In this framework it must be recognized that satisfaction can be achieved in diverse ways and that social limitations have been clearly documented as differing markedly from culture to culture and even from subsociety to subsociety within a culture. If one accepts this view, many of the quibbles over goals shrink to differences among the criteria used to judge and document counseling's efficacy. Behaviorally oriented counselors may speak of symptom reduction or symptom removal as indexes of movement toward personal effectiveness. More existentially oriented counselors use terms more commonly found in discussions of philosophies of life—self-enhancement, personal fulfillment, achievement of personal needs at a highly abstract level—but the terms are all suggestive of achieving personal effectiveness.

Needless to say, a whole spectrum of counseling goal statements exists, but whether they serve any purpose other than convincing counselors of their own personal effectiveness within a socially approved context is questionable. Counselors must use words—verbal criteria of progress that make sense of their activities—in an effort to make rational to themselves what they do and to convey the meaning of their activities to others. The degree to which they are successful in this pursuit justifies their existence to themselves and the value of their service to others. Undoubtedly, choice of words is crucial, but their importance lies in their acceptance by the consumer. Nevertheless, one must recognize that consumers are not always the only judge of the effectiveness of counseling. Their perceptions and definitions of the help they receive—indeed, the very meaning they assign to it—may bear no relationship to what the counselor is trying to do.

Expectancies and goals compared

What various individuals and groups expect of counseling often differs from the goals expressed by its practitioners. Counseling is usually thought to be something *done to* or for the counselee although goal statements generally specify that it is the recipient who acts, decides, changes, becomes, and so on. Seemingly the assignment and acceptance of responsibility for what takes place in counseling differs sub-

[57] Andrew Thompson and Robert Zimmerman, "Goals of Counseling: Whose? When?" *Journal of Counseling Psychology*, 16 (March 1969), 121–125.

[58] C. H. Patterson, *Theories of Counseling and Psychotherapy*, 2nd ed. (New York: Harper & Row, 1974), p. 525.

[59] Herbert M. Burks, Jr., and Buford Stefflre (eds.), *Theories of Counseling*, 3rd ed. (New York: McGraw-Hill Book Company, 1979), p. 333.

stantially between the two. Perhaps this distinction is too subtle to be communicated to and understood by the public.

Furthermore, expectations indicate that counseling is most appropriate for the individual who is in a crisis situation, whereas counseling goals tend to portray counseling as most appropriate for the person who seeks self-understanding and growth rather than a solution for an immediate, pressing concern. Perhaps the real difference lies in whether counseling is to be viewed as remedial or generative. Expectancies are likely to stress remediation and repair; goal statements imply that counseling should be preventive or generative in nature.

One quality reflected by both expectancies and goals, almost without exception, is that there is little or no limitation on what counseling can do. It is almost as though counseling is the answer to all manner of societal and personal difficulties. One wonders sometimes whether either the public or the practitioners of counseling are concerned about clearly defining situations where counseling may be most appropriate. The problem of setting appropriate boundaries for counseling takes on an ever-increasing urgency with the continued expansion of this service into more and more settings.

Issues

Issue 1 What clients expect of counseling influences the process and outcome of counseling.

Yes, because
1. Their behavior in counseling is in accord with these expectations and they judge counselor behaviors by this perceptual set.
2. Clients' previous experiences with other professionals, and their needs, values, and feelings combine to shape their expectancies of counseling, ranging from direct intervention to subtle emotional support. Similarly, these expectations influence what counselors do and affect the results obtained from counseling.

No, because
1. Although client expectations may influence initially that which both clients and counselors do, these client expectations can be changed by counselors who provide information

about ideal client functioning and the nature of the relationship.
2. It is the counselor's artful structuring of the relationship that determines process and outcome.

Discussion Counseling is a relationship established between counselor and client; therefore, it is influenced by whatever each brings or fails to bring to the encounter. There is no doubt that the client's past experiences, present feelings, values, commitments, apprehensions, expectations all come into play in the counseling relationship and that the same holds equally for the counselor. The preconceptions held by clients about counseling—about what they are to do, about what counselors do, about what the process is all about—often serve as a barrier to counseling or at least determine the nature of the first few sessions. Whether positive or negative, these feelings are mixed and often difficult to sort out. The feelings are directed toward the counselor, the counseling process, or inward on clients. Many clients who come to counselors for the first time are likely to be apprehensive and distrustful. Some are afraid that others may find out that they have sought out a counselor. For any one of several reasons, patience and understanding are required of counselors as they help clients understand and cope with these conditions.

Ploys are often used by clients to cover their expectations. Some cloak their apprehensions by a brash "Go to work, I'll answer any question" attitude. Others employ psychological jargon in an attempt to avoid getting down to counseling or engage the counselor in questions about the efficacy of counseling or manage in some fashion to keep their communications about the purposes of life at an intellectual level so as to avoid any exploration of feelings, conflicts, apprehensions.

The expectations and attitudes brought by clients to counseling may be viewed as a test for counselors. For this reason, the first few sessions are particularly critical and counselors must be alert to the implications. Responding inadequately to the client's expectations, attitudes, and needs may cause them to discontinue counseling. Without doubt, initial and early counseling sessions require all the skills, sensitivity, and understanding a counselor can muster.

Issue 2 Counseling goals are determined by clients rather than by counselors.

True, because
1. The clients are the ones who have brought their problems, feelings, indecisions, or situations to the counselor.
2. They differ in their situations and the behaviors to be changed, therefore, goals sought through counseling are rightfully theirs.
3. Imposition of goals by the counselor violates fundamental counseling principles or at the very least the counselor's goals may not be relevant to the client.

False, because
1. Most clients who come to counseling do not know what they want and are unable to establish goals for a process yet to be experienced or yet little understood.
2. The orientation or theory practiced by the counselor sets forth goals in the form of ideal human functioning that are to be achieved through the counseling process.
3. Counselors have achieved expertness in the process and are, therefore, responsible for formulating and generating goals for clients.

Discussion This issue has long been debated in the counseling field, most recently by C. H. Patterson and John Krumboltz (see pages 84–85). Many have come around to the view that specific counseling goals or objectives are to be established mutually by counselor and client.

Two comments are in order here. First, counselors often unwittingly impose their goals on clients; they often want their clients to alter their behaviors to an extent and at a pace set by the counselor. Counselors should know and recognize their own needs and goals for clients as well as those held by clients if counseling encounters are to be managed satisfactorily. Second, in certain rare instances, clients may desire to achieve goals that counselors are unwilling to work toward. In such situations, counselors must help clients understand the undesirable consequences of such goals or objectives.

Annotated references

Arbuckle, Dugald S. *Counseling and Psychotherapy.* 3rd ed. Boston: Allyn and Bacon, 1975. 504 pp.
The first part (pp. 173–189) of Chapter 8 concentrates on the objectives of counseling. Arbuckle points out that coun-

selors in preparation must come to some understanding of the basic purpose of the profession they plan to enter.

Gottman, John Mordechai, and Sandra Risa Leiblum. *How to Do Psychotherapy and How to Evaluate It.* New York: Holt, Rinehart and Winston, 1974. 184 pp.
Chapters 1 through 5 (pp. 15–63) describe how it feels to be in counseling and discuss client expectancies, therapist expectancies, problem assessment, negotiating contracts, and establishing objectives. The authors' ideas are presented and illustrated clearly and concisely.

Nay, V. Robert. *Behavior Intervention: Contemporary Strategies.* New York: Gardner Press, 1976. 384 pp.
Chapter 1 (pp. 9–13) presents an effort to merge the phenomenological and behavioral points of view. Nay views the merging of these seemingly divergent views as more characteristic of the recent literature in the field. Nay's discussion relates to clarifying and reducing the gap between goals derived from polarized philosophical positions seemingly inherent in the phenomenological-behavioral counseling controversy.

Patterson, C. H. *Relationship Counseling and Psychotherapy.* New York: Harper & Row, 1974. 207 pp.
Chapter 2 (pp. 15–30) discusses goals and values in relationship counseling. Patterson focuses directly on the issue of who determines the goals of counseling. He views counseling goals as value statements.

Whitely, John M., ed. "The Behavior Therapies—Circa 1978." *The Counseling Psychologist,* 7, No. 3 (1978).
On pages 1–50 of this issue of The Counseling Psychologist *is an extensive review of the status of the behavior therapies by Carl Thoresen and Thomas Coates followed by eleven reactions to their article. This issue is informative regarding the current status of the behavioral approaches and stimulating because of the variety of views presented.*

Further references

Carter, Jean. "Impressions of Counselors as a Function of Counselor Physical Attractiveness." *Journal of Counseling Psychology,* 25 (January 1978), 28–34.

Cerio, James E. "Structured Experiences with the Educational Growth Group." *Personnel and Guidance Journal,* 57 (April 1979), 398–401.

Claiborn, Charles D., and Lyle D. Schmidt. "Effects of Pre-session Information on the Perception of the Counselor in an Interview." *Journal of Counseling Psychology*, 24 (July 1977), 259–263.

Clarke, Joanna, and Henrietta Waters. "Counseling and Culturally Deprived: A Survey of High School Counselors' Opinions and Attitudes." *The School Counselor*, 19 (January 1972), 201–209.

Dyer, Wayne W., and John Vriend. "A Goal-Setting Checklist for Counselors." *Personnel and Guidance Journal*, 55 (April 1977), 469–471.

Fremont, Ted S., Fred H. Wallbrown, and Eunice D. Nelson. "Social Misperception and Its Implications for Counseling." *Personnel and Guidance Journal*, 57 (November 1978), 149–153.

Glicken, Mary D. "Counseling Effectiveness Assessment: A Practical Solution." *The School Counselor*, 25 (January 1978), 196–198.

Graf, Robert W., Danish, Steven, and Austin, Brian. "Reactions to Three Kinds of Vocational Educational Counseling." *Journal of Counseling Psychology*, Vol. 19 (May, 1972), pp. 224–228.

LaCrosse, Michael B. "Comparative Perceptions of Counselor Behavior: A Replication and Extension." *Journal of Counseling Psychology*, 24 (November 1977), 464–471.

Parish, Thomas S., and Bruno M. Kappes. "Affective Implications of Seeking Psychological Counseling." *Journal of Counseling Psychology*, 26 (March 1979), 164–165.

Scher, Murray. "On Counseling Men." *Personnel and Guidance Journal*, 57 (January 1979), 252–255.

Smith, David L. "Goal Attainment Scaling as an Adjunct to Counseling." *Journal of Counseling Psychology*, 23 (January 1976), 22–27.

5 Counselor and counselee characteristics

The importance of each counselor's characteristics to counseling outcome has been recognized for a long time. It is the counselor who by training and professional obligation is responsible for the counseling relationship. But the counselee's personality structure and expectations (see Chapter 4) have been demonstrated to have a direct effect on the counseling relationship and its outcome. In reality, both personalities interact. Each brings to the relationship his or her preferred method of interacting with others, certain needs, conflicts, and unique lifestyle.

This chapter reviews the major research efforts that have been directed toward identifying counselor and counselee characteristics. The content is divided among seven areas: (1) approaches, techniques, and criteria utilized in studying counselor characteristics; (2) characteristics of counselors; (3) characteristics that distinguish effective from ineffective counselors; (4) characteristics of counselees; (5) similarities of counselor and counselee characteristics; (6) complementary counselor and counselee characteristics; and (7) summary comments. The reader may notice that many of the studies cited employ noncounseling terminology. Such studies frequently are conducted in clinical settings where terminology often differs, but where the activities engaged in are highly similar to counseling as it is broadly defined.

Approaches, instruments, and criteria for studying counselor characteristics

Approaches utilized

Usually, investigations of counselor characteristics have been approached in four ways. Each of these will be identified and a brief description given of selected literature that illustrates it.

SPECULATION Many have speculated about the characteristics considered essential in an effective counselor. In 1949 the National Vocational Guidance Association issued a statement that counselors, ideally, were interested in people, patient, sensitive to others, emotionally stable, objective, respectful of facts, and trusted by others.[1] In Mowrer's judgment, personal maturity is the most important characteristic for counselors, but he noted that there is no valid way to assess it.[2]

The Association for Counselor Education and Supervision has indicated that a counselor should have six basic qualities: belief in each individual, commitment to individual human values, alertness to the world, open-mindedness, understanding of self, and professional commitment.[3] Parker has asserted that the counselor should possess a sensitivity to others, the ability to analyze objectively another's strengths and weaknesses, an awareness of the nature and extent of individual differences, and the ability to identify (diagnose) learning difficulties.[4] Stone and Shertzer cite (1) tolerance for ambiguity; (2) acceptance of self; (3) interest in people; (4) willingness to experiment, change, and improve; and (5) above average verbal ability as qualities of "good" counselors.[5]

All these lists of counselor traits reveal considerable agreement. All want the counselor to be a psychologically healthy person. They tend to reflect an idealized personality. It should be noted that essentially the same qualities apply equally well to ideal teachers, physicians, social workers, and so forth. Cottle pointed out that, although these listings were helpful, they were unsatisfactory because (1) they represented merely the opinions of the people who made them,

[1] National Vocational Guidance Association, *Counselor Preparation* (Washington: The Association, 1949).

[2] O. H. Mowrer, "Training in Psychotherapy," *Journal of Consulting Psychology*, 15 (August 1951), 274–277.

[3] Association for Counselor Education and Supervision, "The Counselor: Professional Preparation and Role," *Personnel and Guidance Journal*, 42 (December 1964), 536–541.

[4] Clyde Parker, "The Place of Counseling in the Preparation of Student Personnel Workers," *Personnel and Guidance Journal*, 45 (November 1966), 259–260.

[5] Shelley C. Stone and Bruce Shertzer, *Careers in Counseling and Guidance* (Boston: Houghton Mifflin Company, 1972), pp. 9–10.

(2) they failed to distinguish the counselor from other professionals, (3) the traits of successful counselors vary so widely that one list never will be sufficient, and (4) it is the interrelations or pattern of characteristics that is important.[6]

Serious study of counselor characteristics has moved from such "armchair" listings to investigating what distinguishes counselors from noncounselors and what the relationship is between counselor characteristics and counselor effectiveness. Both the nature and the complexity of the research have changed as investigators moved from mere speculation to formalized research efforts.

IDENTIFYING EFFECTIVE AND INEFFECTIVE COUNSELORS The second approach to identifying counselor characteristics involves designating effective and ineffective counselors and ascertaining what distinguishes the two groups. A frequently cited study conducted by Stefflre, King, and Leafgren is typical of this approach.[7]

Stefflre, King, and Leafgren used Q-sort judgments by peers as their criterion for designating the nine most effective and nine least effective counselor trainees. The two groups were compared on four dimensions: (1) academic aptitude and performance as measured by the *Miller Analogies Test, Pre- and Post-Tests of Knowledge of Guidance*, grade-point average on undergraduate and graduate pro–NDEA Counseling Institute work, and institute field and class work; (2) interests and values as measured by the *Educational Interest Inventory* and the Social Welfare and Business Contact scales of the *Strong Vocational Interest Blank* (SVIB); (3) personality characteristics as measured by the *Taylor Manifest Anxiety Scale* (TMAS), the *Rokeach Dogmatism Scale*, and the *Edwards Personal Preference Schedule* (EPPS); (4) self-concept as measured by the *Bills Index of Adjustment and Values* and a discrepancy score obtained from the difference between the position trainees thought the average group would give them and the position each was actually assigned. The authors reported significant differences between the effective and ineffective counselor samples on the four dimensions considered in the study.

The effective group earned higher scores on the instruments measuring academic aptitude and performance. They had significantly higher scores on the SVIB Social Welfare scales and significantly higher Deference and Order scores (EPPS) than the ineffective group. Significant differences in the groups' Discrepancy scores suggested that in terms of self-concept the effective counselors underestimated themselves and the ineffective ones overestimated themselves.

HYPOTHESIZED CHARACTERISTICS The third approach consists of ascertaining whether certain characteristics that have been hypothesized as necessary for counseling are in fact present and operative. Typically selected for investigation are those personality characteristics that previous research demonstrates or that counseling theory suggests may be associated with counselor effectiveness. Bandura's research into the relationship between counselor personality and counselor effectiveness is representative of many studies using this approach.[8]

In investigating the relationship between counselor anxiety and counselor effectiveness, Bandura tested the hypotheses that competent psychotherapists (1) are less anxious than those judged to be less competent and (2) possess greater insight into the nature of their own anxieties than do less competent therapists. Forty-two therapists from four clinical settings were the subjects of the study. Subjects rated themselves and all other subjects as to degree of anxiety with respect to dependency, hostility, and sex. The average rating assigned to each subject constituted the anxiety measure. The insight measure was defined as the relative discrepancy between the subject's self-rating and the average group rating for the subject. Supervisor ratings were used as the criterion measure of therapeutic competence. Bandura found support for his first hypothesis, but his second was not confirmed. Anxious therapists were rated less competent than were those low in anxiety, but neither therapist degree of insight into the nature of one's own anxiety nor therapist self-rating of anxiety was significantly related to supervisor ratings of competence. The author concluded that "the presence of anxiety in the therapist, whether recognized or not, affects his ability to do success-

[6] William C. Cottle, "Personal Characteristics of Counselors: I," *Personnel and Guidance Journal*, 31 (April 1953), 445–450.
[7] Buford Stefflre, Paul King, and Fred Leafgren, "Characteristics of Counselors Judged by Their Peers," *Journal of Counseling Psychology*, 9 (Winter 1962), 335–340.
[8] Arthur Bandura, "Psychotherapists' Anxiety Level, Self Insight, and Psychotherapeutic Competence," *Journal of Abnormal Social Psychology*, 52 (May 1956), 333–337.

ful psychotherapy and insight into his anxieties alone is not sufficient." [9]

CORRELATIONAL ANALYSIS The fourth approach to the study of counselor characteristics involves exploring the relationship between certain counselor variables and some criterion measure of effectiveness derived from correlational analysis. A study by Johnson et al. is representative of this highly empirical approach.[10] Johnson and her associates used multiple regression analysis to determine the relationship between five predictor measures of counselor nonintellective characteristics and five criterion measures of counselor effectiveness. The *California Personality Inventory* (CPI), the *Edwards Personal Preference Schedule* (EPPS), the *Guilford-Zimmerman Temperament Survey* (GZTS), the *Minnesota Multiphasic Personality Inventory* (MMPI), and the *Strong Vocational Interest Blank—Male* (SVIB) were used to measure the nonintellective characteristics of ninety-nine counselors. The five criterion measures of counselor effectiveness included (1) the Purdue Q-sort, used to ascertain counselor perception of the client and counselee self-perception; (2) the Counselor Rating Scale (CRS), a five-point, twenty-three-item, three-factor rating scale wherein counselees evaluated their counseling experience; (3) peer ratings, a Q-sort technique with which counselor trainees judged each other in terms of (a) academic effectiveness, (b) counseling effectiveness, and (c) social effectiveness; (4) supervisor grades for performance in the counseling practicum course; and (5) the Graduate Cumulative Index, an average of grades in both didactic and practicum courses in the counselor education program. Multiple regression analysis was used to determine the relative weights of the ten measures.

The analysis suggested that among the combination of predictors, practicum grade appeared to be most useful. Five predictor variables were found by Johnson and her associates to be associated with counselor effectiveness in practicum. The Architect (SVIB) and Well-Being (CPI) scales were identified as male predictors; Schizophrenia (MMPI), Friendliness (GZTS), and Dentist (SVIB) scales were nega-

tively associated with effectiveness for females. Prediction equations using these variables were computed, and counselor trainees were grouped by sex into high (effective), medium, and low (ineffective) groups. The three predictors for females and the Well-Being scale for males were verified by cross-validation using analysis of variance and Newman-Keuls procedures. The authors concluded as follows:

> Effective male counselor trainees may be characterized as confident, friendly, affable, accepting and liking. They appeared to be generally satisfied with themselves and their surroundings. Effective female counselor candidates . . . presented themselves as outgoing and efficient, giving an appearance of confidence. They appeared to be assertive and person- rather than object-oriented. Effective male and female counselor candidates tended to be more like each other than like members of the less effective group of their own sex or both.[11]

Instruments used in assessing counselor characteristics

SELF-REPORT INSTRUMENTS The self-report technique consists of administering selected, usually standardized, self-report personality and interest inventories to the counselor sample. Many of the objective personality and interest inventories have been used. However, dissatisfaction with the available instruments and a desire to gather data that supplement objective personality test data have led researchers to design human relation incidents to which subjects respond in writing or via audio tape.

RATING TECHNIQUES Rating techniques have been used to assess counselor personality in two primary ways: (1) to identify the personal characteristics believed to be related to counselor effectiveness and (2) to assess the relative presence or absence of counselor personality characteristics and certain fundamental counseling skills, that is, empathy, genuineness, and so on. Rating scales, as all forms of observations, are subject to error. Moreover, securing valid mea-

[9] Ibid., p. 337.
[10] Dorothy J. Johnson et al., "The Relationship of Counselor Candidate Characteristics and Counseling Effectiveness," *Counselor Education and Supervision*, 6 (Summer 1967), 297–304.

[11] Ibid., pp. 301–302.

sures and adequate rater reliability have been a persistent problem.[12]

STANDARDIZED TESTS AND INVENTORIES Undoubtedly the most frequently used assessment technique has been comparing counselors on standardized intellective and nonintellective measures. These range from ability tests to personality and interest inventories to moral and values assessments.

Criterion measures of effectiveness

Four types of criteria are most common: supervisor ratings, counselor's peer ratings, client ratings, and Q-sort techniques. These may also be viewed as representing measures of counselor effectiveness that are external and internal to the counseling activity itself. Under this classification scheme, supervisor and peer ratings are considered external observer measures of counselor effectiveness and client ratings and Q-sort techniques performed by clients and/or counselors as internal measures.

SUPERVISOR RATINGS The most widely used criterion of counselor effectiveness appears to be the supervisor rating. Researchers have employed supervisor ratings of observed or taped interviews, supervisor global ratings of counselors based on knowledge of a given counselor's work with several counselees and/or long-term counseling with a single client, and supervisor ratings in the form of practicum grades.

PEER RATINGS Sociometric techniques hold promise as evaluative measures, because groups of trainees presumably have the opportunity to observe each other under more varied circumstances than do supervisors or other individuals who come in contact with members of a trainee group for a limited time and relatively prescribed circumstances. Furthermore, group pressure and interaction among the members influence the individual's behavior. Peers know the limit to which the individual can be pushed and they sometimes test it. Frequently they see the counselor in an un-

guarded moment and hear the chance remark. Peer ratings have been used to identify counselors who were considered effective by Friesen and Dunning,[13] Engle and Betz,[14] and by Bishop.[15]

CLIENT RATINGS Client judgments of counselor effectiveness have not been used as frequently as supervisor or peer ratings, for professional counselors are divided over their importance and validity. Studies using client judgment as a criterion have typically been based on specially developed rating scales.

Linden, Stone, and Shertzer developed a *Counselor Evaluation Inventory* (CEI) to measure clients' reactions to their counseling experiences.[16] The CEI yielded scores on three factors: counseling climate (factor X), counselor comfort (factor Y), and client satisfaction (factor Z). In addition, a total score was demonstrated to be parsimonious in respect to assessing counselor effectiveness.

Myrick and Kelly[17] constructed a scale entitled *Counselor Evaluation Rating Scale* (CERS) for assessing practicum students in counseling and supervision. Three scores were derived from its twenty-seven items: counseling, supervision, and total. Loesch and Rucker[18] subjected the scale to factor analysis and reported six primary factors (general counseling performance, professional attitude, counseling behavior, counseling knowledge, supervision attitude, and supervision behavior). Jones[19] investigating the relationship of CERS

[12] See Carl E. Thoresen, "Constructs Don't Speak for Themselves," *Counselor Education and Supervision*. 16 (June 1977), 296–303.

[13] D. D. Friesen and G. B. Dunning, "Peer Evaluation and Practicum Supervision," *Counselor Education and Supervision*, 12 (March 1973), 229–234.
[14] Kenneth B. Engle and Robert L. Betz, "Peer Ratings Revisited," *Counselor Education and Supervision*, 10 (June 1971), 165–170.
[15] J. B. Bishop, "Another Look at Counselor, Client and Supervisor Ratings of Counselor Effectiveness," *Counselor Education and Supervision*, 10 (March 1971), 319–323.
[16] J. D. Linden, S. C. Stone, and Bruce Shertzer, "Development and Evaluation of an Inventory for Rating Counselors," *Personnel and Guidance Journal*, 44 (November 1965), 267–276.
[17] Robert D. Myrick and F. D. Kelly, "A Scale for Evaluating Practicum Students in Counseling and Supervision," *Counselor Education and Supervision*, 10 (June 1971), 330–336.
[18] Larry C. Loesch and Barbara B. Rucker, "A Factor Analysis of the Counselor Evaluation Rating Scale," *Counselor Education and Supervision*, 16 (March 1977), 209–218.
[19] Lawrence K. Jones, "The Counselor Evaluation Rating Scale: A Valid Criterion of Counselor Effectiveness?" *Counselor Education and Supervision*, 14 (December 1974), 112–116.

counseling, supervision, and total scores and measures of empathy, respect, and genuineness, questioned whether CERS should be used as a criterion measure of counselor effectiveness.

Barak and LaCrosse[20] devised a *Counselor Rating Form* (CRF) to measure perceptions of counselor behavior. The CRF consists of thirty-six 7-point bipolar items designed to measure dimensions of counselor expertness, attractiveness, and trustworthiness. Later, LaCrosse and Barak[21] reported that the CRF differentiated both between and within groups of counselors on the three variables.

Characteristics of counselors

The search for characteristics basic to counseling effectiveness led to the realization that their identification could not be studied independently of the counseling process. Yet in this extraordinarily complex interpersonal process the counselor's personality traits are only one set of variables that interact with other sets of variables. The ideal approach would be the simultaneous investigation of the network of variables manifested in the actual counseling process. However, counseling's fundamental service orientation places severe constraints on "live" data collection. The ethical concern for the individual legitimately limits research efforts. Finally, it should be noted that studies of the counselor's personality *assume* that it is relevant to counselor effectiveness. Many believe that research focused on counselor behavior would be more fruitful.

The material in this section has been organized around some rather arbitrarily established headings selected to convey the essence of research relating to the topic.

Attitudes and beliefs

A key element in any counseling relationship is the *person* of the counselor. An important attitude of that person, ac-cording to Wrenn,[22] is that of *caring*. He has said, "The counselor is a knowing person, but he [or she] is also a caring person. Most people can know all that a counselor knows, but unless a person cares, he is not a counselor. . . . *Counseling is caring*."[23] On the other hand, Brammer suggests ". . . the need to be flexible as a people helper. At times one must be deeply personal, immersing oneself in the relationship, and at other times one must be an objective observer, studying the process carefully."[24]

Beliefs about the nature of the human condition are thought to influence the way counselors respond to and deal with clients. Combs and his colleagues[25] contrasted basic beliefs held about people by various helpers (counselors, teachers, and ministers) and nonhelpers. Helpers, compared to nonhelpers, perceived others as able, dependable, friendly, and worthy. Dole and his associates[26] studied 166 graduate students in counseling psychology, clinical psychology, and vocational rehabilitation programs to determine their philosophies of human nature. They tended to have a neutral or slightly favorable attitude toward other persons and to endorse the belief that human nature is complex and variable. These graduate students did not differ by subspecialty in their responses to the Philosophies of Human Nature scales. However, Ruzicka and Naun reported that coached client interview behavior, but not the counselor's measured philosophy, influenced the range of interviewer verbal behavior.[27]

Counselor attitudes toward women were measured three times over a six-year span in the State of Minnesota by an eighteen-item survey. Englehard, Jones, and Stiggins[28] re-

[22] C. Gilbert Wrenn, *The World of the Contemporary Counselor* (Boston: Houghton Mifflin Company, 1973).

[23] Ibid., p. 248.

[24] Lawrence M. Brammer, *The Helping Relationship*, 2nd ed. (Englewood Cliffs, N.J.: Prentice-Hall, 1979), p. 42.

[25] Arthur Combs with Daniel W. Super et al., *Florida Studies in the Helping Professions*. (Gainesville, Florida: University of Florida Press, 1969), pp. 69–78.

[26] Arthur A. Dole, Jack Nottingham, and Lawrence S. Wrightman, Jr., "Beliefs About Human Nature Held by Counseling, Clinical and Rehabilitation Students," *Journal of Counseling Psychology*, 16 (May 1969), 197–202.

[27] Mary F. Ruzicka and Robert Naun, "Range of Verbal Behavior as a Function of Counselor Philosophy and Coached-Client Role Behavior," *Journal of Counseling Psychology*, 23 (May 1976), 283–285.

[28] Patricia Aver Englehard, Kathryn Jones, and Richard J. Stiggins, "Trends in Counselor Attitude About Women Roles," *Journal of Counseling Psychology*, 23 (July 1976), 365–372.

[20] Azy Barak and Michael B. LaCrosse, "Multidimensional Perception of Counselor Behavior," *Journal of Counseling Psychology*, 22 (November 1975), 471–476.

[21] Michael B. LaCrosse and Azy Barak, "Differential Perception of Counselor Behavior," *Journal of Counseling Psychology*, 23 (March 1976), 170–172.

ported that changes from 1968 through 1971 to 1974 suggested more acceptance of dual role (mother and worker) and broader sex role definitions. Zarski, Sweeney, and Barcikowski[29] reported that counselors' social interest (concept by Alfred Adler) scores were significantly related to clients' scores of satisfaction with counseling, self-acceptance, and sociability.

Race, sex, age

Vontress, in a series of articles, called attention to the impact of racial differences on counseling.[30] He believed that it is difficult for white counselors to establish and maintain relationships with black clients. Similarly, black counselors may find it difficult to relate to black clients unless counselors project themselves as "black." Vontress suggests (1) that it is easier for any counselor to establish a working relationship with what he defined as a "colored" client than it is with either a "Negro" or a "black," (2) that working relationships with black, Negro, or "colored" females can be established more easily than with males, and (3) that rapport can be achieved more quickly with individuals of African descent who live in the South than with those who live in other parts of the country.

Woods and Zimmer[31] examined racial experimenter effects in counselorlike interviews employing a verbal operant-conditioning paradigm. The general objective was to determine whether significant differences in the conditionability of black and white students, as measured by their emission of positive and negative self-reference statements, would be obtained when verbal reinforcement was provided by black and white experimenters. The investigators concluded that the absence of significant differences suggested that race, per se, may not be the most important variable in the counselor-client relationship.

Merluzzi and Merluzzi[32] sought to determine whether racial labels contributed to counselors' assessments of clients. Eighty-six graduate students from six counseling programs read and assessed four intake case summaries. For one group of counselors, the clients in the four cases were labeled black, for a second group they were labeled white, and for a third group there was no racial label. Counselors rated the cases on eleven positive-to-negative dimensions. Black-labeled cases were rated significantly more positive than either those labeled white or with no label. These results led the authors to suggest that counselors may have overcompensated to avoid negative professional bias.

Westbrook and his associates[33] administered a 20-problem survey to 237 black and white students attending a predominantly white university and to 55 black students attending a predominantly black university. The pattern of results showed significant differences on specific problem areas but none between blacks attending universities with different racial make-up or between the groups on variables that typically suggest counseling needs.

Atkinson, Maruyama, and Matsui[34] described two studies in which Asian Americans rated a counselor's performance in a simulated counseling session with an Asian American student. Two tape recordings of a contrived counseling session were used in which the client responses were identical but the counselor responses differed, one depicting a directive counselor approach, the other, a nondirective approach. Each tape recording was paired with two different introductions, one in which the counselor was identified as Asian American, the other identified the counselor as Caucasian American. In the first study, fifty-two Asian American college students were assigned randomly to one of the four introduction approach combinations. In the second study, forty-eight Japanese Americans were assigned randomly to the four combinations. Subjects in both studies rated the directive counselor as more creditable and approachable than

[29] John J. Zarski, Thomas J. Sweeney, and Robert S. Barcikowski, "Counseling Effectiveness as a Function of Counselor Social Interest," *Journal of Counseling Psychology*, 24 (January 1977), 1–5.
[30] Clement E. Vontress, "Racial Differences: Impediments of Rapport," *Journal of Counseling Psychology*, 18 (January 1971), 7–13.
[31] Ernest Woods, Jr., and Jules M. Zimmer, "Racial Effects in Counselor-Like Interviews: An Experimental Analogue," *Journal of Counseling Psychology*, 23 (November 1976), 527–531.

[32] Bernadette H. Merluzzi and Thomas V. Merluzzi, "Influence of Client Race on Counselors' Assessment of Case Materials," *Journal of Counseling Psychology*, 25 (September 1978), 399–409.
[33] Franklin D. Westbrook et al., "Perceived Problem Areas by Black and White Students and Hints About Comparative Counseling Needs," *Journal of Counseling Psychology*, 25 (March 1978), 119–123.
[34] Donald A. Atkinson, Mervin Maruyama, and Sandi Matsui, "Effects of Counselor Race and Counseling Approach on Asian American Perceptions of Counselor Credibility and Utility," *Journal of Counseling Psychology*, 25 (January 1978), 76–83.

the nondirective counselor. The Asian American college students rated Asian American counselors as more creditable and approachable than Caucasian American counselors but the fifty-two Japanese Americans viewed them equally creditable and approachable.

Some years ago, Farson concluded that "the counselor is a woman." [35] His thesis was that counselor behaviors were fundamentally those society traditionally attributed to women: tenderness, gentleness, receptiveness, passiveness. McClain reported that both men and women counselors in his sample appeared to possess in acceptable degrees the tenderness and requisite ego strength that Farson deemed appropriate for the successful counselor.[36] Pointing out that recent research portrays the counselor not only as tender, gentle, and loving but also active, assertive, and able to confront and interpret immediate interactions when they occur, Carkhuff and Berenson[37] suggested that "the counselor is a man and a woman." They set forth the view that, depending on the interaction of counselor, client, contextual, and environmental variables, the counselor usually initiates the relationship with "nurturant responsiveness," but that later in the relationship the counselor shifts to more active, assertive, confronting behaviors to enable clients to act on their own perceptions.

The research literature on the effects of the sex of counselor and client has grown considerably during the past five years. Renewed interest in the topic stemmed, no doubt, from feminists who have advocated female counselors for female clients on the grounds that women clients have problems unique to women. As is often the case, the research results have been equivocal. Simmons and Helms[38] reported that both college and noncollege women preferred female over male counselors. Further, the preferred age of counselors was 35 to 45 for college women and 55 to 65 for noncollege women. Single females were preferred over single males.

Hill[39] examined how sex of client and sex and experience level of counselor affected counseling behaviors. She reported that same-sex pairings had more discussions of feeling by both counselor and client than opposite-sex pairings. Moreover, inexperienced male and experienced female counselors were more empathic and elicited more feelings from clients than did their counterparts.

Johnson[40] explored the responses of forty experienced male and female counselors to video-taped clients. During four vignette stops, the counselors' subjective reactions to the clients were recorded. Two judges rated the verbal material on four dimensions and counselors rated themselves on four other qualities. Multivariate analysis of variance produced two significant counselor-gender effects. Female counselors rated themselves as more empathic than did their male counterparts and female counselors were rated by the two judges as being angrier than were male counselors.

Petro and Hansen[41] had 71 female and 102 male practicing counselors view an *Affective Sensitivity Scale* (measure of empathy) in groups and respond to a multiple-choice scale on the affective status of males and females depicted on the screen. Male and female counselors were reported to be equally accurate in their empathic judgments and no effect of sex pairings was detected. Both male and female counselors demonstrated significantly more affective sensitivity to male than female referents. Scher,[42] too, reported that neither sex nor verbal activity of either clients or counselors predicted therapeutic success. On the other hand, Janda and Rimm[43] observed that female subjects, given assertive

[35] Robert E. Farson, "The Counselor Is a Woman," *Journal of Counseling Psychology*, 1 (Winter 1954), 221–223.

[36] Edwin W. McClain, "Is the Counselor a Woman?" *Personnel and Guidance Journal*, 46 (January 1968), 444–448.

[37] Robert R. Carkhuff and Bernard G. Berenson, "The Counselor Is a Man and a Woman," *Personnel and Guidance Journal*, 48 (September 1969), 24–28.

[38] Janet A. Simmons and Janet E. Helms, "Influence of Counselors' Marital Status, Sex and Age on College and Non-college Women's Counselor Preferences," *Journal of Counseling Psychology*, 23 (July 1976), 380–386.

[39] Clara E. Hill, "Sex of Client and Sex and Experience Level of Counselor," *Journal of Counseling Psychology*, 22 (January 1975), 6–11.

[40] Marilyn Johnson, "Influence of Counselor Gender on Reactivity to Clients," *Journal of Counseling Psychology*, 25 (September 1978), 359–365.

[41] Carole Smith Petro and James C. Hansen, "Counselor Sex and Empathic Judgment," *Journal of Counseling Psychology*, 24 (July 1977), 373–376.

[42] Murray Scher, "Verbal Activity, Sex, Counselor Experience and Success in Counseling," *Journal of Counseling Psychology*, 22 (March 1975), 97–101.

[43] Louis H. Janda and David C. Rimm, "Type of Situation and Sex of Counselor in Assertive Training," *Journal of Counseling Psychology*, 24 (September 1977), 444–447.

training in making complaints, small talk, and saying no to unreasonable requests, who were "seen" by a male counselor changed significantly more than those seen by a female counselor. Sweeney and Cottle[44] examined the influence of sex and major field of graduate study on nonverbal acuity. Subjects were 100 male and female university students enrolled in graduate programs in either counselor education or business management. Nonverbal acuity was assessed by asking subjects to identify nonverbal information about emotional states from 150 pictures. Females were significantly more accurate than males but contrary to expectations, no significant difference existed between counselors and noncounselors.

Despite arguments, sound as they are, for a male counselor in some situations or a female counselor in others, most research suggests that the sex of the counselor is secondary. The personal qualities of the individual counselor have greater impact with regard to effectiveness than does sex.

Hopke and Rochester reported that effective counselors were younger and had fewer years of teaching experience than their less effective counterparts.[45] In a later study, Rochester[46] held sex and age variables constant in an investigation of attitude changes (based on Porter's *Test of Counselor Attitudes*) of some 229 counselor students at the beginning and end of a year-long preparation program. Female students differed from male students in that they were more accepting of probing attitudes at the onset of their program. Pre-post comparisons of age classifications revealed that (1) students age 23 to 27 became more accepting of probing attitudes, and less accepting of evaluative attitudes. Because peer counseling has increased rapidly, Dooley and his associates[47] examined the effects of age, sex, and labeling on

the verbal response styles of children and adolescents in a counseling analogue setting. Boys and girls of three grade levels (fifth–sixth, seventh–eighth, and tenth) responded in writing to video-taped, role-played problem vignettes as though they were in actual contact with the speakers (five males and five females, aged 7 to 15 years) who were identified as being either normal or troubled youngsters. Compared to younger respondents, the oldest ones made more negative statements, more advisements in general, fewer advisements to seek help from a third person, and fewer disclosures. Female subjects gave more advisements, aimed at solving problems verbally, and fewer advisements in general than male subjects. Age is another human dimension—like sex—to which people may respond with preconceived notions or stereotypical attitudes.

Such variables as race, sex, and age are there as facts of the counselor . . . and client . . . even though they may not seem to get in the way. Whether they interfere with counselor effectiveness probably depends largely on how the counselor handles feelings that issue from conditions over which neither counselor nor client has control.

Expertness, attractiveness, persuasiveness

Social psychologists have demonstrated that attractive communicators were more effective than unattractive ones in influencing attitudes. Perceived attractiveness, expertness, and persuasiveness have been set forth as important attributes of counselors. The research literature on these variables has proliferated since 1968 when Strong[48] conceptualized counseling as an interpersonal influence process. Fundamental to this view is that counselors present themselves in such a way that clients see them as attractive, trustworthy, and expert. According to Strong these characteristics influence the client, and those counselors so perceived by their clients are more influential than those counselors who are not. Schmidt and Strong[49] defined perceived counselor attractiveness as the counselor's perceived

[44] Mary Anne Sweeney and William C. Cottle, "Nonverbal Acuity: A Comparison of Counselors and Non-counselors," *Journal of Counseling Psychology*, 23 (July 1976), 394–397.

[45] William E. Hopke and Dean E. Rochester, "Characteristics of Effective and Use of Effective Counselors," *Illinois Guidance and Personnel Quarterly*, 33 (Fall 1969), 24–28.

[46] Dean E. Rochester, "Sex and Age as Factors Relating to Attitude Changes," *Counselor Education and Supervision*, 11 (March 1972), 214–218.

[47] David Dooley, Carol K. Whalen, and John V. Flowers, "Verbal Response Styles of Children and Adolescents in a Counseling Analog Setting: Effects of Age, Sex, and Labeling," *Journal of Counseling Psychology*, 25 (March 1978), 85–95.

[48] Stanley R. Strong, "Counseling: An Interpersonal Influence Process," *Journal of Counseling Psychology*, 15 (May 1968), 215–224.

[49] Lyle D. Schmidt and Stanley R. Strong, "Attractiveness and Influence in Counseling," *Journal of Counseling Psychology*, 18 (July 1971), 348–351.

similarity to a client, the client's perceptions of the counselor's positive feelings for the client, desire to gain approval and desire to be more similar to the counselor. Most often, expertness has been defined as the possession of formal training and experience as evidence of special knowledge. The idea is that the more qualified or expert the client believes the counselor to be, the greater the probability that the client will perceive the counselor as helpful. Expertness is thought to create a perceptual set within which the counselor's actions are viewed. An *expert set* makes the counselor more attractive and influential; it can offset effects of undesirable counselor behavior and, thereby, give the counselor more latitude within role behavior. La Crosse[50] defined persuasiveness as the degree to which what a counselor does has the effect of inducing the client to believe some attitudinal and/or behavioral change might be beneficial. Spiegel[51] reported that suggestions of counselor expertness to 311 undergraduate students led to higher evaluations of counselors. Her findings support the importance of counselor credentials in influencing clients' *initial* impressions of counselors.

Cash and his colleagues[52] reported that a male counselor in a physically attractive condition was perceived favorably by both sexes (more intelligent, friendly, assertive, trustful, competent, and warm) and was rated higher on possible counseling outcomes than the same counselor in an unattractive condition. The counselor wore the same clothes in both conditions. In the attractive condition he was mesomorphic, tanned, clear complexioned, with moderate, stylish black hair, whereas in the unattractive condition he was endomorphic, had shadows under his eyes, a mole on the side of the nose, and less stylishly groomed hair. Lewis and Walsh[53] examined the effects of physical attractiveness on thirty male and thirty female subjects' perceptions of a female counselor. Subjects viewed the video-taped professional self-descriptions of a presumed counselor who was either physically attractive or unattractive. Subjects recorded their impressions of the counselor on twelve traits and their expectancies of her helpfulness for fifteen personal problems. The attractive female counselor was perceived more favorably by female subjects than her unattractive counterpart on such measures as competence, professionalism, assertiveness, interest, and ability to help with problems of anxiety, shyness, career choice, and so on. Two control groups who listened to the tapes but were unaware of the counselor's appearance did not differ in their ratings of the two tapes.

Long[54] examined the effects of wearing a uniform (nun's habit) and religious status of counselors on 128 male and female Catholic and non-Catholic high school and university subjects. He reported that these subjects spent more time talking to nuns dressed in a habit, that female subjects responded more conservatively than males, that Catholic subjects responded more conservatively than non-Catholic, and that all subjects responded more conservatively to nuns than non-nuns.

Atkinson and Carskaddon[55] had subjects rate a counselor's performance on two video tapes that were identical except for the level of psychological jargon employed by the counselor. Each videotape was preceded by either a high- or low-prestige introduction. The counselor's knowledge of psychology was rated higher when abstract psychological jargon was used rather than concrete lay language. The subjects were more likely to rate the counselor as someone they would see for counseling if they were given the high-prestige introduction, but not all populations (for example, drug abusers) were equally impressed by either jargon or by prestige.

An unexpected finding by Claiborn and Schmidt[56] that low-status expert introductions produced significantly

[50] Michael B. La Crosse, "Nonverbal Behavior and Perceived Counselor Attractiveness and Persuasiveness," *Journal of Counseling Psychology*, 22 (November 1975), 563–566.

[51] Sharon Baron Spiegel, "Expertness, Similarity and Perceived Counselor Competence," *Journal of Counseling Psychology*, 23 (September 1976), 436–441.

[52] Thomas F. Cash et al., "When Counselors Are Heard but Not Seen: Initial Impact of Physical Attractiveness," *Journal of Counseling Psychology*, 22 (July 1975), 273–279.

[53] Kathleen N. Lewis and W. Bruce Walsh, "Physical Attractiveness: Its Impact on the Perception of a Female Counselor," *Journal of Counseling Psychology*, 25 (May 1978), 210–216.

[54] Thomas J. Long, "Influence of Uniform and Religious Status on Interviewees," *Journal of Counseling Psychology*, 25 (September 1978), 405–410.

[55] Donald R. Atkinson and Gaye Carskaddon, "A Prestigious Introduction, Psychological Jargon and Perceived Counselor Credibility," *Journal of Counseling Psychology*, 22 (May 1975), 180–186.

[56] Charles D. Claiborn and Lyle D. Schmidt, "Effects of Presession Information on the Perception of the Counselor in an Interview," *Journal of Counseling Psychology*, 24 (July 1977), 259–263.

higher expertness ratings than high-status expert introductions was attributed by them to differences in response set in the use of the counselor rating form. Kerr and Dell[57] reported that only counselor role behavior significantly affected students' perceptions of interview attractiveness, whereas perceptions of expertness seemed to have been affected jointly by role and attire.

The influence of counselor behavior (defined by levels of the facilitative conditions) and of counselor status (as indicated in an introduction) on 120 male and female undergraduate psychology students' perceptions of the counselor was examined by Scheid.[58] The counselor's behavior produced a main effect on each of sex-dependent measures, whereas counselor introduction produced a main effect on only two measures, competence and comfort.

Strong and Matross[59] elaborated on earlier theoretical formulations by Strong by defining the change process in terms of impelling and restraining forces within a lower-dependence relationship. Therefore, change in counseling is to be viewed as a function of the impelling forces (demonstrated by the counselor's power and the client's need) and restraining forces (the client's opposition and resistance to change). Strong and Matross represented the relationship between impelling and restraining forces by the equation $\Delta B = P + (O + R)$ where a change in Behavior (ΔB) is a function of the impelling forces (P) as well as the restraining forces (O+R). To the extent that the impelling forces, power base, and client need exceed the restraining forces, opposition (O) and resistance (R), the client will be susceptible to the counselor's influence.

Two counselor power bases believed to contribute to the impelling forces are *expert* and *referent* power bases. In the expert power base, the client perceives in the counselor special knowledge and abilities to meet his or her needs with the least amount of cost. In the referent, the client perceives similarities between the counselor and self that can be used to resolve psychological inconsistencies. The counselor can use those similarities to maximize his or her ability to influence the client.

Tolerance for ambiguity

Ambiguity tolerance has been defined by Budner[60] as the tendency to perceive ambiguous situations as desirable. An ambiguous situation is one that cannot be adequately structured or categorized by an individual because sufficient cues are absent. It is believed that counselors who have a high tolerance for ambiguity are able to process greater numbers of stimuli than counselors who have a low tolerance for ambiguity.

Tucker and Snyder[61] reported that counselors with high levels of ambiguity tolerance exhibited more effective interview behaviors than counselors with low levels of ambiguity tolerance. Chasnoff[62] investigated the influence of differences in ambiguity tolerance and the effects of exposure to a video-taped model on counselor-trainee interview behavior. She reported only limited support for the hypothesis that high ambiguity tolerance and exposure to a model produced significantly more effective interview behaviors.

Dogmatism

Highly dogmatic counselors are believed to be less effective because they are thought to be more critical and less empathic of their clients than their less dogmatic counterparts. Wright[63] reported that dogmatism was an unstable characteristic of counselors during counseling. Those counselors

[57] Barbara A. Kerr and Donald M. Dell, "Perceived Interview Expertness and Attractiveness: Effects of Interview Behavior and Attire and Interview Setting," *Journal of Counseling Psychology*, 23 (November 1976), 553–556.
[58] August B. Scheid, "Clients' Perception of the Counselor: The Influence of Counselor Introduction and Behavior," *Journal of Counseling Psychology*, 23 (November 1976), 503–508.
[59] Stanley R. Strong and P. R. Matross, "Change Process in Counseling and Psychotherapy," *Journal of Counseling Psychology*, 20 (January 1973), 25–37.

[60] Stanley Budner, "Intolerance of Ambiguity as a Personality Variable," *Journal of Personality*, 30 (March 1962), 29–59.
[61] Robin C. Tucker and William U. Snyder, "Ambiguity Tolerance of Therapists and Process Changes in Their Clients," *Journal of Counseling Psychology*, 21 (November 1974), 577–578.
[62] Selina Sue Chasnoff, "The Effects of Modeling and Ambiguity Tolerance on Interview Behavior," *Counselor Education and Supervision*, 16 (September 1976), 46–51.
[63] Wilbur Wright, "Counselor Dogmatism, Willingness to Disclose and Clients' Empathy Ratings," *Journal of Counseling Psychology*, 22 (September 1975), 390–394.

who were low on dogmatism appeared to show higher levels of psychological insight during counseling than "high dogmatic counselors." He concluded that the psychological state of the client determined, to a great extent, whether highly dogmatic counselors were effective.

Wittmer and Webster[64] studied forty-nine counselor trainees prior to their practicum experience and found that those with teaching experience were more dogmatic than those with no teaching experience. Age and sex differences were not significant, although older students tended to be more close-minded. Heikkenen [65] replicated the study by Wittmer and Webster and reported results in agreement with the original findings. However, age was found to be related to close-mindedness among Heikkenen's subjects as well as the combined samples of the two studies.

Humor

Some armchair speculation, but little empirical research, has been applied to uncovering the effects of humor as a part of the counselor's pattern of reaction to the client. Greenson[66] observed that the best therapists possessed a good sense of humor and had ready wit. Labrentz[67] presented data suggesting humor was an important clinical variable.

Three observations have been made about humor in the counseling situation. First, use of humor by the counselor may be a mask for hostility and therefore destructive. Second, the humor of a stimulus is believed to be related directly to the degree to which the perceiver can empathize and take on the role of the character presented in the humor situation. Third, appreciation of humor can serve as an adaptive function by reducing anxiety.

Roberts and Johnson[68] reported that subjects' humor ratings of cartoons correlated significantly with their scores on empathy questionnaires and with clinicians' ratings of their potential capacity for empathy. Hickson[69] sought to measure the relationship that existed between humor appreciation responses and facilitative abilities (empathy, respect, genuineness, concreteness) of graduate counselor trainees. Her measure of humor was obtained by scores on the *Institute for Personality and Ability Testing Humor Test*, Form A. She reported that counselor trainees who exhibited more intelligence, anxiety, introversion, antiestablishmentism, and flirtatious behavior than other trainees were able to communicate at a more facilitative level. One humor measure, general intelligence, was the single most important predictor of facilitative functioning, accounting for 63 percent of the variance.

Profanity

Nonstandard English is the rather neutral term used by the American Psychological Association[70] to describe profane language. Arbuckle[71] and Perls,[72] among others have acknowledged use of profane statements in counseling. Each counselor response containing a four-letter word in a Carkhuff teaching guide[73] was rated above 3.0, the minimum facilitative level. Heubusch and Horan[74] sought to study the effect of the counselor's use of profanity in initial counseling interviews. Volunteer clients of both sexes were exposed

[64] Joe Wittmer and G. B. Webster, "The Relationship Between Teaching Experience and Counselor Trainee Dogmatism," *Journal of Counseling Psychology*, 16 (November 1969), 499–504.
[65] Charles A. Heikkenen, "Another Look at the Teaching Experience and Close-Mindedness," *Journal of Counseling Psychology*, 22 (January 1975), 79–83.
[66] Ralph R. Greenson, *The Technique and Practice of Psychoanalysis*, Vol. I (New York: International Universities Press, 1967), p. 386.
[67] Helmut L. Labrentz, "The Effects of Humor on the Initial Client Counselor Relationship," (Ph.D. diss., University of Southern Mississippi, 1973). *Dissertation Abstracts International*, 34 (1973), 3875.
[68] Allyn F. Roberts and Donald M. Johnson, "Some Factors Related to the Perception of Funniness in Humor Stimuli," *Journal of Social Psychology*, 46 (August 1957), 57–63.
[69] Joyce Hickson, "Relationship Between Humor Preferences and Facilitative Skills of Counselor Trainees," *Journal of Counseling Services*, 1 (Fall 1977), 15–20.
[70] American Psychological Association, *Thesaurus of Psychological Terms* (Washington, D.C.: The Association, 1974).
[71] Dugald S. Arbuckle, "Comment," *Personnel and Guidance Journal*, 54 (April 1976), 434.
[72] Fritz S. Perls, *Gestalt Therapy Verbatim* (Lafayette, California: Real People Press, 1969).
[73] Robert R. Carkhuff, *Helping and Human Relations: A Primer for Lay and Professional Helpers* (New York: Holt, Rinehart and Winston, 1969).
[74] Norbert J. Heubusch and John J. Horan, "Some Effects of Counselor Profanity in Counseling," *Journal of Counseling Psychology*, 24 (September 1977), 456–458.

to one of two treatment conditions. In the first condition, counselors used four profane words and in the other condition, profanity was not used. These two researchers reported that counselors who used profanity were judged by their clients to be less effective and satisfying.

Teaching experience

Kehas and Morris[75] investigated the way in which counselors who had taught were influenced by their earlier experience, and concluded that having been a teacher (1) was useful to the counselor in understanding and working with counselees and teachers on student-teacher problems and (2) was dysfunctional to the extent that it (a) gave rise to ambivalent feelings about the teaching and counseling role, (b) demanded change in perspective toward the student, the school system, and teachers and (c) caused conflict by the necessity of changing the appeals, rewards, and punishments used with students. In a second article[76] these investigators reported on their twelve subjects' intrarole conflict about, and motivation for, changing from teaching to counseling. They pointed out that the expectations of the counselor held by others are bewildering, diverse, and contradictory. In such intrarole conflicts, previous teaching experience can be a help or hindrance depending on whether the counselor views the expectations as legitimate. These twelve subjects' motivations for becoming counselors stemmed primarily from their dissatisfaction with the total educational process and their desire for personal growth. In becoming counselors, some sought to become expressive leaders.

Transparency

Successful counseling facilitates counselee self-disclosure and self-exploration. It is successful because the individual verbalizes and comes to know his or her beliefs, motives, fears, relationships to others and life's decisions. Truax and Carkhuff have presented research supporting a significant relationship between counselor transparency and counselee self-disclosure.[77] They reported that the greater the self-exploration, the greater the constructive personality change. An exception to this finding was the delinquent adolescent involved in group psychotherapy; for that individual the less self-exploration, the greater the positive personality change.

Branan[78] varied the rates of counselors' self-disclosure to groups of graduate students, but reported that this did not bring about more student self-disclosure, not did it affect the students' ratings of their counselors' genuineness, empathy, or self-disclosure. However, Strong and Schmidt[79] reported positive student reactions to interviewer self-disclosures. Jourard and Jaffe[80] sought to determine whether subjects would follow the leader and emulate the disclosing behaviors of an experimenter, not only in terms of variety of content but also in direction of self-revealing remarks. The experimenter openly and honestly discussed her thoughts and feelings regarding each of twenty topics, and elicited the reactions of forty female subjects. The treatment of the four groups of subjects varied only in the length of attention to different topics. Jourard and Jaffe reported that when the experimenter spoke briefly, the subjects spoke briefly; when the experimenter spoke at length, the subjects spoke significantly longer. Contrary to expectation, the subjects tended to talk longer on highly intimate topics.

Schmidt and Strong[81] and Strong and Dixon[82] instructed interviewers to reveal experiences and feelings either similar

[75] Chris D. Kehas and Jane L. Morris, "Perceptions in Role Change from Teacher to Counselor," *Counselor Education and Supervision,* 9 (Summer 1970), 248–258.

[76] Chris D. Kehas and Jane L. Morris, "Perceptions in Role Change from Teacher to Counselor: Intra-Role Conflict and Motivation for Change," *Counselor Education and Supervision,* 10 (Spring 1971), 200–208.

[77] Charles B. Truax and Robert R. Carkhuff, "Client and Therapist Transparency in the Psychotherapeutic Encounter," *Journal of Counseling Psychology,* 12 (Spring 1965), 3–9.

[78] John M. Branan, "Client Reaction to Counselor's Use of Self Experience," *Personnel and Guidance Journal,* 45 (February 1967), 568–572.

[79] Stanley R. Strong and Lyle D. Schmidt, "Trustworthiness and Influence in Counseling," *Journal of Counseling Psychology,* 17 (May 1970), 197–200.

[80] Sidney M. Jourard and Peggy L. Jaffe, "Influence of an Interviewer's Disclosure on the Self-Disclosing Behavior of Interviewees," *Journal of Counseling Psychology,* 17 (May 1970), 252–257.

[81] Lyle D. Schmidt and Stanley R. Strong, "Attractiveness and Influence in Counseling," *Journal of Counseling Psychology,* 18 (July 1971), 348–351.

[82] Stanley R. Strong and David R. Dixon, "Expertness, Attractiveness and Influence in Counseling," *Journal of Counseling,* 18 (November 1971), 562–570.

or dissimilar to those expressed by subjects. Similar disclosures resulted in warmly positive reactions whereas the outcome of dissimilar disclosures was negative reactions. Murphy and Strong[83] reported that sixty-four college males were interviewed individually for twenty minutes about how college had altered their friendships, values, and plans. The interviewers disclosed experiences and feelings similar to those revealed by the students zero, two, four, and eight times during the interviews. The interviewers' self-disclosures impressed the students with the interviewers' willingness to be known as persons, and increased the students' feelings of warmth, friendliness, and of being understood. These investigators suggest that the timing of self-disclosures is as important as their frequency in the interview.

Counselor activity

Hill and her associates[84] reported that counselors responded more to clients whose problems were viewed as serious, those whom the counselor believed best able to benefit from counseling, and those whom the counselor deemed more desirable with whom to work. Smith and Martinson[85] investigated the effects of counselors' and counselees' learning styles on interview interaction behavior. Various combinations of counselors and clients were used whose learning styles suggested preferences for unstructured learning (called *impulsive learners* because they were friendly, changeable, quick thinking, and quick acting) and counselors and clients whose learning styles suggested preference for structured learning (called *constricted learners* because they were reserved, conscientious, and conservative). Their findings were that impulsive counselors differed from constricted counselors only in directive behavior when both interviewed impulsive clients. The two types did not differ in re-

spect to nondirective behaviors, leading behaviors, clients' following behaviors, or clients' positive or negative feelings about the interviews.

Presumably, the counselor's gestures and body movements have an impact on the client's reactions and verbal communications. Such gestures and body shifts are believed to either accentuate or deny the counselor's verbal expression. Strong and his associates[86] explored the extent to which exposure to counselors' verbal and nonverbal behavior prompted different descriptions of counselors by clients than exposure to counselors' verbal behavior alone. Their thesis was that if the counselor's verbal and nonverbal expressions are congruent, then counselors need not be concerned about nonverbal behavior. If, however, nonverbal cues alter the significance of verbal cues, then counselors must control their nonverbal behavior to avoid a contradictory impact on clients. Their findings were that subjects who saw and heard counselors described them more negatively than subjects who only heard them. Presumably, some visual cues disrupted the subjects' positive image of the counselor. The counselor who moved frequently, changed body position, smiled, frowned, gestured, and so on, provoked more positive descriptions than the counselor who remained as still as possible.

Self-concept and awareness

Fullmer and Bernard[87] stress the reality of "habitual patterns of behavior" with which an individual approaches interpersonal encounters, including counseling. An individual's behavior patterns, whether they be those of the counselor or counselee, are not "isolated in time and place," but are used habitually in relating to other individuals. Aware as counselors may be that they are functioning as professional counselors, they must be themselves to be effective. The way counselors function during the process of counseling is undoubtedly different, at least to some degree, from the way they function when not counseling. But underlying and intertwined with the professional self is a personal self that

[83] Kevin C. Murphy and Stanley R. Strong, "Some Effects of Similarity Self-Disclosure," *Journal of Counseling Psychology*, 19 (March 1972), 121–124.
[84] Clara E. Hill et al., "Counselor Reactions to Female Clients: Type of Problem, Age of Client and Sex of Counselor," *Journal of Counseling Psychology*, 24 (January 1977), 60–65.
[85] William D. Smith and William D. Martinson, "Counselors' and Counselees' Learning Style in Interview Behavior," *Journal of Counseling Psychology*, 18 (March 1971), 138–141.

[86] Stanley R. Strong et al., "Nonverbal Behavior and Perceived Counselor Characteristics," *Journal of Counseling Psychology*, 18 (November 1971), 554–561.
[87] Daniel W. Fullmer and Harold W. Bernard, *Counseling: Content and Process* (Chicago: Science Research Associates, 1964), p. 126.

must respond in a personal way. The professional self and the personal self cannot—and should not—be separate entities.

The dictum "know thyself" long has been a truism for counselors. Accurate self-knowledge is viewed as a condition necessary for counselors to enter their clients' perceptual fields and to be perceptive about behavior. Benjamin[88] asserts that counselors who are aware of themselves can understand better and appreciate the behavior of others. However, Loesch and Weikel[89] had 107 counselor-education students estimate their need levels and then complete the *Personality Research Form* (PRF). Significant differences between their perceived and measured need levels were found for ten of the fourteen PRF Scales. Loesch and Weikel concluded that counselor-education students were unable to assess accurately their own needs. Age, sex, and number of graduate hours completed were not significant factors in these students' abilities to assess their need levels. Selfridge and Vander Kolk[90] compared client ratings of thirty-three school counselors' communication of facilitative conditions (empathy, regard, congruence, trust) to these counselors' scores on a measure of self-actualization. They reported that a strong relationship existed between self-actualization and counselor effectiveness as rated by clients.

A study of counselor self-concept that receives frequent citation was completed by Kazienko and Neidt.[91] They investigated the personality characteristics of male counselor trainees enrolled in twenty-five summer NDEA Counseling and Guidance Institutes who were identified by the professional staffs as being in the top and bottom 25 percent of their institute groups. Using the *Bennett Polydiagnostic Index*, subjects described themselves in terms of self-concept, motivating forces, values, and feelings about others. The good and poor counselor trainee groups' descriptions of themselves were compared. In terms of self-concept,

the good counselors perceived themselves as serious, earnest, patient, soft spoken; aware of personal self-centeredness; more domestic than social; and not of mechanical or industrial inclination. The poor counselors did not recognize qualities of seriousness or patience in self, tended toward loudness of voice, were not aware of any personal self-centeredness, and saw self as normally domestic and social and as of mechanical and industrial inclination. Descriptions of motivation suggested that the good counselor was concerned about possessing a measure of security but inclined to reject need for wealth, whereas the poor counselor was neither moved nor unmoved by prospects of security and riches. In the area of values, the good counselor group was found to reject cunningness and shrewdness, to feel that people should have the right to be different, and to place little value on severity and strictness. The poor counselor group was found to emphasize conformity and tended toward strict adherence to rules. With respect to feelings about others, the good group viewed people as possessing an adequate measure of intellectual ability though self-centered, whereas the poor group gave others no particular credit for intellectual assets.

Characteristics distinguishing effective from ineffective counselors

Much work has been directed to identifying the characteristics of effective counselors. The literature suggests that effective counselors can be separated somewhat from their less effective counterparts on three dimensions: experience, type of relationship established, and nonintellective factors. However, nonintellective measures have not consistently discriminated between the two groups. Distinctions seem due to differences in intensity rather than to the presence or absence of given characteristics.

Experience

There is substantial evidence that experience is an important variable in counselor effectiveness. Fiedler's investigations indicated that (1) better-trained therapists of varying therapy orientations agreed more highly with each other in their concept of an ideal therapeutic relationship than they

[88] Arthur Benjamin, *The Helping Interview*, 2nd ed. (Boston: Houghton Mifflin Company, 1974), p. 6.
[89] Larry C. Loesch and William J. Weikel, "Perceived and Measured Needs Levels of Counselor Education Students," *Counselor Education and Supervision*, 16 (September 1976), 59–65.
[90] Fred F. Selfridge and Charles Vander Kolk, "Correlates of Counselor Self-Actualization and Client-Perceived Facilitativeness," *Counselor Education and Supervision*, 15 (March 1976), 189–194.
[91] Louis W. Kazienko and Charles O. Neidt, "Self Descriptions of Good and Poor Counselor Trainees," *Counselor Education and Supervision*, 1 (Spring 1962), 106–123.

agreed with less well trained therapists within their own orientation,[92] and (2) the therapeutic relationship created by experts of one orientation resembled more closely that created by experts of other schools than it resembled relationships created by nonexperts in the same school.[93]

Rogers demonstrated that more experienced counselors offered more congruence, empathy, and unconditional positive regard than did their less-experienced counterparts and were more successful in communicating these conditions to their clients.[94] Experienced counselors were perceived by their clients to offer a higher level of those conditions, and their clients showed more change over the course of counseling.

Dogmatism

Foulds sought to pinpoint the correlation between dogmatism (as measured by the *Rokeach Dogmatism Scale*) and ability to communicate facilitative counseling conditions (as measured by the Carkhuff scales) of thirty graduate students in an initial counseling practicum.[95] Trained judges observed the degree of empathic understanding, positive regard, and facilitative genuineness extended to clients by the thirty students. Because no significant correlation emerged from the study, Foulds suggested that more than one type of dogmatism may exist; that is, a "benevolent" dogmatism may not interfere with a person's ability to communicate facilitative conditions, whereas a "nonbenevolent" type would destroy such conditions. In an earlier investigation[96] Foulds reported that certain personality characteristics believed associated with self-actualization were related significantly to the ability of the counselor to communicate

empathic understanding and facilitative genuineness. Logically, those counselors who are psychologically healthy should be able to extend high levels of facilitative conditions to clients. However, Winborn and Rowe[97] replicated the Foulds study but could not confirm his findings.

Nonintellective factors

Studies of the relationship between counselor effectiveness and personality show that effective counselors can be distinguished from less effective counselors in regard to (1) self-concept, motivation, values, feelings about others, and perceptual organization and (2) performance on certain standardized personality and interest inventories. Further, counselor effectiveness is associated with tolerance for ambiguity, understanding of the client, maturity, ability to maintain an appropriate emotional distance from the client, and ability to establish good social relationships with nonclients.

According to Wicas and Mahan, high-rated counselors were anxious, sensitive to the expectations of others and society, patient and nonaggressive in interpersonal relationships, and concerned about social progress but always with appropriate self-control.[98] Although many of their findings indicated a pleasant, stable, dedicated person, they also reported undesirable traits such as low originality, rejection of contemplation, lack of persistence, and a conservative orientation to social problems.

Rickenbaugh, Heaps, and Finley[99] examined sixty-seven college students who were on academic probation to determine their perception of the counselor's comfort, the counseling climate, and their counseling satisfaction (as measured by the *Counselor Evaluation Inventory*). The counselors' effectiveness rating was based on degree of positive change in their clients' academic performance. Of the

[92] Fred E. Fiedler, "The Concept of an Ideal Therapeutic Relationship," *Journal of Consulting Psychology*, 14 (August 1950), 239–245.
[93] Fred E. Fiedler, "A Comparison of Therapeutic Relationships in Psychoanalytical, Nondirective and Adlerian Therapy," *Journal of Consulting Psychology*, 14 (December 1950), 436–445.
[94] Carl R. Rogers, "The Interpersonal Relationship: The Core of Guidance," *Harvard Educational Review*, 32 (Fall 1962), 416–429.
[95] Melvin L. Foulds, "Dogmatism and Ability to Communicate Facilitative Conditions During Counseling," *Counselor Education and Supervision*, 11 (December 1971), 110–114.
[96] Melvin L. Foulds, "Self-Actualization and the Communication of Facilitative Conditions During Counseling," *Journal of Counseling Psychology*, 16 (March 1969), 132–136.

[97] Bob B. Winborn and Wayne Rowe, "Self-Actualization and the Communication of Facilitative Conditions—A Replication," *Journal of Counseling Psychology*, 19 (January 1972), 26–29.
[98] Edward A. Wicas and Thomas W. Mahan, Jr., "Characteristics of Counselors Rated Effective by Supervisors and Peers," *Counselor Education and Supervision*, 6 (Fall 1966), 50–56.
[99] Karl Rickenbaugh, Richard A. Heaps, and Robert E. Finley, "Counselor Comfort, Counseling Climate and Client Satisfaction; Client Ratings and Academic Improvement," *Counselor Education and Supervision*, 11 (March 1972), 219–223.

three factors described above, only the client's perception of the counselor's comfort was found to be significantly related to counselor effectiveness. The investigators concluded that counselor effectiveness varies as a function of counselor comfort and that counselors tend to become more comfortable with experience.

Tinsley and Tinsley[100] separated counselors into three groups labeled *relatively effective counselors* (N=32), *relatively ineffective counselors* (N=30), and an indeterminant group (N=12) based on practicum supervisors' assessments. The two extreme groups were compared on the *Strong Vocational Interest Blank* (SVIB-M for men; SVIB-W for women), the *General Aptitude Battery* (GATB), and the *Minnesota Importance Questionnaire* (MIQ). Tinsley and Tinsley reported that effective counselors measured significantly higher than ineffective counselors on the GATB verbal aptitude scale. Further, *ineffective counselors* had stronger needs (based on *Minnesota Importance Questionnaire*) than effective counselors to (1) make use of their abilities, (2) attain feelings of accomplishment, (3) tell others what to do, (4) be paid well, (5) do things for other people, (6) have a boss who would back them up, (7) have a boss who would train them well, and (8) have good working conditions. Effective female counselors, according to Tinsley and Tinsley, scored higher than their ineffective counterparts on SVIB-W scales that reflect interest in artistic, verbal-linguistic and verbal-scientific types of occupations. Relatively ineffective female counselors appeared to be more interested in occupations in which concrete, routine, physical skills of a repetitive or semirepetitive nature were required and they seemed to have stronger vocational needs.

Characteristics of counselees

The personality, expectations, and experiences of counselees increasingly are coming to the forefront in explaining counseling success and failure. Like counselors, clients bring to counseling all they are up to the time of the encounters; their attitudes and values; their experiences and feelings about themselves, their family, and friends; their past successes and failures; their aspirations and disappointments; their habits, concerns, feelings, and uncertainties; and their beliefs about and expectations for counseling.

Sex and race

Tyler[101] points out that counselees—and counselors, too, for that matter—hold "general attitudes toward broad categories of people," and the most obvious and universal is that of sex. From early childhood on individuals learn different expectations of males and females. And it is difficult—if not impossible—to think that counselees entering a counseling room do not notice whether the counselor is a man or woman. At this encounter, whether it be the initial interview or any one of subsequent interviews, their attitudes toward males and females come into play, subtly or obviously, to enhance or to hamper the interaction.

Some years ago, Heilbrun[102] investigated personality differences between male and female counseling subjects who discontinued therapy relatively early versus those who continued. For most of the personality variables he found a "sex by stay" category interaction. One of his inferences was that the nonstay client, male or female, conformed most closely to the cultural and personal stereotype appropriate to his or her sex. Nonstay female clients as compared to females who stayed were less achieving, autonomous, and dominant and more deferent and abasing. Heilbrun's explanation was that the more masculine, independent male finds it difficult to accept the subordinate status of a client, whereas the more feminine male has less difficulty in playing such a role. Further, in the case of the effeminate male client there is an increased likelihood of early identification and a greater bond with the male counselor.

More recently, Heilbrun[103] tested two alternative explanations for the early termination of female counseling clients. One explanation was that dependent, self-disclosing females were frustrated by nondirective, initial interviews

[100] Howard E. A. Tinsley and Diane J. Tinsley, "Different Needs, Interests, and Abilities of Effective and Ineffective Counselor Trainees: Implications for Counselor Selection," *Journal of Counseling Psychology*, 24 (January 1977), 83–86.

[101] Leona E. Tyler, *The Work of the Counselor*, 3rd ed. (New York: Appleton-Century-Crofts, 1969), pp. 55–56.

[102] Alfred B. Heilbrun, Jr., "Male and Female Personality Correlates of Early Termination in Counseling," *Journal of Counseling Psychology*, 8 (Spring 1961), 31–36.

[103] Alfred B. Heilbrun, Jr., "Interviewer Style, Client Satisfaction and Premature Termination Following the Initial Counseling Contact," *Journal of Counseling Psychology*, 21 (September 1974), 346–350.

that failed to provide the structure needed to formulate their problems. Consequently, dissatisfaction leads to discontinuation of counseling. The second alternative explanation was that nondirective, initial interviews were satisfying because they provide dependent, self-disclosing females with the opportunity for cathartic relief. Consequently, they terminate because they feel better. Evaluations of counselor directiveness and interview satisfaction were obtained from twenty-four female clients immediately following the initial interview. Those most likely to defect (did not return for a second session) expressed greater satisfaction with nondirective interviewing; therefore the catharsis alternative appeared to be the more persuasive explanation.

Gamboa, Tosi, and Riccio[104] investigated the effect of race and counselor climate on the preferences for a counselor among delinquent girls. Their findings included that the strongest preference for a counselor among delinquent girls was when counseling was related to educational matters and that white subjects preferred the black counselor over the white counselor when personal-social problems were concerned.

Brooks[105] reported that (1) male interviewees disclosed more to females, whereas females disclosed more to males; (2) dyads containing a female resulted in more disclosure than all male dyads; (3) males revealed more to high-status interviewers, whereas females disclosed more to low-status interviewers; and (4) high- as opposed to low-status male interviewers elicited more disclosure from all subjects, whereas status of female interviewers resulted in no significant difference.

Smith[106] asked 512 secondary school counselors to predict the academic success and choose an appropriate career for four hypothetical cases. The sex and ethnic group designation of the cases were varied systematically to determine whether counselors' evaluations of clients were influenced by these variables. She reported that variation in sex and ethnic group designation did not produce variations in counselor evaluations and that sex of counselor was not related to systematic variance in evaluations.

Little evidence appears to support the notion that girls and women relate better to female counselors or that boys and men relate better to male counselors. Occasionally a client states a preference with regard to sex of the counselor. Sometimes, a female counselee may prefer to talk with a woman "about this particular matter" or a male client may wish "this time" to see a male counselor. For the most part, however, counselees do not seem to view the counselor only as a male or female, but as an individual.

Expectations and perceptions

Considerable research, during recent years, has gone into investigating the relationship between counselee expectations regarding counselors and gains to be made in counseling or counseling outcomes. The beliefs and expectations that clients hold about counselors and the counseling process influence in no small way that which takes place in counseling, particularly the initial sessions. Research on the effects of client expectancies has delved into clients' perceptions of problems appropriate for counseling, how confidential their disclosures will be kept, what the counselor's behavior will be like, and whether they discontinue counseling early, to cite but a few areas. In general, many studies suggest that counselees view problems of an educational and vocational nature as most appropriate for discussing with counselors, whereas those regarding school or college routine and problems of adjustment have been viewed as relatively less appropriate. Clients expect the counselor to be warmly interested in them, to be highly trained and expert, and to be confident of helping them. Clients expect the counselor to be problem centered on a personal level, thoroughly prepared for each interview, to be at ease with them and their individual problems, and to maintain confidentiality.

Gottman and Leiblum[107] point out that although the exact nature of the relationship between client expectations and counseling outcomes has not been established clearly,

[104] Anthony M. Gamboa, Jr., Donald J. Tosi, and Anthony J. Riccio, "Race and Counselor Climate in the Counselor Preference of Delinquent Girls," *Journal of Counseling Psychology*, 23 (March 1976), 160–162.
[105] Linda Brooks, "Interactive Effects of Sex and Status on Self-Disclosure," *Journal of Counseling Psychology*, 21 (November 1974), 469–474.
[106] Mary Lee Smith, "Influence of Client Sex and Ethnic Group on Counselor Judgment," *Journal of Counseling Psychology*, 21 (November 1974), 516–521.

[107] John W. Gottman and Sandra R. Leiblum, *How to Do Psychotherapy and How to Evaluate It* (New York: Holt, Rinehart and Winston, 1974), pp. 19–21.

the evidence collected so far suggests that it is a curvilinear relationship, that is, people with moderate expectancies may improve more than those with extremely high or low expectancies. Further, they catalogue six models descriptive of what clients may expect when they come for counseling. Paraphrased here, the models include (1) an *adjustment* model in that clients expect counselors to help them accept their feelings, problems, and limitations; (2) a *personality* model in which clients expect to remold their personality into a new profile; (3) a *medical* model in which clients have little involvement but will be told by an expert what to do; (4) a *witchcraft* model in which their evil thoughts, feelings, and actions will be exorcised and replaced with good ones; (5) a *moral* model in which the counselor is expected to be a good person who will teach them right ways of acting; and (6) a *replacement* model in which the counselor replaces a friend, father, lover, and so on, missing in their lives.

Kaul and Parker[108] point out that (1) the expectations of the client are potential therapeutic agents, (2) expectations are learned and can be modified, (3) one index of successful counseling is the client's acquisition of a new conceptual scheme for understanding behavior, (4) the similarity of the client's new conceptual scheme to that of the counselor will affect the judged degree of counseling success, and (5) the client's faith in the counselor is more important than the validity of the counselor's techniques. They evaluated the effects of suggestibility and expectancy in a counseling analogue. Suggestibility was assessed both objectively and subjectively by the *Baker Suggestibility Scale.* Some 126 upper-division and graduate students were classified as highly suggestible, middle in suggestibility, and low in suggestibility within each method (objective and subjective). Two levels of expectancy were established. Subjects were paired into homogeneous objective suggestibility and expectancy dyads. The dyads completed the ten programs of the general relationship program that served as the counseling analogue. Three criterion measures (semantic differential scales, content test, and client satisfaction rating scales) were employed. Kaul and Parker reported that subjectively experienced suggestibility was more closely related to at-

titude change than objective suggestibility, and that the generalized expectancy treatments were ineffective in influencing criterion scores.

The client's trust in a counselor was investigated by Kaul and Schmidt.[109] Some thirty-two senior and graduate students viewed twenty-four short video-taped scenes of interviewers who exhibited combinations of trustworthy and untrustworthy content and manner, then rated the interviewer's trustworthiness. Analysis of the ratings indicated that the interviewer's manner influenced trust ratings more than the content of his or her remarks. Kaul and Schmidt suggest that the training of counselors should include attention to manner as well as content of communication with the client.

Hypothesizing that counseling effectiveness is a result of clients' confidence in the ability of the system used to help them deal with their problems, Bednar and Parker[110] investigated whether two different counseling methods were equally effective in helping similar clients. They reported that (1) different counseling-treatment procedures were equally successful in effecting change of equivalent magnitude, but in divergent directions; (2) there was no difference between the two counseling treatments in client satisfaction despite the opposite directions of change; (3) susceptibility to persuasion and heightened expectations did not significantly influence the magnitude of change; and (4) subjects who were classified as highly persuasible viewed the counseling treatments as more valuable to themselves and others, and expressed greater interest both in continuing treatment and attempting new behaviors.

Doubtless an important component in the client's expectations of counseling is the trust placed in the counselor. Clients who trust counselors presumably believe that they are expert. Expertness is often communicated by such factors as status introductions, prestige symbols, degrees, and so forth. Schmidt and Strong[111] explain that "The client's

[108] Theodore J. Kaul and Clyde A. Parker, "Suggestibility and Expectancy in a Counseling Analogue," *Journal of Counseling Psychology,* 18 (November 1971), 536–541.

[109] Theodore J. Kaul and Lyle D. Schmidt, "Dimensions of Interviewer Trustworthiness," *Journal of Counseling Psychology,* 18 (November 1971), 542–548.
[110] Richard L. Bednar and Clyde A. Parker, "Client Susceptibility to Persuasion and Counseling Outcome," *Journal of Counseling Psychology,* 16 (September 1969), 415–420.
[111] Lyle D. Schmidt and Stanley R. Strong, " 'Expert' and 'Nonexpert' Counselors," *Journal of Counseling Psychology,* 17 (March 1970), 115–118.

perception of the counselor's expertness is one of the factors which moderates the degree to which the client will change his [or her] views to those of the counselor rather than discredit the counselor." They reported that counselors identified as expert (actually the inexperienced counselors) were viewed as relaxed, interested, friendly, attentive, and confident. Conversely, the nonexpert counselors (actually the experienced ones) were viewed as awkward, tense, uneasy, and nonconfident.

Guttman and Haase[112] investigated the effects of an experimentally induced set of expertness on thirty-one male college freshmen clients' evaluations of brief vocational counseling. They reported that these clients responded more favorably to relationship aspects of the interview with a counselor who was introduced as an nonexpert, that informational recall was greater for clients interviewed by expert counselors, and that global ratings did not differentiate between expert and nonexpert counselors. Guttman and Haase contend that expertness as an enhancing quality in counselors has been overemphasized.

Tinsley and Harris[113] investigated the expectancies held by college students for counseling. Their subjects seemed to believe that counseling is generally helpful, but were somewhat doubtful that it could ever be helpful to them personally. Their respondents' strongest expectancies were of seeing an experienced, genuine, expert, and accepting counselor they could trust.

Investigations by Gelso and Karl[114] and Gelso and McKenzie[115] unfortunately have indicated that clients may hold negative perceptions, some of which may provide artificial limitations on the effectiveness of the counselor. The presence of these potentially dysfunctional beliefs

among counselees suggests that the value of initial counselor-client contact may be increased if the counselor shares relevant and important information with the client. Savitsky, Zarle, and Keedy[116] investigated the effects that several kinds of information about a counselor might have on an initial interview. Some sixty-four female undergraduates (first- and second-year students) were randomly assigned to four experimental conditions. They were told their counselors (1) had happy pasts and were trying to help, (2) had happy pasts, not trying to help, (3) had unhappy pasts, trying to help, or (4) had unhappy pasts, not trying to help. Interviewee ratings indicated that interviewers who were described as trying to help others were viewed as more competent. The effect of those interviewers described as having a happy background but as not trying to help others was to suppress self-disclosure. However, neither type of information influenced actual liking between the interview participants.

Dreman[117] studied one hundred college clients' preferences of counselor characteristics and behavior. He reported that (1) client preferences and expectations were highly congruent and (2) clients wanted the counselor to be more active in verbalizing and changing behaviors than they expected a professional to be. Previously, Dreman and Dolev,[118] investigating the preferences and expectations held by nonclients, reported that nonclients *wanted* counselors to be more active than they expected them to be. Further, nonclients believed clients suffered more from psychological and interpersonal problems than they did.

Strong, Hendel, and Bratton[119] reported that counselors, compared to psychiatrists, were perceived by students as warm, friendly, and polite people to talk with, although not

[112] Mary A. Julius Guttman and Richard F. Haase, "Effect of Experimentally Induced Sets of High and Low 'Expertness' During Brief Vocational Counseling," *Counselor Education and Supervision*, 11 (March 1972), 171–177.

[113] Howard E. A. Tinsley and Donna J. Harris, "Client Expectations for Counseling," *Journal of Counseling Psychology*, 23 (May 1976), 173–177.

[114] Charles J. Gelso and Norman J. Karl, "Perceptions of 'Counselors' and Other Help Givers: What's in a Label?" *Journal of Counseling Psychology*, 21 (May 1974), 243–247.

[115] C. J. Gelso and J. D. McKenzie, "Effect of Information on Students' Perceptions of Counseling and Their Willingness to Seek Help," *Journal of Counseling Psychology*, 20 (September 1973), 406–411.

[116] Jeffrey C. Savitsky, Thomas H. Zarle, and Nathan S. Keedy, "The Effect of Information About an Interviewer on Interviewee Perceptions," *Journal of Counseling Psychology*, 23 (March 1976), 158–159.

[117] Solly B. Dreman, "Expectations and Preferences of Clients for a University Counseling Service," *Journal of Counseling Psychology*, 24 (September 1977), 459–462.

[118] Solly B. Dreman and A. Dolev, "Expectations and Preferences of Non-Clients for a University Student Counseling Center," *Journal of Counseling Psychology*, 23 (November 1976), 571–574.

[119] Stanley R. Strong, D. D. Hendel, and J. C. Bratton, "College Students' Views of Campus Help Givers: Counselors, Advisers and Psychiatrists," *Journal of Counseling Psychology*, 18 (May 1971), 234–238.

very bright or knowledgeable. Gelso and Karl[120] compared perceptions held by a sample of 240 students of counseling psychologists, college counselors, high school counselors, advisers, clinical psychologists, and psychiatrists. Greater differences were found within the counseling specialties than between counseling psychologists and either clinical psychologists or psychiatrists. None of the groups was viewed as "nice guys" in relation to psychiatrists or clinical psychologists. Finally, Doster[121] investigated interviewee expectancies about self disclosure held by fifty-seven male and fifty-five female introductory psychology subjects who differed on measures of defensiveness and anxiety. Those subjects who measured low on defensiveness and anxiety were most successful in their overall interview participation. Subjects who were low on defensiveness but had high anxiety comprehended the role requirements of an interview but were restrained in their approach. Subjects who had high defensiveness but were low in anxiety failed to acquire an accurate impression of their role behavior. Contrary to expectation, high-defensive, high-anxiety subjects were motivated to comply with situational demands and were not most avoidant.

Likability

Some years ago, client likability was studied by Stoler, who presented taped segments of interviews to ten raters.[122] His data suggest that client likability may be related to success in therapy.

Mullen and Abeles investigated the relationship of liking, empathy, and therapist experience to positive change in therapy.[123] They reported that high liking and high empathy together did not necessarily produce a successful outcome,

though a post hoc analysis of their data showed a positive relationship between high empathy alone and successful outcome. Inexperienced therapists were generally less empathic. Empathy and liking were not related to successful outcome for experienced therapists, but were for inexperienced therapists.

Similarity of counselor and counselee characteristics

The interaction of two personalities, involving both verbal and nonverbal behavior, takes place in counseling. The process is influenced by what each one is and how each perceives himself or herself and views the other. A counselor who is more similar to a client is expected to be more influential than one who is highly dissimilar. A counselor and a client may be alike by virtue of attitudinal similarity or membership group similarity; furthermore, it is assumed that attitudinal similarity is inferred from membership group or background similarity.

Study of the effect of similarity of counselor and client goes back to Whitehorn and Betz[124] who reported that therapists who had high success rates with schizophrenic patients (*A* therapists) were different from therapists who had low success rates with schizophrenics (*B* therapists).

Because success with one kind of patient did not correlate very highly with success with another type of patient, they assumed that the difference was the result of the interaction between a certain type of patient and a certain type of therapist. The A therapists approached patients' problems in a personal way, gained a trusted confidential relationship, and participated more actively with the patient. The B therapists were more interested in the psychopathology, were passively permissive, and attempted to develop insight by interpretation. In a later report (1960) the same researchers investigated the distinguishing personality characteristics of the A and B therapists,[125] using the *Strong Vocational Interest Blank*. Interest patterns of A and B therapists

[120] Charles J. Gelso and Norman J. Karl, "Perceptions of 'Counselors' and Other Help Givers: What's in a Label?," *Journal of Counseling Psychology*, 21 (May 1974), 243–247.
[121] Joseph A. Doster, "Individual Differences Affecting Interviewee Expectancies and Perceptions of Self-Disclosure," *Journal of Counseling Psychology*, 22 (May 1975), 192–198.
[122] Norton Stoler, "Client Likability: A Variable in the Study of Psychotherapy," *Journal of Consulting Psychology*, 27 (April 1963), 175–178.
[123] John Mullen and Norman Abeles, "Relationships of Liking, Empathy and Therapists' Experience to Outcome of Therapy," *Journal of Counseling Psychology*, 18 (January 1971), 39–43.

[124] J. C. Whitehorn and B. Betz, "A Study of Psychotherapeutic Relationships Between Physician and Schizophrenic Patients," *American Journal of Psychiatry*, 111 (November 1954), 321–331.
[125] J. C. Whitehorn and B. Betz, "Further Studies of the Data as a Crucial Variable in the Outcome of Treatment with Schizophrenic Patients," *American Journal of Psychiatry*, 117 (September 1960), 215–223.

were validated on another group of therapists. The basic difference was an attitude of expecting and respecting spontaneity rather than restricting it. Also the A therapists emphasized solving of individual problems for achieving goals with broadly interpreted social mores and expectations. This facilitated the patient's discovering and solving problems and participating in life. The authors suggest that "compatibilities and incompatibilities between physicians and patients become a relevant framework of reference for studying the intrinsic nature of the recovery process."[126]

An attempt was made by McNair, Callahan, and Lorr to validate the Whitehorn and Betz findings on a group of nonschizophrenic outpatients.[127] They identified A and B therapists by their responses to the twenty-three SVIB items reported by Whitehorn and Betz. Using therapists' and patients' reports, they found that patients treated by B therapists improved significantly more than patients of A therapists—just the opposite of the Whitehorn and Betz results. The authors explain that the twenty-three-item A-B scale could be unreliable. Also an internal consistency analysis of the scale indicated that B therapists had more interests in common with the patients and more similar life backgrounds and experiences. Despite the disagreement of the results, both studies indicate that different counselors achieve different results with different counselees, and that similarity of interests, life background, and experiences appear to be significant factors in the counseling relationship and interaction.

Boyd[128] reported that while A and B counselors' interviews contained the same type of verbal content, Bs' clients produced interviews containing more speculative, confrontive, challenging, and thought-provoking statements than As' clients. He suggests that counselor behavior is to some extent under the control of the client.

Kunce and Anderson[129] studied the assignment of clients to counselors. Some sixty-three graduate students were given summaries of seven client cases. Each counselor was ranked by his or her colleagues according to competence in handling each of the cases. Counselors were then classified into two groups: those given clients who were agitated (anxious, tense), and those given clients who were constrained (cool, pessimistic). Clinical interpretations of the *Minnesota Multiphasic Personality Inventory* scores of counselors to whom agitated clients were referred revealed them to be often academically or esthetically oriented, tending to be self-sufficient and interested in other people.

Edwards and Edgerly[130] hypothesized that the counselor and client who are cognitively similar in the meaning they attach to relevant concepts would make more progress. Accordingly, they matched clients to counselors and assessed outcomes. But the clients who were different from their counselors changed significantly and more consistently than those who were similar to their counselors. Accordingly, they suggest that certain types of counselors are more effective with some types of clients than others.

Mendelsohn and Geller matched counselor and client for similarity on judgment-perception, thinking-feeling, sensation-intuition, and extroversion-introversion.[131] Similarity was linearly associated with greater length of counseling; that is, the greater the client-counselor difference score for each dimension, the fewer the sessions. Mendelsohn replicated the study and reported that although client personality affects the decision to seek counseling, client-counselor matching is a more important determinant of its outcome.[132] In a different study the same authors investigated the relationship between client-counselor similarity and counseling outcome.[133] Criterion variables were evaluation, comfort-rapport, and judged competence. Client-

[126] Ibid., p. 218.

[127] Douglas M. McNair, Daniel M. Callahan, and Maurice Lorr, "Therapist 'Type' and Patient Response to Psychotherapy," *Journal of Consulting Psychology*, 26 (October 1962), 425–429.

[128] Robert E. Boyd, "Whitehorn-Betz A-B Score as an Effector of Client-Counselor Interaction," *Journal of Counseling Psychology*, 17 (May 1970), 279–283.

[129] Joseph Kunce and Wayne Anderson, "Counselor-Client Similarity and Referral Bias," *Journal of Counseling Psychology*, 17 (March 1970), 102–106.

[130] Billy C. Edwards and John W. Edgerly, "Effects of Counselor-Client Cognitive Congruence on Counseling Outcome in Brief Counseling," *Journal of Counseling Psychology*, 17 (July 1970), 313–318.

[131] Gerald A. Mendelsohn and Marvin H. Geller, "Effects of Counselor-Client Similarity on the Outcome of Counseling," *Journal of Counseling Psychology*, 10 (Spring 1963), 71–77.

[132] Gerald A. Mendelsohn, "Effects of Client Personality and Client-Counselor Similarity on the Duration of Counseling: A Replication and Extension," *Journal of Counseling Psychology*, 13 (Summer 1966), 228–234.

[133] Gerald A. Mendelsohn and Marvin H. Geller, "Structure of Client Attitudes Toward Counseling and Their Relation to Client-Counselor Similarity," *Journal of Consulting Psychology*, 29 (February 1965), 63–72.

counselor dyads were classified as high, middle, and low similarity and as same or opposite sex. The effects of similarity on outcome varied with the criterion used. More specifically, (1) evaluation is curvilinearly related to similarity, middle similarity producing the highest scores; (2) comfort-rapport scores are related to high similarity for freshmen but to middle similarity for nonfreshmen; (3) on both dimensions low similarity leads to more favorable ratings by nonfreshmen but to less favorable ratings by freshmen; (4) in general, the effects of similarity are more pronounced in opposite than same-sex matchings, particularly for nonfreshmen; and (5) high ratings of judged competence seem to be associated with the extroversion-introversion and thinking-feeling dimensions of client personality rather than with client-counselor similarity.

Cheney[134] studied the effect of attitude similarity and topic importance on attraction in a natural setting by exposing seventy-five prison inmates, incarcerated for public intoxication, to varying attitudes of a male psychotherapist prior to hearing him in a taped therapy session. The therapist's attitudes were either similar or dissimilar to the subject's and pertained to either alcohol (important) or general (unimportant) issues. A group of control subjects received no attitude information. Cheney reported that subjects were more attracted to the therapist after hearing his attitude toward alcohol regardless of degree of similarity expressed.

Ewing[135] obtained client evaluations of precollege counseling interviews from black and white students counseled by three experienced black counselors and eight experienced white counselors. He reported that black students, compared to their white counterparts, tended to react more favorably to counseling but that racial similarity of client and counselor was not an important factor in these counseling interviews.

Cox and Thoreson,[136] investigating the effect of congruent Holland personality orientations between clients seeking career counseling and counselors, obtained results that supported client-counselor similarity hypothesis. Finally, Tessler[137] reported that relationship-centered client satisfaction was significantly greater when clients perceived themselves as similar rather than dissimilar to the counselor in terms of values or lifestyle preferences and when the counselor was informal rather than formal. Further, problem-centered client satisfaction was significantly greater when the counselor was reputed to have had years of professional experience rather than being a novice.

Complementary characteristics

Research focused on the effects of counselor-counselee similarity was followed soon by investigations of complementary characteristics. *Similarity,* as used in the preceding section, means resemblance or being nearly alike, while *complementary,* as discussed here, refers to counselor-counselee characteristics that mutually make up what is lacking in the other. The idea behind complementary characteristics is that the counselor and client have a reciprocal impact on each other; that is, a particular behavior by one elicits a specific response from the other. Certain behaviors—dominance followed by submissiveness, submission followed by dominance, friendliness followed by friendliness, hostility followed by hostility—have been demonstrated to occur frequently in this sequence of elicitation-response. These interaction sequences have been viewed as *complementary,* and, as such, reinforcing to both participants because they reduce anxiety and promote a sense of relatedness.

Divergent hypotheses have been formulated about the effects of complementary counselor-client characteristics on counseling outcomes. One point of view is that successful client change comes because the counselor responds in noncomplementary ways. The client experiences the counselor's noncomplementary responses as nonreinforcing and thus is stimulated to experiment with new ways of behaving. The opposing point of view is that complementary relationships are harmonious and satisfying for both parties and therefore most successful.

[134] Thomas Cheney, "Attitude Similarity, Topic Importance and Psychotherapeutic Attraction," *Journal of Counseling Psychology,* 22 (January 1975), 2–5.

[135] Thomas W. Ewing, "Racial Similarity of Client and Counselor and Client Satisfaction with Counseling," *Journal of Counseling Psychology,* 21 (September 1974), 446–449.

[136] Jennings G. Cox and Richard W. Thoreson, "Client-Counselor Matching: A Test of the Holland Model," *Journal of Counseling Psychology,* 24 (March 1977), 158–161.

[137] Richard C. Tessler, "Client Reactions to Initial Interviews: Determinants of Relationship Centered and Problem-Centered Satisfaction," *Journal of Counseling Psychology,* 22 (May 1975), 187–191.

Among early research on the effect of complementary characteristics was that by Snyder.[138] His research extended over four years with twenty therapy cases, each of whom averaged twenty-five interviews. Snyder analyzed data on the three personality continua of "affect," "control," and "disclosure." Outcome criterion was to label clients as either "better" or "poorer." The relationship and interaction appeared to be better when the client and therapist complemented each other on the three personality characteristics. Heller, Myers, and Kline attempted to see whether the behavior of the therapist is influenced in any way by the interview behavior of the client.[139] Their clients were four student actors who were interviewed by thirty-four counselors in training. The dimensions of behavior studied were control and affect. The hypotheses were as follows: (1) dominant client behavior will evoke dependent interviewer behavior; (2) dependent client behavior will evoke dominant interviewer behavior; (3) hostile client behavior will evoke hostile interviewer behavior; (4) friendly client behavior will evoke friendly interviewer behavior; and (5) hostile client behavior will evoke interviewer anxiety. All hypotheses were tenable except the fifth, implying complementarity on the control dimension and similarity on the affect dimension.

Dietzel and Abeles[140] studied effects of client-therapist complementarity upon outcome by examining 120 tape-recorded sessions representing early, middle, and late interviews with twenty clients. Clients were divided into successful (n = 10) and unsuccessful (n = 10) outcome groups. Dietzel and Abeles reported that comparisons between outcome groups showed no difference in therapist complementarity (dominance followed by submissiveness, submissiveness followed by dominance, and so on) during the early stage of therapy; a significantly lower level of therapist complementarity for the successful group during the middle stage; and no difference during the last stage of therapy. Finally, the two investigators predicted and demonstrated that more disturbed clients elicited greater therapist complementarity during the early stage of the relationship.

Summary comments

Long, complex chapters deserve short summaries. Review of the material presented in this chapter leads to the following concluding remarks about the characteristics of counselors and counselees.

1. Tolerance for ambiguity, maturity, self-understanding, ability to maintain an appropriate emotional distance from the counselee, and ability to maintain good interpersonal relationships are characteristics demonstrated to be *associated* with counselor effectiveness. While psychometric data reflect that, as a group, counselors exhibit greater needs on variables such as succorance, intraception, exhibitionism, affiliation, and the like, nonintellective measures have not consistently discriminated between so-called effective and ineffective counselors. Distinctions between the two groups seem due to differences in the intensity of characteristics rather than to the presence or absence of a given characteristic in an individual counselor. Further, the discriminating traits found are not independent of the particular design, analysis procedure, and effectiveness measures employed in the study.

2. Counselee personality variables—expectancies concerning counseling, motivation, need to change, potential for self-appraisal, emotional responsiveness, introspective attitude, intelligence, flexibility, range of interests, level of personality integration, and social conformity—influence the direction, length, and outcome of the counseling relationship.

3. Experienced counselors are more effective than inexperienced ones.

4. For the most part, sex, race, and age are secondary considerations in clients' views of individuals as counselors.

5. Clients' perceptions of counselor expertness influence favorably initial counseling outcomes.

6. Researchers have measured the personality characteristics of counselors and counselees by a great variety of techniques. Standardized self-report personality and interest inventories have been used frequently but have been harshly

[138] William U. Snyder, *The Psychotherapy Relationship* (New York: Macmillan Co., 1961).

[139] Kenneth Heller, Roger A. Myers, and Linda V. Kline, "Interviewer Behavior as a Function of Standardized Client Roles," *Journal of Consulting Psychology,* 27 (April 1963), 117–122.

[140] C. S. Dietzel and Norman Abeles, "Client-Therapist Complementarity and Therapeutic Outcome," *Journal of Counseling Psychology,* 22 (July 1975), 264–272.

criticized, chiefly because of their unsuitability for testing psychologically knowledgeable trainees and clients and because of their lack of sensitivity. The diversity of the methods employed in published studies of counselor and counselee characteristics and effectiveness attests to a lack of satisfaction with the results obtained. Intimately related to this dissatisfaction is the problem of the definition and measurement of adequate effectiveness criteria for assessing counseling activity. Despite these crucial factors, some criteria do appear to be more promising than others. Those who use sociometrics and the Q-sort techniques have expressed the belief that they are fruitful methods worthy of continued investigation. Ratings by expert judges, supervisors, and peers typify other useful though limited criteria.

7. Attempts to surmount measurement and criterion problems are suggested by certain trends in the study of counselor and counselee characteristics. One is toward the use of multiple measures of personality. Another is toward author-developed methods for assessing personality variables and counselor effectiveness. Finally, internal and external multiple criteria in assessing counselor effectiveness are being used.

8. Investigations of the connection between counselor personality and effectiveness need to be directed not only toward identifying distinguishing characteristics but toward providing empirical and/or theoretical bases for explaining how differences in characteristics are related to differences in effectiveness. There is also a need for identifying personality characteristics associated with effectiveness rather than with lack of effectiveness. The latter type of descriptions provides criteria for judging ineffectiveness rather than effectiveness. The existing data imply that absence of undesired characteristics rather than possession of desired accounts for effectiveness.

9. An untapped reservoir for studying practicing counselor characteristics, rather than those of counselor trainees, lies in elementary and secondary schools. Study of the relationship between counselor characteristics and effectiveness utilizing counselors in these settings should examine methods of assigning students to counselors.

10. At the present time, the counseling profession is unable to demonstrate consistently that a single trait or pattern of traits distinguishes an individual who is or will be a good counselor. Good counseling, like good teaching, is a highly complex activity that is situationally dependent on the counselor, the counselee, the setting, the topic, and the conditions under which it is conducted.

Issues

Issue 1 Personal characteristics rather than skills, techniques, or practices account for counseling success.

Yes, because
1. Counseling is an interpersonal relationship dependent on people being together. Attentiveness, awareness, warmth, acceptance, genuineness, caring, and sensitivity, are personal qualities that constitute the essence of effective interpersonal relationships.
2. These personal qualities, derived from living, the appreciation of relating to others, not skills or techniques taught or learned, are that which engage the other person and interact with his or her qualities to produce, for better or worse, the counseling relationship and its outcomes.

No, because
1. Personal qualities, as other variables, have to be communicated—sent and received—to be influential. Communication is a skill that is and can be taught and learned.
2. Regardless of personal qualities, the counselor has to initiate and respond, to say and do things adeptly if counseling is to succeed.

Discussion This issue crops up in many forms such as the statement "counselors are born, not made" and undoubtedly will emerge again and again. Both logic and research support the notion that a counselor's personal characteristics are important ingredients in the counseling relationship and influence its outcomes. Similarly, both logic and research support that counselor competencies depend on using skills and an understanding of clients and the world in which they live. Counseling competence, therefore, derives from a judicious blend of the counselor's personal qualities, understandings, and skills.

The fundamental problem in attempts to establish what contributes most—the counselor's skills or personal characteristics—to counseling success long has been known. It is that these components not only interact among themselves but differentially in relation to other persons. Consequently, isolation of any component in its pure form is complex and almost impossible to achieve.

Issue 2 Continuing research efforts applied toward identifying personal characteristics of effective counselors should result in better selection of candidates to become counselors.

Yes, because
1. Counselor educators will translate and apply these research outcomes to both criteria and procedures for selecting candidates for counselor preparation.
2. The intellective and nonintellective qualities demonstrated to be important in counselor competence are present in sufficient numbers of the population that the pool of potential candidates remains more than adequate.

No, because
1. The personal characteristics of counselors identified to be important in counselor success vary so widely under diverse conditions that no one pattern can be used to establish criteria for selecting counselors.
2. Instrumentation for identifying these characteristics is undeveloped and weak.
3. Actual factors that influence selections—budgets, the pool of candidates available, the amount of time and seriousness accorded to the process by counselor educators, to cite but a few—are many and varied and outweigh implementation of research findings.
4. Appointment as a counselor or use of the title is insufficiently regulated to assure that such research efforts will inevitably produce better counselors.

Discussion Research efforts directed toward uncovering the personal characteristics, particularly those of a nonintellective nature, unique to effective counselors have many potential benefits, including use in selecting candidates for counselor preparation. For some years now it has been the fond hope of counselor educators that nonintellective criteria could be successfully used to screen applicants who seek to become counselors. Thus, not only would there be greater assurance that most institutions' ever-restricted graduate resources were being invested in those most likely to benefit but the quality of counselors available to the labor market would be improved.

A tremendous amount of effort and energy has gone into investigating this area. The results to date are mixed, and no doubt disappointing to many. In truth, no clear-cut personality pattern has emerged that could be used with assurance in the selection of counselor candidates. This is not to say that the results have been entirely negative, because much more is now known regarding the characteristics of counselors as a total group and of those who seek entry to preparation programs.

Annotated references

Eisenberg, Sheldon, and Daniel L. Delaney. *The Counseling Process.* 2nd ed. Chicago: Rand McNally, 1977. 247 pp.
Chapter 1 (pp. 1–11) identifies and discusses characteristics of effective helpers. Some eleven abilities and characteristics are set forth as descriptive of counselors.

Patterson, Cecil H. "The Selection of Counselors." In *Research in Counseling.* Ed., John Whitely. Columbus, Ohio: Charles E. Merrill, Inc., 1967.
The content, although somewhat dated, is an evaluation of the research on counselor characteristics. The implications of applying research findings and directions are presented.

Wrenn, C. Gilbert. *The World of the Contemporary Counselor.* Boston: Houghton Mifflin Company, 1973. 294 pp.
Chapter 7 (pp. 270–287) discusses counselor functions and some of the characteristics that should be considered in selecting counselors. Prominent among these is the individual's ability to listen.

Further references

Barak, Azy, and Don M. Dell. "Differential Perceptions of Counselor Behavior: Replication and Extension." *Journal of Counseling Psychology,* 24 (July 1977), 288–292.

Bruch, Monroe A. "Client Fear of Negative Evaluation and Type of Counselor Response Style." *Journal of Counseling Psychology,* 26 (January 1979), 37–44.

Childers, John H., and William D. Burcky. "The School Counselor and School Policy Involvement: A Report of Perceptions," *The School Counselor,* 24 (March 1977), 235–242.

Dreman, Solly B. "Expectations and Preferences of Clients for a University Student Counseling Service." *Journal of Counseling Psychology*, 24 (September 1977), 459–462.

Duckro, Paul N. and Clay E. George. "Effects of Failure to Meet Client Preference in a Counseling Interview Analogue." *Journal of Counseling Psychology*, 26 (January 1979), 9–14.

Elliott, Robert. "How Clients Perceive Helper Behaviors." *Journal of Counseling Psychology*, 26 (July1979), 285–294.

Fretz, Bruce R., Roger Corn, Janet M. Tuemmler and William Bellet. "Counselor Nonverbal Behaviors and Client Expectations." *Journal of Counseling Psychology*, 26 (July 1979), 304–311.

Highlen, Pamela S., and Grady K. Baccus. "Effect of Reflection of Feeling and Probe on Client Self-Referenced Affect." *Journal of Counseling Psychology*, 24 (September 1977), 440–443.

Hoffman, Mary Ann, and Gregory P. Spencer. "Effect of Interviewer Self-Disclosure and Interviewer-Subject Sex Pairing on Perceived and Actual Subject Behavior." *Journal of Counseling Psychology*, 24 (September 1977), 383–390.

LaCrosse, Michael B. "Comparative Perceptions of Counselor Behavior: A Replication and Extension." *Journal of Counseling Psychology*, 24 (November 1977), 464–471.

Lavelle, John J. "Comparing the Effects of an Affective and a Behavioral Counselor Style on Client Interview Behavior." *Journal of Counseling Psychology*, 24 (May 1977), 173–177.

Loesch, Larry C., and Barbara B. Rucker. "A Factor Analysis of the Counselor Evaluation Rating Scale." *Counselor Education and Supervision*, 16 (March 1977), 209–216.

Petro, Carole Smith, and James C. Hansen. "Counselor Sex and Empathic Judgment." *Journal of Counseling Psychology*, 24 (July 1977), 373–376.

Sue, Derald Wing, and David Sue. "Barriers to Effective Cross-Cultured Counseling." *Journal of Counseling Psychology*, 24 (September 1977), 420–429.

Tinsley, Howard E. A., and Diane J. Tinsley. "Different Needs, Interests and Abilities of Effective and Ineffective Counselor Trainees: Implications for Counselor Selection." *Journal of Counseling Psychology*, 24 (January 1977), 83–86.

Wachowiak, Dale, and Roger F. Aubrey. "The Changing World of Gilbert Wrenn." *Personnel and Guidance Journal*, 55 (October 1976), 75–85.

Wright, Jarvis A., and Ben O. Hutton. "Influence of Client Socioeconomic Status on Selected Behaviors, Attitudes and Decisions of Counselors." *Journal of Counseling Psychology*, 24 (November 1977), 527–530.

6 Counselor role and function

During the 1960s the topic of counselor role and function increasingly engaged the attention of counselors and counselor educators. This interest led to a proliferation of articles in the counseling literature, but during the 1970s, the flow of role and function articles decreased to a trickle. Examination of that trend leads to the conclusion that the issue of who counselors are as professionals had been taken as far as it could be until new forces, ideas, or experiences could be uncovered and brought to bear on the matter.

For some counseling practitioners, analysis of counselor role is threatening and anxiety provoking because all too often a gap is revealed between an ideal and the reality of their position. For others, analysis of counselor role is viewed as an authentic search for professional identity. Still others wonder why counselors are so concerned about role and function because effective professionals do not search for identity but live it.

This final chapter in Part One defines certain basic concepts of role and function, explores role theory and counselor role, identifies the major reasons for counselor role variability, and presents some current descriptive statements of counselor role and function.

The concepts of role and function

For the most part, the words *role* and *function* have been used, perhaps erroneously, almost synonymously in the literature and in informal discussion by counselors. The word *role* has been adopted by social psychologists and sociologists to designate the customary complex of behavior associated with a particular status or position. Perhaps it will be meaningful at this time to identify and clarify certain terms used in discussing counselor role and function. Clarifying terms is one of the oldest duties of the methodologist and, unfortunately, one that never ends.

Definition of role

The position of counselor should be viewed as an inherent part of a social system. *Social system* does not refer to society or to a state or even necessarily to a large aggregate of people; it means any group of individuals who live and interact with one another, such as a community, a school, or even a classroom within a school. The interactional network of relationships between and among offices, positions, or statuses is referred to as the structure of the society. It is the means of interrelating and regulating individuals and groups. Position is defined as a location or a unit of the social structure. Positions denote the statuses of an individual with reference to other members and are attained in various ways. If they are sought and attained through striving and competitive mastery of the rights and obligations linked to them, they may be termed *achieved* positions or statuses. Other positions, called *ascribed,* devolve on the individual by virtue of certain attributes: race, sex, age, or pre-existing social affinities such as parents' status. One position is distinguished from another by the functions performed for the group and carries with it special rights and obligations. In a high position or status the rights and obligations command prestige, which when translated into action means power or the capacity to influence and direct the behavior of others.

There can be no position without a role and no role without a position. Role is often defined by the individual's behavior in performing the rights and obligations associated with a position. Because in life situations every individual has multiple positions, each person plays many different roles. In one sense, each person is to some degree an actor or a poser, for living in society may be viewed as a playing of roles. At different times, therefore, different roles become prominent. Several roles may be operative simultaneously, but the intensity of their demands for effective fulfillment varies.

Social psychologists have drawn an important distinction between position and role. Role is expected behavior that is approved for the occupant of a defined position. A position is a unit of society or a location in a social structure. Yinger defined role in these words: "*Role* is a unit of culture; it refers to the rights and duties, the normatively approved patterns of behavior for the occupants of a given position."[1]

When counselors put into effect the obligations and responsibilities of their positions, they are said to be performing their roles. A role is a prescription for behavior "inferred from how various persons behave in particular positions, how others behave toward them, and how they all describe the rights and duties in verbal behavior."[2] Parsons and Shils have defined role in this way:

> The role is that organized sector of an actor's orientation which constitutes and defines his participation in an interactive process. It involves a set of complementary expectations concerning his own actions and those of others with whom he interacts. Both the actor and those with whom he interacts possess these expectations.[3]

Bentley, in criticizing us for our loose usage of the term *role*, has urged that it be defined as the way individuals actually perform in a given position as distinct from how they are supposed to perform. He has sought to restrict usage of the term to denote "what a person actually does."[4] But Ivey and Robin have pointed out that role is a normative concept: "Roles are the sets of norms or expectations of behavior that are assigned by significant others to a specific position. Another way of understanding this concept and its function is to note that roles provide a method of organizing expectations by reference to a social structure."[5] And Yinger points out that "we can say that a role is the list of what

most members of a social group believe a position occupant should and should not, may and may not, do. It is not a list of what most occupants of a position in fact do."[6] Yinger adds that role requirements range from those that are mandatory (the absence of which would indicate that the role was not performed at all) to those that are optional (ways of behaving that are permissible). It would seem that what Bentley defined as role, Yinger defined as internalized role, and that Ivey and Robin, in turn, regard what an individual taking a position actually does as *role behavior*. Perhaps all that these differences indicate is that the concept *role* is frequently used in different ways and that consensus as to what it means is lacking. The role of the counselor is most simply defined as the image derived from the expectations and directives for behavior connected with the position. As such, it is the counselor's blueprint for action.

Role expectations

Occupants of any given role are not passive agents. They perform in interactive situations with other individuals who perceive and react to them. These individuals have certain expectations based on needs or conditions of existence that must be secured and maintained if they and the social unit are to function. Their expectations form the "normatively approved patterns of behavior" referred to in Yinger's definition of role.

Other individuals in the social structure interact with and desire certain behavior from role occupants. They anticipate that incumbents will act in ways considered appropriate to their role. Role expectations constitute a definition of behavior that is proper for the role. Both the individual who enacts the role and others with whom he or she interacts expect that the incumbent will act in particular ways. Sarbin and Jones believe that role expectations arise in this way:

> A role expectation is a cognitive structure inferred, on the stimulus side, from the person's previous commerce with regularities in others' behaviors, and, on the response side, from the person's tendency to group a

[1] J. Milton Yinger, *Toward a Field Theory of Behavior* (New York: McGraw-Hill, 1965), p. 99.
[2] Ibid., p. 100.
[3] Talcott Parsons and Edward A. Shils, eds., *Toward a General Theory of Action* (New York: Harper & Row, 1962), p. 23.
[4] Joseph C. Bentley, "Role Theory in Counseling: A Problem in Definition," *Personnel and Guidance Journal*, 45 (September 1965), 13.
[5] Allen E. Ivey and Stanley S. Robin, "Role Theory, Role Conflict and Counseling," *Journal of Counseling Psychology*, 13 (Spring 1966), 30.
[6] Yinger, *Toward a Field Theory of Behavior*, p. 100.

number of descriptions of actions and qualities together with the name of a specific social position.[7]

Their comment indicates that expectations spring from previous contact with others who held the position as well as from notions of what the individual occupying the position should do.

Role expectancies sometimes conflict. Differences may occur (1) between what the individual expects to be able to do and what others expect of that person and (2) between the expectations the person holds for the role and the demands of the role.

Role perceptions

Roles are complementary or interdependent in that each role derives its meaning from other related roles within a social setting. No role is performed in exactly the same way by any two individuals. Performance depends on how each person perceives, interprets, and acts on the obligations and rights of a position. It also depends on the individual's perceptions of others' expectations for his or her behavior in the role. Normally, enactment of a role can only approximate the performance of previous role incumbents.

The occupant's idiosyncratic personality is brought to the role. One's personal expectations, needs, goals, attitudes, achievements, and skills shape one's responses to role demands and subsequently influence performance. The role is stamped by the individual's unique pattern of behavior. Yinger uses the term *internalized role* to refer to

. . . a given individual's tendencies to perform a role in a given way. This is clearly different from the role itself, which is a cultural construct. Internalized role has a particular person's mark or style imprinted on it, for it is affected by all the positions he occupies, by the ways in which he learned the role, and by the total personality system in which it is embedded.[8]

Internalized role results from *role perceptions*—ways the occupant personally views and defines the rights and obligations of the position.

An individual's perceptions may lead one to emphasize certain dimensions of the role and de-emphasize others. Variation in role performance may result from how incumbents internalize the role or may occur because their other roles intrude on it.

Much speculation has gone into how personality variables influence role behavior. Yinger identifies four self-related variables that affect it:

1. Differences in internalized role. We are unlikely to be successful in predicting role performance until we know, among other things, how the individuals involved define the rights and duties.
2. The significance of the position to the individual's self-identification. This affects readiness to accept the role definition of others. If the position is relatively unimportant, few other personality forces are drawn into the performance; if the position is at the center of the individual's identity, however, other personality tendencies, not related to the role, will influence the performance.
3. Other positions being occupied. If the selection process draws persons into position A who have highly dissimilar position constellations (one occupying B, C, and D; another occupying E, F, and G, etc.), role performance is likely to vary more widely than if all those in position A share positions B, C, and D as well.
4. The degree of similarity in personality tendencies not related to the role. Individuals who vary in authoritarianism, intelligence, level of energy, and values, for example, are likely to perform the same role in different ways.[9]

Role conflict

Conflict may occur whenever expectations cannot be harmonized. Gross, Mason, and McEachern, have defined role conflict as "any situation in which the incumbent of a position perceives that he is confronted with incompatible ex-

[7] Theodore R. Sarbin and Donald S. Jones, "An Experimental Analysis of Role Behavior," in *Readings in Social Psychology*, ed. Eleanor E. Maccoby, Theodore M. Newcomb, and Eugene L. Hartley (New York: Holt, Rinehart and Winston, 1958), p. 465.
[8] Yinger, *Toward a Field Theory of Behavior*, p. 99.

[9] Ibid., p. 112.

pectations. . . ."[10] They also present the various meanings ascribed to role conflict by different social scientists, summarized here as (1) any incompatible expectation to which an individual is exposed, whether aware of the conflict or not, (2) situations in which the actor perceives incompatible expectations, (3) exposure to conflicting expectations because the individual occupies two or more positions simultaneously, and (4) contradictory expectations derived from an actor's occupancy of a single position.

Ivey and Robin believe that role conflict occurs when there is systematic difficulty in assuming, maintaining, or functioning in a role situation.[11] These authors have identified and presented four types of possible role conflict for the school counselor. A brief summary of their discussion of these conflicts follows:

1. *Role conflict stemming from role definers.* In some situations, legitimate role definers disagree about the normative content of a role. An example would be those principals who believe counselors should supervise study halls but counselors do not agree.

2. *Role conflict internal to the role.* The definers of a role may be in agreement and what they specify for the role may be congruent, yet the various *expectations* confronting the role taker are such that the *obligations* associated with the role cannot be fulfilled. An illustration of this conflict is the counselor who is expected simultaneously to be a confidant of the client and an administrator enforcing rules.

3. *Role conflict stemming from the role in interaction with the social system.* Two forms of conflict are involved here. First, a "functional" role conflict takes place when the normative role prescriptions are not sufficient to permit the role taker to perform the functions expected by those within the larger social system in which the role is situated. Illustrative of this conflict is the school where the counselor is limited to brief contacts with each client, thereby making impossible the positive counseling outcomes expected by various people within the system. The second form of conflict arises because of the multiplicity of roles an individual assumes. Some elements in separate roles are incom-

patible, for example, in some school districts an individual is expected to be a teacher or a coach in addition to being a counselor.

4. *Role conflict stemming from the interaction of the individual and the role.* That which must be performed in the role exceeds the role taker's capacity or conflicts with personal needs and characteristics. Resisting forces erupt from counselors' needs to safeguard their own well-being or psychological integrity. The individual's personal beliefs or behavior is incongruent with the role and as a result, the role is not performed competently. For example, an authoritarian individual finds his or her efforts to establish a productive relationship with counselees unsuccessful because they are afraid.

Yinger differentiated between internal and external role conflict.[12] Internal role conflict takes place when a person has internalized a role that incorporates contradictory expectations or when an individual holds two or more positions that carry incompatible role expectations, whether recognized or not. External role conflict occurs when one is faced with incompatible expectations from two or more individuals. Yinger's definition is broader than that of Gross, McEachern, and Mason, who refer only to perceived incompatibilities. Yinger notes that when role conflict is limited to only perceived incompatibilities, important aspects of conflict are excluded because unperceived conflicts in others' expectations affect *their* behavior.

Role conflict can spring from expectations that are legitimate or illegitimate. Gross, McEachern, and Mason differentiate a legitimate from an illegitimate expectation on the basis of whether the incumbent of a position believes others have or do not have a right to hold the expectation.[13] Legitimate expectations are called perceived obligations, whereas illegitimate expectations are called perceived pressures.

Role versus functions

It was previously noted that in the counseling literature *role* and *function* often have been used synonymously. Distinc-

[10] N. C. Gross, W. S. Mason, and A. W. McEachern, *Explorations in Role Analysis: Studies of the School Superintendency Role* (New York: John Wiley & Sons, 1958), p. 448.
[11] Ivey and Robin, "Role Theory" p. 30.

[12] Yinger, *Toward a Field Theory of Behavior*, p. 115.
[13] Gross, McEachern, and Mason, *Explorations in Role Analysis*, p. 448.

tions between the two terms are not easy or clear-cut. Role has been defined as the expectations and directives for behavior connected with a position, whereas function is usually defined as the activities assigned to a role. Wrenn has stated that the distinction between the two may be conceptualized as one of purpose (role) and process (function) or as one of ends (role) and means (function).[14] He noted too that many individuals and groups have an investment in defining the role of the counselor, regardless of employment setting, but that functions are the exclusive domain of the professional counselor.

Role theory and counselor role

The previous section has indicated that (1) role is a complex of behavior resulting from multiple expectations and institutional directives and (2) many forces and factors influence role enactment. An adequate treatment of role theory is much beyond the scope of this volume. For those who are interested, an extensive formulation of role theory is provided by Parsons and Shils and their associates.[15]

Getzels' schematic model of role theory is presented here as Figure 6.1 to help the reader visualize in their entirety the interrelationships among the various facets.[16] The important aspect of the figure is that it utilizes three dimensions—anthropological, sociological, and psychological—in seeking to understand and present human behavior. Any behavioral act is conceived of as deriving simultaneously from all three dimensions. Behavioral interaction between one individual and another results from their attempts to cope with an environment consisting of patterns of expectations for both that are consistent with their own independent value orientations. Values interact with expectations and need dispositions. Institutions and individuals are surrounded by cultural mores and values. The character of both the institution and the individual is to some extent determined by the

FIGURE 6.1 **Behavior as a function of social system**

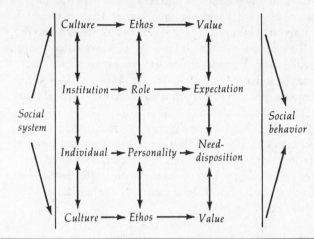

SOURCE: Jacob W. Getzels, "Conflict and Role Behavior in the Educational Setting," in *Readings in the Social Psychology of Education*, ed. W. W. Charters, Jr. and N. L. Gage. Copyright © 1963 by Allyn and Bacon, Inc., Boston. Reprinted by permission.

ethos of the social group. Each institution has expectations for the individuals who occupy certain positions and enact certain roles, and each individual has a particular set of need dispositions. Role expectations and need dispositions are derived from the values of the culture.

For purposes of discussion only, the anthropological and sociological dimensions (upper two in Figure 6.1) taken alone define acceptable institutional behavior. They are useful in understanding the role of the counselor or any other role within an institution, such as the school. As a social institution the school exists for a purpose. Although the purpose may vary somewhat from school to school, it is derived from the culture. But using only the upper two dimensions results in a dehumanized, oversimplified, and somewhat mechanical picture of the total situation. The psychological or idiographic dimension (third level in Figure 6.1) introduces the flesh-and-blood aspect. True, the upper two dimensions may in large part prescribe the functions performed by the role incumbent, but it is the individual who gives life and meaning to these activities. It is one's unique, personalized interpretation and perception of role expectancies that culminate in manifest behavior.

[14] C. Gilbert Wrenn, *The Contemporary World of the Counselor* (Boston: Houghton Mifflin Company, 1973), p. 270.

[15] Parsons and Shils, *Toward a General Theory of Action*.

[16] Jacob W. Getzels, "Conflict and Role Behavior in the Educational Setting," in *Readings in the Social Psychology of Education*, ed. W. W. Charters, Jr., and N. L. Gage (Boston: Allyn & Bacon, 1963), pp. 309–318.

FIGURE 6.2 **Determinants of counselor role**

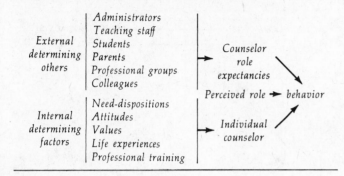

Understanding the counselor role

Understanding the counselor role

Figure 6.2 portrays the major factors involved in understanding individual behavior in the counseling role. The role of the counselor is determined not only by institutional prescriptions and proscriptions but also by the expectations that "external determining others" in the institutional environment hold for the individual in that role. These significant others translate self and institutional requirements into expectations and evaluate counselor behavior according to them. Thus the individual who occupies the position of counselor does so by virtue of certain internal determining factors that contribute to one's personal makeup and subsequently to the enactment of one's role. It should be understood clearly that each of the external determining others listed in Figure 6.2 is influenced by the same internal determining factors as is the counselor.

Counselor's perception of role

The reader would do well to remember that perceptions of counselor role—and ultimately behavior—are influenced by internal determining factors cited in Figure 6.2. Although it is true that Figure 6.2 identifies elements involved in *school* counselor role, similar elements are involved, regardless of the counselor's employment setting. The elements contributing to the helping relationship (see Chapter 1) and the research relating to counselor characteristics and effectiveness (see Chapter 5) testify to the variety of factors imping-

ing on individuals in their efforts to define and enact their roles.

Many observers (see Chapter 5) assert that the self of the counselor is an important ingredient in counseling transactions. Presumably, counselors who are aware of their needs, the expectations held of themselves and others, their values, and so on, perceive and enact their roles differently than those who are unaware. However, because such factors interact with the other variables presented in the upper section of Figure 6.2, further examination of them brings a fuller understanding.

Others' perceptions

Many sources document the commonalities and differences existing among influential persons who perceive and affect the counselor's role. Most of this literature indicates a long history of conflict and misunderstanding as well as positive views of counselor role. The others listed in the upper portion of Figure 6.2 hold expectations based on what they think the counselor is and does, make demands on the counselor in an effort to have their personal needs met, and evaluate the counselor's success as a counselor through their own highly individualistic perceptual screen.

Understandably, conflict occurs when the counselor behaves in a way that is inconsistent with what is anticipated. It is equally obvious that counselors who behave successfully must work toward resolution of potential conflicts. Resolution comes through a mixture of acknowledging and meeting the demands of others, educating others, creating accurate and legitimate expectations in them, and adequately coping with personal views regarding their role.

A research paradigm for counselor role

Ivey and Robin have presented a paradigm for researching the role of the school counselor.[17] It aids in analyzing counselor role and functions and identifies possible sources of role conflict. These authors point out that determiners of the school counselor's role are school boards, administrators, teachers, students, counselors, parents, community

[17] Ivey and Robin, "Role Theory," pp. 31–35.

FIGURE 6.3 **School counselor role definers**

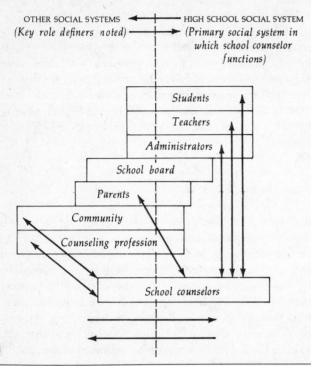

SOURCE: Allen E. Ivey and Stanley S. Robin, "Role Theory, Role Conflict, and Counseling," *Journal of Counseling Psychology*, 13 (Spring 1966), 31. Copyright 1966 by the American Psychological Association. Reprinted by permission.

pressure groups, and the counseling profession, all interacting and influencing one another in their definitions of the counselor's role while simultaneously being influenced by interaction with the counselor. Ivey and Robin have schematically patterned these interactions, as shown in Figure 6.3. Three key concepts should be noted. First, because students, teachers, and administrators are more involved than others in the school social system, they constitute primary reference groups in defining the counselor's role. Second, the arrows between "other social systems" and "high school social system" through the dotted line separating the two represent the constant flow of people and ideas between the school and the world at large. Third, the arrows from the school counselors to the service groups represent patterns of mutual interaction. These groups have the same type of interaction with one another.

FIGURE 6.4 **The school counselor(s) role**

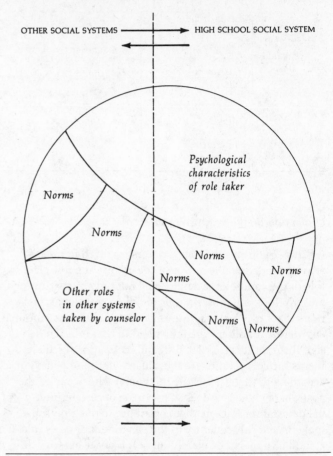

SOURCE: Allen E. Ivey and Stanley S. Robin, "Role Theory, Role Conflict, and Counseling," *Journal of Counseling Psychology*, 13 (Spring 1966), 31. Copyright 1966 by the American Psychological Association. Reprinted by permission.

Ivey and Robin's schematic presentation of the specific role of the counselor is shown in Figure 6.4. Here is the counselor's inner world. In essence it is what underlies role conflicts, decisions, and resolutions of school counselors in general. The authors make a number of relevant comments about this graphic representation. First, each counselor operates both within the school social system and in other social systems; these systems interact and affect the counselor, who in turn affects the systems. Second, many factors influence the counselor's role behavior—one's personality, for example, and the role expectations of others. Third, the counselor's internalization of the expectations constitutes his or her perceptions for role behavior.

Ivey and Robin suggest that their research paradigm would be useful in (1) assessments of attitudes and expectations that significant others have for counselor role; (2) examining counselors' personal characteristics, their perceptions of their role, and their perceptions of others' expectations; and (3) the application of role theory, particularly the concept of role behavior, to counseling process and interpersonal interview interaction. In their view, moreover, counselor role will not be clarified until dimensions of role conflict are identified and taken into account. They recommend that research be conducted into (1) conflict stemming from role definers, (2) conflict internal to the role, (3) conflict stemming from role interaction with the social system, and (4) conflict stemming from the interaction of the individual and his role.

Forces and factors causing counselor role variability

The two preceding sections of this chapter have made it clear that (1) a precise definition of counselor role has not yet been achieved and (2) many individual forces and factors are involved in counselor role definition. Inquiry is now directed to the forces and factors that are related to or affect counselor role variability.

Strivings for professionalization and career commitment

Entry into a profession demands specific behaviors from the aspirant. An occupation, such as counseling, that is striving for professional status, appears to demand certain characteristics. Criteria by which to judge professional status have resulted from endeavors to analyze the difference between occupations classified as professions and those not so classified. Uppermost among these criteria are: (1) that an occupational group possess some unique skill or service, and (2) that it establish a priority or monopoly in the meeting of a social need. Ethical codes, training standards, entry requirements and the indoctrination of new members soon follow these criteria. As this process becomes formalized, the individual worker is increasingly tied more closely to the group and tends to identify with those who epito-

mize the established worker. The willingness of currently aspiring counselors to identify with the role projected as the professional image appears to be a source of some role variability.

The motives of those who seek entry into counselor preparation have not been subjected to sophisticated research, but invariably they are a source for questions asked applicants. Many applicants state that they seek to become counselors because they like people or desire to work with people or have been told they were good at helping others or want to get out of classrooms (for any one of several reasons). Some years ago, Schutz and Mazer[18] investigated the occupational choice motives of 153 graduate students in counseling and identified both adient or positive and aversive or negative motives. Adient motives involved entering counselor preparation because it represented (1) a search for personal status, (2) helping others, (3) opportunities for research, (4) a ladder of success, (5) an opportunity to listen to others and thereby learn about oneself, (6) a means to extend personal influence, (7) an opportunity for creativity, and (8) a means to maintain school relationships. Aversive motives, on the other hand, involved (1) the fear of personal threat, (2) avoidance of the business world, (3) dislike of physical labor, (4) avoidance of competition, and (5) maintenance of present health. The outcomes of this study suggest great heterogeneity in entry motives as well as variation in the characteristics of those who enter counselor preparation.

Kehas and Morse characterized the motives that led twelve teachers with an average of twelve years teaching experience to become counselors as "passive" and "ambivalent." However, it was the two investigators' opinion that teachers enter counseling primarily because ". . . they see it as a possible way of fulfilling an inner desire for personal growth toward what they perceive as their ideal role in education."[19]

Stevic,[20] for his doctoral research, studied school counselor role, commitment, and marginality. Two instruments

[18] R. E. Schutz and Gilbert E. Mazer, "A Factor Analysis of Occupational Choice Motives of Counselors," *Journal of Counseling Psychology*, 11 (Fall 1964), 267–271.
[19] Chris D. Kehas and Jane L. Morse, "Perceptions in Role Change from Teacher to Counselor: Intra-Role Conflict and Motivation for Change," *Counselor Education and Supervision*, 10 (Spring 1971), 200–208.
[20] Richard R. Stevic, "The School Counselor's Role: Commitment and Marginality" (Ph.D. diss., Ohio State University, 1963).

were developed to assess commitment preferences and actual commitment as evidenced by the subjects' present counseling function. Rankings of counseling activities and the correlation between preparation and commitment, as well as the effect of environmental press on counselor preferences, were investigated. The subjects believed that the counselor's main functions were to provide services to individual students and to foster and maintain staff relationships. However, the acceptance of professional responsibility was seen as being least important for the practitioner. The amount of graduate training was demonstrated to correlate with commitment. Likewise, the number of years of counseling experience was an effective predictor of commitment. Stevic noted that certain situational pressures affect the degree of counselor investment and goal-striving behavior toward the ideal role. He concluded that these pressures might be altered if the counselor was militant. Stevic recommended additional graduate training to increase commitment and an analysis of personal ideals and goals.

Gahlhoff surveyed 406 individuals six years after they graduated from twenty counselor preparation programs. Based on data obtained from them, Gahlhoff generalized:

> . . . for every 100 counselors prepared, 45 will enter the field directly and remain in it. Presumably, these individuals may be viewed as committed to the field. It may be inferred that their preparation "took," i.e., was meaningful and sustaining for them. An additional 45 of the 100 counselors either do not enter the field or enter and withdraw. . . . The remaining 10 of the 100 theoretically prepared counselors (those who do not enter field but do so later) encounter difficulty in entering the field directly following preparation.[21]

Gahlhoff's generalizations were based on data obtained in 1968 and do not incorporate current employment problems hindering graduates from entering counseling positions. Moreover, Gahlhoff's generalization that only 45 of 100 counselors enter immediately after preparation and remain in the field may have been overly severe, for Fujinaka and Stone[22] reported that 472 (70 percent) of 680 individuals were counselors or directors of guidance seven years after attaining either state certification in school counseling or graduating from one of twenty counselor education institutions. The two investigators suggested that counselor educators falsely assume that all students admitted to counselor education programs are eager to enter counseling practice. Because some students, even at point of admission, never intend to enter the field as counselors, Fujinaka and Stone recommend that those engaged in counselor preparation build an awareness of career commitment among students.

Marginal status

Many school counselors hold other positions along with their counseling position. Some are counselor-teachers, counselor-coaches, counselor-principals. This dual status led Arbuckle to comment as follows:

> It is interesting to note that of all these groups [teachers, administrators, and special service administrators], it is only the school counselor who is willing to accept the part-time, dual-role status. Other professional workers may spend only part of their time in the services of the school, but they are not part-time doctors, or part-time nurses, or part-time psychiatrists. They are medical doctors, or nurses, or psychologists, or psychiatrists. Like pregnancy, "they are or they ain't," and there is no in-between status. We have no doctor-teacher, or nurse-principal, or psychologist-janitor, but we have thousands of teacher-counselors, or even more absurd, principal-counselors, and even, horror added upon horror, superintendent-counselors. Even worse, this schizophrenic fellow doesn't seem to mind this dual or triple status, and goes blithely walking off in several directions, at the same time, quite unaware that one set of feet is falling over the other.[23]

[21] Peter E. Gahlhoff, "An Analysis of the Personal and Situational Factors Influencing School Counselors' Career Problems" (Ph.D. diss., Purdue University, 1969), p. 86.

[22] Larry Fujinaka and Shelley C. Stone, "Counselor Commitment and Career Development," *Counselor Education and Supervision*, 14 (September 1974), 47–53.

[23] Dugald S. Arbuckle, "The Conflicting Functions of the School Counselor," *Counselor Education and Supervision*, 1 (Winter 1961), 56.

Surely if counseling is not seen as a lifetime career, only marginal commitment can be made to the role. Although today the pattern shows some signs of breaking up, an all too obvious career pattern for counselors is that they become counselors on their way to becoming administrators. Excluding the increased financial rewards realized by traveling this route, it should be noted that certain subtle motivations contribute to this pattern, which culminate in specific undesirable outcomes. Stefflre has charged that such a career line represents "waste" recruitment for the profession:

Many counselors remain counselors only a few years while they gather their strength for the climb to the next plateau. Former counselors who are now administrators, supervisors, or college instructors are all evidence of "waste" recruitment in the sense that they did not have a lasting and firm identification with the occupation of the school counselor. It seems clear that at the present time most of the school counselors in America do not identify with this occupation. Less than a third of them, for example, are members of the national organization devoted to their special emphasis—the American School Counselor Association. They think of themselves as teachers who are temporary refugees from the classroom or as potential administrators waiting in the wings for their cues.

One of the causes of this lack of identification is illuminated by the concept of the marginal man. In education, the most recognized, valued, and consensually accepted roles are those of the classroom teacher and the administrator. The counselor role is not as clear, nor as well validated by educational history, and the other workers in schools may have some difficulty in clarifying this marginal position. Is this marginal man—the school counselor—simply a teacher who has a new assignment; is he a psychologist who has strayed temporarily from his clinic; is he a sub-administrator who has managed to place himself on the administrative salary schedule; or is he a kind of office worker who is giving prestige and dignity to what are essentially clerical tasks?[24]

[24] Buford Stefflre, "What Price Professionalization?" *Personnel and Guidance Journal*, 42 (March 1964), 654. Copyright © 1964 American Personnel and Guidance Association. Reprinted with permission.

Despite the fact that the lines from Arbuckle and Stefflre were written some few years ago, the conditions they address have not altered to any great degree. Too, the implications of these conditions for clarifying counselor role remain ever present. In part-time, dual-role assignments the counselor is neither fish nor fowl and cannot identify professionally with either role. Many of the some 60,000 present-day school counselors are teacher-counselors because either they or the administrative officers of the school want it that way. Why? Speculation is that those counselors who prefer to be teacher-counselors do so because they do not want to leave their classrooms or they are unsure of whether the role of counselor fits them. In short, they did not achieve an identity as a counselor in their preparation program. Some administrators retain part-time, dual-role counselors because of 1) tradition, 2) costs, and 3) outmoded ideas about counseling. Still other administrators do so because they do not want to take the chance that counselors will become powerful or popular with teachers or too frequently sought after by students. Full-time counselors are a threat in that they could dim the shining spotlight traditionally accorded administrators in the school. By dividing counselor functions, by draining away the time of counselors in a multiplicity of activities, the administrator makes counselors marginal workers and renders them ineffective and less of a threat. Consequently, many counselors who find themselves in dual positions often do precisely what the administrator hopes they will not do. They leave the marginal position for the more clearly defined, more influential role of administrator.

Social forces

An array of social forces—legislative acts, custom, public attitudes, judicial decrees—influence conceptions of counselor role and hinder its clarification. Counseling is a relatively new profession, therefore, those who practice it experience what all new professionals must cope with: lack of understanding of their functions, lack of acceptance among the public, and discouraging confusion, even among professionals in allied fields.

A major consideration that should not be overlooked in any attempt to clarify the role of the counselor is the fact that it takes place in public institutions. Counselors are under the general direction of a lay governing board. Those who establish policy for any public institution are involved in defining the functions of those employed within it.

Other pervasive changing social forces currently at work in American society influence—some adversely, others positively—attempts to clarify and consolidate counselor role. Adverse influences include strained budgets, widespread questioning of the value of public institutions, the lack of consensus as to the variables in schooling that contribute to later success, and youth unemployment, to cite but a few. Positive influences include increasing demands for career counseling, more and more federal legislation that gives financial support to counseling, expansion of counseling in settings other than education, implementation of equal opportunity programs, conceptualizing learning as a lifelong process, and so forth.

Reluctance to change

One deterrent to clarifying counselor role is the resistance to change among counseling practitioners. Some cling inexorably to the crust of custom, tradition, and inertia. Their interest is best served by lack of role clarification. This type of resistance is an old story and can likewise be seen in other professions, such as medicine and law. The sense of consistency and security experienced by individuals who are habituated to a particular role concept makes it difficult for them to accommodate a new conception. When they are subjected to the demands of a different role definition, the potential failure to achieve a personal accommodation to it looms large. Transition from the old to the new has its perils, for when people give up the assurance of old certitudes, frequently they fear they may never attain such assurance in the new. Wrenn has written that "in this process [changing values] people may become confused and see the present situation as ambiguous. The struggle to maintain the past while one is living in the present can be frightening indeed."[25]

Professional isolation

There is no doubt that the counselor's work setting is associated with counselor role definition. The work setting of

one counselor may be shared by other counselors, whereas that of another counselor may include teachers and administrators but no other counselor.

Some years ago, Wasson and Strowig noted that "a rapidly growing body of research and theory regarding social conformity, reference group processes, and cognitive dissonance appears to offer plausible support to certain differentiations between professionally isolated and unisolated counselors."[26] They sought to determine (1) whether the isolated counselor (no other counselor in the school) was distinguished from the nonisolated counselor, (2) whether isolated counselors were more satisfied with their jobs than nonisolates, (3) whether isolated counselors believed that teachers and administrators were more supportive of guidance, and (4) whether isolated counselors were less active in professional organizations than their nonisolated counterparts. Their subjects were counselors in forty Wisconsin secondary schools (twenty with more than one counselor and twenty with but a single counselor). Isolates rated their positions as more satisfying than did nonisolated counselors (P < .05). Isolated counselors perceived their administrators and faculties as more supportive of guidance than did nonisolates (P < .01). Nonisolated counselors used the counseling profession as a source of leadership in their work and reported more professional reading than did isolated counselors (P < .01). However, no significant difference was found between the two groups' participation in professional organizations. Wasson and Strowig report that professionally isolated counselors tend to use teachers and administrators as reference groups more than do those who work in schools with other counselors.

Kaplan has also stated that "new counselors who work 'alone' as the only counselor on the staff in a school system report a greater number of problems in performing their duties than do other new counselors."[27]

Determining others

It has been said many times in this book and elsewhere that the expectations of others in the counselor's work situation

[25] C. Gilbert Wrenn, "Values and Counseling in Different Countries and Cultures," *The School Counselor,* 24 (September 1976), 6.

[26] Robert M. Wasson and R. Wray Strowig, "Professional Isolation and Counselor Role," *Personnel and Guidance Journal,* 43 (January 1965), 457–460.
[27] Bernard A. Kaplan, "The New Counselor and His Professional Problems," *Personnel and Guidance Journal,* 42 (January 1964), 473–478.

bear on role definition. Although these determining others do not all share equally in role definition, their conflicting expectations are another reason why consensus has yet to be reached in defining counselor role. The most frequently mentioned groups include counselor educators, state guidance supervisors, state license officials, school administrators, professional organizations, students, parents, teachers, school board members, and community laymen.

The expectations these groups hold for the counselor have been the subject of considerable research inquiry. Kehas[28] has summarized and analyzed the research on the role of the school counselor. He points out that two models have been used almost exclusively in conducting research on counselor role. One is that of relating the counseling position to one other position (dyadic model). Examples of research efforts using the dyadic model include examining the expectations of counselors held by either students, teachers, principals, parents, or counselor educators. The other model is to study the counselor's position as related to two or more other positions (position-centric model). Kehas noted that research on counselor role approached from a *systems model* was conspicuous by its absence. He concluded that the research on counselor role—representing some fifteen to twenty years of work—was wanting and that a national policy regarding school counseling could not be advocated on the strength of current research on counselor role.

We have presented previously summaries of the expectations held by various publics of the counselor,[29] therefore, no attempt will be made to cover that topic exhaustively here. However, some comments are in order: counselor educators are much involved in defining counselor role through the preparation program. State directors of guidance and those who certify school counselors significantly influence counselors. Every state requires certification of school counselors. State directors of guidance are instrumental in determining the criteria by which counselors and their schools will be supported by state and federal funds. Herr, in one of the few studies of state guidance directors, substantiates the leadership, advocacy and support roles

enacted by this particular group.[30] Erpenbach,[31] too, states that the group, though few in number, is recognized in federal law and given broad responsibilities for the preparation and work of school counselors. Recent legislation, the Education Amendments of 1978, placed authority with state guidance directors to develop plans to coordinate all school-delivered counseling and guidance efforts on a state-by-state basis. Local school administrators who nominate, select, and recommend to the school board the appointment of school counselors are influential; all too often, they are the ones who direct counselors' day-to-day efforts and thus do more to define who and what counselors are than any other single individual. Teachers and other school workers hold expectations for counselors that often conflict with the counselor's own role perceptions. Students and parents have definite ideas about the counselor that must be taken into account; the effect of their expectations on actual counselor functioning has yet to be established, but more and more attention is being paid to the matter. Professional guidance organizations have appointed committees and task forces to formulate statements of counselor role.

Using two previous studies that examined the perceptions of counselor educators and of school counselors relative to role determinants as a basis, Herr and Cramer examined the degree of congruity in rank order determinants between these two groups.[32] The earlier studies were those of Cramer,[33] who polled 131 counselor educators of wide geographic dispersion, and Mayer,[34] who used a similar questionnaire with 400 New York State public school counselors. Table 6.1 reproduces Herr and Cramer's rank order of role determinants as perceived by selected counselor

[28] Chris D. Kehas, "What Research Says About Counselor Role," in *Guidance: Strategies and Techniques*, Herman J. Peters and Roger F. Aubrey, eds. (Denver, Colorado: Love Publishing Company, 1975), pp. 45–61.

[29] See Bruce Shertzer and Shelley C. Stone, *Fundamentals of Guidance*, 3rd ed. (Boston: Houghton Mifflin Company, 1976), pp. 141–145.

[30] Edwin L. Herr, "Nationwide Perspectives on State Guidance Office Functions," *Counselor Education and Supervision*, 10 (Spring 1971), 309–319.

[31] William J. Erpenbach, "State Supervisors and Counselor Educators: Can We Get Our Act Together?" *Counselor Education and Supervision*, 16 (June 1977), 305–309.

[32] Edwin L. Herr and Stanley H. Cramer, "Counselor Role Determinants as Perceived by Counselor Educators and School Counselors," *Counselor Education and Supervision*, 5 (Fall 1965), 3–8.

[33] Stanley H. Cramer, "A Collation of the Roles of the Secondary School Counselor and the School Psychologist as Perceived by Educators of Counselors and Educators of School Psychologists," (Ph.D. diss., Teachers College, Columbia University, 1964).

[34] Frank C. Mayer, "An Investigation of Role Perception of Secondary School Guidance Counselors in New York State," (Ph.D. diss., Teachers College, Columbia University, 1963).

TABLE 6.1 **Perceptions of counselor role determinants by selected counselor educators as compared to New York State school counselors**

Counselor educators Determinant (Cramer)		New York State school counselors Determinant (Mayer)	
Rank	(N = 131)	Rank	(N = 400)
1.5	Counselor educators	1	Principal
1.5	Abilities of counselor	2	Abilities of counselor
3	Principal	3	Guidance supervisor
4	Superintendent	4	Students
5	Guidance supervisor	5	Superintendent
6	Community	6	Teachers
7	Board of education	7	Parents
8	Students	8	Board of education
9	Teachers	9	Community
10	Professional organizations	10	Counselor educators
11	Parents	11	State education department
12	State education department	12	Professional organizations

SOURCE: Edwin L. Herr and Stanley H. Cramer, "Counselor Role Determinants as Perceived by Counselor Educators and School Counselors," *Counselor Education and Supervision,* 5 (Fall 1965), 4. Copyright © 1965 American Personnel and Guidance Association. Reprinted with permission.

educators compared to counselors working in New York State public schools.

The similarities and differences between the two groups in their perceptions of counselor role determinants seem self-evident. More fundamental is why disparities exist. Herr and Cramer speculate that counselor educators lack objectivity in their perception of training as a prime determinant because they are threatened and seek to justify their importance in the subsequent life of practicing school counselors. It may be, they also add, that counselor educators lack sufficient experience in secondary schools and maintain little contact with counselors after they complete training; hence they are unfamiliar with issues and pressures existing in the school situation. Haettenschwiller points out that while counselor educators are responsible for communicating the professional attributes of the counselor's role, they lack the power of sanctions to ensure that counselors enact role behaviors in accordance with the pro-

fession's views. Rather, it is the principal who is able to apply positive sanctions (such as praise, providing secretarial help, salary increases) or negative sanctions (criticism, termination of contract, and the like).[35] The low ranking given to professional organizations and state education departments as role determinants was seen by Herr and Cramer as stemming from the lack of consensus on what school counselors should be doing. The low ranking of students as role determinants by counselor educators raises questions as to whether student needs so often cited in the literature are realities or illusions to the group.

Present conceptions of counselor role and function

Answering the ubiquitous questions "Who am I?" (role) and "What do I do?" (function) is a provocative, urgent, and continuing challenge to every individual in the counseling profession. The role of the counselor as an adequately educated, professionally competent, functioning person reacting and relating to the needs of those served is but in the formative stage in most work settings. Clarification of the role will lead to commitment to the tasks of the occupation. It will enable school counselors, for instance, to differentiate their services to students from the services provided by others—psychologists, teachers, and so on. Counselors, individually and collectively, retain the responsibility for functionally differentiating their services from those provided by others.

This is not to say that all counselors will work in identical fashion. One counselor's functions will differ somewhat from those of another because of differences in personality, training, and experience. But despite some diversity within individual activities, commonalities do exist among that which counselors do, and make possible a generalized definition of role. If counselors themselves do not take primary responsibility for this definition, others, by default, will do so. The definition must be firm enough to provide counselors a basis for professional identity but at the same time sufficiently flexible to encourage growth and change within the profession.

A counselor's commitment to provide counseling is far too often conspicuous by its absence in actual performance. Many counselors describe their work in terms of handling

[35] Dunstan L. Haettenschwiller, "Control of the Counselor's Role," *Journal of Counseling Psychology,* 17 (September 1970), 437–442.

papers about clients, engaging in management functions, sponsoring social activities, and doing *some* counseling. In study after study counselors have indicated that their actual role behavior fell short of an idealized role definition. Among the reasons speculated to account for the gap between the ideal and the real role definition are that counselors have been too willing to assume any task to gain acceptance within the institutions that employ them, exhibit undue striving to please others, and are victimized by conflicts stemming from previous work experience.

Formulating and articulating a role enables counselors to specify more precisely the various objectives of their work. In turn, counselor functions then can be selected that are congruent with the role, representing the means to reach the objectives. Although progress has been slow in developing a counselor role statement acceptable to those within the profession, nevertheless change has taken place. Over the years, numerous statements depicting counselor role have been presented. These descriptions will be identified and described here.

The counselor as a quasi administrator

Traditionally, the role enacted by many counselors was that of a quasi administrator or an administrative handyman. The school counselor, for example, often served as administrator when the principal was out of the building, took disciplinary action, was responsible for extracurricular activities, sponsored the student council, assigned teachers and students to classes, administered schoolwide achievement and ability tests, and enrolled new students; when students were interviewed individually, it was usually only for program-planning purposes. Presumably, few counselor education programs prepared individuals for this burden but the situation demanded that they shoulder it. Counselors often were given or assumed the title "dean of boys" or "dean of girls." Facilitating the goals of the institution was the priority of counselors who enacted roles defined as quasi administrators. Their work did not feature any unique objectives because their goals did not differ from those of the school.

Until 1960 this role description was the most frequently encountered one in American secondary schools. It stressed little counseling contact with students, leaning, rather, toward efficient administrative management of the student body. Hidden beneath tiers of officialdom, bureaucracy, and

formality, the student was often forgotten. Apparently there was not time, opportunity, or interest to provide the individual contact necessary to implement counseling services as such in the school. Because counselors lacked the requisite skills and educational experiences, the comfortable role of administrative student body management was both attractive and fitting as they entered the field. Although vestiges of this outmoded concept remain, marked change began with the entry in 1960 of counselors prepared under the NDEA Counseling and Guidance Institutes. The change was due to many factors, but a most instrumental one was the requirement of a counseling practicum in the entry-level preparation of counselors. The institute program certainly stimulated full-time counselor study and greatly upgraded counselor education.

Counselor defined as a generalist

The counselor defined as a generalist gives priority to orientation, group guidance, registration, class scheduling, course changes, cumulative record development, testing and other appraisal, special class placement, scholarship and college application information and procedures, and so on, in addition to some counseling. Those who view counselors as generalists contend that their task is to counteract the harmful effects of specialization and impersonality. Their objective is to facilitate individual learning, personal planning, and decision making and to be the prime advocate urging attention to individual differences. Essentially, those who view counselors as generalists believe that they coordinate and administer services and resources. They give less time to counseling and more time to improving the relationships among teachers, administrators, parents, community resource personnel, and students. Advocates of a generalist's role for counselors believe that their preparation lacks sufficient depth to enable them to perform in any other than a preventive, developmental way.

Effective discharge of the responsibilities frequently attributed to the generalist would demand a social scientist possessing uncommon background and preparation. In effect this role would overlap the roles of even more of the school personnel than at present. The role would, by definition, not only preempt responsibilities of teachers and mental hygiene workers but duplicate the efforts of curriculum specialists, principals, and perhaps even superintendents. Many believe that a more restricted role would be more suitable.

Counselor defined as a specialist

The counselor defined as a specialist gives counseling priority over all other activities and ideally would counsel exclusively. Those who advance this counselor role claim that the generalist role spreads counselors so thinly that they have little or no impact on clients. Further, teachers and others with preparation different from the counselor's could conduct many of the services performed by a generalist. Finally, the need is great for intensive, therapeutic counseling to foster individual development.

Some fifteen years ago, Knowles and Shertzer devised an attitude scale containing eighty items that reflected the specialist and generalist viewpoints.[36] It was submitted to a random sample of 500 members of the Association for Counselor Education and Supervision (ACES), 500 members of the American Association of School Administrators (AASA), and 500 members of the American School Counselor Association (ASCA). Usable returns were received from 291 (58 percent) ACES members, 287 (57 percent) AASA members, and 289 (58 percent) ASCA members. Factor analysis was used to arrive at an empirical grouping of the eighty items that provided a further basis of comparison among the different professional groups. While ACES, AASA, and ASCA members clustered around the middle of the scale, significant differences were found among the groups in their attitudes toward the secondary school counselor's role. These differences were explained in terms of experience and training; that is, those who had many courses in guidance, counseling, and psychology favored the specialist position, whereas those with more secondary school experience and less course work tended toward the generalist position. These results led the investigators to conclude that counselors are probably trained to be specialists but hired to be generalists in the school setting. Counselors themselves take a middle-of-the-road position, although their attitudes toward their roles resemble more closely the

individual who trains them than the individual who hires them. No doubt, these differences are a source of continued tension because each group has conflicting expectations about counselors.

Later the same two authors administered the scale to a random sample of 123 members of Division 16 of the American Psychological Association.[37] Usable returns were received from 74 members (60 percent). School psychologists perceived counselors as being generalists more than did ACES members $(P < .001)$ and even ASCA $(P < .05)$. However, they did not see the counselor as a generalist as much as did school administrators $(P < .001)$. The question arises as to why school psychologists did not follow the pattern expected on the basis of training and experience since these two variables had earlier been shown to be significant. The explanation given by Knowles and Shertzer was fashioned from role perceptions. Individuals are apt to survey the roles of others from a perceptual framework in which their own role serves as the center. If another person's role overlaps one's own, the defensive tendency is to emphasize role differences in order to maintain a consistent role perception. The result is a clear formal perceptual differentiation of roles despite the fact that in reality they may not be so clearly distinct.

Counselor defined as an agent for change

Among role formulations is that of the counselor as an agent for change. In this view counselors not only are experts in learning theory—they know the barriers that prevent and the conditions that facilitate learning—but they are able to communicate their knowledge meaningfully to others. They are sophisticated in the features and consequences of social change and can make innovations in the institution in which they are employed.

The late C. Harold McCully, Specialist in Guidance, U.S. Office of Education, was one who regarded the counselor as an agent for change. He cited four shortcomings in American social processes and two in the schools that he believed provided mandates for defining the school counselor as an

[36] Richard T. Knowles and Bruce Shertzer, "Attitudes Toward the School Counselor's Role," *Counselor Education and Supervision*, 5 (Fall 1965), 9–20.

[37] Richard Knowles and Bruce Shertzer, "Attitudes of School Psychologists Toward the Role of the School Counselor," *Journal of School Psychology*, 4 (Summer 1966), 30–36.

agent of change.[38] The social needs or shortcomings included (1) loss of effective methods for inducting youth into full participating membership in adult society, (2) work instability that results from the accelerated change of a rapidly advancing technology, (3) an "overdeveloped" society that needs increasingly more trained workers at the highest levels of intellectual ability and constantly fewer workers at the lowest reaches of mental ability, and (4) an increasingly corporate society that depresses individualism. The shortcomings of the school included (1) its failure to deal with individual differences and (2) its failure to expect and obtain excellence among all pupils.

Almost all of the above societal and school shortcomings are as visible today as when they were identified by McCully. He asserted that they threatened individuality and self-definition, producing an increasing sense of meaninglessness and alienation. Counselor interventions were to combat and arrest these trends, to enable individuals to experience the meaning of freedom and responsibility.

The counselor as a change agent specifies the environment as the primary target of intervention, rather than the individual. Changes to be produced, according to Pine, lie in organizational development; shaping and reformulating the school's curriculum; and program and organization to meet the needs of students, parents, and the community.[39] As such, counselors work directly with teachers, parents, groups, and significant others to create an environment or structures reinforcing and sustaining for the individual. Thus the approach has been viewed as an intervention that trickles down to and, therefore, influences indirectly, the individual.

Shoben[40] was among the first of those who sought to have counselors think of themselves as change agents. In his conception, a counselor should function as a (1) *human feedback mechanism* for assessing the impact of the school and informing its personnel thereof and (2) *catalyst* for clarifying the character of the school as a community and as a source of appropriate models for developing youngsters. The outcome of enacting such a role, according to Shoben, was that the school would have a sharper impact and greater cogency for changing individual students. Shoben believed that an additional benefit of establishing such a role for counselors would be that a new counseling profession would emerge.

Cook has advocated that counselors define their role as change agents. They can enact that role, according to Cook, by serving as *creative critics* (direct their criticism at structures, not persons), *feedback agents* (interpret student needs and attitudes to the system), *sociotherapists* (view society or the school as the patient), *ombudsmen/student advocates* (trouble-shooter for those who need help), *manager of conflict,* and serving as personal *models of an open system.*[41]

Baker and Cramer[42] suggest that counselors are change agents if they move against the status quo when it is damaging to those whom counselors are trying to help. However, they believe that today's counselors cannot be active change agents because there is no power base to support them, either in the school or the profession, and because the status quo forces would retaliate and thwart counselors who constantly promoted changes. These authors believe that the most that can be expected at present is for counselors to help clients choose some course of action that the clients themselves initiate. In so doing, change may be achieved without the counselor risking direct confrontation with status quo oriented people in the institution or profession.

Counselor defined as a psychological educator

Counselors who assume this role would be responsible for developing and implementing systematic curriculum activities and programs designed to facilitate self-development. Many have noted that educational institutions offer courses designed to develop the intellect but few provide systematic ways to facilitate emotional development.

[38] C. Harold McCully, "The Counselor—Instrument of Change," in *Challenge for Change in Counselor Education,* comp. Lyle D. Miller (Minneapolis: Burgess Publishing Company, 1969), pp. 8–15.
[39] Gerald J. Pine, "Troubled Times for School Counselors," *Focus on Guidance,* 8 (September 1976), 1–16.
[40] Edward J. Shoben, Jr., "Guidance: Remedial Function or Social Reconstruction?" *Harvard Educational Review,* 32 (Fall 1962), 431–443.
[41] David R. Cook, ed., *Guidance for Education in Revolution* (Boston: Allyn & Bacon, 1971), pp. 478–483.
[42] Stanley B. Baker and Stanley H. Cramer, "Counselor or Change Agent: Support from the Profession," *Personnel and Guidance Journal,* 50 (April 1972), 661–665.

Ivey and Weinstein[43] described the content of two programs they constructed separately to refocus what counselors do. According to their view, the counselor would be involved in developing a psychological curriculum offered in group settings ranging from year-long elective courses to short, experimental minicourses in self-understanding and human relations. Such curricular activities would help individuals exhibit personal openness, spontaneity, emotional expressiveness, and relaxation.

Mosher and Sprinthall define psychological education as "educational experiences designed to affect personal, ethical, aesthetical and philosophical development in adolescents and young adults."[44] They suggest that a curriculum be fashioned that consists of a series of courses focused on various stages of the human life cycle, from infancy to adolescence to old age. Sprinthall,[45] describing his experiences in formulating and conducting curricular experiences, notes that such a curriculum is best oriented toward crisis prevention and the advancement of the healthy psychological development of adolescents. Ivey and Alschuler,[46] addressing the question of how psychological education was to be incorporated into existing school programs, suggested numerous tactics, including blending it into regular academic subject courses and courses taught by counselors, the content of which was solely psychological. Several models, designed to implement psychological education, in the form of leadership training for teachers, improving teacher-student communications, peer counseling and teacher-counselor classroom activities were reviewed by Carroll.[47]

Goldman[48] has questioned whether attributing the past failures of school counseling to such factors as relying on individual counseling, its remedial orientation, or its information-giving function is accurate. His point is that school counseling oriented toward such factors may have been ineffective because they were not done well. Unless the counselor activities associated with psychological education are done expertly, the chances for success are no greater than previous attempts.

Prominent functions performed in the role of counselor as psychological educator include teaching, training, and consulting. Competence in teaching, curriculum development and sequencing, constructing curricular experiences is stressed over counseling skills. Arbuckle suggests that the emergence of the role of counselors as psychological educators is because "counselors have been won over to the camp of teachers and administrators."[49] This happened, according to Arbuckle, because counselors labored under two false assumptions: the first being that all school personnel are dedicated to the total well-being of the individual child and the second being that counselors represent a unique professional group who possess skills and knowledge that make them effective consultants. Arbuckle thought neither of these assumptions had proven to be valid in the past nor were they likely to be true in the future. Arbuckle presented three major criticisms of counselors as psychological educators. The first was that counselors who became psychological educators were unable to function as advocates of individuals and that psychological education represents a not so subtle means of forcing students to conform to the system. The second criticism was that psychological education relied primarily on change in the system and it is individuals who must change. The third was that defining counselors as teachers and consultants had not worked before and would not work now. In an invited response to Arbuckle's criticisms, Ivey presented a "new vision of the helper's role." Prominent in this vision was that training rather than counseling was to be the counselor's primary and preferred mode of operation.[50]

Counselor defined as an applied behavioral scientist

Counselors increasingly have been portrayed as applied behavioral scientists. Berdie's description of the 1980 coun-

[43] Allen E. Ivey and Gerald Weinstein, "The Counselor as Specialist in Psychological Education," *Personnel and Guidance Journal*, 49 (October 1970), 98–107.

[44] Ralph Mosher and Norman A. Sprinthall, eds., "Psychological Education: A Means to Promote Personal Development During Adolescence," *The Counseling Psychologist*, 2, No. 4 (1971), 9.

[45] Norman A. Sprinthall, "A Curriculum for Secondary Schools: Counselors as Teachers for Psychological Growth," *The School Counselor*, 20 (May 1973), 361–369.

[46] Allen E. Ivey and Alfred S. Alschuler, "An Introduction to the Field," *Personnel and Guidance Journal*, 51 (May 1973), 592.

[47] Peg Carroll, "Special Feature: Training Models in Communication," *The School Counselor*, 21 (September 1973), 22–27.

[48] Leo Goldman, "Psychological Education: Where Do We Go from Here?" *The School Counselor*, 21 (September 1973), 22–27.

[49] Dugald S. Arbuckle, "The School Counselor: Voice of Society," *Personnel and Guidance Journal*, 54 (April 1976), 428.

[50] Allen E. Ivey, "An Invited Response: The Counselor as Teacher," *Personnel and Guidance Journal*, 54 (April 1976), 431–434.

selor outlines an educational program to prepare such practitioners.[51] According to Berdie, the counselor's job will be to apply theory and research derived from the various behavioral sciences to help individuals and institutions achieve their purposes. He predicts that counselors will provide ". . . experiences that will facilitate individual development most efficiently."

The image of counselors as applied behavioral scientists suggests that they arrange experiences so that their clients learn to act on their environment. Matheny[52] urged counselors to make better use of school and community environments to provide concrete experiences so that students can more fully identify their interests, aptitudes, and values Counselors as behavioral scientists would be engaged in formulating and providing clients with real and simulated work as well as social experiences that correct and extend their decision making and interpersonal relationships.

"Systematic counseling," an approach described by Stewart and his associates[53] may best exemplify counselors as applied behavioral scientists, particularly their individual counseling functions. They suggest that skill attained in systematic counseling leads to adapting its use in group counseling, consulting, and management of guidance systems.

Counselor defined as a consultant

During the past few years, increasing emphasis has been given to consultant functions associated with being a counselor. Many suggest that consultation is the key descriptor of the counselor's work, particularly as intervention is directed toward developmental and preventive processes. Kurpius[54] identified The Community Mental Health Center Act of 1963 as the impetus that accelerated the use of consultation in both clinics and educational settings. Passage of that act brought recognition that consultation was a broadly defined helping process and group, organizational, and community consultation emerged as new interventions for influencing desired changes.

Kurpius and Robinson[55] traced the historical development and purposes of consultation. In its early stage, consultation was viewed as a direct service to clients or client systems in that experts were hired to treat difficult cases. But at the end of the 1950s, the consultee (person trying to solve the problem) became active in the process with the consultant and client, establishing the consultant as a trainer, rather than as a diagnostician or critical evaluator of a problem. Consultation was defined by Kurpius as "a process for synthesizing environmental and human adjustments to influence change."[56] Two issues (February and March 1978) of the *Personnel and Guidance Journal* have presented materials particularly helpful in understanding consultant models, descriptions of on-line consulting programs, topical issues such as consultation on conflict resolution, career development, and the like.

The counselor as community psychologist

Goodyear[57] presents the case for defining counselors as community psychologists. Prominent in this identity is that counselors eschew the medical model of remediation and engage in preventive practices that build on clients' strengths and that teach clients life skills necessary for mastering problems. Goodyear noted that prevention was not a unitary concept, and presented three levels of prevention. These levels were depicted in concentric circles, presented here as Figure 6.5. Counselor activities were specified by Goodyear for each level of intervention—primary, secondary, and tertiary—presented in Figure 6.5. For example, deliberate psychological education, career education, parent education, death education, sex education were identified at the primary intervention level. At the secondary prevention level, crisis counseling, marriage and family counseling, brief therapy, and developmental counseling were named and vocational rehabilitation and supportive therapy were suggested as falling within the tertiary domain.

[51] Ralph F. Berdie, "The 1980 Counselor: Applied Behavioral Scientist," *Personnel and Guidance Journal*, 50 (February 1972), 451.
[52] Kenneth Matheny, "Counselors as Environmental Engineers," *Personnel and Guidance Journal*, 49 (February 1971), 439–444.
[53] Norman R. Stewart et al., *Systematic Counseling* (Englewood Cliffs, N.J.: Prentice-Hall, 1978), pp. 48–69.
[54] DeWayne Kurpius, "Introduction to the Special Issue," *Personnel and Guidance Journal*, 56 (February 1978), 320.
[55] DeWayne Kurpius and Sharon E. Robinson, "An Overview of Consultation," *Personnel and Guidance Journal*, 56 (February 1978), 321–323.
[56] Kurpius, "Introduction to the Special Issue," p. 320.
[57] Robert K. Goodyear, "Counselors as Community Psychologists," *Personnel and Guidance Journal*, 54 (June 1976), 512–516.

FIGURE 6.5 **Levels of psychological interventions**

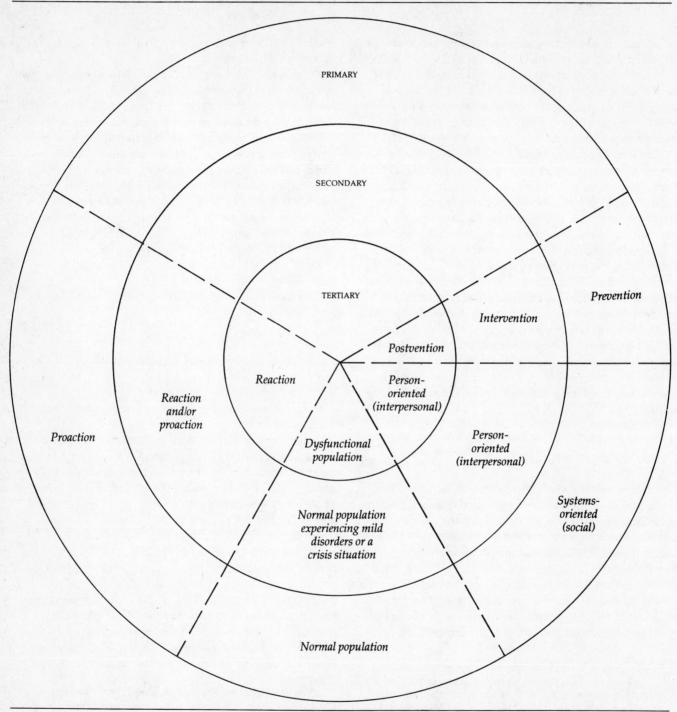

FIGURE 6.5 **Levels of psychological interventions**

The community counselor as a helping professional has been viewed by Lewis and Lewis as an innovative multifaceted approach for delivering helping services. They question reliance on individual counseling and suggest that a developmental or preventive approach is more efficient. The new dimension, in their view, is that the community counselor seeks to "assess and modify the reciprocal relationships between individuals and the social systems in which they interact.[58]

Professional associations' statements

Many statements describing counselor role and functions have been published by divisions of the American Personnel and Guidance Association. Table 6.2 summarizes these statements as well as the views of others. Examination of these counselor role and function statements reveals that they most often define the counselor as a helping professional who advances the personal development of individuals. Although this definition has yet to achieve universal acceptance, it has become increasingly prominent. Functions performed by the professional in the role of counselor as reflected in these statements are (1) counseling individuals and small groups, (2) consulting with those within the institution to instigate change, and (3) conducting training activities that support and augment program objectives. Atkinson and his associates[59] submitted a counselor-role questionnaire to assess attitudes toward twelve counselor functions, ten of which were taken from the American School Counselor Association, to students, parents, teachers, counselors, and administrators associated with four junior and three senior high schools in an urban California school district. The other two counselor functions were ombudsman and change agent. Their most important finding was that these publics—students, parents, administrators, teachers, and counselors—all viewed the twelve functions as appropriate for school counselors. While some functions—program planning, counseling, career planning—received more

support than others, the strength of the support varied across populations surveyed. Stronger support was found for the ombudsman function than for the change agent. Senior high students and parents rated change agent functions higher than did education professionals.

Summary

The task of establishing and integrating a professional identity is difficult. And, no doubt, it is a lifelong process, modified by work experiences, personal interests, and institutional and environmental factors. Verbalizing "this is what I am as a counselor" involves public self-definition and consequently immobilizes some counselors when they are faced with declaring themselves. But more and more are painfully aware of the demand and necessity to do so. Commitment to a role model is often avoided because the individual is aware of internal confusion and does not wish to come to terms with uncertainties, ambivalence, and incompatibilities. For some counselors the lure of an external answer is great indeed. They find it easier to believe that the problem of counselor role lies not with themselves but outside; it is something that exists for others and may perhaps be clutched and made their own.

The array of counselor role and functions that has been presented here attests to the fact that professional identification is diffused. Current thinking about counselor functions goes beyond counseling and consulting and incorporates training, teaching, and organizational change. The *role* of school counselor, long identified as being to help students understand and accept themselves and the world in which they live and to develop a sense of responsibility for and competency in decision making, may be changing to incorporate teaching, training, and social activist endeavors. Whether alterations, often proposed by others, become part of professional counselor identity, or whether counselors select a model for themselves from among themselves rather than looking elsewhere remains unclear at this time. Wrenn has proposed a statement of the functions of counselors, regardless of setting, that remains highly valued. He stated that:

The function of the counselor in any setting is (a) to provide a *relationship* between counselor and counselee, the

[58] Judith A. Lewis and Michael D. Lewis, *Community Counseling: A Human Services Approach* (New York: John Wiley & Sons, 1977), p. 11.

[59] Donald R. Atkinson et al., "The Role of the Counselor as a Social Activist: Who Supports It?" *The School Counselor,* 25 (November 1977), 85–91.

TABLE 6.2 **Major features of statements of counselor role and functions in various settings**

Feature/setting	Elementary schools	Middle/junior high schools	Secondary schools	Post-secondary schools
Rationale	Concerned with children in the developmental process of maximizing their potentials	Early adolescents have special physical, emotional, social needs	Assist students by identifying and meeting their needs in the educational, vocational, and personal-social domains	Integral part of total institution; major concern with normal developmental needs of students
Context	Leadership in guidance; functioning effectively depends on interaction of children's self-concepts and their influences and experiences	Part of guidance program	Guidance as part of pupil personnel services	Are members of student services
Purpose of counseling	Find identity; make choices and decisions	Facilitate self-development; gain self-understanding and identity	Assist students in developing decision-making competence and in formulating future plans	Assist students in acquiring information and developing insights, attitudes, and understanding about themselves and their environment
Nature of relationships	Concerned with each child's perceptions of the present and how they relate to present and future	Not specified	Respect integrity of counselee; keep information confidential; make counseling available to all students	Educational, career, and personal social counseling
Functions identified	Individual and group counseling; consulting with teachers, other staff members, and parents; evaluating counselor and guidance programs; career education; interpret counseling to public	Individual and group counseling, staff consultation, parental consultation, community contacts; orientation to junior and senior high schools; career development activities	Individual and group counseling; staff consultation; parental assistance; student self-appraisal; information and planning; referral; public relations	Individual and group counseling; consultation; orientation; testing; articulation with other institutions; institutional and professional research; interpreting program to public
Professional relations identified	Students, parents, referral personnel	Students, parents, teachers, administrators, agency personnel	Students, parents, teachers, administrators, community agency personnel	Students, faculty, administrators
SOURCES:	American School Counselor Association, "The Unique Role of the Elementary School Counselor," *Elementary School Guidance and Counseling*, 8 (March 1974), 219–224. (Revised August 1977).	American School Counselor Association, "The Unique Role of the Middle/Junior High School Counselor," *Elementary School Guidance and Counseling*, 8 (March 1974), 216–220. (Revised August 1977).	American School Counselor Association, "The Role of the Secondary School Counselor," *The School Counselor*, 24 (March 1977), 228–234.	American School Counselor Association, "The Role and Functions of Post Secondary Counseling," *The School Counselor*, 21 (May 1974), 387–390.

TABLE 6.2

Community agencies	Employment service	Veterans' rehabilitation services	Correctional institutions and agencies
Prevent mental illness by changing community; multifaceted approach	Help clients to higher levels of vocational adjustment; career decision making; job choice; job change; job adjustment; equal opportunity to develop and use talents for betterment of self; life-long process; work meaningful expression of self concept and values; client advocacy needed in some situations	Help clients with disabilities to gain optimum vocational adjustment	Treatment and control
Human services; developmental and preventive programs that are experiential or environmental	Testing; training and retraining; counseling and placement; define and correct employment problems	Work within medical limits and those limits associated with different occupations	Develop human potential in residential, community, and institutional settings
Work with "whole" persons to gain skills to help themselves; improve individual's capacity to cope and achieve	Help client become optimally employable by correction of vocational problems; client can choose, change, or adjust to a vocation	Restore handicapped to fullest physical, mental, social, vocational, and economic usefulness; modify attitudes and behavior; vocational planning	Clarify present situation; vent hostility toward society; gain insight into problems; prepare for re-entering society; prevent recidivism
Develop client's ability to accomplish tasks for independent living, set personal goals; work out positive relations with others; enhance community environment	Short-term to effect changes in values, work attitudes, and personal characteristics	Assessment; personal and vocational counseling; vocational planning; educational training; placement; and follow-up	Individual and group counseling, establish work habits, sense of identity and accomplishment
Consultation; counseling; intensive and extensive experiential and environmental programs, including education about community; training in skill building; create self-help and volunteer programs; crisis help and prevention; community planning and action for change; individual and group advocacy	Collect labor-market information; screen, evaluate, and classify applicants; placement of applicants; identify trainees	Coordinate all services—medical and community agencies—for their clients; arrange employment for clients; provide financial assistance; counseling where personal or emotional problems are involved	Classifying public offenders; serve as a change agent to open up community as a closed system; develop resources linking public offenders and community; therapist dealing with behaviors of offenders who seek to relate to community
Psychologists, social workers, human services specialists, mental health workers, volunteering paraprofessionals	Applicants, employers, training program personnel	Medical and nursing staff members; employers	Program staff members, wardens, employers, medical staff members, education and training personnel
Judith A. Lewis and Michael D. Lewis, *Community Counseling: A Human Services Approach* (New York, John Wiley & Sons, 1977). William Gellman and Herman Murov, "The Broad Role of the Community Agency Counselor," *Personnel and Guidance Journal*, 52 (November 1973), 157–159.	National Employment Counselors Association, "Role of Employment Counselors," *Journal of Employment Counseling*, 12 (December 1975), 148–153.	Edward C. Roeber, "Roles and Functions of Professionally Trained Counselors," in *Counselor Development in American Society*, ed. John F. McGowan (Washington, D.C., U.S. Department of Labor and U.S. Office of Education, June 1965).	Allen E. Ivey, "Adapting Systems to People," *Personnel and Guidance Journal*, 53 (October 1974), 137–139.

most prominent quality of which is that of mutual trust of each in the other; (b) to provide *alternatives* in self-understanding and in the courses of action open to the client; (c) to provide for *some degree of intervention* with the situation in which the client finds himself [or herself] and with "important others" in the client's immediate life; (d) to provide leadership in developing *a healthy psychological environment* for . . . clients, and, finally, (e) to provide for *improvement of the counseling process* through constant individual self-criticism and (for some counselors) extensive attention to improvement of process through research.[60]

Issues

Issue 1 Who and what should determine counselor functions?

The counselor and the work setting, because
1. The professional counselor is prepared to exercise judgment in determining how best to utilize his or her skills and qualifications.
2. Settings vary both subtly and dramatically. Specific functions, therefore, should match the existing situation if they are to be effective.

The administration and public, because
1. The employer hires someone to perform a specific set of well-defined tasks.
2. The consumers of a service are in the best position to determine what they want from the employee.

Discussion An important point to be noted here is that functions differ from role. A role is legitimately viewed as a set of expected behaviors. Consumers, therefore, have a stake in defining the role through their expectancies. Functions are seen as the activities in which professionals engage in performing their role. Therefore, judgment of the functions to be performed remains the prerogative of profession-

als as long as they fulfill appropriate normative expectations of the role.

Functions differ from setting to setting and within a given setting from individual to individual. For example, a counselor in a setting characterized by stable, goal-directed student behavior may perform quite different functions from those undertaken in a school with a high delinquency rate. Even within the latter setting, the counselor may be confronted with two delinquent boys, one of them emotionally disturbed, the other merely conforming to that part of society in which he must live. The approach and procedures employed would differ to best serve the individuals involved and the settings.

Issue 2 Are school counselors essentially psychologists or educators?

Educators, because
1. They are employed in an educational institution that has certain expectations of all employees.
2. The clientele they serve is not universally restricted to a defined population.
3. The major thrust of their work is directed not toward the repair of long-term disability but toward facilitating learning.
4. Their undergraduate and graduate preparation does not entitle them to be called psychologists.

Psychologists, because
1. The success of their contact work with students depends on how well they understand human behavior.
2. Their preparation in counseling consists of instruction in interpersonal relationships, use of tests in counseling, personality and counseling theory, group processes, and so on, all of which fall within the domain of psychology.

Discussion The issue as just stated has been cast in the form most commonly presented among practicing counselors and educational personnel. At the outset it should be made clear that, so stated, it represents a meaningless and false beacon in the field, which generates more heat than light. The pros and cons confuse setting and function, as well as place of work and activity. At least implicitly involved are overtones of an extremely parochial and outdated

[60] C. Gilbert Wrenn, "Crisis in Counseling: A Commentary and a Contribution," in *Counselor Development in American Society*, ed. John F. McGowan (Washington, D.C.: U.S. Department of Labor and U.S. Office of Education, June 1965), p. 237.

view of the training and background of practitioners of both psychology and counseling. Moreover, if a work setting is structured in a particular direction, status and success follow conformity to the demands of the work situation. Perhaps even more importantly, such mistaken and overly simplified concepts needlessly encourage divisionists and establish hostile camps.

There would seem to be little argument that school counselors function in an educational setting, are recruited almost exclusively from the ranks of education, and are charged with facilitating the self-development of children. It is equally obvious that the means they use to meet their obligations, the training they receive during counselor preparation, and their personal inclinations require them to function very much like psychologists. These two views are not, and should not be, incompatible. Extremists of either camp frequently drag forth this issue as a defensive smoke screen for their inability to understand and perform those tasks that are commonly accepted as appropriate for counselors. Extremists at the educational pole expect the counselor to function as a teacher without a classroom or in a tutorial manner with a highly restricted population. The activities of the counselor, they think, should consist of presenting occupational information, encouraging conformity to the institutional milieu through manipulative disciplinary procedures, evaluating students so that decisions can be made about and for them (rather than with them), and, in general, not letting the student off the end of that famous Mark Hopkins log until all is orderly, precise, and decided. Extremists at the other pole expect counselors to confine their contacts to a select group of deviant students, avoid the thought of even dealing with anything that is not highly emotionally charged, completely forgo the use of any kind of information, educational, vocational, or whatever, and totally ignore the educational pond in which the log of learning floats. Not even Sigmund Freud would last in Admiral Rickover's school! The humanistically oriented counselor would stand little chance in a school operated by the traditional advocates of basic education. By the same token, little reward would await the educationalist counselor who attempted to work in a permissive, child-centered setting emphasizing individual development.

Issue 3 Should counseling activities or guidance activities constitute the major focus for the school counselor?

Counseling activities, because
1. Counselors spend the bulk of their time in individual or small group student contacts.
2. It is only through counseling that the goals of guidance are achieved.
3. Other personnel can be utilized in performing most guidance activities.

Guidance activities, because
1. Particular kinds of information are needed by large numbers of pupils.
2. Training limitations do not permit individuals to function effectively as counselors.

Discussion Imbedded in this issue is whether counselors are generalists or specialists. Historically, they have been generalists and frequently even occupied multiple roles by simultaneously teaching and counseling. Increasingly, the contemporary counselor holds a full-time position and concentrates on the counseling function from among the usual services falling under the umbrella of "guidance." A sound argument could be made that guidance services such as the informational service and student appraisal service should exist and be emphasized only to the degree that they contribute to improving the counseling service. This is not to be misinterpreted to mean that the mere giving of these kinds of information should be called counseling. Rather, concern here is for effective and sophisticated use of these valuable types of information as part of true counseling.

Also involved is whether counselors should be called *school counselors* or *guidance specialists*. Title can influence expectancies. To the consumer, the title often conveys the deed. Many who would balk at being guided might readily accept the services of a counselor. It is to be hoped that the title *school counselor* will be fully accepted and come to reflect the kind of service it implies. Those who practice under this title will truly perform the function of counseling and not employ it as a mask for information giving and individualized instruction.

Issue 4 Can the counselor serve the school both as an agent of change and as a counselor?

Yes, because
1. The factors responsible for success in both functions are essentially the same: understanding people and understanding institutions.
2. The counselor is most likely to have a unique kind of access to students which provides that professional with intimate knowledge of concerns and difficulties arising directly from the institution.
3. Many students cannot solve their problems through counseling alone because the problems are rarely entirely internal to but stem also from the individual's interaction with the environment. Consequently, counselors are sometimes required to effect modification in the environment.

No, because
1. Few counselors possess the needed knowledge of or have the authority to influence the power structure of the school and community to effect change.
2. Counselors are usually temperamentally unfit to undertake the struggle to instigate and complete a change cycle in a setting.
3. Leadership for effecting institutional change lies in the sphere of administration.

Discussion Within the past few years many have urged the counselor to be the school's agent of change. Seemingly, their case is built on the assumption that administrators are increasingly alienated from their traditional role of educational leadership and more and more isolated from students and staff. Administrators are viewed as devoting the majority of their time to budgets, buildings, and public relations. Unquestionably their activities create a leadership vacuum into which some seem eager to thrust school counselors by making them responsible for change.

This effort is not without merit, nor would such an assignment be unattractive to one who seeks power and influence. However, in view of the usual administrative hierarchy found in education, assumption of this role is presumptuous. Further, counselors who are now being urged to become agents of institutional change frequently lack certain essential personal characteristics for doing so: aggressiveness, persuasiveness, persistence in the face of disinterest and lethargy, belief in the art of compromise, and political acumen. Needless to say, this list of attributes hardly characterizes the school counselor, who has other, equally positive traits necessary for working intimately with individuals.

It should be noted that some see the counselor's background and training as eminent qualifications. This view, however, often derives from the distorted idea of the counselor in the thoroughly distasteful image of a hidden persuader, maneuvering and manipulating to accomplish devious ends.

Perhaps the more legitimate view would be that of a counselor as a catalyst of change rather than the agent of change. In this case counselors serve a consultative function and bring to bear their unique, intimate knowledge of the school setting derived from knowledge of the students and teachers who populate it, and their contacts with parents, employers, and the community. Essentially the difference here lies in regarding counselors as those whose role in identifying and conceptualizing areas of change, providing justification for legitimately needed modifications, and transmitting their ideas to leaders who are responsible for effecting change.

Annotated references

Hansen, James C., ed. *Counseling Process and Procedures.* New York: Macmillan Publishing Company, Inc., 1978. 501 pp.

Chapter 8 (pp. 419–452) presents four articles that treat counselor role and counselor ethics. Chapter 9 contains an article by Edwin L. Herr (pp. 478–491) that discusses counselor accountability and creditability.

Johnson, Dorothy E., and Mary J. Vestermark. *Barriers and Hazards in Counseling.* Boston: Houghton Mifflin Company, 1970. 244 pp.

Part One (pp. 7–86) presents some of the blocks that prevent the counselor from being effective. Treatment is given to the counselor's self-image and professional role, the effects of time and physical setting on the counselor and the many commitments involved. These two authors have presented some very vivid barriers and hazards that face a counselor.

Peters, Herman J., and Roger F. Aubrey, eds. *Guidance: Strategies and Techniques.* Denver: Love Publishing Company, 1975. 551 pp.

Part I (pp. 7–62) and Part II (pp. 63–171) set forth counselor functions within guidance program development. Articles from several notable authors—Ralph Mosher, Norman Sprinthall, Chris Kehas, Roger Aubrey, to cite but a few—address changes in school counselor functions.

Further references

American School Counselor Association. "The Role of the Secondary School Counselor." *The School Counselor,* 24 (March 1977), 228–234.

Arbuckle, Dugald S. "The School Counselor: Voice of Society." *Personnel and Guidance Journal*, 54 (April 1976), 426–431.

Atkinson, Donald R., Terry Froman, John Romo, and Daniel M. Mayton, II. "The Role of the Counselor as a Social Activist: Who Supports It?" *The School Counselor,* 25 (November 1977), 85–91.

Bartlett, Jane C. and James V. Wigtil. "School Counselors and Political Action." *The School Counselor*, 26 (May 1979), 299–306.

Berry, Elizabeth. "Guidance and Counseling in the Elementary School: Its Theoretical Base." *Personnel and Guidance Journal*, 57 (June 1979), 513–521.

Engen, Harold B. "Toward Updating and Renewal of School Counselors." *The School Counselor,* 25 (September 1977), 24–30.

Gamboa, Anthony M., Jr. "The Humanistic Counselor in a Technocratic Society." *The School Counselor,* 19 (January 1972), 160–166.

Goodyear, Rodney K. "Counselors as Community Psychologists." *Personnel and Guidance Journal*, 54 (June 1976), 512–516.

Hickey, Dolores F. "School Counselors' Attitudes Toward Behavior Modification." *Personnel and Guidance Journal,* 55 (April 1977), 477–480.

Humes, Charles W., II. "School Counselors and PL 94-142." *The School Counselor,* 25 (January 1978), 192–195

Ivey, Allen E. "An Invited Response: The Counselor as Teacher." *Personnel and Guidance Journal,* 54 (April 1976), 431–434.

Jones, Vernon L. "School Counselors as Facilitators of Healthy Learning Environments." *The School Counselor,* 24 (January 1977), 157–164.

Kahnweiler, William M. "The School Counselor as Consultant: A Historical Review." *Personnel and Guidance Journal,* 57 (April 1979), 374–380.

Kuh, George D. "Entry-Level Employment Prospects for Women in College-Student Personnel Work." *Personnel and Guidance Journal*, 57 (February 1979), 296–298.

Mickelson, Douglas J., and Jerry L. Davis. "A Consultation Model for the School Counselor." *The School Counselor,* 25 (November 1977), 98–103.

Penn, Roger. "A Dollar's Worth of Counseling and a Lifetime Guarantee." *Personnel and Guidance Journal*, 56 (December 1977), 204–205.

Sprinthall, Norman A. "A Curriculum for Secondary Schools: Counselors as Teachers for Psychological Growth." *The School Counselor*, 20 (May 1973), 361–369.

Part two
Counseling approaches

In the substantive body of knowledge that counselors are expected to be able to use are insights about humankind drawn from the social sciences and explanations of what takes place in counseling provided by counseling theorists. The four chapters in Part Two are directed to them.

Increasing recognition has been given to the fact that counselor skills should be based on theory and research in the social and behavioral sciences. The intent in Chapter 7 is to identify and describe the contributions that related disciplines—religion, philosophy, political science, anthropology, psychology, economics, sociology—have made to counseling. There is no pretense that each is comprehensively treated. Although these disciplines are presented in separate sections for clarity and emphasis, the unity and interrelationships of their contributions are of paramount importance.

Chapters 8 and 9 deal with eleven counseling viewpoints. To report even briefly all counseling approaches is beyond the scope of this book. Nor is it possible to treat comprehensively the eleven selected for discussion here. Rather, these two chapters have three primary aims: (1) to introduce the fundamental aspects of what eleven theoretical viewpoints believe occurs in a counseling relationship, (2) to encourage counselors in preparation to examine the differences and similarities that exist among these theories, and (3) to encourage counselors to sift through theories to ascertain their own stands vis à vis various theoretical positions. Although experience is always much richer than the language of science can make allowance for, counseling theories are attempts to organize what occurs in counseling into a coherent pattern. The assumptions or postulates in counseling theory are approximate generalizations usually based on empirical observations. Some incompleteness is always present but is accepted for the sake of greater simplicity. The point is that although counseling theories are incomplete, counselors cannot wait until perfection is attained. They must operate on the evidence available to them. Examining conflicting theories is sometimes a traumatizing experience. Closer reflection may reveal, in some cases, that theories complement rather than contradict each other.

Chapter 10 shows how the understandings drawn from the social sciences and counseling theories are utilized by the counselor to develop a personalized philosophy of counseling. Building such a philosophy is a continuous process for those who counsel. The theory and philosophy evolved by counselors will depend on their understanding of themselves, their views of humankind, and their experiences.

7 Counseling and the social sciences

by S. Samuel Shermis

The theory and practice of counseling has been expanded and refined both by practitioners within the field and through the use of insights from that group of disciplines known as the social sciences. Psychology, sociology, economics, anthropology, and political science have, particularly during this century, provided both data and comprehensive hypotheses that have been used by counselors. It is the author's belief that a nontechnical discussion of the social sciences, some of their salient characteristics, and their relationship to counseling will assist the future counselor.

What are the "social sciences"?

The social sciences arose in the last two centuries as thinkers applied the method of the physical and natural sciences to understanding human behavior. Since about the sixteenth century scientists had made astounding progress in explaining the behavior of chemicals, planets, machines, and animals. It appeared to some that if the basic mode of inquiry employed by chemists, astronomers, physicists, and biologists could be used to study human behavior, perhaps a body of information could be built up that was just as accurate and dependable. For most of recorded history, observations of human behavior had been made by discerning and intelligent persons. But such observation, made almost exclusively by poets, novelists, and philosophers, seemed unsystematic, often inaccurate, and sometimes distorted by biases. If the *method* of hypothesis construction, detailed and recorded observation, experimentation, and mathematical analysis could be applied to human social interactions, society could perhaps gain useful insights into why and how people behaved the way they did.

From the perspective of the second half of the twentieth century it now appears that social scientists cannot as yet provide the dependability or accuracy of chemists and physicists. It is now felt by many, that the insights of artists are irrelevant. With the humility forced by a century of experience, social scientists can claim to offer only modest and limited generalizations about human behavior. These are, nevertheless, exceedingly useful. For example, thanks to economists, we know enough to prevent the kind of depression that forced our economy to grind almost to a standstill in 1929. The sociologist's observations required a rather drastic change in our way of looking at the constitutional provision for equal protection: the *Brown* vs. *Topeka Board of Education* Supreme Court decision of 1954 was based on psychological and sociological data about the effects of segregation. According to historians it was, in part, the information of anthropologists who advised General MacArthur in 1945 that enabled the occupation of Japan to proceed more smoothly than it might have. It may be asserted that the systematic and tested knowledge of social scientists—although clearly lacking the precision of physical scientists—has allowed societies to operate with fewer crises and dislocations and less friction than in previous centuries. What, then, are the characteristics of that mode of inquiry that has provided this limited but useful knowledge?

The social sciences are a collection of disciplines that have in common, first, a concern for the study of collective human behavior, and second, an intentional application of the scientific method to the study of human behavior. By *collective* we mean that social scientists study human behavior not as it is exhibited by individual human beings but as it takes place in groups. The groups may range in size from a handful of subjects to an entire culture.[1] The emphasis is on *patterns* of behavior. The social sciences are also scientific in the sense that they use the scientific method of knowing; that is, they make use of hypotheses, perform experiments, collect empirical data, utilize mathematics in the analysis of the data, make predictions, formu-

S. Samuel Shermis is Associate Professor, Department of Education, Purdue University. The authors are pleased to present his treatment of this topic.

[1] See, for example, Clyde Kluckhohn, *Mirror for Man* (New York: McGraw-Hill Book Co., 1944).

late theories, and modify them in the light of more and better data. The social sciences are scientific in another sense. Their procedures are characterized by openness, flexibility, precision, willingness to change interpretations, disinclination to generalize recklessly, and a desire to follow data to conclusions that may not be particularly pleasant.

Which disciplines are clearly social sciences is arguable, although most would agree that economics, anthropology, sociology, political science, and psychology are social sciences.[2] Before we deal with these, the discussion will first turn to philosophy and religion, for certain philosophical and theological tenets have been incorporated into the method and assumptions of the social sciences. That is, from many years of philosophical and theological thought there has emerged a body of assumptions that influence the intellectual climate in which social scientists work. Many social scientists are not able to identify their intellectual atmosphere and their philosophical assumptions; few would disagree that there is a system of unarticulated beliefs, positions, attitudes, and values that influence thinking. It is to theology and philosophy that we must turn to see what some of them are and how they have functioned.

Religion and philosophy

This section is entitled "Religion and Philosophy" even though many will object to coupling the two concepts. To some, religion has to do with the worship of a supernatural deity whereas philosophy is concerned with rational analysis of problems of knowledge and value. Such an oversimplification ignores the fact that until fairly recently there was no clear difference between the two activities. Historically, the sharpened distinction between theology and philosophy is a nineteenth-century phenomenon.

The development of Western philosophy did not take place apart from the Judeo-Christian religious tradition. Concern for individualism, problems of knowing, value issues, and theories of human nature are not simply philosophical; they were also of interest to those who considered themselves basically religious. The best illustration is

the history of the concern for individualism in our own society. Some of the most articulate spokesmen for the inherent importance of the individual were Thomas Jefferson, Henry Thoreau, and John Dewey. Although not usually identified with a formal religion, all three derived their inspiration from religious sources: Jefferson was a Deist, Thoreau was part of New England religious transcendentalism, and Dewey was strongly influenced by his parents' Congregationalism and by the religious reformers of his time.

The point is that positions of interest to counselors have long historical roots in a Western tradition that was at the same time a religious and a philosophical one. Now, let us consider the concept *individualism*.

Individual importance

From religion and philosophy in Western civilization have emerged a number of beliefs that are more correctly described as attitudes than positions. First is the importance accorded the individual. Slowly, over thousands of years, the idea has evolved that individuals matter, not for what they can accomplish, not for their services to the state, but because they have value in and of themselves. This attitude, usually designated individualism, has several implications. People may develop their uniqueness and emphasize their individuality—provided this does not conflict with other values.[3] Individuals ought to be encouraged by significant persons to develop their uniqueness and, under certain circumstances, should be given positive assistance.

Although individualism is important in American society, there are values that oppose individualism. Thus, though American culture permits and encourages certain differences—and in theory even celebrates them—there are pressures on individuals to conform, or in common parlance, to "get along," to be "one of the gang," or "play on the team." One of the reasons simple, prescriptive counseling approaches—"you should begin to do this" or "you must avoid that"—are unpopular among professionals is that the client may well be caught in a bind between contradictory

[2] Whether history is or ought to be a social science or a member of the humanities is likely to depend on the outlook of a given historian.

[3] In many societies, particularly preliterate ones, group cohesiveness is so important that what we would call harmless individualism is seen as dangerous, group-threatening, aberrant behavior.

cultural patterns. And in this case, the counselor may find it quite risky to do more than assist the client to reach an autonomous decision.

Although this may seem an obvious position, it should be pointed out that in another culture people with problems may be told that their troubles lie in their antisocial attitudes, that if they were to obey the elders, stop rebelling against authority, or observe the regulations more closely, their troubles would cease. In this culture a counselor may take the position that what an individual needs is encouragement to make a more independent, autonomous decision. To encourage an individual to make an autonomous decision implies that one has the right to be unique, to make decisions independently, and to be respected in so doing. Such a view reflects one important strand of religious and philosophical belief in Western civilization.

Rationalism

Another important assumption is that rationality provides a more adequate solution to personal problems than irrationality. Again, such an attitude is not universally held. For instance, anthropologists indicate that in some cultures people with a serious psychiatric or physical disability will consult a witch doctor, who may offer incantations, perform dances, or encourage the afflicted to say special prayers on their own behalf.[4] Social scientists who have taken a new look at these irrational methods concede that they may be quite effective.[5] However, counseling in the dominant culture is based on the assumption that rationality offers the most reliable means of solving problems.

Rationality here refers to the belief that there is a cause-and-effect relationship in the world, that by ordinary deductive and inductive procedures, and by thinking consecutively, one may make accurate diagnoses and formulate desirable solutions. Consecutive, logical, rational thought has been regarded by most philosophers from Aristotle to the present as the preferred mode of problem solving. To attribute problems to bad luck, the intervention of hostile

spirits or fate, or to substitute wishful thinking or magic for logical analysis of events is—from the standpoint of Western rationalistic philosophy—not a productive way of dealing with human problems. Therefore, for many counselors, much of activity involves asking questions designed to relate cause and effect, distinguish between or among consequences, ask for rationales, and/or ask the client to speculate about antecedents. All of this is part of the process of rationalism applied to personal concerns.

Two approaches

From philosophy has developed an awareness that humans can look at themselves in two different ways. Employing *introspection* they can search within themselves. They can ask themselves what they have seen and experienced and, by reflection, decide what their experiences mean. Or they can *observe the behavior of others* and, by classifying different or similar kinds of behavior, attempt to arrive at reliable generalizations.

These approaches have had a long and somewhat conflicting history. The tendency has been to choose one or the other as exclusive modes of inquiry. Socrates, for instance, felt that objective observation was so inherently unreliable that it could yield only deception, or at best second-order truths. In the late nineteenth and early twentieth centuries social scientists, particularly psychologists, turned away from introspection and began to think not only that it was possible to observe objectively and make completely accurate reports of observed behavior but that this was the most scientific avenue to truth. The feeling seemed to be that introspection, perhaps appropriate for poets or dramatists, was irrelevant to science.[6]

With the recent emphasis on creativity and the rise of existentialism or neophenomenalism,[7] many counseling

[4] See Ari Kiev, *Magic, Faith, and Healing* (New York: Free Press of Glencoe, 1964).
[5] Ibid.
[6] See the section on natural law in S. Samuel Shermis, *Philosophic Foundations of Education* (New York: American Book Company, 1967) and the same topic in Young Pai and Van Cleve Morris, *Philosophy and the American School: An Introduction to the Philosophy of Education* (Boston: Houghton Mifflin Company, 1976).
[7] *Phenomenalism* is a late nineteenth- and early twentieth-century school of both philosophy and psychology in which the emphasis is on human experience as the starting point in the search for truth.

theoreticians are showing a renewed interest in introspection—although the term *introspection* is not usually employed. To many social scientists, it seems clear that the reports of how individuals perceive their world or the way they feel about themselves constitutes an important source of valid evidence about them. This does not deny that data about a person secured by objective tests may also be a source of considered evidence. At present, counselors make use of both kinds of evidence—objective information and reports of personal feelings—although it may be hard to know when to employ each kind of evidence. The point, however, is that most counselors assume that the evidence of introspection—data concerned with the counselees' subjective feelings about their situation—is considered as valid as evidence obtained from standardized tests.

Value theory

Though certain social scientists have often rejected—and even ridiculed—philosophy,[8] many of them have come to see that philosophical analysis, of at least two kinds, is useful and necessary. These two types of analysis, called technically *ontology* and *axiology*, are concerned, respectively, with perceptions of *reality* and with *value theory*. Both entire cultures and individuals within cultures seem to have distinctive ways of looking at reality. For instance, if we compare the medieval world, with its belief in the literal existence of supernatural powers (ghosts, spirits, imps, devils) and the twentieth century, which tends to deny supernatural manifestations and leans heavily on experimental science, we see a contrast in modes of perceiving reality. To the medieval world spirits sent by the devil to plague God-fearing men were as real as molecules are to us.[9] Perhaps be-

[8] It has been held that philosophy was simply speculation and had little to do with observation, data gathering, testing, and mathematical analysis. Probably the more recently trained and more sophisticated social scientists realize that their philosophical assumptions influence not only the way they perceive the world but also the conclusions they reach.
[9] For a general introduction to the topic see Rossell H. Robbins, *Encyclopedia of Witchcraft and Demonology* (New York: Crown Publishers, 1959) and for the problem in an anthropological context see the witty and absorbing work by Marvin Harris, *Cows, Pigs, Wars and Witches; The Riddle of Culture* (New York: Random House, 1974).

cause of an awareness of theories of reality and of differing perceptions social scientists have largely abandoned the search for absolutes—that is, never-changing and completely permanent truth.

Awareness of value theory has also influenced both the method and the content of the social sciences. Social psychologists and sociologists have recently been studying values, primarily by looking closely at the wants, preferences, and desires of individuals, cultures, subcultures, and even civilizations. For instance, although Americans are prone to perceive the suppression of individual freedom in communist or socialist countries as a very bad thing, they often fail to realize that free expression is simply not seen by them as a dominant value. Soviet observers of the American scene are equally dismayed at what they look on as our obsession with private property and profit, which they are likely to consider harmful and corrupting. In other words, Soviet and American value structures are different. Although stating it this way may appear to be a platitude, the inability of members of each culture to perceive the other's value structure has engendered considerable suspicion and perhaps endangered world peace.

Counselors can make direct use of a number of philosophical constructs in the area of values. Some philosophers have categorized two kinds of values: *conceived* and *operative.* A conceived value is one that an individual verbalizes. An operative value is what one is observed to desire. For instance, counselors may express health as a conceived value; they say that they believe it is important to stay healthy. These same individuals may smoke heavily even though they "know" they are probably injuring their health. The counselor will frequently note that a client is suffering from a personal problem that on analysis may be diagnosed as a conflict between a conceived and an operative value. One may simultaneously say that it is a good thing to obey authority yet in fact experience constant friction with parents because one feels they are unreasonable.

Or, in another situation, counselors may note that clients talk about an operational value such as success. However, some clients do not really exert the kind of effort that "success" is thought to require. What may be happening is that the client really wishes fulfillment, a cultural value that, in recent years, has begun to loom important in the lives of many people. The phenomenon—perhaps growing more frequent—of college students receiving a B.A. in business administration and then abandoning the field to live what others may view as a marginal existence as a leathercraft worker suggests that traditionally defined norms of success are losing some of their appeal. In this instance we can perhaps appreciate the growing awareness of philosophy by counselors. The boy or girl who has strife-ridden relationships with parents or other authorities provides a problem that counselors tend to analyze in psychological terms; and of course it is a psychological problem. But the problem may also be approached with the philosopher's insights, and to see the distinction between an operative and a conceived value may enhance both understanding of the problem and treatment of it.

Philosophical and psychological integration

Another illustration of the bearing of philosophy on counselors is shown in the similarity between an integrated personality and an integrated philosophical system. There seems to be some agreement that in a healthy personality the different elements are integrated. The individual's perception of self is in harmony with reality; desires match the moral code; value structure is so arranged that one knows not only what one wants but how much it is wanted. In philosophical terms, one has an integrated axiological position—a harmonious relationship between all parts of wants, wishes, and desires.

In American culture this is extremely difficult, for most Americans prefer an eclectic outlook, assuming that the opposite of eclecticism is dogmatism or rigidity. Counselors should recognize that, given such a preference, many of us tend to be in a constant conflict, for the culture tells us to prefer all values—tact and self-assertion, generosity and self-interest, gentleness and toughness, innocence and sophistication—without providing us with techniques for resolving inevitable conflict.

From philosophy—particularly some schools of philosophy—we have come to see that it is possible to put together either a piecemeal, haphazard, eclectic patchwork of philosophical positions or a unified, harmonious, consistent position. Realization of this fact by counselors suggests that the goal of counseling may be phrased in philosophical terms: to assist individuals to reach the maximum use of

their potential requires that they develop a consistent philosophical outlook.

Philosophy as a plan for living

The last point suggests that one definition of philosophy is of potential interest to counselors. Philosophy has been defined as a plan for living. Behind this very short and simple definition lie some fairly profound meanings. Philosophy is in part an analysis of what people do. It is an analysis not of a given action at one particular time and place but rather of the generalized *meaning* of that action. To analyze human behavior in philosophical terms is to ask serious questions about what people value, whether they should value it, whether this value fits in with a pattern of values, whether the valuing of something hampers or assists other important values. Further, philosophy asks questions about existence and reality; for example, "What do I take to be real, and what is the meaning of this reality?" This last question suggests another philosophical category, theories of knowledge. Theories of knowledge have to do with types and validity of knowledge. Important questions are, "How do I know what is true?" "How can I be certain?" "Is it possible to arrive at certain knowledge, or is all knowledge uncertain and shifting?"

These questions are precisely the ones individuals ask when they face a problem and begin to think about some of its deeper meanings and implications. Adult clients who come to talk to a counselor about midlife career changes will, if they wish to think in a considered, reflective fashion, ask questions about reality, values, and knowledge. Why? Because they must ask, "What career shift should I choose that will satisfy my values and meet my needs?" "If this new career requires x number of years of training, do I want it badly enough to expend the time, energy, and money?" "How do I *know* that I have the necessary abilities and personality for this new career?" And in the asking of these questions, they will possibly come to see that their answers depend on what they *take* to be real. Counselors should probably take the conceptualization of philosophy as a plan for living more seriously and not be tempted to think of philosophy as an academic abstraction. To take this concept seriously would mean, at the very least, that counselors concentrate on helping clients make decisions; becoming aware of alternatives and consequences.

Sociology and anthropology

Sociology and anthropology arose in the nineteenth century as certain investigators began systematically to study the social interactions of cultures both present and past.[10] Cultural (or social) anthropologists tend to look at what they call *cultural universals*—behavior that may be found in all known cultures—such as religion, technology, the family, music, art, written or folk literature, and others. Although anthropologists differ somewhat at the theoretical level, there seems to be some agreement that their function is to investigate cultural patterns in order to see how the collective behavior forms a unity. Sociologists have many of the same concerns and use the same procedures as anthropologists, but they are likely to emphasize particular institutions within a culture. Studies by sociologists have ranged across areas as diverse as the Hollywood movie industry, socioeconomic status, foreman-worker relations, Puerto Rican slum dwellers, the function of dance studios, the John Birch Society, and the current interest in UFOs.

Relativism

From the methods of investigation of these two disciplines—assisted perhaps by philosophers—has developed relativism. In previous centuries social thinkers tended to assert that there were indeed good and true values and whatever varied from these values was undesirable, dangerous, or evil. In the last century it was recognized that the supposedly eternally true and good absolute was, in fact, the particular preference of a particular group at a particular time. Values, it was seen, not only varied from place to place but changed slowly even within a certain geographical location. The inability to see one's own values in relation to others' or to perceive that values within a given place do change had resulted in equating the values of one's own culture with absolutes.

The theory that values were related to culture, historical time, and geographical location flowed from the sociologists' and anthropologists' study of behavior *among* and *within* cultures. Not only does behavior vary considerably, but even a particular kind of behavior is perceived differently by different persons. For instance, sexual patterns are not uniform. All cultures, say anthropologists, have rules and regulations about sexual behavior, but what is believed good in a Polynesian culture may be thought reprehensible in another culture.

All too often, relativism is equated with the intellectually questionable idea that one value is about as good as another, that one cannot "prove" any choice better or worse, or that "everything" reduces to a matter of "mere opinion." However, relativism, from its inception with the American Pragmatists shortly before the turn of the century, is a more profound position than this stereotype. Relativism, in part, means that (1) any value is relative to some other value, (2) values are chosen in a context, and (3) people ought to make choices with an awareness of consequences. Many counselors—whether knowingly or not—act as if they had adopted a relativistic framework. They constantly ask clients questions such as, "What does this mean to you?" "Would you rather . . . ?" "What might happen if . . . ?" "Do you think you could live with a decision to . . . ?" "How do you think *x* feels about this?" Such questions form a pattern and this pattern conforms to the three characteristics of relativism enumerated above.

Sociologists have uncovered often disturbing differences within our culture. It is widely believed that economic self-interest is an absolutely dependable motivation; people work because they wish to accumulate money in order to buy possessions, gain status, and so on; to motivate someone, we offer money as a reward. However, the Appalachian mountaineers do not hold money in the same esteem as the dominant culture does. A person may find a job but work for only a few weeks, just long enough to earn the money to visit a cousin in the next county. Such individuals value a

---

[10] It will help readers relatively unfamiliar with the social sciences if they will think of anthropology and sociology—and all other social sciences—as a circus tent containing a number of big shows and numerous side shows. Anthropologists, for instance, may engage in the same activities as biologists, geneticists, chemists, archeologists, statisticians, and philosophers. That is, the interests and methods of inquiry of investigators in the field of anthropology owe much to other disciplines.

certain kind of personal relationship much more than they value money. Their perception of money is different from that of the dominant culture and their value structure is different. They are not motivated by what is thought to be a powerful incentive.

By the same token, there are differences in perceptions of education. Education is held by the dominant culture to be an unqualifiedly good thing; it not only liberates one and ex pands one's horizons, but it is also the means of "rising" in the world. However, some segments of society believe that education is actually detrimental: it makes one less warmly human; it turns children away from their parents; it fills minds with weird ideas and—among some religious funda-mentalists—education is believed to make people ungodly and irreligious.

The differences in the perception of values have impor-tant implications for psychologists, sociologists, social workers, teachers, and counselors. Helping professionals have not found it effective to express indignation or de-liver lectures on their clients' faulty attitudes. Despite the seeming inappropriateness or self-defeating results of such attitudes counselors know that individuals have learned them in much the same way that counselors have learned theirs. Another implication is that counselors will be inef-fective unless they can somehow enter the frame of refer-ence, the value structure, of their clients. Presumably, looking at attitudes, values, beliefs, and behavior from an external, supposedly objective viewpoint does not seem to assist the counselor very much in dealing with the client's problems.

To understand that values differ and that counselors need to view the perceptions of clients in a more sensitive and sympathetic light does not, of course, eliminate the problem of deciding which values are to be preferred. It is useful to understand that the child from another cultural background views work differently from the way a middle-class child in the United States does, and it is valuable to realize that not all children have a repugnance for physical conflict, but the value issue is not thereby settled. However, when coun-selors are aware that clients do have a value structure and do not see parts of the world the same way they do, coun-selors are in a better position to establish a closer working relationship with them. When values and behavior no longer seem perverse, outlandish, or immoral, some of the barriers that prevent effective interaction have been removed.

Another implication of the method and findings of an-thropologists, sociologists, and biological scientists is that human behavior is not determined in advance by heredity, nor is an individual a passive object to be shaped by the en-vironment. Neither environmental determinism nor its op-posite, hereditarianism, is seen as a particularly fruitful way of fully explaining behavior. Human beings are the product of an interaction between their biological inheritance and their social and physical environment.[11] In recent years, the nature-nurture, heredity-environment conflict has risen again. Also popular in the last decade or so is the notion that humankind is naturally aggressive.[12]

To gain a relatively adequate description of what a person is and does requires that we examine him or her both as an individual and as a member of a group. Studying a unique individual yields data different from, but not necessarily contradictory to, the kind of data derived from looking at that person as a group member.

The significance of this position can be seen only if it is contrasted with the nineteenth-century view of humans and their behavior. The tendency then was to insist either that humankind was "formed" by its environment or that its destiny was irrevocably sealed by heredity. Those who took the former stand suggested that all one needed to do was change the conditions of the environment and a person could be changed in any desired direction. Those who be-

[11] Although—and this is frustrating—precisely what is an inherited characteristic and what is clearly the function of environment be-comes increasingly less and not more clear!

[12] Scholarly literature on aggression dates back many years. An early although still interesting work is Edwin R. Guthrie, *The Psychology of Human Conflict* (New York: Harper & Brothers, 1938). The re-nowned ethologist Konrad Lorenz has authored many works on the subject, of which *On Aggression* (New York: Harcourt Brace Jovanovich, 1966), an English translation, is one of the best known. A good summary of the topic is Anthony Storr, *Human Aggression* (New York: Bantam Books, 1970). A popular writer on the subject is Desmond Morris, *The Naked Ape: A Zoologist's Study of the Human Animal* (New York: McGraw-Hill, 1967). Another popular writer—not a social scientist but a playwright—is Robert Ardrey, whose *Territorial Imperative: A Personal Inquiry into the Animal Origins of Property and Nations* (New York: Atheneum, 1966) was widely read during the 1960s but who has modified his position somewhat. In general, anthropologists do not accept the notion of innately aggressive human beings, preferring to believe that what is called "aggression," "belligerency," or other synonyms is learned rather than innate.

lieved the latter felt that no amount of environmental change could affect people, for they would be precisely whatever they would be. There seemed no other course, therefore, but to ignore either inherited influences or environment.

With the shift to an interactive position it became possible for social and biological scientists to study human beings in their totality. Anthropologists could investigate cultural patterns, sociologists began to look at class structure, both of them could concentrate on value structure and on the ways values are altered. Another significant change flowing from this new view of human nature was that social scientists from different disciplines merged their knowledge and methods in a combined approach known as the *interdisciplinary* method. What have been some of the findings of this approach, and how can they be utilized by counselors?

Class and status

In the 1920s, sociologists such as Robert Lynd and Helen Merrell Lynd and W. Lloyd Warner became interested in the phenomenon of social class.[13] Their findings are, by now, a standard part of every introductory sociology course. But the implications of their findings have yet to be widely known or understood. Despite the belief that the United States was a one-class society, it was demonstrated that there was a large lower socioeconomic and a small but powerful upper class. The lower class was seen to be impoverished, politically powerless, and very much at a disadvantage in terms of education, housing, and the law. The young people of the lower socioeconomic class have tended not to value education, to leave school before graduation, to exhibit hostility to teachers and other school officials, to settle disputes with physical violence, to be indifferent to cleanliness, and to be in trouble with the law. In short, we discovered precisely what was not supposed to be there: a large part of society did not share in the dominant American values and, despite official dogma, faced barriers to vertical mobility.

As sociologists began to look at the behavior associated with socio-economic class membership with some objectivity, they also focused on the response of schools to impoverished youth—who frequently are also members of ethnic minorities. They discovered that teachers, either middle class themselves or inclined to identify with middle-class values, were often indifferent or hostile to their lower-class students. School administrators were somewhat puzzled by these children. They could cope with misbehaving middle-class students by the usual means, but threats to fail or expel children who were indifferent to grades and who actively disliked school did not avail. Nor was it altogether clear to counselors what their practices should be, for discipline was frowned on by most counseling theorists. More recently, counselors have been asking how they can better work with culturally different clients.[14]

At the other end of the socioeconomic spectrum, sociologists began to illuminate motives that proved to be embarrassing. The exertion of effort to gain status or prestige is widely regarded as stemming from less pure motivation. Thus, if scientists work long hours in a laboratory, their efforts will be approved as beneficial for humanity—the discovery of a new drug, say, or a new inoculation process. They are not likely to say that they are working for recognition, fame, or status; if they do, they will be regarded as improperly motivated. Similarly, it may be seen but denied that a very powerful motivant for students is status: the status that accrues when one makes A grades, is a member of the football squad, or is accepted by one of the "better" colleges.

Counselors are often pressured to see that a student take a college-prep curriculum or to pull wires so that the student is admitted to Princeton. They may succumb to such pressures, although reluctantly, because they know that the student cannot handle a college-prep curriculum and should not apply to Princeton. To refuse to knuckle under to the pressures is perhaps to invite the criticism that one is not doing all one can for the students. The point is that, although one may talk of getting a "quality" education for a child, the real motivation may be to acquire status. The real motive, the acquisition of status, is concealed from oneself.

[13] W. Lloyd Warner, *Yankee City* (New Haven, Conn.: Yale University Press, 1963), and Robert Lynd and Helen Merrell Lynd, *Middletown* (New York: Harcourt, Brace & Co., 1929).

[14] See, for example, Paul B. Pederson, ed., "Special Feature: Counseling Across Cultures," *Personnel and Guidance Journal*, 56 (April 1978), 457–484.

Behavioral change and continuity

Social scientists have revealed that behavior is likely to persist over a long period of time. Although individuals are relatively flexible—in the sense that behavioral change does take place—the patterns of a given culture, subculture, or other group tend to resist change. It is the failure to realize this that has defeated so many well-intentioned attempts by counselors and teachers.

Influenced by the prevailing norms of one's environment, an individual does not drop them when entering a different environment with different norms. Having learned a code of behavior in the home for the first six years, one does not typically make a radical change to accommodate the new environment. For many economically poor children the school is a new environment, and much in it is at variance with what they have learned as proper and desirable. Thus the school's attempt to change their behavior fails. They grow up to become the kind of adults their parents are—and tend to raise their own children in much the same way. That is, the behavior patterns of the poor can endure from decade to decade. If counselors and teachers wish to have some effect on behavior, they seemingly must understand more about the mechanics of behavioral persistence and change.

Research on social class, caste, ethnicity, and similar concepts is now more than half a century old. Recent cultural experiences suggest that such research is more, not less, relevant to the present and that issues that affect social class, ethnicity, status, race, and so forth, are more rather than less pressing. For instance, government policy, especially since the Kennedy-Johnson years of the 1960s is based on the assumption that more federal spending and better nationwide social programs will somehow "help" the poor and the "less fortunate." For reasons that are not clear, the results of these national policies have been less than encouraging. Despite many millions of dollars, the poor still continue to swell statistics on delinquency, unemployment, violence, alcoholism, family instability, and so forth.

Although we do not face—at least in the immediate future—the likelihood of social class resentment exploding in violence, problems associated with disadvantaged youth still tend to plague schools and especially counselors. Counselors have discovered over the years that goals that motivate middle-class youth—that is, success follows effort and self-denial—have not had the same effect on the disadvantaged. In effect, what this means is that while middle-class children do their classwork and assignments without too much overt rebellion, many other children tend to become discouraged, to become defiant and unruly and then to drop out. Once again, teachers and counselors learn that any and all social-economic problems become *school* problems where, in fact, they are not amenable to an educational solution, by itself.

Another kind of problem, resulting from behavior rigidity, is essentially the dilemma of confused sexual role. The behavior expected of a boy or girl is not, as anthropologists have pointed out, unvarying. Sexual roles are defined by each culture: this particular activity, this manner of dress, this kind of behavior are deemed masculine or feminine, and the definition of masculinity or femininity is by no means as universal as is usually believed. In past years the woman in our culture was supposed to be a subservient wife, a demure helpmate who bore and raised children and submitted patiently to her husband. The husband was expected to be the chief breadwinner and the head of the household. This description sounds quaint now, for much has happened to alter the traditional roles of husband and wife—including more education for girls. Girls are encouraged to take an academic major, to go to college and graduate school, to choose "exciting" careers, and, in general, to create an existence for themselves independent of motherhood.

Unfortunately, as women are emancipated from the older roles and trained for new ones, all girls or women are not able to make a clear identification with either. Thus, although a young girl may be encouraged to develop her talent by going to college, she is also pushed toward "going steady," engagement, marriage. Whichever choice she makes, judged by one set of values, is wrong. Too, the proper role of the well-educated wife and mother is by no means clear. She is told to find "fulfillment" in marriage, but the usual child raising, conventional community affairs, and entertainment often seem most unfulfilling.[15]

[15] See Betty Friedan, *The Feminine Mystique* (New York: W. W. Norton & Company, 1963) and Betty Yorburg, *Sexual Identity: Sex Roles and Social Change* (New York: Wiley-Intersciences, 1973). For an introduction to the subject, see F. A. Guerard "Sexism and Education" in Maurice P. Hunt, *Foundations of Education, Social and Cultural Perspectives* (New York: Holt, Rinehart and Winston, 1975).

The counselor who cannot convince the mathematically talented girl to take trigonometry because, in the girl's eyes, math and science are not "girls' subjects" is a victim of cultural conflict. At one time mathematics and science were *not* "girls' subjects" because girls were not thought to have sufficient intellect to profit by intellectually demanding studies. That they can is a matter of psychological fact, that the *perception* of their inadequacy, born of a time when women were regarded as morally and intellectually inferior, has changed but little is also a matter of fact. What is at fault is described as the *social* or *cultural lag:* technological conditions have changed, but habits and beliefs from previous times persist—and conflict with the cultural patterns engendered by technology.

In recent years, there have been some important but by no means dominant shifts in marriage, family form, and sex roles. First, the notion of monogamy coupled with the nuclear family, although not dead, is facing competition with such innovations as stable premarital cohabitation, group marriage, swinging, open marriage, and short-term noncommittal relationships. Similarly, what constitutes "proper" sex role and sexual identification is undergoing what appears to be considerable change. The notions of man as the dominant, aggressive breadwinner and woman as the gentle, domesticated, family-centered "homemaker" are clearly changing as more and more couples experiment with different roles. Thus, men are staying home and raising children while women pursue careers. The implications of such changes are by no means clear. Certainly, they do have implications for such traditional practices as assigning girls to home economics and boys to industrial arts, of investing most or all of the athletic budget on boys' and but token amounts on girls' competitive sports; of scheduling smart boys into science, mathematics, and other college prep courses and girls into general education or vocational training. Schools are beginning to recognize such important changes and altering their structure to cope with them.

The scientific method

Counselors, as we have seen, have learned a great deal from the content of anthropology and sociology. Information about social class, cultural patterns, the hidden motivation of status, and the cultural lag has much bearing on what

counselors do. However, equally important is the method by which knowledge is acquired. Although the scientific method of attaining knowledge has been built up by all of the social, physical, and natural sciences, we are particularly indebted to sociology and anthropology. The last fifty years have seen the replacement of absolutistic, one-sided (for example, hereditarian *or* environmentalist), and sentimental views of humans and society by much more dependable and fruitful outlooks.

Just as it is no longer acceptable for a teacher or counselor to say, "Well, of course Joe flunked all of his subjects; what else could one expect of someone with his background?," it is no longer reasonable to assert, "We'd better install a vocational curriculum and counsel these students into it because they are not going to be helped by anything else." The patent absurdity of these two statements is essentially a testimony to the method and content of the social sciences and to the effect they have had in forcing us to substitute empirical data for wishful thinking, romanticism, and tradition.

Political science

Political science concerns itself with the examination of political power. This oversimplified statement conceals both the complexity of political power and the variety of methods employed by political scientists to investigate the subject. Political scientists' interests include Congressional behavior, the collection of financial contributions to political parties by industry, the voting patterns of various population blocks, the oratory of partisan politicians, the distribution of power in corporate conglomerates, and the public school as a political institution. A good many political scientists do not gather empirical data or observe particular institutions but interpret and analyze the mass of material collected by others. They are called political theorists, and their mode of inquiry is almost indistinguishable from that of philosophers.

Power—what is it?

Investigators of industry and government early in this century became aware of the difference between the symbol of power and the actual reality. Those who were supposed to command, those who had the appearance of power, were not always the ones who actually exercised power. The prime minister, king, or school superintendent, it was discovered, frequently did not make decisions, nor was he or she able to insist that others comply with his or her decisions. This observation led to a definition of power which, in simplified terms, is the actual and effective use of authority such that when one gives a command, it will, in fact, be obeyed. The *nominal* holder of power—the mayor, senator, principal, or chamber of commerce leader—may or may not be the real wielder of power. The latter may be unknown to the public, may consist of a small oligarchy, may deny that he or she has any power, or may be identical with the nominal holder of power.

The power structure

The political scientist's concentration on power and those who control it has led to a construct known as *power structure*. According to the democratic mythology, the people always hold power; only leaders elected by them may exercise power and then in but a limited way. To talk about a power structure—a power "elite," in the words of the late C. Wright Mills—seems a flat contradiction in a democracy. However, a power structure does exist, is clearly operative in any community, and has much relevance to public schools and social agencies.

School counselors frequently complain because they are relegated to quasi-administrative tasks or even clerical jobs. Although they have been told that their job is to counsel students, they spend more and more time in checking attendance, seeking scholarships, sponsoring student government, or doing other jobs distantly related to counseling. Yet they are reluctant to tell administrators that they are counselors and that they cannot or will not be an arm of the administration. They seem to feel that administrators are "in charge" of the school, that they have authority, and that they have no choice but to accede to their wishes. This attitude ignores two questions: where, exactly, does an administrator's authority stop? Does an administrator have the authority to assign a counselor jobs that simply do not fit within the latter's professionally defined responsibilities? If these questions are asked, it may be seen that the administrator does not have anything like unlimited power.

Of crucial concern to counselors, regardless of setting in which employed, is the relationship of the school or agency to the community and the power structure. Those within education have expressed approximately the same grievances and the same beliefs for a century.[16] Changes in schools, when they do arrive, come so slowly that they are almost invariably too little or too late. One analysis of the relatively slow improvements holds that real power does not lie in the hands of professional educators. Quite typically it lies in the hands of the power structure *outside* education, at both the local and the state levels. Thus, local boards of education, consisting almost always of upper-middle-class or upper-class lay leaders, make decisions as to curriculum, salary, personnel, standards, and so on, that are often contrary to the desires of professional school people. At the state level, certification or licensure commissions—which grant licenses or certificates to administrators, counselors, psychologists, teachers, and others—are staffed entirely by nonprofessionals. Indeed, a number of state constitutions specifically prohibit professional persons from serving on certification commissions. To be blunt, the raising of standards for a number of professionals (for example, counselors) is hampered in several states. On the face of it, no one could conceivably advance a rational argument for supporting low standards. Yet reflection will disclose that the higher the licensing standards, the higher the salary; the higher the salary, the more money required to support education. It is the property tax—which falls most heavily on large property owners who are most likely to be the power structure—that largely finances education. The power structure, therefore, can act against schools whenever the schools wish to engage in activities that are perceived to be against its interests.[17]

Recently, teachers' organizations—the distinction between professional associations and unions has dimin-

---

[16] On the unlikely assumption that the reader is not aware of them, we list: low salaries, unstable tenure, inadequate facilities, too little opportunity to introduce innovations, lack of academic freedom, lack of support for the teacher in enforcing discipline, too much time spent on clerical details, and a plethora of rules and regulations that have little to do with teaching or learning.

[17] In a town in which the author lived the power structure threw its weight behind an enrichment program and a stronger college-prep curriculum. It defeated a program to strengthen remedial reading, vocational training, and the counseling program. The latter improvement would have benefited disadvantaged students who were in the numerical majority.

ished—have become increasingly militant. Teachers, along with police officers, firefighters, and other government employees, have shown little hesitation to strike and to engage in "job actions." As a related phenomenon, courts have ruled that students have constitutionally protected rights to express themselves and to disagree with their elders in school newspapers, even if such disagreement is blunt, tactless, and offensive. Such phenomena have rearranged the power distribution so that administrators and school boards no longer exert almost exclusive control. Counselors are caught somewhere in the ambiguous middle of such change. One cannot easily predict what counselors might or should do; but more and more seem to be positioning themselves as a separate profession and exerting efforts to have their goals and demands realized.

The point is not that the power structure behaves in an unethical or illegal manner—although it may at times. The point is that there is a power structure, which is not supposed to exist and the operations of which tend to be ignored, particularly by school people. For this reason counselors have the responsibility of understanding and using political power.

Democracy

Democracy was not invented by political scientists, but political scientists and historians have devoted much time to describing it and theorizing about it. A good deal of what has been written and said in an attempt to relate democracy to education is a mixture of hollow verbalisms and clichés. The tendency is to confuse democracy with freedom or liberty—it is associated with freedom but is not the equivalent of it—or else to state the democracy *requires* social equality, economic opportunity, education, or a number of other values.

Democracy is simply a sociopolitical form of organization in which the people make basic decisions and elect those who govern them. In addition, there is an implication that whatever decision is made, unless it is rescinded or modified, all will abide by it equally.

In reality, a democracy does not require any specific amount or kind of education. In some democracies public education has been undeveloped; in others it is widespread. It does not seem to be defensible to state that because we have a democracy everyone must go to school.

However, it does seem justified to say that, given the complexity of the decision-making process in this country, decision-making skills are required. They can be learned in classrooms as teachers show students how to use information, formulate hypotheses, spot logical fallacies, and learn the values of compromise and adjustment. It is precisely the emphasis on decision making that should distinguish schools in a democracy from those in a nondemocratic or a totalitarian country—although American teachers are often hard put to explain just why this is so.

Viewed from this framework, the counselor in a democracy has an analogous function. In American democracy, which is characterized by a considerable degree of freedom and openness, emphasis is also placed on independent decision making in other than political contexts. Persons are generally called on to make choices about vocation; future education and training; mate; number of children; location, size, and cost of a dwelling; and an almost infinite variety of other matters.[18] Counselors, therefore, are seemingly required to help their clientele to be more thoughtful and reflective—that is, to be more skillful in decision making.

Counselors function not to help an individual become more competent at making this or that decision, although counselors may be called on for advice or help on a particular problem. The counselor, many theoreticians (see Chapters 8 and 9) assert, is supposed to help individuals be more autonomous, more independent, more intelligent as individuals. The assumption is that as a result of counseling a person does not become more effective in simply one area, say about vocational goals, but becomes more effective in all areas of life.

Definitions of counseling and the many theoretical systems that are used to describe the role of counselors are discussed elsewhere in this book. Suffice it to say here that, by any definition of counseling, the end result is an individual who is able to think about his or her problems in a more competent or effective way than before. It is the focus on decision making or problem solving and its relation to democracy and counseling that appears to be most important.

It has occurred to this writer that there is a particularly confusing and complex situation that makes it difficult for

[18] In other societies one's vocation may be inherited or chosen by the government. The children may be raised by the state in nursery schools. One's parents may arrange one's marriage. Or children may be raised in a particular predetermined, prescribed manner.

teachers and counselors to function in a democratic manner. There seem to have been two different and unrelated cultures, which are called the Verbal Culture and the Classroom Culture.[19] The former consists of the oughts and shoulds of philosophers and social critics and revolves around such concepts as democratic self-rule, "growth," "creativity," and the like. The Verbal Culture has told teachers and counselors what ought to be done and how they should behave as professionals. However, the Classroom Culture is quite different. It has to do with the actual authoritarian, subject matter–centered, ground-covering approach. It has appeared that school people have talked about growth, democracy, and autonomous decisions but have tended to behave in the opposite manner. The notion of two cultures, distantly related then, is perhaps accurate.

In the first edition of this book, I wrote "Schools therefore have the unique responsibility of helping future adults become more proficient at decision making. From this point of view, counselors are persons who, working in a one-to-one relationship, assist in the improvement of decision making." There is no valid reason to disavow such a view now, but it should be pointed out that school structure and practices will need to change before such a goal is implemented in any consistent fashion. Clearly, if decision making is important in American society—and it is—then traditional school structure and practices must change.

Economics

Economics is that social science that studies the pattern of human production, consumption, and distribution. As may be inferred from the preceding examination of sociology, anthropology, and political science, it is a discipline whose members pursue many different specialties. Some economists, called *econometricians*, specialize in the compilation and analysis of economic statistics. Others study the economic history of a particular country or even of a particular industry. Some economists specialize in a particular part of the world, as, for instance, Soviet Russia or

Latin America. Some study one institution, such as money and banking. Some share the same interests as political scientists or sociologists, and others work closely with anthropologists. The father of modern-day economics, Adam Smith, thought of himself as philosopher, and a number of economists today are essentially philosophers.

Humans as economic beings

Humans everywhere are economic beings. They produce things, have systems for distributing them, and consume them. Some economic systems are extremely complex—our own, for example, or Soviet Russia's or that of any highly industrialized society. Others are comparatively simple, such as that of the Australian aborigine, who has very little in the way of technology and is a nomadic hunter and food gatherer. In the process of producing, distributing, and consuming, different cultures devise rather elaborate systems and procedures, which have implications for much more than economic activities. For instance, the accumulation of economic power in our society—and many others—almost always generates political power, and this, as we have seen, creates political problems. Or, in the process of devising a monetary and banking system to finance complex factories, there are ramifications extending to much more than factories. Likewise, the system of long-term financing of industry and agriculture, called the stock market, has raised a host of ethical problems relating to the honest sale of stocks and bonds.

Few today are able to stand aloof from economic activities. By the very existence of the need to satisfy their wants for food, shelter, clothing, and other things, all individuals are enmeshed in an economy. But, what is important from our standpoint, the way people theorize about economic activities also constitutes a set of influences, and it is the influence of economic theorizing that we propose to examine.

Economic theory

Economist John Kenneth Galbraith, Harvard professor, has advanced an explanation of economic theory as it affects

[19] The author has developed this idea in "Education as Culture: An Exploration into a Fragile Partnership" (unpublished manuscript, Purdue University, 1978).

production and consumption.[20] The classical economists who wrote in the late eighteenth and early nineteenth centuries operated under the assumption that production would always be unable to satisfy consumption. That is, human wants would always outstrip the capacity of factories and farms to meet them. An economy of scarcity was implied, in which most would be in need, famines would always threaten, and poverty would be the norm. However, in this country in particular, a happy combination of abundant natural resources, a useful system of waterways, the presence of a large labor force that became increasingly better trained, a steady supply of fertile inventors, and a relative absence of destructive and costly wars has made possible what was unimaginable a hundred or more years ago: an economy of abundance. Our factories and farms have been able to produce more than we can consume. (I am aware that this hypothesis does not account for the fact that we, too, have a large number of people without sufficient purchasing power to buy what they want or need. Nevertheless, we have enormously increased the capacity of factories and farms to produce.)

Thus, we have something of a paradox: we are operating on an economic theory of a century ago, which held that human wants would never be met adequately by the means of production; but in fact, our technology has enabled us to produce goods in numbers larger than most of us can consume. One would imagine, if the basic tenet of capitalism were entirely true, that factory owners would simply produce fewer products, just enough to meet consumer need. However, says Galbraith, this is not the case. Given the capacity of factories to produce more than can be consumed, we have *increased* our productive capacity and trained the populace to consume ever more and more. Advertising, for instance, is designed to whet our appetites for things that, in all probability, we could easily exist without. Designing products deliberately to malfunction after a certain period of time, or changing styles on expensive commodities such as refrigerators, ranges, and automobiles (called *planned obsolescence*) is a device, apparently, to get consumers to dispose of their products and buy new ones. Another such economic technique includes long-term installment buying.

With such extremely effective production, the result is a materialistic philosophy and large numbers of people who perpetually generate desires for material objects and status. Both are of direct concern to counselors, who must work with value conflicts. The materialistic philosophy may be seen in the pervasive, continual, and seemingly irrational desire to own things. Some recent studies have noted a close correlation between high school student possession of automobiles and poor academic grades. In view of the many millions of dollars automobile manufacturers spend to create a desire for their product,[21] it is to be expected that individuals will look for after-hours jobs in order to buy and maintain cars. The problem is of course compounded by the fact that, once the cars are bought, students apparently drive them in preference to studying.

A materialistic philosophy would not be inappropriate if there were no other contending philosophies. However, there is also the philosophy emphasizing the importance of the intangibles—good character, cooperation, self-denial, studying for its own sake. Young people growing up in our culture are faced by a very basic value conflict in that they simply do not know what is good. Should they exhibit expensive and stylish clothing or is it better to study for its purely intellectual values? Counselors, in one sense, sometimes contribute to this value conflict, for at the same time that the administrator and the teacher talk about the values inherent in knowledge for its own sake counselors display charts comparing the lifetime salaries of those who do and do not go to college.

Much attention has been paid recently to the hostility, uncooperativeness, and antiauthoritarian attitudes of the economic "have-nots" in American society. Investigations have been made and a wide variety of causes have been adduced to explain these behaviors. However, a relatively ignored factor is frustration—the frustration of having one's appetite for goods and status whetted and then being unable to gratify it. Other cultures have large masses of poor

---

[20] Economics has been called "the dismal science," possibly because the prose of economics is depressingly difficult to read. In addition to Heilbronner, Galbraith is one of the few exceptions. Readers unfamiliar with economics who wish to inquire further into Galbraith's theories should consult his *The New Industrial State*, 2nd ed., rev. (Boston: Houghton Mifflin Company, 1971) and *Almost Everyone's Guide to Economics* (Boston: Houghton Mifflin Company, 1978), coauthored by Nicole Salinger.

[21] For a popular treatment see Vance Packard, *The Waste Makers* (New York: David McKay Co., 1966), and Ralph Nader, *Unsafe at Any Speed* (New York: Grossman Publishers, 1965).

people, larger and poorer than our own. But our poor are told from infancy that one must own things, that possessions lend status, yet for a number of reasons they are unable to purchase what is held up as supremely desirable. It does not seem far-fetched to conjecture that some of the rebelliousness and aggressiveness often directed at teachers and school property is simply displaced aggression against a society that expertly and systematically frustrates the poor.

Many other instances could be cited wherein our economy predisposes to value conflicts. One more fairly simple one will suffice. Cigarette smoking is uniformly denounced by schools, and sufficient scientific evidence has been gathered to show causal relationship between cigarette smoking and diseases ranging from cancer to emphysema. Notwithstanding this and the propaganda barrage directed against cigarettes in social studies, biology, and health classes, students continue to find themselves in trouble with the vice principal for smoking illegally on school grounds. Again, the millions of dollars spent on advertising by tobacco manufacturers have paid off by convincing young people that smoking is sophisticated. If one asks a basic question—why does our society tolerate and even encourage the tobacco industry by means of agricultural subsidies?—the answer is not difficult to find. The growing, manufacture, and distribution of tobacco is a billion-dollar industry, and harming the tobacco industry would, it is held, wreak havoc with our economy. The point is that the decision to perpetuate the tobacco industry is one in which the value of health is weighed against an economic value, and the economic value, at least up until now, has clearly prevailed. Given the extremely high cultural value placed on the alleged economic desirability of selling cars and cigarettes, it behooves counselors to think more seriously about the importance of economic values in our way of life.

Economic motivation

The discussion above leads us naturally into a consideration of the meaning of economic motivation. To say that all of us respond to economic motivation is too simple. The history of Western civilization has seen a rather ambiguous attitude toward it. During the early Christian and medieval eras, the official belief was that good people were those who spent their time contemplating God and withdrawing from the world, for love of money, status, wealth, and possessions

was at the root of all evil. A desire either to realize a profit from one's investment in time or money or to own possessions was considered incompatible with a good life. With the rise of capitalism, however, grew the belief that not only was economic motivation legitimate but the good person was one who finished life as the successful entrepreneur, owner of a large fortune, and possessor of many goods. Today, both traditions exist side by side: we are told that it is desirable to live in tranquillity and to be happy with our lot, and we are also told that it is better to be ambitious, work hard, make more money, and increase our supply of goods. Counselors would do well to understand this cultural contradiction because it is often internalized by their clients and appears to be a factor in predisposing toward intrapersonal conflict.

The same thing is a factor in the life of counselors. One reason counselors have been undercompensated for so long is the public's feeling that an educator's greatest compensation comes from a sense of satisfaction, that the job of counselor, like that of preacher, is a "calling," and that only a poorly motivated person would make an issue of wages and working conditions. This seemingly widespread cultural belief, disappearing now as public school people become more militant, has probably been a barrier to raising salaries. After all, if one is supposed to be impelled by basically altruistic motives, if one's chief aim is to "help" others, why be concerned about the things that motivate union members and others with regrettably worldly goals?

Counselors should, therefore, recognize economic motivation as a factor in their own careers and also assist their clients to appraise it in their lives. There appears to be little or no point for counselors who deal with career problems to ignore, play down, or disguise the meaning of economic motivation. It is something all individuals ought to begin to understand, for it comprises an important part—whether or not consciously ignored—of one's basic value structure.

The key to understanding or appraising the meaning of economic motivation does not lie in the oversimplified procedures of half a century ago. At that time, says educational historian Raymond Callahan, the methods and values of the business world were extended to schools. Efficiency became the goal of education. Schools emulated businesses and applied the same yardsticks and criteria that factories used. The assumption that criteria appropriate for a profit-making institution were also appropriate for public schools was indeed a revolutionary one. Unfortunately, fifty years later this assumption is still very much alive and appears to be another factor in the underfinancing of public education in general and of salaries in particular. We know how to reward successful salespeople: on the basis of how many sales they have made. But, using the same yardstick, how does one adequately compensate the teacher or counselor—on the basis of students' scores on the *Iowa Tests of Educational Development* or how many students were counseled that day? Such quantitative criteria are obviously absurd, but if not these, precisely which ones should be used?

As already indicated in the discussion of democracy, the changes in cultural values that have affected the society as a whole are also affecting teachers and counselors. Recently, the author heard the bitterness of some teachers in California who objected strongly to the governor's pronouncement that school people have a kind of "psychic income" from their vocation and somehow ought to be satisfied with that in preference to simple salary and fringe benefits. School people have traditionally enjoyed the feeling that derives from working with young people but in recent years they have given powerful indications that such is not enough; that they deserve and will demand higher salaries, better fringe benefits, and improved working conditions. In so demanding, school people are in line with the economic motivations of the rest of society.

Another issue—already mentioned on pp. 151–152—has to do with the conflicting values of success, on the one hand, and something called "fulfillment" on the other. "Success" values seem to be intimately tied to the traditional American notion that performance is an all important value. And performance and success are also tied in with the idea that people should strive to "get ahead" and that getting ahead is denoted by the size of one's house, car, and salary, the length and distance of one's vacations, and other such tangible signs. What has happened is that such values, although still powerful among the dominant society, are being replaced for some by other values that emphasize community, sharing, satisfaction, working with one's hands, and the like. The culture quite clearly is changing and counselors need to be attuned to such changes if they wish to function effectively.

To conclude, then, counselors are motivated by the same forces that motivate others. These forces are, in part, economic. And although they have only recently been recognized, it is also the case that other cultural values, in sharp opposition, are being asserted. What this seems to point to is

that counselors need to become aware of the meaning of economic motivations in the life of the culture.

Psychology and psychiatry

Identification

Psychology is that branch of the social sciences that studies human behavior and its interaction with the environment. It is, in a sense, a more general discipline than other social sciences because it does not confine itself to economic or political behavior but takes *all* human behavior as its subject. Psychiatry, although sharing many of the same concerns as psychology, is a branch of medicine. The primary concern of psychiatry is with abnormal human behavior; to put it another way, psychiatry deals with emotional problems that are considered severe.

Psychologists may specialize in physiological psychology, a discipline that borrows heavily from biology and emphasizes such phenomena as the relationship between endocrine flow and behavior or the neurological bases of behavior. Some psychologists are essentially mathematicians or statisticians and assist other experimenters in setting up what are called *experimental designs* and interpreting complex data. Some psychologists will study the behavior of particular groups (for example, industrial psychologists) or become specialists in the psychological aspects of aerospace medicine. Some will study a particular kind of behavior as it is observed in many groups—for example, learning, memory. Counseling psychologists are concerned with the solution of emotional problems and may work in institutional settings or practice privately. Social psychologists study much the same phenomena as political scientists and sociologists. As a social science, psychology is therefore a rather wide-ranging discipline.

When the focus of attention is on disturbed human behavior or emotional problems, psychiatrists and psychologists may combine their skills and backgrounds in order to improve diagnosis and therapy.[22] Although psychiatry is

---

[22] However, relationships between psychologists and psychiatrists are not always sweet. Psychiatrists, because their work is a branch of medicine, often feel that they are better trained, whereas psychologists often feel that they know more about human behavior. The jockeying for status between the two in institutions is a wonder to see and has supplied enough data for several dissertations—done, we might add, by social psychologists.

much older than psychology, specialists in the two fields have been extremely productive during the last seventy-five years, and from a study of their contributions emerge a number of patterns.

Complexity

Like other disciplines, psychology and psychiatry have revealed that human behavior is very complex. Sigmund Freud, the Austrian neurologist and psychiatrist, suggested that the most important human motivations occur at an invisible level, the level of the unconscious or subconscious. Freud felt, and much evidence has confirmed, that what happens in a child's early life—which is almost always consciously forgotten—is crucial to later development. The motivations Freud described, and it is to be recalled that he lived at the end of the Victorian era, involved the hitherto prohibited topic of sexuality.

In psychological laboratories all over Europe and the United States it was also demonstrated that the reasons for people's behavior were not widely recognized. The notion of self-concept was introduced as psychologists learned that the way individuals perceive themselves strongly influences their behavior. A school of theoreticians known as gestalt or field-theory psychologists discovered that whether there is some kind of reality independent of individuals is simply not of psychological value; how people perceive reality constitutes reality for them. Joining forces with sociologists, psychologists found that status and prestige were also important factors in motivating behavior.

These experiments and many others have revealed that human behavior is extraordinarily complex, that people act for reasons that are difficult to describe, and that any simple, unqualified generalization about behavior is probably either wrong or incomplete.

Purpose

At about the turn of the century psychologists began to suggest that human beings were nothing more than clever, complex machines. Just as there were laws that applied to the physical universe (gravity, centrifugal force, and so on), there were also laws that applied to human beings, laws that

governed behavior. Once these laws were discovered, human behavior could be described and predicted completely and perfectly. This somewhat simplistic notion of behavior has since given way to a more complex one. That biologists and physiologists may make important contributions to the study of human behavior is undoubtedly true but human beings are not *reducible* to machines. They have purposes and goals that are not explainable simply by reference to endocrine secretions. If we can understand these goals—and there was a clear implication that in order to do so we must study people in interaction with their physical and social environment—we have a more fruitful means of understanding behavior.

This insight was and still is not accepted by all social scientists, but it is of particular use to counselors. People may exhibit behavior that at first glance appears to be bizarre or irrational. A very bright boy or girl, with a previous record of good grades and cooperative behavior, appears before the counselor, sent by a bewildered teacher who cannot understand why the child is failing all schoolwork and has become defiant. Usually some probing by the counselor reveals that, strange as the behavior is, it is meant to realize some purpose or goal, often one that is not known to the child. For example, the defiant behavior may appear after the birth of a new brother or sister, and despite the fact that the child may be punished severely, it does indeed pay off: obtaining the recognition sought, even if it is of an unpleasant and negative kind.

Another illustration of purpose appears in a witty book called *Games People Play* by Eric Berne, a psychiatrist.[23] Berne describes a large number of apparently weird and self-defeating "games" wherein one person, with the active help of one or many others, repeats a pattern of destructive behavior. In the game *schlemiel*[24] the visitor unendingly spills soup on the host's rug, burns cigarette holes in furniture, or trips over the canapés. The *schlemiel* apologizes profusely and is forgiven by the host. Berne suggests that the *schlemiel* has a purpose, if an unconscious one: the oafishness is simply behavior designed to get forgiveness—in Berne's terms, to achieve a particular "payoff." Although

---

[23] Eric Berne, *Games People Play* (New York: Grove Press, 1964).
[24] "Schlemiel" is a Yiddish word that denotes inept and clumsy people whose lack of coordination or foresight constantly gets them in trouble.

Berne has drawn on psychopathology (serious deviation from a norm of mental health), his ideas have relevance for counselors. If counselors wish to probe beyond the obvious, behind the overt behavior, they may first ask, "What payoff, what purpose, does this person hope for when this is done?"

Probing for purpose is obviously difficult. Often individuals are unaware of their purposes because purposes are part of goal structure. And if social psychologists are correct, we absorb goals almost by osmosis, without much awareness *that* values are being learned or *what* the values are. Further, as most counselors who work with adolescents know, purposes are likely to be conflictual. For instance, many adolescents articulate a strong desire to be independent, that is, to be free of the presumably meddlesome interference of their parents. However, such independence is mitigated by sporadic dependence or by lack of dependable knowledge of how to be independent. Thus, the adolescent who asserts that he or she is going to drop out of the eleventh grade and get some "real" work and live alone and do what he or she wants is likely to be blissfully unaware that (1) jobs with the salary expected are few and far between; (2) it is quite literally impossible to pay for the cars, entertainment, clothes, stereos, and so on, wanted on the salaries available; (3) employers, foremen, and so on, are just as demanding as parents—perhaps more so, because employers can fire one. Thus, the culture tantalizes young people with visions of independence and material plenty while either denying or obscuring the realities that are required to realize the goals.[25]

Conflict

Psychologists describe two kinds of conflict, *interpersonal* and *intrapersonal. Inter*personal conflict is that between or among people. *Intra*personal conflict is the suffering individuals undergo when they have two conflicting desires that they are unable to resolve. When the NAACP and the Ku Klux Klan are at odds with each other, it is a case of interpersonal between-group conflict. When individuals are mis-

erable because they cannot decide whether to obey their parents and go to college, which they do not want to do, or go to work, which they do want to do, they experience intrapersonal conflict. This is conflict *within* an individual, and it arises out of the inability to make a satisfactory decision.

As psychologists have studied the research of anthropologists and sociologists, they have come to realize that intrapersonal conflict is very often the result of *internalizing* conflicts already existing in the culture. The individual who cannot decide whether to attend college or go to work has internalized two conflicting cultural values. It is good to obey authority, to do as one's parents wish; it is also good to do what one wants, to fulfill oneself by choosing the vocation that is most satisfying. Unhappily, one cannot always do both, and sometimes compromise is out of the question. One has to choose either/or. The inability to choose, to establish a clear preference for one value, is at the root of many different conflicts. From one standpoint, the neurotic is a person who is perpetually unable to make a choice without suffering guilt or anxiety.

Learning

Perhaps the most important contribution of psychologists and psychiatrists is their data and theories on learning. In a sense, learning theory is as old as Aristotle and Plato, the Athenian philosophers who addressed themselves to the question of how and why people learn. Other philosophers—Locke, Kant, Rousseau, and Dewey—were concerned with learning, but not until the second half of the nineteenth century did psychologists attempt to study learning systematically and objectively. Unfortunately for counselors, psychologists interested in learning divided into two schools. "Unfortunately" because there is considerable difference between the schools, and most textbook authors have recently tended to ignore it. Both schools, the older associationist, represented by such psychologists as Edward Lee Thorndike and more recently B. F. Skinner, and gestalt or field theory, represented by Kurt Koffka, Max Wertheimer, Wolfgang Kohler, and Kurt Lewin, have attempted to describe learning in specific terms—specific enough so that counselors know what happens when someone learns or does not learn.

[25] See the poignant book by Paul Goodman, *Growing Up Absurd: Problems of Youth in the Organized System* (New York: Random House, 1960) and "Youth Culture in Education" in Hunt, *Foundations of Education*, pp. 71–86.

Briefly, and in a much oversimplified manner, the associationists describe learning as essentially a mechanical matter best detailed in physiological terms. Thorndike, for instance, believed that learning takes place as an organism responds to a stimulus; hence the term *stimulus-response*, or S-R. As the response moves through the neural pathway, an individual may be said to have learned. In recent years the Harvard psychologist B. F. Skinner has considerably refined Thorndike's original position, and his work with pigeons has impressed many.

However, interesting as Skinner's experiments are, some counseling theorists have objected to them on the ground that learners are essentially passive, possessing little insight into the meaning of their acts. That is, the criticism made of Skinner is couched in philosophical terms: the person is manipulated and has lost the freedom to comprehend the significance of what is being done to him or her. For this reason some counseling theorists use a variant of gestalt theory. With its emphasis on insight, gestalt theory holds that it is desirable to encourage independent and autonomous thought. What gestaltists mean by insight is, roughly, a realization or awareness of a certain relationship. At first, insight was thought to be sudden. The early experimentation with apes suggested that individuals who get insight "catch on" in a rapid, almost dramatic fashion. It is now believed that insights may arrive slowly. An insight may be deep or shallow, and there is no guarantee that an insight is necessarily accurate.

When counselors employ the theory of insight, they do not behave like Skinnerian "conditioners," who reinforce correct responses. The counselor as conditioner would probably, in a manner unknown to counselees, encourage the latter to behave the way the counselor wanted them to. Counselors who believe in the validity or importance of insight, however, attempt to get their clients to utilize their own intellectual and emotional resources to become aware of certain feelings, relationships, or attitudes. There needs to be a prior assumption that counselees have sufficient intelligence to solve their own problems and that the role of the counselors is to provide a sympathetic or helpful environment for this purpose. When counselees develop insight— that is, see a certain pattern of relationships—into themselves and their problems, then they may take the next step: decide what is to be done and, finally, how to do it.

Although psychiatrists have not been particularly interested in learning theory, at least one of Freud's constructs bears on this problem. Freud believed that the unconscious is able to prevent certain learning, as, for instance, when a repressed feeling "blocks" the sounding of a word, the memory of a face, or the learning of a subject. For some reason Freud's rather seminal discovery of the role of the unconscious in blocking learning has not been followed up to any considerable extent by educational psychologists. However, many teachers report instances of seemingly irrational forgetting or nonlearning, and it seems reasonable to believe that some kind of unconscious process is operative.

There is good reason for emphasizing incompatibility and inconsistency in this section and in the previous section on conflict. A coherent learning theory, therefore, is useful precisely because it explains how individuals learn, how and why they learn inconsistent patterns of desire, and also how individuals may learn to reconcile conflict and arrive at workable solutions to intrapersonal problems. As we have stated frequently, conflict in individual belief structures, values, or feelings usually derives from inconsistent cultural patterns. The individual has learned—to re-emphasize the point, without awareness—many values that prove to be inconsistent and/or conflicting. One's outlook, feelings, purposes, and so on, then, are likely to be confused because they are inconsistent. Because it is impossible to satisfy equally conflicting goals, individuals in our culture are often beset by self-doubt, guilt, confusion, and similar negative feelings. The kind of self-exploration that counselors encourage in counselees is therefore designed to uncover the usually conflicting and unconscious pattern of desires that characterize many of us much of the time.

Conclusion

In one sense psychology is to the counselor as physiology and anatomy are to the physician. It would be possible for physicians to make a diagnosis and prescribe a pill without knowing these two subjects. But if physicians did so, we would call them technicians, persons who operate in a limited way by rule-of-thumb prescriptions and without deep understanding. For practicing counselors, an understanding of the dynamics of human behavior is a sine qua non, an indispensable element, without which their treatment is superficial. For counselors to deal effectively with their clientele, for counselors to become professional, they must have an understanding of human behavior.

By the same token, an awareness of the social sciences, their structure, and the principles and data that have arisen from this structure, is also a necessary part of the professional education of counselors. If we assume that a distinctive characteristic of a profession is that it possess an intellectual rationale, surely the rationale includes the insights of the social sciences. To obtain the knowledge to work most effectively with their clients, counselors require an understanding that is both broad and deep. A knowledge of human behavior is a key element of this understanding.

Annotated references

Alexander, Franz, and Sheldon F. Selesnick. *The History of Psychiatry*. New York: Harper & Row, 1966.

This is a comprehensive history of psychiatry from primitive times to the present. Theories, history, case studies, and interpretation are effectively combined to paint a readable picture of psychiatry.

Beals, Ralph L., and Harry Hoijer. *An Introduction to Anthropology*. 3rd ed. New York: Macmillan, 1965.

This is an introductory textbook that covers both cultural and physical anthropology.

Birket-Smith, Kaj. *The Paths of Culture*. Madison: University of Wisconsin Press, 1965.

A comprehensive introduction to cultural anthropology, this work provides a detailed interpretation of anthropology and its methods.

Cornford, Francis M. *From Religion to Philosophy*. New York: Harper & Brothers, 1957.

This scholarly essay on the transition from religion to philosophy puts particular emphasis on the difference between magico-religious and rational speculation.

Dewey, John. *Reconstruction in Philosophy*. New York: Henry Holt & Co., 1917.

One of Dewey's best-known works, this is an attempt to relate the development of philosophy to the social matrix.

Friedan, Betty. *The Feminine Mystique*. New York: W. W. Norton & Company, 1963.

This book is the author's analysis of the "problem that has no name"—the plight of the intelligent, college-trained woman who is stifling in the middle-class suburbs.

Heilbronner, Robert. *The Worldly Philosophers*. New York: Simon & Schuster, 1953.

Here is a rarity—an extremely readable work on economic theory. The author presents some of the most important economic theoreticians, describes their positions, and assesses their contributions. This is perhaps the best place to begin a study of economic theory.

Joad, C. E. M. *Philosophy*. New York: Fawcett World Library, 1962.

Designed for laymen, this is a most interesting introduction to philosophy. See especially Chapters I and II, "On Reading Philosophy" and "Subject Matter and Scope."

Kluckhohn, Clyde. *Mirror for Man*. New York: McGraw-Hill, 1944.

This readable work, an introduction to American culture for beginners, was one of the first attempts by anthropologists to study the United States as a culture.

Lieberman, Myron. *The Future of Public Education*. Chicago: University of Chicago Press, 1960.

In this controversial work on educational sociology the author analyzes the problem of teacher impotence and (in the last chapter) makes a number of specific recommendations—some of which have received considerable attention.

Further references

Bayles, Ernest E. *Democratic Educational Theory*. New York: Harper & Brothers, 1961.

Berne, Eric. *Games People Play*. New York: Grove Press, 1964.

Bigge, Morris, and Maurice P. Hunt. *Psychological Foundations of Education*. New York: Harper & Row, 1968.

Bronfenbrenner, Urie. "Soviet Methods of Character Education: Some Implications for Research." *American Psychologist*, 17 (August 1962), 550–564.

Drucker, Peter. *The Concept of a Corporation*. New York: Mentor Books, New American Library, 1964.

Freud, Sigmund. *New Introductory Lectures on Psycho-Analysis of 1932*. New York: W. W. Norton & Company, 1933.

Galbraith, John Kenneth. *American Capitalism: The Con-*

cept of Countervailing Power. Boston: Houghton Mifflin Company, 1962.

Haley, Jay. *Strategies of Psychotherapy.* New York: Grune & Stratton, 1963.

Kiev, Ari. *Magic, Faith, and Healing.* New York: Free Press of Glencoe, 1964.

Lieberman, Myron. *Education as a Profession.* Englewood Cliffs, N.J.: Prentice-Hall, 1956.

Lynd, Robert, and Helen Merrell Lynd. *Middletown.* New York: Harcourt, Brace & Co., 1929.

Maxey, Chester C. *Political Philosophies.* New York: Macmillan, 1950.

Mead, Margaret. *Coming of Age in Samoa.* New York: Mentor Books, New American Library, 1949.

Mead, Margaret. *Growing Up in New Guinea.* New York: Mentor Books, New American Library, 1953.

Mills, C. Wright. *The Power Elite.* New York: Oxford University Press, 1957.

Nader, Ralph. *Unsafe at Any Speed.* New York: Grossman Publishers, 1965.

Packard, Vance. *The Waste Makers.* New York: David McKay Co., 1960.

Robbins, Rossell H. *Encyclopedia of Witchcraft and Demonology.* New York: Crown Publishers, 1959.

Rogers, Carl R. *Client-Centered Therapy.* Boston: Houghton Mifflin Company, 1951.

Rogers, Carl R. *On Becoming a Person. A Therapist's View of Psychotherapy.* Boston: Houghton Mifflin Company, 1961.

Shermis, S. Samuel. *Philosophic Foundations of Education.* New York: American Book Company, 1967.

Shipley, Thorne, ed. *Classics in Psychology.* New York: Philosophical Library, 1961.

Tawney, R. H. *Religion and the Rise of Capitalism.* New York: Mentor Books, New American Library, 1942.

Warner, W. Lloyd. *Yankee City.* New Haven, Conn.: Yale University Press, 1963.

Whyte, William H. *The Organization Man.* New York: Simon & Schuster, 1956.

8 Cognitively oriented counseling approaches

The content presented in this and the next chapter is labeled in most counseling textbooks *Theories of Counseling* or *Counseling Models* or *Approaches to Counseling* or *Counseling Points of View*. The latter two terms will be used here because they seem more appropriate in view of the formal meaning attached to *theory* and *model*, particularly as applied to speculations about counseling. However, *theory*, *model*, and *approach* will often be used interchangeably in the discussion that follows for no other than stylistic reasons.

The diverse points of view discussed in this chapter and the next represent a considerable sweep of the helping relationship. Many who separate counseling from psychotherapy on any one of several dimensions would argue rather persuasively that what is presented are theories of psychotherapy rather than counseling. If this reasoning is valid, few "theories" of counseling exist. Perhaps an even more forceful argument is that the content presented may be viewed as applications of personality theories or behavior theories. Counseling deals with behavior, therefore, it would seem inevitable and logical that a counseling theory incorporate or be built on a theory of behavior.

Although more will be said in Chapter 10 about theory, its nature, function, and purposes, basically it is a practical means or framework for making systematic observations and explaining phenomena. Counseling theory attempts to explain and provide understandings of what happens in the counseling relationship. Some years ago, Shoben and his associates remarked that those who deal directly with clients use theoretical ideas and that "their choice is not one of theory versus no theory, but between notions of human conduct that are explicit and formalized against those that are implicit and the inarticulate product of experience."[1]

Little or no compelling evidence exists that counseling success depends definitely on the extent and explicitness of a counselor's theoretical orientation, or that one theory is superior to another. Smith and Glass, for example, coded and integrated statistically 400 controlled evaluations of counseling and psychotherapy. Few significant differences in effectiveness among ten types of psychotherapy (psychodynamic, Adlerian, eclectic, transactional analysis, rational emotive, gestalt, client-centered, systematic desensitization, implosion, behavior modification) were established. Virtually no difference in effectiveness was observed between the class of behavioral (systematic desensitization, and so on) and nonbehavioral (rational emotive, and so on) therapies. Smith and Glass concluded that "Despite volumes devoted to the theoretical differences among different schools of psychotherapy, the results of research demonstrate negligible differences in the effects produced by different therapy types. Unconditional judgments of superiority of one type or another of psychotherapy, and all that these claims imply about treatment and training policy, are unjustified."[2]

Extensive effort within recent years has gone into theory construction. It is to be hoped that some day unification of the multiplicity of theories will take place. However, as Black has pointed out, resolution of theoretical differences may come through the critical analysis of the process rather than the promotion of a particular point of view.[3]

Examination of counseling points of view indicates great diversity. Yet each viewpoint can teach something if one evaluates the facts and opinions behind it. Basic issues cut across all approaches, and differences often appear to exist largely in emphasis and convictions.

This chapter and the next will summarize eleven counseling viewpoints. We would be hard pressed to defend against the charge that some major ones in the field have been excluded. The reason for choosing these eleven is that

[1] Edward J. Shoben, Jr., et al., "Behavioral Theories and a Counseling Case: A Symposium," *Journal of Counseling Psychology*, 3 (Summer 1956), 107–124.

[2] Mary Lee Smith and Gene V. Glass "Meta-Analysis of Psychotherapy Outcome Studies," *American Psychologist*, 32 (September 1977), 752–760.

[3] J. D. Black, "Common Factors of the Patient-Therapist Relationship in Diverse Psychotherapies," *Journal of Clinical Psychology*, 8 (July 1952), 302–306.

they represent clear-cut and important formulations. To date, those excluded do not seem to have attained the eminence or excited the interest of those included. The omitted ones also tend to overlap with one another and with the more polar theories presented here. It is essential for the student to realize that the clear dichotomy indicated is an exaggeration used for convenience of comparison, contrast, and discussion. Much understanding is to be found in the theories not presented. In our opinion, such understanding will come more easily if it is based on the content of this and the next chapter.

How best to organize the presentation of these viewpoints remains a difficult decision. A case could be made for ordering it chronologically, according to the following continuum:

	Trait/	Self	
Psychoanalytic	Factor	Theory	Existential
1900		1950	2000

But this plan would give little more than some notion of the historical development of a counseling theory. Patterson has grouped existing theories into five categories ranging from cognitive to affective, as follows:[4]

Rational	Learning	Psychoanalytic	Phenomenological	Existential
COGNITIVE				AFFECTIVE

Within categories, no attempt was made to base theories on the dimensions of the continuum. Perhaps the merit of Patterson's scheme is that it moves from the relatively simple to the more intricate, although all theories of human behavior are complex because people are complex. The order followed in this and the next chapter is based somewhat on a similar continuum.

Two excellent volumes[5] devoted entirely to counseling theory have been published; therefore, no attempt will be made here to present counseling theories in their entirety. The student is referred to these two sources and to other

relevant books and articles throughout the discussion that follows. For each viewpoint there will be identification and discussion of (1) its proponents and relevant sources, (2) the major concepts it embodies, (3) the counselor and the counseling process, and (4) the major criticisms of it and the contributions it has made. Treatment is devoted, then, to the broad dimensions of the viewpoints rather than to the deviations, details, or refinements connected with them.

Each individual in counselor preparation is urged to develop a personal theory of counseling; consequently, it would seem necessary to know existing viewpoints in counseling and why they exist. Each student is then in a better position to evolve, through practice and study, the approach most appropriate for him or her.

Trait and factor viewpoint

Proponents and sources

The best-known proponents of the trait and factor point of view have been associated with the University of Minnesota. They include Walter Bingham, John Darley, Donald G. Paterson, and E. G. Williamson. Most renowned is Williamson (1967 APGA president), who served as Dean of Students at the University of Minnesota from 1941 to 1970. While this point of view has been expounded in a number of journal articles and books, the most definitive treatments by Williamson are contained in *How to Counsel Students,*[6] *Counseling Adolescents,*[7] and *Vocational Counseling.*[8] Relevant source material also appears in two chapters written by Williamson—one in a monograph entitled *Counseling Points of View*[9] and the other in a volume edited by Stefflre and Grant.[10] Information useful in understanding both trait

---

[4] C. H. Patterson, *Theories of Counseling and Psychotherapy*, 2nd ed. (New York: Harper & Row, 1973).

[5] Ibid. and Virginia Binder, Arnold Binder, and Bernard Rimland, eds., *Modern Therapies* (Englewood Cliffs, N.J.: Prentice-Hall, 1976).

[6] E. G. Williamson, *How to Counsel Students* (New York: McGraw-Hill, 1939).

[7] E. G. Williamson, *Counseling Adolescents* (New York: McGraw-Hill, 1950).

[8] E. G. Williamson, *Vocational Counseling* (New York: McGraw-Hill, 1965).

[9] E. G. Williamson, "Some Issues Underlying Counseling Theory and Practice," in *Counseling Points of View*, ed. Willis E. Dugan (Minneapolis: University of Minnesota Press, 1959), pp. 1–13.

[10] E. G. Williamson, "Vocational Counseling: Trait-Factor Theory," in *Theories of Counseling*, 2nd ed., ed. Buford Stefflre and W. Harold Grant (New York: McGraw-Hill, 1972), pp. 136–176.

and factor counseling and its principal contributor has been presented by Ewing.[11]

The trait and factor point of view is sometimes called *directive counseling* and *counselor-centered* theory. As is true of all dynamic viewpoints it has undergone change since its origin as a vocational counseling approach. It has been broadened to include a concern for total development, not solely vocational development.

Major concepts

Advocates of this viewpoint explain personality as a system of interdependent traits or factors such as abilities (for example, memory, spatial relations, verbal, and so on), interests, attitudes, and temperament. Development of the individual progresses from infancy to adulthood as these factors are energized and mature. Numerous attempts have been made to categorize people in terms of various trait dimensions. Scientific study of the individual has included (1) assessing one's traits by psychological tests and other means, (2) defining or portraying a person, (3) helping one to know and understand self and environment, and (4) predicting probable success in certain ventures. Fundamental to trait and factor counseling is the assumption that individuals seek to use self-understanding and knowledge of their abilities as means of developing their potentialities. Achievement of self-discovery results in intrinsic satisfaction and reinforces efforts to become all that one is able to become.

Williamson notes that "the foundation of modern concepts of counseling rests on the assumption of the unique individuality of each child and also upon the identification of that uniqueness through *objective* measurement as contrasted with techniques of *subjective* estimation and appraisal."[12] Psychologists long have tried to develop instruments capable of objectively assessing individuals for purposes of counseling them about educational and vocational decisions. Elaborate probability tables utilizing one or more intellective and/or nonintellective variables have been constructed to enable counselors to help their clients select courses, programs of study, a college, and so forth, rationally and presumably with some probability of success.

In Williamson's opinion the purpose of counseling is to facilitate the development of excellence in all aspects of human life. He further asserts that "the task of the trait-factor type of counseling is to aid the individual in successive approximations of self-understanding and self-management by means of helping him [or her] to assess his [or her] assets and liabilities in relation to the requirements of progressively changing life goals and his [or her] vocational career."[13] In his early work Williamson referred to clinical counselors "who diagnose and counsel in such problem areas as mental hygiene, reading and studying difficulties, and vocational and educational orientation."[14] Counseling—by assisting the individual to modify or eliminate defects, disabilities, and limitations—facilitates personality growth and integration. It is believed that in the counseling relationship the individual is able to face, clarify, and solve immediate problems. Presumably one learns from the process and can apply this learning to future conflict situations.

ASSUMPTIONS UNDERLYING THE VIEWPOINT Williamson has identified eight assumptions regarding personality, work, and society that undergird trait and factor counseling.[15] Five are summarized here:

1. Because every individual is an organized, unique pattern of capabilities and potentialities and because these qualities are relatively stable after adolescence, objective tests can be used to identify these characteristics.
2. Personality and interest patterns correlate with certain work behavior. Consequently, identification of characteristics of successful workers is information that is useful in helping individuals choose careers.
3. Different school curricula require different capacities and interests and these can be determined. Individuals will learn more easily and effectively when their potentials and aptitudes are congruent with curriculum demands.

[11] Dorlesa B. Ewing, "Direct from Minnesota—E. G. Williamson," *Personnel and Guidance Journal*, 54 (October 1975), 77–87.
[12] Williamson, *Vocational Counseling*, p. 56.
[13] Williamson, "Vocational Counseling: Trait-Factor Theory," p. 198.
[14] Williamson, *How to Counsel Students*, p. 56.
[15] Williamson, "Vocational Counseling: Trait-Factor Theory," pp. 194–195.

4. Student and counselor diagnoses of student potential should precede placement in a curriculum and/or work setting. Diagnosis prior to instruction would facilitate instruction because modifications could be made based on what is known about the individual.

5. Each person possesses the ability and the desire to identify cognitively his or her own capabilities. Individuals seek to order and maintain their lives and to utilize their capabilities in achieving satisfying work and home life.

NATURE OF HUMANKIND Williamson has urged counselors to examine continuously their philosophic orientation and has noted that provisional answers rather than tribal dogma are best. He has posed and responded to such questions about the nature of being human, the nature of human development, the nature of the "good life," who determines what is good, and the nature of the universe and a person's relationship with it.[16] In respect to the nature of humankind, he believes that people are born with the potential for both good and evil. The meaning of life is to seek good and reject or control evil. He said that counselors should be optimistic about humankind and must believe that individuals can learn to solve their problems, particularly if they learn to utilize their abilities.

In respect to the nature of human development, Williamson believes that "man may not be fully capable, autonomously in the Rousseauan pattern, of becoming his potentiality *without* human assistance; rather does he need other persons to aid him to achieve his full development of potentiality."[17] Responding to what is the nature of the "good life," he states,

It is one thing to accept and advocate self-actualization or *becoming* one's full potentiality. It is another and not identical assumption that the nature or form of one's full potential and self-actualization will thus be the "best possible" or "the good" form of human nature. Indeed, man seems to be capable both of becoming his "best bestial and debasing self," as well as those forms of "the best" that are of high excellence.[18]

Williamson identifies *excellence* as one dimension of the *good* and believes that because counselors serve as role models for their clients they should strive for excellence in all things.

In respect to who determines the "good," Williamson rejects dictating the form of determination and feels that the search for the good may well constitute the good life. He has noted that conceptions of the universe and the individual's relationship to it often take the form that either (1) the individual is alone in an unfriendly universe or (2) the universe is friendly and favorable to the individual and his or her development. Williamson urges counselors to develop their own "personal cosmology."

The counselor and the counseling process

The trait and factor viewpoint holds that the counselor actively influences the development of the client. Williamson contends that the individual's freedom "to become" includes self-destructive and antisocial forms of individuality as well as positive development.[19] Because of this possibility, the counselor seeks openly and frankly to influence the direction of development. Counseling help is sought because people do not possess the personal resources to determine their own individuality. Because they do not fully understand themselves, externally known diagnostic data are collected by the counselor to supplement clients' perceptions of themselves. The counselor uses these data to formulate hypotheses for understanding the individual. They are tentative and have to be checked and verified.

Williamson recognizes that students who come voluntarily for counseling are easier to help, but he doubts that the completely voluntary relationship is the only possible one for counseling. He urges that counselors not sit in their offices and wait for students, but he does not advocate "forcing" or "compelling" students. "In every school surely there are many, many situations in which a little inventiveness in working out a roundabout way of persuading people to want to do what they 'ought' (or need) to do, would produce effective results and would be of great use to teachers."[20] The counseling objectives set forth by William-

---

[16] Williamson, *Vocational Counseling*, pp. 181–189.
[17] Ibid., p. 183.
[18] Ibid., p. 185.

[19] Williamson, "Some Issues Underlying Counseling Theory and Practice," p. 3.
[20] Ibid., p. 10.

son include (1) helping individuals feel better by acceptance of their perceived self and (2) helping individuals think more clearly in resolving their personal problems so that they can control their own development through rational problem-solving methods.

Counselors who use a trait-factor viewpoint are active in the learning situation represented by counseling. They are involved in diagnoses, presenting information, clarifying issues, and the like. They collect and evaluate data. They sort and appraise life history data to help counselees understand themselves. Because counselors are older or more mature and have special skills, their major role in counseling is essentially that of a teacher, with the subject matter being the counselee and his or her pattern of behavior. The task of the counselor is to teach counselees how to learn about themselves and their environment whereas the counselee's task is to learn how to understand oneself and to use this learning rationally to achieve a productive life.

The work of trait-factor counselors was divided into six steps by Williamson.[21] *Analysis* involves collecting data from a wide variety of sources to obtain an understanding of the client. *Synthesis* refers to the summarizing and organizing of the data to determine the client's strengths and liabilities. *Diagnosis* is the counselor's conclusions about the problem causes and characteristics. *Prognosis* refers to the counselor's prediction of the counselee's future development or the implications of the diagnosis. *Counseling* means the steps taken by counselor and counselee to bring about adjustment and readjustment. *Follow-up* includes whatever the counselor does to assist the counselee with new or recurring problems as well as evaluation of the effectiveness of counseling.

The counselor's techniques were placed in five general categories by Williamson:[22] (1) forcing conformity, (2) changing the environment, (3) selecting the appropriate environment, (4) learning needed skills, and (5) changing attitudes. Five stages of counseling were conceptualized by Williamson:[23] (1) establishing rapport, (2) cultivating self-understanding, (3) advising or planning a program of action, (4) carrying out the plan, and (5) where appropriate, making referral to other personnel workers. In respect to advising,

trait and factor counselors could engage in (1) *direct advising,* which means that they state their opinions openly and frankly, (2) the *persuasive method,* wherein the evidence is marshaled in such a fashion as to lead the individual to understand the outcomes of alternative actions, or (3) an *explanatory method,* which refers to explaining the significance of diagnostic data and pointing out possible solutions.

Criticisms and contributions

Common criticisms of the trait and factor viewpoint may be summarized briefly:

1. The viewpoint was developed in an educational setting and its clientele was restricted primarily to students who possessed varying degrees of maturity and self-responsibility.
2. The viewpoint overemphasizes counselor control and results in the counselee's becoming dependent on the superior being of the counselor for direction and definition.
3. The counselee's affective concerns are at best minimized and at worst ignored or relegated to the domain of psychotherapists.
4. Too much reliance is placed on objective data. The overuse of and overconfidence in these data are not justified because of their present limited reliability, validity, and completeness.
5. A dilemma exists for the counselor, who is urged to make sure that the counselee actualizes potentialities but must do this without undue exhortation or persuasion.

The contributions often cited for the trait and factor viewpoint are as follows:

1. It has sought to apply the scientific approach to counseling. Particularly at its origin, the trait and factor viewpoint represented a protest against the prevailing shoddy practices of untrained personnel.
2. Its emphasis on the use of objective test data led to improvements in test development, their predictive uses, and the collection and use of environmental data.
3. The emphasis given to diagnosis called attention to problems and their sources and led to the creation of techniques to deal with them.

[21] Williamson, *How to Counsel Students,* p. 57.
[22] Williamson, *Counseling Adolescents,* p. 215.
[23] Ibid., p. 224.

4. The emphasis on cognition and cognitive forces counter-balanced other viewpoints that stressed affect and emotional states.

Rational-emotive viewpoint

Proponent and sources

Albert Ellis, a clinical psychologist specializing in the field of marriage and family counseling, has set forth the basic tenets of rational-emotive psychotherapy in three books.[24] In the first one, *Reason and Emotion in Psychotherapy*, he outlined the origin of the viewpoint and the second and third books amplified on its practices. After becoming dissatisfied with the outcomes of his work in marriage and family counseling, Ellis completed psychoanalytic training and practiced psychoanalysis. He soon came to believe that orthodox analytical procedures with their emphasis on insight were not sufficient to enable his clients to overcome their deep-seated fears and hostilities. Drawing on his experiences as a private practitioner and his knowledge of behavioral learning theory, he formulated rational-emotive therapy.

Major concepts

Ellis has stated that he views humans as both rational and irrational. People behave in certain ways because they believe that they should or must act in these ways. People possess a high degree of suggestibility and negative emotionalism (anxiety, guilt, and hostility). Emotional problems lie in illogical thinking. By maximizing one's intellectual powers one can free oneself of emotional disturbances. The rational-emotive practitioner believes that no person is to be blamed for anything he or she does, but each person is responsible for his or her behavior. Blame and anger are viewed as dysfunctional and irrational feelings.

A major element in rational-emotive therapy is the assumption that thinking and emotion are not two disparate processes. Ellis believes that the two overlap and that, for all practical purposes, thinking and emotion are the same thing. Drawing on Stanley Cobb's work, emotion is defined as:

> . . . (1) an introspectively given affect state, usually mediated by acts of interpretation; (2) the whole set of internal physiological changes, which help (ideally) the return to normal equilibrium between the organism and its environment, and (3) the various patterns of overt behavior, stimulated by the environment and implying constant interactions with it, which are expressive of the stirred up physiological state (2) and also the more or less agitated psychological state (1).[25]

Emotions, according to Ellis, can be controlled in four ways:

> (a) by electrical or biochemical means (e.g., electroshock treatments, barbiturates or tranquilizing or energizing drugs); (b) by using one's sensorimotor system (e.g., doing movement exercises or using yoga breathing techniques); (c) by employing one's existing emotional states and prejudices (e.g., changing oneself out of love for a parent or a therapist); and (d) by using one's cerebral processes (e.g., reflecting, thinking or telling oneself to calm down or become excited).[26]

While noting that these four processes are highly interrelated, Ellis stresses that emotion is caused and controlled by thinking. Emotion is biased and prejudiced thought or an intrinsically attitudinal and cognitive process.

Ellis believes that which is usually labeled *thinking* consists of less personalized, dispassionate appraisals of a given situation, and that which is usually labeled *emoting* is composed of slanted, biased, highly personalized, passionate evaluations of some person or object. Ellis summarizes this by stating that "one's thinking often *becomes* one's emotion; and emoting, under some circumstances, *becomes*

[24] See Albert Ellis, *Reason and Emotion in Psychotherapy* (New York: Lyle Stuart, 1962), 442 pp.; *Humanistic Psychotherapy: The Rational-Emotive Approach* (New York: Julian Press, 1973), 273 pp.; and Albert Ellis and Russell Grieger, *Handbook of Rational-Emotive Therapy* (New York: Springer Publishing Company, 1977), 433 pp.

[25] Stanley Cobb, *Emotions and Clinical Medicine* (New York: W. W. Norton & Company, 1950).

[26] Ellis, *Reason and Emotion in Psychotherapy*, p. 40.

one's thought."[27] Although an emotion may exist briefly without thought, Ellis has stated that ". . . it appears to be almost impossible to sustain an emotional outburst without bolstering it by repeated ideas."[28] Therefore the difference between feelings and emotions is that feelings are largely sensory appraisals (feeling good about eating ice cream) while emotions stem from cognitive sensory states (eating ice cream and thinking good things of the person who supplied it).

Particularly important to the rational-emotive viewpoint is the concept that much of the individual's emotional behavior stems from "self-talk" or internalized sentences. That which individuals tell themselves *is* or *becomes* their thoughts and emotions. If individuals tell themselves "that would be awful" or "that would be wonderful" in connection with a situation, their calm thinking is changed into excited emoting. Ellis states ". . . that every human being who gets disturbed really is telling himself a chain of false sentences—since that is the way that humans seem almost invariably to think in words, phrases and sentences. And it is these sentences which really are, which constitute his neuroses."[29]

Sustained emotion stems from self-verbalizations, therefore, a conscious effort must be made to change this internalized talk that creates negative emotions. Those people who rarely do so, according to Ellis, refrain because "(a) they are too stupid to think clearly, or (b) they are sufficiently intelligent, but just do not know how to think clearly in relation to their emotional states, or (c) they are sufficiently intelligent and informed but are too neurotic (or psychotic) to put their intelligence and knowledge to good use."[30]

Ellis has explained neurosis as consisting of stupid behavior by a nonstupid person:

> . . . a neurotic is a potentially capable person who in some way or on some level of his functioning does not realize that (or how) he is defeating his own ends. Or else he is an individual who (in rare cases) has full understanding of or insight into how he is harming himself but who, for some irrational reason, persists in self-sabotaging behavior. In any case, we may say that the neurotic

is emotionally disabled because he does not know how to (or does not care to) think more clearly and behave less self-defeatingly.[31]

The major illogical ideas held and perpetuated by men and women that invariably lead to self-defeat and neurosis have been set forth by Ellis and are reproduced here.

Irrational Idea No. 1. The idea that you must—yes, *must*—have sincere love and approval almost all the time from all the people you find significant.
Irrational Idea No. 2. The idea that you must prove yourself thoroughly competent, adequate, and achieving; or that you must at least have real competence or talent at something important.
Irrational Idea No. 3. The idea that people who harm you or commit misdeeds rate as generally bad, wicked, or villainous individuals and that you should severely blame, damn, and punish them for their sins.
Irrational Idea No. 4. The idea that life proves awful, terrible, horrible, or catastrophic when things do not go the way you would like them to go.
Irrational Idea No. 5. The idea that emotional misery comes from external pressures and that you have little ability to control your feelings or rid yourself of depression and hostility.
Irrational Idea No. 6. The idea that if something seems dangerous or fearsome, you must become terribly occupied with and upset about it.
Irrational Idea No. 7. The idea that you will find it easier to avoid facing many of life's difficulties and self-responsibilities than to undertake more rewarding forms of self-discipline.
Irrational Idea No. 8. The idea that your past remains all-important and that because something once strongly influenced your life, it has to keep determining your feelings and behavior today.
Irrational Idea No. 9. The idea that people and things should turn out better than they do; and that you have to view it as awful and horrible if you do not quickly find good solutions to life's hassles.

---

[27] Ibid., p. 49.
[28] Ibid., p. 49.
[29] Ibid., p. 28.
[30] Ibid., p. 54.

[31] Ibid., pp. 54–55.

Irrational Idea No. 10. The idea that you can achieve happiness by inertia and inaction or by passively and un-committedly "enjoying yourself."

Irrational Idea No. 11. The idea that you must have a high degree of order or certainty to feel comfortable; or that you need some supernatural power on which to rely.

Irrational Idea No. 12. The idea that you can give your-self a global rating as a human and that your general worth and self-acceptance depend upon the goodness of your performances and the degree that people approve of you.[32]

Ellis contends that these ideas are taught by parents, ab-sorbed from social agencies, and are the cause of most people's emotional disturbances. Although childhood ex-periences strongly influence a person to think illogically, the illogical thinking can be reversed. That, of course, is the responsibility of the rational-emotive therapist: to show clients that their illogical thinking is the cause of their un-happiness and to help them change their self-sabotaging internal remarks and attitudes into rational behavior.

The A-B-C-D-E theory of personality

Ellis has formulated a theory of personality identified as the A-B-C-D-E theory, represented in the following column.[33] Personality, according to Ellis, consists primarily of beliefs, constructs, or attitudes. He stresses the importance of hu-man values. When an individual has an emotional reaction at point C (the emotional Consequence), after some acti-vating agent, event, or experience has occurred (point A), it is caused by the belief system (point B). A does not cause C, but the belief system that is held about A causes C. Ellis has stated that:

> Your first set of Beliefs has rationality because, since your basic value system includes *wanting* to stay alive,

External event	A	Activity *or* Action *or* Agent
Self-verbal-izations	iB	Irrational beliefs directed at ex-ternal event (A) *or* Inappropriate beliefs directed at external event (A) (cannot be empirically supported)
	rB	Rational beliefs (can be empiri-cally supported)
Consequent affec-tive emotion	C	Irrational consequences inap-propriately ascribed to A *or* Inappropriate consequences in-appropriately ascribed to A *or* Rational consequences appro-priately ascribed to rB *or* Reasonable consequences ap-propriately ascribed to rB
Validate or invalidate self-verbalizations	D	Dispute irrational beliefs
Change self-verbalizations	cE	Cognitive effect of disputing iB
Change behavior	bE	Behavioral effect of disputing iB

feel happy, and gain acceptance from others, you *will* find rejection unfortunate and you'd *better* feel appropriately sad about it. Your second set of Beliefs has little ration-ality because you only *define* rejection as "awful" (meaning *more* than unfortunate). You *can* bear it—though you'll rarely like it. And it doesn't make you a slob or a worthless individual—but at worst a person with some slobbish traits.[34]

[32] From Albert Ellis, *How to Live with a Neurotic* (New York: Crown Publishers, 1975); Albert Ellis and Robert A. Harper, *A New Guide to Rational Living* (Englewood Cliffs, N.J.: Prentice-Hall and Hollywood: Wilshire Books, 1975); and Albert Ellis, *Reason and Emotion in Psychotherapy* (New York: Lyle Stuart, 1962).

[33] Presented in Kenneth T. Morris and H. Mike Kanitz, *Rational-Emotive Therapy* (Boston: Houghton Mifflin Company, 1975), pp. 9–10.

[34] Albert Ellis, "Rational-Emotive Therapy," in *Modern Therapies*, ed. Virginia Binder, Arnold Binder, and Bernard Rimland (En-glewood Cliffs, N.J.: Prentice-Hall, 1976), p. 22.

The counselor and the counseling process

The task of the counselor, according to Ellis, is to work with individuals who are unhappy and troubled and "to show them (a) that their difficulties result largely from distorted perceptions and illogical thinking and (b) that there is a relatively simple, though work-requiring, method of reordering their perceptions and reorganizing their thinking so as to remove the basic cause of their difficulties."[35] Ellis contends that all effective counselors teach or induce their clients to reperceive or rethink life events. Clients, by doing so, modify their illogical thought, emotion, and behavior.

The main goal of rational-emotive therapists is to demonstrate to clients that their self-verbalizations have been and currently are the source of their emotional disturbances. Rational-emotive practitioners uncover their clients' past and present illogical thinking by "(a) bringing them forcibly to [their] attention or consciousness, (b) showing [them] how they are causing and maintaining [their] disturbance and unhappiness, (c) demonstrating exactly what the illogical links in [their] internalized sentences are, and (d) teaching [them] how to rethink, challenge, contradict, and reverbalize these (and other similar sentences) so that [their] internalized thoughts become more logical and efficient."[36] Further, the rational-emotive therapist not only corrects the client's specific illogical thinking, but also disputes (see D in personality theory) the main irrational ideas so that the client will not fall victim to one or more of them at a later time.

Advocates of rational-emotive therapy use relationship techniques, insight-interpretative techniques, and supportive techniques mainly as preliminary strategies designed to gain the client's trust and confidence. These techniques are useful, according to Ellis, to demonstrate that the individual is illogical and how he or she became that way. But relationship techniques fall short because they fail to show clients how they maintain their illogical thinking and how it can be changed.

Ellis encourages use of a wide assortment of techniques by rational-emotive therapists. Desensitizing techniques, operant conditioning procedures, didactic teaching, use of bibliotherapy, and philosophic discussions are among those used, but the most important is homework by clients. Ellis believes that homework is the missing ingredient in other therapies and accounts for their poor outcomes. Individual homework is almost always applied in rational-emotive practice, no matter what procedure or technique is involved. A homework report has been designed by Ellis (presented in Chapter 12).

Tosi[37] has described several techniques associated with rational-emotive counseling, including (1) rational-emotive modeling (rem), (2) the Premack principle of reinforcement (see p. 285), (3) rational-emotive-assertive-training (reat), (4) new cognitive control techniques, (5) rational-emotive imagery, (6) systematic written homework, (7) systematic desensitization and relaxation training (rec), (8) tape listening, and (9) rational-emotive counseling in groups. Morris and Kanitz have described in considerable detail three rational-emotive techniques: bibliotherapy, rational-emotive imagery, and the techniques for Desensitizing Irrational Beliefs (DESIBELS).[38]

The rational-emotive therapist attacks the specific and general irrational ideas and induces the client to adopt more rational views. The therapist does so in two main ways:

(a) The therapist serves as a frank counter-propagandist who directly contradicts and denies the self-defeating propaganda and superstitions which the patient has originally learned and which he is now self-instilling. (b) The therapist encourages, persuades, cajoles, and occasionally even insists that the patient engage in some activity (such as doing something he is afraid of doing) which itself will serve as a forceful counter-propaganda agency against the nonsense he believes.[39]

Ellis has pointed out that the rational-emotive therapist must deal with the individual's *basic* irrational thinking processes that *underlie* all kinds of fears. Otherwise treatment of one specific fear will not prevent another illogical fear from cropping up at a later time. Because therapists are supposed to be emotionally stronger and healthier than clients, they should be able to take the risk of attacking their

[35] *Reason and Emotion*, p. 36.
[36] Ibid., pp. 58–59.
[37] Don J. Tosi, *Youth: Toward Personal Growth* (Columbus: Charles E. Merrill, 1974).
[38] Morris and Kanitz, *Rational-Emotive Therapy*, pp. 28–30.
[39] Ibid., p. 95.

clients' defenses or resistances to changing their illogical thinking. Ellis believes that passivity on the part of counselors encourages clients to take advantage of them and enables clients to avoid facing and working on their basic problems.

Contrary to orthodox psychoanalysis, rational-emotive therapists do not create a transference neurosis with their clients, but when normal transference and countertransference relations appear, they are either directly interpreted or dealt with or simply noted but not interpreted to the clients. The therapist spends considerable time in the interview, according to Ellis, analyzing and observing the philosophic basis of illogical beliefs. The counselor then attacks the foundations of these beliefs. Counselors use, where appropriate, suggestion, persuasion, activity, homework assignments, and other directive methods of therapy.

Ellis has responded to charges and criticisms (1) that rational-emotive therapy is too unemotional, intellectualized, and oververbal, (2) that the use of reason is essentially limited in human affairs and psychotherapy, (3) that rational-emotive therapy is a superficial, suggestive form of psychotherapy, (4) that rational-emotive therapy is too directive, authoritarian, and brainwashing, and (5) that rational-emotive therapy does not work with extremely disturbed or mentally limited clients.[40]

Type of clients

In his first book Ellis cites cases where rational-emotive therapy was used to treat premarital and marital problems, frigidity, impotence and homosexuality, psychopathy, and borderline schizophrenia. He has repeatedly stressed its value in treating neurotics and individuals who do not believe they are emotionally disturbed but who know they are not functioning adequately in some area of their lives. Ellis has pointed out that psychotic individuals are the most difficult kind of clients and that therapeutic results with them are quite discouraging. He believes that this is due, not because they were reared to be the way they are, but because they were born with distinct psychotic tendencies exacerbated by their upbringing. However, Ellis believes they

can be helped, but rarely truly cured, by intensive psychotherapy, including rational-emotive therapy.[41]

Rational-emotive theory was designed originally for treating fairly disturbed people but it has wide applications. According to Ellis, it can help many people experience less anxiety and hostility and is useful in actualizing their growth potential. Ellis[42] has stated that rational-emotive theory is particularly applicable to the work of school counselors because it is an educational rather than a medical or psychodynamic model. He believes that school counselors could use rational-emotive theory in working with "normal" students, "disturbed" children, parents, and teachers experiencing emotional crisis.

Outcomes

In a very forthright way, Ellis has stated that all (including himself) who present a system of counseling or psychotherapy describe clients who are treated successfully whereas those with whom therapy has been ineffective are rarely publicized. Some reasons why people act self-defeatingly and resist therapy have been given by Ellis. They include (1) the human being's prolonged period of childhood, (2) difficulty in unlearning, (3) inertia, (4) short-sightedness, (5) the prepotency of desire over what individuals should or should not do in their own best interest, (6) oversuggestibility, (7) overvigilance and overcaution (stemming from fears), (8) grandiosity and overrebellion (individuals feel the universe revolves around them), (9) extremism rather than moderation, (10) tendencies toward change, oscillation, erraticness, and unbalance, (11) automaticity and unthinkingness, (12) forgetfulness, (13) wishful thinking, (14) ineffective focusing and organizing, (15) unsustained effort, (16) overemphasizing injustice, (17) overemphasizing guilt, (18) stress-proneness, (19) lack of self-perspective, (20) discrimination difficulties, (21) overgeneralization tendencies. These are some of the many conditions that make therapy ineffective or unsuccessful.[43]

Ellis has stated that when he practiced classical analysis he helped about 50 percent of his total patients and 60 per-

---

[40] Ellis, *Reason and Emotion*, pp. 331–374.

[41] Ibid., p. 266.
[42] Albert Ellis, "Rational-Emotive Therapy and the School Counselor," *The School Counselor*, 22 (March 1975), 236–242.
[43] Ellis, *Reason and Emotion*, pp. 375–419.

cent of his neurotic ones. When he practiced analytically oriented psychotherapy (1952–1955), he helped 63 percent of his total patients and 70 percent of his neurotic patients to distinctly or considerably improve. With respect to rational-emotive therapy, Ellis states that ". . . my own experience, as well as that of several of my associates, tend to show that whereas about 65 per cent of patients tend to improve significantly or considerably under most forms of psychotherapy, about 90 per cent of the patients treated for 10 or more sessions with RT tend to show distinct or considerable improvement. . . ."[44]

Criticisms and contributions

Major criticisms of rational-emotive therapy—that it relies too heavily on intellectual techniques and shortchanges emotions—have been identified and responded to by Ellis. Among the contributions attributed to the rational-emotive viewpoint is its emphasis on extending treatment procedures outside the counselor's office and the active involvement of the counselor in the process.

Eclectic viewpoint

Proponent and sources

The leading proponent of the eclectic viewpoint is Frederick C. Thorne, who in 1945 founded and edited the *Journal of Clinical Psychology*. Thorne earned his doctorate in psychology (Columbia University, 1934) and his M.D. degree (Cornell, 1938) and is a Diplomate in Clinical Psychology of the American Board of Examiners in Professional Psychology. His position has been presented in four books: *Principles of Personality Counseling*,[45] *Principles of Psychological Examining*,[46] *Clinical Judgment*,[47] and *Personality: A Clini-*

cal Eclectic Viewpoint.[48] Recently, Brammer presented a statement advocating an "emerging eclecticism" as a view of counseling appropriate for most practitioners.[49]

Major concepts

The word *eclectic* means to select, to choose appropriate doctrines or methods from various sources or systems. The eclectic believes that a single orientation is limiting and that procedures, techniques, and concepts from many sources should be utilized to best serve the needs of the person seeking help. True eclectics maintain that they have a consistent philosophy and purpose in their work and that they employ techniques for reasons that are as well verified as possible rather than completely by trial and error. From his or her knowledge of perception, development, learning, and personality, the eclectic counselor develops a repertoire of methods and selects the most appropriate for the particular problem and the specific individual.

The sequence by which counselors develop an eclectic viewpoint has been described by Brammer. First, the counselor resists emphasizing theory exclusively by observing and assessing client and other counselor behaviors. Second, the counselor studies the history of counseling and psychotherapy to build on what is known. Third, the counselor who evolves an eclectic viewpoint knows his or her own personality. He or she is aware of personal interacting styles with particular kinds of clients.[50]

Thorne has attempted to analyze the contributions of all existing schools of counseling and to fit them together into an integrated system, retaining the best features of each. He refers to how the methods are combined and used as the "art of clinical practice."[51]

Eclecticism as perceived by Thorne would require an assessment of clients in respect to their past history, present situation, and future possibilities. This evaluation would utilize methods of understanding personality development

[44] Ibid., p. 38.
[45] Frederick C. Thorne, *Principles of Personality Counseling* (Brandon, Vt.: Journal of Clinical Psychology, 1950).
[46] Frederick C. Thorne, *Principles of Psychological Examining* (Brandon, Vt.: Journal of Clinical Psychology, 1950).
[47] Frederick C. Thorne, *Clinical Judgment* (Brandon, Vt.: Journal of Clinical Psychology, 1961).

[48] Frederick C. Thorne, *Personality: A Clinical Eclectic Viewpoint* (Brandon, Vt.: Journal of Clinical Psychology, 1961).
[49] Lawrence M. Brammer, "Eclecticism Revisited," *Personnel and Guidance Journal,* 48 (November 1969), 193–197.
[50] Ibid., pp. 195–196.
[51] Thorne, *Principles of Personality Counseling*, pp. 27–28.

contributed by the biological and social sciences. It would require the counselor to possess direct and intimate knowledge of the individual's manifestations and activities.

Both affective-impulsive and rational-intellectual concerns are dealt with as they are encountered in the counselee. Eclectic counseling theory and practice are built on the need for maximizing the individual's intellectual resources to develop problem-solving behavior. Maladjustment is believed to result from clients' failures to learn to use their intellectual resources, as they were supposed to do early in life.

Counseling is viewed as a process of re-education and treatment and is conceptualized as training the individual. If emotions block training, they may have to be resolved but this is not an inevitable step since training may take place under unfavorable conditions. "The goal of therapy is to replace emotional-compulsive behavior with deliberate rational adaptive behavior based on the highest utilization of intellectual resources."[52]

Counseling and psychotherapy are conceived of as learning processes. The learning process, according to Thorne, involves

... (a) diagnosing the etiologic psychodynamic factors in the disorder in order to formulate the problem to be learned, (b) arranging optimum conditions for learning, (c) outlining and guiding the steps of education and re-education, (d) providing opportunities for practice, and (e) giving the subject insight into the nature of the process and its results in order to increase motivation and incentive to learn.[53]

Counseling is defined as a "face-to-face relationship in which the counselor, a person competently trained in psychological science, consciously attempts by attitudes and verbal means to help others solve problems of life in which personality factors are the primary etiologic agents."[54] Further, it is concerned with the personality problems of normal people with intact personality resources and is regarded as a method of dealing with more superficial personality problems rather than defect or disorder.

Thorne believes that individuals seek counseling assistance because they have problems with which they are unable to cope alone. Counselees expect the counselor to be more intelligent and to have more training and experience than they do. Consequently, a dominance-submission relationship is present in every counseling relationship, no matter how nondirective the counselor.

The direction of counseling lies on an active-passive continuum and is the responsibility of the counselor. Any degree or multiple degrees of this continuum may be used with a counselee according to the indications in the situation.

Direction is an attribute of behavior indicative of specific function and variously expressed in terms of needs, drives, goals, purposes, and other concepts descriptive of integrated behavior. . . . Until such time as the person demonstrates his ability to regulate his behavior within the limits of what is socially acceptable, he is subjected to varying degrees of direction or regulation from the environment. The general rule may be stated that *the need for direction is inversely correlated with the person's potentialities for effective self-regulation*, i.e., the healthier the personality, the less the need for direction; the sicker the personality, the more the need for direction.[55]

Training and experience let the counselor know when to utilize directive or nondirective methods. And the skill with which the method is used is the critical factor, not the method per se.

Thorne believes that an individual's personality is formed and reflected as he or she interacts with the environment. It is characterized as a process of changing or becoming. Personality dynamics include a series of drives: (1) the drive for higher organization (actualization, perfect functioning, integration), (2) the drive to achieve and maintain stability (self-preservation, homeostasis, control, life goals, lifestyle), and (3) the drive to integrate opposing functions so as to avoid imbalance. There is "a constant striving for unity manifesting itself in efforts to maintain the unity of the system of organization self-consistently."[56]

[52] Ibid., p. 24.
[53] Ibid., p. 28.
[54] Ibid., p. 85.

[55] Ibid., pp. 87–88.
[56] Thorne, *Personality: A Clinical Eclectic Viewpoint*, p. 65.

An individual's lifestyle is based on characteristic patterns of achieving unification of his or her strategy in satisfying needs and coping with reality. Consciousness is "considered the main organizing, integrating and unitizing mechanism determining and making possible higher level personality functioning."[57] Emotional status and disturbances in behavior result from disturbances of consciousness. Self-image is defined as what one thinks oneself to be whereas the self-concept is defined as the evaluative core of one's self as the individual believes it appears to others. "From the eclectic viewpoint, personality development is regarded as a struggle to transcend affective-impulsive-unconscious determination of behavior by learning and perfecting rational-logical-voluntary control of behavior."[58]

Past experience may place limits on an individual but a person transcends the past by the ability to imagine and manage the future. Logic and rationality are the individual's best means for becoming better and healthier.

The counselor and the counseling process

The counselor's major objective is to safeguard mental health. This is achieved by either preventing or modifying causative factors producing maladjustment or mental disorder. Although individuals come for help (1) to avoid future maladjustment, (2) to gain relief, (3) to avoid pressure or punishment, or (4) to gain success or avoid failure, the counselor is primarily interested in causes and secondarily in symptoms.

Thorne has stated that the basic problem in counseling is to assist the individual to learn to adapt more efficiently. Learning involves

. . . (a) the diagnosis of the causes of personality maladjustment, (b) the making of a plan for modifying etiologic factors, (c) securing proper conditions for efficient learning, (d) stimulating the client to develop his own resources and assume responsibility for practicing new modes of adjustment, and (e) the proper handling of related problems which may contribute to adjustment.[59]

Eclectic counseling is indicated, Thorne believes, for those persons

. . . (a) who are motivated enough to seek psychological help and to enter and remain in the counseling relationship long enough to receive help, (b) with whom a satisfactory contact (rapport) can be established so that the client feels free in expressing his problems, (c) who are sufficiently articulate to deal with problems on verbal levels, (d) whose difficulties are not organic in the sense of requiring medical or psychiatric care, (e) whose personality resources are sufficient so that some solution can be worked out, and (f) who are sufficiently stable and not dangerous either to themselves or to society so that treatment outside an institution is safe.[60]

Personality counseling is contraindicated for uncooperative clients, inaccessible (dull, disturbed, confused, or disoriented) clients, dangerous (suicidal, homicidal, or felonious) clients, inarticulate clients, and those who are unavailable for prolonged periods of time, who have psychopathic personalities, or who are very young or very old.

The eclectic counselor is one who possesses superior intelligence and judgment. Counselor training should be in the basic and applied sciences as these relate to the human organism. Ideally it is coupled with intensive training in clinical psychology, psychiatry, and psychoanalysis and augmented by clinical experience in which exposure is given to all known types of psychopathology.

FACTORS DETERMINING CHOICE OF METHODS Eclectic counseling is based on a rational plan that involves appropriate measures for (1) opening the relationship, (2) dealing with causes and symptoms, and (3) terminating therapy. Passive techniques are generally used unless definite indications exist for more active methods. Thorne has discussed the factors on which choice of techniques depends.[61] They are paraphrased here:

1. *Specificity of action needed.* Direct curative action on the causes of disorder is preferred.
2. *Economy of action.* Briefer methods are considered before expensive, lengthy methods.

---

[57] Ibid., p. 86.
[58] Ibid., p. 184.
[59] Thorne, *Principles of Personality Counseling,* pp. 88–89.

[60] Ibid., p. 91.
[61] Ibid., pp. 106–108.

3. *Natural history of the disorder.* Behavior disorders follow definite patterns of development including prodromal stage characterized by vague, undefined symptoms, syndromal stage without client insight but apparent to others, and syndromal stage with client insight.

4. The *distributive principle.* The counselor directs treatment in a plastic, adaptive manner along directions that offer most promise of results.

5. The *total push.* Every possible influence is brought to bear on the individual.

6. *Failure of progress.* Blind experimentation using any and all methods available.

Eclectic counseling requires counselors to be sensitive to the developing situation so that they can evaluate the indications and contraindications for the application of any method. This does not imply that counselors work without a plan. However, their ability to alter plans or approaches is a hallmark of eclectic counseling. As the situation changes so should the plan. Thorne has stated that the counselor formulates a plan after becoming familiar with case details and identifying causative factors, depending on (1) knowledge of the various levels of functional integration as related to normal adjustment or disease, (2) ability to evaluate the counselee's status in relation to what is possible to accomplish, and (3) ability to estimate goals and the possibility of attaining them.[62]

ACTIVE VERSUS PASSIVE TECHNIQUES   A most relevant issue for the eclectic counselor is the degree of activeness or directiveness to be employed in working with a counselee. After tracing the history of basic trends of thought concerning the role of the counselor, Thorne makes the following generalizations concerning the use of directive or nondirective methods:

1. In general, passive methods should be used whenever possible.

2. Active methods should be used only with specific indication. In general, only a minimum of directive interference is necessary to achieve therapeutic goals.

3. Passive techniques are usually the methods of choice in the early stages of therapy when the client is telling his story and to permit emotional release.

4. The law of parsimony should be observed at all times. Complicated methods should not be attempted (except with specific indications) until simpler methods have failed.

5. All therapy should be client-centered. This means that the client's interests are the prime consideration. It does not mean that directive methods are contra-indicated. In many cases, the client's needs indicate directive action.

6. It is desirable to give every client an opportunity to resolve his problems non-directively. Inability of the client to progress therapeutically, using passive methods alone, is an indication for utilizing more directive methods.

7. Directive methods are usually indicated in situational maladjustment where a solution cannot be achieved without the cooperation of other persons.

8. Some degree of directiveness is inevitable in all counseling even if only in reaching the decision to use passive methods.[63]

PHASES OF TREATMENT   Thorne has also outlined the stages developed in the course of treating a disorder:

1. *Stage of Incipient Maladjustment.* Minimal evidences of maladjustment with no insight. Usually recognizable only by a trained psychologist or psychiatrist.

2. *Stage of Overt Maladjustment.* Here the fact of maladjustment becomes apparent, usually to others first, but as yet its seriousness is not comprehended.

3. *Stage of Reactive Personality Disorder.* The person develops secondary emotional reactions usually in the form of defense mechanisms intended to conceal or compensate for the maladjustment.

4. *Stage of Bewilderment and Trial and Error Behavior.* The person is now dimly aware that something is wrong but does not know what. Usually rationalizes in terms of projective devices. This is the lowest level of insight that something is wrong. Here the person develops a need for help.

5. *Stage of Insight into Psychological Nature of Disorder.* With some degree of shock and embarrassment, the person learns that his [or her] problems may be "mental."

6. *Stage of Reactive Depression and Discouragement.* Following the basic insight that the disorder is psy-

[62] Ibid., p. 109.

[63] Ibid., pp. 112–113.

chological, or after . . . a full "confession" of painful things, there is frequently a stage of reactive depression with feelings of futility. The person is shocked with the realization of "how could this have happened to me?" and of embarrassment [in looking] forward to contact with people again.

7. *Stage of Symptomatic Relief.* Some superficial improvement occurs but no alleviation of basic etiological causes has yet been accomplished.

8. *Stages of Growth and Recovery.* Following release of negative emotions and acquisition of further insights, recovery processes get under way. This stage is associated with improved feeling tone and optimism. Here the specific etiologic factors are identified and remedied through use of appropriate methods.

9. *Stage of Relapse.* In practically all cases the recovery process does not have a uniform positive acceleration but is associated with "backsliding" and relapses. These relapses may be ignored if the general trend continues in the direction of improvement. The client may even be warned to expect relapses.

10. *Stage of Cure.* The client is relieved of symptoms, understands himself better, learns more adequate solutions of problems and reestablishes his position of independence.[64]

DIAGNOSIS AND USE OF CASE HISTORY Eclectic counselors advocate that a comprehensive case history be taken and that objective information be obtained from many sources. Thorne has noted that marked discrepancies may exist between the history taken from the counselee and information obtained elsewhere for any one of three reasons: "(a) the nature of the client's illness, (b) conscious or unconscious withholding or falsification of facts, and (c) disordered viewpoints of the client or informants due to the difference between phenomenological viewpoints."[65] Accurate case histories are significant because of their potential diagnostic yield. Psychological diagnosis involves determining the sequence of cause-effect relationships. This permits evaluation as to whether the behavioral disorder is environmentally stimulated or organic in nature.

CLOSING PHASES OF COUNSELING Terminating counseling requires as careful attention as beginning the process. Terminal stages are characterized by problem-solving behavior on the part of the counselee. The counselor may engage in more directive activity compared to the first half of the process. Premature termination may occur because of (1) counselee relief from symptoms, (2) failure to achieve rapport, (3) crude direction by the counselor, (4) improper handling of transference by the counselor, (5) client financial problems, (6) uncontrollable environmental factors, and (7) client resistance.[66] Thorne has stated that adequately treated clients (1) express their affective-impulsive life more effectively, (2) have better control, (3) perceive themselves and their environment more realistically, (4) think more logically, (5) have values, beliefs, and attitudes that are more internally consistent, (6) no longer indulge in mechanisms of repression or suppression, and (7) can be said to have grown, to have become more emotionally mature and more intellectually adequate.[67]

Criticisms and contributions

Some of the more common criticisms of eclectic counseling are the following:

1. The present state of scientific progress does not permit detailing differential treatments for various diagnostic conditions.
2. Achieving facility in a few counseling methods is difficult, let alone achieving skill in a multiplicity of methods.
3. Counselees will be uneasy with changes in methods, and change may only be a counselor's rationalization because the selected method fails.
4. It is doubtful if the counselor can determine the correct or most appropriate method on the basis of immediate client reaction.

The contributions often cited include the following:

1. An attempt at systematization of counseling in itself is valuable and worthwhile.

[64] Ibid., p. 116.
[65] Ibid., p. 132

[66] Ibid., pp. 155–156.
[67] Ibid., p. 150.

2. The eclectic approach deals with a wider range of etiologic factors than any single method.
3. Dogma and emotional involvement associated with a single orientation are minimized or reduced.

Psychotherapy by reciprocal inhibition

Proponent and sources

Because counseling is concerned with effecting behavioral changes, there have been attempts to interpret and explain what occurs in the process in the light of one or more of the several available learning theories. Reinforcement and conditioning theories have been applied very frequently. Ivan Pavlov's classic conditioning theory and B. F. Skinner's concepts and principles[68] have influenced many counseling theorists and practitioners.

Joseph Wolpe was educated in South Africa and received his M.D. degree from the University of Witwatersrand, Johannesburg (1948). He has served as Professor of Psychiatry at the University of Virginia (1960–1965) and Temple University (1965). The name of his conditioning therapy, "psychotherapy by reciprocal inhibition," also serves as the title for the volume he produced to describe the method.[69] In the Preface, Wolpe traces the evolution of his interest in counter-conditioning methods beginning in 1944 when as a medical officer he read enough to cause him to question the universality of Freud's Oedipal theory. His interest turned from Pavlov to Hull and from Hull to studies of experimentally induced neuroses. The book was written during 1956–1957 while Wolpe was a fellow at the Center for Advanced Study in the Behavioral Sciences, Stanford, California.

Another source of information is *The Conditioning Therapies,* a report of the papers presented and the resulting discussion at the University of Virginia Conference,[70] and *The Practice of Behavior Therapy.*[71]

[68] B. F. Skinner, *Beyond Freedom and Dignity* (New York: Alfred A. Knopf, 1970), 225 pp. and B. F. Skinner, *About Behaviorism* (New York: Alfred A. Knopf, 1974), 256 pp.
[69] Joseph Wolpe, *Psychotherapy by Reciprocal Inhibition* (Stanford: Stanford University Press, 1958).
[70] Joseph Wolpe et al., eds., *The Conditioning Therapies* (New York: Holt, Rinehart and Winston, 1964).
[71] Joseph Wolpe, *The Practice of Behavior Therapy* (New York: Pergamon Press, 1969), 314 pp.

Major concepts

The logic of Wolpe's approach has been briefly stated by him:

> Only three kinds of processes are known that can bring about lasting changes in an organism's habit of response to a given stimulus situation: growth, lesions, and learning. Since neurotic behavior demonstrably originates in learning, it is only to be expected that its elimination will be a matter of unlearning.[72]

Wolpe conducted experimental observations on cats in which neurotic anxiety had been induced and was later removed by having the animals eat in the presence of initially small but progressively larger doses of anxiety-evoking stimuli. When anxiety was intense, feeding was inhibited. Transient inhibition of anxiety occurred at time of feeding because the reduction of the hunger drive "stamped this in." The experiments suggested to Wolpe that human neurotic anxieties might be handled similarly, and he concluded that "fundamental psychotherapeutic effects follow reciprocal inhibition of neurotic responses."[73] Rather than applying feeding responses to overcome human neuroses, Wolpe uses more convenient anxiety-inhibiting responses such as assertion, relaxation, and desensitizing responses inside and outside the consultation room.

Learning takes place, according to Wolpe, if "a response has been evoked in temporal contiguity with a given sensory stimulus and it is subsequently found that the stimulus can evoke the response although it could not have done so before."[74] Reinforcement is defined by Wolpe as the process of learning. An individual's behavior can be judged as either *adaptive* (progress toward satisfaction of need or avoidance of possible damage or deprivation) or *unadaptive* (expenditure of energy or occurrence of damage or deprivation). Neurotic behavior was defined by Wolpe as "any persistent habit of unadaptive behavior acquired by learning in a physiologically normal organism. Anxiety is usually the central constituent of this behavior, being invariably present in the casual situations."[75] Unadaptive responses are usually ex-

[72] Wolpe, *Psychotherapy by Reciprocal Inhibition,* p. ix.
[73] Ibid., p. ix.
[74] Ibid., p. 19.
[75] Ibid., p. 32.

tinguished; it is their persistence that is a feature of neuroses.

ANXIETY Wolpe has defined anxiety as "the autonomic response pattern or patterns that are characteristically part of the organism's response to noxious stimulation."[76] He makes no differentiation between fear and anxiety, because there is no physiological difference in the response aroused by a stimulus associated with an objective threat such as a rattlesnake and unadaptive fear such as that aroused by a kitten. Neurotic behavior thus is learned. Stimuli previously incapable of provoking anxiety may acquire the power to arouse it if they happen to act on the organism when anxiety is evoked by other stimuli. Neuroses arise from the exposure of the individual either to ambivalent stimuli or to noxious stimuli (pain, discomfort), and these situations can induce high anxiety. However, not only well-defined stimuli but the ever present properties of the environment (light, shade, noise, and so on) may condition anxiety responses. If they do, the individual often suffers from pervasive anxiety.

> Since each of these enters into most, if not all, possible experience, it is to be expected that if any of them becomes connected to anxiety responses the patient will be persistently, and apparently causelessly anxious. He will be suffering from what is erroneously called "free-floating" anxiety, and for which a more suitable label would be *pervasive anxiety.*[77]

Conditions that predispose to neuroses include (1) direct evocation of anxiety (conditioned stimuli such as war experiences), (2) conflict (such as in difficult discriminations), and (3) confinement (spatial or environmental confinement).[78]

PRINCIPLE OF RECIPROCAL INHIBITION Reciprocal inhibition is the inhibition, elimination, or weakening of old by new responses. The principle was stated by Wolpe: "If a response antagonistic to anxiety can be made to occur in the presence of anxiety-evoking stimuli so that it is accompanied by a complete or partial suppression of the anxiety responses, the bond between these stimuli and the anxiety responses will

be weakened."[79] Wolpe points out that the bonds may be weakened by other means although when experimental extinction was sought, it was singularly ineffective. Poor extinction of anxiety responses was thought to be due to (1) the small amount of reactive inhibition generated by the autonomic response and (2) the reinforcement of anxiety responses by drive reduction when the individual is passively removed from anxiety-evoking stimuli.

The counselor and the counseling process

Individuals come for counseling because they suffer. Later they appraise therapy in terms of the relief experienced. The methods employed, according to Wolpe, should be assessed using several criteria.

> The primary criteria relate directly to the well-being of the patient. Is the suffering alleviated? If so, how quickly, how completely, and how enduringly? And how free is the accomplishment from disadvantageous sequelae? Secondary criteria are the amount of time and effort demanded of the therapist, and the cost of the treatment to the patient.[80]

INITIAL INTERVIEWS Wolpe has given a full account of the way interviews are conducted. The first interview lasts an hour, later ones forty-five minutes. The patient faces the therapist across a desk, and notes are taken openly at every interview. Everything a patient says is accepted without question or criticism. An outline of early interviews (first 10–15) is abstracted from his remarks:[81]

1. The patient gives name, address, age, telephone number.
2. A detailed history is taken of patient's difficulties, symptoms, precipitating events, and factors that aggravate or ameliorate symptoms.
3. Individuals who are unable to recall anything of the onset of neurotic reactions are urged to think back more carefully, but if nothing significant is produced, the point is not pressed. Wolpe tells such patients that "to overcome . . .

[76] Ibid., p. 34.
[77] Ibid., p. 83.
[78] Ibid., pp. 78–82.

[79] Ibid., p. 71.
[80] Wolpe et al., eds., *The Conditioning Therapies,* p. 5.
[81] Wolpe, *Psychotherapy by Reciprocal Inhibition,* pp. 105–113.

neurotic reactions it is of greater relevance to determine what stimuli do or can evoke them at the present time."[82]

4. Attention is directed to the patient's life history, starting with the circumstances in which he or she grew up (attitudes and relationships with parents, siblings, and others; religious training; fears).

5. Patient gives educational experiences.

6. An occupational history is taken.

7. Patient is questioned about sex life and marital history.

8. Bernreuter's self-sufficiency questionnaire is completed by the patient as homework.

9. Willoughby's questionnaire (a test for neuroticism) is administered in the interview situation.

10. Wolpe interprets how inhibitions or phobias or fears are learned.

11. From the patient's history, experiences that have led to present sensitivities are explained.

12. The patient is told that measures have to be taken to break down anxious habits and that some measures are applied in the consulting room whereas others are engaged in the life situation.

13. Methods are then introduced to inhibit anxiety and weaken neurotic habits. These include (a) assertive responses, (b) sexual responses, (c) relaxation responses, (d) respiratory responses, (e) "anxiety-relief" responses, (f) competitively conditioned motor responses, (g) "pleasant" responses in the life situation (with drug enhancement), and (h) interview-induced emotional responses and abreaction.

METHODS   The choice of responses depends on the anxiety-evoking stimuli.

> In general, assertive responses are used for anxieties evoked in the course of direct interpersonal dealings, sexual responses for sexual anxieties, relaxation responses for anxieties arising from any source whatever but especially from stimulus configurations that do not allow of any kind of direct action (e.g., inanimate objects), and respiratory responses for pervasive (free-floating) anxiety.[83]

These four techniques are briefly described here.

Assertive responses refer not only to more or less aggressive behavior but also to feelings of friendliness and affection. Assertive responses are used to treat anxieties arising from interpersonal relationships (for example, inability to express one's opinion to friends lest they disagree).

> The essence of the therapist's role is to encourage appropriate assertiveness, the outward expression, whenever it is reasonable and right to do so, of the feelings and action tendencies that anxiety in the past inhibited. In other words, the therapist instigates "acting out." Each act of assertion to some extent reciprocally inhibits the anxiety, and in consequence somewhat weakens the anxiety response habit.[84]

Techniques for instigating assertive behavior include (1) use of analogies, (2) behavior rehearsal in which the therapist takes the role of the persons toward whom the client has a neurotic anxiety reaction and instructs the client to express the inhibited feelings, and (3) pressure interviews, in which individuals are given a task to perform while verbal demands are simultaneously made on them. Appropriate pressure is applied to motivate the individual to engage in the requisite behavior outside the consulting room. Wolpe has warned that assertive acts should never be instigated that have punishing consequences for the client.

Sexual responses refer to measures used to inhibit anxiety responses conditioned by various aspects of sexual situations. Sexual inhibition varies by definable properties within the situation. Wolpe indicates the essential nature of the techniques employed:

> There are occasional patients of either sex in whom so high a degree of anxiety has been conditioned to individual women (or men) or classes of women (or men) that the mildest embrace or even close proximity may produce great disturbance; and if there is pervasive anxiety, as may be expected in patients so sensitive, its level is raised. Such a patient is instructed to expose himself only to sexual situations in which pleasurable feelings are felt exclusively or predominantly. The decision regarding the suitability of a situation is made *on the basis of the feelings experienced when the situation is in prospect.*[85]

[82] Ibid., p. 105.
[83] Ibid., p. 113.

[84] Wolpe et al., eds., *The Conditioning Therapies*, p. 11.
[85] Wolpe, *Psychotherapy by Reciprocal Inhibition*, pp. 130–131.

Relaxation responses are methods that involve giving patients intensive training in the practice of relaxation to enable them to keep relaxing muscles not in use. Differential relaxation (tension kept to a minimum in the muscles required for an act along with relaxation of other muscles) is used. Wolpe gives training in relaxation in seven sessions to most of his patients.[86]

Respiratory responses are those used for individuals suffering from pervasive anxiety. After being shown how to empty and fill the lungs, the individual empties the lungs and then inhales a gas mixture usually consisting of 65 percent carbon dioxide and 35 percent oxygen. Between one and four inhalations are given at a session.[87]

SYSTEMATIC DESENSITIZATION Most well known among Wolpe's techniques is that of systematic desensitization. Three sets of operations are involved in systematic desensitization: training in deep muscle relaxation, construction of anxiety hierarchies, and counterposing relaxation and anxiety stimuli from the hierarchies. The individual makes up a list of stimulus situations to which he or she reacts with graded amounts of anxiety. The most disturbing items are placed at the top and the least disturbing at the bottom. After being taught to relax, the individual (in some cases) is hypnotized and told to relax. The person is then told to imagine the weakest item in the anxiety hierarchy. If relaxation is maintained, the client is told to imagine the next item, and so on until the strongest item can be encountered. Apparently the relaxation inhibits the anxiety and weakens the anxiety-invoking potential of the stimulus. If a stimulus is too strong and increases sensitivity, scenes are not presented for one or two interviews. The hierarchies of one patient are as follows:

A. Fear of hostility
 1. Devaluating remarks by husband
 2. Devaluating remarks by friends
 3. Sarcasm from husband or friends
 4. Nagging
 5. Addressing a group
 6. Being at social gathering of more than four people (the more the worse)

7. Applying for a job
8. Being excluded from a group activity
9. Anybody with a patronizing attitude
B. Fear of death and its accoutrements
 1. First husband in his coffin
 2. At a burial
 3. Seeing a burial assemblage from afar
 4. Obituary notice of young person dying of heart attack
 5. Driving past a cemetery
 6. Seeing a funeral (the nearer the worse)
 7. Passing a funeral home
 8. Obituary notice of old person (worse if died of heart disease)
 9. Inside a hospital
 10. Seeing a hospital
 11. Seeing an ambulance
C. Fear of symptoms (despite *knowing* them to be nonsignificant)
 1. Extrasystoles
 2. Shooting pains in chest and abdomen
 3. Pains in left shoulder and back
 4. Pain on top of head
 5. Buzzing in ears
 6. Tremor of hands
 7. Numbness or pain in fingertips
 8. Dyspnea after exertion
 9. Pain in left hand (old injury)[88]

OUTCOMES Wolpe followed up 210 individuals he treated and reported 89 percent recovery, which is indeed dramatic. He concludes his comparison of conditioning therapies with psychoanalysis with these words:

> The present position is clear. As far as the evidence goes, conditioning therapies appear to produce a higher proportion of lasting recoveries from the distress and disability of neurosis than does psychoanalysis. Even if a controlled study were to show an equal, or even higher, percentage of recovery for psychoanalysis, the time it requires would remain incomparably greater, and conditioning therapy would therefore deserve preference.[89]

[86] Ibid., p. 136.
[87] Wolpe, *The Practice of Behavior Therapy*, p. 173.
[88] Ibid., pp. 142–143.
[89] Wolpe et al., eds., *The Conditioning Therapies*, p. 15.

Criticisms and contributions

The more commonly cited criticisms and contributions parallel those cited for behavioral counseling (see pp. 191–192). In addition, some psychotherapists claim that recoveries represent only symptom relief rather than lasting modifications of the basic problem.

Behavioral counseling viewpoint

Proponents and sources

John D. Krumboltz, Stanford University; Carl E. Thoresen, Stanford University; Jack Michael and Lee Meyerson, Arizona State University; and Ray E. Hosford, University of California, Santa Barbara, are among those who present behavioral counseling viewpoints. Primary treatment will be given here to the works of Krumboltz, Thoresen, and Hosford. The most relevant sources of information include *Revolution in Counseling*,[90] *Behavioral Counseling*,[91] *Counseling Methods*,[92] five articles by Krumboltz,[93] an article by Thoresen,[94] and an article by Hosford.[95]

[90] John D. Krumboltz, ed., *Revolution in Counseling* (Boston: Houghton Mifflin Company, 1966).
[91] John D. Krumboltz and Carl E. Thoresen, eds., *Behavioral Counseling: Cases and Techniques* (New York: Holt, Rinehart and Winston, 1969).
[92] John D. Krumboltz and Carl E. Thoresen, *Counseling Methods* (New York: Holt, Rinehart and Winston, 1976), 576 pp.
[93] John D. Krumboltz, "Behavioral Goals for Counseling," *Journal of Counseling Psychology*, 13 (Summer 1966), 153–159; John D. Krumboltz, "Behavioral Counseling: Rationale and Research," *Personnel and Guidance Journal*, 44 (December 1965), 383–387; John D. Krumboltz and Wade W. Schroeder, "Promoting Career Planning Through Reinforcement and Models," *Personnel and Guidance Journal*, 44 (September 1965), 19–26; John D. Krumboltz and Carl E. Thoresen, "The Effect of Behavioral Counseling in Group and Individual Settings on Information-Seeking Behavior," *Journal of Counseling Psychology*, 11 (Winter 1964), 324–333; John D. Krumboltz, "Parable of the Good Counselor," *Personnel and Guidance Journal*, 43 (October 1964), 118–124.
[94] Carl E. Thoresen, "Behavioral Counseling: An Introduction," *The School Counselor*, 14 (September 1966), 13–21.
[95] Ray E. Hosford, "Behavioral Counseling—A Contemporary Overview," *The Counseling Psychologist*, 1 (1969), 1–32.

Major concepts

Behavioral counselors define behavior as the function of the interaction of heredity and environment. Observable behavior is what counselors are concerned with and constitutes the criterion against which counseling outcomes are to be assessed. This view excludes virtually all hypothetical constructs such as those found in self-theory and in Freudian theory. "Man is not at the mercy of his 'unconscious' or his drives; for these entelechies, if they exist, can be expressed in many ways." [96]

Although there are wide divergencies in the specifics of behavioral viewpoints, fundamental agreement exists regarding the fact that most human behavior is learned. Behavior is modifiable by manipulation and the creation of learning conditions. Basically, the counseling process becomes the judicious and expert arrangement of learning or relearning experiences to help individuals change their behavior in order to solve whatever problems they manifest or select for presentation to the counselor.

Thoresen has characterized behavioral counseling with a fivefold statement:

1. Most human behavior is learned and is therefore subject to change.
2. Specific changes of the individual's environment can assist in altering relevant behaviors; counseling procedures seek to bring about relevant changes in student behavior by altering the environment.
3. Social learning principles, such as those of reinforcement and social modeling, can be used to develop counseling procedures.
4. Counseling effectiveness and the outcome of counseling are assessed by changes in specific student behaviors outside the counseling interview.
5. Counseling procedures are not static, fixed, or predetermined, but can be specifically designed to assist the student in solving a particular problem.[97]

More recently, Thoresen and Coates stated that the behavior therapies share a distinguishing characteristic: "they

[96] Jack Michael and Lee Meyerson, "A Behavioral Approach to Counseling and Guidance," *Harvard Educational Review*, 32 (Fall 1962), 395.
[97] Thoresen, "Behavioral Counseling," p. 17.

individual sufficiently to continue performing the behavior being reinforced. The second is that the reinforcement must be applied systematically. Third, the counselor must know when and how to reinforce, and fourth, the counselor must be able to elicit the behavior planned to reinforce.[113]

Imitative learning or social modeling is applied in that the counselor can arrange for the counselee to observe models of more adaptive behavior. If clients have little idea of what constitutes appropriate behavior, models in the form of tape recordings, programmed instruction, video tapes and films, people, and autobiographies may induce imitative behavior, which can then be reinforced. Krumboltz and Thoresen point out that social models should be prestigious, competent, knowledgeable, attractive, and powerful, and that clients may be influenced more when the social model they view is similar to them in some characteristics.[114] Hosford states that social modeling techniques work with groups as well as with individuals. He believes that when clients need to learn completely new or highly complex behaviors, social modeling or combinations of social modeling and operant conditioning can best be used to promote the desired change.[115]

Cognitive learning supplies methods that include verbal instruction, contracts between counselor and counselee, and role playing. *Emotional learning* has application in that individuals with severe feelings of anxiety can be systematically relaxed when the stimuli that produce anxieties are paired with more pleasant stimuli.

The techniques employed by the behavioral counselor depend on many variables. Among those cited by Hosford are (1) the client's behavioral assets and deficiencies, (2) the type of problem for which the client sought help, (3) the type and value of the various reinforcements available in the client's environment, and (4) the significant others in the client's life who might assist the counselor in promoting the desired behavior change.[116]

EVALUATION OF COUNSELING Krumboltz believes that counseling in its totality cannot be evaluated. Evaluation consists of specifying the kind of client problem, the direction of change desired by the client, the precise counseling procedure used, and the circumstances under which it is used. "What we need to know is which procedures and techniques, when used to accomplish what kinds of behavior change, are most effective with what kinds of clients when applied by what kind of counselors."[117]

Criticisms and contributions

Some of the commonly cited criticisms of both behavioral counseling and Wolpe's model include:

1. Behavioral counseling is cold, impersonal, and manipulative and relegates the relationship to a secondary function.
2. Behavioral counseling has concentrated on techniques, but the ends to which counseling is directed are equally important.
3. Although behavioral counselors say they accord counselees the freedom to select counseling goals, they are often predetermined by the counselor.
4. Although behavioral counselors assert that each client is unique and requires a unique, specific treatment, the problems of one client are often similar to the problems of another client and therefore do not require a unique counseling strategy.
5. The constructs of learning developed and adopted by behavioral counselors are not sufficiently comprehensive to explain learning and should be viewed only as hypotheses to be tested.
6. That client changes are but symptoms removed that emerge later in other forms of behavior.

Among the contributions to the field by behavioral counselors are these:

1. They have advanced counseling as a science because they have engaged in research and applied known knowledge to the counseling process.
2. They have called attention to the fact that, if counseling outcomes are to be measured, specific behaviors will have to be made explicit.
3. They have illustrated how limitations in environments can be removed or reduced.

[113] Hosford, "Behavioral Counseling," pp. 9–10.
[114] Krumboltz and Thoresen, *Behavioral Counseling*, p. 164.
[115] Hosford, "Behavioral Counseling," pp. 20–21.
[116] Hosford, "Behavioral Counseling," p. 8.

[117] Krumboltz, *Revolution in Counseling*. p. 22.

4. They have stressed that counseling should be focused on current rather than historical determinants of behavior.

Issues

Issue 1 A theory of counseling has yet to evolve.

True, because
1. That which is presented as counseling theory does not meet the criteria designated for use of the word *theory*. Such criteria include the presence of a coherent, integrated set of interrelated hypotheses that explain relationships between characteristics, conditions, or events; operationally defined terms that can be observed and measured, and so on.
2. The so-called counseling theories are really personality theories.
3. That which is presented as counseling theory is actually a theory of psychotherapy and does not describe counseling or counselor or client behaviors.

False, because
1. That which is presented as counseling theory seeks to make explicit that which takes place in counseling. It represents a framework for making observations and explaining phenomena of client behavior. Crude though the framework may be, it is a source of suggestions and hypotheses for further counselor action, research, testing, and modification.
2. Counseling is a process of changing behaviors, therefore, personality theory is a fundamental component of counseling theories. Prediction is an outcome of good theory and counseling theory enables its practitioners to make predictions about human behavior.
3. Whether that which is presented as counseling theory is conceptualized as theories of psychotherapy depends on the definitions ascribed to the terms.

Discussion The word *theory* has various meanings both in science and ordinary use. It may be contrasted with practice as unverified speculation, whether confirmed or not, or it may be restricted to hypotheses that have been confirmed sufficiently to become part of the accepted doctrine of a particular discipline.

A theory, in the strict formal use of the word, is a systematic account of some field, derived from a set of propositions. These propositions may be taken as postulates, as in pure mathematics (theory of functions, and the like), or they may be principles more or less confirmed by experience.

Scientific purists, no doubt, would suggest that current counseling theories fall far short of the elegant theories found in their favorite scientific endeavors. They would be critical that counseling theories are not very systematic or comprehensive in the observations made about counseling, that the terminology employed is quite esoteric, being incapable of standardization and measurement, and that predictions about human behavior generated from counseling theory are extremely limited.

A characteristic of the counseling field is the presence of rival theories, differing in their selection of principles or in the emphasis laid on particular principles. That characteristic, though maddening for the student, augurs well for the field and is best viewed as a mark of vitality for the profession. As the counseling profession, youthful compared to other professions, develops and matures, the part played by theory building will become increasingly important.

Issue 2 An eclectic theory is practiced by most counselors.

True, because
1. Most counseling practitioners will use any technique or method they believe will be beneficial and helpful to their clients.
2. Most counseling practitioners' conceptualizations of client behaviors are drawn from several theories rather than a single explanation.

False, because
1. Selection from among disparate counseling techniques and methods is based primarily on a trial-and-error basis, because a rational, systematized and verified knowledge base of techniques has yet to be developed.
2. The case conceptualizations of a true eclectic, although derived from several relevant theories, are drawn from client behaviors and these explanations are not necessarily internally consistent or coherent.

Discussion The Greek root of the word *eclectic* means "to pick out" and dictionary definitions stress selecting what seems best from various possibilities and combining them harmoniously. A major difficulty experienced by counselors who thought *eclectic* best described their theory and practice was combining harmoniously the best explanations and practices. Bits and pieces selected from among various counseling theories and practices often produced a hodgepodge of contradictory assumptions and incompatible principles, ideas, and methods. Nevertheless, counselors who observe other counselors or interact with them about their beliefs, observations about clients, techniques used, and so on, discover that the propositions and practices associated with one single theory are rarely representative of these counselors. Other counselors say that although theory X seems to give good explanations of human behavior and counseling, it does not fit precisely what their life experiences have led them to believe, therefore, it would be inaccurate for them or their counseling work to be characterized as theory X. They conclude that any departure from theory X means that they must be eclectic.

Still other counselors reason that, for example, only Williamson can be Williamson or that only Ellis can operate from a rational-emotive theory. Any attempt to follow their (or any theorist's) views is, at best, a weak imitation or, at worst, a gross distortion because that theorist has evolved a point of view from singular life experiences. Therefore, the conclusion is that one's own views and style are best described as eclectic.

Brammer has suggested that the term *eclectic* is best used to define those counselors who occupy a middle ground between "looking myopically through research eyes at minute aspects of the counseling experience and, on the other hand, reflecting in sweeping fashion about the relationship of counseling to philosophy, society and the individual."[118] Major characteristics of this "evolving eclectic," according to Brammer were an openness to all counseling research findings and a flexibility to change because of these research findings and to generate questions and hypotheses for more research.

Annotated references

Ellis, Albert. *Humanistic Psychotherapy: The Rational-Emotive Approach*. New York: Julian Press, 1973. 273 pp.

A wide variety of RET methods are presented and the major RET principles applied to psychotherapy have been explained more fully in these pages.

[118] Lawrence M. Brammer "Eclecticism Revisited," *Personnel and Guidance Journal*, 48 (November 1969), 194.

Krumboltz, John D., and Carl E. Thoresen, eds. *Behavioral Counseling: Cases and Techniques*. New York: Holt, Rinehart and Winston, 1969. 515 pp.

Descriptions of behavioral counseling techniques and practices are presented by various authors. The introduction by Krumboltz and Thoresen presents the essential features of behavioral counseling.

Patterson, C. H. *Theories of Counseling and Psychotherapy*. 2nd ed. New York: Harper & Row 1973. 554 pp.

Chapter 2 (pp. 6–48) presents Williamson's point of view and Chapter 20 (pp. 463–518) Thorne's personality counseling. Chapter 6 (pp. 125–156) gives Wolpe's counseling viewpoint. Patterson's coverage of these approaches is extensive and insightful.

Skinner, B. F. *About Behaviorism*. New York: Alfred A. Knopf, 1973. 256 pp.

Skinner presents the case for a technology of psychology based on behavioristic principles and research. He discusses views of human behavior and his ideas about designing a society that accommodates the individual. Chapter 14, "Summing Up," is a rather complete discussion of his views.

Wolpe, Joseph. *The Practice of Behavior Therapy*. New York: Pergamon Press, 1969. 314 pp.

In this volume, Wolpe updates his explanations of psychotherapy by reciprocal inhibition and presents other behavioral techniques.

Further references

Ellis, Albert. "Rational-Emotive Therapy and the School Counselor." *The School Counselor*, 22 (March 1975), 236–242.

Gilmore, Susan K. "Pioneers in Guidance: Leona Elizabeth Tyler." *Personnel and Guidance Journal*, 55 (April 1977), 451–459.

Hickey, Dolores F. "School Counselors' Attitudes Toward Behavior Modification." *Personnel and Guidance Journal*, 55 (April 1977), 477–480.

Hutchins, David E. "Systematic Counseling: The T-F-A Model for Counselor Intervention." *Personnel and Guidance Journal*, 57 (June 1979), 529–531.

Jackson, Barry, and Brenda Van Zoost. "Changing Study Behaviors Through Reinforcement Contingencies." *Journal of Counseling Psychology*, 19 (May 1972), 192–195.

Johnson, Richard H. "Individual Styles of Decision Making: A Theoretical Model for Counseling." *Personnel and Guidance Journal*, 56 (May 1978), 530–536.

Kirkpatrick, J. Stephen. "A Maslovian Counseling Model." *Personnel and Guidance Journal*, 57 (April 1979), 386–391.

Olbrisch, Mary Ellen. "Psychotherapeutic Interventions in Physical Health: Effectiveness and Economic Efficiency." *American Psychologist*, 32 (September 1977), 761–777.

Ponzo, Zander. "Integrating Techniques from Five Counseling Theories," *Personnel and Guidance Journal*, 54 (April 1976), 414–419.

Riedesel, Brian C. "Toward Full Development of the Person." *Personnel and Guidance Journal*, 57 (March 1979), 332–337.

Rosenblatt, Howard S. "How I Counsel," *Personnel and Guidance Journal*, 54 (September 1975), 44–45.

Smith, Mary Lee, and Gene V. Glass. "Meta-Analysis of Psychotherapy Outcome Studies." *American Psychologist*, 32 (September 1977), 752–760.

Sue, Derald Wing. "World Views and Counseling." *Personnel and Guidance Journal*, 56 (April 1978), 458–462.

Sue, Stanley. "Psychological Theory and Implications for Asian Americans," *Personnel and Guidance Journal*, 55 (March 1977), 381–389.

Thoresen, Carl E., and Thomas J. Coates. "What Does It Mean to Be a Behavior Therapist?" *The Counseling Psychologist*, 7, No. 3 (1978), 3–20.

9 Affectively oriented counseling approaches

The previous chapter presented five counseling viewpoints: trait and factor, rational-emotive, eclectic, psychotherapy as reciprocal inhibition, and behavioral counseling. Those included in this chapter will be psychoanalytic, Adlerian, transactional analysis, client-centered, existential, and gestalt therapy.

Psychoanalytic viewpoint

Originator and source material

Psychoanalysis is a method of treating individuals by psychological rather than physical means and is a branch of science. The original body of doctrine was set forth by Sigmund Freud between approximately 1890 and 1939. He won recognition as the first to map the subconscious of the human mind. Freud was born in 1856 in Freiberg, Moravia (Czechoslovakia), and died in 1939 in England. After graduating from the University of Vienna in 1881 he became interested in psychiatry, studied under Jean Martin Charcot, and later worked with Josef Breuer on the use of hypnosis in treating hysteria. His works, excluding those of his students and followers, make up twenty-three volumes and cover a time span of fifty years.[1] Freud's thinking, recognized and unrecognized, permeates many contemporary theories of personality and is the basis for many counseling practices.

Individuals who accepted basic Freudian principles and simultaneously sought to modernize them by attempting to incorporate the findings of contemporary psychology are usually referred to as neo-Freudians. Their ranks include the following:

CARL JUNG (1875–1961) His rupture with Freud occurred in 1912 with the publication of Jung's book *The Psychology of the Unconscious.* Among his disagreements with Freud was

that over the interpretation of the nature of the libido. Jung believed that *libido* (or life force) was primarily sexual in early human history but became desexualized as humans evolved. He accepted an individual unconscious similar to Freud's but posited also a collective unconscious containing racial memories. Within this were emotional stereotypes (archetypes) common to all races. Examples would be the Jovian figure of the "old, wise man" and the "earth mother." Evolving a theory of character, Jung divided people into two types: introverts (interests centered on self) and extroverts (interests turned on external world). Each type was further subdivided into feeling, thinking, intuition, and sensation subtypes.

OTTO RANK (1884–1939) After experimenting with short-term therapy (circa 1920), Rank broke with Freud and moved to Paris and later to New York. It seemed to him that birth trauma (shock of leaving the womb and security) rather than the Oedipal complex was responsible for emotional disturbance. He believed Oedipal feelings came too late to be decisive. Anxiety caused by birth trauma formed a sort of reservoir that should seep away gradually during maturation. If it persisted, then neurosis set in. He evolved a more active therapist role (contrasted to Freud's passive role) and established time limits for therapy. Basic to the Rankian viewpoint is the conception of the will as an expression of the positive and unifying aspects of the individual in developing independence. Dependency strivings are often viewed as blocks to the growth of positive will.

WILHELM REICH (1897–1957) Reich broke with Freud in 1932 in a dispute over the existence of the death instinct and its function in causing masochism. Reich utilized character analysis as a preliminary step (other analysts view it as the chief objective of therapy) prior to the main task of analysis or as education for analysis.

KAREN HORNEY (1885–1952) Trained as a Freudian analyst in Germany, Horney came to the United States in the 1930s

---

[1] James Strachey, ed., *The Standard Edition of the Complete Psychological Works of Sigmund Freud* (London: Hogarth Press, 1964).

and soon founded a separate training institute. She repeatedly insisted that her views were corrective of Freud rather than a new approach. However, she rejected both his structural theory of the mind and his instinct theory. She sought to apply the thinking of anthropologists and sociologists to analysis. Human behavior, according to Horney, stems from the need for security. Basic anxiety results when the child is unable to manage insecurities caused by certain relationships with parents and views the world as hostile and threatening. Horney emphasized the importance of present-life situations in understanding and helping individuals, for the strategies they invent to cope with their aloneness and helplessness assume the character of a drive or need and constitute irrational or neurotic behavior. She modified Adler's concept of neurotic goals because she believed that these contained their own sources of anxiety. Horney identified ten such goals, including need for affection and approval, power, exploitation of others, personal admiration, personal achievement, perfection, and unassailability.

THEODORE REIK (1888–1969) Reik never broke away from Freud, but pursued and extended Freud's explorations into love, guilt, and compulsions. His classical work, *Listening with the Third Ear*, won wide acclaim, for it portrayed the analyst's thoughts and emotions in encounters with clients. Reik, one of the first nonmedical psychoanalysts, founded a training center for such individuals, the National Psychological Association for Psychoanalysis.

HARRY STACK SULLIVAN (1892–1949) Sullivan held that the human individual is the product of interpersonal relationships. The pattern of the child's earliest nonsexual relationships with significant figures largely (but not rigidly) determines the pattern of later interpersonal integration. The goal of human behavior is twofold: the pursuit of satisfaction (biological) and the pursuit of security (cultural). Satisfactions include sleep, rest, sex, food, drink, and close interpersonal contacts; security refers to well-being, belonging, and acceptance. Most emotional problems, argued Sullivan, stem from the pursuit of security. Socialization is the process of becoming a human being, and the individual develops a self with three personifications: "me," "good me," and "not me." If positive experiences bring security the "good me" represents the individual's self-concept.

The theorists who accepted most of Freud's theories but whose contributions are also presented as logical extensions of Freud's ideas rather than separate systems are referred to as ego analysts. Often included in this category are Heinz Hartmann, Anna Freud (Freud's daughter), David Rapaport, and Erik Erikson, who, basically, have sought to understand and study normal human behavior. They believe that antecedents to behavior are more varied than innate psychological events (Freud's instinctual drives) and that some behavior is learned in relation to other events. They have stressed ego functions (behavior by which individuals direct their activity and deal with their environment) such as thought, language, and perceptual and sensory responses. Erikson, for example, has described the development of the normal personality by a series of eight focal problems or dilemmas (see Chapter 3).

Among the secondary sources available for study of the psychoanalytic viewpoint are Brill,[2] Arlow and Brenner,[3] Ford and Urban,[4] Harper,[5] Beck,[6] and Alexander.[7]

Major concepts

Freud originated elaborate theories of the structure of personality and of the causes of psychological disorders. His ideas long were disregarded or attacked, partly because they were derived from clinical rather than experimental observation, partly because they often seemed rather incredible, and partly because of shock and distaste regarding what Freud stated he had discovered. Over time, however, personality research has validated parts of Freud's theories.

OBJECTIVE OF PSYCHOANALYSIS The major objective of psychoanalytic therapy is to help individuals achieve an en-

[2] A. A. Brill, *The Basic Writings of Sigmund Freud* (New York: Modern Library, 1938).

[3] Jacob A. Arlow and Charles Brenner, *Psychoanalytic Concepts and the Structural Theory* (New York: International Universities Press, 1964).

[4] Donald H. Ford and Hugh B. Urban, *Systems of Psychotherapy*. (New York: John Wiley & Sons, 1963), pp. 109–178.

[5] Robert Harper, *Psychoanalysis and Psychotherapy* (Englewood Cliffs, N. J.: Prentice-Hall, 1963).

[6] Carlton E. Beck, *Philosophical Foundations of Guidance* (Englewood Cliffs, N.J.: Prentice-Hall, 1963).

[7] Franz Alexander, *Fundamentals of Psychoanalysis* (New York: W. W. Norton & Company, 1963), 312 pp.

during understanding of their own mechanisms of adjustment and thereby to help them resolve their basic problems. It is designed primarily for the treatment of neurosis but has been used with a variety of psychological disorders.

NATURE OF HUMANKIND   A fundamental influence attributed to Freud is that of antirationalism, which stresses unconscious motivation, conflict, and symbolism as its primary concepts. Freud believed that humankind is essentially biological, being born with certain instinctual drives, and that behavior is a function of reacting in depth to these drives. Human beings are irrational, unsocialized, and destructive of themselves and others. Most notable is the drive toward self-gratification. A person's basic psychic energy, or libido, is equated with sexual energy by using the word *sex* broadly to stand for all pleasure. The libido (Eros or life force) drives the individual in search of pleasure. In about 1920 Freud also proposed that another drive existed in addition to Eros. This was the death wish or *Thanatos* and referred to the individual's aggressive drive. Harper points out that there are two hypotheses from which Freud never departed and that serve as guides to understanding his theories. The first is the concept of psychic determination (each psychic event is determined by those that precede it) and the second is the idea that consciousness is the unusual rather than the usual characteristic of mental processes.[8]

PERSONALITY THEORY   Freud formulated (circa 1900) a *topographic theory* of how the mind functions that has been discussed by Arlow and Brenner.[9] The following is based on their presentation. Mental processes derive no more by chance or are no more arbitrary or disconnected than physical processes. Many mental processes, including some of the more important determinants of behavior and conscious thought, occur without conscious awareness. In Freud's topographic theory the mental apparatus was divided into three systems. The *unconscious (Ucs.)* system contains mental elements accessible to consciousness only with difficulty or not at all. The *preconscious (Pcs.)* system includes those elements readily accessible to consciousness. Finally, the *conscious (Cs.)* system includes whatever is conscious at any given moment. Between the unconscious and precon-

scious systems an intersystemic censor operates to enable the preconscious to exclude objectionable elements from the conscious system. For an unconscious element to become conscious it must first become preconscious. Freud conceptualized the systems *Ucs.* and *Pcs.* in terms of energy discharge and potential. Unconscious elements function according to what he labeled the *primary process* whereas preconscious and conscious elements function according to *secondary processes.* The primary process, characteristic of young children, features complete discharge of mental energies without delay, and immediate gratification is uninhibited by reality factors. By contrast, in the secondary process emphasis is on delay of wish fulfillment, recognition of reality, and cognizance of environmental factors that are favorable or unfavorable to the discharge of psychic energy.

Freud discarded the topographic theory, according to Arlow and Brenner,[10] because he found it inadequate to explain, among other things, how the anti-instinctual forces may be accessible to consciousness if the sexual wishes they repress are not. He replaced it with the structural theory, which divided the mind into the *id*, the *ego*, and the *superego.* More precisely, the mind was divided into two parts, the id and ego, the id being the source of instinctual drives, the ego regulating or mediating between the drives and environmental demands. The moral functions in the ego separate from the other functions and constitute the superego.

These three terms simply represent convenient concepts for summarizing major aspects of personality, and no clear line exists among them. The id, as Freud conceived it, is the repository of the libido (life force) or unlearned physiological motives and unlearned primitive reactions for satisfying them. Left to itself, the id would seek immediate gratification for motives as they arose without regard to the realities of life or to morals of any kind (would in effect be governed by the pleasure principle).

The emerging human personality develops, out of intimate contacts with others in families and groups, the elements of a conscious "self" that is perceptive, adaptable, and self-seeking; this is the ego. The ego bridles the id. The ego includes the elaborate ways of behaving and thinking that have been learned for dealing effectively with the world. Governed by the reality principle, the ego delays

[8] Harper, *Psychoanalysis*, p. 13.
[9] Arlow and Brenner, *Psychoanalytic Concepts*, pp. 9–23.
[10] Ibid., p. 28.

satisfaction of motives or channels them into socially acceptable outlets. Seemingly, Freud's view was that a person's motives are basically those of beasts overlaid and modified (but in no sense expunged) by the history of interaction with others, from whom each learned *you* and *yours* and the meaning of *me* and *mine*. As a result, human beings become equally capable of purposeful social effort but also indulge in vanity, greed, and cruelty.

The superego corresponds to conscience and is ruled, not by the pristine seeds of passion and egotism, but by the morality principle. Into the superego component is built those socially acquired restraints, redirections, and sublimation of impulse without which people are less than human. The superego may condemn as wrong things that the ego might do in the service of satisfying the id's motives. How did this conscience come about? Concern with virtue is presumably a concomitant of awareness of vice and a sense of guilt over acts that are "wrong." The first acts judged wrong were doubtless those that threatened the survival of the group. Perhaps primitive cannibalism initiated such sentiments as people dimly saw that the killing and eating of one another was potentially a road to death for all. Freud's thesis was that in the "primal horde," ruled by an elder male with a plurality of wives and a multiplicity of offspring, the maturing sons sought to kill the jealous and all-powerful father, to eat his flesh, and to fight to the death among themselves for the females. Patricide, incest, and fratricide spelled ruin to the group and consequently were at some point condemned, renounced, and guarded against through elaborate taboos on murder and incest, totemic myths, and rigid rules of exogamy as a means of survival. Freud thus derived conscience from these postulated relationships.

DOCTRINE OF INFANTILE SEXUALITY   Freud formulated the doctrine of infantile sexuality in which the libido, or basic psychic energy, drives the individual in search of pleasure. While the libido is primarily sexual in nature, it includes all things that stand for pleasure. Beginning in infancy the individual is pushed by the libido toward the achievement of mature development. If no serious obstacle is encountered, one progresses through certain phases. If frustrated, one persists or becomes *fixated* at a particular phase.

The infant's first search for gratification is limited to release of hunger tension. Freud considered this the beginning of the child's sexuality because the desire to suck is partly the desire for the mother's breast or the first of a long series of sexually desired objects. The *oral* phase characterizes the first year of life, and libidinal energy is centered around the mouth. In the second or *anal* phase satisfaction comes from defecation. The child's pleasures during this phase (ages 1 to 3) are concentrated on self (narcissistic), and satisfactions lie in achieving body control and mastery over objects.

Around the third or fourth year the genitals become a major focus of libidinal energy; this is the *phallic* phase. The penis and clitoris become a source of pleasure and a matter of pride. Any threat to their existence or functioning may result (among boys) in a fear of castration. The girl, in her exploration, discovers that she is without a penis and may deprecate all men—"penis envy." Sexual exploration and interest in the parents begin and the *Oedipal* period is initiated (ages 3 to 7). During this phase the child becomes interested in the opposite-sexed parent, desires to possess him or her sexually, and views the other parent as a hostile rival. All of this, of course, is a matter of private fantasy. Because children soon learn that such sexual interest is forbidden, they seek to resolve the situation. Freud believed that resolution of the situation was the crucial factor in the development of personality. Resolution could be accomplished by (1) repressing the wishes and thoughts, (2) destroying them, or (3) identifying with the same-sexed parent. If strong feelings of anxiety and guilt developed, serious personality disturbances evolved.

Following the Oedipal period is the *latency* phase (age 7 to about ages 12–14), characterized by decrease in sexual interest and energy. But with the onset of puberty the intensity of biological sex energy increases again and Oedipal feelings are reactivated. If the Oedipal feelings were previously resolved satisfactorily, the healthy individual becomes interested in opposite-sexed persons outside the family and goes on to mature sexual fulfillment. The libido, therefore, reaches its original goal, the *genital* stage of development.

Harper identifies four important concepts derived by Freud from his theory of personality development.[11] They are summarized here:

1. *Concept of bisexuality of human beings.*   No male is devoid of some strong wishes of a feminine nature, and no female is without some underlying masculine tendencies.

[11] Harper, *Psychoanalysis*, pp. 16–18.

At a conscious level such homosexual inclinations are very strongly repudiated, but unconsciously bisexuality (and guilt and anxiety regarding it) is of paramount importance in understanding human behavior.

2. *Concept of bipolarity of human emotions.* This process is known as ambivalence: feelings of a positive nature toward a person or group are almost invariably accompanied by negative feelings. Often negative feelings are repressed from consciousness. Examples of ambivalence include the parent who consciously loves his or her child but is unconscious of accompanying feelings of hostility toward the child.

3. *Concept of sublimation.* Freud believed that a certain amount of libido that is originally devoted to a sexual focus may be directed into ostensibly nonsexual channels. In other words, a substitute activity that conforms to personal and social definitions of acceptability is used to gratify a motive. Frustrated sexual urges could be partially gratified by being channeled into art, music, or some other aesthetic activity that is socially acceptable.

4. *Concept of displacement.* In his analysis of dreams, Freud discovered that the object or goal of a motive is often disguised by substituting another one in its place. That is, when one idea or image is substituted for another that is emotionally (not necessarily logically) associated with it, displacement has occurred.

NATURE OF ANXIETY Freud first believed that anxiety resulted from undischarged, accumulated libido but later considered anxiety biologically inherited rather than culturally acquired. Anxiety arises from two sets of circumstances: traumatic situations and danger situations. Harper's description of these situations will be discussed here.[12] An example of a traumatic anxiety is the birth experience. Examples of signal or danger anxiety include (1) loss of a loved object or (2) loss of the object's love or (3) disapproval and punishment by superego. In the danger situations the individual learns to recognize and anticipate trouble and reacts to the anticipation with anxiety.

Freud distinguished three types of anxiety. In *real* or *objective* anxiety the source of danger is external to the individual (for example, loss of job or loss of wife). *Neurotic anxiety* results from an unsuccessful attempt to achieve

[12] Ibid., pp. 32–35.

harmony between id and ego (for example, the individual is overwhelmed by an uncontrollable urge to commit some act that the ego defines as harmful). Neurotic anxiety could take three forms: free-floating, phobic, and panic. The free-floating form is exemplified in the nervous person who is apprehensive but the source of anxiety is vague, transitory, and ill defined. The phobic form is characterized by specific irrational fear (claustrophobia). The panic form arises when individuals act out their impulses (murder, suicide, rape). *Moral anxiety* derives from a threat from the superego or is the result of being punished by one's conscience.

DEFENSE MECHANISMS Freud noted that, to cope with frustration and its accompanying anxiety, general defenses were utilized by the individual—a change in focus of attention, fantasy, or other means of neutralizing the energy of the dangerous drive. Defense mechanisms were formulated by Freud while treating patients with conversion hysteria (individuals who have symptoms such as blindness or paralysis without organic cause) who appeared unable to remember certain traumatic experiences, yet could recall these experiences after undergoing psychotherapy. Defense mechanisms are learned and operate to some degree in normal behavioral functioning as well as in pathological ways. Although taken up singly below, they often function together or in multiple forms.

1. The most basic mechanism in reacting to anxiety is *repression*, a reaction in which a person rejects from consciousness impulses or thoughts that provoke anxiety. The person refuses to recognize or admit the motives or memories that make him or her anxious and consequently avoids or reduces anxiety.
2. A common defense mechanism, *reaction formation* covers conversion of unacceptable hostility into cloying solicitousness, seen in many do-gooders and some overprotective mothers who unconsciously reject their children. In other words, a motive is expressed in a form that is directly opposite to its original intent.
3. In employing *rationalization* people explain their own behavior so as to conceal the motive it expresses and assigns it to some other motive. Many examples exist in everyday affairs—the student who is motivated to have a good time rationalizes failing grades as being due to inadequate instruction or unfair teachers, for instance.

4. By use of *projection* the individual disguises the source of conflict in oneself by ascribing motives to someone else. The woman who will not leave her house because she is sure that men are waiting to attack her may be suspected of projecting her own thwarted sex desires. She projects her impulses on men as a group.

5. *Introjection* is the reverse of projection. In the example of the woman cited in the above paragraph, if through fantasy the woman identifies with a movie actress who is in the embrace of a man, she can partially achieve her wish fulfillment but successfully keeps out of consciousness the fact that she has such a sexual desire.

6. In *displacement* the object or goal of a motive is disguised by substituting another one for it. If a man who becomes angry at his employer but dares not tell him off goes home and berates his wife, he is making use of displacement.

7. *Regression* is a retreat to earlier or primitive forms of behavior. It is a relapse to habits learned earlier, or it takes the form of a more simple, less intellectual approach to problem solution.

8. Sometimes it is possible to gratify a frustrated motive, at least in part, by resorting to daydreaming. *Fantasy* is common among most people, particularly adolescents. As a form of adjustment it rarely leads to constructive action but can produce certain amounts of satisfaction. It becomes serious when it interferes with effective ways of dealing with frustrated needs.

9. *Denial of reality* is readily observable in severe pathological cases. The brain-injured person who suffers from leg paralysis, for instance, does not "see" the limb if it is brought into the area of vision. Denial of reality may be a special form of repression.

A fundamental weakness of defense mechanisms is that they are directed at anxiety, not at the motivational conflicts that give rise to it. They often conceal or disguise the real problem, leaving it ever present and operative. Their inadequacy is also bound up in the fact that they may allay anxiety from one cause but increase anxiety from another cause.

When a relatively stable balance among the id, ego, and superego is achieved, the existing state, according to Freud, constitutes the person's character structure. If people are relatively happy and well adapted to their environment, they are considered healthy. If their capacity for pleasure is relatively restricted and their adaptation to the environment is impaired, they are said to have a pathological character structure or a character disorder or character neurosis.

NEUROSES AND PSYCHOSES A two-fold classification exists to divide illnesses into psychoneuroses (more commonly called neuroses) and psychoses. Psychoneurosis, in Freud's terms, is caused by the ego's failure to control id impulses, in which case the ego works out a compromise. Neurotics use defense mechanisms to such a degree that their functioning is impaired and they become too anxious or incapacitated in their work and relationships with others. Neuroses are usually classified into (1) hysterias, (2) psychasthenias, and (3) anxiety reactions. Psychoses, on the other hand, are grouped into functional (no known disease) and organic (originating from damage or disease). Three functional categories of psychoses include (1) manic-depressive, (2) paranoia, and (3) schizophrenia. Several organic types of psychoses exist, including (1) involutional melancholia, (2) senile and alcoholic psychoses, and (3) general paresis. For several years questions have been raised as to whether the "manic" or bipolar depressive psychosis is functional. More and more evidence suggests that it is organic.

The process

Classic psychoanalytic treatment required the patient to recline on a couch with the analyst seated behind the patient's head. Literally and figuratively, the analyst occupied the role of unquestioned authority. Freud's work with Breuer uncovered the fact that a hypnotized patient was helped by talking out emotional difficulties that apparently arose from early events that could not be remembered previously. Although Breuer abandoned the talking out (catharsis) process because of its sexually laden content, Freud began to utilize it in a waking state (free association). After the analyst explains the general procedures, aims, and purposes of therapy, patients are told that their behaviors and attitudes may depend on emotional factors of which they are unaware and that these must be traced back to their unconscious motivations if they are to be understood and dealt with effectively. The analyst is generally passive and silent, offering no advice and speaking only to prod the patient into uncovering more nuggets from the inner resources of the mind.

FREE ASSOCIATION An important tool of psychoanalysis is the use of free association. The individual tells all that comes to mind (free associating) especially about early trauma (or shock) regardless of how irrelevant or objectionable it may seem. Because infancy and much of childhood are consciously forgotten, the patient may persist or fail to produce any words, ideas, or thoughts. *Resistance* is an inability to remember important past events or to talk about anxiety-charged subjects. It is the analyst's task to deal with resistances.

INTERPRETATION Situations cannot be forced, but the analyst may interpret the resistance to clear the path of the associations and provide a flow for further understanding. Interpretations are tentative and are revised as free association continues.

DREAM ANALYSIS During the course of analysis the patient may report dreams, which often recapture childhood experiences. Dreams are considered important because they may provide a means of understanding the unconscious. The manifest content (reported dream product) is not as important as the latent content or motivational conflicts symbolized in the dreams. Although a dream is often a wish fulfillment, there is no absolute symbolism (snakes may be phallic symbols to one dreamer but to another simply reminiscent of a trip to a zoo) and consequently no universal key to the meaning of dreams.

TRANSFERENCE At the core of psychoanalytic therapy is the transference that develops as analysis proceeds. Transference is the re-enactment of previous relationships with people and principally of the parent-child relationship. This attachment of the patient to the analyst may actually be seen as a form of displacement since the analyst becomes the proxy for love or hatred unconsciously attached to a significant person. The therapist may become, emotionally, a father figure for the patient. When the emotions directed toward the therapist are those of affection and dependence, the transference is positive; if a hostile attitude is dominant, the transference is negative. Handling transference requires great adroitness on the part of the analyst, who normally meets the transference reaction boldly but treats it as unreal. Success in the analysis is dependent on using the transference to understand the patient's resistance.

USE OF PARAPHRASES AND WIT Freud often used "slips of tongue" and wit or humor as an aid in understanding unconscious motives. They were seen as individual ways of releasing pent-up energy attached to repressed wishes.

TERMINATION OF THERAPY Termination is indicated when the patient gives evidence of having cleared up childhood memories that have served as resistances for important motives. Another indication is that the transference situation has been resolved and a normal relationship between analyst and patient has been established.

Criticisms and contributions

Some major criticisms of psychoanalysis include the following:

1. Freud's deterministic view pictures human beings as ugly and driven too much by animalistic instincts, needs, and wants. Humankind is seen erroneously as being composed of two parts, the mental and physical (both derived from and dependent on laws of cause and effect).
2. Too much stress is placed on early childhood experiences. It tends to erode individual responsibility because it makes an individual's life seem totally determined and beyond any personal power to alter.
3. It is doubtful that behavior is determined by a reservoir of psychic energy. Rather, it is probably manifested under certain situational events and not others.
4. Freud minimized rationality.
5. Treatment in analysis is too rational in its approach and too dependent on reasoning as a therapeutic influence.
6. Research data do not indicate that the system results in a better percentage of recovery and improvement than occurs among groups whose members have had no treatment.

Among the many contributions of psychoanalysis are the following:

1. Freud made it plain that human beings are often motivated in thought and in behavior by impulses they do not recognize or admit.
2. Freud's bold and insightful observations yielded the first substantial theory of personality and the first effective technique of psychotherapy.

3. Freud's identification of early influences that shape the development of personality had far-reaching implications for child rearing and stimulated research in the area.

4. Freud established a model in the use of the interview as a therapeutic vehicle. He was among the first to identify the function of anxiety in neurosis and in therapy and to emphasize the critical nature of interpretation, resistance, and transference in the therapeutic process.

5. Freud was one of the first to stress the importance of a nonmoralizing attitude on the part of the therapist.

6. Psychoanalysis represents a system in which there is a high degree of correspondence between theory and technique.

Individual psychology

Proponents and sources

Individual psychology was originated by Alfred Adler who represented the system as a comparative means of understanding individuals in relation to their social environment. Adler was born in 1870 near Vienna, the third child (second son of six children) of parents in comfortable circumstances. In 1911, he resigned from the Vienna Psychoanalytic Society, breaking with Freud who said, "I made a pigmy great." Adler's split with Freud came primarily because he rejected the sexual etiology of neurosis. Adler came to the United States in 1926 and later served as a visiting professor at Long Island College of Medicine. He died (1937) in Scotland while on a lecture tour.

Prominent practitioners of Adlerian psychology include Rudolph Dreikurs (1897–1972), Martin Sontesgard, and Donald Dinkmeyer. An original source of information about the theory is Adler's volume[13] translated by Paul Radin and a secondary source volume is that by Ansbacher and Ansbacher.[14]

Major concepts

A major construct of individual psychology is that human behavior is best viewed as compensation for inferiority

feelings. Inevitably, feelings of weaknesses and helplessness arise and become intensified because children live among adults or perceive their body organs as being deficient. Adler believed this fundamental principle of motivation by compensating for inferiority feelings explained almost all human behavior. Humans are dismayed by their feelings of inadequacy and imperfection, therefore, they react to this unpleasantness by attaining excellence, greatness, perfection, and supremacy. Reacting to deficit conditions, the organism strives for equilibrium by compensating for the inferiority. The goal of superiority lies at the heart of psychic life and explains why people are motivated to win at games or war, to make money, to dominate others, to demonstrate power over a sexual partner, to achieve immortality. Individuals who overcompensate for feelings of inadequacy develop an *inferiority complex*, a term Adler created to convey that repressed (unconscious) fear or resentment of being inferior, particularly in some feature or organ of the body, produced distorted behaviors.

The inferiority complex, according to Adler, originated in any of three sources. One was organ inferiority and the other two sources were associated with childhood: (1) spoiled, pampered children and (2) rejected (neglected, unwanted, ugly, and "wrong sex") children. Certain adults, coddled as children, believe they are inferior because they cannot adjust to other adults, whereas still other adults, rejected as children, believe they are inferior because they were unloved.

Adler proposed that an individual with a sizable inferiority complex often overcompensated to achieve unparalleled superiority (similar to Freudian compensation as an ego-defense mechanism; see pp. 199–200). Those with a superiority complex believe themselves to be extraordinarily gifted and accomplished. They are vain, arrogant, snobbish, boastful, domineering, and deprecate others.

Adler suggested a novel (at that time) device for the compensation of a severe inferiority complex. He noted that society equated femininity with inferiority and masculinity with superiority. Therefore, superiority may be gained by embracing masculinity and rejecting femininity. Masculine endeavors make men seem superior and feminine endeavors make men seem inferior. On the other hand, masculine endeavors make women more superior, so that some women with acute inferiority complexes tend to renounce their femininity, to assume masculine roles and to compete with men. Adler termed this *masculine protest*, offering it as an alternative explanation to Freud's *penis envy*.

---

[13] Alfred Adler, *The Practice and Theory of Individual Psychology*, trans. Paul Radin (London: Routledge and Kegan Paul Ltd., 1923).
[14] Heinz L. Ansbacher and Rowena R. Ansbacher, eds., *The Individual Psychology of Alfred Adler* (New York: Basic Books, 1956).

Another important construct in individual psychology is its social situational conception of behavior. The individual is a holistic organism; a unified unconscious-conscious entity; there is no reduction to components; there is no id, ego, superego as presented in the Freudian conception. Adler states that "by starting with the assumption of the *unity of the individual*, an attempt is made to obtain a picture of this unified personality regarded as a variant of individual life-manifestations and forms of expression."[15] People are basically social and seek to find a place in society.

Another major construct is that Adler viewed this unified organism as goal oriented. Strivings for superiority are directed by the individual's unique goal. Both biological and environmental factors influence the individual's goal but mainly it is created (an ideal, therefore a fiction) by the individual. Adler wrote that "we cannot think, feel, will, or act without the perception of some goal. Every psychic phenomenon can only be grasped and understood if regarded as a preparation for some goal."[16] Adler's emphasis on goal-directed behavior differed considerably from Freud's concept of drive-impelled behavior. Individuals strive for mastery, superiority, totality and this striving is directed by these "fictions." Individuals are socially driven to move from a state of perceived inferiority to a state of perceived superiority. Although influenced by parental attitudes, family conditions, and family constellation (birth order), each individual has a creative self that is responsible for choices of thoughts, actions, and feelings. A goal remains unknown to the individual. Because it is not understood or known it represents unconsciousness.

Human beings, as viewed by Adlerian psychology, never act at cross purposes with themselves as set forth by Freud. Both conscious and unconscious psychic factors strive for the same ends; however, consciousness may conflict with unconsciousness over the means to an end. Adler viewed both the conscious and the unconscious as determined by subjective values and interests, being ideals or "fictions" created by the individual. The individual is not separate from the social situation. Person and situation are embedded. These views have been labeled a *soft determinism* compared to Freud's *hard determinism.*

Another major construct is that the individual is a self-consistent organization. Adler states that "all psychical powers are under the control of a directive idea and all expressions of emotion, feeling, thinking, willing, acting . . . are permeated by one unified life plan."[17] At about 3 to 5 years old, children assess their life circumstances and lay down a prototype or life plan of action. Once this plan (rarely understood consciously) has been formulated, meanings are ascribed to experiences thus forming a *lifestyle.* People experience reality as they perceive it and according to their own private logic. Behavior that appears contradictory to the lifestyle is best viewed as being an adaptation of different means to the same end. The individual's sense of identity, views of the world, interpretations of the relationship between the individual and the environment are facets of the lifestyle and influence behavior. The lifestyle takes root in the nature of the family constellation. Such contingencies as the birth position of individuals, whether they are an only child, or the only boy in a family of six children, necessarily influence the kind of prototype likely to be formed.

Another important construct is that *community interests,* an inherent quality in human beings, are to be cultivated. Community or social interests (tenderness, love, friendship) represent the antidote to selfish strivings for superiority. If humans feel inferior, they equally are able to feel empathy for others. Strivings for *perfection* rather than *superiority* can be altruistic and represent not just fictions but facts of life. Humankind is evolving into a higher state and each individual has the responsibility to further this end by striving for perfection.

Maladjustment, according to individual psychology, can be understood as behaviors used as substitutes to gain a feeling of superiority. Anxiety arises as a result of an individual's concentration on achieving personal superiority to the exclusion of considering needs of others. Neurotics are unable to harmonize what they believe are opposite tendencies—power and submission—in their natures. They live a *life lie* in that their movements are to play one side against the other, sidestepping life's problems, cooperation, social adaptation, and community responsibilities. A neurotic has an inferiority complex as well as a superiority complex. Psychotics, according to Adler, withdraw to a fantasy world, construct a delusional belief system, hallucinating to help justify failures and obtain sympathy from others.

[15] Adler, *Practice and Theory,* p. 2.
[16] Ibid., pp. 3–4.
[17] Ibid., p. 17.

The counselor and the counseling process

The first rule in counseling, according to Adler, is to secure the confidence of the client and the second rule is not to worry about success for to do so means that success will be forfeited. Counselors serve as skillful coparticipants in the process, but responsibility for change is placed squarely on clients.

Counseling strategy usually involves uncovering the present life pattern and then working backward until both counselor and client are clear about the latter's superiority goal. Ansbacher and Ansbacher[18] identify three major components used by Adler in treating specific cases. The first is that of *gaining an understanding of the specific lifestyle* of clients, their specific problems and symptoms through counselor empathy, intuition, and guessing. This enables counselors to form a hypothesis of the client's lifestyle and situation. Adler believed there were variations of lifestyles. Examples included individuals with (1) inferiority complexes, who do not feel strong enough to solve life's problems in a socially useful way, (2) Oedipus complexes, who have been pampered so that their mothers are the goals they cannot forgo, (3) proof complexes, who are terrified of committing errors and seek to intimidate others by constantly asking for immediate proof of anything said, (4) redeemer complexes, who go through life trying to save or redeem others for some presumed drawback, (5) predestination complexes, who fear nothing because they believe nothing can happen to them or fail to plan because everything is the same in the end, (6) leader complexes who stick to their guns and cut their own swaths in life because they view themselves as "out front," (7) spectator complexes, who want to be near the action of life but not to participate or take the lead, and (8) "no" complexes, who oppose all change because they are conservative and fearful and must contradict whatever is said in their presence.

The second component of the process is to *explain clients to themselves*. The counselor's hypothesis of the client's lifestyle must be interpreted and communicated to the client so that it will be accepted, despite initial negativism and lack of cooperation. Individual psychology stresses the importance of providing clients with insight into their con-

dition. Uncovering the life plan enables clients to understand themselves. The counselor's explanations should be simple and direct and so clear that clients know and feel their own experience instantly. It was Adler's belief that a true insight by the client always aroused affect.

The third component of the counseling process is to *strengthen the social interests* of clients by confronting them as equals, by demonstrating interest and concern for them.

Adler's concept of transference worked in an opposite direction from that described by Freud. Rather than clients transferring unhealthy features of their lifestyles onto the therapist, Adler believed that therapy worked through the process of the counselor transferring healthy features of the relationship back into the lifestyles of clients. Accordingly, counselors served as teachers mediating between the selfish, secretive goals of superiority held by clients and the broader community or socal interests.

The Adlerian approach to counseling proceeds on the assumption that clients have formulated mistaken styles of life and their conceptions of reality are out of focus. The counselor must help them achieve a reinforced and more correct view of reality. The Adlerian practitioner confronts the superiority mechanisms that are reflected in the power strivings and encourages clients to work on the cultivation of social interest.

Length of therapy varies considerably but Adler usually said to clients that time depended on their willingness to cooperate but that improvement should be noted at the end of three months. Frequency of contacts varied according to the needs of the client, from daily contacts through weekly or even monthly contacts.

Counselor practices

Adlerian counselors make use of a *comparative technique*. Through empathy, counselors begin the process of comparison by trying to imagine the goal they would seek if they were the client. They examine the way clients present themselves on first contact (handshakes), the chairs they select, general posture. In taking clients back in time to draw out psychological attitudes and physical handicaps that may have contributed to their formation of a lifestyle, the Adlerian therapist compares each bit of information

[18] Ansbacher and Ansbacher, *The Individual Psychology*, pp. 326–327.

with another (handshake against presenting complaint). Life-history data are compared with contemporary events in the client's life.

Adler made use of the client's dreams to ferret out the lifestyle. Dreams reflect goals because they are related to what is desired in the future. Dreams occur because of some frustration in life. Dreams of falling, which Adler found to be the most common theme reported, invariably deal with the anxiety experienced by the individual who is losing a sense of worth.

Adlerians never routinely evaluate birth order but believe birth order does show definite trends. In a multiple-child family, for example, the eldest or first-born child often looks after younger children, thereby becoming an extension of parental authority. The second born, confronted by an older sibling who is more adept at things as well as losing the limelight of being the baby if younger children arrive, sometimes develops a jealous and predatory nature. Third, fourth, and later children must be examined as a result of a combination of factors such as opportunities to share a bit of the family spotlight, time between children. Above all, the total situation facing the client must be understood.

School application

Adler's close association with teachers in adult education and his founding of individual psychology clinics in Vienna combined to give his orientation a kind of educational flavor. He was among the first to advance the idea that school failures are often life failures as well. He spoke of the therapeutic task as being re-education in the art of living. Dreikurs and Cassel[19] present an Adlerian approach to discipline. Children who misbehave in classrooms are believed to be discouraged, acting on mistaken private logic that the only way to find a place in the classroom is through misbehavior. The goals of misbehavior include attention, power, revenge, and adequacy. Once these goals are recognized, counselors are in a position to begin helping children understand the mistaken private logic on which they base their behavior. Dreikurs and Cassel suggest that confronting children with these goals is the first step toward helping them change. They recommend that this confrontation

be couched in tentative terms, take place at a time other than that of the conflict and use a format such as the following:

"Could it be that you want special attention?"
"Could it be that you want your own way and hope to be boss?"
"Could it be that you want to hurt others as much as you feel hurt by them?"
"Could it be that you want to be left alone?"

Even though counselors might expect one goal to be the right one, they wait for what Dreikurs and Cassels call the "recognition reflex," the glimmer in the eye that says, "You guessed it." When the goal is revealed in this way, the mistake can be pointed out and alternatives can be explored that lead to cooperation.

The fundamental assumption of Adlerians that people are decision makers responsible for the consequences of their own decisions is made most obvious in the concept of logical consequences. Dreikurs and Grey[20] distinguish between natural and logical consequences. *Natural consequences* follow solely from an act of the child. An example would be the child who climbs a high fence, falls and scrapes a knee. *Logical consequences*, on the other hand, are arranged by an adult, parent, or teacher. An example of this might best be seen in the child who comes home late for dinner and is not permitted to eat. Logical consequences teach the child the reality of the social order, that there is a logical relationship between the act and the consequence. In the school setting, teachers need to point out existing relationships and to make it clear that the result of the behavior is related to what the child is doing rather than to what has been done in the past: "I see you do not want to work properly now, so we will meet to get the work done during recess." The use of logical consequences is viewed as particularly helpful in dealing with attention-seeking behavior.

Counseling goals

The goals of Adlerian counseling include reduction of the intensity of inferior feelings, correction of erroneous habits

[19] Rudolph Dreikurs and P. Cassel, *Discipline Without Tears* (New York: Hawthorne Books, 1974).

[20] Rudolph Dreikurs and Loren Grey, *A New Approach to Discipline: Logical Consequences* (New York: Hawthorne Books, 1968).

of perceiving, alteration of life objective, development of affection for others, and increase in activity. Clients must achieve insight about their mistaken style of life, confront their superiority mechanisms and cultivate social interests.

Criticisms and contributions

Among the criticisms of individual psychology are the following:

1. It relies heavily on intellectual insight to bring about change.
2. It overemphasizes "soft" determinism, that is, subjective experiences, values, and interests determine behavior.
3. It minimizes biological factors and past history.
4. It places heavy responsibility on the practitioner's diagnostic skills.

Among the contributions to be noted for individual psychology are the following:

1. Its optimistic belief that anybody can change, can accomplish anything; the direction of human evolution is positive.
2. Its emphasis that the counseling relationship represents an important mediator of client change.
3. Its stress that societies were not sick or in error, only people were. Individual solutions to human problems take care of the social ills.
4. Its emphasis that power (ego) is as central as sex or any other factor in motivating behavior.

Transactional analysis

Originator and source material

Transactional theory, an attempt to account for a process by defining the setting, the participants and the goals, has a considerable history. Eric Berne has been one of the pioneers who has sought to apply transactional analysis (TA) to psychotherapy. In doing so, the relationship between the client and the counselor is viewed as transactional (interactions, actions taken, conversation) in that it is within an environment that includes participants relating to each other as a function of certain goals. Each acts on the other in reciprocal and cyclical processes of initiating, responding, and feedback. Transactions, according to Berne, are the manifestations of social intercourse.

Berne (1910–1970), the son of a physician, was born in Montreal, Quebec, Canada. His B.A. and M.D. degrees were earned at McGill University and he studied at Yale Psychiatric Clinic (1936–1938), New York Psychoanalytical Institute (1941–1943), and San Francisco Psychoanalytical Institute (1947–1956). He served in the U.S. Army during 1951–1954.

Major sources of information about transactional analysis applied to psychotherapy include four works of Berne's[21] and a volume by Harris.[22] These works will be the principal sources drawn on for the material that follows.

Major concepts

As a rationale, Berne[23] divides conventional psychotherapies into two groups: one group consisting of those that involve suggestions, reassurance, and other "parental" functions; the other group includes those "rational" approaches using confrontation and interpretation, such as nondirective therapy and psychoanalysis. He suggests that the structural-transactional approach overcomes fundamental weaknesses associated with each class. A defect of the "parental" approaches is that they overlook and override archaic (childhood) fantasies of the client resulting in the therapist losing control of the situation. A shortcoming of the rational approaches is that they require a long time for clients to establish inner controls and in the meantime, their family and associates have to put up with their injudicious behavior. Transactional analysis, according to Berne, increases rapidly clients' ability to tolerate and control their anxieties and

[21] See Eric Berne, *Transactional Analysis in Psychotherapy* (New York: Ballantine Books, a div. of Random House, 1961); *Games People Play* (New York: Ballantine Books, 1964); *Principles of Group Treatment* (New York: Ballantine Books, 1966), and *What Do You Say After You Say Hello?* (New York: Ballantine Books, 1970).
[22] Thomas A. Harris, *I'm OK—You're OK* (New York: Harper & Row, 1969).
[23] Berne, *Transactional Analysis*, pp. 1–2.

enables them to circumscribe acting out while permitting the therapist to remain fully aware of the archaic elements within clients' personalities.

The theory of transactional analysis is based on exposing the manifestations and patterns of behavior in the transactions between therapist and client. Berne states as follows:

> The unit of social intercourse is called a transaction. If two or more people encounter each other . . . sooner or later one of them will speak, or give some indication of acknowledging the presence of others. This is called the *transactional stimulus.* Another person will then say or do something which is in some way related to the stimulus, and that is called the *transactional response.*[24]

Transactional analysis examines these transactions, determines roles and ego states characteristic of each person, and systematizes the information from the transactions.

THE HUMAN CONDITION Adherents of transactional analysis posit a multiple nature as being representative of humans. Each person has multiple selves, is viewed as being of intrinsic value, and is one whose personhood is important not only to self but also to others. Humans, being subject to fears and emotional tensions, are capable of and engage in both rational and irrational behaviors. Although much of human behavior is determined by childhood experiences, people can change. They live in an open and evolving universe about which not enough is known but can be explored by individuals emancipated sufficiently from the past. Humans choose and change, and in doing so society changes. Human beings, through thought, are capable of looking to the future and estimating probabilities.

PERSONALITY Individuals exhibit three different and inconsistent ego states (states of mind that denote related patterns of behavior), shift from state to state, and can manifest two states simultaneously. Childhood ego states exist as relics (are archaic) in grownups that under certain circumstances can be revived and cause spontaneous activity in daily waking life. Everything in an individual's conscious awareness is recorded and stored in the brain and is capable of being "played back" in response to the present. Harris states

FIGURE 9.1 **Personality as depicted by transactional analysis theory**

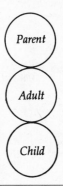

that ". . . the brain functions as a high-fidelity recorder, putting on tape, as it were, every experience from the time of birth, possibly even before birth."[25]

Three ego states, called parent, adult, and child exist in all people, and are depicted in Figure 9.1.

Berne intuitively put the parent in Figure 9.1 at the top and the child at the bottom. The intuition had moral origins for the parent is the guide for ethical aspirations; the adult is concerned with earthly realities of objective being; and the child is a purgatory for archaic tendencies. The *parent* state is composed of the unquestioned or imposed external events experienced by individuals during their early years. Its content, according to Harris, comes from examples and pronouncements of parents and consists of everything children see their parents do and everything children hear their parents say, recorded "straight" without editing.[26] The *parent*, at its most benevolent, is the confident self that knows which fork to use, which temptations to resist. At its worst, the *parent* may crush all joyousness. The *child* state is composed of internal events consisting of responses of a seeing, feeling, hearing, and understanding nature to that which is seen and heard as a child. Fixated in early childhood, the *child* state may be charming in its spontaneity or embarrassing in its willful folly. The *adult* state comes into being at about ten months of age when children's ability to manipulate objects and engage in movement enable them to do

[24] Berne, *Games People Play*, p. 29.

[25] Harris, *I'm OK—You're OK*, p. 9.
[26] Harris, *I'm OK—You're OK*, p. 19.

FIGURE 9.2 **Gradual emergence of the adult beginning at ten months**

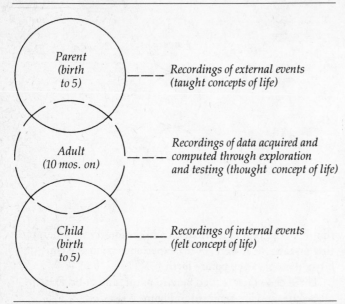

Parent
(birth
to 5)   — — —   *Recordings of external events*
                   (taught concepts of life)

Adult
(10 mos. on) — — — *Recordings of data acquired and*
                     computed through exploration
                     and testing (thought concept of life)

Child
(birth
to 5)   — — —   *Recordings of internal events*
                   (felt concept of life)

SOURCE: From *I'm OK—You're OK* by Thomas A. Harris, M.D. Copyright © 1967, 1968, 1969 by Thomas A. Harris, M.D. Reprinted by permission of Harper & Row, Publishers, Inc.

something evolving from their own awareness. The *adult* files, updates, transforms, and processes information from the parent and child states to make decisions. It is the ego state that is autonomously directed toward objective appraisal of reality. Harris suggests that a major function of the adult is probability estimating.[27] Berne makes clear that parent, adult, and child (P-A-C) are not concepts, like superego, ego and id, but phenomenological realities and that cathexis (psychic energy) flows from the child into the adult and vice versa, the boundaries being conceived as semipermeable under most conditions.[28] Harris discusses factors associated with each ego state and depicts them, presented here as Figure 9.2.

Harris contends that as people sort through their experiences they arrive at one of four emotional positions that influence everything they do. Harris[29] identifies and de-

scribes each of these four possible life positions held with respect to oneself and others. Paraphrased here, these include:

1. *I'm not OK—you're OK.* Being at the mercy of others, children need recognition, or stroking from others and initially conclude that they personally are inferior to others, hence, not OK. They are eager, willing and compliant to the demands of others.
2. *I'm not OK—you're not OK.* Individuals whose parents ceased demonstrating their love for them and whose comforts are abandoned or outweighed by hurts and punishments come to the conclusion that neither they nor others are worthwhile. They give up, have no hope, and often exhibit withdrawal and regressive behavior.
3. *I'm OK—you're not OK.* Children who are brutalized sufficiently long enough by their parents switch to this third position. The conclusion "I'm OK" comes because the child engages in self-stroking brought on through experiencing a sense of comfort as wounds heal.
4. *I'm OK—you're OK.* This position is a conscious decision, being based on thought, faith, and the wager of action.

Harris believes that by the end of the second or third year of life, most children have become fixed on one of the first three positions and they stay there. That position governs what they do until they later, consciously change, if they do, to the fourth position. Furthermore, unlike ego states, people do not shift back and forth.

Positions become *life scripts* by which life is fashioned. Berne defines a script as a "complex set of transactions, by nature recurrent, but not recurring, since a complete performance may require a whole lifetime."[30] Script analysis is used to uncover the early decisions, made unconsciously, as to how life is to be lived.

MALADAPTION Berne[31] sorts pathology into two classes: structural pathology brought about by either exclusion or contamination of the ego states and functional pathology being brought about by the lability of cathexes and the permeability of ego boundaries. The constant parent, constant adult, and constant child result primarily from defensive ex-

[27] Ibid., p. 33.
[28] Berne, *Transactional Analysis*, p. 4.
[29] Harris, *I'm OK—You're OK*, pp. 37–53.

[30] Berne, *Transactional Analysis*, p. 117.
[31] Ibid., p. 47.

clusion of the complementary aspects in each case. Berne suggests that the excluding parent is classically illustrated in "compensated schizophrenics" and occurs because exclusion is the principal defense against confused archaeo-psychic activity. *Contamination* is illustrated by certain types of prejudice and by delusions. For example, part of the parent intrudes into the adult and is included within the adult ego boundary.

Neurotic symptoms, according to Berne,[32] are exhibitions of a single well-defined ego state, although they may be manifestations of complex conflicts. Character disorders and psychopathies are manifestations of the child, but structurally they have the cooperation of the adult.

The process and the counselor

A fundamental feature of transactional analysis applied to counseling is that each transaction (stimulus statement by one person and response statement by another) is analyzed to discover which ego state (parent, adult, or child) brings about each stimulus and response. First, clients are taught the language and ideas of transactional analysis. The process is viewed as a learning experience by which individuals discover how to sort out data that go into their decisions. Counselors explain the process and often apply the concepts to their own transactions with clients so that they can know and use the same techniques. Diagnosis of ego states comes through observation and intuitive sensitivity. Berne[33] identifies and describes certain key elements that aid in diagnosing ego states including the client's demeanor, gestures, voice, and vocabulary. Also, he suggests that diagnosis proceeds clinically through the parent, the adult, and then the child ego states and that the adult is the least understood of the three. Harris[34] presents a list of physical and verbal clues reflecting that which is recorded in parent, adult, and child.

Harris has described the process of the initial hour. The first half is devoted to hearing clients' describe their problems and the second half is used to teach them the basics of P-A-C. After an understanding of P-A-C is gained, their

[32] Ibid., p. 55.
[33] Ibid., pp 62–64.
[34] Harris, *I'm OK—You're OK*, pp. 65–70.

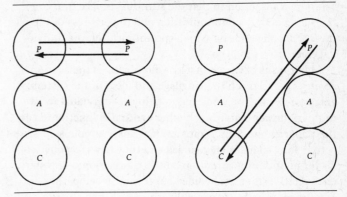

FIGURE 9.3 **Complementary transactions**

problems are discussed again, using the concepts they have learned. Adult-adult interpretations are made at each appearance of the child. A contract or statement of mutual expectations held by both the counselor and client is settled on by the participants. Length of time depends on client progress. A client usually agrees to ten sessions followed by another ten, if needed. Average length of time in group counseling is twenty hours. Transactions are examined to determine whether they are complementary or crossed. Complementary transactions are depicted in Figure 9.3; crossed transactions are presented in Figure 9.4. When stimulus and response make parallel lines, the transaction is complementary and communication takes place, but crossed

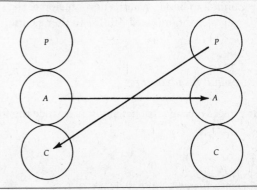

FIGURE 9.4 **Crossed transactions**

transactions stop communications. Harris[35] also identifies a *duplex* transaction in that the stimulus transaction contains a secondary communication and the progress of the transaction depends on which communication the individual elects to respond to.

Major tasks of the counselor who practices transactional analysis are to teach the language and ideas of the system, to diagnose the transactions and to help the individual to live more in the adult state with other ego states functioning at their appropriate time. Transactional analysis counselors are active, long silences are avoided and they have responsibility for maintaining attention on the transactions. Transference relationships are avoided but if they develop, they are counteracted by broad generalizations from the client's transactions. Transactional analysis has been applied to both individual and group counseling. For many, the preferred mode is group treatment. Training programs are readily available for those who seek to build competencies in its application.

Goals of transactional analysis

A major objective of transactional analysis is to assist counselees in programming their personalities in order to allow the proper ego state to function at the proper time. The goal of transactional-analysis therapy is to enable people to be expert in analyzing their own transactions. Harris states that "the goal of treatment is to *cure* the presenting symptom, and the method of treatment is the freeing up of the Adult so that the individual may experience freedom of choice and the creation of new options above and beyond the limiting influences of the past."[36] "Psychoanalytical cure," according to Berne, "means deconfusion of the Child with a largely decontaminated Adult as a therapeutic ally."[37]

Advantages and disadvantages

The advantages of transactional analysis include the following:

[35] Ibid., p. 89.
[36] Ibid., p. 199.
[37] Berne, *Transactional Analysis*, p. 172.

1. Its simple terminology can be learned easily and applied immediately to describe complex behavior.
2. Clients are expected and encouraged to experiment in relationships outside the counseling room to change self-defeating behaviors.
3. "Here-and-now" client behaviors serve as the means to bring about client improvement.
4. It emphasizes not only early experience but also the social environment.

Among the shortcomings attributed to transactional analysis are:

1. It represents little more than "warmed-over," simplified psychoanalytical theories.
2. Few specific details about actual counselor behaviors and practices are given to determine precisely why or how transactional analysis brings about benefits to clients.

Client-centered counseling viewpoint

Originator and source material

Client-centered counseling is also often called self-theory counseling, nondirective counseling, and Rogerian counseling. Carl R. Rogers, its originator, labeled it "client-centered therapy." Like many others, Rogers thinks distinctions between counseling and psychotherapy are artificial and unnecessary.

Rogers received his B.A. degree from the University of Wisconsin (1924) and his M.A. (1928) and Ph.D. (1931) from Columbia University. He is a Diplomate in Clinical Psychology of the American Board of Examiners in Professional Psychology.

Other proponents of the self-theory viewpoint include C. H. Patterson (University of Illinois), Nicholas Hobbs (Vanderbilt), and E. T. Gendlin (University of Chicago).

Rogers' theory of therapy evolved first, followed by a theory of personality. During the years 1930–1961 he presented his views in numerous professional journal articles, contributing chapters, films, and seven books. Needless to say, all are important in attaining an understanding of his viewpoint. Particularly useful in amplifying and enriching the discussion contained in this chapter are *Coun-*

seling and Psychotherapy,[38] *Client-Centered Therapy*,[39] *Psychotherapy and Personality Change*,[40] *Person to Person*,[41] and *On Becoming a Person*.[42] Three other publications noteworthy for their contributions to understanding client-centered counseling include two works by Patterson[43] and a book by Wexler and Rice.[44]

Client-centered counseling originated in America. Many in the helping professions, eager for new concepts and tools, readily accepted it for use not only with adults and adolescents but also with children. It has also been utilized widely in group therapy.

Harper cites five reasons for the prominence achieved by Rogers' viewpoint: (1) it fitted into the American democratic tradition because the client is treated as an equal rather than as a "patient"; (2) its optimistic philosophy emphasized the individual's potentiality for constructive change and was reflective of the optimistic American culture; (3) it appealed to young, insecure therapists as an easy approach; (4) it held promise of being a swifter route to personality change than did psychoanalysis; (5) it was better understood by American psychologists because of its philosophical postulates, its respect for research, and its lack of foreign terms and methods.[45] An examination of the professional counseling journals makes abundantly clear the impact of Rogers' thinking. Many counselors and therapists have adopted the client-centered approach and others have modified their methods to incorporate features of it that appealed to them.

Major concepts

This approach stresses the ability of clients to determine the issues important to them and to solve their problems. The most important quality of the counseling relationship is the establishment of a warm, permissive, and accepting climate that permits clients to explore their self-structure in relation to their unique experiences. Individuals are thus able to face their unacceptable characteristics without feeling threatened and anxious; they move toward acceptance of themselves and their values and are able to change those aspects of themselves that they select as needing modification.

CONCEPT OF SELF Fundamental to understanding both client-centered counseling and self-theory are the concept of self and the concept of becoming or self-actualizing growth. Attention is first given to the concept of self, which will be identified and traced back to previous thinking on the topic.

Rogers states that the central construct of client-centered counseling is the self, or the self as a perceived object in a phenomenal field.

> The self-concept, or self-structure, may be thought of as an organized configuration of perceptions of the self that are admissible to awareness. It is composed of such elements as the perceptions of one's characteristics and abilities; the percepts and concepts of the self in relation to others and the environment; the value qualities that are perceived as associated with experiences and objects; and goals and ideals that are perceived as having positive and negative valence.[46]

The *self* is a learned attribute constituting the individual's picture of himself or herself. It is the "I" or "me" but is not used by Rogers as a synonym for organism. Rather it stands for *awareness* of one's being or functioning.

Freud originated the concept of the developing organism whose behavior was dynamic (motivated). To this organism he attributed drives that were inborn biological needs and postulated psychic wishes (reactions in depth). Freud also conceived of the *ego*, or that construct that interacted with the real world. Jung, it may be remembered, differed from Freud in believing that behavior was determined by

[38] Carl R. Rogers, *Counseling and Psychotherapy* (Boston: Houghton Mifflin Company, 1942).
[39] Carl R. Rogers, *Client-Centered Therapy: Its Current Practice, Implications and Theory* (Boston: Houghton Mifflin Company, 1951).
[40] Carl R. Rogers and Rosalind F. Dymond, eds., *Psychotherapy and Personality Change* (Chicago: University of Chicago Press, 1954).
[41] Carl R. Rogers and Barry Stevens, *Person to Person: the Problem of Being Human* (New York: Pocket Books, 1971).
[42] Carl R. Rogers, *On Becoming a Person* (Boston: Houghton Mifflin Company, 1961).
[43] See C. H. Patterson, "A Current View of Client-Centered or Relationship Therapy," *The Counseling Psychologist*, 1 (Summer 1969), 3–6, and C. H. Patterson, *Relationship Counseling and Psychotherapy* (New York: Harper & Row, 1974), 207 pp.
[44] David A. Wexler and Laura N. Rice, eds., *Innovations in Client-Centered Therapy* (New York: John Wiley & Sons, 1974), 517 pp.
[45] Harper, *Psychoanalysis*, pp. 83–84.
[46] Rogers, *Client-Centered Therapy*, p. 136.

aims and aspirations as well as individual and racial history. He postulated the *collective unconscious* (characterized as the shadow), which was composed of archetypes (a universal idea containing large elements of emotion), one archetype being the self. This self was life's goal, a goal that people strive for but rarely reach. Equally important in tracing the development of the concept of self is the gestalt view of the perceptual field or psychological environment, defined by Hall and Lindzey: ". . . the way in which an object is perceived is determined by the total context or configuration in which an object is embedded. Relationships among the components of the perceptual field rather than fixed characteristics of the individual components determine perception."[47] Kurt Lewin might express this as B = f (L). In this context a need is a motivational concept within the life space (L), which determines behavior in accord with its value in the environment. Stated simply, one's perception of "me," "myself," and "I" is a result of the perceptual framework of one's past, present, and future. Finally, William James and his concept of self, which included the pure ego or "a stream of thought that is one's sense of personal identity,"[48] led to the modern concept of self. This concept is viewed as self-as-object (attitudes, feelings, perceptions) or self-as-process (thinking, perceiving). Such dualism has contributed to a definite controversy, and various theorists adhere to one or the other notion or both. All agree, however, that the concept represents awareness: "self-theory represents a serious attempt to account for certain phenomena and to conceptualize one's observations of certain aspects of behavior."[49]

SELF-ACTUALIZATION   Rogers has defined the actualizing tendency as "the inherent tendency of the organism to develop all its capacities in ways which serve to maintain or enhance the organism."[50] The concept of self-actualization growth goes back, at least in part, to Otto Rank and his followers Jessie Taft and Frederick Allen. Rank rejected the idea that human beings were pulled and pushed by impersonal forces; he spoke of "will," recognizing the positive, creative, directional nature of human striving. In this view the neurotic was someone whose positive will conflicted with the fear of the consequences of willing. On the other hand, the healthy individual could be oneself without fear.

This self-actualizing characteristic, according to Patterson, means that human behavior is motivated by this single master motive or drive—enhancement of the self and actualization of potential—rather than multiple motives or drives. Patterson does not believe that Abraham Maslow's hierarchy of motives is needed because all are secondary to this basic tendency. Moreover, self-actualization should not be construed as being self-centered or antisocial. Humans, being social animals, need others to actualize themselves.[51]

THEORY OF PERSONALITY   In marked contrast to Freud's irrational and unsocialized human, Rogers' humankind is "basically socialized, forward-moving, rational and realistic."[52] Deep down, in the core of their beings, humans have no desire to strike back or to wound but rather want to rid themselves of such feelings. Although negative feelings may be and often are expressed in counseling, beneath the bitterness and hate is a self that is positive, constructive, and concerned about others. The assumption is that "the subjective human being has an importance and a value which is basic: that no matter how he may be labeled or evaluated he is a human person first of all, and most deeply. He is not only a machine, not only a collection of stimulus-response bonds, not an object, not a pawn."[53]

Rogers has presented his theory of personality in the form of nineteen propositions. They are given here, but the reader is urged to study Rogers' discussion and clarification of each proposition.

1. Every individual exists in a changing world of experience of which he is the center.

2. The organism reacts to the field as it is experienced and perceived. This perceptual field is, for the individual, "reality."

3. The organism reacts as an organized whole to this phenomenal field.

---

[47] C. S. Hall and G. Lindzey, *Theories of Personality* (New York: John Wiley & Sons, 1957), p. 206.

[48] Ibid., p. 468.

[49] Ibid.

[50] Carl R. Rogers, "A Theory of Therapy, Personality, and Interpersonal Relationships," in *Psychology: A Study of Science, Study I,* ed. S. Koch, "Conceptual and Systemic," Vol. 3, *Formulations of the Person and the Social Context* (New York: McGraw-Hill, 1959), p. 194.

[51] Patterson, *Relationship Counseling*, pp. 36–39.

[52] Rogers, *On Becoming a Person*, p. 91.

[53] Rogers and Barry, *Person to Person*, p. x.

4. The organism has one basic tendency and striving —to actualize, maintain, and enhance the experiencing organism.

5. Behavior is basically the goal-directed attempt of the organism to satisfy its needs as experienced, in the field as perceived.

6. Emotion accompanies and in general facilitates such goal-directed behavior, the kind of emotion being related to the seeking versus the consummatory aspects of the behavior, and the intensity of the emotion being related to the perceived significance of the behavior for the maintenance and enhancement of the organism.

7. The best vantage point for understanding behavior is from the internal frame of reference of the individual himself.

8. A portion of the total perceptual field gradually becomes differentiated as the self.

9. As a result of interaction with the environment, and particularly as a result of evaluational interaction with others, the structure of self is formed—an organized, fluid, but consistent conceptual pattern of perceptions of characteristics and relationships of the "I" or the "me," together with values attached to these concepts.

10. The values attached to experiences, and values which are a part of the self-structure, in some instances are values experienced directly by the organism, and in some instances are values introjected or taken over from others, but perceived in distorted fashion, as if they had been experienced directly.

11. As experiences occur in the life of the individual, they are either (a) symbolized, perceived, and organized into some relationship to the self, (b) ignored because there is no perceived relationship to the self structure, (c) denied symbolization or given a distorted symbolization because the experience is inconsistent with the structure of the self.

12. Most of the ways of behaving which are adopted by the organism are those which are consistent with the concept of self.

13. Behavior may, in some instances, be brought about by organic experiences and needs which have not been symbolized. Such behavior may be inconsistent with the structure of the self, but in such instances the behavior is not "owned" by the individual.

14. Psychological maladjustment exists when the organism denies to awareness significant sensory and visceral experiences, which consequently are not symbolized and organized into the gestalt of the self-structure. When this situation exists, there is a basic or potential psychological tension.

15. Psychological adjustment exists when the concept of the self is such that all sensory and visceral experiences of the organism are, or may be, assimilated on a symbolic level into a consistent relationship with the concept of self.

16. Any experience which is inconsistent with the organization or structure of self may be perceived as a threat, and the more of these perceptions there are, the more rigidly the self-structure is organized to maintain itself.

17. Under certain conditions, involving primarily complete absence of any threat to the self-structure, experiences which are inconsistent with it may be perceived, and examined, and the structure of self revised to assimilate and include such experiences.

18. When the individual perceives and accepts into one consistent and integrated system all his sensory and visceral experiences, then he is necessarily more understanding of others and is more accepting of others as separate individuals.

19. As the individual perceives and accepts into his self-structure more of his organic experiences, he finds that he is replacing his present value system—based so largely upon introjections which have been distortedly symbolized—with a continuing organismic valuing process.[54]

No pretense will be made of covering adequately Rogers' theory of personality. Rather, discussion will be limited to three fundamental concepts. First, perception (translation of knowledge of one's environment into mental processes such as judgment, reasoning, and memory) is an active process. Individuals attach meaning to their experience and do not merely recognize meanings inherent in the situation. What is perceived constitutes reality for the individual, and one attends to or responds to the focus of that reality (behaves) as a total organized system. The individual does not want to be controlled but moves with struggle and pain toward self-government, self-regulation, and autonomy.

Second, as the individual develops, a portion of the perceptual field is differentiated and represents an awareness of

[54] Rogers, *Client-Centered Therapy*, pp. 483–524.

one's own personality. In other words, one learns to differentiate one's body and behavior from other objects in the environment and becomes aware of one's being. When experiences and needs appear that have not been symbolized and that are inconsistent with the self, they are, in Rogers' words, *disowned* by the individual. The unconscious mind has little place in Rogers' theory of personality. Self-perception is influenced by the ways others perceive one and the way one perceives self-defining references. Values assigned to these experiences are based on either introjection of others' references or direct involvement. The individual needs to be regarded positively by others. From one's experiences flows the need for self-regard or worth as an individual.

The fundamental need underlying all behavior is to preserve and enhance the self. Brammer and Shostrom have pointed out that

Although the "self actualizing tendency" is postulated as being biologically determined, the direction of the growth tendencies is assumed to be culturally determined by parents, peers, teachers, and other persons significant to the child. Since the individual tends to deny perceptions which conflict with his self concept, these growth forces often become distorted in the developmental process. This condition often gives the picture of a person devoid of positive growth motives. There seems to be a strong belief on the part of the self theorists that the positive growth forces will ultimately triumph. For example, independence will supersede dependence; integration will overcome disintegration; social behavior will replace anti-social behavior.[55]

Third, the need for self-regard may lead to perceiving experiences selectively so that they are in accord with one's conditions of worth. If incongruity develops between self and experience, serious adjustment problems arise because the individual is constantly called on to explain away evidence that is incompatible with self-views. This incongruity is subceived as threatening and, if symbolized into awareness, introduces inconsistency into behavior, leads to anxiety, and leads to perceptual rigidity or inaccurate views of reality.

THE FULLY FUNCTIONING SELF The healthy person is one who can incorporate without distortion most of the data of living, and among the most significant are one's organic reactions to experiences. Rogers has stated that the individual strives to become himself or herself. One seeks to find the pattern or underlying order existing in the flow of one's experience. The individual who becomes fully functioning (1) is open to experience, (2) lives fully each moment, and (3) trusts one's own judgments and choices and depends less on others' approval or disapproval.[56]

THE NATURE OF ANXIETY Vulnerability or anxiety occurs when there is discrepancy between the experiencing organism and the concept of self. Trouble comes when events perceived as having significance for the self are incompatible with the organization of self. In this case the events are either denied or distorted to the point of acceptability. The important point is whether they are consistent with the self. When the experiences are inconsistent, says Rogers,

Conscious control becomes more difficult as the organism strives to satisfy needs which are not consciously admitted, and to react to experiences which are denied to the conscious self. Tension then exists, and if the individual becomes to any degree aware of this tendency or discrepancy, he feels anxious, feels that he is not united or integrated, that he is unsure of his directions.[57]

The healthy or "self-accepting" person can admit without distortion to awareness and symbolize sensory experiences arising from internal or external forces. "The emotionally maladjusted person, the 'neurotic,' is in difficulty first, because communication within himself has broken down, and second because, as a result of this, his communication with others has been damaged."[58] In effect, the neurotic acts before all the data are in. Figure 9.5 is an attempt to depict adjustment and maladjustment from the self-theorist viewpoint. Brammer and Shostrom[59] point out that *congruence*, the close matching of awareness and experience, is important in client-centered counseling. Incongruence between the individual's potential and attainments, between ideal and func-

[55] Lawrence M. Brammer and Everett L. Shostrom, *Therapeutic Psychology*, 3rd ed. (Englewood Cliffs, N.J.: Prentice-Hall, 1977), pp. 51–52.
[56] Rogers, *On Becoming a Person*, pp. 187–192.
[57] Rogers, *Client-Centered Counseling*, p. 511.
[58] Rogers, *On Becoming a Person*, p. 33.
[59] Brammer and Shostrom, *Therapeutic Psychology*, p. 50.

FIGURE 9.5 **Maladjustment and adjustment from the self-theorist's viewpoint**

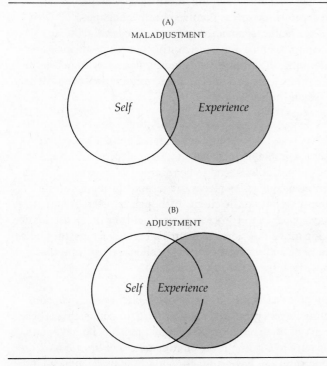

(A)
MALADJUSTMENT

Self *Experience*

(B)
ADJUSTMENT

Self *Experience*

SOURCE: Lawrence M. Brammer and Everett L. Shostrom, *Therapeutic Psychology*, 3rd ed. (Englewood Cliffs, N.J.: Prentice-Hall, 1977), p. 50.

tioning selfs, between actual and possible selfs bring lowered self-esteem, guilt, and anxiety. For the counselor, the implication is that help will be provided to clients to face the incongruence between their awareness and their experience so that their communication of real experiences is not defensively distorted.

The counselor and the counseling process

Client-centered counseling focuses on the experiencing individual. In a process of disorganization and reorganization of self, it tries to reduce to a minimum perceived threat to the self and to maximize and sustain self-exploration. Change in behavior comes through releasing the potential-ity of individuals to evaluate their experiences, permitting them to clarify and gain insight into their feelings, which presumably leads to growth. Through acceptance of the counselee, the counselor enables that person to express, examine, and incorporate previously consistent and inconsistent experiences into the self-concept. By redefinition, the individual gains in self-acceptance and learns to accept others and to become a more fully functioning person.

Interviews are usually for one hour and are scheduled once or twice a week. Every effort is made to prevent the development of a dependent relationship. In general, in client-centered counseling (1) the individual, not the problem, is the focus; (2) feelings, rather than intellect, are attended to; (3) the present is given greater attention than the past; and (4) emotional growth takes place in the counseling relationship.

THE COUNSELOR The effective counselor is one "who holds a coherent and developing set of attitudes deeply imbedded in his personal organization, a system of attitudes which is implemented by techniques and methods consistent with it."[60] According to Rogers, it is the attitudes of counselors, rather than their techniques, that facilitate therapy, and it is their basic operational philosophy that determines how long they will take to become skillful counselors. Primary among counselor attitudes is functioning behavior with others—that of according them worth, dignity, respect, right of self-direction, and the like. "We may say that the counselor chooses to act consistently upon the hypothesis that the individual has a sufficient capacity to deal constructively with all those aspects of his life which can potentially come into conscious awareness."[61] The counselor does not try to shift his role to a more directive one or undertake responsibility for the counselee's reorganization, for it is believed that in doing so the counselor will confuse and defeat the counselee.

Although the counselor has values, insofar as possible they should be kept out of the counseling relationship to avoid their introjection by the counselee. That view, originally set forth by client-centered theory, is no longer accepted, according to Patterson. He notes that "indeed, it is now recognized that the therapist's values cannot be kept

[60] Rogers, *Client-Centered Therapy*, p. 19.
[61] Ibid., p. 24.

out of therapy, if only because goals are values and all therapists are concerned with goals."[62]

The counselor's role in client-centered counseling is not, as many believe, passive or laissez-faire. Passivity would probably be experienced by the counselee as lack of interest. Laissez-faire could be interpreted by the client as implying that he or she is not regarded as a person of worth. Rogers has also warned (in a nondirective way, of course) that formulating the counselor's role as one of clarifying and objectifying client feelings is too intellectualistic. If taken literally, objectifying such feelings would mean that only the counselor knows what the feelings are and would be interpreted by the client as disrespect. Rogers has formulated the role in these words: ". . . it is the counselor's function to assume, in so far as he is able, the internal frame of reference of the client, to perceive the world as the client sees it, to perceive the client himself as he is seen by himself, to lay aside all perceptions from the external frame of reference while doing so, and to communicate something of this empathic understanding to the client."[63]

Hobbs has presented the activities of client-centered counselors involved in counseling:

1. The therapist attempts to understand what the client is saying with reference to content, feeling, and import to the client and to communicate this understanding to the client.
2. The therapist interprets what the client has said by offering a condensation or a synthesis of the expressed feelings.
3. The therapist simply accepts what the client has said with an implication that what he has said has been understood.
4. The therapist defines for the client, at moments when the issue is relevant from the client's point of view, the nature of the therapeutic relationship, the expectancies of the situation, and the limits of the therapist-client relationship.
5. The therapist attempts to convey to the client, through gestures, posture, and facial expression, as well as through words, a sense of acceptance and of confidence in the ability of the client to handle his problems.

6. The therapist answers questions and gives information when such responses are relevant to treatment, but he may refrain from giving information when the issue of dependency seems involved in the question.
7. The therapist actively participates in the therapy situation, keeping alert, attempting to pick up nuances of feeling, interrupting the client if necessary to make certain that the therapist is understanding what the client is saying and feeling.[64]

Diagnosis is viewed as not only unnecessary but unwise. Use of test data and counselor-stated opinions about the client's problems is thought to foster dependency because the counselor will tend to be regarded as an expert. Client-centered counseling places the responsibility not on the counselor but on the client. Although transference attitudes may appear in the process, Rogers believes they will not develop into a transference neurosis because counselor understanding and acceptance leads to client recognition that these feelings are not the counselor's.

THE COUNSELEE In his first book on client-centered counseling Rogers presented eight criteria for counseling. These required that the client (1) be under tension, (2) have some capacity to cope with the circumstances of life, (3) have an opportunity to have contact regularly with a counselor, (4) be able to express conflicts verbally or through other media, (5) be "reasonably independent . . . of close family control," (6) be "reasonably free from excessive instabilities, particularly of an organic nature," (7) be dull-normal or above average in intelligence, and (8) be of suitable age—"roughly from ten to sixty."[65] Rogers now believes that these conditions no longer apply or are of little importance. Research and clinical experience have tended to disprove some of them, and client-centered counseling presumably has been found effective with a wide range of individuals and problems.

STEPS IN THE COUNSELING PROCESS In outlining the development of the counseling process, Rogers pointed out that these steps are not discrete. Processes mingle and shade into

---

[62] Patterson, *Relationship Therapy*, p. 22.
[63] Rogers, *Client-Centered Therapy*, p. 29.
[64] Nicholas Hobbs, "Client-Centered Psychotherapy," in *Six Approaches to Psychotherapy*, J. L. McCary (New York: Dryden Press, 1955), p. 16.
[65] Rogers, *Counseling and Psychotherapy*, pp. 76–77.

one another and occur only approximately in the order given. He has described and illustrated each step, but here the twelve steps will only be identified.

1. The individual comes for help.
2. The helping situation is usually defined.
3. The counselor encourages free expression of feelings in regard to the problem.
4. The counselor accepts, recognizes and clarifies these negative feelings.
5. When the individual's negative feelings have been quite fully expressed, they are followed by the faint and tentative expressions of the positive impulses which make for growth.
6. The counselor accepts and recognizes the positive feelings which are expressed, in the same manner in which he has accepted and recognized the negative feelings.
7. This insight, this understanding of the self and acceptance of the self, is the next important aspect of the whole process.
8. Intermingled with this process of insight—and it should again be emphasized that the steps outlined are not mutually exclusive, nor do they proceed in a rigid order—is a process of clarification of possible decisions, possible courses of action.
9. Then comes one of the fascinating aspects of such therapy, the initiation of minute, but highly significant, positive actions.
10. There is, first of all, a development of further insight —more complete and accurate self-understanding as the individual gains courage to see more deeply into his own actions.
11. There is increasingly integrative positive action on the part of the client. There is less fear about making choices, and more confidence in self-directed action.
12. There is a feeling of decreasing need for help, and a recognition on the part of the client that the relationship must end.[66]

Later Rogers sought to further identify the directions evident in the counseling process.[67] He conceptualized the following trends, which we paraphrase:

1. Clients experience their potential self in the security of the counseling relationship.
2. Clients learn to experience and accept fully and freely the positive feelings of the counselor.
3. Clients not only accept themselves, they actually come to like themselves.
4. Clients discover that hate does not lie in the core of personality, but rather a self that is deeply positive and socialized.
5. Clients do not continually act in terms of the form of behavior imposed on them or they do not act in accord with the opinions and expectations of others. Rather, they come to act on the basis of the meaning of their experiences—the realistic balancing of the satisfactions and dissatisfactions that any action will bring them. They become.

NECESSARY CONDITIONS OF THERAPEUTIC PERSONALITY CHANGE Rogers has addressed himself to the psychological conditions believed necessary and sufficient to bring about personality change. Change means either surface or deep changes in the personality structure, change from less conflict or immature behavior, or change in the sense of utilizing more energy for effective living. He believes that if the following conditions are maintained over a period of time, constructive personality change will take place:

1. Two persons are in psychological contact.
2. The first, whom we shall term the client, is in a state of incongruence, being vulnerable or anxious.
3. The second person, whom we shall term the therapist, is congruent or integrated in the relationship.
4. The therapist experiences unconditional positive regard for the client.
5. The therapist experiences an empathic understanding of the client's internal frame of reference and endeavors to communicate this experience to the client.
6. The communication to the client of the therapist's empathic understanding and unconditional positive regard is to a minimal degree achieved.[68]

OUTCOMES Since the early 1950s, Rogers and others have devoted considerable time and energy to assessing changes

[66] Ibid., pp. 30–45.
[67] Rogers, *On Becoming a Person*, pp. 74–106.

[68] Carl R. Rogers, "The Necessary and Sufficient Conditions of Therapeutic Personality Change," *Journal of Consulting Psychology*, 21 (April 1957), 95–103.

brought about by client-centered counseling. Among the findings were that (1) profound changes occurred in the client's perceived self, (2) the client's personality characteristics and structure changed, (3) the direction of change was toward personal integration and adjustment, and (4) the client's increased maturity was observed by friends.[69] At a special conference on research problems in psychotherapy Rogers said he believed that "progress has been made in conceptualizing the outcomes of psychotherapy" in ways "which are specific, measurable and rooted in a context of theory."[70] However, most of the other conferees were not so optimistic. It should be noted that when Rogers uses the word *change* he does not necessarily mean *success,* or *cure.* He believes these latter two words are undefinable, constitute value judgments, and are not amenable to the application of scientific research.

A CURRENT PERSPECTIVE   In 1974, Rogers identified and discussed certain concepts, discernible in the past and present of client-centered counseling, that to him pointed to the future. The key ideas, paraphrased here, included that (1) the confidence of the client-centered counselor lies in the *process* by which truth is discovered, achieved, approximated and, hence, such a counselor is relatively free of dogmatism; (2) the client-centered orientation is that the unique, subjective inner person is the honored and valued core of human life; (3) the emphasis on the potential of the individual is, in effect, to give permission to clients to be themselves, who, therefore, *become* more of their potentialities; (4) although not strongly present at the inception of client-centered counseling, it meets and responds to a widely held need for a deep human relationship in which the individual is fully known and accepted; and (5) the belief that life is *lived now* (rather then being determined) has been a major element in its success.[71]

[69] Ibid., p. 231.
[70] Carl R. Rogers, "A Tentative Scale for the Measurement of Process in Psychotherapy," in *Research in Psychotherapy,* ed. E. A. Rubinstein and M. B. Parloff (Washington: American Psychological Association, 1958), Vol. I, p. 277.
[71] Carl R. Rogers, "Remarks on the Future of Client-Centered Therapy," in *Innovations in Client-Centered Therapy,* ed. David A. Wexler and Laura North Rice (New York: John Wiley & Sons, 1974), pp. 7–13.

Criticisms and contributions

The following are among the major criticisms of the client-centered viewpoint:

1. It emphasizes the affective, emotional, feeling determinants of behavior but ignores or denies the intellective, cognitive, rational factors.
2. The use of information to help counselees is conspicuously absent from the theory. Wexler's work could be viewed as an effort to correct this criticism.[72]
3. Because it has the same goal for all clients—maximizing self—it is so broad, general, and sweeping that assessment for any one individual is impossible.
4. It specifies that the counselee sets the goal, but counseling goals are sometimes established by the setting in which the counselor and counselee are located.
5. Although some evidence indicates client-centered counseling is effective with a wide range of individuals and problems, that evidence is not systematic or complete enough, particularly in respect to clients who accept little responsibility for their problems.
6. While client-centered counselors are expected to be neutral, it is impossible to be valueless in an interpersonal situation.

   The most frequently cited contributions to the helping relationship are the following:

1. It has established the counselee, rather than the counselor, as the center, focus, or deciding agent of the counseling process.
2. It has identified and emphasized the counseling relationship as the primary agent in facilitating personality change.
3. It has placed in perspective the importance of the counselor's attitudes, rather than techniques, in affecting the counseling relationship.
4. It has offered a wealth of research findings and stimulated quantitative investigations among other points of view, all of which have led to far better understanding of the process than ever before achieved.

[72] David A. Wexler, "A Cognitive Theory of Experiencing, Self-Actualization, and Therapeutic Process," in *Innovations in Client-Centered Therapy,* pp. 49–116.

5. It has emphasized that counseling is properly concerned with emotion, feeling, and affect.

The existential viewpoint

Proponents and source material

The history of existentialism closely parallels that of psychoanalytic theory. Its origin, however, predates Freud's analytic views, lying in an extremely productive period of philosophical thought and accompanied by the rise and dominance of late nineteenth- and contemporary twentieth-century science. The existentialist viewpoint—taken broadly during the last hundred years—is a meld of theology, philosophy, psychiatry, and psychology involved in a tremendous effort to understand human behavior and emotions. Among the earliest individuals associated with the existentialist concept of man and his behavior was Søren Kierkegaard, the nineteenth-century Danish philosopher and theologian. His works treating the relationships among humankind, the universe, and deity are commonly considered in the forefront of existential thought.

Because of its diverse origins and the complicated contributions to it from a variety of fields, existentialism remains staggeringly difficult to understand, let alone discuss with clarity and precision. Adequate appreciation of this conceptualization of the individual requires a truly educated person, knowledgeable in all the disciplines that have contributed to its present state.

The very nature of existentialism makes it impossible to distinguish clearly and concisely among its proponents, and distinctions by contributing field are also difficult to maintain. Such theologically oriented proponents as Kierkegaard and Paul Tillich, philosophical contributors such as Martin Heidegger and Jean Paul Sartre, and psychiatric and psychological contributors like Eugene Minkowski, Ludwig Binswanger, and Rollo May have all added substantially to a highly complex theory. Indeed, this approach struggles against fractionating humans in an attempt to understand them, using instead a truly holistic approach in order to grasp the reality and essence of being human. Humans are thought of as being and becoming, as a dynamic process, as a complex organism in relation to the universe. Though humans belong in the world of natural things, they alone can reflect, make free decisions, and set goals. Each person must learn to act as a free person rather than as a part of a crowd.

Contributors to existential thought

SØREN A. KIERKEGAARD (1813–1855) Kierkegaard was a philosopher and Protestant theologian who championed religious existentialism. He believed that God could be known only through faith, not through reason. He urgently pursued the issue of becoming an individual, formulated truth as a relationship, and emphasized the necessity of commitment. Perhaps the most notable from among his over two dozen books are *Either-Or* (1834) and *The Concept of Dread* (1844), the latter a penetrating analysis of anxiety.

PAUL TILLICH (1886–1965) Tillich was a German-American theologian who left Germany when Hitler came to power in 1933. Most reflective of his views is *The Courage to Be* (1952), which employs existentialism as an approach to actual living crises. Both reason and religion are utilized.

MARTIN HEIDEGGER (1889–1976) Heidegger is often regarded as the major contributor to present-day existential thought. His main work, *Being and Time* (1927), is cited by many as source material for psychiatrists and psychologists who apply existential concepts in understanding the individual.

JEAN PAUL SARTRE (1905–) Sartre is a French philosopher, novelist, and playwright who became a leader of French intellectual life during the 1940s. His is a nihilistic, subjective existentialist point of view, stressing that the world has little or no meaning and that individuals must find some direction and meaning for their own personal lives. Individuals develop a sense of responsibility for their own decisions or actions and through this means become free. Sartre's existential despair has been expressed in many novels (*Nausea*, 1928), short stories (*The Wall*, 1939), plays (*The Flies*, 1943), and autobiography (*The Words*, 1964).

EUGENE MINKOWSKI (1885–) Minkowski was born in Poland, completed secondary studies in Warsaw, and received his medical degree at the University of Munich (1909). After World War I he practiced psychiatry in Paris and conducted studies in phenomenological psychiatry. Among his contributions is a different view of the concept of time. He challenged the traditional idea that patients cannot relate to the future because of their disorder and proposed instead that the basic disorder is that of distorted attitudes toward the future that give rise to anxiety and depression.

LUDWIG BINSWANGER (1881–1966) Binswanger studied under Jung at the University of Zurich and served as an intern under Bleuler. He was among the first to apply existential analysis to deepen basic concepts of psychoanalysis. He sought particularly to interpret human beings through their personal relations with others and the individual in relation to self. The individual was conceived as one existence communicating with another. He termed his formulations *Daseinanalyse* ("being who is there").

ROLLO MAY (1909–   )   May, a well-known psychoanalytic therapist, has contributed much to interpreting existential psychotherapy to American psychology. He is the author and editor of *Existence* (1958) and other existential works.

VIKTOR E. FRANKL (1906–   )   Frankl founded *logotherapy* (*logos* is usually translated as "speech" or "reason" but is defined by Frankl as "meaning"). Frankl rejects (1) Freud's view that humans are driven mainly by sexual energy, (2) Adler's emphasis on power drives, (3) Jung's archetypes, and (4) conditioning theories that define humans as nothing but machines. To Frankl, the search for meaning in life is the tap root of human striving and the search is at an intellectual rather than instinctual level. "Meaning" is the individual's own, unique to that person in his or her situation at a given moment and contrasts to values that are shared among many people.

Some resource materials that will help the reader better understand existential thought include books by Beck,[73]

May et al.,[74] and Ofman[75] as well as journal articles by Dreyfus,[76] Vaughan,[77] Arbuckle,[78] Landsman,[79] and Kemp.[80]

Major concepts

The factors that led to the development of existentialism have been identified by May, who sees its fundamental basis as an attempt to understand individuals as they really are, to know them in their reality, to see their world as they see it, to comprehend that they move and have a being which is unique, concrete, and quite different from abstract theory.[81] May indicates that the existentialist movement sprang up spontaneously in different parts of Europe among different schools of thought and cannot be credited to any single person. Among the apparent stimuli for its application to psychotherapy were an inability to understand why cures did or did not occur, dubious theories of man, and blind spots within existing theories. In essence it was an attempt to arrive at a structure from which all therapeutic systems could be understood. It is perhaps unique among therapeutic approaches in that it has not created a new leader and does not purport to found a new "school of therapy."

May cites several factors that have tended to create resistance to the acceptance of existentialism.[82] Among these is the assumption that older therapies are sufficient to explain human nature and all that is needed is to sketch in the de-

[74] Rollo May, Ernest Angel, and Henri F. Ellenberger, eds., *Existence* (New York: Basic Books, 1958).

[75] William V. Ofman, *Affirmation and Reality: Fundamentals of Humanistic Existential Therapy and Counseling* (Los Angeles: Western Psychological Services, 1976), 203 pp.

[76] Edward A. Dreyfus, "The Counselor and Existentialism," *Personnel and Guidance Journal,* 43 (October 1964), 114–117.

[77] Richard P. Vaughan, "Existentialism in Counseling: The Religious View," *Personnel and Guidance Journal,* 43 (February 1965), 553–557.

[78] Dugald S. Arbuckle, "Existentialism in Counseling: The Humanist View," *Personnel and Guidance Journal,* 43 (February 1965), 558–567.

[79] Ted Landsman, "Existentialism in Counseling: The Scientific View," *Personnel and Guidance Journal,* 43 (February 1965), 568–573.

[80] C. Gratton Kemp, "Existential Counseling," *The Counseling Psychologist,* 2, No. 3 (1971), 2–30.

[81] May et al., eds., *Existence,* p. 4.

[82] Ibid., pp. 7–9.

[73] Carleton E. Beck, *Philosophical Foundations of Guidance* (Englewood Cliffs, N.J.: Prentice-Hall, 1963).

tails. A second form of resistance lies in the position that existentialism represents an encroachment of philosophy on psychiatry and psychology; it erodes disciplines viewed as sciences. Finally, other therapeutic methods tend to be preoccupied with technique and to prefer not to grapple with fundamental questions posed by an existential approach to therapy.

Beck, tracing the emergence of existential analysis, indicates that because phenomenology did not provide a framework wide enough and vital enough to meet therapy requirements, *Daseinanalyse* emerged. *Phenomenology* as a theoretical point of view advocates the study of direct experience taken at face value. It asserts that behavior is determined by experience rather than by external objective reality. It differs from the presuppositions of *Daseinanalyse,* according to Beck, in these particulars:

1. *Daseinanalyse* emphasizes the fact that, because of existential anxiety, one may live in two or more mutually exclusive worlds; phenomenology emphasizes the centrality or unity of the experiences of the organism. The *Daseinanalyse* theorist feels that the latter statement may be true of lower forms of life, but that [humans] partake of a different mode of existence (termed *Dasein*) and therefore faces meanings which often complicate . . . life meanings.
2. *Daseinanalyse* attempts to reconstruct the meaning-structure of the world of the individual, or the conflicting structures of his two or more worlds of meanings and influences; it explores how and why meanings have changed. Phenomenology stresses the present field of influences.
3. Phenomenology stresses awarenesses, consciousness, perceptions. *Daseinanalyse* is concerned with the total meaning-structure of the client: . . . life style, . . . views of life and death, . . . word choices, and all aspects of . . . relating to life.[83]

CONCEPT OF BEING AND NONBEING Existentialism endeavors to understand humans—most simply, to understand them as being and becoming. The grasping of another's being occurs on a different level from that of knowledge of specific things about him or her. "This is the classical distinction between *knowing* and *knowing about*. When we seek to know a person, the knowledge *about* him must be subordinated to the over-arching fact of his actual existence."[84] In this context, existentialism seeks to understand the individual at greater depth than that represented by the subject-object dichotomy that has permeated Western thought since the Renaissance. It tries to see the individual as a meaningful whole. Unless one focuses on the fundamental fact of a person's existence and being, one cannot understand drives and behavior. All lose meaning unless viewed from the dynamic point of being and becoming.

Being is one's awareness of who one is, the individual's definition of self, what one makes of self. The healthy individual is open to reality and creating meaning. The most obvious form of *nonbeing* is death. However, the real therapeutic issue of nonbeing focuses on live nonbeing represented by total conformity, absorption by collective society —in short, loss of uniqueness and individual identity.

CONCEPTS OF ANXIETY AND GUILT From the existential point of view, anxiety and guilt are central in understanding existence. May states that "anxiety is *the experience of the threat of imminent non-being.*"[85] As individuals confront the fulfillment of their potentiality, they experience anxiety. If they deny their potentiality or fail to fulfill it, their condition is guilt. May identified four characteristics of ontological (things that exist) guilt. First, because people never really fulfill their potentialities, everyone feels guilt. Second, guilt is not totally culturally determined through failure to meet the demands of society's rules; rather it stems from the realities of choice—choosing one type of behavior precludes choosing another. Third, ontological guilt differs from neurotic guilt in that it is a condition of existence. Finally, ontological guilt is to be viewed as a constructive force in human personality leading to humility, sensitivity in personal relationships, and creative utilization of one's potentialities.[86]

CONCEPT OF TIME Some existentialists differ with the traditional concept of time as analogous to space and seek to understand the client's existential meaning of time. Min-

[83] Beck, *Philosophical Foundations*, p. 107.

[84] May et al., eds., *Existence*, p. 38.
[85] Ibid., p. 50.
[86] Ibid., p. 55.

kowski, it may be remembered (see p. 220), proposed that distorted attitudes toward the future brought manifestations (for example, delusions) rather than that delusion prevented the individual from relating to the future. Because individuals are always in the process of becoming, they can never be defined at a static point as though they were objects at a particular spot. One can project oneself backward and forward in time and thus is able to transcend the present and act and react in these dimensions. People may become disturbed or anxious because they come to believe that they do not have a future.

> Repression and other processes of the blocking off of awareness are in essence methods of ensuring that the usual relation of past to present will not obtain. Since it would be too painful or in other ways too threatening for the individual to retain certain aspects of his past in his present consciousness, he must carry the past along like a foreign body *in* him but not *of* him, as it were, an encapsulated fifth column which thereupon compulsively drives to its outlets in neurotic symptoms.[87]

The future rather than the present or past is the most dominant mode of time. Personality is best understood as a projection of the individual's future. Explorations into the immediate future mold and move the individual in distinctive ways.

CONCEPT OF TRANSCENDING THE IMMEDIATE SITUATION Humans have the ability to transcend (climb over or beyond) their immediate situation. They seek to stand out and by their ability to think abstractly they can orient themselves to project what they can be.

CONCEPT OF FREEDOM Some existentialists see humans as becoming, as having choice and will, and, therefore, as exercising freedom. This view is diametrically contrary to that of some behaviorists who regard humans as being controlled by their environment and think of their behavior as governed by law. For some existentialists the self is the determiner of man's culture. Although determinism may be part of the world, it does not apply to humans. "The free man lives within the laws of his culture, but he is not bound by

them. They do not control him, but, rather, his self transcends them."[88] Although people are not free from conditions, they are free to act upon or take a stand toward them. It is the individual who decides what his or her existence is to be, not the environment.

CONCEPT OF HUMANKIND Beck has given thirteen propositions that he believes constitute a credo for counselors. In them human nature, as seen from the existentialist viewpoint, is evident.

1. Every man, not mentally incompetent, is responsible for his acts.
2. Man can do little to change most of the physical universe, the given, but he can predict it and make his life happier by facing reality.
3. Each man must aid others and try to understand their feelings, for mankind is left alone in an uncaring world.
4. Man creates his own nature. This is an individual choice.
5. Man should act toward others as he would want them to act toward him.
6. Decisions shall be made only by the criterion, "What is the effect on humankind?" Man must be treated with dignity; his status as a past-and-future-experiencing being, the only creature so endowed, makes this mandatory.
7. Determinism applies to physical laws; choice is a fact of human existence within the framework of the given surroundings.
8. Man counsels because no man can meet all problems alone.
9. Choices must be made by the counselee, for the counselor cannot claim omniscience.
10. The end of counseling is enabling fellow creatures better to bear the buffets of life, better to seek happiness and individual fulfillment.
11. Man must operate as if he is alone in the universe with his fellows; it is futile to argue about supernatural creation; there is no proof.
12. Man's suffering can be relieved by suggestions from those who have traveled the road before, or a road like it.

---

[87] Ibid., p. 68.

[88] Arbuckle, "Existentialism in Counseling," p. 560.

13. It would be an act of cruelty not to try to benefit others; they are involved with us in life.[89]

Prominent among some existentialists' conceptions of man is the "throwness" of life. Illustrations of this condition are the casting of dice or seeds being thrown on the ground. "Thrown" represents aspects of life beyond an individual's control. Although one does not have any choice of the ground, choice is possible, within the thrown limits, in what one becomes. Being born a male or a female is a "thrown" condition but deciding to accept or reject one's "maleness" or "femaleness" is a choice exercised by the individual. Kemp's comment about the concept is relevant here:

> Many of us also are aware of the contingency of life, its "throwness." Too, many of us have wondered why we are here, not there; why it was a friend, a wife or husband [to whom something happened] and not ourselves. We would like to have a satisfying understanding but find none, and sometimes, to still our disquietude, we take refuge in some superficial explanation of time and space.[90]

The counselor and the counseling process

Individuals seek counseling for any one of several reasons. Nevertheless, Dreyfus points out, the counselor assumes that clients seek to expand their psychological world in one way or another.[91] The client's world is unique and must be understood by counselors if they are to give assistance. The premise underlying the existential viewpoint is that "the client is a figure standing out from his ground, the ground being the world of other peoples, creatures and objects. The goal of counseling is the elucidation of this client's uniqueness."[92]

The problem presented by the client may be only a socially acceptable excuse to obtain help. Consequently, the counselor encourages clients to unfold their world in their encounter so that both of them can begin to understand it and the counselee can act on the possibilities inherent in it.

Dreyfus maintains that the existential counselor "does not offer interpretations in terms of the client's past, but rather in terms of the client's present being-in-the-world."[93]

Existentialists view the counseling relationship as an encounter. Ofman[94] suggests that "engaged encounter" is more descriptive of that which takes place in the relationship. He has depicted four types of relationships (including the engaged encounter) and how each can be engaged, denied, or broken. His diagram has been presented here as Figure 9.6. Ofman identifies the basic tactic as being that clients assume a "falsely-safe" omnipotence, take control, and are unwilling to see that they exist in the world and that others are free entities in their own right. Further, a ". . . healing relationship is one based on mutuality, on a conclusion that the person is the way he is and that there is a unifying, underlying meaning to his existence, a meaning that he chooses to hold onto in the face of the aversive consequences attending his project."[95]

Honesty or authenticity is an essential characteristic of an encounter; therefore, counselors must expose themselves and cannot view the client as an object to be manipulated or exploited. The counselor's ability to be human enables clients to become aware of similar qualities in themselves. It is through this process that clients will realize their potentialities and achieve self-growth because that becomes their responsibility.

The emphasis placed on understanding the individual by existential counselors relegates counselor techniques to secondary importance. This is contrary to traditional views, which state that understanding follows technique. The counselor's basic task is to enter the world of clients and participate with them in its realities. In the special relationship—the encounter—that comes to exist between counselor and counselee the latter is no longer an object but becomes a "thou." The intent of the encounter, according to Vaughan, is threefold: to foster freedom within clients, to improve their encounters with others, and to discover meaning for their existence.[96]

The existential counselor's techniques are flexible, and their application is based on what is believed will enable

[89] Beck, *Philosophical Foundations*, pp. 124–125.
[90] Kemp, "Existential Counseling," p. 6.
[91] Dreyfus, "The Counselor and Existentialism," p. 115.
[92] Ibid., p. 114.

[93] Ibid., p. 116.
[94] Ibid., p. 123.
[95] Ibid., p. 153.
[96] Vaughan, "Existentialism in Counseling," p. 555.

FIGURE 9.6 **Possible positions or tactics in a relationship**

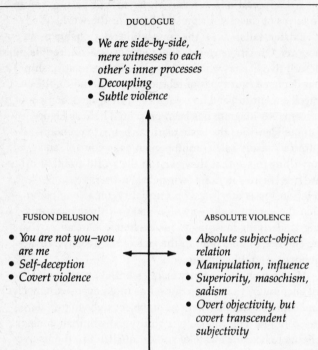

DUOLOGUE

- *We are side-by-side, mere witnesses to each other's inner processes*
- *Decoupling*
- *Subtle violence*

FUSION DELUSION

- *You are not you—you are me*
- *Self-deception*
- *Covert violence*

ABSOLUTE VIOLENCE

- *Absolute subject-object relation*
- *Manipulation, influence*
- *Superiority, masochism, sadism*
- *Overt objectivity, but covert transcendent subjectivity*

ENGAGED ENCOUNTER

- *Two gods openly struggling with their subjectivity, constantly asking "How can we permit each other to enter into the other's system for a while, for as long as is possible"*
- *I-Thou*
- *Affirmation*
- *Authenticity*
- *Struggle toward the establishment of mutual process and the essential we*
- *Avowal of implicit symmetry*

SOURCE: Copyright © 1976 by Western Psychological Services. Reprinted from *Affirmation and Reality* by William V. Ofman by permission.

counselees to reveal their existence. Repression and resistance are seen as manifesting rejection of potentialities. The counselor's presence provides an experience for clients so that their existence becomes real to them.

In existential counseling, knowledge and insight are presumed to follow commitment. The assumption generally accepted in other counseling approaches is that decision comes after insight or knowledge. "We use the term decision as meaning a *decisive attitude toward existence,* an attitude of commitment. In this respect, *knowledge and insight follow decision rather than vice versa.*"[97] Finally, most existentialist counselors do not believe a person is divided into conscious and unconscious parts. They hold that what is often called the unconscious is part of the individual's being and that the unconscious is too often used as a frivolous means of rationalizing behavior and responsibility, and as a way of avoiding the realities of one's existence. The aim of psychotherapy is to enable clients to accept responsibility for themselves.

Criticisms and contributions

Three contributions of the existentialists to the helping relationship may be cited:

1. They have moved the philosophical issues of goals, values, and existence to the forefront of the helping relationship and postulated them as the source of conflict. They have emphasized that a person's identity, or self-awareness, is a basic antecedent of behavior.
2. They have initiated behavioral study from a subjectively observable methodology (sensations and feelings) which may yield certain scientific facts that can be verified and communicated to others.
3. They have emphasized the importance of the self of the counselor rather than techniques.

Criticisms include the following:

1. Terminology is often incomprehensible and employed in disparate ways.

[97] May et al., eds., *Existence,* p. 88.

2. The approach utilized is not systematic, and little attention is given to methods or techniques to implement its concepts. In short, the existential viewpoint is nonscientific.

Gestalt therapy

Originator and source materials

Frederick S. Perls (1894–1970) originated and developed gestalt therapy. He has described his approach in two major publications: *Gestalt Therapy Verbatim*[98] and *In and Out of the Garbage Can.*[99] The material presented here will be drawn from these two publications and a recent article by Passons.[100] Perls was associated with the Esalen Institute, Big Sur, California at the time of his death in 1970. He views gestalt therapy as existential in nature and asserts that it is in harmony with medicine, science, and the universe.

Major concepts

The word *gestalt* has long been used to mean "wholes." Those who advocate gestalt theory believe that a response to a situation is a whole response to the whole situation. The whole is more than the sum of its parts. They deny that behavior consists of separate responses to a combination of separate stimuli. Gestaltists believe that specific components serve as important *figures* rather than as distinct elements. Accordingly, "parts" derive their meaning from their membership in the whole. Learning, according to gestalt theory, takes place, not by accretion, but by insight through reorganization.

VIEW OF THE HUMAN CONDITION Perls believes that individual human beings always work as a whole. Each person is not merely a summation of parts (such as liver, lungs, brain,

and so on), but a coordination of all parts. Health is viewed "as an appropriate balance of the coordination of all of what we are."[101]

When a person encounters another, the two seek through their communications to establish a world in which both have a common interest. The "I" and "you" changes to "we," an ever-transforming boundary. Their encounter produces change that comes about because of dissatisfaction.

Humans are viewed as a whole, therefore, the organism cannot be separated from the environment. The boundary between the individual and the environment, according to Perls, is experienced simply as what is inside the skin and what is outside the skin. The *ego boundary* is the differentiation between self and others. *Identification* and *alienation* are two components involved in Perls' use of ego boundary. Identification means that the "I" is more prized than "others." A person identifies with his family, group, or profession. This identification results in cohesion, love, cooperation inside the ego boundary. Alienation, the other pole in the ego boundary, comes from strangeness, conflict, unlikeness. Alienation is the outcome of excluding or disowning that which is threatening to the individual. Perls has stated that "the whole idea of good and bad, right and wrong, is always a matter of boundary, of which side of the fence I am on."[102]

PERSONALITY Each individual is tortured by contrasting, conflicting, inner forces. Perls believes that Freud did not go far enough in his conception of personality. Although Freud posited the superego or conscience, he never formulated its actual opposite. Perls labels the superego the "topdog" and describes its opposite as the "underdog." The former is righteous, authoritarian, perfectionistic, and knows best. The topdog manipulates the individual with its "oughts" and "shoulds" and threats of catastrophe. The underdog manipulates with good intentions and by being defensive and apologetic. Perls states that "the underdog is the Mickey Mouse. The topdog is the Super Mouse."[103]

Within each individual, topdog and underdog struggle for control. This inner conflict, never complete, is a form of

[98] Frederick S. Perls, *Gestalt Therapy Verbatim* (New York: Bantam Books, 1971).
[99] Frederick S. Perls, *In and Out of the Garbage Can* (New York: Bantam Books, 1970).
[100] William R. Passons, "Gestalt Therapy Interventions for Group Counseling," *Personnel and Guidance Journal*, 5 (November 1972), 183–190.

[101] Perls, *Gestalt Therapy Verbatim*, p. 6.
[102] Ibid., p. 9.
[103] Ibid., p. 18.

persistent self-torture. Perls describes this struggle in these words:

> If the person tries to meet the topdog's demands of perfectionism, the result is a "nervous breakdown," or flight into insanity. This is one of the tools of the underdog. Once we recognize the structure of our behavior, which in the case of self improvement is the split between the topdog and the underdog, and if we understand how by listening, we can bring about a reconciliation of these two fighting clowns, then we realize that *we cannot deliberately bring about changes in ourselves or in others.*[104]

A fundamental concept in gestalt therapy is the clash between social and biological existence. Too many people try to actualize what they "should" be like rather than actualize themselves. For Perls, this difference between self-image-actualizing and *self*-actualizing is very critical. The former, the curse of the ideal, leads to the notion that one should not be what one is. Each person lives on two levels. The first is the public (or doing) level that can be observed and verified. The second is the private (or thinking) level. On the latter, the individual rehearses or prepares for future roles.

Perls suggests that the *situation* should control a person's actions or behavior. Those individuals who lack confidence in themselves, or who are not in touch with themselves or the world, react by wanting to exert control, rather than reacting spontaneously to the whole. Perls distinguishes between *end-gain* and *means-whereby* behavior. Needs of the organism determine the end-gain whereas means-whereby are matters of choice. Once the organism is integrated, control of the means-whereby produces satisfaction for the individual.

FRUSTRATION Developing individuals are confronted with two choices. They either learn to overcome frustration or they are spoiled by their parents. Perls views frustration as a positive element for it forces individuals to mobilize their own resources, to discover their potential, and to manipulate the environment.

CHARACTER Individuals who are not sufficiently frustrated use their potential to control adults and to create dependencies. In so doing, they acquire character. Perls does not appear to use the word *character* in its conventional sense of moral fiber. His use of the word seems to refer to rules and proscriptions that inhibit individuals from achieving their potential. He believes that the development of character leads to rigidity in responding, loss of the ability to cope freely and spontaneously, and produces predetermined behaviors. Character demands directional support from parents, teachers, and other adults. It forces the individual to play stupid and to establish dependency games. The individual expends energy in manipulating the world rather than using energy for development. The outcome, according to Perls, is that "the more character a person has, the less potential he has."[105]

PATHOLOGY Pathology occurs when a person's thoughts and feelings are so unacceptable that they are disowned. The cost of remaining intact by disowning parts of oneself, of one's experience, or one's properties is high, for the individual's power, energy, and ability to cope with the world become less and less. The person becomes more fragmented, rigid, and patterned.

Prominent among Perls's conception of pathology is the concept of self-regulation versus external regulation. Self-regulation is achieved as a result of becoming *aware* that one can trust oneself. Environment control or self-manipulation that interferes with or interrupts "organismic self-control" leads to pathology.

NEUROSIS A neurosis, according to Perls, is a disturbance in the individual's development. He has said that a neurotic individual is one who is confused and who fails to see the obvious.

MATURING Maturation is defined by Perls as ". . . the transcendence from environmental support to self-support."[106] The critical point is the *impasse,* which is the point where environmental support stops but authentic self-support has

[104] Ibid., p. 20.

[105] Ibid., p. 35.
[106] Ibid., p. 30.

yet to be generated. He illustrates the impasse with these words:

> The baby cannot breathe by itself. It doesn't get the oxygen supply through the placenta any more. We can't say that the baby has a choice, because there is no deliberate attempt of thinking out what to do, but the baby either has to die or to learn to breathe. . . . The "blue baby" is the prototype of the impasse which we find in every neurosis.[107]

The healthy personality is not one who adjusts to society but rather one who assimilates, understands, and relates to whatever happens. Moreover, responsibility for behavior is accepted.

ANXIETY Perls defines anxiety as the gap between the now and the later. Individuals experience anxiety because they leave the surety of the now and become preoccupied with the future and the roles they will play. Preoccupation with future performances reflects stage fright more than existential anxiety. Stage fright comes from expecting bad things to happen in our role or patterned behavior. Realizing that this type of anxiety is only an inconvenience or unpleasantness, and not a catastrophe, is the beginning of coming into one's own.

The counselor and the counseling process

The aim of gestalt therapy is to assist individuals to discover that they need not depend on others; rather, they can be independent. The process enables individuals to discover that something is possible for them. The therapist helps clients remove blocks that keep them from being authentic.

A major focus in gestalt counseling is that of helping the individual make the transition from environmental support to self-support. The therapist does this by identifying the impasse. The gestalt therapist serves as a screen for clients who project that which they cannot mobilize in themselves. In projecting on the therapist, clients discover that neither they nor the therapist is complete, that everyone has holes

in his or her personality. What is missing is a center. According to Perls:

> Without a center, everything goes on in the periphery and there is no place from which to work, from which to cope with the world. Without a center, you are not alert. . . . This achieving the center, being grounded in one's self, is about the highest state a human can achieve.[108]

The missing parts of the personality in this conception by Perls are those that the individual has alienated or given up to the world. The therapist frustrates clients so that they are forced to find their own way or to develop their own potential. The client discovers ". . . that what he expects from the therapist, he can do just as well himself."[109] That which is disowned can be recovered. Recovery comes by understanding, playing, and becoming those parts that the individual has disowned.

A major symptom of what is disowned by the individual is *avoidance.* Some illustrations of avoidance are phobias, escapism, changing of therapists, changing of spouses. Individuals who are confused, frustrated, or blocked are in an impasse. They have to discover the means of survival within themselves. The surprising thing, according to Perls, is that the impasse is mostly a matter of fantasy. An impasse occurs because they prevent themselves from using their resources by ". . . conjuring up a lot of catastrophic expectations."[110] Prominent in these expectations are feelings that people won't like one, of doing something foolish, of dying, and so forth. These catastrophic expectations stifle living, prevent the person from taking reasonable risks, and exclude *being.*

Perls points out that an individual rarely wants to get beyond an impasse. It is easier to maintain the status quo. In his words: "Very few people go into therapy to be cured, but rather to improve their neurosis."[111] It is awareness of how a person is stuck that starts recovery.

An important concept in gestalt therapy is the *here and now.* According to Perls:

[107] Ibid., p. 31.

[108] Ibid., p. 40.
[109] Ibid.
[110] Ibid., p. 42.
[111] Ibid.

The *now* is the present, is the phenomenon, is what you are aware of, is that moment in which you carry your so-called memories and your so-called expectations with you. Whether you remember or anticipate, you do it *now*. The past is no more. The future is not yet. . . . Some people make a program out of this. They make a demand, "you should live in the here and now." And I say it's *not possible* to live in the here and now, and yet, nothing exists except the here and now.[112]

That which exists in the here and now is often an unfinished situation or an incomplete gestalt. Perls's example of a common unfinished situation is that of children who never forgive their parents. They blame them and make them responsible for all their problems. It is only by letting go of one's parents and forgiving them that one becomes responsible for *being*.

Perls suggests that gestalt counselors use the *now* and the *how* rather than the *why* in their work with clients. The *why* only leads to rationalizations and never to understanding. *Now* includes all that exists, for the past is no more and the future is not yet. *How* is the structure or behavior and includes all that is going on. The therapist seeks to help the client to understand the *"how—how* do you behave *now, how* do you sit, *how* do you talk, all the details of what goes on *now."*[113] Above all, the therapist tries to find out what the client avoids or is unwilling to suffer.

Perls emphasizes that the gestalt therapist does not analyze, but integrates attention and awareness. Attention is defined as a deliberate way of listening to the foreground figure or that which is unpleasant. Awareness is experiencing or being in touch with the self and the world.

Prominent among Perls' techniques is to have clients relive their dreams. He maintains that little value comes from interpreting dreams, but by having clients act on their dreams (viewed as a fragment of one's personality) individuals can put the different fragments of their personality together. They reown their personalities and their hidden potentialities.

Passons has identified some techniques used by gestalt therapists. Some, but not all, of his techniques are summarized here:

1. *Enhancing awareness.* Clients are helped to attend to that which they are presently experiencing.
2. *Personalizing pronouns.* Clients are asked to personalize their pronouns to increase their personal awareness. Personalizing pronouns enables individuals to own their experience by projecting it.
3. *Changing questions to statements.* Encouraging clients to use statements rather than questions forces them to express themselves unambiguously and to be responsible for their communications.
4. *Assuming responsibility.* The client is asked to substitute the use of the word *won't* for *can't.* Experimentation in this substitution often uncovers the dynamics involved in the impasse and leads individuals to feel that they are in control of their fears.
5. *Asking "how" and "what."* Asking "why" leads to intellectualizations rather than experiencing and understanding. "How" and "what" enable individuals to get into the experience of their behavior.
6. *Sharing hunches.* Rather than using overt interpretation of client behaviors that too often cause defensiveness, the therapist encourages exploration by tentatively introducing insights as "I see" or "I imagine."
7. *Bringing the past into the now.* Much of that which is dealt with in counseling is concerned with past events. Rather than rehashing the past, previous experiences or feelings can be brought to the now.
8. *Expressing resentments and appreciations.* The individual who is beset with resentments also experiences appreciations; otherwise there would be no need to retain that which was resented. The gestalt counselor helps individuals to identify and express their resentments and appreciations, for they are often part of the individual's "unfinished situations."
9. *Using body expressions.* The counselor observes the client's body expressions and focuses attention on these to facilitate the individual's awareness.[114]

Counseling goals

Perls has stated that gestalt therapy seeks to promote clients' growth processes and to help them develop their human potentials, to take a stand. In his words "We have a very specific aim in Gestalt Therapy, and this is the same

---

112 Ibid., p. 44.
113 Ibid., p. 48.

114 Passons, "Gestalt Therapy Interventions," pp. 184–189.

aim that exists verbally in other forms of therapy, in other forms of discovering life. The aim is to mature, to grow up."[115]

Criticisms and contributions

The contributions imputed to gestalt therapy tend to parallel those cited for existentialism. Stress is placed on the wholeness and unity of behavior. Related to this is that the approach recognizes the importance of nonverbal behavior as an integral source of knowledge that reveals the individual.

Criticisms include:

1. The terminology tends to be idiosyncratic to the system. Although not as esoterically or philosophically based as that of existentialism, it incorporates a jargon that must be thoroughly understood to be properly used. This shorthand language often uses phrases that capture complex patterns of human behavior.
2. Little or no research exists to demonstrate its effectiveness empirically.

Issues

Issue 1 Cognitive rather than affective behaviors properly serve as the primary object of the counselor's attention, action, and processing.

Cognitive, because
1. Successful counseling lies in what clients *do* rather than *feel.*
2. Affect occurs only because the client's cognitive processing produces feelings and emotions.
3. Affect is most likely to be present when cognitive information processing causes change, disorganization, or disruption in the structure of the client's phenomenological field.

Affective, because
1. Identifying and clarifying the attitudes and feelings actually experienced by the client lead to behavioral changes.
2. Understanding of feelings, emotions, and attitudes ex-

[115] Perls, *Gestalt Therapy,* p. 28.

perienced by clients enables them to organize, process, and differentiate better the meanings associated with cognitions in their phenomenological field.

Discussion At the heart of this issue lies the question of whether cognitive based counseling theories are superior to affective counseling theories. The evidence amassed about the issue to date does not enable either side to claim victory. But above and beyond the question of superiority of theories, the issue is important to the counseling profession for it raises the question of what counselors should use to guide them in selecting what to respond to and what to ignore in their client contacts.

To some it may seem that the issue represents nothing more than a chicken-egg controversy now couched in emotion-action terms. And debate about which comes first—experiencing emotion (E) or visceral physiological changes (V) or overt responses to the environment (O)—has raged since 1884 when William James argued persuasively for what came to be called the James-Lange theory that V really preceded E followed by O. Many suggest that the soundest of positions is to recognize the interdependence of the three factors and that the counselor judge what to respond to according to client verbalizations. Essentially, the response by the counselor represents an integrating form providing a focus and organization absent in client behavior. By doing so, the counselor evokes a basis for the client useful in differentiating meanings that emerge when they attend to their experiences conceptualized as either cognition or feelings. In short, the dualism between feelings and behavior, between internal and external experience, can be viewed as originating from the same source, that which the client experiences.

Issue 2 It is the relationship established between counselor and counselee rather than the counselor's methods that is the source of gain.

True, because
1. The relationship, composed of different modes of participation, takes counselees where they want to go.
2. Relationship variables remove threat and thus permit clients to differentiate and integrate the meanings and directions associated with their abilities, attitudes, and behaviors.
3. It is how counselor and client relate to each other in

specific ways rather than using a specific method or procedure that produces gain.

False, because
1. It is the conversation content, what is talked about, rather than the relationship between counselor and counselee that produces changes in behavior.
2. The relationship established is as much a function of counselor methods as it is a function of counselor and counselee personalities or attitudes.
3. It is what the counselor does, not what either feels or thinks, that influences clients and brings about behavioral changes.

Discussion In many ways, this issue, if pursued to its logical conclusion, presents two extreme views of the counselor. At one extreme is the unfeeling, impersonal counselor who administers only methods or procedures. The opposite extreme is an unthinking, but highly personal counselor who provides only caring and warmth. Stated as these extreme positions, counselors, no doubt, would suggest that neither extreme is logical in understanding or explaining the benefits or the burdens of counseling.

Considerable evidence has been presented in recent years that relationship variables—empathy, genuineness, respect, concreteness—are ingredients found in effective levels of counseling. Few doubt that individuals will disclose themselves unless they receive positive, friendly and caring responses from others. But both relationships and methods are important and bear on outcomes produced. In any given case, they form a unique interaction with situational or contextual variables that serve as ingredients for facilitating change. Resourceful counselors invest themselves in both relationship and methods and use their skills, understandings, and insights to improve counselee level of functioning.

Issue 3 Client insight is necessary to bring about behavioral change.

Yes, because
1. Thinking it through (insight), understanding, examining, being aware of and attending inner and external situations enable clients to modify responses or to enact correct behaviors.
2. Maladaptive behavior stems from lack of insight or fail-

ure to observe subjective responses and examine their relationships with other responses and situational events.
3. The very act of insight or understanding is a precondition of new modes of cognition, feelings and change.

No, because
1. Individuals need not discover for themselves causes for their problems because correct responses to situations can be taught and learned by imitation and become part of acquired behavior.
2. Grasping or recognizing the relationship between A and B, between thoughts and feelings, between situations and their perceptions, comes after behavior is enacted.

Discussion The function of insight long has been a source of controversy in learning, whether in the classroom or the counseling room. Various theorists assign it differential importance, ranging from insight being central to being peripheral or nonessential in bringing about changes in human behavior. Some counseling theorists postulate that client insight is the target of their intervention and once that target is reached, change of behavior is automatic. Other theorists believe that insight or thoughtful understanding is valuable only if it is discovered by clients after observing their responses. Still others believe that the development of thoughts describing what is happening, though not essential, is better ideally because conscious control will then be brought to bear on behavioral changes. These authors believe this controversy about insight and its function will continue until agreement is reached as to what insight is and how it is to be defined operationally.

Annotated references

Alexander, Franz. *Fundamentals of Psychoanalysis.* New York: W.W. Norton & Company, 1963. 312 pp.

Alexander's presentation of psychoanalysis is comprehensive, concise, and knowledgeable. The basic theoretical concepts of the theory and its application are treated.

Beck, Carlton E. *Philosophical Foundations of Guidance.* Englewood Cliffs, N.J.: Prentice-Hall, 1963.

Chapter 4 (pp. 95–138) introduces certain basic philosophic questions that counselors must seek to answer, traces the history of existential psychology, and presents the Daseinanalyse *point of view. Beck cites some of the implications of existential thought for the future of counseling.*

Fisher, Seymour, and Roger P. Greenberg. *The Scientific Creditability of Freud's Theories and Therapy.* New York: Basic Books, 1977. 376 pp.

In ten chapters, the authors have organized data assembled from a wide range of sources that bear on Freudian theory. They assess the relevance of this evidence for contemporary Freudian theory and therapeutic constructs. They demonstrate how specific concepts have or have not been substantiated.

Patterson, C. H. *Relationship Counseling and Psychotherapy.* New York: Harper & Row, 1974. 207 pp.

Patterson presents the reasons why the term relationship counseling *is preferred over* client-centered counseling. *He identifies and discusses counseling goals, elements of therapeutic conditions, and the counselor and client in the counseling process. Application is made of relationship counseling to groups.*

Perls, Frederick S. *Gestalt Therapy Verbatim.* Moab, Utah: Real People Press, 1971. 306 pp.

Perls describes his views of the nature of man, learning, anxiety, and therapeutic practices. The publication is drawn from audiotapes made at weekend seminars and gives some of the flavor of Perls at work.

Rogers, Carl R. *Client-Centered Therapy.* Boston: Houghton Mifflin Company, 1951.

This book is a fundamental source for understanding client-centered counseling. It is divided into three parts: views of client-centered therapy, application of therapy, and the self-theory of personality. The second section—application—treats play therapy, group psychotherapy, leadership and administration, student-centered teaching, and the training of counselors and therapists.

Wexler, David A. and Laura North Rice, eds. *Innovations in Client-Centered Therapy.* New York: John Wiley & Sons, 1974. 517 pp.

Each of the fifteen chapters has been written to explore ideas and developments within client-centered counseling of the 1970s. The chapter authors were reported to be faculty members or graduate students at the University of Chicago Counseling and Psychotherapy Research Center where and when Rogers shaped client-centered theory, practice, and research.

Further references

Abbott, Anne H. "Individual Counseling with High-Risk Students: A Practical Approach." *The School Counselor,* 25 (January 1978), 206–208.

Collison, Brooke B. "The Mrs. Lincoln Response." *Personnel and Guidance Journal,* 57 (December 1978), 180–182.

Combs, Jeanne M. and Robert C. Ziller. "Photographic Self-Image of Counselors." *Journal of Counseling Psychology,* 24 (September 1977), 452–455.

Coven, Arnold B. "Using Gestalt Psychodrama Experiments in Rehabilitation Counseling." *Personnel and Guidance Journal,* 56 (November 1977), 143–147

Goodstein, Leonard D. and Russell, Scott W. "Self-Disclosure: A Comparative Study of Reports by Self and Others." *Journal of Counseling Psychology,* 24 (July 1977), 365–369.

Hendricks, Gaylord. "What Do I Do After They Tell Me How They Feel?" *Personnel and Guidance Journal,* 55 (January 1977), 249–252.

Hill, Clara E., Terri B. Thames, and David K. Rardin. "Comparison of Rogers, Perls and Ellis on the Hill Counselor Verbal Response Category System." *Journal of Counseling Psychology,* 26 (May 1979), 198–203.

Krumboltz, Helen Brandhurst and Johanna Shapiro. "Counseling Women in Behavioral Self Direction." *Personnel and Guidance Journal,* 57 (April 1979), 415–418.

Neufeldt, Susan A., Jules M. Zimmer, and Daniel M. Mayton, II. "Client Cognitive Levels and Counseling Approaches." *Journal of Counseling Psychology,* 24 (September 1977), 448–451.

Newton, Fred B. "How May I Understand You? Let Me Count the Ways." *Personnel and Guidance Journal,* 54 (January 1976), 256–261.

Pyke, Sandra W. "Cognitive Templating: A Technique for Feminist (and Other) Counselors." *Personnel and Guidance Journal,* 57 (February 1979), 315–318.

Roney, Anne M. "TA and Sex Stereotypes." *Personnel and Guidance Journal,* 54 (November 1975), 165–166.

Wright, Logan. "Conceptualizing and Defining Psychosomatic Disorders," *American Psychologist,* 32 (August 1977), 625–628.

10   Building a personal theory of counseling

Chapter 7 presented some of the counseling contributions and insights available from disciplines related to counseling. Chapters 8 and 9 outlined eleven counseling theories. This chapter seeks to discern the personal meaning of the content presented in Chapters 7, 8, and 9. Consideration will be given first to the characteristics and functions of theory, second to how counseling viewpoints diverge and converge, and finally to the evolution of a personal philosophy of counseling.

Characteristics and functions of theories

Theory is usually defined in a dictionary as a statement of general principles supported by data offered as an explanation of a phenomenon. It is generally pointed out that theory is a statement of the relations believed to prevail among a comprehensive body of facts. Theory is often contrasted to a hypothesis, the distinction being that the latter has less evidence to support it. Furthermore, in contrast to a law, theory covers a wider range of relationships.

Characteristics of theories

Stefflre and Matheny envision theory as a human convention for keeping data in order and say that theory would be unnecessary if human memories were better than they are. Memory is both limited and fallible, therefore, theories are needed to enable people to reduce complexities to manageable proportions. "To perform this function, a theory must consist of data plus an interrelating structure which tells us how one piece of information relates to another. . . ."[1]

The fundamental purpose of theory, then, is to describe and explain phenomena. Many visualize theory as apart from practice—as something remote, vague, impractical, and idealistic. Others more correctly think of it as going hand in hand with practice. Baffled by a problem, they employ theory to enlarge the range of circumstances to which attention should be paid to derive a solution. In basing practice on theory, one must closely observe the consequences of practice in order to determine whether it corroborates the theory. If corroboration occurs, the theory is verified; if not, the theory must be rejected or modified.

The terms *paradigm* and *conceptual model* are sometimes loosely substituted for *theory* in current literature. A paradigm is a model that exhibits all the variable forms of a phenomenon; a conceptual model is a diagrammatic representation of a complex concept. A model is a schematic representation of the relationships postulated within a theory. According to Rychlak, models are useful for the generation of hypotheses but not for verification of theories.[2] Hall and Lindzey define theory as a cluster of relevant assumptions systematically related to each other and to a set of empirical definitions.[3]

Stefflre and Matheny point out that most theories have two elements in common: reality and belief.[4] Reality is the data of behavior that are observable and for which explanations are sought whereas belief involves the way individuals try to make sense out of data by relating what is observed to conceivable explanations

BASES OF THEORIES   A theory is not generated in isolation but has personal, historical, sociological, and philosophical bases. It reflects the personality of its builder—his or her needs—and is a product of the time in which it appears and is used. Temporal and social forces impinge on theory builders, determining to some extent their interest and selection of factors in the theory. Finally, their philosophy influences

---

[1] Buford Stefflre and Kenneth Matheny, *The Functions of Theory in Counseling,* Houghton Mifflin's Professional Guidance Monographs (Boston: Houghton Mifflin Company, 1968), pp. 2–3.

[2] Joseph F. Rychlak, *Introduction to Personality and Psychotherapy,* (Boston: Houghton Mifflin Company, 1973), p. 8.
[3] Calvin S. Hall and Gardner Lindzey, *Theories of Personality* (New York: John Wiley & Sons, 1957), p. 11.
[4] Stefflre and Matheny, *Functions of Theory,* p. 3.

the theories they construct, either explicitly or implicitly. For these reasons, theory, especially in social science, is rarely purely scientific. Tyler has described the sources and procedures involved in generating her own personal theory of counseling: physiological and psychological laboratories, psychiatric consulting rooms, observations of people in their natural settings, the realm of formal philosophy and religion.[5]

FORMAL ATTRIBUTES Stefflre and Matheny have cited five formal attributes that should be present in a theory.[6] A theory can be judged by how well it meets these criteria. First, a good theory is clear. It is understandable, and its general principles are not self-contradictory. Second, a good theory is comprehensive. A theory that explains the most phenomena is preferred over the one that explains a single phenomenon. Third, a good theory is explicit. Precision is evident in its terms and relationships, and its rightness or wrongness can be tested. Fourth, a good theory is parsimonious. It explains data simply and clearly without unnecessary diversions. Finally, a good theory generates useful research. Measured against these criteria, almost all counseling theories fall short and are imperfect. Those who construct them usually see them as partial and incomplete.

Functions of theory

The major functions of theory may be summarized in a fourfold statement:

1. Theory summarizes and generalizes a body of information. It is used as a sort of scientific shorthand. The principle of reinforcement—that people and animals must have some kind of reward or punishment in order to learn—is an example of a theory that may not be entirely correct but is useful because it gives the essence of literally hundreds of learning studies. Hence, to the extent that it states laws or principles, a theory is a useful way of summarizing facts.
2. Theory facilitates understanding and explanation of complex phenomena. This function is somewhat related to the summarizing and generalizing function just cited. Theory points out that which may be most pertinent among a confusing array of facts and observations. It orders and relates data and thereby creates a comprehensible body of information that otherwise would tend to remain random data.
3. Theory is a predictor. It permits one to foretell what will happen under certain conditions. Prediction is an essential objective of all science. If science and/or theory were but the collection of facts and if prediction could never be made from them, little value would accrue to their collection. A well-developed theory is like a road map that depicts many, but not all, features of a geographical area. Its main purpose is to tell how the area may be traveled. In similar fashion a theory lays out in advance certain important features of an area of knowledge. A good theory presents a good approximation of the facts it encompasses. However, there need not be prediction of every detail.
4. Theory stimulates further research and fact finding. Even if inaccurate or wrong, it leads to more theorizing. It was a theory about the nature of the atom that led to experiments culminating in the atomic bomb and uses of atomic energy. Theories are guides for research and often constitute the basis for deciding next steps in fact collecting.

Theory and the counselor

The functions described above apply equally well to counselors confronted with a client. Counselors attempt to apply, either implicitly or explicitly, the theory or theories with which they are conversant. Their purpose is to give meaning and life to whatever they do in that situation.

It has been said that theory summarizes and generalizes a body of information. Thus counselors must somehow summarize the data provided to them by a particular client. These data are both complex and confusing. Whether or not they engage in diagnosis, counselors must make comparisons between the body of unique data supplied by a client and the larger body of generalizations about human behavior.

In respect to the second function, all counselors stress understanding as fundamental to the counseling process.

[5] Leona E. Tyler, "Theoretical Principles Underlying the Counseling Process," *Journal of Counseling Psychology*, 5 (Spring 1958), 3–8.
[6] Stefflre and Matheny, *Functions of Theory*, pp. 5–6.

Understanding must go beyond merely comprehending moment-by-moment verbal interchange, although even this is often a complex task. In the helping relationship, understanding involves grasping a larger part of the individual's life situation. Clients present many facets, self-perceptions, feelings, self-descriptive statements, and the like that counselors must comprehend and explain, at least to themselves. Their efforts at understanding this array of information can be usefully based on a theory.

In respect to the third function, counselors predict at many levels. Somewhat informally, they predict as they select approaches and even as they select among alternative responses those stimuli to be presented to the client. Presumably, these are not random activities but stem from a theory about the counselee. More formally, counselors engage in prediction when they speculate, either alone or with a client, about the effects of certain courses of action available to the client. These more formal predictions derive from knowledge of the client, theories of human behavior and the environment.

Finally, theory frequently tells counselors what facts they lack to achieve understanding of an individual. It may also help to point out the shortcomings of their own efforts. In the latter context, if counselors view their work in relation to a theory of counseling, often they are able to identify reasons for success and failure both with particular clients and over·time with all their clientele.

Comparison of counseling viewpoints

Chapters 8 and 9 dealt with major aspects of eleven counseling viewpoints. Table 10.1 shows the general positions of these approaches with regard to ten important characteristics. As is true of any attempt like this, some violence may have been done to the nuances and subtleties of the theories. The intent here is to point up basic agreed-on characteristics in which the various counseling approaches are similar and different. The information presented in the 110 cells of the table will not be recapitulated since in large part this information has been treated in Chapters 8 and 9. Rather, attention will be drawn to the broader issue of similarities and differences among the eleven counseling viewpoints.

Nature of humankind

The eleven theories differ on the role of rationality and volition in determining human behavior. At one extreme, psychotherapy by reciprocal inhibition and the behavioral approach tend to view human beings as reactive and basically impotent in relation to their environment. The orthodox Freudian approach takes an equally bleak view of humankind's rationality and volitional capabilities but for an entirely different reason. Those who operate within the Freudian context believe that humankind's incapacities stem not from an overwhelming, unchangeable environment but from unconscious forces over which they exert little if any power. Adler departed from this, but at the other end of the continuum, the client-centered and existential viewpoints see people as rational and striving to determine their own destiny. Seemingly, the trait and factor viewpoint is also built on the implicit assumption that, given the necessary facts about oneself and the environment, the individual is capable of independent functioning. Although these views tend to use different terminology, they share the basic assumption that humankind strives for self-actualization, freedom, and self-responsibility.

The freedom-determinism issue has long been troublesome for most counselors. Gelso, in a perceptive analysis, reconceptualizes the dilemma.[7] He holds that strict determinism and free will are both valid and necessary assumptions in any complete conception of human behavior. Whether and at what times determinism or freedom is valid depend on the source of information used. On the one hand, human actions are best understood as determined when one *objectively* observes one's own functioning or when one attempts to observe other individuals and seek reasons for their behavior. On the other hand, belief in freedom is both necessary and possible, according to Gelso, when people *subjectively* experience themselves or empathically experience another person. Gelso suggests that counselors have to live with this paradox. Exclusive use of a freewill model of humankind would not permit counselors to gain a causal understanding of their clients, and further, it would exacerbate inappropriate guilt in their clients because they would

[7] Charles J. Gelso, ''Two Different Worlds: A Paradox in Counseling and Psychotherapy,'' *Journal of Counseling Psychology*, 17 (May 1970), 271–278

view their misbehaviors as their fault alone. Gelso says that exclusive use of a deterministic model would make it difficult for counselors to empathize with their clients. Further, such a model would reinforce the client's feelings of being a pawn manipulated by external forces.

The Adlerian and client-centered approaches consider humans as trustworthy, reliable, and "good." Individuals will move toward the good for themselves and others because they have self-enhancing tendencies. The Freudian view, note Burks and Stefflre, is less sanguine about basic nature: "Evil is seen as not only something done *by* people but as something natural *to* them. Counseling, then, has the function of the proper housekeeping for the part of our nature that loves to romp."[8]

An interesting dichotomy has been presented by Ford and Urban.[9] Certain counseling theories view individuals, either implicitly or explicitly, as pilots whereas others view them as robots. Those (client-centered and existentialist) who take the "pilot" position see the person as exercising control over one's own behavior and life situations and able to choose and be responsible. Those (reciprocal inhibition, behavioral, Freudian analysis) with the "robot" image cite the automaticity of behavior. Ford and Urban point out that the data emphasized, the observational settings and procedures, and the concepts and propositions differ according to whether the individual is seen as pilot or robot. Neither image appears in pure form in any counseling system, but all tend to stress that behavior is characterized by automaticity and by choice making, and excessive stress on the individual as pilot or as robot leads to theoretical weaknesses.

Despite the apparently negativistic view of humankind in relation to their environment found in the strongly behavioristic approaches (reciprocal inhibition and behavioral) it is clear that all approaches share some optimism for humankind given its difficulties. Obviously all must accept to some degree the belief that humans are pliable and can change their condition; otherwise there would be no reason for the existence of counseling theories or counselors! Perhaps Chenault's view is more useful:

The question of man's nature is not clearly amenable to the goal of generalization. Were that goal achieved, the question may still remain unanswered. At least when our quest of defining man seeks commonality among men, it must take care not to define out the *commonality of idiosyncrasy.* It must not define away man's literal uniqueness, especially in a field dealing with the one-to-one relationship.[10]

Major personality constructs

Optimism about changing humans is not independent of the various concepts of the nature of humankind. For each position, this philosophical base colors its conceptualizations of personality, called personality constructs in Table 10.1. They are hypothetical constructs that in reality are never actually observed.

All agree that much behavior is learned in the sense that developmental events influence any image of humankind at any point in time. Again the degree of emphasis placed on prior learning varies from viewpoint to viewpoint. In some approaches (transactional analysis, behavioristic) prior learning becomes the central focus as well as the mechanism for bringing about change. In others learning is dealt with as primarily that which has brought people to their current state and shapes their perceptions of their life situation.

Anxiety

Virtually all viewpoints assign a central position to anxiety. They differ on the source of anxiety but agree that it is unpleasant or undesirable. Anxiety, fear, tension, and conflict are seen as critical in the development of disorder or as interfering with the individual's functioning. To the behaviorists, anxiety emanates from situational events of all kinds, including concrete objects, whereas Rogers stresses the acquisition of conflicting evaluations and the existentialists point to the conception of nonbeing. Rogers believes that anxiety is a consequence of the attention to and symbolization of certain kinds of conflict whereas Freud first

[8] Herbert M. Burks and Buford Stefflre, "A Summing Up," in *Theories of Counseling*, 3rd ed., ed. Herbert M. Burks and Buford Stefflre (New York: McGraw-Hill Book Co., 1979), p. 289.

[9] Donald H. Ford and Hugh B. Urban, *Systems of Psychotherapy* (New York: John Wiley & Sons, 1963), pp. 595–599.

[10] Joann Chenault, "Counseling Theory: The Problem of Definition," *Personnel and Guidance Journal*, 47 (October 1968), 113.

TABLE 10.1 **Comparison of eleven counseling approaches**

Characteristic	Trait/Factor	Rational-Emotive	Eclectic counseling	Reciprocal inhibition	Behavioral counseling
1. Nature of humankind	A rational being with potentialities that may be developed in either positive or negative directions; people not capable of developing autonomously but need assistance of others to achieve full potentiality	Humans subject to powerful biological and social forces, have potential for being rational. Can rid self of emotional difficulty by maximizing rational thinking	Humans both rational and irrational but having asocial tendencies; normal person, by conscious use of intellectual resources, acquires self-regulatory abilities through training	Humans shaped by environment; no volition, no free will, but only learned reactions; impossibility of being rational or objective; all thinking affected by conditioned feelings and needs and is thus rationalization	Depends on theorist but humans viewed primarily as mechanistic, or responding to an environment over which they have little control, living in a deterministic world, have little active role in choosing their destiny
2. Major personality constructs	Each person an organized, unique pattern of capabilities and potentialities seeking to organize and maintain one's life by utilizing one's unique traits	Psychological states largely result of thinking illogically; thinking and reasoning are not two disparate processes; humans rewarded or punished by their own thinking or self-talk	Personality the changing states of coping with environment; drive to achieve and maintain stability, integrate opposing functions, maximize self; lifestyle consists of characteristic ways of unifying strategies for satisfying needs and coping with reality; development consists of perfecting rational and voluntary control	Behavior law-conforming; change a result of (a) growth, (b) lesions, (c) learning	Behavior lawful, and a function of its antecedent conditions
3. Nature of anxiety	Uncertainty over utilization of one's potentialities	Overgeneralizing that an event will be catastrophic	Not explicitly described; repressed emotional conflict	Unadaptive behavior acquired by learning; unlearned anxiety characteristic response to noxious or threatening stimuli; situations requiring difficult discriminations or conflict	Learned reactions to cues involved in certain situations which operate as secondary or acquired drives; learned reaction to an originally neutral stimulus
4. Counseling goals	To aid the individual in successive approximation of self-understanding and self-management	Elimination of anxiety, fears, etc., and the attainment of rational behavior, happiness, self-actualization	Independent self-regulation; attainment and preservation of mental health	Relief of suffering and removal of causes	Solution of whatever problems (within ethical limits) client brings to counselor
5. Major techniques	Forcing conformity, changing environment, selecting appropriate environment, learning needed skills, and changing attitudes	Use of relationship techniques to establish rapport followed by teaching, suggestion, persuasion, confrontation, prescription of activities designed to rid the client of irrational ideas	Active to passive techniques employed	Assertive, respiratory, sexual, and relaxation responses including systematic desensitization	Reinforcement techniques, social modeling, desensitization techniques
6. Use of tests and appraisal devices	Extensively used	Limited use	Limited use of standardized tests; projective techniques used as clinical data to be integrated with other data	Limited use	May be used if needed
7. History taking	Necessary before an individual can be counseled	Relatively little use of historical clarification	Important for diagnostic reasons	Therapy begun with history taking to uncover anxiety	Necessary to identify contingencies
8. Diagnosis and prognosis	A necessary step	Used to uncover illogical ideas	Cornerstone of all clinical work; the basis for counseling approach adopted	Part of counselor activity	Necessary to assess (a) role of anxiety in symptoms and (b) client's capacity to handle anxiety and to extinguish it
9. Clientele	"Normal" individuals who wish to become prepared to solve their adjustment situations before self-conflict develops	No limitation but notes that psychotics rarely completely cured	Normal people with intact personality resources who have personality problems	No limitation placed on types of clients other than that disorders must be learned	Individuals who can think about and attend to the events in their environment
10. Activity of counselor	Active role	Highly active	Ranges for passive to active role depending on nature of problem and client's resources	Active role	Counselor warm and friendly but highly active

Freudian analysis	*Adlerian psychology*	*Transactional analysis*	*Client-centered counseling*	*Existentialism*	*Gestalt therapy*
The individual is both animalistic and human; shaped by biological needs, sexual drives, and aggressive instincts; behavior primarily determined by unconscious processes that are motivational and goal-directed	Humankind naturally good, its evolution positive	Determined by childhood experiences, but can change	The individual is rational, good, trustworthy; moves in self-actualizing directions or toward growth, health, self-realization, independence, and autonomy	The individual is required to shoulder tasks set by life and hence to define meaning of life; strives for freedom from instincts and environment; individually unpredictable; free and responsible to self	Human beings not independent from their environment but work as a whole. Individual not sum of parts but a coordination
Personality a system composed of id, ego, and superego and a result of genetic relationship between ego functions in later life and those of infancy and childhood; outcome of a mutual interaction among tendencies of id, ego, and superego	Behavior springs from meanings or fictions; people establish a life plan at early age; make their own law of movement according to plan; compensation for feelings of inferiority	Conceptualized as three ego states—Parent, Adult, Child—and four life positions	Self-concept a regulator of behavior and perceptual field is reality for the individual; behavior a function of perceptions and organized with respect to self-concept	Behavior motivated by attempts to find meaning; not driven but pulled by one's values	Individual is considered a system in balance. He or she lives in a public (doing) level and a private (thinking) level. Imbalance is experienced as a corrective need. Awareness permits self-regulation and self-control
Conflict between id impulses, superego demands, and ego defenses	Stems from feelings of inferiority	Results from conflicts, concerts, or contaminations between ego states	Incongruence between self-concept and experience; conditions of worth violated; need for self-regard frustrated	Lack of meaning in life or threat of nonbeing	The gap between the *now* and the *then*; unfinished situations
Personality reconstruction and reorientation	Change mistaken lifestyles; confront superiority mechanisms; cultivate social interest	Cure presenting problem; enabling people to experience freedom of choice	Self-direction and full functioning of client who is congruent, mature, and open to experience	Experiencing of existence as real so that individual can act on one's potentialities and develop a commitment	To mature, to grow up, to take responsibility for one's life, to be in touch with one's self and with the world
Free association, use of dreams, transference, interpretation, etc.	Relationship techniques; diagnosis of life plan; explanation to achieve insight; comparisons	Diagnosis and analysis of transactions	Limited use of questioning, reassurance, encouragement, suggestion, but technique a way of communicating acceptance, respect, understanding	Psychoanalytic techniques often used, including free association, interpretation, transference, but emphasis on therapist's presence and patient's being	Confrontative; provide situations in which client experiences frustrations; focus attention on body posture, gestures; enactment of dreams
Projective techniques often employed	Limited use	Limited use	Extremely limited use; tends to be seen as inimical	Limited use	Limited use
Detailed history usually not taken	Necessary to go back for comparisons	Limited use	Inimical to counseling process	Most believe essential	Limited use
Necessary for interpretation	Diagnosis of life plan	Diagnosis of ego states to determine executive power, adaptability, mentality, etc.	Inimical to counseling process	Seen as necessary step by most existentialists	Limited use
Therapy contraindicated for schizoid personalities, paranoid states, severe hypochondriasis; extremely guarded for marked conversion symptoms	No limitation noted	No restriction noted	Currently no restriction placed on clientele	No restriction noted; most believe approach has wide applicability and utility	No limitation stated
Initially passive; moves toward active, interpretive role as treatment progresses	Counselor very active	Counselor very active	Counselor active in providing facilitative conditions	Therapy seen as partnership, with therapists risking themselves and clients encouraged to be themselves	Highly active

thought anxiety was due to conflict and then changed to conceptualize it as the antecedent motive producing conflict.

Ford and Urban state that

. . . the diversity of viewpoints becomes quite impressive. Many of the theorists are employing the same concept-labels—anxiety, conflict, negative self-evaluative thoughts, unawareness, to cite a few. Thus, they tend to sound the same, and therefore some might conclude that they are all saying the same thing about disorder and its development. But the similarity is sometimes found to be superficial, since analysis reveals that they are employing the same terms to refer to different combinations of events.[11]

Counseling goals

Most counseling goals are expressed in abstractions rather than precise behavioral descriptions (see Chapter 4). The behavioral approach is the exception, and of all views it is most likely to utilize behavior as an outcome characteristic.

The approaches differ mainly in regard to range and variety of goals: from symptom removal to personality reorganization to self-actualization. There appears to be common agreement that individuality and responsibility are desirable. Behavioristically oriented approaches, although stressing symptom removal, generally posit this outcome as an intermediate step to assisting the individual to function better and achieve increasing freedom and expressiveness.

Major techniques

Variation in the use of major techniques centers around the emphasis placed on reasoning and problem solving versus stressing the individual's affective life and experiencing. Another source of variation lies in the degree to which counseling activity is restricted to the session itself as opposed to moving beyond the relationship between counselor and client. Some approaches rely on environmental intervention, directly urging their clientele to engage in the ap-

plication and testing of themselves in anxiety-provoking situations outside the counseling room. Wolpe clearly requires this by urging patients to practice desensitizing techniques in real-life situations. Others generally work almost entirely within the relationship itself and leave clients to choose their own means of applying what they learn of themselves to their lives.

In those approaches that rely heavily on the counselor-client relationship a great deal of similarity has been demonstrated among experienced therapists regardless of their theoretical orientation. Substantiation of this assertion may be found in the work of Robert Wrenn and others. Wrenn sought to determine whether theoretical orientation or situational factors affected counselor responses. His findings supported earlier findings that theoretical orientation has little influence on the manner in which experienced counselors respond.[12]

London has differentiated the approaches into insight therapies (client-centered, existential, and psychoanalysis) versus action therapies (behavioral). Although noting that differences exist among the insight viewpoints, London believes that two commonalities stand out:

1. The single allowable instrument of the therapy is talk, and the therapeutic sessions are deliberately conducted in such a way that, from start to finish, the patient, client, analysand, or counselee does most of the talking and most of the deciding of what will be talked about.
2. The therapist operates with a conservative bias against communicating to the patient important or detailed information about his [or her] own life, that is to say, the therapist tends to hide his [or her] personal life from the patient.[13]

The action therapies are more concerned with symptoms, behaviors, or actions. According to London the action therapist "cares not a whit what the patient does or does not say about himself or even know about himself insofar as such *behaviors* have concrete and demonstrable value for producing change."[14] There are two major characteristics of action therapies:

[11] Ford and Urban, *Systems*, p. 654.

[12] Robert L. Wrenn, "Counselor Orientation: Theoretical or Situational?" *Journal of Counseling Psychology*, 7 (Spring 1960), 40–45.
[13] P. London, *The Modes and Morals of Psychotherapy* (New York: Holt, Rinehart and Winston, 1964), p. 45.
[14] Ibid., p. 78.

1. The therapist assumes a much greater influence over the detailed conduct of the treatment sessions, and possibly over the outside life of the patient, than Insight therapists would.

2. The therapist is much more responsible for the outcome of treatment, that is, for whatever changes take place in the patient, than are Insight therapists.[15]

Despite the fact that all approaches describe and presumably employ fairly specific techniques, most theories seemingly consciously avoid clear prescriptions of what should be done in the counseling process. This curious de-emphasis of technique apparently exists because, regardless of orientation, counselors generally eschew viewing the client as an object to which something is done. Even when objective techniques are stressed, theorists usually insist on maximum flexibility since they prize the uniqueness of each client. Related to this latter point is the consensus that the client must be respected as an individual and that critical and derogatory statements by the counselor are to be avoided.

The de-emphasis on counselor techniques led Ford and Urban to comment as follows:

One wonders why these theorists as a group have specified so little in the way of principles and techniques for producing behavioral change. Some have expressed concern that published techniques might come to be misused by uninformed people (Freud). Rogers started out by specifying technique but abandoned this when he realized that the same statements made by different therapists could have different effects. In his instance, we think he erred in concluding that further specification was not possible. A more appropriate conclusion would have been that since his original degree of specification was inadequate, certain other variables must be considered: tone of voice or the context of statements. More specification, rather than less, was required. Several other theorists have discussed in very general terms what the therapist should feel toward the patient and how he should think about the patient's problems. The issue is often dropped at this point, as if appropriate actions or techniques would follow automatically. We think such

an assumption is untenable and encourages one to evade the difficult task of specifying technique. It is what the therapist does, not what he [or she] thinks and feels, that directly affects the patient.[16]

Appraisal, history taking, and diagnosis

Although appraisal, history taking, and diagnosis are presented in Table 10.1 as separate entries, discussion here will apply to all three at once because they are closely related. The intent of appraisal (including life history) is to derive a diagnostic and prognostic statement permitting counselors to form a working image of their clients. Considerable variety exists among the approaches as to the kinds of data necessary to arrive at this image. A notable exception is client-centered counseling, which regards the procedures described as unnecessary and harmful to the counseling relationship. The client-centered view stresses understanding of the client's internal frame of reference whereas other approaches place greater emphasis on the counselor's achieving a kind of external understanding apart from the relationship itself. Approaches that rely heavily on external understanding of the client invariably affirm the tentative and partial nature of their understanding and also are likely to claim that the reason for formal assessment is the mutual planning of counseling activities.

Clientele

The trait/factor and the eclectic approaches restrict their services to so-called normal individuals who exhibit adjustment problems but retain the resources necessary to cope with their difficulties. The other approaches place no limitation on their clientele except to exclude those incapable of benefiting from treatment, for example, the extremely disturbed psychotic or those suffering from severe organic disorders. In actual practice most counselors, regardless of theoretical orientation, work with individuals having temporary situational problems, neurotic personalities, and mild neuroses. Selection criteria appear to focus on whether the client retains the personal resources necessary to indicate

[15] Ibid.

[16] Ford and Urban, *Systems*, p. 667.

hope for favorable treatment outcome. Lowe points out the following:

> The criteria that therapists use in selecting clients are typically highly personal and require value judgments by the therapist.
>
> In choosing his clients the therapist first judges whether they will be able to relate and to communicate meaningfully. Counselors and therapists typically require that clients meet such objective criteria as having above-average intelligence and being between adolescence and early middle age. In addition they are likely to make more subjective judgements of client suitability, and they often insist that clients possess a working conscience, a tendency to introspection, and motivation for self-improvement.[17]

All approaches seemingly prefer self-motivated clients who voluntarily seek help and cooperate by consenting to the rules and procedures employed with them. Almost all point out that counselees come for counseling because they desire change in their life situation, which is in itself a kind of self-selection. Practitioners of every approach believe that they can help those who seek their assistance, providing there is no clear indication that their professional help cannot be utilized. Few pretend to help everyone who seeks their assistance.

Counselor activity

All approaches postulate certain common conditions in a counseling relationship. These tend primarily to describe the counselor-client relationship and include warmth, acceptance, and understanding. Variations exist in the way each approach attempts to provide these conditions and the degree to which certain activities are seen as fostering or working against them. Although the focus in Table 10.1 is on active versus passive counselor behavior, a comparison of approaches on this basis should not be stretched too far. Although in general the extent of counselor activity and

passivity is related to particular approaches, activity and passivity within an approach may change during a series of contacts with a given client. Another difference lies in where responsibility resides. The first, sixth, ninth, and tenth approaches assume that the counselor is responsible for the course of action; it is the professional's task to determine what is wrong and what is needed to produce change. Client-centered and existentialist counselors, on the other hand, believe that the responsibility lies chiefly with the client, who is able to determine what is wrong and what is needed because of the conditions inherent within the relationship. This distinction is a crucial one and accounts for much of the difference between these two approaches and the other approaches in a variety of characteristics descriptive of the counseling process. The philosophic assumptions concerning the nature of humankind cited for the eleven counseling viewpoints clearly bear on this issue.

Burks and Stefflre, commenting on the common elements among theories, present ten facets of counseling that are common to all.[18] Their remarks are particularly appropriate to end this section and are paraphrased here. First is *flexibility*, and they noted that the hallmark of experienced counselors was their ability to fit their style to the unique character of the client and the relationship. Second is *motivation*; individuals who want counseling are more likely to profit from it. Third is *relationship*, generally seen as the base on which the structure of counseling is built. Fourth is counselor *respect* for the individuality, humanness, and complexity of the individual. Fifth is *communication* between counselor and client, whether through words or nonverbal cues. Sixth is *learning*, present to some degree in all theories in that clients learn more about themselves and their world and therefore perform better. Seventh is *direction* of the client by the counselor, recognized by most theories; Burks and Stefflre noted that concern has shifted from the presence or absence of direction to the extent, method, and purpose of direction. Eighth, the counselor's presence, interests, and activities are seen by all approaches as giving *support* to the client. Ninth, the counselor *rewards* clients for their presence and for some of their behavior. Finally, in respect to *purposes* of counselors, all seek a free, informed, responsible person.

[17] C. Marshall Lowe, *Value Orientations in Counseling and Psychotherapy* (San Francisco: Chandler Publishing Company, 1969), p. 39.

[18] Burks and Stefflre, "A Summing Up," pp. 330–333.

Building a personal philosophy of counseling

Philosophical orientations examined

Philosophy is a broad term. It is used throughout the following discussion in the narrower sense of professional philosophy. Counseling behavior is the product of one's philosophy, theoretical orientation, technique, and self-concept. At some early point in their thinking, counselors must answer for themselves: "What significance do I attach to this person?" Beck[19] has set forth the following philosophical questions that need to be discussed by counselors:

What is the nature of reality?
What is man's place in the universe?
What is knowledge?
How free is man?
What things (events, people) are of most worth?
Are there mandatory goals for society? For individuals?

A philosophical orientation

Some years ago, C. Marshall Lowe[20] described and criticized four value orientations, each of which he suggests tends to exclude the others, and each of which has been offered as an orientation for counseling. His article will serve as a basis for the discussion here.

NATURALISM By *naturalism* Lowe says he means "positivism, scientism, behaviorism, and hedonism." The word *positivism* refers to the philosophical position of A. J. Ayer and the linguistic analysts for whom the only statements that have any meaning are those that can be empirically verified or logically induced from empirical data. *Scientism* is related to positivism and is characterized by the validation of statements by control and prediction of observed phenomena. This philosophy is eloquently expressed in B. F. Skinner's *Walden Two*. The expression of *scientism*

in the field of psychology is often referred to as *behaviorism*. It insists on validation by observable and measurable stimulus-and-response experimental techniques. It tends, therefore, to disregard concepts like *consciousness* and *freedom* as terms to which no scientific meaning can be attached. Many criticisms of psychotherapeutic techniques have come from this source, particularly through H. J. Eysenck,[21] who quotes Raimy with relish: "Psychotherapy is an unidentified technique applied to unspecified problems with unpredictable outcomes. For this technique we recommend rigorous training." The word *hedonism* refers to the characterization of all human behavior in terms of the pursuit of pleasure, the relief of tension, or the satisfaction of needs. Joseph Samler[22] argues for the establishment of a validated system of values, the basic data of which, he maintains, will come from humankind's "increasing scientific knowledge." He holds that such values will be translatable, without undue difficulty, from an examination of human needs. What humans value, it seems, is to be equated with what is needed, and that is saying a great deal more than that individuals value what they need.

Naturalism in counseling has been reflected in a wide range of developing trends over the last half-century. The Freudian and prescriptive schools of an earlier era rested on deterministic foundations. More recently phenomenology has provided a framework within which deterministic views of human behavior have been set forth. Mathewson employs the phenomenological model, but strenuously rejects determinism: ". . . to discard the intuitive-artistic view of life might tend to relegate man to the position of a determinable unit in a mechanistic world. . . ."[23] Carlton Beck, who quotes Mathewson at length, rightly points out, however, that phenomenology is essentially a mechanistic psychological model. More recently still, naturalism has been reflected in the techniques advocated by such people as Wolpe, Krumboltz, and Michael and Meyerson. Thus, "observable behavior is the only variable of importance in the counseling and guidance process, and it is the only criterion

[19] Carlton E. Beck, *Philosophical Foundations of Guidance* (Englewood Cliffs, N.J.: Prentice-Hall, 1963), p. 96.
[20] C. Marshall Lowe, "Value Orientations: An Ethical Dilemma," in *Counseling: Readings in Theory and Practice*, ed. John McGowan and Lyle Schmidt (New York: Holt, Rinehart and Winston, 1962), pp. 119–127.

[21] H. J. Eysenck, "The Effect of Psychotherapy," in *Handbook of Abnormal Psychology*, ed. H. J. Eysenck (New York: Basic Books, 1961), pp. 697–725.
[22] Joseph Samler, "Changes in Values: A Goal in Counseling," *Journal of Counseling Psychology*, 7 (Spring 1960), 32–39.
[23] Robert Hendry Mathewson, *Guidance Policy and Practice*, 3rd ed. (New York: Harper & Row, 1962), p. 141.

against which the outcome of the process may be evaluated."[24]

Although the objectivity, replicability, and predictability of behavioristic techniques are a valuable contribution to research into counseling techniques, naturalism as a philosophy for counseling is viewed as too limiting by many counselors. Carl Rogers makes the particular point that scientism is unable to answer questions about the profound subjectivity of human experience. Objectivity in the physical sciences is necessary and sufficient for validation; in the field of human relationships it is insufficient. What point is there, for example, in showing parents that love is a necessary condition for the healthy nurture of children, unless the parents subjectively experience love in their own existences? Paul Halmos[25] believes that the behaviorists (referred to by Halmos picturesquely as "the mechano-therapists") fail to distinguish the operational and attitudinal aspects of love. Halmos points out that Lazarus conceptualizes *handling* as "overt love." It is a truism, however, that love cannot be successfully imitated by the unloving, even in response to the most precise operational description available from behavioristic psychology.

This single criticism seems to be sufficient to show that naturalism, as a philosophical orientation to humankind, fails to "grapple with ultimate questions," or to reach "the ground of our being" in the words of Paul Tillich. There is some implication of an acknowledgment of this in Wolpe's use of terms such as *sympathetic acceptance.* Such a term certainly rests on unverifiable underlying concepts such as *consciousness* and *person,* unless it is being used in a highly metaphorical sense. It is more likely, as Halmos says, that "mechanotherapeutic techniques" can only be applied against the secure background of person-to-person relationships, an element that is unacknowledged simply because it is unamenable to scientific dismemberment.

CULTURALISM *Culturalism* is also mentioned in Lowe's article. He quotes the American Psychological Association, whose ethical statements indicate that "the psychologist's ultimate allegiance is to society." It seems that Caiaphas

and the Athenian City Fathers might have enrolled the help of the APA against Jesus and Socrates. Lowe cites Adler, Sullivan, and Horney as leading theorists who have defined neurosis in terms of social isolation and cure in terms of adjustment to society. Culturalism as a philosophical orientation is therefore the pursuit of what most people want, normally.

Among counseling professionals E. G. Williamson[26] speaks for some form of culturalism. In his article "Value Orientation in Counseling" he argues that the counseling relationship is one between client and "mentor." For the mentor, certain "outer limits" of the counselor's freedom for influencing the client are defined which will allow the counselor to pursue on behalf of the client a variety of "loose fitting" values appropriate to a pluralistic and democratic society.

The logical fallacy in all of this is that of arguing from "what is" to "what ought to be." The possibility of "progress" is logically precluded in that "normality" is what is valued, and most people are "normal," by definition, already. Lowe rejects culturalism as a value orientation, quoting Lindner's observation that culturalism involves humans in the exchange of their freedom for the doped security of accepting things as they are, and adds his own caustic remark, "normality is nothing to brag about."

Normality is, in any event, a vague concept, and one of the reasons it is so vague is that the concept of society is itself a highly reducible one, logically. What is valued by society will depend on what is thought to be the origin and function of society. There is no unanimity on either of these points. In order to approach "the ground of our being" a question must be asked prior to "What is normal?" and that is "What principles of human behavior underlie social organization?" This is perhaps what C. G. Wrenn meant when he said that counselors can never be loyal to society until they are loyal to something more than society.

HUMANISM The third value orientation mentioned by Lowe is *humanism.* By this he means a basic commitment to the idea that humans are self-sufficient. He quotes Rogers and Fromm as proponents of the view.

[24] Jack Michael and Lee Meyerson, "A Behavioral Approach to Counseling and Guidance," *Harvard Educational Review,* 32 (Fall 1962), 395.

[25] Paul Halmos, *The Faith of the Counsellors* (New York: Schocken Books, 1966), pp. 67–74.

[26] E. G. Williamson, "Value Orientation in Counseling," *Personnel and Guidance Journal,* 36 (November 1957), 175–183.

Carl Rogers[27] argues that the direction of therapy is toward the discovery that the core of the personality is positive. He quotes Maslow in support of the point that destructive behavior arises from the frustration of constructive behavior. Later in his book Rogers specifically identifies Søren Kierkegaard's statement, "to be that self which one truly is," with the movement of the client in the therapeutic situation. This involves movement away from facades and subjection of the self to the group and movement toward self-direction and trust of self.

Such a philosophy chooses to disregard the basic propositions of St. Paul, the Reformation, and Freud, although this need not necessarily be thought of as a criticism. Lowe, however, does make two further criticisms. One is the general observation that the most dignified self is the self least concerned with one's own dignity. Certainly a re-emergent theme in philosophy is that of the ultimate futility of pursuing self-fulfillment for its own sake. "Happiness," Aristotle wrote, "is like the bloom on the cheek of an athlete." By this he may be taken to mean that happiness is achieved only by pursuing something more important than happiness, as such. Somewhat more recently, Bertrand Russell has condemned the "cosmic impiety" of the individualism of our romantic age. Jesus maintained that "whoever would lose his life for my sake, he will save it!" The pursuit of self-fulfillment does not appear to have been recommended very highly by several of the world's major minds.

A further criticism made by Lowe, and one that is more readily amenable to objective validation, is that Rogers' intense individualism is closely similar to, and may be a product of the pathology of American, middle-class, achievement-oriented society. Rogers himself says that the successful completion of therapy would mean "the establishment of an individualized value system having considerable identity with the value system of any equally well adjusted member of the human race." The question is: "Adjustment to what? To the values of American Suburbia and Mrs. Hillside?"

If counselors are to "grapple with ultimate questions" they must ask Rogers why he values independence and self-realization above other possible values. Naturalism and culturalism can attempt to provide some criteria for evaluating the ideals that they pursue. Rogers provides none of any substance beyond the correspondence theory of truth quoted above, which is a form of culturalism. He might be said to be concerned for a "being" for which he provides no "ground."

Rogers' identification of a philosophy for client-centered counseling with the thinking of Kierkegaard is not mentioned by Lowe, who omits any reference to existentialism from his article. The existentialist implications of his orientation are not pursued with much emphasis by Rogers himself, perhaps because Kierkegaard and his successors have been much less optimistic about mankind than Rogers The existentialist theme is pursued at length, however, by Carlton Beck.[28] He argues that guidance has outgrown formerly fashionable prescriptive and phenomenological models and that it now rests on a weak philosophical framework. He recommends that the movement in the United States should follow that in Europe toward *Daseinanalyse* or existentialist therapy. Existentialism in psychology, according to Beck, is an extension of phenomenology in the direction of attributing to man a mode of experience, termed *dasein,* which is beyond animal experience, and raises humans above the deterministic conceptions attributed to them by phenomenology. *Dasein* means "little aware of itself," which the existentialists regard as the basic existential concept of humankind, inexplicable in operational terms.

At the heart of existentialism is Sartre's affirmation that individuals are nothing but what they make themselves. One's acts define one's limits; one's existence defines one's essence. Concepts of *dasein* and freedom elaborate this basic affirmation. The writings of Buber, Maritain, and Jaspers further elaborate this theme. Jaspers in particular makes a characteristic distinction between the empirically known, predictable psychological and biological self that is the proper object of scientific study and the "authentic self" that contains the source and meaning of life. On such a distinction rests Buber's description of the "I-Thou" relationship. May's *Existence*[29] develops an appropriate theme for counseling, the thesis being that "the grasping of the being of another person occurs on a quite different level from our knowledge of specific things about him."

[27] Carl R. Rogers, *On Becoming a Person* (Boston: Houghton Mifflin Company, 1962), pp. 73–106.

[28] Beck, *Philosophical Foundations of Guidance.*
[29] Rollo May, *Existence* (New York: Basic Books, 1958), p. 38.

Like humanism, existentialism has a profound sense of the worth and dignity of humankind. "Man is free," says Carlton Beck. "This is at once a pleasant heady luxury and also the source of his discontent."[30] Certain philosophical absolutes are admitted, that is, the belief in the freedom and dignity of the "authentic" self because people are ends, not means. Certain mandatory goals are conceived, that is, empathy, sympathy, and genuine free action. The philosophical basis for all oughts, it is claimed, is not an a priori universal, but "to further the race of man and his existential amelioration."[31]

The Christian existentialist does, of course, accept certain a priori assumptions. Although the secularists strenuously deny that they make any such assumptions, a belief in the dignity of the authentic self is not supported by the existentialists any more than it is by Rogers. Just why the "existential amelioration of man" deserves to be considered the basis of all oughts they do not say; they provide the ground of our being.

THEISM   Lowe deals with theism as the fourth of his value orientations. He defines theism as a commitment to the view that life has objective meaning. He argues that religion should become part of psychotherapy because it is wholly based on love, which Allport says is "incomparably the greatest therapeutic agent."

Many counselors find theistic arguments inferential. Inferential they must be because by definition they place the locus for evaluation of the individual outside what can be fully comprehended by human experience. Though the theistic argument may be inferential it could be maintained that the inference of theism is a necessary one. Lowe maintains that the counselor is faced with a range of orientations each of which excludes the others. Here it is argued that the various kinds of orientations attach various kinds of significance to humans, that is, as the object of scientific study, as a member and product of society, as a creative individual, as a unique member of the creature kingdom, and that each of these evaluations has its validity, none necessarily excluding any others. Each of them may therefore be regarded in some degree as a necessary part of a total evaluation of human beings. What is probably more accurate

is that none of them, taken separately or together, is a sufficient evaluation because none of them reaches "the ground of our being." The further step that is necessary is a speculative extrapolation, an inference that cannot be entirely validated empirically. Such a step appears to be necessary if a complete, irreducible, and rounded attribution of the significance to humans is ever to be made.

That a religious orientation appears to rest at the heart of counseling is the argument of Paul Halmos.[32] He maintains that "counsellors" (a term he uses in a very broad sense) are committed to the "faith," a "tendermindedness" in which "spiritual solace, sanity, a state of grace, or merely adjustment" are sought for the client. He draws attention to what he calls the "ideological cramp" that has overtaken modern societies: a paralysis in the face of the seemingly insoluble complexities of modern problems. He regards scientific objectivism and individual personalism as escape routes from moral ideology. But he also regards professionalism as an escape route, or at least as a means whereby Christian *agape* can be conveniently camouflaged. Nowhere in his book does Halmos attempt a systematic philosophical analysis of what he regards as the "faith of the counsellors." However, to express this faith he frequently uses the Greek word *agape*, translated as "love" in modern versions of the New Testament.

Formulations equating God with any other kind of concept are rare in biblical tradition. Indeed, Hebrew-Christian thinking is notable for its unwillingness to conceptualize God in any but metaphorical terms. The statement "God is love" does appear, however, in the First Epistle of John, and it is to be understood as a realization that the experience of interpersonal brotherly love springs from the "ground of our being" and therefore deserves to be equated with the universalized, objectified concept of God. The first part of such a statement would receive a great deal of support from recent research into the effects of psychotherapy. The second part is an inference, but it is one that has the experiential completeness, the logical irreducibility, and the philosophical roundedness that have not been found in any of the orientations so far considered.

Lowe criticizes theistic orientations in terms of their blandness, superstition, unrealism, optimism, and prolongation of dependence. The shortcoming of this kind of criti-

---

[30] Beck, *Foundations*, p. 134.
[31] Ibid., p. 133.

[32] Halmos, *The Faith of the Counsellors.*

cism is that it fails to take account of the kind of distinction made above between institutionalized and existential awareness. Institutional religion is prone to all the static blandness of culturalism. Indeed, Paul Halmos appears in one place to suggest that the operation of *agape* grows in inverse proportion to the strength of the ecclesia. He points to a simultaneous increase in the number of people per clergy member and decrease in the number of people per member of the medical or paramedical professions. Such an argument is too facile, but many cannot accept that Lowe's charges may not be fairly leveled against the Jesus philosophy. For many, Jesus' teachings were not bland, unrealistic, or prolonging of dependence. They were not dependent either on whatever superstitious thought-forms were employed to express them in the first century A.D., although the process of demythologization is not yet complete. Certainly in the mind of Tillich, the encounter with the "ground of our being" was no bland, unrealistic, or dependent experience. Indeed, "the pain of looking into one's own depth is too intense for most people."

It is sometimes argued that religious counseling ought to be separately retained. This is the sense of an article by William C. Bier.[33] He maintains that "spiritual ends" require "spiritual means," and that the religious counselor ought to be retained in order to help the client to be right in the life to come. Paul Tillich makes a similar kind of distinction in saying that existential anxiety grows out of the threefold threat of death, meaninglessness, and guilt and is properly a priestly concern. Pathological anxiety he concedes as the province of the psychotherapists. In his way, Carlton Beck also argues for the separation of religious and secular counseling. "By what criterion," he asks, "could it be said that a priest or a minister is closest to such problems as the question of vocational choice in a complex industrial society?"[34]

It is a false reading of life itself to imagine that experiences can be divided between two self-contained categories. Any problem can be viewed from a number of different points of view and probed to a number of significances. "Why do I choose this profession?" may be honestly answered in a number of different ways. As Paul Tillich has it,

"Look at an uneducated worker who performs a mechanical task day by day, but who suddenly asks himself, 'What does it mean for my life?' 'What is the meaning of life?' Because he asks these questions, that man is on the way into depth." At any moment in an interview, counselors may find themselves in the presence of a client making profound self-observations. It is the poorly equipped counselor who is unprepared to appreciate their significance and to respond to them at the level of being from which they emerge.

The comments here attempt to demonstrate that philosophic orientations to counseling are often shortsighted. Each of them eventually reaches an impasse, a point beyond which it cannot progress without, in some way, stepping outside the limits it has defined for itself. As Halmos more colorfully puts it, "When counsellors don the garb of the sceptic their moral underwear shows."[35] Where that impasse is met and ignored the orientation either fails to meet the full range of human experience (as does naturalism); or defines itself as reducible and therefore at ambiguous levels (as does culturalism); or simply omits any philosophical framework at all (as does Rogers); or provides a philosophical basis that is inadequate because it leaves certain basic questions unanswered (as do existentialism and theism). Other criticisms might have been made, but the purpose here has been to point out current failures to "grapple with ultimate issues."

The process of building a counseling philosophy

Counselors in training are frequently urged to develop a personalized view of themselves as counselors. In some respects this amounts basically to achieving a fairly thorough self-understanding. It is a person's own experience, personality, and view of the nature of humankind that influence the very choice of the theory he or she will operate under. One cannot accept and internalize what is foreign and repulsive to one's personal makeup. One cannot operate maturely and professionally in borrowed clothes. Preferably one's suit is tailor-made with the cloth and style selected on the basis of individualistic taste.

It is unlikely that counselors will accept all aspects of any one theory; it is essential, however, that they be able to

[33] William C. Bier, "Religious Counseling: The Roman Catholic Church," in *The Yearbook of Education*, 1955, ed. R. K. Hall and J. A. Lauwerys (Yonkers: World Book), pp. 354–362.
[34] Beck, *Foundations*, p. 56.
[35] Halmos, *The Faith of the Counsellors*.

commit themselves to its fundamental tenets even though disagreeing with some of its specifics. Presumably the choice of a theory or a way of operating as a counselor begins with and is strongly influenced by one's training, experience, and of course one's own traits influence the impact of training. Early commitment to a counseling approach, moreover, is frequently highly tentative and subject to considerable modification as the individual moves through the common sequence of didactic course work, supervised counseling experience and actual practice. It is a fact of life that the true fit of a theory to individual counselors cannot be determined until they attempt to practice what they claim to believe. Actual practice is what exposes discrepancies between the theory chosen and the practitioner's personality and philosophy of life.

It would be naive to assume that any theoretical approach, like any ready-made suit of clothing, could fit an individual without some minor alterations. Perhaps it would be even more naive to assume that a suit once fitted, even if it never wore out, would conform to the changing characteristics of a counselor over time. The length might, but the girth and other parts would surely begin to bind and probably appear out of date and ludicrous. What is needed is constant refitting of the suit (theory). No argument is made for totally discarding it, although this sometimes may be necessary.

Many counselor educators would argue that a counselor's attempts to choose bits and pieces from diverse theories lead only to a hodgepodge of contradictory assumptions and incompatible techniques. On the other hand, others would just as strongly assert that adoption of a single counseling viewpoint is parochial, because the theorist was bound by a time frame, clientele, personality, and society. Little doubt exists that most counselors adopt portions of various viewpoints in developing and articulating what are called counseling behaviors. The important element is that counselors, by continuously struggling to formulate their comprehensive point of view, give meaning to their counseling experience and slowly evolve a counseling style that fits them.

Finally, counselors in preparation should not make the error of thinking that they can operate atheoretically. Any counselor's activities must be based on some set of assumptions, some set of organizing principles, some core of beliefs. These could well be labeled *theories,* and the issue would be whether they are openly and explicitly recognized as such or whether counselors choose to deny their existence while deluding themselves that theory has no place in their world.

Issues

Issue 1 It is logical and sound, both educationally and psychologically, to expect counseling students to study in depth and exhibit a comprehensive grasp of one counseling theory rather than a variety of counseling approaches.

True, because
1. It is too much to expect a person to learn several counseling theories; concentration on one during the preparation period leads to better mastery of the theory. By doing so, one would gain an understanding of how and why one agrees or departs from its explanations.
2. An instructor cannot teach or present all theories comprehensively, impartially or objectively; therefore, the theory taught and learned should be confined to one that is espoused by the instructor.
3. Concentration on one theory permits students to acquire knowledge of a depth and breadth sufficient to start client contacts.

False, because
1. The research evidence about outcomes produced by practitioners of different theories does not make possible selection of one theory over another.
2. Students should explore and learn a variety of counseling approaches because that knowledge coupled with their philosophical beliefs provides the base for them to decide what fits them and/or to construct their own personal approaches.

Discussion Each side of this issue has strong arguments including some not cited above. Moreover, the issue and the pros and cons parallel, at least to some degree, the issues presented at the end of Chapter 8. We believe that students should be taught and learn a variety of counseling theories for the reasons stated above plus some other very practical considerations to be noted here. Most students who apply to and are admitted by a graduate counselor-education institution do not possess sufficient prior knowledge of counseling theory to make an informed choice of an institution that confines its teaching and practice to but one counseling theory. If the counseling theory presented and implemented in the program did not fit students, the graduate education experience for them would be unhappy to say the least.

Another reason for believing that individuals who are preparing to be counseling professionals should be formally presented and expected to learn a variety of counseling theories lies in the principle that educational efforts should start where learners are, not from the point of development at which the institution would like to find the hypothetical average student. Most students who begin graduate study in counselor education have made a commitment to entering a helping profession. They expect, in the time they are at the institution, to master the competencies and the body of knowledge that will enable them to occupy an entry level position. Many have an idea that a particular setting fits them because of their experience, background, aspirations, and so on, but expect to test out that idea during practice. However, a few current students are at that point of development where they could say that it is best for them to concentrate on behavioral counseling theory or client-centered counseling theory. Courses designed to survey counseling theories are necessary to take students to that point of making informed decisions about their implementation of a theory or the usefulness of a counselor theory. Beyond that point lies the concentration on a particular theory.

Issue 2 Students in counselor education spend too much time and effort studying counseling theories.

True, because
1. Effective counselor behaviors are based on or evoked from individual client behaviors, not some hypothetical individual.
2. Counseling practitioners are but technicians who tinker with but merely make but small adjustments in complicated equipment (clients).
3. Actual counseling practice is atheoretical.
4. Students need only to be taught counseling methods demonstrated to be efficient.

False, because
1. Theory informs practice and serves as a model for counselor behaviors.

2. Methods could not be selected and applied without ordering and understanding client behaviors made comprehensible by theory.
3. Learning the formal counseling theories stimulates counselors to inquire, seek additional information, and to perfect their knowledge and competencies.

Discussion Many students in counselor education complain that their preparation is long on theory and short on practice. Others criticize the education of counselors for being overly concerned about how-to techniques while shortchanging students on the "why" of what they do. These contradictory views represent a paradoxical situation that is difficult to resolve satisfactorily.

Our observation is that more, not less, time ought to be given in preparation programs to mastering counseling theories and to theory building by the student. Most institutions in a year-long preparation program offer but one course in counseling theory. That represents but one tenth or less of the course work taken by most masters degree students. And even that course is often a mixture of theory and techniques. Although it is believed here that studying theory and techniques together is logical, more time is needed by students to explore, assimilate, and implement a theory.

Annotated references

Ford, Donald H., and Hugh B. Urban. *Systems of Psychotherapy.* New York: John Wiley & Sons, 1963. 712 pp.

Section III (pp. 593–690) presents a comparative analysis of ten systems of psychotherapy—how they view the development of normal behavior and the development of disordered behavior, the goals of therapy, conditions for producing behavioral change, and evaluation of behavior change in therapy.

Lowe, C. Marshall. *Value Orientations in Counseling and Psychotherapy.* San Francisco: Chandler Publishing Company, 1969. 305 pp.

The purpose of the book, according to Lowe, is to relate the theory and practice of counseling to the broad social, philosophical, and historical issues. Particularly useful to students is his discussion of the moral overtones in counseling and psychotherapy (Chapter 2, pp. 35–51).

Patterson, C. H. *Theories of Counseling and Psychotherapy.* 2nd ed. New York: Harper & Row, 1973. 554 pp.

The divergences and convergences among several counseling approaches are discussed in Chapter 21 (pp. 521–542). Treatment is centered on philosophy and concepts, counseling process, and goals and objectives. Patterson also has a brief but sophisticated presentation on integration of theories.

Burks, Herbert M., and Stefflre, Buford, eds. *Theories of Counseling.* 3rd ed. New York: McGraw-Hill Book Co., 1979. 352 pp.

Eight counseling theories are presented, each written by a different author. In Chapter 8 Stefflre sums up the eight approaches. The nature of humankind, behavioral change, counseling goals, counselor role, crucial determinants of an approach, and common elements are analyzed.

Further references

Herrnstein, R. J. "The Evolution of Behaviorism." *American Psychologist,* 32 (August 1977), 593–603.

Highlen, Pamela S., and Grady K. Baccus. "Effect of Reflection of Feeling and Probe on Client Self-Referenced Affect." *Journal of Counseling Psychology,* 24 (September 1977), 440–443.

Kelly, F. Donald, and Thomas P. Byrne. "The Evaluation of Filmed Excerpts of Rogers, Perls and Ellis by Beginning Counselor Trainees." *Counselor Education and Supervision,* 16 (March 1977), 166–171.

Kirkpatrick, J. Stephen. "A Maslovian Counseling Model." *Personnel and Guidance Journal,* 57 (April 1979), 386–391.

Moreland, John R. "Some Implications of Life-Span Development for Counseling Psychology." *Personnel and Guidance Journal,* 57 (February 1979), 299–303.

Oblas, Arthur S. "Rampant Passivity." *Personnel and Guidance Journal,* 56 (May 1978), 550–553.

Ponzo, Zander. "Integrating Techniques from Five Counseling Theories." *Personnel and Guidance Journal,* 54 (April 1976), 414–419.

Randolph, Daniel Lee, Everett E. Caston, and Jarvis Wright. "Personality Needs as Predictors of Functional Specialty of Counseling Psychologists." *Journal of Counseling Psychology,* 24 (November 1977), 531–533.

Smith, Darrell, and James Peterson. "Values: A Challenge to the Profession." *Personnel and Guidance Journal,* 55 (January 1977), 227–231.

Sue, Derald Wing. "Counseling the Culturally Different: A Conceptual Analysis." *Personnel and Guidance Journal,* 55 (March 1977), 422–425.

Turoc, Art. "Effective Challenging Through Additive Empathy." *Personnel and Guidance Journal,* 57 (November 1978), 144–148.

Warnath, Charles F. "Relationship and Growth Theories and Agency Counseling." *Counselor Education and Supervision,* 17 (December 1977), 84–91.

Part three
Counseling: content, process, and practice

MARRIAGE COUNSELING

CHILD ABUSE THERAPY

SEX COUNSELING

DRUG & ALCOHOL REHABILITATION

YOUTH COUNSELING

CAREERS

SENIORS GROUP SESSION

Part Three explains the major content of and practices utilized in the counseling process. Practices evolve from experience and represent certain ways of behaving in particular situations that have stood the test of time.

Chapter 11 describes the core elements—empathy, rapport, understanding, acceptance, and the like—that affect counseling. Chapter 12 presents the basic techniques employed in the counseling relationship. Chapter 13 discusses diagnosis, test interpretation, referral practices, and other counseling practices. And Chapter 14 discusses counseling practices with some special focus and populations. Chapter 15 deals with counseling in groups.

The acquisition of counseling skills and techniques can be accomplished only partially through didactic examination. Basically, they develop into personal work skills through counseling experience and eventually blend to create a personal counseling style.

11　Core elements that facilitate counseling

Chapter 10 indicated that establishment of a satisfactory relationship between counselor and counselee(s) was one element common to virtually all theories. The counseling relationship is a blend, a complex, and derives its distinctiveness from many factors of varying intensity. A symposium of counselors organized to draw out its essence would discern numerous different ideas, meanings, generalizations, rhythms, and patterns.

This chapter will take up first the significance of privacy, confidentiality, and setting to the counseling relationship. Second, the part played by counselor attitudes in facilitating the relationship will be considered, including how values, understanding, and acceptance influence it. Finally, the additional factors of empathy, rapport, genuineness, attentiveness, and their effect on the relationship will be examined.

The topics discussed in this chapter are pertinent not just to the initial counseling contact but to the whole process. In many instances the initial counseling session will be the final one if these factors are not continuously present.

External conditions influencing counseling

The setting in which counseling is conducted undoubtedly has some bearing on whether the relationship will be facilitated or thwarted.

Physical setting

The room should be comfortable and attractive. Although counseling offices may be impressive and beautiful, neither monumental character nor artistic expression is mandatory. Counseling facilities should be designed for comfort and relaxation. Pictures, draperies, carpet, plants, and the like are usually viewed as conducive to creating an unhurried climate in which clients may express themselves. Little corroborating data exist for any assertion that a sterile physical atmosphere reduces a counselee's willingness to talk, but it is axiomatic that people tend to derive a sense of well-being from a pleasant environment.

The general appearance of a counseling facility depends on color, decor, lighting, arrangement of equipment and furnishings, and noise control. Furnishings should be harmonious and comfortable, and the decor is usually subdued but not depressing. Light, quiet colors are often used to give a feeling of friendliness. By attention to features such as these tensions are eased, feelings of warmth and comfort are engendered, and rapport and contact are encouraged. Needless to say, the same features that lead to an aesthetically pleasing environment for the counselee enable the counselor to function better.

Proxemics

Recently, a rash of investigations has explored the effects of physical distance between counselor and client, seating arrangements, furniture, and so on, within the counseling office. "The manner in which man regulates the spatial features of his environment and conversely the impact of that environment on his subsequent behavior" is defined as *proxemics* by Haase and DiMattia.[1] They investigated the seating arrangement preferred by ten counselors, ten administrators, and ten clients. These subjects used the *Semantic Differential Scale* to respond to photographs that depicted four proxemic seating arrangements common to counseling. Their findings confirmed conventional wisdom: the seating position preferred by all three subject groups was across the corner of the desk.

Widgery and Stackpole sought to determine whether desk position influenced the interviewer's "perceived credibility" among high- and low-anxiety subjects. Forty-four subjects

---

[1] Richard F. Haase and Dominic J. DiMattia, "Proxemic Behavior: Counselor, Administrator and Client Preference for Seating Arrangements in Dyadic Interaction," *Journal of Counseling Psychology*, 17 (July 1970), 319–325.

were interviewed separately for four minutes by a professor of communication. The interviewer sat behind the desk during interviews with half the subjects; with the other twenty-two he sat facing each with no desk between. Highly anxious subjects recorded the interviewer's credibility as higher with no desk between whereas low-anxiety subjects responded inversely.[2]

That people have a personal space within which they are comfortable in their interactions with another person is not only well known, but has been documented by considerable research. The comfortable space or distance between two persons has been ascribed to cultural background, the relationship between the two parties, the sex of the participants, the topic of their conversation, and their relative status. Haase investigated the relationship of sex and specific instructional set (academic advising or personal counseling) of counseling to students' reactions to five interpersonal interaction distances. His findings revealed that males did not differ from females in preferred distance nor did it matter whether the session was for academic advising or personal counseling. Subjects believed that distances of 30 and 39 inches represented the close and far phases of the space between counselor and client. Haase notes that this range of distance is usually reserved for interaction between closely related people (husband-wife, intimate friends).[3] More recently, Haase and DiMattia manipulated such factors as room size, distance, and furniture arrangements to determine their effects on interviews conducted according to a standard, verbal operant-conditioning paradigm. Room size was reported as the most significant variable; smaller rooms (7.67m²) tended to inhibit the duration and length of self-reference statements.[4] Because most proxemic research has been conducted in simulated settings, the full impact of seating arrangements, physical distance between participants, and other physical features on the counseling relationship and, even more important, its outcomes are still unknown.

Privacy

A most important perquisite of the physical setting is privacy. If the confidence of the counselee is to be secured, the feeling of security engendered by privacy cannot be overemphasized. Individuals desire and have a right to both *auditory* and *visual* privacy from peers, teachers, and others when they enter into a counseling relationship. Nothing can limit the relationship more quickly than knowing that others are able to hear what is being said or watch what is taking place. The experienced counselor knows how hard it is for a counselee to state why counseling was sought if privacy is not assured. Holahan and Slaikeu[5] investigated the effects of reduced privacy in a counseling setting on client self-disclosure. Some seventy-four subjects were assigned randomly to three experimental conditions characterized by varying degrees of privacy. The investigators reported that reduced privacy decreased client self-disclosure and that although spatial dividers improved clients' perceptions of privacy, self-disclosure failed to increase.

The provision of auditory and visual privacy is basic to the ethical standard that counselors will safeguard the confidentiality of the relationship. The communication between counselor and client is privileged in that the confidence in which it is given will not be violated. According to the APGA Code of Ethics, "The counseling relationship and information resulting therefrom must be kept confidential consistent with the obligations of the member as a professional person."[6] Since more extensive discussion of the matter of confidentiality will be found in Chapter 16, it is sufficient to state here that confidentiality is an essential condition for counseling and that physical facilities that safeguard it also encourage the development of the counseling relationship.

[2] Robin Widgery and Cecil Stackpole, "Desk Position, Interviewee Anxiety and Interviewer Credibility: An Example of Cognitive Balance in a Dyad," *Journal of Counseling Psychology*, 19 (May 1972), 173–177.
[3] Richard F. Haase, "The Relationship of Sex and Instructional Set to the Regulation of Interpersonal Interaction Distance in a Counseling Analogue," *Journal of Counseling Psychology*, 17 (May 1970), 233–236.
[4] Richard F. Haase and Dominic J. DiMattia, "Spatial Environments and Verbal Conditioning in a Quasi-Counseling Interview," *Journal of Counseling Psychology*, 23 (September 1976), 414–421.

[5] Charles J. Holahan and Karl A. Slaikeu, "Effects of Contrasting Degrees of Privacy on Client Self-Disclosure in a Counseling Setting," *Journal of Counseling Psychology*, 24 (January 1977), 55–59.
[6] American Personnel and Guidance Assocation, *Ethical Standards* (Washington, D.C.: The Association, 1974), p. 3.

Tape-recording

For the past thirty years the mechanical recording of counseling interviews has been common practice. Particularly since the 1950s it has been widely used in counselor preparation because of its training value. Counselors prepared in such programs often continue to record some of their counseling sessions in order to evaluate their own work. Questions continue to be raised, however, regarding the desirability of sound-recording procedures.

In recent years video taping has been used with increasing frequency. The same basic issues are involved. Originally much clamor centered around the ethics of mechanically reproducing the contents of counseling sessions, apparently quelled by the assurance that such material receives the same safeguards as any information acquired in the counseling setting. One proviso attached to the question of ethics is that all recordings are made with the counselee's permission and that subsequent use of recordings is made only with the counselee's written consent.

A continuing controversy is whether recording interferes with or negatively affects the counseling process. This issue is commonly raised among students in training. While the question is legitimate, raising the issue frequently is tinged with insecurity and embarrassment experienced by fledgling counselors who are forced to defend their words and deeds. In a very real sense, they often feel they must present evidence that may prove them guilty and lead to their own condemnation.

Whatever the effects of recording on the counselor, determining its impact on the counseling process remains difficult. The fact that relatively little research has been done in this area may in itself indicate that these procedures are generally accepted. Research by Roberts and Renzaglia clearly supports the contention that sound recording does influence certain counseling interaction variables.[7] In an experiment in which recordings were made sometimes by machines in the counseling room and at other times by hidden equipment without counselor or client knowledge, clients produced more favorable self-references when they knew they were being recorded and more unfavorable self-

references when secret recordings were made. The counselors, despite exposure to what the authors describe as client-centered counseling style, tended to be less client centered when recording was open. Implementation of client-centered counseling seemed to take place when secret recording was used. The investigators suggest that this rather unusual finding may have occurred because the student counselors used in the study felt freer to use the client-centered style in sessions they believed were not being recorded.

Two serious questions may be raised about this particular study. (1) Despite the care taken by the investigators to conduct their research in a highly ethical manner, the procedures they employed were criticized on ethical grounds by Leona Tyler in a comment immediately following their article. Tyler freely admits that her objection may stem from a narrower view of the ethical practices involved. (2) The experience level of the counselor sample may have influenced the results. There would appear to be little question that the greater the experience and security of counselors, the greater the likelihood that they will behave consistently whether recorded or not.

Our experience indicates that the reaction of counselees to recordings tends to be highly individual. The vast majority raise no objection to recording when given the opportunity to (1) not have the session recorded and (2) discontinue the recording at any point in the session. On the other hand, a few counselees do object, either at the outset or when they approach highly sensitive material. Because their wishes are respected, there is no chance to determine whether refusal to stop the recording would influence the outcome.

In the authors' experience, the sigh of relief when the recorder is stopped generally comes from the counselor in training rather than from the counselee. Probably all counselor educators are accustomed to a disproportionate number of malfunctioning machines reported by a small number of highly threatened trainees. Although this situation is sometimes treated jokingly with specific individuals, it can become a serious problem that must be actively coped with in supervision of the trainee.

Yenawine and Arbuckle compared and contrasted the effects of audio-tape and video-tape recordings on counselor trainees' practicum experiences. The fourteen student subjects kept a log of their counseling and supervisory experiences from which data were abstracted. Their findings sug-

[7] Ralph R. Roberts, Jr., and Guy A. Renzaglia, "The Influence of Tape Recording on Counseling," *Journal of Counseling Psychology*, 12 (Spring 1965), 10–16.

gested that, of the two media, the video tape was superior for (1) it produced more complete, relevant material for review, (2) it increased the likelihood that a counselor-centered focus as opposed to a client-centered focus would be maintained in supervisory sessions, and (3) it provided a more objective basis for evaluating interviews. These investigators reported that initial anxiety and resistance were higher among those who video-taped than those who audio-taped. However, initial anxiety soon yielded to enthusiastic acceptance. Yenawine and Arbuckle state that the vividness and completeness of video-tape recordings tend to make it difficult for students to become emotionally involved in the critique of a fellow counselor's work. Presumably, the completeness of the video tape may foster a situation with which peers are unable to cope fully. Therefore, they concluded that student counselors identify more easily and completely with counselor performances recorded on audio tape than video tape.[8] Feedback from either or both is not only desirable but highly necessary for developing and improving counselor skills and attitudes.

After reviewing the few available research reports about recording effects on counseling, Gelso concluded, among other things, that (1) consent by clients to be recorded does not reveal whether they will be affected by the procedure; (2) recording (especially video) appears to inhibit client self-expression and to increase defensiveness; (3) recording effects persist across sessions; (4) clients expect recording to be much more inhibiting than it actually is; (5) both video and audio recordings inhibit self-exploration in educational-vocational clients, although only video recording inhibits personal-adjustment clients; and (6) counselors, too, are affected by recordings, but are insensitive to recording effects on their clients.[9]

Client characteristics influencing counseling

There is no doubt that many additional factors, external to the process itself, influence counseling. Prominent among these are the characteristics of the client. The experiences, cultural background, and expectations for counseling held by clients are clearly brought with them and influence the process. Additionally, economic conditions, the environment of the community, and characteristics of the institution in which counseling takes place—all have an impact on the client and therefore on the process. Detailed treatment of these conditions may be found in Chapters 3, 4, 5, and 14.

Counselor attitudes that influence counseling

The attitudes of counselors, their approaches to the individual, and what they do all influence the counseling relationship to a marked degree. The counselor is the key to the initiation and development of the relationship.

Some key concepts

This section briefly treats two components of the philosophical orientation of the counselor: beliefs and values. Distinctions between these two terms are not easily made. Beliefs generally are seen as emotionally accepted doctrines based on unexamined, implicit grounds. Values, although closely related to beliefs, usually represent what some social scientists call "oughtnesses" or "conceptions of the desirable" that influence behavior.

BELIEFS Many of the beliefs that people hold most dear may be called myths. "Every society is held together by a myth-system, a complex of dominating thought-forms that determines and sustains all its activities," says MacIver. "All social relations, the very texture of human society, are myth-born and myth-sustained. . . . Wherever he goes, whatever he encounters, man spins about him his web of myth, as the caterpillar spins his cocoon."[10] Myths can be very powerful. People, it is said, possess thoughts, but myths possess people.

Myths vary from culture to culture and from age to age. The myths of modern men and women in today's "civilized" societies are perhaps more sophisticated than those of an-

[8] Gardner Yenawine and Dugald S. Arbuckle, "Study of the Use of Videotape and Audiotape as Techniques in Counselor Education," *Journal of Counseling Psychology*, 18 (January 1971), 1–6.
[9] Charles J. Gelso, "Effects of Recording on Counselors and Clients," *Counselor Education and Supervision*, 14 (September 1974), 5–12.

[10] R. M. MacIver, *The Web of Government* (New York: Macmillan, 1947), pp. 4–5.

cient Greece, but they are still myths. Myths are neither necessarily false nor evil. The word is neutral. "We include equally under the term 'myth' the most penetrating philosophies of life, the most profound intimations of religion, the most subtle renditions of experience, along with the most grotesque imaginations of the most benighted savage."[11] The great religious and political beliefs of the Western world make up a large part of our own myth system. We think our religious faiths and our democratic ideals are true. We know they are noble. Nevertheless they remain myths.

Myths are even more powerful than logic because they usually cannot be refuted. They must be taken on faith. They come in all shapes and sizes. Some are central to our whole system of beliefs; others are of lesser importance. Most basic to or central in the mythology of counselors is their belief that the counselee must be accorded dignity, equality, and individuality. The emphasis on the supreme worth of the individual has been an unbroken thread in democratic thought. It can be found in the writings of Thomas Jefferson, especially in the Declaration of Independence, where he eloquently proclaimed that all people have been endowed by their Creator with certain unalienable rights and that governments are created to secure these rights. This doctrine of individualism (not to be confused with the doctrine of laissez-faire) is the belief that there is something of supreme value in every human being.

The "rights of individuals" are coming increasingly under examination. *Rights* imply laws or a *law giver* to confer them, and rights that purport to transcend positive law imply the existence of a transcendent system of law. To the authors of the American Declaration of Independence this presented no difficulty: "We hold these truths to be self-evident, that all men . . . are endowed by their Creator with certain unalienable Rights, that among these are Life, Liberty and the pursuit of Happiness." A few years later the preamble to the French constitution of 1791 omitted reference to the Creator but could assume the self-evidence of natural law in which were grounded the "rights of man." Those who framed the United Nations declaration in 1948, "The Universal Declaration of Human Rights," however, could invoke a common assumption neither about a Creator nor about the reality of natural law. The status of the rights they enumerated is accordingly nebulous.

[11] Ibid., p. 5.

It is possible, of course, to regard all these declarations simply as specifying aspirations. In that case, their force depends on their ability to kindle the imaginations and direct the purposes of the people of their times. If that is so, it must be confessed that the ringing brevity of the eighteenth-century documents (three rights were enough for America, four for France) is superior to the prolixity of the United Nations—thirty articles of two or three items each, descending to such banalities as "everyone has the right to participate in the cultural life of the community." And the impact is not sharpened by the proliferation of subsidiary declarations, conventions, and covenants, elaborating or refining the original.

But the United Nations is not content to regard its work as a summary of aspirations. One purpose of these subsidiary instruments is to bind national governments to make their laws conform to "universal" principles formulated by the United Nations and its agencies. They also contain another development, which is perhaps more interesting. Rights depend on laws for their recognition, but on tribunals for their enforcement. And there has been some progress toward the establishment of international tribunals to vindicate rights that are internationally declared. The European Court of Human Rights furnishes one example. Another, more tentative, is found in the Convention on the Elimination of All Forms of Racial Discrimination, which has not yet come into force. In certain circumstances complainants who do not get satisfaction from a domestic tribunal may be heard by an international tribunal established for that purpose under the convention.

Perhaps the above statement that "rights imply laws . . . ," though meant to be unexceptional, is not really so. Rights (in the sense of the word used in the various declarations) imply that others have duties to those who are said to have rights. Some duties are legal, others moral, and it is reasonable enough to distinguish similarly between legal and moral rights. Although one kind of ethical theory describes morality as "the moral law," there is no necessity to think that moral duties or moral rights "depend on laws for their existence." Discussion of moral rights often implies that they are not but ought to be a subject of law. That certain moral rights ought to be turned into legal rights is the main point of declarations of human rights.

Fundamental among the counselor's philosophical attitudes is a belief in the worth and value of each counselee.

People everywhere, of almost all faiths, proclaim a generalized acceptance of brotherhood. Almost all people preach liberty, equality, fraternity, personal dignity, and social justice. But many of these same people are so entangled in the loves and hates stemming from particular myths, ideologies, and their own self-interest that they seem quite unable to practice what they expound on an individual-to-individual basis. Recurrent experiences of frustration, fear, and misery so shape motives that many people attempt to serve the interests of all by directing their worry and rage against those they see as odious because their ways are different, disturbing, or heretical.

Another important part of the counselor's philosophic orientation is the belief in the need for freedom. Erich Fromm says that people have freed themselves from the old bonds of slavery and feudalism and become individuals, enjoying certain rights and liberties, but have not gained freedom in the positive sense of realizing their intellectual and artistic possibilities.[12] The individual has gained too much freedom *from* traditional controls, too little freedom to live actively and spontaneously. Fromm sees the root of this problem in the nature of modern industrial civilization—in its large-scale organization, its mobility and competitiveness, its impersonality, its sheer bigness. Gone is the old framework of custom and authority, of life in small groups and stable communities. The machine age has made people rich in material things, but in the face of today's vast problems and responsibilities they feel insecure, helpless, isolated, powerless, and lost. Individuality is an illusion.

Value conflicts exist in today's society. As cited in Chapter 7, religion teaches us to love each other whereas economic philosophy teaches rivalry. Modern Western culture, with its stress on individual liberties and its comparative lack of religious faith, leaves people insecure, confused, and lacking in purpose. Under such conditions people seek succor from someone who can help them establish control over their environment and permit them to believe in something or somebody.

A third cardinal principle of the counselor is the belief in the desirability of liberty, the conviction that freedom is good. *Liberty* and *freedom* are slippery abstractions, and the words are used here interchangeably to mean maximum opportunity to select one's own purposes in life and the means to accomplish them. The core of liberty is self-determination. Liberty means more than the absence of external restraint. It includes the power to act positively to achieve one's chosen goals. To the counselor, the freedom to make choices and to act on them is essential to developing those characteristics that make one a human being. Denied this freedom, the individual becomes something less than human. Perhaps it is the ability to make rational choices, to distinguish the good from the bad, to decide whether to seek the good, that separates humans from the other animals. In exercising their freedom they develop responsibility and self-restraint and can exploit their full capacity for growth.

Finally, most counselors are committed to the belief that counselees possess the ability to deal constructively with their problems. They believe that humans make their world and are capable to changing it, that their problems are soluble.

Arbuckle presented five philosophical issues in counseling.[13] The first deals with the relationship between the counselor's self-concept, objectives, and methods. The self-concept and attitudes of counselors toward the client are reflected in what they do in the counseling session. If they believe that the client must be directed because the client lacks the capacity for growth, or conversely if they believe that the client can be trusted to take action or to move in directions that are socially acceptable, this belief will be transmitted in their techniques and in turn be present in their own self-concept.

Arbuckle's second issue considers whether a religious orientation of counselors acts as a controlling agent in their relationship with the counselee. There might be, he thought, differences in attitudes but not in actions toward counselees. It was hoped that there would not be differences in attitudes because counseling goals should not be affected by religious orientation.

Arbuckle's third issue involves the counselor's concept of human nature. The person who is optimistic about human beings and their possibilities transmits these beliefs in contacts with counselees, just as the one who regards human nature as hostile and carnal reflects that view in contacts with others.

[12] Erich Fromm, *Escape from Freedom* (New York: Rinehart and Company, 1941).

[13] Dugald S. Arbuckle, "Five Philosophical Issues in Counseling," *Journal of Counseling Psychology*, 5 (Fall 1958), 211–215.

Arbuckle's fourth issue deals with confidentiality. The counselor has to decide when silence about confidential information is too great a price for society to pay. Arbuckle noted that few school counselors erred on the side of maintaining too much confidence.

The final issue discussed by Arbuckle is whether counselor education could in fact prepare a counselor to use certain techniques and methods. Essentially the issue is what kind of experience is needed in counselor education for the individual to become accepting of deviant behavior, sensitive to attitudes and procedures, aware of self and what one is attempting as a person and counselor.

Arbuckle's 1975 volume presents the systems of several counselors and psychotherapists and strongly stresses the philosophic orientation of each contributor.[14] The initial chapter in this valuable work sketches Arbuckle's own analysis of the philosophical bases of counseling, and his final chapter gives an overview of the fundamental philosophical issues presented by the other contributors.

VALUES Should counselors convey their values to a counselee? For many years, client-centered counselors held the opinion that they should have no value orientation and maintain a neutral role while counseling. They sought to appear nonmoralizing and ethically neutral in counseling. For them it was the client's values that determine counseling's direction, focus, and purposes.

Williamson has called repeatedly for abandonment of this position in favor of an open and explicit value orientation in counseling.[15] He said that to try to be neutral in regard to social standards leads to the danger of appearing to accept the client's unethical behavior and actually condoning if not approving it. Counselors cannot be indifferent to social and moral standards, he feels, and should not attempt to be so.

It was Samler's opinion that change in values constituted a counseling goal and that the counselor's values must be held in awareness. He proposed that counselor intervention in the client's values was an actuality to be accepted as a necessary part of the process and urged counselors to de-

velop testable hypotheses relative to the values to be supported in counselor-client interactions.[16]

Patterson points out that the counselor's values influence the ethics of the counseling relationship, the goals of counseling, and the methods employed in counseling. Noting the growing opinion that it is impossible for the counselor to avoid influencing the client, Patterson cited evidence for the assertion that, no matter how passive and valueless the counselor appears, the counselee's value orientation is unconsciously influenced and comes to approach the counselor's. However, counselors are not justified, Patterson believes, in consciously and directly manipulating or influencing clients because (1) each individual's philosophy of life is different, unique, and unsuited to adoption by another; (2) all counselors cannot be expected to have a fully developed, adequate philosophy of life; (3) the appropriate places for instruction in values are the home, school, and church; (4) an individual develops a code of ethics, not from a single source or in a short period of time, but over a long time and from many influences; (5) one ought not to be prevented from developing one's own unique philosophy because it will be more personally meaningful; and (6) the client must have the right to refuse to accept any ethic or philosophy of life.[17]

Dreyfus asks a penetrating question: "Does it really matter what the therapist *does* so long as he establishes a relationship with his patient?"[18] He points out that if in the therapy hour the patient learns to incorporate certain aspects of the therapist's intact ego, the patient becomes like the therapist with regard to values, mannerisms, and behavior. Counselors cannot play-act the way they feel.

Play-acting, then, gives the patient but a facade to emulate and serves to reinforce the inauthentic behavior of the patient, supplanting the patient's playing-acting-in-the-world with the therapist's. That is, the patient learns to become inauthentic . . . through the therapist who is being inauthentic. If the therapist responds in a genuine fashion to the patient, freely revealing and giving of him-

[14] Dugald S. Arbuckle, ed., *Counseling and Psychotherapy: An Existential-Humanistic View*, 3rd ed. (Boston: Allyn & Bacon, 1975).
[15] E. G. Williamson, "Value Orientation in Counseling," *Personnel and Guidance Journal*, 36 (April 1958), 520–528.
[16] Joseph Samler, "Change in Values: A Goal in Counseling," *Journal of Counseling Psychology*, 7 (Spring 1960), 32–39.
[17] C. H. Patterson, *Relationship Counseling and Psychotherapy* (New York: Harper & Row, 1974), pp. 22–26.
[18] Edward A. Dreyfus, "Humanness: A Therapeutic Variable," *Personnel and Guidance Journal*, 45 (February 1967), 573–578.

self, the patient then can learn to respond to the world in his own unique manner, and hence is potentially capable of becoming even more human than the therapist.[19]

Dreyfus stated that humanness is the most important variable in the counseling process. In response to the question as to what it means to be human he wrote,

> . . . we must add that it is not only the ability to be warm, kind, supportive, etc., but also to be angry, sad, guilty. Being human does not mean loving everyone all the time, but rather recognizing that one cannot love everyone all the time and cannot be loved all the time by everyone. Being human is the capacity, willingness, and ability for self-disclosure . . . with the acceptance and expression of all the feelings within the human emotional spectrum.[20]

There is no longer any doubt that counselors will *expose* their values to the counselee. Because counselors are individuals who are present in an intimate relationship with another, their values (either consciously or unconsciously) will be brought into play. There should be no pretense that they do not possess a value system or that they are something other than they are. The real issue is whether or to what degree counselors *impose* their values on the counselee. Some would argue that counselees, by agreeing to counselor intervention, have given their consent to be influenced in any ethical way that will enable them to establish meaning in their lives. Some years ago Wrenn formulated some principles of human relationships that have direct application in any consideration of values. Some pertain to the relationship between counselor and counselee and perhaps place in perspective the responsibilities one human being has for another.

1. I shall strive to see the positive in the other person and praise it at least as often as I notice that which is to be corrected.
2. If I am to correct or criticize someone's action I must be sure that this is seen by the other as a criticism of a specific behavior and not as a criticism of himself [or herself] as a person.
3. I shall assume that each person can see some reasonableness in his [or her] behavior, that there is meaning in it for him [or her] if not for me.
4. When I contribute to another person's self-respect I increase his [or her] positive feelings toward me and his [or her] respect for me.
5. To at least one person, perhaps many, I am a person of significance, and he [or she] is affected vitally by my recognition of him [or her] and my good will toward him [or her] as a person.[21]

Acceptance

Within the language of counseling *acceptance* and *understanding* have become somewhat platitudinous. But like all platitudes they are relevant, particularly as they apply to the counseling process. Some authors classify acceptance and understanding as skills or techniques, others as attitudes. Whether they are techniques or attitudes and whether they can be developed in training or originate in the individual's experiences in responding to people, the important point is that they are essential to any facilitating relationship.

DEFINITION OF ACCEPTANCE Acceptance of another derives from the basic attitudes held toward humankind in general and toward an individual specifically. Acceptance requires respect for the individual as a person of worth. Rogers defined acceptance in the following way:

> By acceptance I mean a warm regard for him as a person of unconditional self-worth—of value no matter what his condition, his behavior or his feelings. It means a respect and liking for him as a separate person, a willingness for him to possess his own feelings in his own way. It means an acceptance of and a regard for his attitudes of the moment, no matter how negative or positive, no matter how

---

[19] Ibid., p. 575.
[20] Ibid., p. 576.

[21] C. Gilbert Wrenn, "Psychology, Religion and Values for the Counselor," *Personnel and Guidance Journal*, 36 (January 1958), 331–334.

much they may contradict other attitudes he has held in the past.[22]

CHARACTERISTICS OF ACCEPTANCE   Tyler identified two components of acceptance. The first was a "willingness to allow individuals to differ from one another in all sorts of ways" and the second was "a realization that the ongoing experience of each person is a complex pattern of striving, thinking, and feeling."[23] Acceptance is a direct outgrowth of the ability of counselors to be nonjudgmental. They do not have normative or judgmental standards against which counselees are matched, balanced, and found wanting as persons. They assign no condition to be met before extending help. They do not attach "if" clauses—if you study, if you behave, if you apologize, then I will consider you a worthwhile person.

Acceptance is a nurturing, lifting attitude manifested in the counselor's verbal and nonverbal behavior. It wells from the depths of one's value orientation. It is a prizing of the individual that reflects a desire to help but not to control.

Rejecting behavior can be unintentionally demonstrated through inappropriate use of assurance and adherence to the counselor's frame of reference rather than the client's. Acceptance of the client by counselors is not only indicated by their words, but also by their gestures and posture. For example, clients who perceive their counselors as relaxed and attentive rather than agitated and bored build such a perception on cues that are both verbal and nonverbal.

The counselee experiences acceptance as a feeling of being unconditionally understood, liked, and respected. Acceptance—a positive tolerant attitude on the part of the counselor—is part of the condition that enables the counselee to change.

Finally, to be accepting of the counselee, counselors must accept and understand themselves. What they see themselves to be as persons may or may not be what they really are as counselors. A critical factor is the awareness by clients that they are accepted by the counselor. Virtually all counselors recognize the need of this acceptance and strive to provide this quality in the relationship. Admittedly, there are times when they fall short of the ideal communication of acceptance or are unable to transmit it as adequately to the client as they would like.

Understanding

Everyone wants to be understood. It is through understanding that help can be given. The counselor must understand the counselee if the relationship is to be fruitful.

UNDERSTANDING DEFINED   Understanding is the ability to perceive another's relationships, meanings, content, and structure. Tyler[24] defined understanding as "simply to grasp clearly and completely the meaning the client is trying to convey." Acknowledging that no human being fully understands another, Tyler said that understanding was essentially a sharing process. In this process what the client verbalizes enables the counselor to grasp its meaning and to put that meaning into words in order to clarify it for both of them.

CHARACTERISTICS OF UNDERSTANDING   The counselee's verbal behavior is only part of what the counselor seeks to understand. Equally important, if not more so, is the counselor's ability to understand the meanings behind the words, however much disguised or hidden. The understanding counselor "feels with" or "experiences" meanings from the counselee's vantage point. Among the elements of such experiencing identified by Gendlin are the following five: (1) experiencing is felt, rather than thought, known, or verbalized; (2) experiencing occurs in the immediate present; (3) experiencing can be directly referred to by the individual; (4) experiencing guides conceptualization; and (5) experiencing is implicitly meaningful.[25]

Understanding is not a magical process. It comes through being free to attend carefully to the client. The importance of understanding as a dimension in the counseling process has been pointed up by Fiedler's description of the ideal relationship, based on studies of therapeutic sessions:

1. The therapist is able to participate completely in the patient's communications.

---

[22] Carl R. Rogers, *On Becoming a Person* (Boston: Houghton Mifflin Company, 1961), p. 34. Copyright © 1954 the Trustees of Oberlin College.
[23] Leona E. Tyler, *The Work of the Counselor*, 3rd ed. (New York: Appleton-Century-Crofts, 1969), p. 34.

[24] Ibid., p. 36.
[25] Eugene T. Gendlin, "Experiencing: A Variable in the Process of Therapeutic Change," *American Journal of Psychotherapy*, 15 (April 1961), 233–245.

2. The therapist's comments are always right in line with what the patient is trying to convey.
3. The therapist is well able to understand the patient's feelings.
4. The therapist really tries to understand the patient's feelings.
5. The therapist always follows the patient's line of thought.[26]

LEVELS OF UNDERSTANDING Understanding occurs at several levels. Some years ago, Davis, in a penetrating analysis, identified four levels. The first kind of understanding is knowledge *about* other individuals—their behavior, their personality, their interests, and so on—but it is accompanied by evaluations or judgments. A second kind of understanding is composed of two parts, a verbal or intellectual understanding and a behavioral or operational one. Davis points out that although individuals are able to learn an operation intellectually they may still be unable to perform it. The third level of understanding is derived directly from individuals themselves and is an attempt to step into their perceptual world, to know their internal world, their fears, loves, and anxieties. This kind of understanding is more intense, personal, and meaningful than the others. The fourth level is self-understanding, and to attain this requires much exploration within and usually in the company of another.[27]

Internal conditions that influence counseling

Four conditions—rapport, empathy, genuineness, and attentiveness—can either further or inhibit the counseling process. These components are based on and intimately related to acceptance and understanding.

Rapport

Rapport is described most simply as a condition essential to a comfortable and unconditional relationship between counselor and counselee. It is established and maintained through the counselor's genuine interest in and acceptance of the client. It cannot be forced or contrived. It is a bond characterized by interest, responsiveness, and a sensitive emotional involvement.

All too often rapport is referred to as the outcome of techniques counselors use in the initial interview that put counselees at ease and help them to express their feelings. True, some individuals have difficulty in discussing their purpose in seeing a counselor and need help in stating why they are there. But rapport means more than opening the interview smoothly and effectively. It is a quality, a mutual understanding, a respect, and a sustained interest that should be communicated from the first through the last contact.

Rapport is generated by the smoothness (lack of awkwardness, bumbling) with which the counselor opens and interacts within the relationship. Recognizing that the counselee may experience some reluctance in the beginning, the counselor usually opens the conversation by focusing on some neutral topic or event known to both. However, artful judgment based on cues received from the client is required since trite conversational leads may result in an increase in strained feelings.

Published suggestions for establishing rapport are abundant. Most of them emphasize the necessity of being friendly, being attentive, and demonstrating interest to reduce counselee resistance. But beginning counselors should not make the mistake of implying that the weather, sports, or activities are what the counselee wants to discuss with them. Counseling is not a social call, and the opening conversation should be brief. Focus should be on the reason for the counselee's being there. The counselor might say, "How may I help you?" or "Would you like to tell me what brings you here?" or "What would you like to talk about?" or "I've asked you to come in because. . . ." A natural, straightforward and tactful approach that helps counselees verbalize why they are there and enable them to begin is best used. It leads to communication and encourages commonality of interest. Versatility, flexibility, and relatability are all essential factors in establishing rapport.

But it is to be underscored that rapport is more than a pleasant greeting and putting the counselee at ease. Unfortunately, rapport is an intangible entity characterized by pleasantness, confidence, cooperation, sincerity, and interest—all qualities difficult to measure, impossible to turn

[26] F. E. Fiedler, "The Concept of the Ideal Therapeutic Relationship," *Journal of Consulting Psychology*, 14 (August 1950), 239–245.
[27] Donald A. Davis, "Understanding is *Not* Enough!," mimeographed (APGA address, April 10, 1963).

on in a mechanical way, and difficult to initiate by recipe or by a bag of tricks. Patterson believes that small talk as a rapport-building technique is neither necessary nor desirable. Small talk reflects insecurity on the part of the counselor and Patterson believes that when it is used, it misleads clients in terms of structuring. Further, the shift from conversational pleasantries to the work of counseling hinders the process.[28]

Basically, rapport means that an appropriate working relationship has been established and maintained between counselee and counselor. As it develops, this relationship is experienced by counselees as being one of trust, acceptance, and understanding such as they never before may have encountered with any human being. It is rapport or the working relationship that will enable their counselees to examine themselves and concerns, rid themselves of their fears and conflicts, and achieve a better understanding of themselves and connections with others. The length of time required to establish a good working relationship will depend on the counselor's skills and on client motivation. Although no counselor is capable of establishing rapport with all individuals, he or she should, with adequate training and personal inclination, be able to relate to most of those who come for help. Competence in intervention techniques fosters confidence. By conveying an attentive and accepting manner through facial expressions and gestures and by asking pertinent questions, restating, summarizing, and using other techniques, counselors demonstrate that they are interested, understanding, and observant. No doubt the reputation of the counselor partially influences the establishment and maintenance of rapport. Consequently, counselors should be consistent in their work with counselees in order to build a reputation of honesty, competence, and trust in keeping of confidences. But most of all they nurture rapport by being sensitive to the client's needs, moods, and conflicts.

Empathy

Typically, empathy has been described as putting oneself in the other person's shoes. Many meaningful experiences are instances of empathy. *Empathy*, from the German *Ein-* *fühlung,* means "feeling into" and plays a significant part in counseling communication. Most definitions indicate that empathy is comprehending the emotions of another person without feeling completely (as in sympathy) what he or she feels. If the counselor enters the client's internal frame of reference, perceives the client's world and how the client perceives self, that counselor is said to be empathic with the client, capable of taking the role of the client.

Evidences of empathy may be observed every day: for example, the mother who, while nursing her baby, makes similar mouth motions; the golfer who leans one way as the ball approaches the hole; the racing crowd that swoops with the car as it moves around a curve; the football player who unthinkingly comes off the bench to make a defensive tackle. All these examples illustrate *imitative* phenomena because the observer introjects or takes on from the person acting that which he or she perceives and in some way identifies with and imitates the action.

Dymond called empathy "the imaginative transposing of oneself into the thinking, feeling and acting of another and so structuring the world as he does,"[29] or "the ability to feel and describe the thoughts and feelings of others."[30] Her definitions reflect that empathy is an interrelationship between two people and is dependent on mutual agreement on the experience being shared. Empathy may be said to exist when counselors recognize the feeling a client presents as being the client's and not their own, and are able to communicate back to the client the same feeling so the client can recognize its similarity to the one expressed. Empathy was one of the six necessary conditions in counseling set forth by Rogers who defined it as sensing the client's private world "as if it were your own, but without ever losing the 'as if' quality."[31]

The emphasis in the remarks by Dymond and Rogers is on *transposition,* but not imitation. One does not do exactly what the other person does, yet one makes that individual aware that one understands the thoughts, feelings, and actions being expressed. This is done imaginatively with one's affect and intelligence.

---

[28] Patterson, *Relationship Counseling,* p. 106.

[29] Rosalind F. Dymond, "A Scale for the Measurement of Empathic Ability," *Journal of Consulting Psychology,* 13 (April 1949), 127.

[30] Rosalind F. Dymond, "A Preliminary Investigation of the Relation of Insight and Empathy," *Journal of Consulting Psychology,* 12 (July–August 1948), 232.

[31] Rogers, *On Becoming a Person,* p. 284.

Other terms for empathy are *synchronicity* (H. S. Sullivan) and *recipathy* (H. S. Murray). Both convey the idea of mutuality. Buchheimer uses the word *confluence,* rather than *empathy,* because it reflects the quality of counselor-counselee interactions.[32] Buchheimer identified five dimensions of empathy: (1) *tone,* an expressive and nonverbal dimension reflected when two people interact in expressive harmony and unity; (2) *pace,* or appropriate timing of counselor leads; (3) *flexibility,* or the counselor's ability to discard previously thought out tactics or goals if they do not fit the counselee's situation; (4) perception of the counselee's *frame of reference,* or the ability to abstract the core of the counselee's concern and to formulate it objectively and palatably so that the person can elaborate; and (5) *repertoire of leads,* or the resourcefulness with which counselors vary their leading in appropriate ways to apply to both manifest and dynamic content of the counselee's expression.

Empathy as a counseling variable has been the subject of considerable research. O'Hern and Arbuckle use the term *sensitivity,* and their definition of it embodies many of the characteristics found in definitions of empathy.[33] They developed an instrument to assess the degree of sensitivity possessed by potential counselors. The instrument (tape-recorded counselor remarks) was administered to 212 counselors in training. Counselors judged most sensitive tended to be younger and employed for fewer years in their present position. Sex, religion, occupation, personal security, and intelligence did not differentiate between the most and the least sensitive groups.

Campbell and his associates concluded that empathy is a trait that is measurable, that individuals have this trait in varying degrees, and that empathy is subject to change by training.[34] Haase and Tepper reported that nonverbal behaviors were significant in the counselor's communication of and the client's perception of empathy. Their research indicated that nonverbal behaviors had twice the effect on perception of empathy as verbal messages of empathy.[35] Payne and his colleagues demonstrated that empathy could be taught by "modeling" procedures and by supervisors who used such didactic approaches as giving examples of responses that were empathic.[36]

In 1969, Carkhuff[37] published a scale to measure the construct, empathy, that has had wide use. Later he entitled it *empathic understanding* (EU), and defined it as "the ability to recognize, to sense and to understand the feelings that another person has associated with his behavioral and verbal expressions and to accurately communicate this understanding to him."[38] Each of the five levels of empathic understanding is differentiated by the extent to which the helper adds or subtracts from the feelings and meaning of the client's expression.

The five levels of empathic understanding were defined by Carkhuff as follows:

Level 1—The verbal and behavioral expressions of the helper either *do not attend to* or *detract significantly* from the verbal and behavioral expressions of the helpee(s) in that they communicate significantly less of the helpee's feelings than the helper has communicated.

Level 2—While the helper responds to the expressed feelings of the helpee(s), he does so in such a way that he *subtracts noticeable affect* from the communications of the helpee.

Level 3—The expressions of the helper in response to the expressions of the helpee(s) are essentially *interchangeable* with those of the helpee in that they express essentially the same affect and meaning.

Level 4—The responses of the helper *add noticeably* to the expressions of the helpee(s) in such a way

[32] Arnold Buchheimer, "Empathy in Counseling," (APGA address, March 28, 1961), mimeographed.

[33] Jane S. O'Hern and Dugald S. Arbuckle, "Sensitivity: A Measurable Concept?" *Personnel and Guidance Journal,* 42 (February 1964), 572–576.

[34] Robert J. Campbell, Norman Kagan, and David R. Krathwohl, "The Development and Validation of a Scale to Measure Affective Sensitivity (Empathy)," *Journal of Counseling Psychology,* 18 (September 1971), 407–412.

[35] Richard F. Haase and Donald T. Tepper, Jr., "Nonverbal Components of Empathic Communication," *Journal of Counseling Psychology,* 19 (September 1972), 417–424.

[36] Paul A. Payne, Stephen D. Weiss, and Richard A. Kapp, "Didactic, Experimental, and Modeling Factors in the Learning of Empathy," *Journal of Counseling Psychology,* 19 (September 1972), 425–429.

[37] Robert R. Carkhuff, *Helping and Human Relations,* Vol. I: *Selection and Training* (New York: Holt, Rinehart and Winston, 1969).

[38] Robert R. Carkhuff, *The Development of Human Resources* (New York: Holt, Rinehart and Winston, 1971), p. 266.

as to express feelings a level deeper than the helpee was able to express himself.

Level 5—The helper's responses *add significantly* to the feeling and meaning of the expressions of the helpee(s) in such a way as to accurately express feeling levels below what the helpee himself was able to express or in the event of ongoing deep self-exploration on the helpee's part, to be fully with him in his deepest moments.[39]

Avery and his associates[40] sought to determine if different units of analysis of client-therapist interaction would affect ratings assigned empathic understanding. Interaction units consisted of a client statement (C1), therapist response (T1), and client response (C2) and part interaction units consisting of C1 and T1, T1 and C2, and T1 only. A significant overall difference was found among the rating units on the level of EU, however, post hoc tests of the differences among means revealed that it was primarily the client's initial statement rather than the client's response to the therapist that contributed to its significant effect. They contended that the higher EU ratings for excerpts of the therapist alone supported the view that the ratings scales were not measuring EU, but rather something found only in the actions of the helper. They challenged the construct validity of the EU scale for they concluded that the rater might be more important than the client in judging the helper's response.

Horwitz[41] asserted that the accuracy of ratings of EU must depend on the perceived correspondence between a client's expression and a counselor's responses. In short, the data reported by Avery and his associates support the construct validity of EU ratings, but not their challenge. Thoresen[42] examined both statements and concluded that both Horwitz and Avery and associates appeared reasonable and

that neither party was wrong, nor necessarily right! The situation, according to Thoresen, simply demonstrated that an infinite number of theoretical explanations exist for any finite set of data. To extend an empathic relationship counselors must be able, during the interview, to free themselves of their own problems so they do not interfere with their becoming congruent with the counselee. The counselor has to be able to "see" with the eyes of counselees and "hear" with their ears if the counselor's responses are to approximate the counselee's. The responses by counselors are inferences as to the counselee's thoughts and feelings, and their communication of this understanding is done in such a way that counselees can reasonably accept it and know that they are being understood.

Hackney traced the evolution of the construct *empathy*, and discussed its use by various groups within the profession. He noted that counselor educators define empathy as "training to be spontaneous in one's response to the affective state of a second person." For practicing counselors empathy was regarded as a self-disciplinary process designed to screen out their world so that the client's world can invade their consciousness. Empathy to the epistemologist meant an event that happened within an individual rather than between two people. Hackney concluded that empathy, like love, was a qualitative response to people, a potential possessed by the counselor that can be inhibited or encouraged.[43]

Counselor congruence or genuineness

Experience and research demonstrate the importance of the counselor's congruence or genuineness in the counseling relationship. Rogers' description of this condition is that "... it means that he [the counselor] is *being* himself, not denying himself."[44] He defines congruence more fully in the following statement. "By this we mean that the feelings the counselor is experiencing are available to him, available to his awareness, that he is able to live these feelings, be them

[39] Carkhuff, *Helping and Human Relations*, pp. 174–175.
[40] Arthur W. Avery, Anthony R. D'Augelli, and Steven J. Danish, "An Empirical Investigation of the Construct Validity of Empathic Understanding Ratings," *Counselor Education and Supervision*, 15 (March 1976), 177–183.
[41] Michael B. Horwitz, "A Comment on 'An Empirical Investigation of the Construct Validity of Empathic Understanding Ratings,'" *Counselor Education and Supervision*, 16 (June 1977), 292–295.
[42] Carl E. Thoresen, "Constructs Don't Speak for Themselves," *Counselor Education and Supervision*, 16 (June 1977), 296–303.

[43] Harold Hackney, "The Evolution of Empathy," *Personnel and Guidance Journal*, 57 (October 1978), 20–22.
[44] Carl R. Rogers, "The Interpersonal Relationship: The Core of Guidance," in *Person to Person*, Carl R. Rogers and Barry Stevens (Lafayette, California: Real People Press, 1967), p. 90.

in the relationship, and able to communicate them if appropriate."[45]

Congruence implies honesty and candor with oneself while functioning as a counselor. Counselors do not pretend to be something they are not; they do not play a role, they are genuinely themselves. Role playing differs from congruence in its emphasis on the attempt to be that which one is not. Indeed, "playing" a role implies acting or attempting to create a facade or an illusion that is damaging to the counseling relationship. Congruence demands authenticity and transparency of the counselor.

Patterson[46] has discussed some distortions of the genuineness concept that are relevant here. He makes two major points. First, genuineness does not mean that "anything goes," because some expressions of counselor feelings may be damaging to and nonfacilitative for the client. A notable example of these are expressions of boredom or hostility toward the client. Second, genuineness does not mean total self-disclosure by the counselor. It does mean that those aspects of oneself that the counselor reveals must be honest. The counseling relationship requires sincere, spontaneous verbal interactions to avoid the pitfall of role playing by the counselor. The burden and opportunity for self-disclosure lie with the client, for the reverse raises the question of who is counseling whom.

Truax[47] developed a five-point scale for assessing genuineness, or counselor self-congruence. Carkhuff revised the scale and its five levels are described here in his words.

Level 1—The helper's verbalizations are clearly unrelated to what he is feeling at the moment, or his only genuine responses are negative in regard to the helpee(s) and appear to have a totally destructive effect upon the helpee.

Level 2—The helper's verbalizations are slightly unrelated to what he appears otherwise to be feeling at the moment, or when his responses are genuine they are negative in regard to the helpee and he does not appear to know how to employ

his negative reactions as a basis for inquiry into the relationship.

Level 3—The helper provides no "negative" cues between what he says and what he feels, but he provides no positive cues to indicate a really genuine response to the helpee(s).

Level 4—The helper presents some positive cues indicating a genuine response (whether positive or negative) in a nondestructive manner to the helpee(s).

Level 5—The helper appears freely and deeply himself in a nonexploitative relationship with the helpee(s).[48]

Concreteness

An important element in the relationship is the accuracy and specificity of the counselor's responses to the client. Sometimes labeled *concreteness*, the counseling interaction requires that the counselor's responses convey the specific feelings, experiences, and behaviors emitted by the client rather than any generalities or abstractions of them. Carkhuff and Berenson indicate that this behavior accomplishes three ends. First, concreteness enables the counselor to remain close to the client's level of feelings and experiences. Second, it eliminates misunderstandings and permits clients to correct distortions in their expressions. Third, it fosters client attention to specific problem areas.[49]

A scale to measure concreteness, one originally proposed by Truax and Carkhuff,[50] has been revised by Carkhuff. His description of the five levels is presented here.

Level 1—The helper appears to lead or allow all discussion with the helper(s) to deal only with vague and anonymous generalities.

Level 2—The helper frequently appears to lead or allow even discussions of material personally relevant to the helpee(s) to be dealt with on a vague and abstract level.

[45] Ibid.
[46] C. H. Patterson, *Relationship Counseling and Psychotherapy* (New York: Harper & Row, 1974), pp. 63–65.
[47] Charles B. Truax and Robert R. Carkhuff, *Toward Effective Counseling and Psychotherapy* (Chicago: Aldine, 1967), pp. 68–72.
[48] Carkhuff, *Helping and Human Relations*, Vol. 1, pp. 184–185.
[49] Robert R. Carkhuff and Bernard G. Berenson, *Beyond Counseling and Therapy* (New York: Holt, Rinehart and Winston, 1967), p. 30.
[50] Truax and Carkhuff, *Toward Effective Counseling.*

Level 3—The helper is open and at times facilitative of the helpee's discussion of personally relevant material in specific and concrete terminology.

Level 4—The helper appears frequently helpful in enabling the helpee(s) to fully develop in concrete and specific terms almost all instances of concern.

Level 5—The helper appears always helpful in guiding the discussion so that the helpee(s) may discuss fluently, directly, and completely specific feelings and experiences.[51]

Respect or caring

It may be remembered (see p. 217) that unconditional positive regard was one of the six conditions established by Carl R. Rogers as being necessary to bring about constructive personality change. Further he suggested that positive regard is unconditional in that it does not depend on client behaviors. Respect for the client as a person of worth is demonstrated by nonjudgmental, nonevaluative attitudes on the part of counselors, despite client imperfections.

Wrenn uses the word *caring* to convey respect for the individual or unconditional positive regard. He has defined *caring* as being, among other things, "concern for the person," "your attitude toward yourself and others," "trust," and "sharing."[52] Truax[53] developed a scale to measure positive regard, called *nonpossessive warmth.* Carkhuff revised the scale and labeled it *respect.* The five levels of the scale have been defined by him, as follows:

Level 1—The verbal and behavioral expressions of the helper communicate a clear lack of respect (or negative regard) for the helpee(s).

Level 2—The helper responds to the helpee in such a way as to communicate little respect for the feelings, experiences, and potentials of the helpee.

Level 3—The helper communicates a minimal acknowledgment of regard for the helpee's position and concern for the helpee's feelings, experiences, and potentials.

Level 4—The helper communicates a very deep respect and concern for the helpee.

Level 5—The helper communicates the very deepest respect for the helpee's worth as a person and his potentials as a free individual.[54]

Attentiveness

Fundamental to all counselor skills is attentiveness. As used here the term implies maximum involvement by the counselor in the client's communications. Attentiveness requires skill in listening and observing, through which the counselor comes to know and understand the core of content and feeling presented by the counselee. The information thus "collected" can then be utilized in the helping relationship, as clients realize that they are *received* within the relationship.

Hackney, Ivey, and Oetting use the term *attending behaviors* to describe attentiveness.

Attending implies that the counselor is emitting both verbal and nonverbal behaviors which communicate that he hears the messages emitted by the client. It implies further that the counselor is not dividing his attention between the client's messages and extraneous variables which remain unidentified to the client. Indeed, nonattending lapses by the counselor are likely to be revealed by behaviors such as frequent breaks in eye contact, intonation and vocal pitch, or characteristically, topic-jumping verbal behavior. Such inconsistencies reflect a decrease or absence of attending to the client.[55]

For many counselors, particularly those who have been teachers, listening is hard to learn since they have been accustomed to being listened to. By consciously making an effort to attend closely to what the counselee is expressing (verbally and nonverbally), counselors are able to participate in the counselee's communication. Through this means they understand not only *what* the counselee says but *how* it is said and *why.* Moustakas says this about listening:

---

[51] Carkhuff, *Helping and Human Relations,* Vol. 1, pp. 182–183.

[52] C. Gilbert Wrenn, *The World of the Contemporary Counselor* (Boston: Houghton Mifflin Company, 1973), pp. 248–250.

[53] Truax and Carkhuff, *Toward Effective Counseling,* pp. 58–68.

[54] Carkhuff, *Helping and Human Relations,* pp. 178–179.

[55] Harold L. Hackney, Allen E. Ivey, and Eugene R. Oetting, "Attending, Island and Hiatus Behavior: A Process Conception of Counselor and Client Interaction," *Journal of Counseling Psychology,* 17 (July 1970), 343–344.

Listening is a magnetic and strange thing, a creative force. . . . The friends that listen to us are the ones we move toward, and we want to sit in their radius as though it did us good, like ultraviolet rays. . . . When we are listened to, it creates us, makes us unfold and expand. Ideas actually begin to grow within us and come to life. . . . It makes people happy and free when they are listened to. . . . When we listen to people there is an alternating current, and this recharges us so that we never get tired of each other. We are constantly being recreated.

Now there are brilliant people who cannot listen much. They have no in-going wires on their apparatus. They are entertaining but exhausting too. I think it is because these lecturers, these brilliant performers, by not giving us a chance to talk, do not let us express our thoughts and expand; and it is this expressing and expanding that makes the little creative fountain inside us begin to spring and ease up new thoughts and unexpected laughter and wisdom.

I discovered all this about three years ago, and truly it made a revolutionary change in my life. Before that, when I went to a party I would think anxiously: "Now try hard. Be lively. Say bright things. Talk, don't let down." And when tired, I would have to drink a lot of coffee to keep this up. But now before going to a party, I just tell myself to listen with affection to anyone who talks to me, *to be in their shoes when they talk*; to try to know them without my mind pressing against theirs, or arguing, or changing the subject. Now my attitude is: "Tell me more. This person is showing me his soul. It is a little dry and meager and full of grinding talk now, but presently he will begin to think, not just automatically to talk. He will show his true self. Then he will be wonderfully alive. . . ."[56]

Listening is the means by which counselors sustain, extend, and deepen their knowledge of the client. Listening in counseling is different from the partial listening one gives to a lecturing professor. In the latter instance people listen with but one ear while simultaneously thinking about something else, or they are engaged in pro and con reactions to what is being said. Superficial listening is most often observed in social interactions where "listeners" can hardly

wait for the speaker to pause so that they can present their own dazzling comments.

The counselee wants the full attention of the counselor. The counselor's listening tells the client that the counselor is interested in and sensitive to the nuances of what the client seeks to convey. When counselors are "tuned in," their inferences will be more accurate, their observations will be more acute, and their responses will contribute more to fostering a relationship. By listening they will understand the meaning an experience has for a counselee and to perceive the experience as the counselee does.

But listening is not enough. Confrontation occurs in virtually all forms of counseling and unquestionably contributes to the quality of the relationship as well as enriching the data available to the counselor. Both participants watch as well as listen to each other. Those who have listened to sound recordings of counseling sessions can fully appreciate the fact that many subtleties of the process are lost when one is unable to observe the physical interaction between the participants.

Obviously many of the skills and attitudes of counselors are transmitted to the counselee through their nonverbal behavior: facial expressions, posture, eye contact, and the like. It is equally obvious that the counselor learns much of the feeling components through observations of the client. Frequently it is the counselor's recognition of the appearance and physical expression of a mood by clients that lets clients know they are being attended to and understood at a level more meaningful than words alone can convey.

The counselor's nonverbal behavior is of extreme importance in establishing and maintaining a relationship. Many clients are quite able to describe counselor discomfort and, perhaps more important, perceive it as a cue to avoid certain content or perhaps even the counseling situation itself. Even the valued counselor behavior of maintaining eye contact can be carried to such an extreme that it seems to the client a hostile stare rather than friendly attentiveness. Much literature has been produced about nonverbal behavior, which will be treated more extensively in the next chapter.

Counseling relationship—the common denominator

Most theories and approaches stress the relationship between participants as the common ground for the helping process. Although viewpoints differ in the amount of em-

[56] Clark E. Moustakas, *The Authentic Teacher* (Cambridge, Mass.: Howard A. Doyle Publishing Co., 1966), pp. 42–43.

phasis and in how they treat this topic, most agree that the relationship is a necessary condition for bringing about change in the individual. The elements discussed earlier in this chapter—external conditions, attitudes, and skills—blend to foster it, and presumably these ingredients—provided or withheld, consciously or unconsciously used, or varied in quantity or quality—influence its nature.

The construct *counseling relationship* is elusive, more amenable to description than definition. Even descriptive terms vary markedly from theory to theory, each counseling practitioner knows what is meant yet is often hard put to communicate verbally the personal and private meaning to others. If counselors attempt to approach its description through, for example, Freudian terminology such as *transference* and *countertransference*, they risk a negative reaction from those of a different persuasion.

The interpersonal relationship present in counseling is basically a reciprocal influence of the participants. Its characteristics were discussed in Chapter 1. Chapter 4 delineated the reasons for one participant's seeking help and the other's attempting to provide it. This chapter has sketched the elements that interact to produce a relationship.

It should be recognized that the counselor's attitudes and skills develop over a span of years and are a product of training and experience. Each counselor tries to provide some optimal set of conditions that facilitate the counseling relationship with most individuals. The particular mix of attitudes and skills will not always be helpful to all clients, but it is hoped that with additional experience a given counselor can work effectively and flexibly with a larger and larger variety of counselees.

Issues

Issue 1 Neither sound nor video recordings should be made of counseling sessions.

True, because
1. Recordings invade the client's privacy and increase the probability that confidentiality of the relationship will be broken.
2. Recordings of any kind, including note taking, cause clients to be guarded, inhibit self-expression and increase defensiveness.

False, because
1. By the act of coming to a counselor, the client gives assent to intervention. Electronic recordings of this intervention can be safeguarded and duly protected from third-party use.
2. Most clients . . . and counselors . . . soon forget the presence of recording equipment.

Discussion Little doubt exists but that the presence of electronic recording equipment has an effect on the behavior of both the client and novice counselor. And that effect is undoubtedly adverse, creating anxiety, for most people are not accustomed to having their words or their verbal and nonverbal behavior recorded. How long the adverse effect lasts has never been determined. Based on the authors' own experiences and observations drawn from supervising many students in counseling practicum situations and their clients, the answer would be that the effects do not last long. Most clients seem to forget recordings after the first ten to twenty minutes as they become engrossed in the relationship. Others—client or counselor—take somewhat longer.

The gains from recording more than offset this adverse, temporary effect. Electronic recording of counseling sessions enables both counselors and clients to hear and/or see the nuances of the session not heard and/or seen while it was taking place. Recordings are the means by which observation and supervision of counselors can be delivered with precision and concreteness. In short, recordings enable the counselor to develop the competence and confidence to be helpful to clients.

Issue 2 Counselors should be ethically neutral or value free within the counseling relationship.

True, because
1. Clients should develop their own values, rather than "borrowing" them from counselors.
2. Other institutions—church, home, school—are more appropriate places for instilling values or instructing individuals about what is "right," "good," "true," or "fitting."

False, because
1. Counselors, being human, cannot be ethically neutral or value free. Any transaction they have with clients is influenced by values.

2. Being ethically neutral means condoning immoral, un-ethical, illegal behaviors of clients.

Discussion Discussion of this issue evolved with the advent of client-centered counseling. It is still a source of lively debate, at least among students in preparation programs. And rightly so, for it is a complex issue.

Abundant evidence exists (see Chapter 5) that counselors influence the values of their clients. In any relationship of any length, counselors would find it difficult, if not impossible, to refrain from giving an impression that they favor certain values. It should be remembered that extending help to another who seeks to resolve personal difficulties or to facilitate self-development is a value in itself. Some have even suggested that if counselors were to remain completely silent, the silence would represent judgmental attitudes and be interpreted judgmentally by the client. Disclosure of values, then, occurs in counselors' communications, whether they are aware of it or not. Considerable research (see Chapter 6) has even demonstrated that, at termination of counseling, clients whose values approximate or become like those of their counselor, were rated as improved, whereas those rated as unimproved tended to have values less like their counselors.

Few question that counselors *expose* their values in their transactions with clients, but many are less certain that their values should be directly *inculcated* by or *imposed* on counselees. If the latter were to be done, then the question becomes which values, specifically, constitute the set usefu to clients? And to specify the set is more than identifying being purposeful and responsible, for it would necessitate stipulating values associated with thought (truth and understanding), feeling (happiness), and will (virtue). The very complexity of doing so is compounded by the absence of a satisfactory theory of values needed to uphold objectivity.

Annotated references

Avila, Donald L., Arthur W. Combs, and William W. Purkey, eds. *The Helping Relationship Sourcebook.* 2nd ed. Boston: Allyn & Bacon, 1977. 253 pp.

Some twenty articles, authored by different individuals, present the helping process, the professional helper, beliefs, values, and goals in counseling and ways of being helpful.

Selections by Rogers, Combs, Patterson, Kelly, and Maslow are especially useful.

Benjamin, Alfred. *The Helping Interview.* 2nd ed. Boston: Houghton Mifflin Company, 1974. 167 pp.

The author presents the external factors that influence helping relationships, opening interviews, recording interviews and attitudes and behavior of the interviewer. Interview extracts are presented throughout the book.

Kennedy, Eugene. *On Becoming a Counselor.* New York: The Seabury Press, 1977. 337 pp.

Part 2 (pp. 63–136) sets forth practical considerations of interviewing such as appointments, physical arrangements, what to call the client, to name but a few. Treatment is given to resistant or reluctant clients, counselor involvement, diagnosis, and other factors.

Further references

Amidon, Edmund, and Raphael R. Kavanaugh. "The Observation of Intimacy in Groups." *Personnel and Guidance Journal*, 57 (May 1979), 464–468.

Bath, Kent E., and Robert O. Calhoun. "The Effects of Professional Counselor Training on Empathy: Continued Cause for Concern." *Counselor Education and Supervision*, 17 (December 1977), 98–106.

Bruch, Monroe A. "Client Fear of Negative Evaluation and Type of Counselor Response Style." *Journal of Counseling Psychology*, 26 (January 1979), 37–44.

Easterly, Jean L. "Assisting Middle School Students to Assess Their Own Values." *The School Counselor*, 25 (September 1977), 52–55.

Fridman, Myron S., and Shelley C. Stone. "Effect of Training, Stimulus Context, and Mode of Stimulus Presentation on Empathy Ratings." *Journal of Counseling Psychology*, 25 (March 1978), 131–136.

Gulanick, Nancy, and Ronald R. Schmeck. "Modeling, Praise and Criticism in Teaching Empathic Responding." *Counselor Education and Supervision*, 16 (June 1977), 284–290.

Kimball, Heber C., and Bert F. Cundick. "Emotional Impact of Videotape and Reenacted Feedback on Subjects with High and Low Defenses." *Journal of Counseling Psychology*, 24 (September 1977), 377–382.

Motto, Jerome A. "Recognition, Evaluation, and Management of Persons at Risk for Suicide." *Personnel and Guidance Journal*, 56 (May 1978), 537–545.

Murphy, Harry B., and Warren Rowe. "Effects of Counselor Facilitative Level on Client Suggestibility." *Journal of Counseling Psychology*, 24 (January 1977), 6–9.

Scher, Murray. "The Little Boy in the Adult Male Client." *Personnel and Guidance Journal*, 57 (June 1979), 537–539.

Seay, Thomas A., and Michael K. Altekruse. "Verbal and Nonverbal Behavior in Judgments of Facilitative Conditions." *Journal of Counseling Psychology*, 26 (March 1979), 108–119.

Smith, Darrell, and James Peterson. "Values: A Challenge to the Profession." *Personnel and Guidance Journal*, 55 (January 1977), 227–231.

Smith-Hansen, Sandra S. "Effects of Non-Verbal Behaviors on Judged Levels of Counselor Warmth and Empathy." *Journal of Counseling Psychology*, 24 (March 1977), 87–91.

Studi, E. W., and James McKelvey. "Ethics and the Law: Friend or Foe?" *Personnel and Guidance Journal*, 57 (May 1979), 453–456.

12　Counseling techniques and practices: I

This chapter identifies and describes the more concrete techniques and practices utilized by counselors. Some rather specialized methods are used only occasionally, when the situation is appropriate. Some techniques are employed by some counselors and avoided by others because of personal inclination, differences of opinion as to their effectiveness, or incompatibility with their philosophy. Many practices are difficult to distinguish clearly from one another and undoubtedly represent differences in emphasis rather than in method.

A curious paradox exists in respect to the attention given to counseling techniques. Practitioners frequently have been criticized for being technique ridden—a popular charge and one common to most professions. Those who make it believe that counselors should be more knowledgeable about the "why" of the relationship. Typically, they urge counselors to concentrate more on attitudes of relating to individuals, the counseling process, or how the self of the counselor affects counseling. On the other hand, close examination of the counseling literature reveals that its theoreticians and practitioners have done little to specify the conditions under which techniques should or should not be used, have failed to organize techniques and practices into a meaningful system, and are unable to predict what behavioral outcomes will be produced by certain techniques. Furthermore, those who have formulated theoretical approaches have been very imprecise about the specific procedures to be used to secure behavioral change.

As one examines the wide assortment of techniques that follow, several observations should be borne in mind:

1. Techniques are tied to counseling theory and philosophy. What counselors do or say directly or indirectly reflects their theory and philosophy.
2. Counseling techniques may be seen as a personal invention—personal in the sense that they work for a particular individual at a specific time given his or her attributes and training and given the client being counseled.

3. The variables dealt with in counseling are myriad, complex, and ever changing. The subject matter is the individual being—a person—possessing all the foibles common to humans.
4. Effective counselors adapt their repertoire of techniques to the particular problem and individual involved. Although different counselors subscribe to particular theories, they use techniques because of the client and the situation at hand more than because of counseling orientation.
5. Investigations seem to indicate that many counselors possess or use too few interviewing techniques. Hoffman reported that (a) they tended to use a limited repertoire of techniques, regardless of change in counselee or type of problem; (b) techniques were usually determined early in the contact; (c) some techniques were used more often than others; and (d) the average number of techniques used per interview was 5.9.[1]
6. Regardless of training, counselors develop a style of counseling and adapt particular techniques to their way of responding, their experiences, current attitudes, and methods of speech. Above all, most counselors try to be themselves rather than play a role.
7. Generally, research demonstrates that (a) counselors employ rather consistent techniques with each counselee and across counselees and (b) expertness and experience produce variability of approach.

Structuring the counseling relationship

Structuring was defined in Chapter 1 as the way the counselor defines the nature, limits, roles, and goals within the counseling relationship. It is an orientation to what counseling is about and what takes place. Its fundamental purpose is to reduce the counselee's anxiety originating from concern about the ambiguity and newness of the counseling

---

[1] A. E. Hoffman, "Analysis of Counselor Sub-Roles," *Journal of Counseling Psychology*, 6 (Spring 1959), 63–65.

situation. Controversy exists as to whether the counselor needs to define the relationship explicitly. Some argue that the relationship is more beneficial if the structure remains implicit and emerges naturally from the situation rather than being provided by the counselor. They believe that an implicit structure permits the client more flexibility in expressions of thought and feeling. Others urge counselors to outline the counseling process verbally during early contacts with clients. Two reasons for doing so include: (1) to let the client know what to expect from the counselor and (2) to give the client some idea of what is involved in counseling methods and purposes.

Structuring originates in and is guided by the particular self-system of clients—the way their reality is constructed and the perceptions they hold of themselves. Each client serves as the pacesetter with the counselor gearing to interview to that pace. Consequently, that which takes place in the relationship is a function of the self-reference clues provided by counselees and perceived by counselors as a result of their own self-system. The counselor's responsibility is to provide the conditions so that the client's self-system may be perceived and understood. The counselor aids in this unfolding and participates in the building and rebuilding of organizations of personal constructs.

Structuring by the counselor is especially important when counselees (1) do not have a clear image of what takes place in counseling, (2) have erroneous ideas of what is expected of them, or (3) are reticent about entering the process or fearful of its consequences. The counselor's explanations should be in broad terms. One value of providing some structure to counselees is that common misconceptions about counseling such as "psychoanalyze me and tell me what's wrong," magical cures, advice giving, unreasonable expectations, and the like, can be alleviated. Another value is that anxiety can be reduced so that clients will not feel that their task is formless or purposeless.

Brammer and Shostrom identify five types of structure that are paraphrased here:[2]

1. *Contracts.* Formal contracts often list privileges extended, responsibilities incurred, bonuses or sanctions, and how and by whom the contract is to be monitored. Contracts focus on what clients are expected to do, set forth expected outcomes and rewards for fulfilling the terms.

2. *Time limits.* Explaining how much time is available for each interview or estimating the time required for counseling provides some structure for the counselee.

3. *Action limits.* Although the counselor does not limit verbal expression in any way, most counselors would not permit the counselee to break windows or destroy furniture or equipment. An explanation of such limits provides structure.

4. *Role limits.* Counselors who also serve in another capacity such as teacher or administrator may find it necessary to clarify for their clients the capacity in which they are being interviewed. This clarification of authority provides structure.

5. *Procedural or process limits.* The counselee has to accept the responsibility for carrying on the major share of the interview. Certain values evolving from the process either are stated by the counselor or, because of attitudes exposed, come to be understood by the client. These include six suggested by Ingham and Love: (a) that it is appropriate and good to investigate ourselves, (b) that it is better to investigate than to blame, (c) that emotions are to be regarded as real and important realities, (d) that freedom of expression is complete, (e) that investigation of the past leads to an understanding of the present, and (f) that the client's present view of the world is a basis for change.[3]

Most people who come for counseling are uncertain how to begin. They will remark, "I don't know where to begin" or "I'll be glad to answer any questions you ask" or "I've never done this before and I don't really know what I'm supposed to do." At this point several options are available to counselors. They can suggest content, explain the kind of service they offer, or respond to the feeling involved. They might respond in this fashion:

You find it hard to know where to begin. Many find it helpful to start by telling why they wanted to see a counselor. You're free to talk about anything you like. Many discuss the things that concern or bother them. Whatever

[2] Lawrence M. Brammer and Everett L. Shostrom. *Therapeutic Psychology*, 3rd ed. (Englewood Cliffs, N.J.: Prentice-Hall, 1977), pp. 194–197. Copyright 1968. Reprinted by permission of Prentice-Hall, Inc.

[3] H. V. Ingham and R. Lemore Love, *The Process of Psychotherapy* (New York: McGraw-Hill, 1954), pp. 79–81.

you say will be kept confidential, will be just between the two of us. Most people find that if they discuss those things that are of concern to them the counselor can help in clarifying their feelings and behavior so that they can understand themselves and others better or they can decide on a direction or plan of action. You might begin by telling why you wanted to see me.

The definitional process is important. Conveying the essence of the relationship without engaging in a miniature lecture is most essential. When the situation calls for structuring, counselors would do well to remember that there is no substitute for simplicity, modesty, and sensitivity in their definitions.

Degree of lead by counselor

Previously it was mentioned that the discovery and development of a counseling style is related to the personal characteristics of the counselor. Effective counseling requires understanding the counselee, understanding oneself, and understanding the process involved.

The exchanges between counselor and counselee represent behavioral interaction with both immediate and latent effects. The interaction, present and past, stimulates the counselee's choice of content—kind, quality, and sequence. The way counselors lead (their statements or responses as well as their actions and feelings) the counselee affects the direction of the interview. Each counselor lead has meaning for counselees and triggers response patterns for them. The counselee's responses, in turn, have reciprocal impact on the counselor.

The term *lead* means a teamlike working together in which the counselor's remarks seem to clients to state the next point they are ready to accept. *Lead* is used in this fashion to refer to communications made by the counselor. It should be recognized that *lead* can also refer to the extent to which the counselor is ahead of or behind the counselee's thinking and to how much the counselor directs or pushes the client into accepting the counselor's remarks.

Brammer and Shostrom cite three principles to guide the counselor's leads:

1. . . . *Lead only as much as the client can tolerate* at his present level of ability and understanding.

2. . . . *Vary the lead.*
3. . . . *Start the counseling process with little lead.*[4]

Buchheimer and Balogh[5] have classified counselor leads into categories of techniques. These leads, the techniques they reflect, what is communicated, and the role the counselor assumes in the communication are presented in Table 12.1.

Much can be learned of techniques and practices by close study of audio and video tapes of counseling sessions. The following remarks serve only to introduce readers to gross analysis of techniques presented in Table 12.1. It is hoped that they will be stimulated to try analyzing their own behaviors through role playing and tape critique methods. Such activities are highly valuable learning experiences because they enable individuals to make reasonable, informed judgments about the effects of their counseling behavior.

Below is a statement made by a counselee immediately after being seated in the counselor's office. The counselor had not met the student before. Different leads or counselor responses are given and classified.

Miss Jones told me to come down here and talk to you—I don't know why! She said I couldn't come back to class until I learned to stay awake. . . . I work at a filling station until one every night and I'm tired. Anyway, who could stay awake in there—she bores you to death.

Among the responses the counselor could make are the following:

You were bored, fell asleep, and Miss Jones asked you to leave. *(Restatement of content)*
What does she do that you find boring? *(Questioning)*
You feel put upon. *(Reflection of feeling)*
I bet that something can be worked out in this situation. *(Reassurance)*
Do you think that you might be disowning responsibility for what happened? *(Interpretation)*

These and other techniques will be briefly described.

[4] Brammer and Shostrom, *Therapeutic Psychology*, pp. 217–218.
[5] Arnold Buchheimer and Sara Carter Balogh, *The Counseling Relationship* (Chicago: Science Research Associates, 1961).

TABLE 12.1 **Degree of leading and kinds of leading**

Description of leads	Types of communication	Counselor role
Techniques designed to elicit feeling:		
Silence	Take your time; there's no rush.	Receiving
Restatement of manifest content or feeling	This is what you said . . . *or* You say you feel . . .	Accepting
Reflection of content	In other words, it's this way . . .	Understanding
Reflection of feeling	In other words, you feel . . .	Understanding
Reflection of core	In essence, you've said this . . .	Understanding
General leads	Tell me more about it.	Searching
Techniques designed to facilitate self-understanding:		
Summarization	So far, you've said this . . .	Understanding
Tentative analysis	You seem to mean . . .	Clarifying
Interpretation	What seems to be operating is . . .	Interpreting
Direct question	What do you mean? What have you done?	Investigating
General leads	Tell me more.	Searching, understanding
Reassurance	Things could be worse. You're not alone . . .	Explaining, supporting
Assurance	You can do this; the prognosis is good.	Predicting
Information giving	The facts are . . .	Explaining
Techniques designed to facilitate action:		
Encouragement	You will get along.	Predicting
Specific suggestion	You might do this . . .	Advising
Urging	You ought to do this . . .	Advising
Cajoling	Ah, come on . . .	Directing

SOURCE: *The Counseling Relationship: A Casebook* by Arnold Buchheimer and Sara Carter Balogh. Copyright © 1961 by Science Research Associates, Inc. Reprinted by permission of the publisher.

Restatement of content

Counselor leads that restate the content of the counselee's communications attempt to convey understanding either by simple repetition of or by rephrasing the communication. Usually little or no attempt is made to organize, clarify, or interpret it, and such a technique departs the least from the client's statement.

Questioning

Questioning is a common and often overused counseling technique. It indicates the counselor's intent to seek further information and asks the counselee to elaborate on a point. Ideally, questions used by counselors are open-ended and require more than a yes or no response; otherwise they get nowhere and only stifle discussion. However, in fact-finding interviews, questions posed by the interviewer should be straightforward, clear, and precise.

The overuse of questions in counseling runs the risk of causing counselees to conceptualize the situation as an inquisition in which they need only sit back and direct their thinking along the lines indicated by the questions. Questions rarely probe or respond to the counselee's basic feelings, most often they force attention on cognitive matters. One question leads to another and that leads to another.

Even more important, extensive questioning draws counselees into a passive position in which they wait for the counselor to solve their problems.

Perhaps more to the point, counselors who put their questions accusingly or suspiciously arouse fear and suspicion, not cooperation. Manner and tone of voice may be more important than the wording of the questions. Unnecessary probing to satisfy an interest in the esoteric is always unjustified. The counselor's safeguard in the use of questions is a true interest in understanding and aiding the individual. That interest can be conveyed in the counselor's manner and tone. Questioning is best used (1) to obtain specifically needed information and (2) to direct the client's conversation to more fruitful channels. In the latter instance it encourages the counselee to talk further in relevant areas where the going may be difficult, and leading questions that cannot be answered by a yes or no are preferred. They stimulate the individual to talk freely and avoid the danger of supplying ready-made answers.

Reflection of feeling

Rogers has defined *reflection of feeling* as an attempt "to understand from the client's point of view and to communicate that understanding."[6] Reflection of feeling, then, indicates the counselor's intent to show that he or she understands correctly what the client feels or is experiencing. Reflection techniques consist of verbalizing the core of the client's attitudes. Because it is nonthreatening when properly done, reflection of feeling enables counselees to think of their feelings as part of themselves rather than external to or apart from them. It may be used immediately after a feeling has been expressed, or a summary reflection may be used. In the latter instance, the counselor attempts to tie together in one statement several feelings expressed by the client.

Reflection techniques serve not only to surface client feelings and attitudes but also to bring problems into awareness without making clients feel that they are being pushed by the counselor. The intent is to mirror clients' attitudes so that they can be clarified and understood. Brammer and Shostrom have given counselors a note of caution about client feelings as well as an explanation.

A common misconception arising from an emphasis on feeling is that the expression and identification of feelings have in themselves some intrinsic merit. The conclusion often drawn is that feelings are more important than intellectualizations. Expression of feelings is encouraged by the reflection technique. Its effectiveness, however, seems to reside in the idea that the expression of feeling is a means to self-confrontation and not an end in counseling.

Feelings are thought by the client to be subjective and not to be trusted. They tell him of danger when there is no danger, of presence of symptoms when he is tired and discouraged. The expression of feeling, therefore, is to make possible the discovery of the idea which underlies or is attached to the feelings. The client should be taught to *trust* the expression of his feelings.[7]

Most counselors find it hard to acquire and implement techniques that reflect feelings. Too often the reflection is simply the content or intellectual component of the counselee's expression rather than underlying attitudes or feelings. Perhaps skill in the use of reflection techniques comes from a combination of intuition and experience in paying attention to the feeling tone of what is being expressed. Our experience in supervising counselors in counseling practicum and internship activities indicates that they are more adept in responding to counselees who express negative feelings toward parents, teachers, or rivals than in helping to bring to conscious expression hostile feelings toward themselves or the counselor. In the latter situations, counselors are inclined to rise to the defense of the counselee because of sympathy or react defensively because their ability as a counselor is challenged.

Brammer and Shostrom cite seven errors or difficulties in the use of reflection techniques.[8] They are paraphrased here.

1. A common error is made in reflection when the counselor uses a stereotyped introductory phrase, such as "You feel . . ."
2. If many feelings are expressed, counselors sometimes err by waiting for the client to stop talking before they reflect rather than interrupting to focus on significant feelings that might be overlooked.

[6] Carl R. Rogers, *Client-Centered Therapy* (Boston: Houghton Mifflin Company, 1951), p. 452.

[7] Brammer and Shostrom, *Therapeutic Psychology*, p. 183.
[8] Ibid., pp. 185–189.

3. The counselor's choice of feelings to be reflected, selected from among a variety of feelings presented by the client, may be inaccurate or not properly worked through.
4. Reflecting content in the same words rather than getting below its surface is a common error.
5. Reflecting feelings either too shallowly or too deeply causes difficulty for the client.
6. Adding to or taking away from the meaning of the client's statement is another error.
7. Finally, error occurs when the counselor uses inappropriate terminology or language that is overinterpretative or pedantic.

Brammer and Shostrom have also identified and elaborated on the reasons why reflective techniques are effective in achieving the goals of counseling. Here the reasons are given, and the reader is urged to examine the commentary on them.

1. Reflection helps the individual to feel *deeply understood.*
2. The reflection technique helps to break the so-called neurotic cycle, often manifested in marital counseling and expressed by such phrases as, "She won't understand me and therefore I won't understand her."
3. Reflection impresses clients with the inference that *feelings are causes of behavior.*
4. Reflection causes the *locus of evaluation* to be in the client.
5. Proper reflection gives . . . the feeling that [the client] . . . has the *power of choice.*
6. Reflection *clarifies the client's thinking* so that . . . the situation [can be seen] more objectively.
7. . . . It helps communicate to the client the idea that *the counselor does not regard him* [or her] *as unique and different.* (The counselor is not shocked.)
8. Reflection helps clients to *examine their deep motives.*[9]

The point has been made that reflective techniques depend on an alert counselor, responsive to feelings and attitudes recognized in the client's verbal expression. Recognizing and verbalizing attitudes implied but not yet expressed by the counselee can either be constructive and speed the course of counseling or create a threat for the

counselee and lead to harmful resistance and resentment. Finally, it is not enough for counselors simply and correctly to identify and understand the counselee's feelings. They must convey their understanding to clients so that it is sensed by them. It is equally important for counselors to recognize that pretending to understand when they do not is dangerous because it leads eventually to confusion and distrust. Although it is probably impossible for counselors to understand completely the attitudes and feelings contained in the counselee's statements, if they are unsure or uncertain they can ask for clarification by saying, "I'm not quite sure what you mean, but as I understand it the essence of what you feel is. . . ."

Reassurance

Reassurance goes beyond acceptance and serves as a reward or reinforcing agent. It often is used to support counselee exploration or ideas and feelings or the testing out of different behaviors. It may be helpful in reducing anxiety generated within the counseling relationship or in controlling it outside the relationship. As an example of the latter instance the counselor might reassure the counselee who has expressed anxiety about responding in class as follows: "Because you really know the material that is being discussed tomorrow, you can talk about the westward expansion."

Reassurance may be expressed directly by the counselor. For example, the counselee enters and says, "Late again" and the counselor responds, "That's all right." It should be noted that in this instance reassurance may have been used unwisely because the counselee may have a hard time going beyond the impasse created by the counselor's remark. Reassurance may be given through predicting outcomes such as the backwash effects of discussing problems with the counselor.

Some counselors take the categorical position that reassurance techniques should never be used and are inappropriate in counseling because they show disrespect for the counselee. Client appeals for support from the counselor are best met with reflective responses. Thorne, on the other hand, believes that reassurance techniques, though admittedly palliative, are warranted.[10] He has described eight types of reassurance, paraphrased here.

[9] Ibid., pp. 189–191.

[10] Frederick C. Thorne, *Principles of Personality Counseling* (Brandon, Vt.: Journal of Clinical Counseling, 1950), pp. 201–202.

1. The counselor may reassure clients that their disorder is very common.
2. Reassurance may be given that the disorder has a known cause and something can presumably be done about it.
3. Reassurance may be given that symptoms are annoying but not dangerous.
4. Reassurance may be given that specific methods of treatment are available.
5. Reassurance may be given that cure is possible.
6. The counselor may need to reassure clients that their condition will not lead to insanity.
7. Reassurance may be given that relapses are sometimes inevitable but do not mean that the client is getting worse.
8. Clients may need reassurance that their disorder is not a result of sinful action.

Reassurance techniques can be misused. An easy error is to offer false reassurance. Such remarks as "I know you'll get a scholarship" and "Everything will be all right" are far from reassuring and usually cause the counselee to doubt the counselor's understanding of the situation and ability to help. To tell individuals who are describing how bad things are for them that others have the same problem or that their problems are not unusual gives the impression that the counselor is unsympathetic or, worse, minimizes the counselee's problems. To dismiss as unimportant a counselee's complaints that represent responses to inner conflict may be viewed as the counselor's failure to grasp what is at stake. The outcome is frustration, lack of confidence in the counselor, and premature termination.

Finally, the counselor's use of reassurance must be attuned to the counselee's level of development and emotional maturity. Clients may need to know that the counselor is committed to help them through the experiences that are encountered in counseling. Understandably, they may need reassurance and encouragement to discuss their feelings and attitudes rationally to come to grips with them.

Interpretation

Interpretation in counseling involves two types of data: *external* or test results and *interpersonal* data obtained through counseling communication. Test interpretation will be discussed in the next chapter. Here the concern is with interpretation of counselee remarks.

Interpretative techniques are those that identify and conceptualize patterns of relationships and explain meanings behind client statements. For some, interpretation is the sine qua non of achieving counseling goals; through it individuals become cognizant of their underlying feelings and/or attitudes and achieve integration of feeling and action. The counselor who uses interpretation infers a relationship or a meaning from what has been said or done by the counselee. Causation is generally implied or indicated in interpretative techniques.

As counselees reveal more and more of themselves, the counselor's insight deepens so that he or she can suggest motives, purposes, relationships, or patterns of reactions that are evident from what has been stated. In making interpretations the counselor gambles that the inference is accurate and will be accepted by the counselee. If the interpretation is unacceptable to counselees (goes beyond what they are willing to face at the time), anxiety may be created. Counselors can gauge their use of interpretation by how well they know the counselee and by the counselee's reactions. If the counselee is permitted to accept, modify, or reject the interpretation, the technique may speed client insight and cause little difficulty. Bordin believes, however, that the client's acceptance or rejection of an interpretative remark is a fallacious criterion.

In some cases, the too ready acceptance of an interpretation may mean that the client has succeeded in momentarily achieving an objective view of himself by divorcing this view from the affect with which it is usually associated. Momentarily, he is being rational. However, he has not learned to utilize these resources of rationality on occasions when he experiences the affect. On the contrary, when he is in the affective stage he will revert to anxiety and to the associated need to defend himself against impulse expression.[11]

Bordin suggests two principles for the counselor's use of interpretation. First, whether accepted or rejected, the interpretation will be ineffectual for counselees who are conflicted and who strive to keep affect from awareness and expression. Second, the amount of emphasis on the cognitive aspects of the counselor-counselee interactions should

[11] Edward S. Bordin, *Psychological Counseling*, 2nd ed. (New York: Appleton-Century-Crofts, 1968), p. 171.

be related to the intensity of affect expressed by the client. Further, the more intense the affect, the more cognitive the interpretation can be without causing the client to revert to cognitive processes as a means of repression.[12]

Although interpretative techniques are used by many counselors, client-centered counselors do not favor them because the locus of responsibility is on the counselor. The use of interpretation, moreover, represents an attempt to change individual attitudes by the intellectual means of explaining the causes of behavior. Rogers in an early book cited some admonitions about the use of interpretation that are still germane: (1) interpretation should be avoided if counselors feel unsure of themselves; (2) it is best to use the client's terms and symbols in interpretation; (3) interpretation best deals with attitudes already expressed; (4) nothing will be gained by arguing about the correctness of an interpretation; (5) if genuine insight has been gained, the client will see spontaneously its application in new areas; and (6) after the client has achieved a new insight, temporary relapse may occur.[13]

Some time ago, Colby classified interpretations, by content and technique, into three types. *Clarifications* were statements designed to crystallize the thoughts and feelings of clients around a particular subject or to focus their attention on something requiring further thought. *Comparisons* were interpretations in which the counselor placed two or more sets of events, thoughts, or feelings side by side for comparison—present and past behavior, childhood and adulthood, fantasy and reality, and so on. Patterns of repetitive similarities and recurring contradictions may be compared. *Wish-defense* interpretations were those pointing directly to the wish-defense components of neurotic conflict.[14]

According to Kelly, the material of interpretation is the personal construct—an anticipatory concept or predictive idea—utilized by the individual in coping with life experiences. In interpretation, then, life events are compared and contrasted with the individual's constructs. Kelly's five steps utilized in interpretation are paraphrased here.

1. Clients make generalizations about themselves that they use as constructs to predict their behavioral events. The counselor, in turn, uses six basic questions to obtain comprehension of the construct or complaint: (a) what is the difficulty? (b) when was it first noticed? (c) under what conditions was it first noticed? (d) what has been done about it? (e) what changes have come with treatment or the passing of time? (f) under what conditions is it most noticeable?
2. The counselor relates the responses to these questions to ascertain the similarities and contrasts.
3. The counselor, in *construct elaboration*, focuses on constructs that relate to the events in the counselee's life. These constructs are likely to be dichotomous black-and-white evaluations about life since behavior expresses affirmation and denial.
4. There is *interpretative extension*, or the application of ideas or constructs to new events.
5. Finally, *validation* occurs, or constructs are tested by using them as wagers on the future.

This is an overly simplified presentation of Kelly's system of interpretation, which he has elaborated and illustrated in a two-volume work.[15]

Interpretation may be employed early in the counseling process in respect to the counselee attitudes toward counseling. Usually it is general and tentative and serves only to open up and explain the process. A client who is afraid to talk may be encouraged by a query like "You are not quite sure that I understand?" or by an interpretative question such as "You're afraid that I will blame you as your father always does?" The latter, of course, would be appropriate only if the counselee had previously been able to express feelings of rejection fairly freely.

Timing is most important. Interpretations should not be blindly made; rather, caution should be exercised until the counselor is sure that the client is ready to accept them. Clients can profit from counselor insight only if it also becomes *their* insight. They arrive at their conclusions at their own pace. To be told that they feel anxiety or are expressing rejection or fear will not help them until they themselves recognize the existence of these feelings and voluntarily acknowledge their presence. Thus interpretations are not to be proffered until the counselor understands the counselee—possesses knowledge of his or her anxiety and readiness to consider and work through threatening material.

[12] Ibid., p. 171.

[13] Carl R. Rogers, *Counseling and Psychotherapy* (Boston: Houghton Mifflin Company, 1942), pp. 205–206.

[14] K. M. Colby, *A Primer for Psychotherapists* (New York: Ronald Press, 1951), pp. 83–84.

[15] G. A. Kelly, *The Psychology of Personal Constructs*, Vols. I and II (New York: W. W. Norton & Co., 1955).

Brammer and Shostrom have discussed some guidelines for making interpretations. They are paraphrased here.

1. There should be sufficient evidence for the interpretation.
2. The depth of the interpretation should be appropriate.
3. Whenever possible, the manifest behavior of the interpreted tendency should be specified.
4. The intensity of the interpreted tendency should be estimated.
5. The interpreted tendency should be given a hierarchic position in the total personality picture.
6. The adaptive and pathological aspects of the interpreted tendency should be distinguished.[16]

Interpretations are phrased *tentatively* by the counselor rather than asserted dogmatically. Questions are a common format: "Do you think, then, that you could become an engineer when your interest patterns tend to be markedly dissimilar?" Again, it is emphasized that reactions from the counselee will enable the counselor to gauge any use of interpretations. Techniques of interpretation may be employed throughout the course of the relationship starting with mild interpretations of the counselee's attitudes toward counseling, progressively being used during the middle phases of counseling (after counselor has attained good understanding of counselee), and diminishing and becoming more general toward the closing phases of the process.

Facilitating techniques

Acceptance

Acceptance is an attitude crucial to the counseling process. Most counselors strive through certain mechanisms to communicate their acceptance of the counselee. Communicating acceptance involves the verbal and nonverbal counselor behaviors that tell counselees they are being understood and received. Such behaviors stimulate further discussion and elaboration by counselees, enabling them to continue talking about their perceptions without threat. Verbal responses by the counselor include "Mm-hm," "Yes," "I understand," "I see," and the like. Reflection of at-

[16] Brammer and Shostrom, *Therapeutic Psychology*, pp. 260–270.

titudes and feelings and restatement of the counselee's remarks are frequently used.

The degree to which counselors' techniques will effectively communicate acceptance depends on their tone of voice and their facial expressions and movements (nodding of head, and so on) as well as their posture and distance from the counselee (such as leaning toward clients and whether they sit relatively close to them). All of these elements and others provide cues that the counselee discerns and interprets. Techniques to communicate acceptance are used extensively in the beginning phase of counseling as well as later when clients delve deeply and painfully into their situations.

Clarification

Clarifying techniques are related somewhat to those of reflection and interpretation. *Clarification* is a statement by the counselor that seeks to place the counselee's feeling or attitude in a clearer or more recognizable form for the benefit of both participants. Compared to reflection, clarification goes slightly beyond what the counselee expresses verbally in such a way that the meanings can be more plainly understood and used. But there is no direct effort at interpretation of counselee feelings or implicit references to the cause of the problem.

An example of clarification applied to the counselee's statement presented on page 273 might be "You feel annoyed and angry in this situation."

General leads

General leads are used to encourage clients to continue talking or to elaborate on a point they are discussing. They include such remarks as "Tell me more," "Would you explain that further?" and the like.

Encouragement

Techniques that encourage or give support to the counselee are sometimes used. Related to reassurance, encouragement is designed to counter feelings of inadequacy or to prompt action. It may build on the individual's ego strength. Examples of encouragement are "That's fine," "You can do that," "You are OK," "You will get along," and so on.

Dinkmeyer points out that encouragement, a critical ingredient in the counseling process, is present either explicitly or implicitly in most major counseling approaches. As Dinkmeyer uses the term, encouragement consists of procedures that enable clients to experience and become aware of their own worth. It does not mean that bribes or undue praise or reward are lavished on the client. Rather, encouragement means that the counselor provides positive, honest feedback to clients about their attitudes, assets, goals, directions, changed behaviors, risk taking, and so on.[17]

Information giving

Counselors are often required to give information during the counseling process. Some would argue that counseling has stopped when information is provided by the counselor. But information giving need not involve persuasion or advice. It can mean, for example, clarification of high school courses needed for admission to a particular college, what is assessed by certain tests, and the like.

Advice giving

Counselors serve a wide population. Because counselors are there, some clients come to seek advice, to obtain suggestions, or to get help in formulating rather concrete plans of action. When they ask for advice they *may* expect it to be proffered. Counselors have the problem of deciding how far direction of this type is to be carried. If, in their judgment, the individual is free enough of conflict to be able to accept advice, and the counselor has some to offer, it may be worthwhile to give. In many instances, however, advice is futile because counselees are unable either to accept or to act on it unless it happens to confirm their own opinion.

It is also to be noted that clients frequently ask advice when they neither want nor need it. The array of advice givers—parents, teachers, neighbors, friends—available to

[17] Don C. Dinkmeyer, "Use of the Encouragement Process in Adlerian Counseling," *Personnel and Guidance Journal*, 51 (November 1972), 177–181.

them is great indeed. What they often seek through the socially accepted guise of asking advice is help in freeing themselves from confusion and uncertainty. They are looking for additional insight into their problem and help in utilizing their personal resources to come to a decision. Perhaps it is equally true that any rigid refusal to make suggestions may be interpreted by counselees as unwillingness to help or be interested in them.

Without doubt, some counselees will ask, "What do you think I should do?" In most instances the counter response "What have you thought about?" will reveal several resourceful ideas and plans.

Silence

Silence is difficult to master as a technique for many counselors, and especially for those who have been teachers. They often believe that client silence is synonymous with counselor failure and become uncomfortable when it occurs. Because silence in social situations tends to be looked on as rejection, defiance, or disapproval, this meaning from a different context is quite often transferred to the counseling relationship. When pauses occur, the counselor may be overcome with the desire to break the silence rather than tolerate it.

Overextended or greatly prolonged silence by counselors sometimes appears to be almost sadistic if they refuse to speak merely because they demand the initiation of all expressions from the counselee. The client who becomes embarrassed and appears physically uncomfortable may need and appreciate assistance from the counselor to begin again. Neutral leads or expressions recognizing the client's discomfort can be very useful at such times by stimulating additional interchanges or promoting discussion of the client's embarrassment.

Pauses vary from a few seconds to several minutes. The significance of any counseling pause is dependent on when it takes place and by whom it was initiated. Here are some of the times that silence occurs as well as possible reasons why and by whom it may be broken:

1. During initial contacts clients may become afraid of the impression they have given the counselor or what they think the counselor thinks of them and become silent. Ap-

propriate rapport-building techniques may be used by the counselor in this case.

2. A pause may come because counselees are thinking over what they have just expressed. Interruption by the counselor at this point is inadvisable.

3. Silence may come because either counselor or counselee or both have reached the end of an idea or line of thought and do not know what to say next. Often, but not always, the counselor breaks such a silence.

4. An extended contemplative pause may occur just after initial remarks and during the time in which the two individuals are settling down to the business at hand. The counselor may interrupt by saying, "It's rather hard to get under way today."

5. A pause may mean that counselees are experiencing painful emotions that they are unable to express, yet desperately yearn to share with the counselor. Recognizing this, the counselor could appropriately say, "Feelings are sometimes difficult to put into words, but perhaps expressing them is more important than the exact words."

6. Silence may come because clients are cautious about the process or have a preconceived notion that their responsibility is merely to reply to questions posed by the counselor. It may mean that clients are shy and that they conceptualize silence as rejection of them. Such silence may best be interrupted by the counselor to structure or define the process with a statement like "You don't feel much like talking," "What has brought this silence about?" or "What are you thinking about?"

7. A pause sometimes occurs because the counselee wants some assurance, support, or confirmation from the counselor.

8. Finally, silence may fall just after heavily emotionally laden expression by the counselee. The counselor's quiet acceptance of this pause is, of course, appropriate.

There is no one criterion for gauging whether the counselor should remain silent or interrupt the pause. Operationally, most counselors tend to remain silent when the pause was initiated by the counselee, but sensitivity to silence and judgment about interruption come with experience. Some years ago, Tindall and Robinson classified *counselor* pauses into three types. The first was *deliberate* or one used for emphasis. The second was *organizational*, used to effect transitions. The third was natural *termination*, used

to close counseling. They reported that organizational pauses usually helped to clarify the subject discussed and paved the way for information to be given to the counselee. Counselees, however, generally responded only after deliberate or natural terminal pauses.[18]

As a technique, silence may be productively employed to place responsibility on counselees to face and talk about their problems. It may also be used to slow the pace of the interview if counselee or counselor is moving too fast or pushing too hard. Following a flood of emotional expression, silence often enables the individual to gain insight or achieve integration of feeling. In this respect its value is that it leads to penetration of feelings and understanding of actions. Finally, silence may give less articulate people a feeling of worth and help them to accept themselves for what they are.

The amount of talk is occasionally used as a measure of counseling effectiveness. It is sometimes postulated that the greater the proportion of verbal exchanges engaged in by the counselee, the better the working relationship. Clients who feel responsible for the interview tend to talk more.

Action methods

Carkhuff and his associates[19] have conceptualized helping as consisting of two phases. The first could be termed a *downward* or inward phase during which the client is encouraged to explore and experience various previously denied aspects of self. The second is an *emergent directionality* phase during which the client, given increased levels of self-understanding, begins to translate this understanding into constructive action. Counselors nurture the first phase by offering clients high levels of facilitative conditions (empathy, respect, concreteness) best described as *responsive* methods or conditions. The second phase, emergent

[18] R. H. Tindall and Francis P. Robinson, "The Use of Silence as a Technique in Counseling," *Journal of Clinical Psychology*, 3 (April 1947), 136–141.

[19] See Robert R. Carkhuff and Bernard B. Berenson, *Beyond Counseling and Therapy* (New York: Holt, Rinehart and Winston, 1967); Robert R. Carkhuff, *The Development of Human Resources* (New York: Holt, Rinehart and Winston, 1971); Robert R. Carkhuff, *The Art of Helping*, 3rd ed. (Amherst, Mass.: Human Resource Development Press, 1976).

directionality, is nurtured by *initiative* or *action* conditions or methods and include counselor *genuineness, confrontation,* and *immediacy.*

The three components of the first phase are counselor responses to the client's experiencing within the relationship, whereas the three components of the second phase have been classified as action oriented because they are initiated by the counselor. Empathy, respect, concreteness and genuineness have been described and discussed in Chapter 11. Here, treatment has been given to confrontation and immediacy followed by some other action-oriented methods.

Confrontation

Confrontation is designed to give clients a point of view different from their own so that they can see themselves and their behaviors as others view them. It is useful when clients do not know that their behavior is inappropriate or are unaware of its consequences. The counselor's management of confrontation is not easy. Rude, unmannerly confrontations, especially when clients have not been prepared for such, may degenerate into insults that arouse hostility, defensiveness, or resistance to change.

Carkhuff[20] defines confrontation as "telling it like it is," by pointing out the discrepancies between what clients say and do, how they say they are and how they look, or by calling attention to the fact that the reality of a given situation is different from the way clients present it. Confrontations can range from mild or tentative (open-ended inquiries into discrepancies) to direct counselor statements. Carkhuff points out that confrontation is often viewed as "tearing down" or destructive, but that confrontations can be used to reveal assets as well as deficits, strengths as well as weaknesses. The purpose of using confrontation is to tear down defenses, whether they be defenses against strengths or against weaknesses.

Carkhuff's scale for measuring confrontation has the following five levels (levels 1 and 2 are the same):

1. The verbal and behavioral expressions of the helper disregard the discrepancies in the helpee's behavior (ideal versus real self, insight versus action, helper versus helpee's experiences).

[20] Carkhuff, *The Art of Helping*, pp. 112–123.

2. The verbal and behavioral expressions of the helper disregard the discrepancies in the helpee's behavior.
3. The verbal and behavioral expressions of the helper, while open to discrepancies in the helpee's behavior, do not relate directly and specifically to these discrepancies.
4. The verbal and behavioral expressions of the helper attend directly and specifically to the discrepancies in the helpee's behavior.
5. The verbal and behavioral expressions of the helper are keenly and continually attuned to the discrepancies in the helpee's behavior.[21]

Immediacy

Carkhuff uses the term *immediacy* to refer to the counselor's ability to communicate the different feelings and experiences going on, at the moment, between the counselor and client.[22] Often, clients are unable to understand or discuss openly their relationship with the counselor. This focus on the *here and now* transactions and relationships between counselor and client is useful, according to Carkhuff, because clients, though talking about third parties or situations, are invariably making statements about the counseling situation or the counselor. For example, a client who describes the trouble experienced in taking an examination may be saying something about the here and now feelings of frustration being experienced in the situation with the counselor. In effect, immediacy means that counselors tell the client what is going on so that clients can understand themselves.

The five-level scale designed to measure immediacy represents Carkhuff's revisions of scales presented originally by the Mitchells[23] with modifications by Leitner and Berenson.[24]

[21] Robert R. Carkhuff, *Helping and Human Relations*, Vol. I: *Selection and Training* (New York: Holt, Rinehart and Winston, 1969), pp. 189–190.
[22] Carkhuff, *The Art of Helping*, pp. 130–134.
[23] R. Mitchell and K. M. Mitchell, "The Therapist Immediate Relationship Scale" (Unpublished research scale, Michigan State University, 1966).
[24] L. Leitner and B. G. Berenson, "Immediate Relationship Scale: A Revision" (Unpublished research scale, State University of New York at Buffalo, 1967).

Level 1—The verbal and behavioral expressions of the helper disregard the content and effect of the helpee's expressions that have the potential for relating to the helper.

Level 2—The verbal and behavioral expressions of the helper disregard most of the helpee expressions that have the potential for relating to the helper.

Level 3—The verbal and behavioral expressions of the helper, while open to interpretations of immediacy, do not relate what the helpee is saying to what is going on between the helper and helpee in the immediate moment.

Level 4—The verbal and behavioral expressions of the helper appear cautiously to relate to the expressions directly to the helper—helpee relationship.

Level 5—The verbal and behavioral expressions of the helper relate the helpee's expressions directly to the helper—helpee relationship.[25]

Homework

A technique common to many theories of counseling is the use of homework. Between counseling sessions, clients are asked to try out certain behaviors, to set down their ideas or feelings in certain situations, to practice certain responses, to read certain materials, and so on. These self-directed assignments extend counseling outside the counselor's office and serve to reduce or alleviate dependency feelings placed on the counselor.

Homework assignments should be chosen carefully. They should be designed so that they can be completed successfully and the client understands their purpose. Homework activities sometimes are used to give clients an opportunity to evaluate their progress in practicing new skills or behaviors in real-life situations.

The homework assignment is viewed by Ellis[26] as a prerequisite in rational-emotive therapy, whether treating an individual or a group, and is used to combat irrational beliefs through higher level cognition. He has suggested that homework is the missing "vector" in other therapies. A homework report form used by the Institute for Advance Study in Rational Psychotherapy has been presented here in Figure 12.1. It brings the A-B-C-D comprehensive procedure to bear on undesirable emotional feelings, actions, or habits associated with irrational ideas.

Behavioral modification techniques

Techniques based on behavioral modification principles have forged to the front in the recent literature, convention presentations, and the discussions of counseling practitioners. Krumboltz and Thoresen[27] point out that behavioral counselors employ a variety of techniques; each is used for specific reasons. They urge counselors to experiment continuously and to evaluate systematically their techniques, procedures, and practices. In this way, counselors can determine what works best under what conditions with specific clients.

It may be remembered (see Chapter 8) that goal setting (a mutual undertaking by counselor and counselee) is highly stressed by behavioral counselors. Establishing the goals of counseling depends on identifying target behaviors to be changed. This, in turn, leads to selection of techniques appropriate to changing these behaviors. Another important element in behavioral counseling is the monitoring of changes that occur as a function of the technique or techniques employed. Finally, the outcome of the monitoring procedure is either a modification of counseling techniques or the re-evaluation of the goals.

The following brief description of behavioral counseling techniques draws heavily on those identified and discussed more fully in two books by Krumboltz and Thoresen.[28]

---

[25] Robert R. Carkhuff, *Helping and Human Relations*, Vol. I, pp. 192–193.

[26] Albert Ellis and Russell Grieger, *Handbook of Rational-Emotive Therapy.* (New York: Springer Publishing Company, 1977), p. 424.

[27] John D. Krumboltz and Carl Thoresen, eds., *Behavioral Counseling: Cases and Techniques* (New York: Holt, Rinehart and Winston, 1969), p. 3.

[28] John D. Krumboltz and Carl Thoresen, eds., *Behavioral Counseling: Cases and Techniques* (New York: Holt, Rinehart and Winston, 1969) and John D. Krumboltz and Carl Thoresen, eds., *Counseling Methods* (New York: Holt, Rinehart and Winston, 1976).

FIGURE 12.1 **Sample rational self-help form**

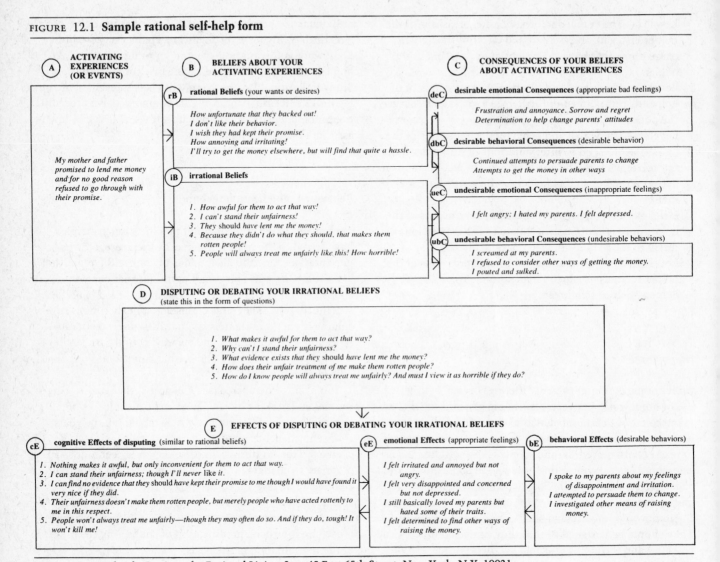

SOURCE: © 1976 by the Institute for Rational Living, Inc., 45 East 65th Street, New York, N.Y. 10021

Reinforcement techniques

The practices employed by behavioral counselors are based on the principle that behavior is a function of its consequences. Basically, these techniques seek to strengthen certain counselee behaviors by positive or negative reinforcement schedules. The stimuli used by counselors to reinforce behavior are many and varied but verbal expressions predominate. Additionally, token or trinkets or some type of a currency system are often used as reinforcers. Tokens (money, chips, tickets, and the like) are presented to subjects as they perform the desired behavior and can be exchanged for whatever reinforcers (candy, privileges, films, trips) they choose or are able to afford.

Krumboltz and Thoresen point out that *timing* is a key element in programming reinforcement consequences for desirable behaviors and in eliminating punishing or the reinforcement for undesirable behaviors. "The reinforcer must be presented immediately following the desired behavior and it must not be presented immediately following undesirable behavior."[29] Another essential factor is the *nature* of the reinforcer. Daley[30] describes a way to gain control over managing contingencies by developing a "menu" of activities based on the Premack[31] Principle (for any pair of responses, the preferred one will reinforce that less preferred one). The menu consists of behaviors that subjects like (eat, jump, telephone, color, and so on). Before engaging in the task to be learned, subjects are presented with the menu and allowed to select an event from it which for them at that moment is a highly preferred event. When they have completed the task to be learned, they are allowed to engage in the selected behavior.

SHAPING Consequences are arranged to develop desirable behavior, such as getting to class on time. The counselor may first reinforce responses that have little resemblance to the desired behavior pattern, but then arranges consequences for responses that are progressively more like the desired behavior. Finally, only the desired behavior is reinforced until it attains suitable strength. An example of shaping techniques is the case presented by Wanda K. Castle[32] in Krumboltz and Thoresen.

FADING Consequences are arranged to change clients' discriminations of the conditions that control their behavior. The counselee develops appropriate discriminations because those stimulus conditions in which the behavior is already highly probable are reinforced. Gradually, the desired behaviors are introduced in these stimulus conditions and come under the counselee's control. An example of fading techniques is the case described by David A. Shier[33] in Krumboltz and Thoresen.

ROLE PLAYING AND REINFORCEMENT Role-playing techniques are sometimes used to enable clients to practice behaviors they want to learn. The client rehearses new behavior, such as to speak out in a classroom situation, with the counselor, who reinforces or encourages the client's attempts and suggests ways the client can improve performances.

BEHAVIOR CONTRACTS Counselors sometimes formulate and draft a contract or written agreement that specifies what the client and counselor or another person will do for a given period of time. The contract, in effect, makes explicit the type of behavior to be performed and its rewards and/or punishments.

Social modeling techniques

Techniques designed to establish new behaviors in clients with behavioral deficits are often based on imitation and observation, or social modeling. Although much remains unknown about social modeling procedures (which clients does it help, with what problems, with which modes of presentation, and so on), Krumboltz and Thoresen state that the social models selected should be prestigious, competent, knowledgeable, attractive, and powerful. Moreover, clients may be more influenced when the social model is similar to them in some characteristics.[34]

LIVE MODELS Live modeling techniques (often referred to as *in vivo* training) have not been extensively used in any systematic manner by counseling practitioners. Little doubt exists that counselors themselves, as well as parents and teachers, serve as models to children and adolescents. Live models have been used to illustrate certain behaviors, particularly those involving complex interpersonal situations such as interviewing for a job, engaging in a social conversation, interacting with a parent or an adult. The best live models are probably one's peers. The major limitations in using live models are (1) controlling the model's behavior so as to demonstrate the desired behavior, and (2) having them physically available precisely when needed.

FILMED MODELS Because of the disadvantages of using live models, the behavior to be imitated has often been

[29] Krumboltz and Thoresen, *Behavioral Counseling*, p. 29.
[30] Marvin F. Daley, "The 'Reinforcement Menu': Finding Effective Reinforcers," in Krumboltz and Thoresen, *Behavioral Counseling*, pp. 42–45.
[31] D. Premack, "Reinforcement Theory" in *Nebraska Symposium on Motivation*, ed. David Levine (Lincoln, Nebraska: University of Nebraska Press, 1965), pp. 128–188.
[32] See Krumboltz and Thoresen, *Behavioral Counseling*, pp. 33–36.
[33] Ibid. pp. 114–123.
[34] Ibid., p. 164.

reproduced on films. Filmed models (examples include how to participate in class discussions, engaging in career exploration) provide the observer-learner with many important auditory and visual cues needed in learning the desired behavior. The advantages of filmed models are that they can be used again and again and have flexibility and utility.

AUDIO TAPE—RECORDED MODELS   Clients can learn new behaviors by listening to others describe how they behave in certain situations, such as selecting a college, exploring occupations, and the like.

SELF-MODELING   Though this technique is probably the least developed or clearly described, it holds much promise for counselors. In self-modeling, clients themselves enact the behavior that they wish to perpetuate. It is recorded either on audio or video tape for playback. Clients are then presented with a desirable form of their own behavior that can serve as a model. An example of this has been described by Ray Hosford[35] who worked with a young boy who stuttered. After audio-taping each interview, Hosford edited out all stuttering, leaving a stutter-free record of the interview. This was played back to the client and, after ten sessions, the client's stuttering within the interview had decreased to a small fraction of its original frequency.

Counter-conditioning techniques

Clients who cope with anxiety, fears, phobias, defensiveness, and other maladaptive behaviors have been helped by counter-conditioning techniques. Such techniques introduce responses that counteract, are incompatible with, or are antagonistic to fears or anxiety. The counter-conditioner, because it is stronger, suppresses and replaces the old response.

SYSTEMATIC DESENSITIZATION   In this technique, the counselor suggests situations that are potentially anxiety producing to a relaxed client. The client is able to imagine the situations without becoming anxious. A more complete de-

scription of this technique is found in Chapter Eight, page 187.

RELAXATION   Methods to relax clients are usually based on Jacobson's progressive relaxation training.[36] The client is instructed by the counselor to relax by successively tensing and releasing gross muscle groups throughout the body. Other relaxation techniques include hypnoses and respiratory inhalations (clients are shown how to empty their lungs and then inhale a gas mixture consisting of 65 percent carbon dioxide and 35 percent oxygen).

SELF-CONTROL   Several self-control techniques have been formulated and tried out to modify the behavioral problems of children and adults. For example, Schneider and Robin[37] describe their use of the "turtle technique" to help children gain self-control over impulsive behaviors. Essentially, the technique consists of (1) practicing the turtle response (pulling arms in close to body and putting head down so that the chin rests on the chest), (2) mastering being able to relax in that position, (3) giving daily ten- to fifteen-minute instruction sessions on social problem solving, and (4) developing peer support for those who are "doing turtle." Thoresen and Mahoney cite the advantages of self-control practices as being that clients are more apt to maintain the new behaviors, assume control of their own lives and become more self-sufficient in solving their future problems.[38]

Kahn[39] describes the application of self-control techniques to a variety of overt and covert behaviors exhibited in both the clinic and the natural environment. The four basic components of any self-management paradigm, according to Kahn, are self-monitoring, self-measurement, self-mediation and self-maintenance. His matrix, presented here as Table 12.2, illustrates the various components and their application to four situations.

[35] Authors' personal communication with Ray Hosford, March 1972.

[36] E. Jacobson, *Progressive Relaxation* (Chicago: University of Chicago Press, 1938).

[37] Marlene Schneider and Arthur Robin, "The Turtle Techniques: A Method for the Self-Control of Impulsive Behavior," in Krumboltz and Thoresen, *Counseling Methods*, pp. 157–163.

[38] Carl E. Thoresen and M. J. Mahoney, *Behavioral Self-Control* (New York: Holt, Rinehart and Winston, 1974).

[39] Wallace J. Kahn, "Self-Management: Learning to Be Our Own Counselor," *Personnel and Guidance Journal*, 55 (December 1976), 176–180.

TABLE 12.2 **The four M's of self-management**

Self-management component	Behaviors of real concern (BORC)			
	Cigarette smoking (excess)	Obesity (excess)	Assertiveness (deficit)	Depression (deficit)
1. Self-monitoring	Excessive coughing, cigarette breath, high cost, comments by others	Clothes too small, high food costs, frequent eating	Can't say no, never get your way, maintain covert hostility	No hobbies, seldom laugh, few friends, no positive self-references
2. Self-measurement	Count average 40 cigarettes smoked per day over 2 weeks	Caloric intake average 4,000 per day over 2 weeks	Said "Yes" on average of 4 times per day when preference was "No"	Count average of 1 positive self-reference per day for 3 weeks
3. Self-mediation	Decrease cigarettes by 5 per day with loss of $5 for each day over goal	Decrease calories by 200 per day, to goal of 2,000 per day. Control "what, when and where" of eating	Increase expressed personal preference by 1 per day and reinforce with natural consequence	Keep personal log of daily accomplishments and review 3 times daily
4. Self-maintenance	When down to 10 cigarettes per day decrease by 2 per day. Money gained used for new skis when hit goal of 0 per day for 7 days	Add exercise component to program, only eat in kitchen, buy new suit when reach goal	Try out assertive responses with a friend before confronting boss, stop 1 per day increase after desired level attained	Review log once per day (evening). Plan 2 pleasant activities per day and initiate 1 weekend activity with another person

SOURCE: Wallace J. Kahn, "Self-Management: Learning to Be Our Own Counselor," *Personnel and Guidance Journal*, 55 (December 1976), 179. Copyright © 1976 American Personnel and Guidance Association. Reprinted with permission.

Cognitive techniques

Cognition refers to the process of knowing, and cognitive techniques in counseling are those designed to help clients know themselves and their environment so that they act more appropriately in future problem situations.

SIMULATION These techniques are used to give clients the opportunity to practice behaviors under conditions that approach reality. Krumboltz[40] has produced simulated materials designed to give high school students practice in solving simple but realistic problems similar to those solved by members of some twenty different occupations.

GAMING This technique places the client in a role. The *Life Career Game*, originally developed by Sarane Boocock of

Johns Hopkins University, and adapted by Barbara Varenhorst as a counseling tool, is an example of a gaming technique. In such roles, the actors make plans, decide on risks, and interact to achieve objectives.

PARADOXICAL INTENTION Although this technique has been reported by Frankl,[41] the existentialist, it shares many characteristics with counter-conditioning and cognitive techniques. The technique is based on the belief that anxiety or fear makes that which one fears come true, and that hyperintention makes that which one wishes impossible. Therefore, clients are urged to "intend" precisely that which they fear. Problems, phobias, and obsessions are treated by intensifying them, enabling clients to see the humor of the situation and put it in proper perspective. Insomniacs have

[40] Krumboltz and Thoresen, *Behavioral Counseling*, pp. 397–398.

[41] Viktor E. Frankl, *Man's Search for Meaning: An Introduction to Logotherapy* (Boston: Beacon Press, 1962), pp. 125–131.

been helped by paradoxical practices that instructed them to practice staying awake, and incessant smokers helped to overcome the habit by being told to smoke more. In simplest terms, paradoxical techniques represent reverse psychology in that to get people to do what is wanted, they are encouraged to do just the opposite.

ASSERTIVE TRAINING Assertive training includes one or more methods such as role playing, rehearsals, and social modeling designed to encourage the client to engage in behaviors that approximate those desired but feared.

The work of Jakubowski-Spector[42] in defining and illustrating differences between assertiveness and aggressiveness and in developing training films and programs has been particularly noteworthy. Wilk and Caplan[43] describe practices they use with participants ranging from corporate executives to students, most of whom were women between the ages of 18 and 60. Shelton observed that considerable differences exist in definitions of assertiveness but common threads running through them include (1) the ability to express all manner of emotion, (2) the capacity to express one's rights without denying rights of others, (3) the confidence to stand up for oneself, and (4) the ability to choose when assertive behavior is appropriate. Assertive training methods, according to Shelton, usually incorporate some combination of microcounseling; homework; feedback, either video or audio; peer feedback; behavioral rehearsal; coaching; prompting; modeling; and imitation and bibliotherapy.[44]

DOUBLE-BINDS Situations are imposed on clients in which any response they make contradicts previously impoverishing experiences and expands their behaviors. Double-bind

techniques have been used in homework assignments or contracts to perform certain actions between counseling sessions.

Analyzing communications

Below are two excerpts of counselee-counselor interactions presented to help the learner develop insight into how attitudes influence counselor responses.[45] In each case the counselee's statements are followed by the counselor's response with but little information given about the nature of the counselee. In brief, you are presented with two isolated client expressions followed in each situation by five counselor responses. You are asked to evaluate each counselor response and to select the explanation from each group of four that you believe best describes the counselor's response as it relates to what the counselee has expressed or implied. It should be remembered that rightness and wrongness of counseling techniques are concepts strictly relative to the counselor's values, training, and experience. Consequently, there is no one correct answer. You are to read the counselee statement, then each counselor's response. From the four alternatives to each counselor response select the one that you think describes the usefulness of the response.[46]

> Situation 1—This excerpt is the opening remark made by a counselee immediately after seating himself in the counselor's office. The counselor has not met the student before.
> "Miss Jones told me to come down here and talk to you—I don't know why! She said I couldn't come back to class until I learned to stay awake. . . . I work at a filling station until one every night and I'm tired. Anyway, who could stay awake in there—she bores you to death."
> Counselor responses:
> 1. "Do you have to work so much at the filling station?"
>   A. A useful statement to help the counselee continue talking.

[42] See Patricia Jakubowski-Spector, "Facilitating the Growth of Women Through Assertive Training," *Counseling Psychologist*, 4, No. 1 (1973), 75–86; Patricia Jakubowski-Spector, J. Parlman, and K. Coburn, *Assertive Training of Women: A Stimulus Film* (Washington, D.C.: American Personnel and Guidance Association, 1973); and Patricia Jakubowski, "Assertive Behavior and Clinical Problems of Women," in E. Rawlings and D. Carter (Eds.) *Psychotherapy for Women: Treatment Toward Equality*, (Springfield, Ill.: Charles C Thomas, 1976), pp. 147–167.
[43] Carole Wilk and Virginia Coplan, "Assertive Training as a Confidence-Building Technique," *Personnel and Guidance Journal*, 55 (April 1977), 460–464.
[44] John L. Shelton, "Assertive Training: Consumer Beware," *Personnel and Guidance Journal*, 55 (April 1977), 465–468.

[45] This material was abstracted from the tapes employed by Jane S. O'Hern and Dugald S. Arbuckle in their research entitled "Sensitivity: A Measurable Concept?" *Personnel and Guidance Journal*, 42 (February 1964), 572–576. Used with the authors' permission, with adaptations by Robert Finley of the University of Utah.
[46] The following were the responses most frequently selected by a group of 200 counselors in training: Situation 1—1B, 2B, 3C, 4C, 5C; Situation 2—1D, 2B, 3C, 4B, 5A.

B. Asks for information that is irrelevant at this time.
C. Implies understanding of the counselee's problem.
D. None of the above.
2. "What does she do that you find boring?"
A. Asks for relevant information that the counselor needs to gain understanding.
B. Ignores the implicit meaning in the counselee's communication.
C. Will help the counselee focus his thought on an important aspect of the situation.
D. Implies interest in the counselee.
3. "Going to sleep in class can get you into trouble, can't it?"
A. Is a pertinent statement because it implies that you understand the counselee's problem.
B. Suggests that the counselor doesn't understand the problem.
C. Is a restatement of an obvious fact.
D. None of the above.
4. "Teachers get angry when we don't behave the way they think we should, don't they?"
A. Indicates that the counselor understands what the problem is.
B. Is an irrelevant statement.
C. Will be useful to help the counselee continue talking.
D. None of the above.
5. "Is this the first time she has called you down for sleeping?"
A. Ignores the implicit meaning of the counselee's statement.
B. Asks for inappropriate information.
C. Both A and B.
D. None of the above.

Situation 2—Taken from the first interview with a counselee who is on the brink of failing college:

"You know it makes me so mad, every time . . . I don't know what is wrong with this university—it seems like they are out to get me. I just keep going down in grade point and everything else—and it's not my fault. I don't know why they have these stupid required courses. It just doesn't make sense. Why do I have to take them when I am in agriculture?"

Counselor responses:
1. "If you put your mind to it and work and study, you could get something out of these courses that you might find useful to you later."
A. Is a reality of life that the counselee must learn.
B. Useful because it helps the counselee learn from the counselor's experience.
C. Shows that the counselor understands what has to be done.
D. None of the above.
2. "You feel that since you are in agriculture you don't need to know anything about literature and history?"
A. Focuses on the counselee's feelings.
B. Focuses on the counselee's beliefs.
C. Asks for needed information.
D. None of the above.
3. "What are your aims in life?"
A. Implies the counselor understands what the counselee's problem is.
B. Asks for information that is relevant at this time.
C. Ignores the implicit meaning in the counselee's communication.
D. None of the above.
4. "What makes you think the university is out to get you?"
A. Is a pertinent question if the counselor is to understand the situation.
B. Misses a more pertinent element for exploration.
C. Suggests the counselor is interested in the counselee's point of view.
D. None of the above.
5. "It sounds to me like you're blaming others for your own inadequacies."
A. Is a bad statement because it implies an insight beyond the counselee's awareness.
B. Is a bad statement because it focuses on an irrelevant element of the counselee's communication.
C. Is a bad statement because it makes an incorrect interpretation.
D. Is a good statement because it states a truth the counselee should recognize and accept.

Bandler and Grinder[47] have presented a step-by-step procedure for analyzing the form of the client's communications.

[47] Richard Bandler and John Grinder, *The Structure of Magic*, Vols. I and II (Palo Alto: Science and Behavior Books, 1975).

Effective counselors, they suggest, have sensitized themselves to hear the structure of verbal communications so as to sharpen their intuitions about the client. They identify three linguistic phenomena that counselors should recognize in client talk and these have been paraphrased here.

1. *Deletions.* Portions of the original experience (the world) or full linguistic representations (deep structure) have been deleted or omitted by the client. Bandler and Grinder suggest that there are three classes of deletions: comparatives and superlatives, "clearly" and "obviously" adverbs, and modal operators (rules and generalizations that clients have developed). Counselors who recognize that a deletion has occurred can ask specifically for what is missing.

2. *Distortions-nominalizations.* Things are represented but twisted in some way (distorted) that limits ability to act or increases pain or clients sometimes are immobilized by turning ongoing processes into events (nominalization). Counselors can recognize distortions or nominalizations by checking nonverbs in client statements, asking themselves if they can think of a verb or adjective closely associated with nonverbs in appearance/sound or meaning.

3. *Generalizations.* Words and phrases that have no referential index and verbs that are specified incompletely can be identified in order for the client's statements to make sense. Generalizations often cause loss of detail and richness of original experiences and prevent clients from making distinctions that give them fuller choices in coping with situations. Counselors who challenge generalizations in client communication enable the client to reconnect with the experience, reduce the experience to something definite that can be coped with, and create choices based on distinctions previously not available to client. Bandler and Grinder urge counselors to challenge generalizations by checking for referential indices for nouns and event words and by checking for fully specified verbs and process words.

A counselor response scale

Kagan[48] has developed a counselor verbal response scale to describe the counselor's communications on four dichoto-

mized dimensions: affect-cognitive, listening-nonlistening, honest labeling–distorting, exploratory-nonexploratory. By the replaying of video-taped interview sessions, each verbal interaction between counselor and counselee represented by a counselee statement and counselor response may be judged on each of the four dimensions of the rating scale. The primary focus in judging the response is on describing how the counselor responded to verbal and nonverbal elements of the client's communication. Figure 12.2 presents the *Interpersonal Process Recall* (IPR) *Counselor Response Rating Scale* developed by Kagan.

Description of IPR rating dimensions

The four dimensions of the IPR rating scale have been described fully by Kagan. Abstracts of his descriptions of each dimension are presented here.

I. *Exploratory-nonexploratory dimension.* This dimension indicates whether a counselor's response encourages clients to stay deeply involved in or to expand on their communications, or whether the counselor's response limits clients, explorations of these concerns.

A. *Exploratory responses.* Exploratory responses encourage and permit client latitude and involvement in responding. They give clients freedom in their responses and encourage them to be active participants in the communication rather than passive receivers of counselor advice and knowledge. Such counselor responses are often open-ended (essaylike) and are delivered in an egalitarian manner, bespeaking a partnership rather than an authoritarian leadership. These responses:

1. Encourage clients to explore their own concerns.

   Examples: Cognitive—"You're not sure what you want to major in, is that it?" Affective—"Maybe some of these times you're getting mad at yourself, what do you think?"

2. Assist clients to explore by providing them with possible alternatives designed to increase their range of responses.

[48] Norman I. Kagan, *Interpersonal Process Recall* (East Lansing, Mich.: Michigan State University Press, 1976).

FIGURE 12.2 **IPR counselor verbal response rating scale**

Judge: _____   Subject: _____   Date: _____

| Responses | DIMENSIONS | | | | | | | | Counselor response evaluation | | |
	Explor-atory	Nonex-ploratory	Listening	Non-listening	Affective	Cognitive	Honest labeling	Distorting	Effective 4 3		Noneffective 2 1
1		√	√		√						√
2											
3											
4											
5											
6											
7											
8											
9											
10											
11											
12											
13											
14											
15											
16											
17											
18											
19											
20											
21											
22											
23											
24											
25											
% of Responses											
TOTAL									TOTAL [ ]		

Examples: Cognitive—"What are some of your other alternatives to a major in history?"
Affective—"In these situations do you feel angry, mad, helpless, or what?"
3. Reward the client for exploratory behavior.

Examples: Cognitive—"It seems that you've considered a number of alternatives for a major, that's good."
Affective—"So you're beginning to wonder if you want to be independent."
B. *Nonexploratory responses.* Nonexploratory responses either indicate no understanding of the

client's basic communication, or so structure and limit the client's responses that they inhibit the exploratory process. These responses give clients little opportunity to explore, expand, or express themselves freely. Although it is sometimes necessary to limit clients' responses (as when specific information is needed), nonexploratory responses discourage clients from pursuing their concerns and limit the scope of their responses. Such responses discourage further exploration on the part of the client.

Examples: Cognitive—"You want to change your major to history."

Affective—"You *really* resent your parents treating you like a child."

II. *Listening-nonlistening dimension.* This dimension indicates whether a counselor's response communicates to the client that the counselor has listened to and sincerely wants to understand the client's basic communication. Listening responses encourage clients to clarify their own thinking so that both they and the counselor understand the nature of client concerns.

A. *Listening responses.* Listening responses communicate to the client that the counselor understands the client's communication—the counselor makes appropriate reference to what the client is expressing or trying to express both verbally and nonverbally—or the counselor is clearly seeking enough information of either a cognitive or affective nature to gain such understanding. Such responses:

1. Directly communicate an understanding of the client's communication.

   Example: "In other words, you really want to be independent."

2. Seek further information from the client in such a way as to facilitate both the counselor's and the client's understanding of the basic problems.

   Example: "What does being independent mean to you?"

3. Reinforce or give approval of client communications that exhibit understanding, but do not judge or accuse.

Example: CL: "I guess then when people criticize me, I'm afraid they'll leave me."

CO: "I see you're beginning to make some connection between your behavior and your feelings."

B. *Nonlistening responses.* By such responses, the counselor fails to understand the client's basic communication or makes no attempt to obtain *appropriate* information from the client. In essence, nonlistening responses often represent jumps to conclusions. Such responses:

1. Communicate misunderstanding of the client's basic concern.

   Example: CL: "When he said that, I just turned red and clenched my fists."

   CO: "Some people don't say nice things."

2. Seek information that may be irrelevant to the client's communication.

   Example: CL: "I seem to have a hard time getting along with my brothers."

   CO: "Do all your brothers live at home with you?"

3. Squelch client understanding or move the focus to another, irrelevant area.

   Example: CL: "I guess I'm really afraid that other people will laugh at me."

   CO: "We're the butt of other people's jokes sometimes."

   Example: CL: "Sometimes I really hate my aunt."

   CO: "Will things be better when you go to college?"

III. *Affective-cognitive dimension.* The affective-cognitive dimension indicates whether a counselor's response refers to any affective component of a client's communication or concerns itself primarily with the cognitive component of that communication.

A. *Affective responses.* Affective responses generally make reference to emotions, feelings, fears, and so on. The rating is based solely on the content and/or intent of the counselor's response, regardless of whether it be reflection, clarification, interpretation. These responses attempt to maintain the focus on the affective component of a client's communication. Thus they may:

1. Refer directly to an explicit or implicit reference to affect (either verbal or nonverbal) on the part of the client and *name* or label that perception.

   Example: "It sounds like you were really angry at him."

2. Encourage an expression of affect on the part of the client.

   Example: "How does it make you feel when your parents argue?"

3. Approve of an expression of affect on the part of the client.

   Example: "It doesn't hurt to let your feelings out once in a while, does it?"

4. Present a model for the use of affect by the client.

   Example: "If somebody treated me like that I'd really be mad." Special care must be taken in rating responses that use the word *feel*. For example, in the statement "Do you *feel* that your student-teaching experience is helping you get the idea of teaching?" the phrase "Do you feel that" really means "Do you think that." Similarly the expression "How are you feeling?" is often used in a matter-of-fact, conversational manner. Thus, although the verb *to feel* is used in both these examples, these statements do *not* represent responses that would be judged affective.

B. *Cognitive responses.* Cognitive responses deal primarily with the cognitive element of a client's communication. Frequently such responses seek information of a factual nature. They generally maintain the interaction on the cognitive level. Such responses may:

1. Refer directly to the cognitive component of the client's statement.

   Example: "So then you're thinking about switching your major to chemistry?"

2. Seek further information of a factual nature from the client.

   Example: "What were your grades last term?"

3. Encourage the client to continue to respond at the cognitive level.

   Example: "How did you get interested in art?"

IV. *Honest labeling–distorting dimension.* This dimension reflects whether the counselor's response is frank without being brutal or whether it tones down or distorts the statement. In essence, honest labeling describes whether the counselor names, or "zeroes in" on the underlying core of the client's communication or distorts it by responding in a general, vague, or peripheral manner. Effective counselors label honestly, but nondefensively, the most intense, bitter, shameful, hurtful of the client's message or the message's impact, even if it is directed to the counselor.

A. *Honest labeling responses.* Such responses focus on the core concerns being presented either explicitly or implicitly, verbally or nonverbally, by the client. Such responses:

1. Delineate or label honestly the client's basic concerns.

   Example: "This vague feeling you have when you get in tense situations—is it anger or fear?"

2. Encourage clients to discriminate among stimuli affecting them.

   Example: "Do you feel——in all your classes or only in some classrooms?"

3. Reward the client for being specific.

   Example: CL: "I guess I feel this way most often with someone who reminds me of my father."
   CO: "So as you put what others say in perspective, the whole world doesn't seem so bad, it's only when someone you value, like Father, doesn't pay any attention that you feel hurt."

B. *Distorting responses.* Such responses indicate that the counselor has not focused on the basic concerns of the client. They avoid, clean up, modify, tone down, or mellow what has been said and communicate that the counselor is not willing to

engage the client. Their effect is to suggest that
the counselor either rejects or is not yet able to
help the client differentiate among various stimuli. Such responses miss the problem area completely (such responses are also nonlistening).
Thus such responses:

1. Fail to label the client's concerns and cannot
   bring them into sharper focus.
   Example: "It seems your problem isn't very
   clear—can you tell me more about
   it?"
2. Completely miss the basic concerns being presented by the client even though the counselor
   may ask for specific details.
   Example: CL: "I've gotten all A's this year and
   I still feel lousy."
   CO: "What were your grades before
   then?"
3. Discourage clients from bringing their concerns into sharper focus.
   Example: "You and your sister argue all the
   time. What do other people think of
   your sister?"

Use of IPR rating scales

Although this book cannot provide a video tape or an audio
tape so that the reader may see and/or listen to counselee-
counselor exchange, the foregoing materials may be employed to rate the counselor responses presented in three
situations.[49] For example, if you believed that the response
of Counselor 1 to Counselee I was more exploratory than
nonexploratory, you would check that column in the IPR
counselor response scale. If you believed that the response of
Counselor 1 reflected more "listening" than "nonlistening"
you would place a check mark in the appropriate column.
The authors' evaluation of the first counselor's remark has
been recorded on the form given as Figure 12.2 to serve as an
example.

[49] Case material used by permission of Jane S. O'Hern. Abstracted
from case materials used in O'Hern and Arbuckle, "Sensitivity."

Counselee I: "I've been sitting here and I have been
seeing you for a long time—for several
months, and usually I thought, well you
kind of understood me, but lately you
haven't—I wonder, maybe I ought to
leave."

Counselor 1: "Why do you feel that I don't understand
you?"
2: "You can't tolerate it when you are not
understood."
3: "Can you explain why you think I don't
understand you?"
4: "It is fine if you want to leave—you're
sure you know why?"
5: "What would you accomplish by leaving?"
6: "What do you expect from me?"
7: "What change has taken place that makes
you think that I don't understand you?"
8: "Let's talk about what I don't understand
and see if I can understand it better."
9: "It's not my understanding that keeps you
from making any progress."
10: "You feel as if you are not being understood—why do you need so much understanding?"
11: "My not understanding you makes you
feel that you aren't worthwhile."

Counselee II: "What the hell are you asking me how it
feels for? If I knew how I felt I probably
wouldn't have come to see you."

Counselor 12: "You're pretty touchy today, aren't you?"
13: "I'm sorry if I intruded on your privacy,
maybe we can talk about something else
if you like."
14: "I am attempting to find out what your
inner feelings are so that I can be of help
to you in some way."
15: "If we are going to solve your problems it
is important that I get to know you better."
16: "How do you think you feel at this time?"
17: "Don't you think it important to consider
your feelings about yourself and your environment in order to determine why you
are having trouble?"

18: "You would like for me to take the responsibility for knowing how you are."

19: "I guess we all have those days, don't we?"

20: "It makes you angry for someone to ask you how it feels—I wonder why."

21: "It is just common courtesy to ask you how you felt."

22: "Why did you come to see me?"

23: "I'm just trying to get you to express how you feel about your problem."

Counselee III: "I was thinking about it the other night and you know my father died when I was fifteen. I was just in high school and you know at the funeral I knew I was supposed to cry and act upset and everything, and I did. I put on a real good act. But you know when they first told me that he died . . . that he was dead and do you know what the first thing was that came to my mind? The first thing that I thought about was—ha, ha—all the restrictions are gone and I can be free."

Counselor 24: "Your father meant some different things to you than what the people thought. Inside you were really glad and you're wondering why these things are bothering you now."

25: "Why do you say 'at last I can be free'?"

26: "Why did you feel that you had to cry to put on a good act?"

27: "Now you think of your father as the restrictions he put on you. You really didn't have any need for him at all."

28: "Do you think this is a bad thought? Do you think people will think badly of you because you think this way? Does everyone love his or her father?"

29: "How do you feel about it now? How are these restrictions?"

30: "Your father's death just sort of lifted off a lot of rules and regulations and you felt that your life was your own?"

31: "You thought your father was the party who kept you from the things you really wanted to do. Without him, you're entirely free with nothing to hold you back."

32: "This bothers you because you went through all the motions socially."

33: "Do you still feel that way?"

Summary

Counseling communication is complex, myriad, and constantly changing. The techniques employed by the counselor reflect his or her personal growth so that each counselor tends to develop a personal style based on experience. Most counselors implement a role that is performed consistently with all counselees. Some twenty-five years ago the use of recorded interviews was originated to study client-counselor interactions. From these early studies and from others now conducted with greater refinement, more understanding is being gained about interview dynamics. Counselees tend to approach their problems from either a cognitive or an affective framework. During segments of an interview a counselor's behavior usually reflects a certain consistency as he or she enacts one or another subordinate role with sensitive adjustment depending on the topic under discussion.

Buchheimer and Balogh have conceptualized the counseling relationship in a highly useful way.[50] They believe that techniques used by the counselor are dependent on the strategy he or she employs or the "set" taken toward the counselee. The set may be either *peripheral* or *central*. If it is peripheral, the counselor takes a third-person view and seemingly possesses an attitude of inquiry. Emphasis is placed on knowing and doing, with little concern for feeling, under the assumption that counselees do not know what they need to know and that once they do, they will be able to act. The counselor, then, is the primary acting person whereas the counselee remains essentially a passive individual who is judged, evaluated, and told. The central counselor, on the other hand, takes a first-person view because he or she feels and thinks within the counselee's point of view. Such a counselor engages in the counselee's affective life, and his or her leads are in "you" terms derived from the

---

[50] Buchheimer and Balogh, *The Counseling Relationship*, p. 12.

"I." Fundamentally, the counselor's aim, expressed through techniques, is to achieve certain goals while simultaneously allowing clients to be responsible for themselves, for their communications, and for their behavior.

Issues

Issue 1 The counselor who is truly a counselor does not advise counselees.

True, because
1. Counselees can get advice from teachers, adults, parents, and peers. The counselor should be seen as different from them.
2. If counselors present advice that clients follow, responsibility for success or failure for their action rests with the counselor.
3. Clients don't seek advice from counselors; they seek to establish a relationship that facilitates self-understanding.

False, because
1. Advice giving is a time-honored function of any relationship in which trust and understanding are present.
2. Advice—predicting the probability of success in a future venture—can be given to clients who exhibit no undue anxiety and possess good self-understanding.

Discussion If advice is defined as providing a ready-made solution, most counselors would tend to avoid this kind of activity. One reason is that providing solutions is likely to defeat achievement of the goals of counseling, which strives for responsible self-sufficiency. Advice giving, on the other hand, fosters dependency and blocks the individual's progress toward mastery of decision-making processes.

Most counselors undoubtedly give advice on occasion. In many instances individuals ask advice because they lack the necessary information to make complex decisions. It is essential that the counselor determine whether a request for advice arises from lack of information or from other, more complicated personal reasons. If the latter is the case, such requests could more properly be labeled a symptom of a problem that may in itself call for longer-term attention.

In essence, each request must be weighed against the incontrovertible fact that advice giving generally frustrates

and sometimes totally prevents the achievement of most commonly accepted counseling goals. In other helping professions, such as law and medicine, practitioners rely heavily on advice giving primarily because these fields encompass a highly complex body of knowledge that is unavailable to their clientele. The equally complex and technical body of knowledge of the counselor is applicable only when combined with a thorough knowledge of the individual counselee. The point is that, for law and medicine, solutions arise from the knowledge on which they are based whereas in counseling the individual's solution stems from self-understanding and awareness.

Issue 2 Counselors should not present information to clients during counseling sessions.

True, because
1. It places the counselor in roles similar to those occupied by teachers and other adults and reinforces the widely held view that counseling is information giving and advising.
2. Presenting information shifts the focus of the relationship from the client to external features.
3. When clients have reached the point that they are ready to absorb and use information, counseling is no longer needed or being conducted.

False, because
1. Information is needed about options considered in planning and choice making.
2. Counselors actually provide information to clients as the two identify alternatives, discuss anticipated consequences of certain actions, or assess implications of behaviors.

Discussion This issue parallels, in many respects, the previous issue of giving advice. Few counselors would deny that they presented information to clients. Equally true, few counselors would relish the image that counseling was merely the dispensation of information. Arbuckle's statement here represents a fitting summary of this issue.

Many of the clients who come in to see the school counselor, of course, are going to be quite capable of using relevant information, *and if they want it, and if the counselor has it*, there would seem to be little reason for withholding it. Even though in the school counseling relationship information will play a very minor role, the school counselor will periodically be called upon to supply information. There would seem to be no reason why he [or she] could not do so and at the same time maintain his [or her] counseling relationship with the client.[51]

Annotated references

Bandler, Richard, and John Grinder. *The Structure of Magic*, Vols I and II. Palo Alto, Calif.: Science and Behavior Books, 1975.

These two volumes are particularly helpful to counselors. They present a model for examining client language, illustrate practices and set out methods to bring about client change.

Cormier, William H., and L. Sherilyn Cormier. *Interviewing Strategies for Helpers.* Monterey, Calif.: Brooks/Cole Publishing Company, 1979. 557 pp.

Numerous helping skills and strategies directed to assessment, treatment, and evaluation are presented and discussed. Both verbal and nonverbal behaviors are set forth as useful for assessment practices.

Krumboltz, John D., and Carl E. Thoresen, eds. *Counseling Methods*. New York: Holt, Rinehart and Winston, 1976. 576 pp.

Some sixty-two presentations by various authors of counseling methods. The methods are organized into three parts, those for altering maladaptive behavior, those for promoting wise decision making and those for preventing problems and developing resourcefulness. A diagnostic table of contents serves to help locate techniques useful for a particular type of problem.

Further references

Berman, Judith. "Counseling Skills Used by Black and White Male and Female Counselors." *Journal of Counseling Psychology*, 26 (January 1979), 81–84.

Coven, Arnold B. "Using Gestalt Psychodrama Experiments in Rehabilitation Counseling." *Personnel and Guidance Journal*, 56 (November 1977), 143–147.

[51] Dugald S. Arbuckle, *Counseling and Psychotherapy: An Existential-Humanistic View*, 3rd ed. (Boston: Allyn & Bacon, 1975), p. 266.

Denney, Douglas R., and Patricia A. Rupert. "Desensitization and Self-Control in the Treatment of Test Anxiety." *Journal of Counseling Psychology*, 24 (July 1977), 272–281.

Elliott, Robert. "How Clients Perceive Helper Behaviors." *Journal of Counseling Psychology*, 26 (July 1979), 285–294.

Fridman, Myron S., and Shelley C. Stone. "Effect of Training, Stimulus Context, and Mode of Stimulus Presentation on Empathy Ratings." *Journal of Counseling Psychology*, 25 (March 1978), 131–136.

Kaplan, Leslie S. "A Matter of LOSS: Living On, Surviving Sadness." *The School Counselor*, 26 (May 1979), 229–235.

Naster, Barry J. "Reciprocity Counseling: A Behavioral Approach to Marital Discord." *Personnel and Guidance Journal*, 55 (May 1977), 515–519.

Nystul, Michael S. "Three Dimensions of a Counseling Relationship." *The School Counselor*, 26 (January 1979), 144–149.

Roark, Albert E. "Interpersonal Conflict Management." *Personnel and Guidance Journal*, 56 (March 1978) 400–402.

Robyak, James E. "A Revised Study Skills Model: Do Some of Them Practice What We Preach?" *Personnel and Guidance Journal*, 56 (November 1977), 171–175.

Ronnestad, Michael Helge. "Effect of Modeling, Feedback, and Experimental Methods on Counselor Empathy." *Counselor Education and Supervision*, 16 (March 1977), 194–201.

Spooner, Sue E., and Shelley C. Stone. "Maintenance of Specific Counseling Skills Over Time." *Journal of Counseling Psychology*, 24 (January 1977), 66–71.

Stokes, Joseph Powell. "Model Competencies for Attending Behaviors." *Counselor Education and Supervision*, 17 (September 1977), 23–28.

Trussell, Richard P. "Use of Graduated Behavioral Rehearsal, Feedback, and Systematic Desensitization for Speech Anxiety." *Journal of Counseling Psychology*, 25 (January 1978), 14–20.

Wilk, Carole A., and Virginia M. Coplan. "Assertive Training as a Confidence Building Technique." *Personnel and Guidance Journal*, 55 (April 1977), 460–464.

13   Counseling techniques and practices: II

This chapter is organized around the following topics: (1) things to look for in counseling, (2) nonverbal behavior, (3) diagnosis, (4) test use and interpretation, (5) nontest adjuncts to counseling, and (6) referral practices.

Things to look for in counseling

The content presented in this section treats some key features that counselors observe and to which they respond. These six features, if put in the form of questions, can be useful to any counselor in reviewing the conduct of a counseling session.

How do I view the association of ideas contained within the interview?

What shifts in conversation occur that might be meaningful?

What content and affect were present in the client's opening and closing statements?

What recurrent references were present?

Did inconsistencies and gaps occur that might be of particular significance?

Does a reconsideration of the session indicate an unconscious effort to conceal or hide that which is of concern to the counselee?

Association of ideas

Careful review of any counseling session, no matter how disjointed or faltering the session may appear, commonly reveals a pattern in the ideas expressed by the counselee. Normally, the pattern is recognized more readily by the counselor after a series of contacts, for fairly obvious reasons. Initially, the counselor seeks and the client attempts to give a great deal of information, much of which may not be of importance later. Especially in earlier contacts much

of what takes place, as Perez indicates,[1] clearly evolves from the mutual interaction of the participants' defense mechanisms.

Presumably, counselees seek the helping relationship because of some concern or problem. They look for relief from a condition that may be relatively simple or tremendously complex. However inept and convoluted the way they approach the situation, they are nevertheless attempting to present their problems as they perceive them. Digressions, defensiveness, and tangential references notwithstanding, in most instances the thread of the problem is embedded in the weave of the material presented. The skillful, perceptive, and experienced counselor is not only able to extract this thread but assists the client in setting it in a less tortuous pattern.

This thread is often referred to as an association of ideas; it is akin to William James' "stream of consciousness." While the term *free association* is sometimes loosely applied to this phenomenon, such mental meanderings clearly contain consistency and logic if viewed from the counselee's frame of reference. The associations are there. What is missing is the grasp of the client's perceptual framework by the counselor. Even the most bizarre human behavior can be thought of as having meaning and purpose to the individual who performs it. The point is that there are two limitations to understanding another: the client's inability to express adequately what he or she wishes to say and the counselor's inability to hear the essence of what is said to him or her. Neither should be taken as a condemnation of the participants. Both are human failings that can be overcome only by repeated contact coupled with recognition of the complexity involved in knowing and understanding communication.

The association of ideas takes place in both counselor and counselee. The counselor who uses what may be an emo-

[1] Joseph F. Perez, *The Initial Counseling Contact*, Houghton Mifflin Professional Guidance Monograph Series (Boston: Houghton Mifflin Company, 1968).

tionally charged word such as *divorce, college, stealing, mother,* or *lying* may simultaneously trigger in the counselee a stream of association that has little to do with the counselor's feelings about these things. Unless counselors recognize their own associations, their unconscious operation may cause them to attribute feelings and emotions to the counselee that he or she does not have.

Shifts in conversation

To the counselor, topical shifts in the counselee's conversation may appear random and purposeless. Review of what was said previously in the interview as well as what comes after may reveal the reason for change. Topical changes may represent any of the following behaviors, or others:

1. Counselees may be trying to make themselves better understood by citing what they consider a relevant situation illustrating the point they are making or the feeling they seek to convey.
2. Counselees may believe that they are revealing too much of themselves. Because they are unsure of how they are being received by the counselor, they may deliberately shift the focus to what they think can be safely communicated and examined.
3. Counselees may be seeking relief from examination of a topic too painful or too sensitive to pursue. This is related to the second point.

Opening and closing remarks

The initial remarks made by counselees may contain much that is helpful in understanding them as well as their perspective on their situation. "The principal sent me down here" bears special study by the counselor as it probably indicates reluctance to be there. The attitudes reflected by counselees in presenting their problem may give significant cues not only to their motivation for change but to how fully they understand themselves. Similarly, concluding remarks are worth study because they often indicate the counselee's view of what has happened. They may give insight both to the meaning they attach to what has been discussed and to their commitment to working on their problems.

Recurrent references

As stated earlier, a consistent theme may be visible in reviewing what has been said in a counseling session. The counselee returns to it again and again. For example, the theme may be the lack of self-acceptance, and counselees will repeatedly refer to their dissatisfaction with their present level of functioning in school, their unhappiness at home, their inability to establish friendships, and the like. Recurring references may indicate an inability to accept or cope with authority. During the interview or its review, then, the counselor is able to discern a pattern of behavior from the counselee's recurring descriptions of situations.

Similar to recurring references is the situation in which the individual "talks in circles." The client talks and talks and talks but fails to move forward. The same ideas, the same complaints, the same explanations are presented over and over.

The very circularity of the verbal content is a stumbling block to the counselor. When such an impasse has been reached, counselors have to devise ways of breaking the circle and transforming it into a spiral. Counselors can do so by inserting something new into the pattern, for example, a new topic for the client to react to, discuss or explain. Or the counselor could ask questions such as "What would you like to do about it?" or "How would you like that person to act toward you?" Such topics or questions may stimulate the counselee to move into new and more profitable areas of discussion.

Inconsistencies and gaps

A counselee's remark may contradict one previously made, or present a picture that contains inconsistencies and gaps. The inconsistencies and gaps, particularly if they are repeated, may be significant to understanding the client. A counselee who describes the members of his or her family but omits mentioning a brother or sister leaves a gap that may contain meaning fundamental to understanding the problem. Similarly, the counselee who remarks that he or she "likes school" but later keeps talking of dropping out has revealed a contradiction to be followed up by the counselor.

Concealed meaning

By listening intently the counselor is often able to discern the concealed meaning behind client statements. Some beginning counselors worry and unduly pursue every client remark in an effort to uncover hidden meaning. The senior girl who "can't tolerate boys" may be concealing her hurt that she has not been dated, and the boy who is lonely may go to great lengths to hide this by explaining that he has "too much to do to seek out and encourage friends." The presence of concealed meaning is usually far from obvious; only through careful attentiveness to the counselee's attitudes, slips of tongue, and other cues does it become apparent.

Nonverbal behavior

The verbal exchanges between counselee and counselor are but part of the communication involved in the counseling relationship. The counselee's nonverbal behavior—gestures, body movements, blushing—supplements and indeed sometimes belies his or her words. Although each counselor's observation of nonverbal behavior is limited by his or her sensitivity and training, the meaningfulness of cues derived from expressive movements adds much to an intuitive understanding of a counselee.

Certainly the occurrence of nonverbal behavior is not random; it derives from elements within the relationship. Expressive gestures and movements are used to either accent or contradict verbal exchanges. Unfortunately for the counselor, there is as yet no codification of the meanings of nonverbal behavior. Weeping is clear and needs no explanation, but most expressive behaviors have yet to be accurately identified in respect to their stimulus situation.

It is still unknown whether gestures have common or unique meanings and under what conditions interpretations of nonverbal behavior can be generalized. Furthermore, a chasm exists between even the present level of understanding nonverbal behavior and the knowledge needed for preparing individuals to master that understanding.

Classifying nonverbal behaviors

Knapp[2] points out that verbal and nonverbal behaviors are so intimately woven and subtly represented that it is difficult to segregate words from gestures, even for research purposes. Based on research directions, he proposed an eightfold classification system of the nonverbal dimensions of human communication. His categories included *body motion* or *kinesic behavior* (gestures, body movements, facial expressions, eye behaviors); *physical characteristics* (nonmovement-bound cues such as physique, attractiveness, body or breath odors, height, weight, and the like); *touching behavior* (stroking, hitting, greetings and farewells, holding); *paralanguage* (voice qualities such as pitch, rhythm, tempo, articulation, resonance and vocal characterizers, qualifiers and segregates); *proxemics* (use of social and personal space); *artifacts* (use of perfume, clothes, lipstick, eyeglasses, wigs, and so on) and *environmental factors* (use of furniture, interior decorating, lighting, smells, colors, temperature, music, noise).

Purposes of nonverbal behaviors

The purposes served by nonverbal behaviors have been classified by Ekman and Friesen.[3] Their first purpose was that of *emblems*. These nonverbal acts portray words or phrases such as gestures to signify "A-OK" or peace. The second purpose was that of *illustrators*. These nonverbal acts accompany speech and are generally hand or other bodily movements that accent what has been said. The third purpose was as *affect displays*. These are facial expressions that repeat, augment, contradict, or are unrelated to verbal affective states (anger, fear, joy). The fourth purpose is as *regulations* that are acts (head nods, eye movements) that maintain or regulate back and forth speaking and listening. Finally there are *adapters* or behaviors (such as leg movements or restless hands) that are believed to have developed in childhood to accommodate needs, manage emotions, perform actions, or develop social contacts.

[2] Mark L. Knapp, *Nonverbal Communication in Human Interaction* (New York: Holt, Rinehart and Winston, 1972), pp. 2–8.
[3] Paul Ekman and W. V. Friesen, "The Repertoire of Nonverbal Behavior: Categories, Origins, Usage and Coding," *Semiotica*, 1 (1) (1969), 49–98.

Nonverbal behavior in counseling

Research in nonverbal communication has been carried on for decades employing a variety of procedures and settings. One mode—and the forerunner to present research—has been the use of photographs to determine whether emotions can be judged correctly. The absence of motion and the lack of information about the behavioral sequence in photographs severely limit the facets their use can uncover. Gestures have also been investigated in such settings as drama, speech, and educational administration. Nonverbal behavior within the confines of the classroom has been examined through film recordings. More recently, study has been made of nonverbal communication in interviews, particularly in respect to the relationship between and among emotional stress and gestures and body movements.

Practicing psychiatrists have developed some literature dealing with nonverbal behavior. They have highlighted the fact that such behavior is significant and constitutes a source of information and insight. Feldman has a comprehensive listing of speech and body mannerisms and their meaning.[4] He believes that certain bodily movements could be traced back to their original use as communicative tools in life struggles. In his book he presents current meanings of gestures. The reader should of course recognize that Feldman's interpretations are at best educated guesses regarding highly idiosyncratic human behavior. Below is a list of representative gestures and the meanings he ascribes to them:

Erect head: self-esteem, self-confidence, courage
Bowed head: humility, resignation, guilt, submission
Touching nose: anxiety, stage fright
Rapid eye-blinking: relief mechanism or displacement from below upward
Artificial cough: criticism, doubt, surprise, anxiety
Whistling or humming: genuine or feigned self confidence
Fixing neckties: demonstrating masculinity
Pressing head with hands: distress, despair, helplessness
Placing head between two palms: sadness, exhaustion, meditation

Placing index finger alongside the nose: suspicion
Closing nostrils with fingers: contempt
Closing ears with hands: don't want to hear
Putting arms akimbo: firmness
Crossing arms over chest: straitjacket
Outstretched arms: call attention, surprise, alarm, blessing
Forming ring with fingers: unity, perfection
Rubbing thumb and middle finger: searching for solution
Finger or knuckle-cracking: frustration, aggression, hostility
Playing with ring or handbag: releasing tension or conflict, decision making
Embarrassed hands: repressed inclination to masturbate, suppression of bad habits

Some years ago, Bronfenbrenner and Newcomb devised a framework within which behavior may be studied as a vehicle of emotional and dispositional expression.[5] The five formal dimensions of bodily movement in clinical situations included (1) *quality* of motion (relaxed, jerky, abortive, controlled, or immobilized), (2) *front* of body contour (closed or open), (3) *locus* of activity (peripheral, medial, central, or integrative), (4) *direction* or plane of movement (vertical, transverse, or lateral), and (5) *body area* of activity (head, mouth, eyes, hands, trunk area, shoulder and back, legs).

Ekman believes that two types of information result from nonverbal behavior: specific direct meaning and information about other behavioral variables. Nonverbal behaviors, either augmenting or contradicting verbal responses, were organized by Ekman into a schema according to the functions served by such behaviors. Five functions were identified: (1) emphasizing or accenting the content of the verbal message; (2) amplifying part of the content of a verbal message; (3) examining a verbal silence; (4) providing information related to the content of the verbal message; and (5) adding new information not in the content of the verbal message by (a) substituting for verbalization, (b) contradicting the verbal message, or (c) providing a context to aid in interpretation of the verbal message.[6]

[4] Sandor S. Feldman, *Mannerisms of Speech and Gesture in Everyday Life* (New York: International Universities Press, 1959).

[5] Urie Bronfenbrenner and Theodore M. Newcomb, "Improvisations—An Application of Psychodrama in Personality Diagnosis," *Sociometry*, 1 (March 1948), 367–382.

[6] Paul Ekman, "Body Position, Facial Expression and Verbal Behavior During Interviews," *Journal of Abnormal and Social Psychology*, 68 (March 1964), 295–301.

Most counseling requires that the counselor talk far less than the client. However, counselors communicate, even when they are not talking, by their nonverbal expressions. Many believe the counselor's nonverbal behaviors are the major source for inducing desirable changes in client behaviors. Because nonverbal behavior interacts with verbal behavior, systematic investigation of it in counseling has been difficult.

FACIAL GESTURES   The primary means used for communicating affect (feelings of joy, sadness, anger, disgust, and so on) has been the face. Hackney[7] investigated the effects of four levels of nonverbal facial gestures on female client verbal behavior in a quasi-interview setting. Each treatment level—head nod, smile, no expression, and combination of head nod and smile—was presented by a male and female experimenter. Hackney reported that the subjects produced progressively and significantly greater amounts of feeling and self-referenced statements for head nods, smiles, and the head nod/smile combination when these stimuli were presented by the female but not the male experimenter.

Sweeney and Cottle[8] reported that graduate students in counseling, alas, were no more proficient than graduate students in business management in identifying fifteen nonverbal pictured emotional states. Female students in their study were more accurate than males.

PROXEMIC BEHAVIOR   Graves and Robinson[9] investigated the inconsistencies between counselor verbal and nonverbal behaviors on client proxemic behavior and ratings of counselor genuineness. Nonverbal behaviors included eye contact, body lean, body orientation, trunk lean, and leg positioning. Verbal content reflected either high or low levels of empathy. The confederate male counselor communicated either contradictory of consistent verbal and nonverbal messages. Graves and Johnson reported that results obtained from eighty college undergraduates indicated that inconsistent messages were associated with greater interpersonal distance, especially when the nonverbal messages were negative and the verbal messages were positive. Inconsistent messages produced lower rating of counselor genuineness.

ATTENDING BEHAVIORS   D'Augelli[10] studied the influence of helpers' nonverbal attending behaviors on clients in helping interactions. Nonverbal attending behaviors observed were smiles, head nods, leans forward, looks down, stares away, stammers, fiddles with something, and interrupts. Therapeutic talent correlated significantly with frequency of smiling and nodding. Frequency of fiddling was associated with being viewed by others as being sad or blue or discontented. Helpee-rated understanding and warmth were related positively with the frequency of head nods.

The investigator concluded that nonverbal attending behaviors were but one of many cues to which a helpee responds, but because no more than 10 percent of the common variance was accounted for in any correlation reported in his study, the critical impact of nonverbal behavior could be questioned.

FACILITATIVE CONDITIONS   One verbal and five nonverbal cues were studied by Tepper and Haase[11] in a multichannel communication paradigm to assess their effect on the communication of empathy, respect, and genuineness. Fifteen counselors and fifteen clients rated thirty-two video-taped interactions between counselor and client, each interaction portraying a different combination of verbal message, trunk lean, eye contact, vocal intonation, and facial expression. Ratings of empathy, respect, and genuineness were that (1) nonverbal cues in the paradigm accounted for significantly greater message variance than the verbal message, (2) counselors and clients differed significantly from one another in perception of the cues and these differences depended heavily on the presence or absence of the remaining cues, and (3) cues of vocal intonation and facial expression proved to be

[7] Harold Hackney, "Facial Gestures and Subject Expressions of Feelings," *Journal of Counseling Psychology*, 21 (May 1974), 173–178.

[8] Mary Anne Sweeney and William C. Cottle, "Nonverbal Acuity: A Comparison of Counselors and Noncounselors," *Journal of Counseling Psychology*, 23 (July 1976), 394–397.

[9] James R. Graves and John D. Robinson, II, "Proxemic Behavior as a Function of Inconsistent Verbal and Nonverbal Messages," *Journal of Counseling Psychology*, 23 (July 1976), 333–338.

[10] Anthony R. D'Augelli, "Nonverbal Behavior of Helpers in Initial Helping Interactions," *Journal of Counseling Psychology*, 21 (September 1974), 360–363.

[11] Donald T. Tepper, Jr., and Richard F. Haase, "Verbal and Nonverbal Communication of Facilitative Conditions," *Journal of Counseling Psychology*, 25 (January 1978), 35–44.

significant contributors to judgments of facilitative conditions. Tepper and Haase reported that facial expression accounted for 26 percent and 40 percent of the message variance in ratings of empathy and respect. The authors conclude that the verbal and nonverbal cues operate as a system and the message perceived depends on a relative balance between and among these variables. Communication is, indeed, a multichannel process.

Smith-Hanen[12] divided a sample of forty subjects into a control and experimental group and controlled nonverbal behaviors involving movement, four arm positions and six leg positions. After viewing forty-eight video segments, the subjects rated the counselor's warmth and empathy. The movement/no movement factor produced no significant effect on counselor warmth or empathy, but various arm positions influenced these two variables. The arms-crossed position was the coldest and least empathic position. The various leg positions significantly affected judged counselor warmth and empathy. Ratings of leg positions were not dependent merely on whether the leg position was open or closed, but far more complex distinctions in leg positions.

Finally, Sue and Sue[13] present several illustrations of how nonverbal behaviors differ between and among races, classes, and cultures. Particular attention is given to differences in personal space and eye contact and the authors conclude that counseling success depends on the counselor's flexibility in using techniques appropriate not only to the cultural group but to the individual as well.

A typology of nonverbal behavior

Kagan and his associates have developed a typology of nonverbal behavior.[14] In their study nonverbal behavior was limited to gestures, particularly arm and hand movements and postural movements limited to the client's position in a chair. They excluded lower leg or foot movements because their video-taped pictures of clients were from the knees up and they also excluded facial expression and eye movement because these have been subjected to much previous research. They first established a common repertoire of client nonverbal behavior by observing numerous clients, then validated the typology by comparing the meaning of nonverbal behavior as implied by the typology with that revealed in recall interviews. Table 13.1 presents the major components of this typology. The description given below is drawn from their report to the U.S. Office of Education.

SOURCE OF NONVERBAL BEHAVIOR Nonverbal behavior was observed as being related either to the verbal interview content or to the client's affective experience within the interview. Although these components occur simultaneously, nonverbal behaviors generally relate only to one or the other and seldom to both simultaneously.

AWARENESS Variation occurred in nonverbal behavior according to the client's degree of awareness of his or her actions. Kagan and his associates cited three categories (see Table 13.1): awareness, potential awareness, and lack of awareness. *Awareness* implies that clients not only know of their behavior but fully intend it. *Potential awareness* occurs when clients could indicate knowledge of their action if attention were directed to it. In this state they neither overtly intend nor overtly suppress the action. *Lack of awareness* means that clients are entirely unaware of their behavior and if their attention were directed to it they would indicate that they were oblivious to the action at the time.

DURATION Nonverbal behaviors arranged themselves in regular fashion by duration (see the items 1 to 6 in Table 13.1), or the extent of each behavior in terms of time. The behaviors ranged from a motion occupying a fraction of a second (item 1) to one lasting ten to fifteen minutes almost uninterrupted (item 6). Kagan and his associates suggest that although an overt gesture may be only momentary, the tension state that produced it is more continuous and occurs either prior to the gesture or as a result of client anticipation of what is to come.

[12] Sandra S. Smith-Hanen, "Effects of Nonverbal Behaviors on Judged Levels of Counselor Warmth and Empathy," *Journal of Counseling Psychology*, 24 (September 1977), 420–429.

[13] Derald Wing Sue and David Sue, "Barriers to Effective Cross-Cultural Counseling," *Journal of Counseling Psychology*, 24 (September 1977), 420–429.

[14] Norman Kagan, David R. Krathwohl, and William W. Farquhar, *IPR—Interpersonal Process Recall. Stimulated Recall by Videotape*, Educational Research Series, No. 24 (East Lansing: Bureau of Educational Research Services, College of Education, Michigan State University, March 1965), pp. III-1–III-22.

TABLE 13.1 **Nonverbal behaviors of clients in counseling interviews: degree of awareness of behavior**

Source of behavior	Unaware	Potentially aware	Aware
Content	1. *Emphasis*. Gestures of shortest duration accompanying particular items of verbal content; function is emphasis.	2. *Facilitation*. Gestures of brief duration accompanying verbal content, serving the function of facilitating clear communication.	3. *Portrayal*. Gestures intended to portray or give example of the topic of verbal content; duration directly related to content.
Affect	4. *Revelation—unaware (unconscious)*. Unconsciously motivated body motion related to feelings.	5. *Revelation—aware (conscious)*. Unconsciously motivated gestures revealing some degree of tension; client is aware of body motion but neither intends nor suppresses it.	6. *Affect demonstration (conscious)*. Intentional demonstration of feeling on client's part.

SOURCE: Norman Kagan, David R. Krathwohl, and William W. Farquhar, *IPR—Interpersonal Process Recall. Stimulated Recall by Videotape*, Educational Research Series, No. 24 (East Lansing: Bureau of Educational Research Services, College of Education, Michigan State University, March, 1965), p. III-10.

Source and awareness, the first two variables, interact to produce six distinct and definable categories of nonverbal behavior. The third element, duration, results from the arrangement of the six categories, each of which is described comprehensively by Kagan and his associates. The following material selected from their commentary outlines the description.

1. *Emphasis.* Gestures used for emphasis are brief and forceful, closely related to particular verbal content in respect to both time and forcefulness. Hands and arms are used primarily, followed by head and leg movements; postural movements are least used for emphasis. Because they are of brief duration (for example, tapping of chair), the client is usually unaware of them.

2. *Facilitation.* Gestures are often used to assist in increasing clarity. Hand and arm gestures (most frequently quick upward and outward motions) seem to be intended to release words from within and to speed them to their purpose. Such gestures were more often used when clients were expressing abstract ideas or were at a loss for words or believed that their verbal expression was inadequate. Clients are generally unaware of gestures for facilitation unless the motions are called to their attention.

3. *Portrayal.* Individuals wish to demonstrate what they mean and gestures can give an example or a picture of what

is being communicated. Those common in ordinary conversation include listing of items on the fingers or motions accompanying statements like "she's about this tall." Clients use similar gestures to illustrate their ideas. The girl in conflict with her mother crosses and recrosses her arms before her. Portrayal and emphasis are the most direct forms of nonverbal communication in our culture; they are most easily understood and frequently used. Portrayal is generally a conscious gesture.

4. *Revelation—unaware.* Tension-motivated behavior of which the client is totally unaware is the most critical nonverbal behavior in counseling situations. In tension-packed sessions clients are concerned more with verbalized content than with their own overt behavior. Such unconsciously motivated gestures or postures originate from feelings about themselves, or the topic (past, current, or potential), or the counselor, or the situation. Gestures may be continuous for an extended period of time or may recur frequently with repeated feelings of anxiety or tension. Kagan and his associates report that only mature, perceptive clients are able to interpret such nonverbal behaviors on recall.

5. *Revelation—aware.* Clients are aware of gestures in this category but attribute them to habit. Though aware of the activity they are unaware of its motivation. Leg swinging, ring twisting, key jingling are examples of common tension-associated habitual behaviors adopted as pacifiers by many adults.

6. *Affect demonstration.* The client who wishes deliberately to demonstrate feelings uses nonverbal behaviors falling in this category. Kagan and his associates cite two reasons for such demonstration: (1) the individual "puts on an act" to deceive the counselor regarding feelings or concerns (sadness is covered by wearing a bright smile or the client appears sober and serious because he or she thinks a "good" client acts that way) or (2) clients have an intense desire for the counselor to know and understand their feelings (use of hands by clients to tell counselors that they have nothing to say). Such nonverbal behavior is intentional and fully within awareness of the client.

Summary

Nonverbal behavior is likely to be interpreted intuitively by counselors. It varies so greatly that generalizations are usually unwarranted. Presumably, the typology by Kagan and his associates gives some specificity of meaning for interpretative value and reflects some degree of universality. These researchers report that confusion in interpreting nonverbal behavior often comes from an assumption that the behavior being observed is an unconsciously motivated manifestation (this behavior would be categorized as revelation—unconscious, category 4). However, such behavior is very often the counselee's attempt to make sure that he or she conveys a particular role to the counselor. In essence, the client is putting on an act, and the problem is to ferret out the nonverbal or verbal clues in the situation that contradict any assumed pose.

Because of the lack of commonality of nonverbal behavior among individuals, caution must be exercised in interpreting nonverbal behavior. More and more research effort is being applied to the topic. As greater understanding is gained, more and more attention will be given it in counselor education so that counselors will develop greater sensitivity to nonverbal behavior. To conclude this section, the following comments of Manoil still have much meaning:

Expressive aspects of behavior appear as dynamic, direct, and immediate communication, consequently unaltered by their crystalization into verbal symbols. What is obtained by avoiding the use of words is, however, not necessarily nearer to the truth since cultural factors and

learning, operating at the nonverbal level, would make expressive behavior also into a symbolic system. And, if expressive behavior to be intelligible and communicable has to be codified, the nature of the problem would shift only from verbal codification to nonverbal codification.

The intuitive character in nonverbal communication can be recognized, however, only as a supplementary relative clue to human interaction.[15]

Diagnosis

Diagnosis has been defined as a summary of the counselee's problems and their causes, description of the individual's personality dynamics, and understanding of the individual. As used in counseling, it generally refers to identification of abnormality by the symptoms presented and classification on the basis of observed characteristics. Williamson defined diagnosis as a "terse summary of problems, their causes and other significant and relevant characteristics of the student, together with the implications for potential adjustments and maladjustments."[16] Thorne, using a different approach, stated that "diagnosis refers to the description of the organism and its behavior by a variety of methods whose basic purpose is to discover the personality dynamics of each individual case."[17] He cited ten objectives of diagnosis including the demonstration of etiological factors, the nature and extent of the morbid process, the determination of prognosis and probable course, and the formulation of a dynamic hypothesis of the process as a rational basis for specific psychotherapy.

In the early days of counseling, diagnosis was accepted as an inevitable and desirable function. It included a statement of the present status or adjustment of the counselee, causal factors, suggested counseling procedures, and a prediction of future adjustment. As a process, diagnosis consisted in reducing case data by eliminating irrelevant material and arriving at a best judgment through formulating and testing

[15] Adolph Manoil, "Review of V.A. Film on Psychotherapeutic Interviewing," Part IV, "Nonverbal Communication," *Contemporary Psychology*, 2 (April 1957), 116.
[16] E. G. Williamson, *Counseling Adolescents* (New York: McGraw-Hill, 1950), p. 178.
[17] Frederick C. Thorne, *Principles of Personality Counseling* (Brandon, Vt.: Journal of Clinical Psychology, 1950), p. 40.

hypotheses. The hypotheses were based on generalizations from research and experience, intuition and insight. The term *best judgment* was used rather than a definite conclusion because it was made on the data then at hand and was revised as counseling progressed.

The advent of client-centered counseling cast doubt on the appropriateness of diagnosis as part of the counselor's behavior. The objections of client-centered counseling to the traditional concept of diagnosis originally formulated by Rogers were that it (1) placed the locus of evaluation in the counselor and thereby increased dependent tendencies of clients by causing them to feel that the responsibility for understanding and improving their situation lay with the counselor and (2) resulted in certain long-range social and philosophical implications (direction of the social control of the many by the few).[18]

But even prior to the introduction of client-centered counseling, questions were being raised as to whether diagnosis could be applied to psychological problems. Medical diagnosis is the *distinguishing* of an illness or disease and its *differentiation* from other diseases. Patterson[19] and Tyler[20] have summarized the difficulties of applying diagnosis to emotional disorders. First, the classification of diseases into discrete, mutually exclusive categories (each of which has a common origin, a common course, and a common prognosis) does not fit psychosocial disturbances. Whereas patients with the same physical disease follow rather closely the same course, those who have been diagnosed as having the same emotional disorder do not necessarily follow the same course. Second, the etiology of physical disease is always a specifiable, and ultimately verifiable, physical or external agent (chemical, bacteriological, or viral) whereas emotional disturbances may be due to multiple factors. Third, specific remedies exist, either known or unknown, for physical disease but none has yet been devised for personality problems.

Still another reason why a medical analogy does not precisely fit diagnosis in counseling can be advanced. The degree of participation by the medical patient and the coun-

selee varies greatly. More reliance is placed on the counselee's active participation in the process, and more weight is given his or her self-report statements. In the medical setting such reports are not ignored, but often actual physical tests can be used to verify them. This view could be extended to the treatment process also. Physicians are able to do things *to* patients whereas to a greater extent counselors must depend on working cooperatively *with* counselees.

Another objection to the heavy emphasis placed on diagnosis is the growing evidence that clinical predictions are insufficiently accurate to serve as a basis for life decisions. Intuitive judgments stemming from all known data have been found to be less accurate than statistical predictions derived from a regression equation based on a few variables, especially for predicting complex behavior in variable situations.

Diagnostic classification systems in counseling

Some years ago, Callis suggested that "the fundamental purpose of diagnosis in counseling is to enable the counselor to make predictions about client behavior from which he in turn constructs his plans for handling the case."[21] Several diagnostic classification systems have been devised. These systems assume, perhaps questionably, that emotional disorders, like physical disorders, are separable into discrete entities and that all emotional disorders are basically similar in nature.

WILLIAMSON'S CLASSIFICATION Since early emphasis in counseling was placed on the area of the individual's life in which the problem arose, Williamson and Darley suggested five categories for describing problems encountered in counseling.[22] A summary of these follows:

1. *Personality problems.* Difficulties in adjusting to social groups, family conflicts, and disciplinary infractions.
2. *Educational problems.* Unwise choice of courses of study, differential scholastic achievement, inadequate general scholastic aptitude, ineffective study habits, reading

[18] Carl R. Rogers, *Client-Centered Therapy* (Boston: Houghton Mifflin Company, 1951), pp. 223–224.
[19] C. H. Patterson, *Relationship Counseling and Psychotherapy* (New York: Harper & Row, 1974), pp. 163–175.
[20] Leona Tyler, *The Work of the Counselor*, 3rd ed. (New York: Appleton-Century-Crofts, 1969), pp. 65–72.

[21] Robert Callis, "Diagnostic Classification as a Research Tool," *Journal of Counseling Psychology*, 12 (Fall 1965), 238.
[22] E. G. Williamson and J. G. Darley, *Student Personnel Work* (New York: McGraw-Hill, 1937).

disabilities, lack of scholastic motivation, over- and under-achievement.

3. *Vocational problems.* Uncertain vocational choice, no vocational choice, discrepancy between interests and aptitudes, unwise vocational choice.

4. *Financial problems.* Difficulties arising from need for self-support in school and college.

5. *Health problems.* The individual's acceptance of his or her state of health or physical disabilities or both.

Obviously the classification is an attempt to describe the individual in terms of adjustment to the demands of the environment.

BORDIN'S CLASSIFICATION Bordin pointed to evidence of overlap among the above categories and proposed an alternate set that would be closer to the basic psychological issues involved and therefore more related to differential treatment.[23] His diagnostic categories are summarized here:

1. *Dependence.* Conflict that immobilizes the client and blocks active efforts to resolve the problem or reach a decision is fundamental to this category. Individuals with problems of this type have not learned to solve their problems and are used to playing a passive role. Such problems include how to plan use of time, how to find a part-time job, whether to take a course this semester or next. Bordin suggests that treatment includes aid in attaining insight and acceptance of the fact of feeling inadequate to cope with the problem and in obtaining experiences that will make it possible to work the problem out.

2. *Lack of information.* Sheer restriction in range or appropriateness of experience or in special opportunities to acquire necessary skills is found in this category. Clients are accustomed to accepting and making decisions but face a decision involving information or special skills out of the reach of their experience. They may lack the opportunities to compare themselves with representative groups necessary to judge their abilities, or lack sufficient information about occupations to set their sights realistically, or lack knowl-edge of appropriate social behavior. Bordin suggests that when the ignorance is real and sufficient to account for the difficulty, treatment can be direct: the information can be given or the client referred to source materials or other individuals.

3. *Self-conflict.* Conflicts between self-concepts or between a self-concept and some other stimulus function are involved here. Individuals who fall in this category are unable to cope with problems arising from conflict between the response functions associated with two or more of their self-concepts or between a self-concept and some other stimulus function. Treatment is by nondirective techniques that enable the client to recognize and accept conflicting feelings.

4. *Choice anxiety.* The need to decide among alternative plans all of which upset present life defines this category. Individuals are usually fully informed of all alternatives open to them but come to the counselor hoping to find an alternative that will represent a way out without unpleasant social consequences. Problems of this type increase in incidence during periods of social upheaval and rapid change (for example, military draft). Bordin suggests that treatment indicated is to let them talk it out and help them face and accept the fact that there is no escape without unpleasantness.

5. *No problem.* Some individuals will seek out the counselor in the same spirit as they visit a doctor once a year for a physical checkup. They are playing safe, or they use the contact as an occasion for making up their minds.

Bordin's categories were based more on *source* of difficulty than on *kind* of difficulty (see Williamson's categories).

PEPINSKY'S CLASSIFICATION Pepinsky modified Bordin's categories and tested them out.[24] For "no problem" he suggested that "lack of assurance" be substituted. Individuals who have made a decision but who wish to play safe by checking with others would fall in this category. Pepinsky added a "lack of skill" category and further subdivided self-conflict into cultural, interpersonal, and intrapersonal.

[23] Edward S. Bordin, "Diagnosis in Counseling and Psychotherapy," *Educational and Psychological Measurement*, 6 (Summer 1946), 169–184.

[24] Harold B. Pepinsky, "The Selection and Use of Diagnostic Categories in Clinical Counseling," *Applied Psychological Monographs*, No. 15 (February 1948).

MISSOURI DIAGNOSTIC CLASSIFICATION According to Callis,[25] Berezin[26] contended that neither the Williamson-Darley categories nor the Bordin-Pepinsky categories were adequate but that a two-way classification scheme utilizing both could be useful in counseling. Berezin constructed such a scheme and tested it against actual case data. Callis also reported that Apostal and Miller modified and simplified Berezin's scheme and again tested it against case data.[27] Callis describes the system and its use. The Missouri Diagnostic Classification is a two-dimensional scheme in which problem-goal and cause are indicated. The problem-goal dimension is (1) vocational, (2) emotional, and (3) educational and specifies not only the type of problem dealt with but also the practical goal of counseling. This dimension refers to the developed problem that the counselor and client agree to pursue; it is not necessarily the presenting problem. Callis' definitions of the three categories of this dimension follows:

Vocational (VOC)—Career choice and planning, choice of college major and similar educational planning which would ultimately implement or lead to a career plan.
Emotional (EM)—Personal and social adjustment problems which have a primary affective component. Problems of adjustment to current situations involving emotions, attitudes and feelings.
Educational (ED)—Lack of effective study skills and habits, poor reading ability or lack of information about institutional policies and regulations. Primarily concerned with adjustment to current academic situations rather than planning for future.[28]

Categories in the other dimension refer to the probable cause of the developed problem and attempt to answer such questions as "Why are clients unable to solve their problem within their own personal resources?" or "What is the inadequacy in the client's behavior repertoire?"

The five categories in this dimension and associated commentary are summarized as follows:

1. *Lack of information about or understanding of self* (LIS). Emphasis is on relatively uncomplicated lack of information. Clients simply do not know enough about themselves in relation to certain groups.
2. *Lack of information about or understanding of the environment* (LIE). Although similar to LIS, this refers to environment rather than self and includes lack of educational and occupational information. LIE may result from lack of experiences, gaps in training, or exposure to incomplete or biased propaganda. Clients who persistently distort available information about the environment would more accurately be diagnosed LIS or CS.
3. *Motivational conflict within self* (CS). Conflicting and competing motivations within self and contradictory attitudes toward self predominate. Intrapunitive attitudes, self-depreciation, anxiety, and depression are suggestive of this category. There is a gap between the client's perceived self and ideal self.
4. *Conflict with significant others* (CO). Conflict with parents, teachers, roommates, girl friends, or boy friends are common in this category. In addition, conflicts with new subcultural groups and movement from one geographic region to another or from one socioeconomic level to another may produce CO.
5. *Lack of skill* (LS). Individuals who lack skill to meet the demands imposed by their particular situation, whether educational, social, or vocational, are diagnosed LS. Poor reading ability, poor study skills, poor social skills are typical, but problems that are primarily motivational are not classified LS.

Callis indicates that because not all counseling cases can be described by one problem and one cause, his scheme makes provisions for indicating multiple problems and multiple causes. Although acknowledging that the ultimate use of any diagnostic classification is in the differential choice of treatment, Callis states that the major use currently being made of his diagnostic plan is in record keeping for both training and research purposes. Some questions that the University of Missouri Testing and Counseling Center are investigating and that depend on a diagnostic classification are: "What is the nature of our case load?" "How much

[25] Callis, "Diagnostic Classification."
[26] Annable G. Berezin, "The Development and Use of a System of Diagnostic Categories in Counseling" (Ph.D. diss., University of Missouri, 1957).
[27] R. A. Apostal and J. G. Miller, "A Manual for the Use of a Set of Diagnostic Categories," mimeographed (Columbia: University of Missouri Testing and Counseling Service Report, No. 21, 1959).
[28] Callis, "Diagnostic Classification," p. 239.

time per case is devoted to different types of cases?" "Do counseling centers serving different kinds of populations (for example, high school, college, hospital, rehabilitation agency) generate a different pattern (proportion) of diagnosis?"[29]

Essential characteristics of a diagnostic scheme

Any diagnostic system must reliably classify subjects among its categories. Different judges should agree in the assignment of subjects. Most current schemes fail in this respect. Even for a gross classification, Hunt and his associates report only 54 percent agreement on classifying patients as psychotic, neurotic, or personality disorder and only 32.6 percent agreement on more specific diagnoses.[30]

Some years ago Bordin cited three characteristics that diagnostic classifications of personality problems should possess.[31] First, the classification should enable the counselor to understand more clearly the significance of the individual's behavior. In this way the counselor can be sensitized and respond more adequately to the feelings of the client.

Second, the diagnostic constructs should be mutually exclusive. Categories should not overlap but should vary independently. The more they vary independently, the closer they are assumed to be to the true causes and the farther from surface symptoms. There should be homogeneity of subjects within categories and heterogeneity of subjects among categories. In other words, a classification system should result in greater variance among categories than within categories. Few current diagnostic schemes meet this requirement because clients within the same category vary almost as much as those with different diagnoses. Thus the basis of classification, that is, symptoms, is not a particularly relevant variable. Classification should permit significant differential predictions about individuals in different categories. This prognostic factor is not normally found in most of the present systems.

Third, the category should form the basis for treatment. This most vital characteristic indicates that significant grouping would point to differences in treatment of subjects based on exact knowledge of the etiology and nature of the disturbance.

Because most diagnostic systems devised to date fail to meet these criteria, it has often been suggested that attempts to construct and to use psychological diagnostic systems be abandoned. But apparently this advice is not strong enough to prevail against the desire to design such a system. Classification reflects man's need to simplify and to reduce complex information. In counseling, it would provide the basis for controlling cases and permit comparison of different treatments.

Diagnosis as a comprehensive picture

Tyler believes that diagnosis should be thought of as a means of obtaining a comprehensive picture of the individual.[32] Used in this fashion, diagnosis would involve understanding the image an individual projects so that intelligent action could be taken. From the first moment of contact, the counselor begins forming a working image of clients. Impressions—of their development to date, of the nature of their interpersonal relationships, of their work—go into this picture and sensitize the counselor to alternate courses of action. The outcomes of tests, interviews, observations, and background data modify the image and fill in the details.

Tyler further suggests that diagnosis may be seen as the counselor's asking such questions as "Shall I continue working with this client?" or "What does he need most?" She points out that the diagnostic act in and of itself does not help. For example, the counselor's knowledge of a person's fears does not remove the fears. Any diagnosis must assume that somewhere, sometime the counselee is going to be able to use that diagnosis.

Structural diagnosis

Diagnosis in counseling has been extended to mean interpreting case data. Williamson used the term to refer to the

[29] Ibid., pp. 241–242.
[30] W. A. Hunt, C. L. Sittson, and Edna B. Hunt, "A Theoretical and Practical Analysis of the Diagnostic Process," in *Current Problems in Psychiatric Diagnosis*, ed. P. H. Hoch and J. Zubin (New York: Grune & Stratton, 1953), p. 51.
[31] Bordin, "Diagnosis in Counseling."

[32] Tyler, *Work*, pp. 65–72.

"pattern of consistency" that helps to explain or describe the client's behavior. After data analysis, the counselor selects, from the mass of case data, the relevant facts that form the basis for a prognosis and a plan for later counseling.

Cautions in using diagnosis

Brammer and Shostrom cite and discuss five cautions in respect to diagnostic endeavor: (1) the tendency of counselors to overextend themselves when data are incomplete or inaccurate, (2) the tendency to become preoccupied with the history of the client and to neglect present attitudes and current behavior, (3) the temptation to utilize tests too quickly to facilitate diagnosis, (4) the tendency to lose sight of the counselee's individuality and to become preoccupied with morbidity rather than healthy behavior, and (5) the tendency to show a judgmental attitude toward the client.[33]

Bordin has rejected Rogers' view of diagnosis as being detrimental to counseling relationships.[34] He believes that diagnosis does not automatically mean being judgmental and nonaccepting. Bordin points out that the client's perceptual awareness is only part of his or her experience and that preoccupation with one's own perceptions may lead the counselor to gain superficial rather than penetrating understanding.

Summary

Whether to diagnose or not is a question that has produced much heated discussion during the past few years. The concept *diagnosis* can be considered from many levels and viewpoints. In its broadest sense, however, a certain amount of informal diagnosis takes place within all counseling relationships. As counselors, for example, give consideration to whether they should continue working with a client or refer him or her for more extensive help they may be said to be engaged in diagnosis. The counselor who gathers information from counselees to help them select a particular

interest or personality test in order to provide needed information may be engaged in diagnosis. Diagnosis, then, is not necessarily used to ascertain a basic cause or to determine the best method of treatment. It may simply be the counselor's succession of hypotheses as to what is taking place in the thinking and attitude changes of the counselee. In this sense, the significance of the affective changes expressed by the counselee would be grasped and responded to by the counselor, and thus the relationship between diagnosis (understanding) and counseling seems close. The two processes generally operate concurrently, with one influencing the other. Diagnosis is a developing process, not a discrete event, and counselors learn about clients as they assist them.

Transference and countertransference

A fundamental process in Freudian psychoanalysis is *transference*, or the process whereby patients project their feelings toward a significant person in their life onto the psychoanalyst. For example, the patient shifts the love or hatred that he or she had experienced for a parent to the analyst. It is essential to recognize that this process goes on in the life of an individual in relationships with others; unresolved negative feelings toward parents may express themselves in a person's relationships with authority figures.

The resolution of transference is crucial in the classical Freudian therapeutic process. The working through of feelings projected onto the therapist is viewed as the key to developing or relearning appropriate and realistic reactions necessary to adequate adjustment. In treatment the patient re-examines previously held attitudes and, through the mechanism of insight, establishes more constructive attitudes and feelings.

Psychoanalysis has long recognized that positive and negative transference may develop in the therapist as well as in the patient. When this occurs, it is referred to as *countertransference*. In countertransference therapists project their biases, prejudices, and attitudes onto the patient. Countertransference may interfere with or be destructive to the patient's progress. Countertransference in the therapist may take a variety of forms, depending on the character structure of the analyst and the content with which he or she deals. In its purest sense, the term is applied only to those situations

[33] Lawrence M. Brammer and Everett L. Shostrom, *Therapeutic Psychology*, 3rd ed. (Englewood Cliffs, N.J.: Prentice-Hall, 1977), pp. 139–140.
[34] Edward S. Bordin, *Psychological Counseling*, 2nd ed. (New York: Appleton-Century-Crofts, 1968), p. 147.

where therapists project feelings unresolved in their own personality onto the patient. Normal reactions of warmth, affection, or anger are excluded from this category unless they become extreme or inappropriate. Countertransference problems in therapy are commonly resolved through insight by the therapist, achieved either independently or in the supervisory process.

Counseling is not "depth therapy" in the same sense as psychoanalysis—that is, therapy directed toward personality reconstruction—therefore, the concepts of transference and countertransference are not directly applicable. However, these concepts do have implications for what occurs in counseling, for the simple reason that the human relationship is involved in both psychoanalysis and counseling.

Counselors do not intentionally foster transference in their clients as do classically oriented psychoanalysts—the latter actively encourage its development as a necessary and integral part of treatment. Unless the counselor has a full Freudian orientation, he or she is far more likely to view what the Freudian sees as transference as a manifestation of dependency or positive and negative attitudes. As such, counselors deal with these attitudes as they would any other attitudes expressed in the relationship. The most common approach is through the use of interpretation that encourages client insight into the inappropriateness of extreme positive or negative feelings toward the counselor. The client-centered counselor views such attitudes as stemming from misperceptions of the relationship, and believes they will correct themselves if the counselor reacts to them with understanding and acceptance. These responses lead to recognition by the client that transference attitudes exist within and have no basis or utility in the reality of the relationship.

Test use and interpretation

This book is not designed to familiarize students with basic measurement principles or to present commonly used tests in counseling. Other books[35] and other courses exist for those functions. Here the concern is with test use and interpretation.

Some counseling viewpoints consider the use and interpretation of tests inimical, or at best of limited value, to counseling. Generally opponents of testing maintain that (1) testing encourages client dependency on the counselor and on an external source for problem resolution, (2) test data prejudice the counselor's picture of an individual, and (3) test data are invalid and unreliable enough so that their value is severely limited. It is sometimes maintained that if tests are used or if a test interpretation is given, counseling as such is interrupted or terminated. But from the huge number sold in the United States it appears that most counselors must be using tests in counseling or in other ways. Not all of them, of course, were sold to or used by counselors.

Goldman views the utilization of tests in counseling as flawed. He likens it to a marriage that failed or, even more colorfully, one that was never consummated. Goldman assigns the failure to the following causes: (1) tests were designed initially for selection rather than prediction purposes, (2) the special environmental handicaps suffered by too many disadvantaged populations make the use of tests useless with them, and (3) too few counselors have the requisite knowledge and competencies to tease out and use the subtle information available from current tests.[36] Needless to say, the panel members—counselors, psychologists, test authors —who heard Goldman's proposition argued strenuously against it by (1) stressing the validity, reliability, and utility of test data; (2) suggesting that the current de-emphasis on testing represents an overreaction to test deficiencies; and (3) recommending more extensive treatment of test and measurement theory and practice in counselor education programs.[37]

Criticisms and harmful consequences

The increasing use of tests has been accompanied by a flow of critical comment, for which we cited the following reasons:

[35] See, for example, Bruce Shertzer and James D. Linden, *Fundamentals of Individual Appraisal* (Boston: Houghton Mifflin Company, 1979).

[36] Leo Goldman, "Tests and Counseling: The Marriage That Failed," *Measurement and Evaluation in Guidance*, 4 (January 1972), 213–220.

[37] "Symposium: Tests and Counseling—The Marriage That Failed?" *Measurement and Evaluation in Guidance*, 5 (October 1972), 394–429.

First, tests in and of themselves vary in quality and are far from perfect measuring instruments. . . . *Second*, tests are sometimes improperly administered. . . . *Third*, test scores are often misused. . . . *Fourth*, test data are sometimes misinterpreted. . . . *Fifth*, in many instances tests are improperly safeguarded.[38]

Ebel has summarized four harmful consequences of testing suggested by critics:

It may place an indelible stamp of intellectual status —superior, mediocre or inferior—on a child, and thus predetermine his social status as an adult, and possibly do irreparable harm to his self-esteem and his educational motivation.

It may lead to a narrow conception of ability, encourage pursuit of a single goal, and thus tend to reduce the diversity of talent available to society.

It may place the testers in a position to control education and determine the destinies of individual human beings, while incidentally making the testers themselves rich in the process.

It may encourage impersonal, inflexible, mechanistic processes of evaluation and determination, so that essential human freedoms are limited or lost altogether.[39]

Functions of tests in counseling

The use of tests in counseling has been advocated for several purposes.

1. Tests may be used to help the counselor decide whether the counselee's needs are within the range of his or her services. Some counseling centers, as part of an intake service, routinely collect precounseling diagnostic data to help determine the locus and severity of the problem. Personality inventories and problem check lists may facilitate this rough screening. Sometimes quick estimates of the individual's intellectual functioning are made.

2. Tests may be used for informational purposes to assist the individual to gain self-understanding. Counselees may request or counselors may decide that tests will be used to help counselees secure information about their abilities, aptitudes, interests, and personal characteristics. Lister and Ohlsen, investigating the extent to which test interpretation improved self-understanding of pupils in grades five, seven, nine, and eleven, reported that at all grade levels interpretation was associated with increased accuracy of self-estimates of achievement, intelligence, and interests.[40]

3. Tests may be used to help the counselor gain a better understanding of the individual. Estimations of the counselee's scholastic ability, school achievement, interests, and personality are often used to support data obtained through other means.

4. Tests may be used to help determine which methods, approaches, tools, and techniques will be suitable. Diagnosis is sometimes aided by the use of personality inventories. The individual's unique patterns of thinking and feeling may be uncovered by tests that indicate basic character structure. Certainly diagnostic tests in such skill areas as reading and arithmetic give information around which to plan remedial help and counseling.

5. Tests may be used to help counselees predict future performance such as college success, work potential—as secretary or clerk, for example—performance in mechanical occupations, and the like. Tests provide an improved basis for prediction regarding the likelihood of success in those activities in which prospective performance can be measured.

6. Tests may be used to help counselees arrive at decisions in planning their educational and vocational futures. This is the major use of tests in counseling. If counseling deals with facts and with the individual's feelings about them, tests can yield information about the individual relative to the facts of an educational or vocational program. For counselees who really mean it when they say "I don't know what to do," test data help identify possible courses of action. They may be used to evaluate two or more alternatives or to help determine or confirm the suitability of a tentative choice, plan, or decision. Test data may reveal limitations of

[38] Bruce Shertzer and Shelley C. Stone, *Fundamentals of Guidance* 3rd ed. (Boston: Houghton Mifflin Company, 1976), pp. 237–238.

[39] Robert L. Ebel, "The Social Consequences of Educational Testing," in *Introduction to Guidance*, ed. Bruce Shertzer and Shelley C. Stone (Boston: Houghton Mifflin Company, 1970), pp. 226–234.

[40] James L. Lister and Merle M. Ohlsen, "The Improvement of Self-Understanding Through Test Interpretation," *Personnel and Guidance Journal*, 43 (April 1965), 804–810.

ability, unexpected assets, or inappropriate interests or aptitudes, all of which are relevant for counseling.

7. Tests may be used to stimulate interests not previously considered in counseling. Many counselors use interest inventories with clients to stimulate further thinking about the work world and their interest in it. Some clients learn from test interpretations about their previously unsuspected potentialities for further education or certain occupations. Or counselors use test-interpretation sessions to communicate their interest in clients and to make known their availability to discuss any matter with the client.

8. Tests are sometimes used to help evaluate the outcomes of counseling. In attempting to assess the worth of their work, many counselors have turned to test data. The usual approach involves testing before and after counseling with the use of appropriate control groups. Psychological measures that have been employed include tests of achievement, social and emotional adjustment, self-concept, and social attitudes.

Guidelines for test use

The individual who reads this book has no doubt been exposed innumerable times to guidelines for the use of tests. Consequently, only a few remarks will be made here. First, if tests are to be part of counseling, the counselor should be very familiar with whatever instrument is to be used—what it measures, its validity, reliability, norm groups, error of measurement, administrative procedures, scoring methods, and so on. Second, the reasons why a counselee or a counselor thinks a test would be helpful should be fully explored. What are the expectations for the data once they are obtained? How will the data be used? Is a test the best, most efficacious means of obtaining the information needed? Third, the counselor should be sure that the counselee possesses at least a gross understanding of what the test measures—ability, interest, personality, or whatever. Fourth, counselees should have some idea of the test's strengths and limitations so that their expectations are appropriate to the data elicited. The explanations of this and the preceding point to the counselee should be given in nontechnical language. Fifth, the administration and scoring should be done carefully and thoroughly. Finally, the use of tests by counselors should be guided by ethical considerations:

counselors provide only those services that they are qualified to render, and consideration is given to the client's well-being and welfare. Most of all, the counselor should remember that the purpose of administering tests is to help counselees understand themselves. Test data are to be used by the counselee because they provide information that is needed and wanted and is relevant to the situation.

Test selection in counseling

In by far the greater number of school situations, schoolwide tests have been given prior to the initiation of a counseling relationship. But many college and agency counseling centers employ a psychometrist who administers needed testing. In such cases, the counseling contact is often interrupted for a period of days or weeks. The concern here is with test selection as part of the counseling relationship. Basically, the same principles—understanding, acceptance, and communication—that characterize the counseling relationship apply equally to test selection.

A frequent response to the counselor's query as to why the client has come to the counseling office is "I'd like to take some tests to find out what jobs I'd be good at" or "My mother said you could give me some tests that would tell me what I could do" or "Mrs. White said that since I wasn't doing too good in algebra I should come down and take some tests to see whether I should stay in it." This heavy reliance on a test orientation confronts counselors in almost every setting. Because individuals think tests will help them, all too often the counselor assumes the same thing and proceeds to test selection. Clearly, careful exploration of the client's request is in order to determine whether tests are really needed or will be useful. If a test is appropriate, client participation in its selection may somewhat alleviate his or her dependency feelings and obviate the prescriptive role fostered when counselors select tests on their own. Client participation in test selection has long been advocated, and Goldman has summarized the arguments for it. The first three of the advantages listed below have been paraphrased from Bordin, the remaining five from Goldman:

1. Clients may not return for further interviews if tests are planned without their participation. (This happens when individuals are not emotionally ready to subject themselves to

realistic scrutiny or are unprepared for reality testing or fail to understand the relationship between the test and their problems.)

2. Clients who feel convinced of the purpose of testing can gain insights from self-observation during testing.

3. Motivation to do one's best on tests is strongest when the individual sees the relationship between them and personal goals.

4. To the extent that clients have participated in the decisions to use tests, they will be more ready to accept later interpretations with a minimum of defensiveness.

5. Where dependency is a problem, complete counselor responsibility for test planning does nothing to deal with the problem of dependency except perhaps to reinforce it.

6. Where indecisiveness is a problem, with clients fearing to make a decision either because of lack of confidence in their judgment or because of lack of successful experience in decision-making, they need the experience of making decisions.

7. The client's reactions to suggestions and descriptions of various tests may provide a wealth of diagnostic data.

8. Finally, a better job of test selection is done in terms of the tests selected.[41]

Goldman has also cited the main arguments against client participation in the selection of tests:

1. All this is much ado about nothing; it makes little difference what process is used so long as the most appropriate tests are administered and skillfully interpreted.

2. Because decisions as to the use of tests require knowledge and competencies which few clients have in this area, they must be made by the counselor.

3. Clients are much too emotionally involved with their problems to make objective decisions as to the testing part of planning.

4. Dependency and indecisiveness are not problems with which the counselor legitimately should deal; they more properly are the domain of psychotherapy.[42]

The effect of counselee participation in test selection in relationship to other variables has received a limited amount of investigation. Generally, the findings are contradictory and inconclusive. Many years ago, Seeman reported that college students who selected tests themselves (counselor described each test's values and limitations in a neutral, nonpersuasive manner) each chose a mean number of 5.71 tests (out of 25 available) whereas a control group took a mean number of 4.70 each.[43] The difference was not significant, but the experimental group took a significantly greater variety of tests, which suggests that they were more discriminating as to their individual needs than were counselors of the controls. Further, tests selected by the student were judged to be suitable (93.2 percent of possible cases) for making either actuarial or clinical predictions of the client's stated objectives. In another article Seeman reports further on these same subjects.[44] Through a questionnaire, subjects were asked to give reactions to the first interview and to make judgments about the value of each test. More students who had selected their own tests than control students reported the first interview different from their expectations, but no significant difference was found in the extent to which they felt positively about the interview. Experimental subjects reported no more learning than control students nor did they rate tests as any more valuable.

Logic would seem to be on the side of encouraging counselee participation if only to demonstrate the counselor's belief in the counselee's ability to make decisions and judgments. But some counselors may find client selection of tests incompatible with their counseling style. The "best" way of test selection is the way in which the counselor feels comfortable and competent so that the operation is not bumbling or awkward. It should be clear that those who advocate counselee participation in test selection do not mean that the counselee decides which specific test is the better measure. This technical responsibility rightfully belongs to the counselor. As Goldman suggests,

An approach that seems to us to have considerable merit is to ask counselees to participate in specifying alternate *courses of action* and *questions* about these alternatives. Some of these questions have nothing to do with tests, as

[41] Bordin, *Psychological Counseling*, pp. 299–301, and Leo Goldman, *Using Tests in Counseling*, 2nd ed. (New York: Appleton-Century-Crofts, 1971), pp. 41–42. Copyright © 1971 by Meredith Corporation.

[42] Goldman, *Using Tests in Counseling*, p. 43.

[43] Julius Seeman, "A Study of Client Self-Selection of Tests in Vocational Counseling," *Educational and Psychological Measurement*, 8 (Autumn 1948), 327–346.

[44] Julius Seeman, "An Investigation of Client Reactions to Vocational Counseling," *Journal of Consulting Psychology*, 13 (April 1949), 95–104.

TABLE 13.2 **Summary of research on modes of test interpretation**

Criterion	Study	Results*
Accuracy of self-knowledge	Folds & Gazda (1966)	I > M (2 of 9 self-estimates of aptitude and achievement) M > I (2 of 9 self-estimates) M > P (2 of 9 self-estimates) I > C, G > C, P > C (5 of 9 self-estimates) I = M = P (5 of 9 self-estimates)
	Forster (1969)	P > I (composite score based on aptitude and achievement)
	Tipton (1969)	I > C (2 of 8 ability concepts on immediate posttest, 3 of 8 on delayed posttest) P > C (7 of 8 concepts on immediate, 2 of 8 on delayed posttest) P > I (2 of 8 concepts on immediate, 1 of 8 on delayed posttest)
	Wright (1963)	I = M, I > C, M > C (aptitude self-estimates) I > M, I > C, M = C (interest self-estimates) I = M, I > C, M > C (achievement self-estimates) I = M, I > C, M > C (total: aptitude + interests + achievement)
Realism of choice	Bivlofsky et al. (1953)	I = M (mean ratings by 4 judges)
	Hoyt (1955)	I > C, M > C, I = M (sum of ratings by 2 judges)
	Wright (1963)	I = M = C (rating agreement by at least 2 of 3 judges)
Certainty of choice	Hoyt (1955)	I > C, M > C, I = M (client self-ratings)
Appropriateness of certainty	Hoyt (1955)	I = M = C (increases/decreases in certainty scored according to judges' ratings of realism)
Satisfaction with choice	Hoyt (1955)	I > C, M > C, I = M (client self-ratings)
Information test score	Wright (1963)	I > C, M > C, I = M (quiz covering testing and test interpretation)
Relaxation rate	Forster (1969)	I > P (rate of decline in skin conductance over interview)
Client ratings of counseling	Folds & Gazda (1966)	I > M, I > P (2 of 4 questionnaire items) I = M = P (2 of 4 questionnaire items) I = M (1 questionnaire item applicable only to interview setting)
Client ratings of counseling (continued)	Wright (1963)	I > M (4 item immediate posttest) I > M (4 item delayed posttest)

*I = individual interpretation
 M = multiple interpretation (2 or more clients in group)
 P = programmed or written materials used for interpretation
 C = control group (no treatment)

SOURCE: Laurel W. Oliver, "Evaluating Career Counseling Outcome for Three Modes of Test Interpretation," *Measurement and Evaluation in Guidance*, 10 (October 1977), 154. Copyright © 1977 American Personnel and Guidance Association. Reprinted with permission.

for example, "What salaries are usual in pharmacy?" or "Which colleges offer courses in hotel management?" For those questions that may be answerable by tests, as "What are my chances of doing well in retailing?" the counselor indicates which tests can provide answers and the nature of the answers. The client can participate in deciding, first, whether this is a question he wishes answered. Second, he can participate in thinking about whether a particular kind of predictive information is already available, in his record or his memory, and if not, whether he then wants to try those tests that would be appropriate.[45]

Test interpretation

Research studies have sought to determine the most effective means of communicating test results. Test information has been presented to clients in one-to-one interviews, in groups, by using audio-visual devices, through written or programmed materials, by computers or by combination of these modes. Similarly multiple criteria have been used to judge the usefulness of providing test information to the client. Oliver[46] summarizes the findings of fourteen studies that compared various modes of presenting test data to clients. His tabular summary has been presented here as Table 13.2. Oliver points out that these investigations demonstrate that clear-cut proof is lacking of the superiority of any one mode of presenting test data. Although some research undertakings have shown individual test interpretation to be superior to group, the majority of such studies have reported no significant difference. Similarly, when programmed interpretation has been compared with counselor interpretation, equivalence of the two modes has been the outcome. Oliver speculated that the reason for inconsistent findings was that both the *mode* and the *content* varied.

Oliver compared the outcome of individual, multiple, and programmed modes of test interpretation of four different vocational tests with the content held constant across treatments. The seventy-five subjects (thirty-five males and forty females) were introductory psychology students who were assigned randomly to one of the three modes. Subjects in the individual condition scored significantly higher than subjects in the other two modes on perceived effectiveness of test interpretation and on career choice certainty, and they preferred it to the other two modes. Subjects in the multiple and programmed conditions did not differ significantly from each other on any dependent measure.

Hills and Williams hypothesized that communication of educational-vocational test results would bring about substantive changes in self-perceptions of counselees engaged in brief counseling contacts. Tests included the *Strong Vocational Interest Blank*, the *Kuder Preference Record*, the *Differential Aptitude Tests*, and other measures when appropriate. Experimental measures were Self-Ideal-Ordinary scores, obtained before and after counseling. The self-perceptions of forty-five subjects who read written summaries of test results and who were given the Self-Ideal-Ordinary evaluation before completing counseling were compared to self-perceptions of other counselees receiving other treatments. The results indicated that communication of test results did not lead to positive changes in self-perception. Test results that differed from clients' preconceived notions of themselves appeared to have a negative effect.[47]

Hopper[48] sought to determine how well parents of fourth- and fifth-grade students remembered the norm groups and standardized test results reported to them in parent-teacher conferences. Parents (N = 84) were interviewed during a two-week period following the conferences and asked to indicate the stanine in which their child had scored on the subtests of the *Stanford Achievement Test*. Some 35 percent of the parents' responses were accurate and 40 percent were off by one stanine. Parents of high-achieving students were most accurate in placing their child's subtest achievement at a proper stanine level and parents of low-achieving students were least accurate. About 20 percent were accurate in

[45] Goldman, *Using Tests in Counseling*, p. 53.
[46] Laurel W. Oliver, "Evaluating Career Counseling Outcome for Three Modes of Test Interpretation," *Measurement and Evaluation in Guidance*, 10 (October 1977), 153–161.
[47] David A. Hills and John E. Williams, "Effects of Test Information upon Self-Evaluation in Brief Educational-Vocational Counseling," *Journal of Counseling Psychology*, 12 (Fall 1965), 275–281.
[48] Gordon Hopper, "Parental Understanding of Their Child's Test Results as Interpreted by Elementary School Teachers," *Measurement and Evaluation in Guidance*, 10 (July 1977), 84–89.

their recollections of the norm groups (national and classroom) to which their child had been compared.

Some years ago Bixler and Bixler identified two crucial aspects of test interpretation: (1) presenting test results and their predictive possibilities in a manner understandable to the client and (2) selecting the methodology of dealing with the client in order to facilitate his or her use of this information. Their paraphrased recommendations follow:

1. Give the client simple statistical predictions based upon the test data.
2. Allow clients to evaluate the prediction as it applies to themselves.
3. Remain neutral toward test data and the client's reaction.
4. Facilitate the client's self-evaluation and subsequent decisions by the use of therapeutic procedures.
5. Avoid persuasive methods. Test data should provide motivation—not the counselor.[49]

What counselors know about a test or an inventory and how they administer and interpret it determine how effectively it will work for their counselees. Professionally competent counselors validate test data against other counselee information secured from records, interviews, observation, and other test situations.

Use of test results by counselees depends on their understanding and acceptance of test data. Because counselees are ill informed about test scores or profiles, the counselor must decide what they are to be told and how test data should be discussed. If the data are to be useful to counselees, they must be able to accept and use them to change behavior or make future choices. Clearly, they can do so only if the counselor's language about the meaning of test scores minimizes threat, which is not uncommonly involved in test interpretation sessions. Basically, this means that the counselor communicates test data objectively, without introducing judgments in the meaning of the test scores.

Some counselors have found it helpful to present personality and interest inventory scores that are above or below the average part of the normative group graphically. For most personality or interest inventories this means scores below the sixteenth percentile and above the eighty-fourth percentile. Such scores vary enough from the norm to reflect ways the individual differs from the middle two thirds of the norm group. A simple expedient is to draw lines across the profile and say, "Unless scores are above or below these lines, they do not describe the individual as being different from most people on whom the inventory was standardized." Most counselees will infer that if their personality or interest inventory score is not in the "normal" group they are abnormal. It is better, therefore, to avoid use of the word *normal* in discussing personality and interest inventory scores.

In interpreting any test—personality, interest, ability, aptitude—beginning counselors may find it helpful to experiment for a while with terms with which they feel comfortable and those that are simple enough to be understood by their counselees. In brief, scores should be discussed and interpretations given in simple, lay terminology. It may be noted that when counselors use the same words over and over to convey the meaning of scores to different counselees they are likely to feel that their interpretations are becoming boring. But they, of course, are the only ones who hear the same description repeatedly. After finding a useful way of describing a score to counselees, they should stick with it.

Whether counselors discuss scores in the third person—that is, "People with scores like these tend to . . ."—depends on their style and perceptions of what the counselee can best accept and use. By evaluating their interview tapes, they can discover suitable interpretative methods. In addition, knowledge of a particular counselee will permit them to judge what the latter will be comfortable in discussing.

After interpreting the meaning of a given score it is advisable to pause to ascertain whether the counselee wants to discuss it in greater detail or understands it. Although observation of the counselee's verbal and nonverbal behavior provides cues to the reception of the information, the counselor may not always be sure, but can ask, "Is this clear?" or "Would you like me to run through that again?"

It should be recognized that not all counselees will accept the test results. The individual may not react in a logical, coherent manner to results that are unfavorable or different from what was expected. Test data may be threatening and reacted to as individuals respond to threat: with anger, rejection, withdrawal, disbelief, and so on. Whatever emotional

[49] Ray H. Bixler and Virginia H. Bixler, "Test Interpretation in Vocational Counseling," *Educational and Psychological Measurement*, 6 (Spring 1946), 145–155.

FIGURE 13.1 **Purdue Guidance Clinic test record profile**

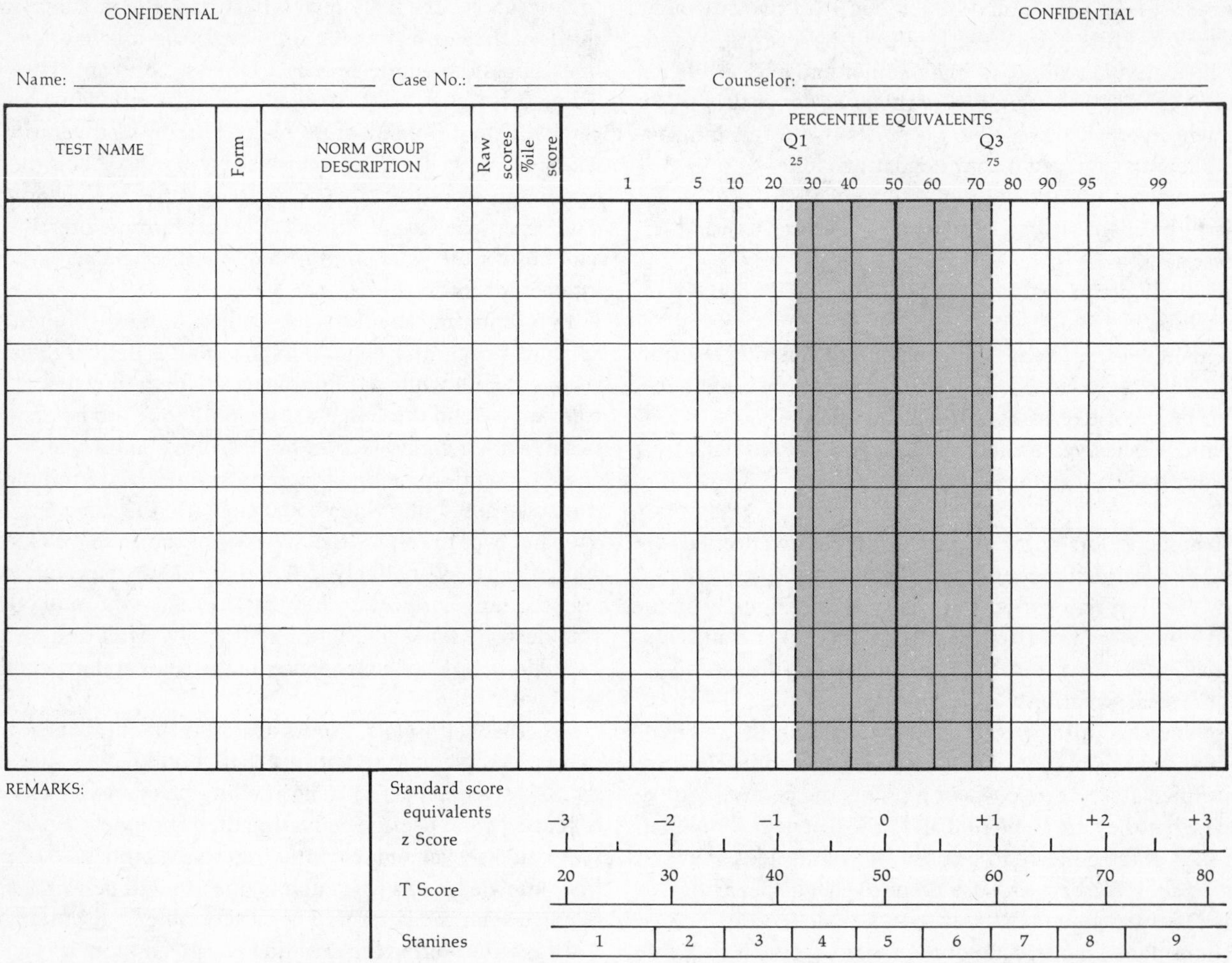
CONFIDENTIAL
CONFIDENTIAL
Name:
Case No.:
Counselor:
TEST NAME
Form
NORM GROUP DESCRIPTION
Raw scores
%ile score
PERCENTILE EQUIVALENTS
Q1
25
Q3
75
1 5 10 20 30 40 50 60 70 80 90 95 99
REMARKS:
Standard score equivalents
z Score
−3 −2 −1 0 +1 +2 +3
T Score
20 30 40 50 60 70 80
Stanines
1 2 3 4 5 6 7 8 9

reaction—satisfaction, doubt, fear—is evoked by the description of test data, it is the responsibility of counselors to deal with these attitudes just as they deal with other emotional components encountered in other counseling situations. Essentially this means that counselees are given an opportunity to verbalize their feelings and attitudes and that the counselor recognizes and responds to them. The counselee's feelings cannot be ignored or responded to by defending the validity of the instrument used. Rather the counselor accepts the feelings as feelings and responds to them in ways that are helpful to the counselee.

Organization of test data is essential if the two problems identified by Bixler and Bixler are to be met with any degree of success. Some means of coherently presenting test data are needed if they are to be incorporated into the counselee's experience, and a test profile form (see Figure 13.1) is one such means. Some counselors have the individual complete the profile as the data are communicated to him or her. Profiles have the advantage of keeping the test results directly in front of the counselee and encouraging integration of the data during the interpretation. They also insure that all the necessary information is discussed and thus serve as a reminder to the counselor to deal with all scores and their interrelationship as well as covering necessary points such as norm groups, type of scores used, and so on. Data are not to be presented all at once. Most beginning counselors err in presenting test results too rapidly as though it were an unpleasant task that they wished to be rid of. The individual has to have time to absorb the meanings and think through the implications.

Goldman has outlined four dimensions of test interpretation and identified the types of test validity associated with each.[50]

The first is *descriptive*. Essentially it provides an interpretation of the kind of person the individual is—how he or she relates to other people, how numerical reasoning is handled, what the person likes to do, or how he or she compares to others. Descriptive interpretation depends on construct, content, and concurrent validities.

The second is *genetic*. It seeks to interpret how and why individuals became the way they are. Predictive validities are used in a postdictive manner—inferences as to what happened previously are made from a present score.

The third type of interpretation is *predictive*, or what is likely to happen to individuals—for example, how they might fare at college. Predictive interpretation is directly linked to predictive validity.

Finally, there is *evaluative* interpretation, which involves advice from counselors or presentation of their judgment as to what choice—to marry, go to this college—the counselee should make. This particular type of interpretation differs from others, not in respect to types of validities on which it is based, but in terms of whether the counselor makes recommendations.

EXPECTANCY TABLES Meaningful and clear interpretations of test data are the counselor's basic aim, and the use of expectancy tables is probably one of the most effective techniques available for providing them. An expectancy table can be constructed very easily by plotting scores on a specific test against scores on another criterion for a group of individuals. Expectancy tables require little mathematical or statistical sophistication for either developing or interpreting them. For example, if the raw scores on test ABC range from 1 to

TABLE 13.3 **Sample expectancy table**

Raw scores ABC test	Third-year English marks				
	F	D	C	B	A
51–60	0%	5%	40%	40%	15%
41–50	10	15	40	25	10
31–40	15	15	50	20	0
21–30	30	30	30	10	0
11–20	80	20	0	0	0
1–10	90	10	0	0	0

60 and the grades in third-year English are available, all that is needed is a listing of the students that have taken the ABC test and their grades in third-year English. Then an expectancy table can be drawn up showing the percentages of students receiving specific grades for the specific scores on the ABC test (see Table 13.3). If a student receives a score of 32 on the test, other students who obtained scores in the same range (31–40) received the following marks: 15 percent F's, 15 percent D's, 40 percent C's, 20 percent B's, and 0 percent A's. (The 0 percent would be the least reliable because there is no score in this area, but it could be pointed out to the student that he or she might be the person to change the percentage.)

A score such as 32 could be interpreted in a number of ways; for example: "Students receiving scores like yours on the ABC test have ranged from B to F; 15 percent failed third-year English and 85 percent passed; 60 percent received marks of B or C." This is obviously more valuable than saying, "Your chances of passing are pretty good."

Sycamore[51] has described the use of expectancy tables in midterm conferences to inform students of their future performance based on their past or current efforts. He notes that the worth of an expectancy table will be obvious to students, vocational advisees, or concerned parents.

COUNSELOR STATEMENTS Byrn has developed examples of counselor statements that may be used to stimulate counselee thinking about test data and self.[52]

[50] Goldman, *Using Tests in Counseling*, pp. 146–150.

[51] James N. Sycamore, "The Expectancy Table: A Tool for Midterm Conferences," *The School Counselor*, 25 (January 1978), 203–205.
[52] Delmont K. Byrn, "The Test Interpretation—Planning Interview," unpublished paper developed for use in training at the University of Michigan.

The test interpretation—planning interview

1. Have confidence in the student's planning ability—even if he or she has shown little.

   Try: "What other information do you need about yourself before you decide?"

   Not: "Maybe we can decide what you should do by taking some tests."

2. Relate immediate plans to future plans—don't try to treat them separately.

   Try: "What can you do this year in high school to prepare for college later on?"

   Not: "Your grades aren't so good now but you have good engineering aptitude."

3. Make alternate plans sound respectable—not like second-rate crash programs.

   Try: "If that doesn't happen to work out, what else could you do?"

   Not: "If you fail in engineering you always could go back to drafting."

4. Encourage students to make their own plans—rather than to agree to yours.

   Try: "How do you suppose you would go about your idea of studying harder?"

   Not: "It looks to me like you've got to study a lot harder."

5. Remind girls of both career and homemaking plans—not just one or the other.

   Try: "How do you plan to work marriage and family into your future plans?"

   Not: "Your future seems all set with college and a career in journalism."

6. Open new educational and vocational doors—don't just close them to the student.

   Try: "There are 20,000 jobs besides engineering, many of which you can qualify for."

   Not: "You won't be able to get into engineering with your low grades."

7. Relate test data to other experiences—don't discuss them as abstractions.

   Try: "How does this fit in with your interests as you know them?"

   Not: "That's the way your interests look. Any questions?"

8. Reflect on a student's rejection of low test scores—don't write off low performance.

   Try: "You don't think this is your real ability? What other clues do you have?"

   Not: "Tests aren't foolproof. There might have been a slip-up."

9. Get students involved in test interpretation—don't just recite the results.

   Try: "What did you think of that test? How do you suppose you did?"

   Not: "On this test you are at the 46%ile. On this one, the 23%ile."

10. Explain the purpose of the test in functional terms—not in psychological jargon.

    Try: "This test allows you to compare yourself with H.S. juniors in numerical ability."

    Not: "This DAT test, like the A.C.E., measures numerical perception."

11. Use test results in context with all other data—not as goals in themselves.

    Try: "Add this test information to everything else you know about yourself."

    Not: "According to these tests you should be in mechanical work."

12. Use test results for student planning—not for the counselor's diagnosis.

    Try: "This allows you to compare yourself with other seniors in ability to learn."

    Not: "This confirms my hunch that you would be able to succeed in college."

13. Refresh the student's memory on each test before discussing it—don't discuss it cold.

    Try: "Remember this one on which you chose which things you liked best and least?"

    Not: "On the Kuder you were high on persuasive and mechanical, low on artistic."

14. Relate scholastic aptitude to the school record—don't look only at test results.

    Try: "With your ability you should be able to do A or B work with average effort."

    Not: "Your grades haven't been good, but you have high aptitude for college."

15. Explain test results simply—don't use elaborate statistical devices.

    Try: "This is high, this low, this average for seniors; here is about how you stand."

    Not: "You fall within these fiducial limits. If you flip a coin 100 times, etc."

16. Express low test performance or unpleasant information honestly—but with perspective.

> *Try:* "You are within the range of successful college students but well below average."
> *Not:* "Only 20% of college students have less scholastic ability than you."

17. Turn test profile sheets so students can read them—don't make them read upside down.

> *Try:* (Read profile upside down yourself or follow along on a duplicate copy.)
> *Not:* "Let's see if we can both read this profile." (both twisting)

18. Clearly establish interests as preferences—don't confuse them with ability.

> *Try:* "You like these activities, dislike those." "Your interest patterns are—"
> *Not:* "You are high in social service, low in mechanical."

19. Remember expressed and demonstrated interests—not just interest inventory results.

> *Try:* "This inventory gives you another kind of picture of your interests."
> *Not:* "This inventory shows where your interests lie."

20. Explain the Strong through occupational comparisons—not directly as with the Kuder.

> *Try:* "You can compare your interest patterns right now (in 400 items) with those of established people in 45 different occupations."
> *Not:* "You like accounting—probably because of math."

21. Regroup complicated profile scores—don't assume the student can assimilate them.

> *Try:* "What are your high areas of interest? Low areas? Average ones?"
> *Not:* "See all these red marks? What do you think of them?"

22. Have students summarize often—don't do all the reviewing and organizing for them.

> *Try:* "How would you summarize your interests as you see them right now?"
> *Not:* "Your interests are highest in this, lowest in that area. Any questions?"

23. Let test interpretation be the beginning of career planning—not the end.

> *Try:* "Now you should study occupations just as you have studied yourself."
> *Not:* "Well, that's what the tests show. Are there any questions?"

Career discussion plan
Compare:

Self	with	*Occupations*
1. aptitudes		4. requirements
2. interests		5. opportunities
3. personality		6. atmosphere

Finally, it should be recognized that test interpretation in actual practice is far from being as logical or orderly as presented in this and other descriptions of it. There is considerable latitude in counselor test interpretative practices. Presumably, variability exists not only from counselor to counselor but from counselee to counselee because of the differing role each enacts during the activity. The extent of counselee participation is dependent not only on counselor style or approach but also on counselee personality and the interaction of his or her personality with that of the counselor.

Nontest adjuncts to counseling

Some principal adjuncts utilized in counseling are autobiography, personal data questionnaires, essays, sentence completion, and play media.

Autobiography

Production of an autobiography sometimes helps clients place in perspective the development of their current situation. The autobiography as a tool for understanding someone reveals not only patterns of behavior but, perhaps even more important, the personal attitudes and emotions behind the behavior. Undertaken in a cooperative manner by the counselee, it may provide insight into the inner person—the experiences and knowledge about oneself. An autobiography is one's own written introspective account of his life.

The autobiography has a long history of providing source information for studying behavior. However, the rise of behaviorism in psychology relegated its use to the fringe area of scientific psychological data.

Most authorities classify autobiographies into two basic types—structured and unstructured. Naturally, it is possible to combine the two or to vary the degree of structure. Some call the two types controlled and uncontrolled; others label them systematic and unsystematic. The unstructured is perhaps the more fruitful for counseling purposes and may reveal many facets of personality not brought to the surface by other techniques. The autobiography is often difficult to interpret, particularly if the client does not present material in an organized way. Basically, the unstructured autobiography presents the individual's life without regard to specific questions. It is the individual's choice to write what has been important to that person and the experiences that have had a bearing on his or her life. The structured autobiography is written according to an outline or in response to specific questions or topics provided by the counselor. It may be more useful for individuals who are not very verbal. Instructions or questions are given to the client to write about family history, personal history, major experiences, aims and aspirations, and the like.

Another way of classifying autobiographies is described by Annis.[53] The first category is *comprehensive*, and individuals cover a wide range of interrelated experiences over a relatively long period of their life. The second is *topical*, and deals with a fairly specific theme, episode, or experience. Annis presents a graphic representation of autobiographies with respect to the degree of structure (see Figure 13.2).

RESEARCH ON AUTOBIOGRAPHIES Years ago, Danielson and Rothney compared structured and unstructured autobiographies written by seventy-eight eleventh-grade students in an English class.[54] Their analysis dealt with the effectiveness of these two approaches in their ability to elicit students' problems in six areas. No significant difference was reported in four of the six problem areas. Significantly greater numbers of problems were found in the family relationships category in unstructured autobiographies and significantly more problems in the education category in the

FIGURE 13.2 **Graphic representation of an autobiographical typology**

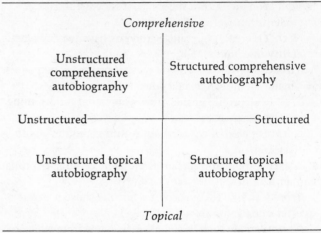

SOURCE: From Arthur P. Annis, "The Autobiography: Its Uses and Value in Professional Psychology," *Journal of Counseling Psychology*, 14 (January 1967), 10. Copyright © 1967 by the American Psychological Association, and reproduced by permission.

structured approach. These authors concluded that selection of the autobiographical form was dependent on the problem areas in which the counselor is interested.

Mueller, Schmieding, and Schultz also have sought to determine which autobiographical form elicits the most useful responses.[55] They investigated the effects of writing structured and semistructured autobiographies in first or third person. From their data the authors concluded that (1) differences existed in self-report data elicited by the four autobiographic forms; (2) semistructured, first person was the most effective form; (3) structured, third person was the least effective; (4) either form of semistructure was superior to a structured form; and (5) differences were clearly less between the first- and third-person forms than between the semistructured and structured forms.

No technique is of value unless it is put to use. Some years ago, Shaffer reported that the autobiography was used by only one fourth of the counselors in large school systems and that only one half of them had ever seen an autobiog-

[53] Arthur P. Annis, "The Autobiography: Its Uses and Value in Professional Psychology," *Journal of Counseling Psychology*, 14 (January 1967), 9–17.
[54] Paul J. Danielson and John W. M. Rothney, "The Student Autobiography: Structured or Unstructured?" *Personnel and Guidance Journal*, 33 (September 1954), 30–33.
[55] Richard J. Mueller, O. A. Schmieding, and John L. Schultz, "Four Approaches to Writing Autobiographies," *The School Counselor*, 11 (March 1964), 160–164.

raphy.[56] Ratings obtained from sixty-eight counselors placed the autobiography next to last in a list of ten sources of data. The rank order was as follows: (1) interview, (2) achievement tests, (3) intelligence tests, (4) anecdotal records, (5) oral teacher reports, (6) grades, (7) written teacher reports, (8) personality tests,(9) autobiographies, and (10)questionnaires. Finally, Shaffer reported that from his study of 500 autobiographies, most appeared to be honest and accurate.

INTERPRETING AUTOBIOGRAPHIES All autobiographies, whether structured or unstructured, are limited by the individual's (1) willingness to self-disclose, (2) self-insight and self-understanding, (3) ability to understand the content of the topic, and (4) ability to communicate in writing. The autobiography is a very intimate technique because it involves the direct expression of an individual. It has the weaknesses inherent in any subjective technique: individuals may overlook their limitations or magnify real or imagined strengths when judging themselves.

Baldwin's personal structure analysis provides a quantitative analysis of autobiographies.[57] He translated content to a table of correspondence that resembles a computational scattergram for a product-moment correlation. The table was interpreted in respect to two basic assumptions. The first was the *frequency* with which an item appeared. This may be used as a measure of its importance. The second was the *contiguity* of two items. The appearance of two items together more often than would occur by chance indicates a relationship to the individual's personality. In addition, Dollard and Mowrer developed a discomfort-relief quotient to assess tension change that they believed was applicable to the autobiography.[58] They reported a scoring reliability of .80 for eight different scorers of a social case record.

There is no quick or easy route to analysis and interpretation of autobiographies. Interpretation takes time, careful attention to detail, and some background knowledge of the individual. The following questions can help guide interpretation by counselors of what they are examining.

1. *What general impression is conveyed by the writer?* Note the variability in tone as writers touch on things that are of vital concern to them. Are impressions of happiness, depression, good mental health present? Observe the use of emotionally charged words such as *love, mother, hate,* and the like. The appearance of the paper, whether it is neatly or carelessly done, has little correlation with behavior patterns

2. *From your knowledge of the client's history, have significant experiences or persons been omitted?* Although autobiographies are not expected to be complete in every detail, significant omissions may be cues worthy of follow-up in counseling. If the individual has avoided mentioning family members or a known event, such omissions should be studied carefully. This does not mean the counselor should expect a blow-by-blow, day-by-day, or week-by-week account. Normally, people write briefly about peaceful, pleasant periods in their lives, concentrating on incidents of major import to them.

3. *What is the length of the autobiography?* Length is dependent on such factors as (1) motivation to write, (2) degree of structure, (3) facility of expression, and (4) degree to which the individual believes help is needed.

4. *How is the autobiography organized?* Naturally, if the individual is given an outline, few clues for interpretation can be obtained from this guideline. However, changes in any prepared outline should be noted. The most common organization for unstructured autobiographies is chronological. Are there gaps and omissions in the material? What has the author chosen to emphasize?

5. *What is the level of expression?* If the individual believes no value will result from the autobiography, he or she may write in a very superficial manner. Students, particularly in upper elementary and junior high school, are likely to report fairly minor events and experiences. Extremely defensive persons may resort to shallowness in writing about their development. Lack of depth or evasiveness characterizes the papers of those who are attempting to hide, or who do not wish to disclose, their concerns or anxieties.

6. *Are there inaccuracies in the autobiography?* Inaccuracies as used here refers to attempts to deliberately falsify experiences or events or to unconscious errors in

[56] E. Evan Shaffer, Jr., "The Autobiography in Secondary School Counseling," *Personnel and Guidance Journal*, 32 (March 1954), 395–398.

[57] A. L. Baldwin, "Personal Structure Analysis: A Statistical Method for Investigating the Single Personality," *Journal of Abnormal and Social Psychology*, 37 (April 1942), 163–183.

[58] John Dollard and O. Hobart Mowrer, "A Method of Measuring Tension in Written Documents," *Journal of Abnormal and Social Psychology*, 42 (January 1947), 3–32.

reporting. Relatively few autobiographies are distorted on purpose; the distortions occur when the writer is not convinced of the value of the autobiography. The ability to detect inaccuracies increases with experience in reading autobiographies as well as with previous knowledge of the individual.

Some years ago, Shaw classified the orientations with which the autobiographer responded to the task.[59] In the first category was the *chronicler*, who cites only the external events of life. In the second was the *self-defender*, who sought to defend his or her activities and points of view. The *confessant* used the opportunity to communicate thoughts never before expressed, and the *self-analyst* used the autobiography as an exercise in self-analysis. Allport, in his classic monograph, specified thirteen motives that usually operate several at a time in the production of any personal document: special pleading, exhibitionism, desire for order, literary delight, securing personal perspective, tension relief, monetary gain, completing an assignment, assisting in therapy, redemption and social reincorporation, scientific interest, public service, and desire for immortality.[60]

SUMMARY The major feature of the autobiography is that it permits clients to tell their own story in their own manner. Baird points out that it is a low-cost technique that helps individuals organize and interpret their experiences in such a way as to see their personal significance.[61] If this is the case, then surely clients will be in a better position to work on their problems. Riccio believes that the autobiography is little used because counselors are more secure and comfortable with test scores.[62] Test scores can be interpreted through reference to norms whereas the autobiography cannot. But perhaps Bonner's criticisms of the autobiography are the most compelling reasons.

The chief defects of the autobiographical method are, first, that it is practically impossible to determine the consistency or stability of its data short of requiring the autobiographer to write still another self-revealing document, with which to compare the first. Second, there is no criterion for evaluating the subject's internal attitudes and feelings regarding the crucial events in his life.[63]

Bonner's criticisms can be applied equally well to any self-report document.

Personal data questionnaires

Personal data questionnaires have long been used to obtain vital information. Usually they contain items regarding the student's home, family, health, educational and vocational plans, current activities, present life situation, and the like.

Their purpose in counseling has been primarily that of obtaining background information. Figure 13.3 presents the Purdue Guidance Clinic form, which has been revised a number of times to obtain the specific kinds of information useful to counselors in helping high school and college students who come to the clinic.

Personal data questionnaires may provide an organized system by which individuals can begin to think about themselves; that is, they supply intake interview information. Essentially, they help the counselor better understand clients as they function in their environment.

Essays

The essay is another personal document yielding material about the counselee's self-perceptions and showing readiness for counseling. The counselee is assigned a specific topic to write about, such as "What I Want from Life," "My Family and Me," "What I'm Like as a Person."

[59] C. R. Shaw, *The Jack-Roller: A Delinquent Boy's Own Story* (Chicago: University of Chicago Press, 1930).

[60] Gordon W. Allport, *The Use of Personal Documents in Psychological Science*, Bulletin 49 (New York: Social Science Research Council, 1942).

[61] C. R. Baird, "The Autobiography," *Education Digest*, 19 (March 1954), 39–43.

[62] Anthony C. Riccio, "The Status of the Autobiography," *Peabody Journal of Education*, 36 (July 1958), 33–36.

[63] H. Bonner, *Psychology of Personality* (New York: Ronald Press, 1961), p. 123.

Sentence completion techniques

Sentence completion techniques have a long history of use in studying intellectual functioning and personality. Some items are as follows: "I am . . . ," "I like people who . . . ," "What worries me is . . . ," "They . . . ." The task of the counselee is to finish the sentences in such a way as to make meaningful statements. Items such as "They . . ." and "I am . . ." are often termed *inventive* items whereas the others are referred to as *selective* items. Inventive items are viewed as being more intuitive and therefore less meaningful but they are useful in generating counselee production of projection.

Sentence completion techniques have a wide variety of purposes, chief among which are screening and diagnosis. Basically, the assumption in their use is that individuals will reflect certain of their needs or attitudes if presented with an ambiguous sentence stem. From the responses, inferences are often made as to their mode of adjustment such as withdrawal, aggression, dependence, and inaction, and the like. A study by Feldhusen and his associates used a sentence completion scale to differentiate "behaving" from "misbehaving" children.[64] The responses not only discriminated between these groups but yielded valuable insight into each child's personal problems.

The reader who is interested in further information about projective methods for assessing personality will find the volume by Rapaport and his associates an excellent introduction to this field.[65]

Play media

Play media are often used by counselors who work with elementary school children. Play media include puppets, modeling clay, dolls, plastic arts, toy telephones, paints, crayons, pipe cleaners, building materials, rubber guns and knives, typewriters, and so on, and they encourage the release of feelings without guilt. For example, children may be able without embarrassment to do violence to a doll representing the father but in an interview situation would never allow themselves to verbalize this feeling. Ginott states that "the child's play is his talk and toys are his words."[66]

The counselor, through play media, may encourage the discussion of fears and other emotional reactions. As Nelson points out, it is in play that the elementary school child (1) develops social relations, (2) tests various roles and concepts, and (3) works through frustrations and concerns.[67] In contrast to the adolescent who can and does *verbalize* frustrations, the child *acts* feelings of love, anger, and acceptance. Nelson believes that the use of play media is less likely to be subject to the rush and hurry of the verbal interview and is a means of facilitating communication. He recommends that elementary school counselors treat play behavior as though it were verbalized behavior and respond to the emotional content of the play behavior rather than extending play behavior into an interpretative realm.

Nelson suggests that if play moves into symbolic avenues beyond the counselor's level of training a referral is in order. Further, he recommends that the *closer the counselor's statements about play behavior relate to actual behavior expressed the more they are preferred.* He cites the following examples, with the second statement preferred in each case.

A child suddenly and violently crumbles a clay figure he has called his brother.
1. "You really hate your brother so you smashed him."
2. "You're very angry so you crushed the clay (or it)."

Ted is calm to outward appearances as he draws a picture showing a plane bombing a city.
1. "You're angry and you wanted the pilot to bomb the city."
2. "You've drawn a man in a bombing plane."

Sue starts to feed her doll, then drinks from the bottle herself.
1. "You want to be the baby now."
2. "The bottle is for you."

[64] John F. Feldhusen, John R. Thurston, and James J. Benning, "Sentence Completion Responses and Classroom Social Behavior," *Personnel and Guidance Journal*, 42 (October 1966), 165–170.
[65] David Rapaport, Merton M. Gill, and Roy Schafer, *Diagnostic Psychological Testing*, rev. ed. (New York: International Universities Press, 1968), pp. 222–521.
[66] H. G. Ginott, *Group Psychotherapy with Children* (New York: McGraw-Hill, 1961), p. 51.
[67] Richard C. Nelson, "Elementary School Counseling with Unstructured Play Media," *Personnel and Guidance Journal*, 45 (September 1966), 24–27.

FIGURE 13.3 **Purdue Guidance Clinic personal data inventory**

Date_____

Counselor_____

It is often useful if your counselor can know a little about your background and present experiences. Therefore, please complete this inventory as carefully as you can. All information which you provide about yourself will be treated confidentially.

Name_____

Last   First   Middle

Address_____

School_____ Grade_____

Age_____ Birthdate_____ Phone_____ Sex_____

School Information:

	Name of School	Grades Attended	Years Attended	Course of Study
Elementary				
Jr. High				
Sr. High				
College				
Other				

Best Liked Subjects_____ Easiest Subjects_____

Least Liked Subjects_____ Hardest Subjects_____

Out-of-school leisure time activities and hobbies_____

What magazines do you read regularly?_____

What types of books do you enjoy?_____

Activities and Hobbies:

School Activity	Number of Years of Participation	Offices Held	Kind of Activity

Class offices held_____

FIGURE 13.3 *(continued)*

Work Experience:

	Job Held	When	What did you like best about it?
1.			
2.			
3.			
4.			

Family and Home:

	Last name-First name	Live at Home	Age	Occupation	Years of Schooling Completed
Father					
Mother					
Bro/Sis					

Health:

Do you have normal eyesight?_____Normal hearing?_____

Briefly summarize important factors in your health history _____

_____

Underline any of the following words which seem to describe you fairly well:

Active, ambitious, self-confident, persistent, hard working, nervous, impatient, impulsive, quick-tempered, excitable, imaginative, original, witty, calm, easily discouraged, serious, easy-going, good-natured, unemotional, shy, submissive, absent-minded, methodical, timid, lazy, frequently gloomy, hard-boiled, dependable, reliable, cheerful, sarcastic, jittery, likeable, leader, sociable, quiet, retiring, self-conscious, often feel lonely.

Plans:

What are your plans for the future? _____

_____

What occupations have you seriously considered as possible goals? Why? _____

_____

What topics would you like to discuss with your counselor? _____

_____

_____

_____

Comments:

_____

Mary's eyes fill with tears after the paint runs on her picture.
1. "That's all right, we'll just get another sheet of paper."
2. "It bothers you when things don't turn out well."[68]

Play media build rapport and facilitate communication with children. For children the world of play is a natural and relaxed place in which they are free to be themselves. Because these factors also characterize the counseling setting, play techniques can contribute to an optimal relationship between the child and the counselor.

Referral techniques

Referral is the act of transferring an individual to another person or agency for specialized assistance not available from the original source. It is important to emphasize that referrals are made for the purpose of obtaining *specialized* service. They do not necessarily mean that the individual has a serious problem but may be due simply to the fact that the problem or concern is beyond the scope of the services provided. For example, high school counselors refer students to employment agencies because the latter are better equipped to assist them with job placement. Or the counselor whose client presents a problem complicated by his or her parents' marital difficulties may work with the parents in an effort to refer them to a marriage counseling service.

The referral decision

The ability to recognize when the needs of a particular individual call for procedures beyond the scope of one's personal resources or those of the employing setting is a professional necessity. At least two misconceptions surround the nature of the referral decision. First, referral is sometimes viewed as occurring only in times of emergency. Second, referral sometimes causes counselors to either unnecessarily prolong or too quickly terminate a relationship. Some counselors see nearly all contacts as being outside their personal resources or in need of others' help. Other counselors are so timid about working with emotional issues at a level appro-

priate to their competencies that they are completely unwilling to discuss substantive personal issues with clients. In part, this timidity has been encouraged by counselor educators and administrators who stress that counselors should not overextend themselves or overstep the bounds of their competencies in the area of personal problems. Forgotten and/or ignored in this situation is the fact that "normal" individuals have emotions that are not necessarily equated to serious emotional problems but do come into play materially in their daily lives.

Counselors who refuse to deal with emotions frequently find it impossible to cope effectively with clients who have more serious emotional disturbances when they are inevitably confronted with them. For clients with disabling emotional problems, the counselor's refusal to work toward even enough understanding to permit appropriate referral is tantamount to negligence. At a safer and less critical level, the counselor's refusal to cope with feeling components forces clients to focus on purely informational factors rather than permitting the motivations and feelings that crucially influence human decisions to come into play.

Ethical and legal considerations almost invariably accompany referral. The ethical standards of the American Personnel and Guidance Association are as follows:

If the member is unable to be of professional assistance to the counselee, the member avoids initiating the counseling relationship or the member terminates it. In either event, the member is obligated to refer the counselee to an appropriate specialist. (It is incumbent upon the member to be knowledgeable about referral sources so that a satisfactory referral can be initiated.) In the event the counselee declines the suggested referral, the member is not obligated to continue the relationship.[69]

The essential question is how or on what criteria counselors decide when they are "unable to be of professional assistance." It is a subjective judgment. Counselors screen their observations of verbal and nonverbal behavior of clients against an image of the kind of person their experiences and beliefs have led them to believe they can help. The counselor considers the nature of the problem, the context or life

[68] Ibid., pp. 25–56.

[69] American Personnel and Guidance Association, *Ethical Standards* (Washington, D.C.: The Association, 1974).

situation within which the problem exists, the amount of anxiety present, and the degree to which functioning is impaired and estimates the length of time required for counseling as well as his or her own competencies.

Although the referral decision is ultimately the counselor's to make, the situation can be discussed with professional colleagues. Counselors can talk the situation over with a professional counseling colleague (client's permission need not be obtained for this) or the situation could be discussed at a staff meeting.

The referral process

When the counselor's judgment suggests referral as the appropriate course of action, discussion with the client is the next step. Making a referral does not indicate a departure from a profound faith in the worth, dignity, and great potentiality of the individual human being. Patterson has called attention to the necessity for maintaining "a fundamental respect for the individual and a fundamental belief that it is best for him to work out his own problems in his own way."[70] The fact that individuals who are referred are likely to be apprehensive, anxious, or somewhat fearful requires the counselor clearly to exhibit acceptance, understanding, and concern as communicated in a willingness to help.

An attitude of reassurance born of confidence that appropriate steps are being taken is a critical ingredient. This is a matter of realistically facing the facts and the related available alternatives. Feelings of remorse for having failed to act sooner on the basis of previous evidence can result in hasty and ill-advised referrals. Naturally, the earliest possible detection and action increase the likelihood of rational and desirable counselor functioning. The critical questions are "What kind of special service does this person require?" "Is it available and if so where?"

It is imperative that the counselor be fully familiar with referral sources before suggesting the possibility of referral to the counselee. School counselors need to include the counselee's parents in their deliberations as soon as possible without violating ethical responsibilities to the counselee. With regard to referral agencies, students, and parents, Patterson's reminders, as adapted from a Michigan State University publication, *How to Make Referrals*, remain timely:

It is unwise and impractical to refer a student to community agencies without the knowledge, consent, and cooperation of his parents. Many child-guidance agencies will not accept students for treatment unless parents cooperate fully and are willing to present themselves for help, too. Check on the policy of your local agencies in this regard.

Further,

When telling students or parents about available services, in the school or in the community, explain both the functions and the limitations of these services. Do not give the impression that any specialist or agency has all the answers and can work wonders.[71]

Successful referral is more likely to be accomplished by offering to arrange for the needed service rather than dwelling on the counselor's inability to continue the relationship or the uncommon problem represented. The suggestion of referral to the individual requires a positive, helpful approach with no condition attached to it. Occasionally direct action is necessitated, but it is usually administrative action, which should not be confused with the counselor's efforts.

The actual presentation should be straightforward and tactful; labels and diagnoses should be avoided. The fact that another service is available that may provide the needed assistance should be included. The counselor should work slowly and carefully. Everything possible should be done to avoid making the referral an emergency or a crisis situation.

Whatever is required in the way of making contacts and arrangements with the referral agency should be offered by counselors. Having provided this information, identified the referral service, and discussed what acceptance of the referral involves, they are responsible for assisting the individual (and his or her family) in deciding what action to take. Rejection of the referral suggestion need not be interpreted as failure on the counselor's part. The very fact that the

[70] C. H. Patterson, *An Introduction to Counseling in the School* (New York: Harper & Row, 1971), p. 318.

[71] Ibid., p. 318.

individual is now openly facing the problem may contribute materially to a more satisfactory resolution. Resistance, doubts, fears, guilt, and defensiveness are factors with which the counselor must be prepared to cope in discussing referral. The conscientious application of skills in these difficult situations may result ultimately in further development of both the counselor and the counselee.

Legal and ethical considerations

Legal provisions for privileged communication and confidentiality of student records vary widely among the fifty states. Even among communities within a given state these conditions vary because of precedent or tradition. Ethical considerations almost inevitably accompany referral situations and should be carefully observed in order to minimize difficulties. It should be a matter of policy for the counselor to obtain from minors and their families written permission to furnish any referral information sought by the new agency. After referral, measures to ensure the confidentiality of the fact that an individual is under the care of an outside person or agency should be taken. Such information should be available to personnel only on a need-to-know basis. A more thorough presentation of ethical and legal matters may be found in Chapter 16.

Communications necessary

Communication channels with other services and community agencies must be established so that referral and outcome information can travel both ways with as little indirect handling as possible. Timing and confidentiality are basic concerns, of course, but administrative cost and efficiency are also involved. The term *reciprocity*, as used in the context of the referral process, applies to the amount and kind of feedback to be expected from another agency. A given agency is usually governed by an established general policy covering this subject that may allow for either fairly comprehensive reports, on the one hand, or none at all, on the other. The central consideration always reflects the need for information rather than the satisfaction of curiosity or administrative routine. Any general policy should be identified in initial contacts with the agency, and in specific

cases the request for a report should be based on clearly defined need.

Agencies vary as to whether they acknowledge acceptance of a referral. Counselors making a referral may not be asked by the agency for a professional opinion. This omission is not a discourtesy. Such a request would be incongruent, since it is not usually necessary, and might contribute to a biased view of the individual. However, acceptance of the referral by an agency will usually be accompanied by a request for objective data about the individual's school performance and behavior.

Most referral agencies do not lack for clients. Providing for ease of counselee access to special services is the counselor's responsibility. This is fundamentally a matter of becoming acquainted with the procedures to be followed in placing the student in contact with the agency. Agency representatives are typically cooperative in explaining their organization and routine to those who take the time to inquire. Certainly, the counselor has to provide clients and their families with accurate instructions and assist in completing the referral. This may mean making telephone calls, obtaining and forwarding request or consent forms, applications, and so on, and even, in rare instances, accompanying the individual to the agency.

Continued working relationships

School and community agencies from time to time share a common clientele. That is, the agency may suggest that the student continue seeing a school counselor during part or all of the time the agency is working with the student. In such cases the agency specialist will discuss with the counselor the purpose of maintaining the school counselor relationship and will usually suggest what its orientation should be. The student may require support for the periods between visits to the agency; the counselor's work with the student may be entirely different from the agency's, so that both may continue without conflict; it may be an active part of therapy or rehabilitation involving assistance in completing school tasks assigned by the agency.

Finally, in such instances two precautions are to be observed: maintaining confidentiality and staying within one's realm of responsibility. The fact that an individual is working with two or more professionally qualified persons, all parties being aware of the fact, does not justify exceptions to the ordinary standards of confidentiality. Clients may precipitate this breach of confidentiality, either intentionally or unintentionally, by discussing their agency experience with their counselor or vice versa.

Issues

Issue 1   Diagnosis is inimical to counseling.

True, because
1. Diagnosis means classification and labeling; clients are viewed more appropriately as individuals with unique situations, needs, and behaviors.
2. Diagnosis leads clients to expect counselors to solve their problems and creates dependency feelings between the two parties that are inimical to the counseling relationship and outcomes.
3. Diagnosis means evaluation of behavior and counselors ought to be nonjudgmental.

False, because
1. Diagnosis means assessing clients to acquire accurate pictures of them, their problems, functioning, assets, and liabilities so that intervention strategies can be designed to help them.
2. Identifying and describing behaviors of clients do not mean that clients are any less real as individuals.
3. Clients come to counselors for help with baffling, stressful situations; analyzing causes of these complex situations is the first step toward change or improvement for clients.

Discussion   This is one of the oldest issues in the counseling field. Much discussion of whether counselors engaged in diagnosis took place in the 1950s. Many counselors agreed with Carl Rogers that diagnosis meant evaluating and labeling clients and that too much of that had been done already to individuals who sought counseling. They argued that such clients really needed an understanding, nonjudgmental, nonlabeling, nonthreatening counselor so that they could come to an understanding of themselves and decide what, if any, changes were to be made in their behaviors.

More recently, arguments have been made that counselors who engage in diagnosis are following a medical model of intervention. Further, that model neither works nor is useful in characterizing counselor functions and behaviors because most clients are concerned with developmental problems and crises rather than remedial, longstanding personality disorders. Finally, diagnosis viewed from the medical model is not useful because treatment designs have yet to be specified for emotional disorders.

Admittedly, any number of attitudes are held about diagnosis in counseling and even more questions exist about the meaning of the word, diagnosis. However, regardless of the theory implemented by counseling practitioners, we believe that most of them engage in some form of client assessment and diagnosis when they seek to understand the ways their clients react and cope under various circumstances. Counselors engage in diagnosis by taking into account everything they know about clients and simultaneously observe their present behaviors so as to form hypotheses about ways of helping them accomplish their objectives.

Issue 2   Clients should be involved in the selection of tests or inventories administered to them.

True, because
1. The client's involvement helps to demystify tests and inventories.
2. Clients who are involved make better use of test information.
3. Clients who are involved are more motivated to do well or to respond more honestly to tests and inventories.

False, because
1. Clients do not possess the technical information necessary to make such decisions.
2. Clients expect counselors, as experts, to make such decisions.

Discussion   Little research has been reported to date that resolves this issue. The few attempts to do so have produced equivocal findings that client participation in test selection leads to greater understanding of test data, more satisfaction with counseling, or greater certainty in decisions that are made.

It should be clear that clients are not expected to decide which specific test of inventory among the many available is to be used. That is the responsibility of counselors.

Rather, the issue addresses the question of whether clients ought to be involved in deciding whether general ability tests or specific ability tests or interest inventories or personality inventories would be useful in gathering information that bears on their particular problems or situations. For clients to be involved means that counselors should give them a description of the category of tests, what they measure, and the relationship between the measures and the problems or decisions to be made by clients.

Annotated references

Brammer, Lawrence M., and Everett L. Shostrom. *Therapeutic Psychology*. 3rd ed. Englewood Cliffs, N.J.: Prentice-Hall, 1977. 476 pp.

Part II (pp. 121–344) consists of seven chapters describing counseling techniques. Psychodiagrams, acceptance, structuring, transference, interpretation, test interpretation, and many more methods are presented in these chapters.

Blocher, Donald H. *Developmental Counseling*. 2nd ed. New York: Ronald Press, 1974. 318 pp.

Chapters 8, 9, and 10 (pp. 146–207) considers diagnosis, prediction, dependency, transference, goal formulation, structuring, and other methods and behaviors in counseling. These concepts and techniques are viewed from a developmental point of view.

Knapp, Mark L. *Nonverbal Communication in Human Interaction*. New York: Holt, Rinehart and Winston, 1972. 213 pp.

Chapter 1 (pp. 1–24) presents perspectives on defining nonverbal communications, their importance, their origins and universality. Chapter 4 (pp. 91–118) treats gestures, postures, and other movements. And Chapter 5 (pp. 119–146) details facial expressions and eye behaviors. The content is interesting reading and useful for counselors.

Further references

Aplin, John C. "Structural Change Versus Behavioral Change." *Personnel and Guidance Journal*, 56 (March 1978), 407–411.

Bauer, David. "Motivation of Aptitude and Achievement Test Performance." *Elementary School Guidance and Counseling*, 12 (December 1977), 77–88.

Bradley, Richard W. "Person-Referenced Test Interpretation: A Learning Process." *Measurement and Evaluation in Guidance*, 10 (January 1978), 201–210.

Carey, Albert R., K. James Black, and Gary G. Neider. "Upping the Odds on the Referral Gamble." *The School Counselor*, 25 (January 1978), 186–191.

Coyne, Robert K. "Environmental Assessment: Mapping for Counselor Action." *Personnel and Guidance Journal*, 54 (November 1975), 150–155.

Dooley, David, Carol K. Whalen, and John V. Flowers. "Verbal Response Styles of Children and Adolescents in a Counseling Analog Setting: Effects of Age, Sex and Labeling." *Journal of Counseling Psychology*, 25 (March 1978), 85–95.

Fretz, Bruce R., Roger Corn, Janet M. Tuemmler, and William Bellet. "Counselor Nonverbal Behaviors and Client Evaluations." *Journal of Counseling Psychology*, 26 (July 1979), 304–311.

Loesch, Larry C. "Flow Chart Models for Using Tests." *Measurement and Evaluation in Guidance*, 10 (April 1977), 18–23.

McLemore, Clinton W., and Lorna S. Benjamin. "Whatever Happened to Interpersonal Diagnosis? A Psychosocial Alternative to DSM-III." *American Psychologist*, 34 (January 1979), 17–34.

Osborne, W. Larry. "I'd Like to Try That, But . . ." *The School Counselor*, 25 (May 1978), 342–345.

Protinsky, Howard. "Children's Drawings as Emotional Indicators." *Elementary School Guidance and Counseling*, 12 (April 1978), 249–255.

Seay, Thomas A., and Michael K. Altekruse. "Verbal and Nonverbal Behavior in Judgments of Facilitative Conditions." *Journal of Counseling Psychology*, 26 (March 1979), 108–119.

Stimac, Michele. "A Model for Evaluation of Decision Passages: A Facet of Self-Assessment." *Personnel and Guidance Journal*, 56 (November 1977), 158–163.

Sycamore, James N. "The Expectancy Table: A Tool for Midterm Conferences." *The School Counselor*, 25 (January 1978), 203–205.

Tepper, Donald T., and Richard F. Haase. "Verbal and Nonverbal Communication of Facilitative Conditions." *Journal of Counseling Psychology*, 25 (January 1978), 35–44.

14 Counseling: special areas and populations

This chapter has a twofold purpose. First, treatment has been given to counseling focused on certain special areas. These include marriage and family counseling, agency or community counseling, crisis intervention, and career counseling. Second, attention has been directed toward some special subgroups within the general population served by many counselors. Included are American Indians, blacks, Spanish-speaking Americans, Asian Americans, women, the exceptional, and the aged.

Special counseling areas

Marriage and family counseling

Probably the most rapid evolution in any of the helping relationship specialties has occurred in the marriage and family counseling field. From its early beginnings as a recognizable subspecialty in the 1930s and 1940s, the field grew rapidly in the 1960s and 1970s. Expansion has taken place in the numbers of practitioners and in the realm of theory and technique. A major stimulus to the explosive growth experienced in this professional field, of course, has been the rather radical and continuing social changes that affect marriage and family structure and relationships. In 1976, divorces in the United States reached the rate of slightly more than one divorce for every two marriages.[1] Instability in marriages and the resultant impact on all family members are among the most pressing problems facing society today.

Norton and Glick,[2] reviewing demographic studies of divorce, reported that age at first marriage, level of income, and level of education were the variables demonstrated empirically to be related to marital stability. McCahan[3] reported a correlation of .47 between self-concept and marital adjustment. Kemp,[4] in a study of fifty-five married university student couples characterized those whose marriage functioned well as having high self-esteem, equalitarian role expectations, attempting to promote growth in each other, and agreeing on the goals of marriage. Dysfunctional marriages related inversely to these characteristics. Birchler, Weiss, and Vincent[5] assessed a total of twenty-four couples as to the recreational and pleasurable activities they experienced during the previous thirty days. Distressed couples had fewer pleasures, more displeasures, more conflicts, fewer recreational activities, fewer positive and more negative reinforcements. But both distressed and nondistressed spouse dyads had fewer positive and more negative reinforcements than a comparison group composed of "stranger" dyads. The investigators concluded that marital distress was a function of the relationship, because partners maintained normal social competency in their interactions with others.

Positing some direction based on research findings is always hazardous, at best. An overview of the research on unhappy marriages seems to indicate that a combination of interpersonal variables, cognitive, and behavioral variables, is associated with marital dysfunctioning. Among these variables are congruity of perceptions and expectations, emotional stability and flexibility, self-concept, positive and negative reinforcements in the marriage, socioeconomic status, and age. Most powerful variables in unhappy marriages appear to be instrumental behaviors of each partner,

[1] U.S. Bureau of Census. *Statistical Abstract of the United States: 1976*, 98th ed. (Washington, D.C.: Government Printing Office, 1977).
[2] Arthur J. Norton and Paul C. Glick, "Marital Instability: Past, Present, and Future," *Journal of Social Issues*, 32 (Winter 1976), 5–20.

[3] George R. McCahan, "Relationships Between Self-Concept and Marital Satisfaction," Dissertation Abstracts International (Ph.D. diss., Columbia University, 1973).
[4] Thomas E. Kemp, "The Two-Student Marriage: An Emerging Non-Traditional Family Form." (master's thesis, Purdue University, 1974).
[5] Gary R. Birchler, R. L. Weiss, and J. P. Vincent, "Multimethod Analysis of Social Reinforcement Exchange Between Maritally Distressed and Non-distressed Spouse and Stranger Dyads," *Journal of Personality and Social Psychology*, 31 (February 1975) 349–360.

experienced as pleasurable or displeasurable, as positive or negative reinforcements. And a powerful determinant of pleasure or displeasure is the way valence is construed by the individual.

Individuals who engage in marital and family counseling may be found in diverse fields. By its very nature it is an interdisciplinary field. Physicians, ministers, social workers, psychologists, counselors, and, to some degree, educators and lawyers find marital and family concerns an important and sizable part of their work. Indeed, professionals from these fields often find that at least some of their effort inevitably involves marriage and/or family situations of those with whom they work.

Glick and Kessler define marital and family treatment as

. . . a professionally organized attempt to produce beneficial changes in a disturbed marital or family unit by essentially interactional, nonphysical methods. Its aim is the establishment of more satisfying ways of living for the entire family, and not only for a single family member.[6]

MARITAL AND FAMILY COUNSELING APPROACHES The growth of marital and family counseling has brought a broadening of the kinds of assistance provided clients. Marital and family counselors are involved in virtually all concerns that evolve in the complex human institutions of marriage and family. Marital problems as such, the initial concern of the field, now form only a part of this type of counselor's work. Included in the field is the whole range of activities from premarital counseling, marital counseling, divorce counseling, parent-child relationships, couple growth and enrichment, sexual problems, counseling focusing on relationship changes occurring across the years of marriage, medical problems in marital conflict situations, and others.

Given the wide variety of professional backgrounds from which marital and family counselors emerge, their theoretical views and treatment roles understandably are diverse. In general, among practitioners agreement exists that counseling should involve the whole family unit and individual treatment is not preferred. Although situations may exist where only one member of a family or of a couple is counseled, the more common approach involves working with both partners or with the several members of a family simultaneously. Also, it is not unusual to find involvement of more than one counselor with the family unit. It should be noted that a variety of arrangements are used ranging from working with a single member of the family through involvement of the entire family either throughout the process or at selected points during the process.

The rapid growth of the marital and family counseling field has been led by a number of theorists and practitioners. Prominent among them are Jay Haley, Don Jackson, Virginia Satir, Nathan Ackerman, John Bell, Salvador Minuchin, and Gerald Zuk. It is beyond the scope of this text to present the theory and practice of marital and family counseling in great detail. However, the conjoint family therapy approach will be described briefly because it has been employed extensively in practice. The interested reader is urged to pursue these topics further, especially in the works cited in the Annotated References at the end of this chapter.

Emerging in the late 1950s, the conjoint approach was practiced during the 1960s. Especially noteworthy has been the work of Virginia Satir.[7] Conjoint family therapy involves the counselor directly with the whole family unit and rests on direct observation of family interactions. Communication patterns and the family system are directly confronted in the process. Maximum interplay between family members is encouraged with the goal of fostering a cooperative effort that will lead to a better, more satisfying family life. Key concepts in the process are the concepts of family homeostasis and the double bind.

Family homeostasis refers to the relatively stable set of interrelationships among family members that effect members' behavior and operate to maintain the status quo in the family system. Troubled families often have established a homeostasis that is detrimental to one or more members and it becomes necessary to intervene in the existing system to alter the interrelationships within the family unit.

The *double bind* concept relates to the existing family communications system. Communications between and among family members are highly complex and frequently convey multiple meanings that are conflicting and confusing. Statements not only often contain multiple meanings but also are shaded by subtleties such as voice tone, facial

[6] Ira. D. Glick and David R. Kessler. *Marital and Family Therapy* (New York: Grune and Stratton, 1974), p. 4.

[7] See, for example, Virginia Satir, *Conjoint Family Therapy*, rev. ed. (Palo Alto, Calif.: Science and Behavior Books, 1967), and *People Making*, (Palo Alto, Calif.: Science and Behavior Books, 1972).

expression, and bodily posture. Confronted with messages having multiple meanings, whether because of verbal content, tone of voice, facial expression or a combination of these factors, the individual receiving the message is caught in a double bind—to what aspect of the message does the individual respond? what reaction does the speaker expect? what behavior is sought by the speaker? The counselor's activities with the family consists of active efforts to clarify the communications taking place within the family.

Satir views the communication process as crucial and in her more recent work describes five ways individuals handle communication at stress points. The five modes of communication—placating, blaming, computing, distracting, and leveling—represent people's survival methods in dealing with others (See Chapter 15). Satir indicates that the first four modes are efforts to survive in the face of threat and, although less desirable than congruent communication, she does not view the first four modes as intended to harm others. The leveling mode in communication does not omit or conceal messages; it consists of messages that avoid double meaning in that verbal content and affect are both present and in agreement. Demonstration through role play of the types of communication modes is used extensively by Satir in her family therapy and in teaching her techniques.[8]

Manus[9] characterized marriage counseling of the 1960s as a technique in search of a theory. He described practice at that time as having no consistent theoretical foundation and making no attempt to test its techniques on empirical grounds. The most common way of conceptualizing marriage problems, he said, was as a pattern of neurotic interactions between partners, based on a psychoanalytic framework.

The decade after Manus's statement was marked by a number of attempts to systematize marriage counseling and test it empirically. An early effort to do this, and the one that probably stimulated the greatest amount of later theorizing and research was by Stuart.[10] His approach was to translate the concept "lack of communication" into behavioral terms, and was based on the assumption that success-ful and unsuccessful marriages can be distinguished by the frequency and range of reciprocal positive reinforcements. Stuart taught four couples contracting procedures and used a token system of reinforcement whereby each partner could increase desired behavior in the other. Conversation and sex increased sharply at the beginning of treatment and continued through a forty-eight-week follow-up.

Although most research and theoretical developments in marriage counseling for several years after Stuart's beginning were based on the operant behavioral-exchange model, there were a few exceptions. For example, Hurvitz[11] suggested an interaction hypothesis model. He posited that marriage partners are always forming hypotheses to understand and explain their own and each other's behavior, and taught partners to form instrumental hypotheses, which allow for the possibility of change and problem solving, as opposed to terminal hypotheses, which would not.

Miller, Corrales, and Wachman[12] reviewed recent developments in practice and noted the emergence of several new dimensions. One is a concern for process—how things are said—rather than for content—what is said. A second addition is attention to growth and development and the learning of skills for solving future problems. A third is that a systems perspective has replaced an individual perspective, and a fourth is a new emphasis on strengths as well as weaknesses. They reported that one of the most important new concepts is that of esteem building. Glisson[13] suggested that current practice has tuned out theory. She pointed out that most research has been based on a tautology: successful marriages are reinforcing, reinforcing marriages are satisfying, and satisfying marriages are successful. But this circular reasoning leaves unanswered the question of how marriages become reinforcing. She also pointed to the lack of sufficient empirical data to test the theories, having located only nine data-based studies between 1968–1976, using a total number of sixty-eight couples.

Besides a movement away from a strict behavioral reciprocity approach, probably the most important develop-

[8] Satir, *People Making*, pp. 59–79.
[9] Gerald S. Manus, "Marriage Counseling: A Technique in Search of a Theory," *Journal of Marriage and the Family*, 28 (November 1966), 449–453.
[10] Richard B. Stuart, "Operant-Interpersonal Treatment for Martial Discord," *Journal of Consulting and Clinical Psychology*, 33 (December 1969), 675–682.
[11] Nathan Hurvitz, "Interaction Hypotheses In Marriage Counseling," *The Family Coordinator*, 19 (January 1970), 64–75.
[12] Sherwood Miller, R. Corrales, and D. B. Wachman, "Recent Progress in Understanding and Facilitating Marital Communication," *The Family Coordinator*, 24 (April 1975), 143–152.
[13] Diane H. Glisson, "A Review of Behavioral Marital Counseling: Has Practice Tuned Out Theory?" *Psychological Record*, 26 (Winter 1976), 95–104.

ment in recent years has been the emergence of the concept of marriage enrichment, as opposed to marriage therapy. Mace[14] describes marriage enrichment as a preventive rather than a remedial approach. Outcome criteria, according to Gurman and Kniskern,[15] have been of three kinds: overall marital satisfaction and adjustment, relationship skills, and individual personality variables. They reported that 60 percent of criteria tests in each category showed positive change, but 84 percent of the measures were based on participant self-reports.

The oldest and largest marriage enrichment program is the Roman Catholic Church's Marriage Encounter, introduced from Spain to the United States in 1967. Empirical research outcome studies have yet to be published, but Genovese[16] reported that the Marriage Encounter national office estimated in 1975 that 100,000 to 200,000 couples had participated. Another widely used program is the Minnesota Couples Communication Program,[17] using Sherwood and Scherer's[18] model for preventive maintenance, based on teaching concepts to increase communication between the couple. In this model the marriage relationship is viewed as going through four phases cyclically: sharing information and negotiating expectations, role clarity and commitment, stability, and disruption. The approach is described as teaching couples skills for self-awareness, for understanding the partner, and for negotiation.

Other marriage enrichment models have been variations on the communications training approach or the behavioral exchange approach, or combinations of both. Friest,[19] for example, used a marriage enrichment handbook that contained structured experiences designed to help couples increase communications by examining their behaviors in terms of choice awareness constructs and the five-choice paradigm originated by Nelson.[20] Seven couples completed an eighteen-hour group-study treatment, seven couples a self-study treatment, and nine couples were in a control group. Each couple was assessed as to how well their marriage was functioning on six dimensions, by a *Marriage Problem Scale*,[21] by the *Caring Relationship Inventory*,[22] and by a locus of control scale. Although many findings were equivocal, significant differences were obtained between treatments groups and the control group on the caring relationship scale. Treatment couples had a higher degree of congruence between their own ideal and actual marriage relationships. Friest concluded that the choice awareness treatment program increased couples' awareness of the alternatives open to them.

SETTING Marital and family counselors work in marriage counseling clinics, family service agencies, counseling centers, mental health centers, courts, and private practice. Virtually any type of setting that provides helping relationships may include one or more individuals who provide marital and family counseling either as their primary or preferred activity or as a part of their general counseling responsibilities.

NUMBERS AND NEED No accurate estimate can be given to the number of marital and family counselors in the nation's labor pool. In part this is true because of the variety of professions that feed into marital and family counseling. This makes it difficult to determine if individuals view their primary occupation as marriage and family counselors. For example, when does a psychologist or a social worker, engaged in general counseling activities that may include some marital or family counseling activities, cease to become a psychologist or social worker and practice as a marriage and family counselor? Except through membership in a professional organization, discussed below, any attempt to cite numbers is potentially misleading.

[14] David R. Mace, "We Call it ACME," *Small Group Behavior*, 6 (February 1975), 31–44.
[15] Alan S. Gurman and David P. Kniskern, "Enriching Research on Marital Enrichment Programs," *Journal of Marriage and Family Counseling*, 3 (April 1977), 3–11.
[16] Robert J. Genovese, "Marriage Encounter," *Small Group Behavior*, 6 (February 1975), 45–46.
[17] See David R. Mace, "Marriage Enrichment: The New Frontier," *Personnel and Guidance Journal*, 55 (May 1977), 520–522.
[18] John J. Sherwood and John J. Scherer, "A Model for Couples: How Two Can Grow Together," *Small Group Behavior*, 6 (February 1975), 11–29.
[19] Wendell Friest, "An Analysis of the Differential Treatment Effects of a Marriage Enrichment Handbook" (Ph.D. diss., Purdue University), 1978.

[20] Richard C. Nelson, *Choosing* (Chicago: Guidelines Press, 1978).
[21] Clifford H. Swensen and A. Fiore, "Scale of Marriage Problems," in *The 1975 Annual Handbook for Group Facilitators*, ed. J. E. Jones and J. W. Pfeiffer (LaJolla: University Associates, 1975), pp. 71–79.
[22] Everett L. Shostrom, *Caring Relationship Inventory* (San Diego: Educational and Industrial Testing Service, 1966).

PREPARATION AND PROFESSIONAL ORGANIZATION Although specific graduate level training programs exist for marital and family counselors it is important to keep in mind that specialty training in this field is often added to prior training in other mental health fields. Hence, many come to specialized training with a previous background in the areas commonly included in the preparation of personnel for the helping professions; for example, personality development, psychopathology, individual and group counseling, and therapy. According to Glick and Kessler, marital and family counseling training programs stress basic seminars covering broad topics such as the family as a social institution, theory of family pathology, family evaluation and study techniques, and techniques of family therapy and intervention. Added to these is an emphasis on clinical work and supervised experience.[23] Formal, structured training usually occurs at the masters degree level although in the case of those holding advanced degrees in related fields no formal degree may be sought.

The American Association of Marriage and Family Counselors (AAMFC) is the major professional organization of practitioners. Founded in 1942, the organization's membership exceeds 5,000 persons in the United States and Canada. The AAMFC sets its membership standards, examines and approves training centers, conducts professional meetings, cooperates with other professional groups in allied fields, and carries on public educational activities. The AAMFC publishes the *Journal of Marriage and Family Counseling*. At the present time relatively few states, approximately six, require certification or licensing for marriage and family counselors. Although interest and efforts continue in many states to mandate certification for marriage and family counselors to protect the public, membership in AAMFC remains the best available assurance to consumers of adequate preparation and experience in the field.

Agency or community counseling

During the latter half of the 1960s and continuing through the 1970s the loosely organized and very broad field of agency or community counseling emerged as a helping profession. Lewis and Lewis describe counseling and the counselors in this field as

. . . responsive and responsible helpers [who] realize that they have a role to play, not in just changing individuals, but in effecting whole communities. They know that the kinds of services offered must be provided in accord with the needs and wants of consumers—not just in terms of traditional and comfortable professional roles. They are aware of the need to find developmental and preventive approaches, so that they can stop allocating their time solely to the remediation of existing problems.[24]

As is true of marital and family counseling, those who engage in agency or community counseling come from diverse fields. The field cuts across many of the conventional subspecialties in the helping professions. Emphasis in community counseling is placed on service delivery through diverse, often nontraditional, means and on preventative rather than remedial activities. Regardless of the individual's original professional affiliation—psychology, social work, school counseling, probation counseling, and so on—stress is placed on outreach to a wide variety of clientele in the hope of altering the environment and conditions that create human distress and problems. Many workers in community counseling may be agency based. That is, they may, for example, be employed as school counselors or social workers, hold the title of probation counselor in a juvenile court, be titled drug counselor in a community mental health service. In truth, agency or community counseling describes a setting rather than a separate occupational role within the helping professions. Those who work in the field either move into community activity from their original training base or, in the case of paraprofessionals, receive their training on the job.

Counselors employed in mental health agencies have created a definition of their work by stating that they assist individuals or groups through a helping relationship to achieve optimal mental health. Seiler and Messina have set forth the dimensions of mental health counseling including promotion of healthy lifestyles, identifying and reducing

[23] Glick and Kessler, *Marital and Family Therapy*, pp. 156–160.

[24] Judith A. Lewis and Michael D. Lewis, *Community Counseling: A Human Services Approach* (New York: John Wiley & Sons, 1977), p. ix.

stressful elements for individual functioning, and preserving and restoring mental health.[25]

AGENCY COUNSELING APPROACHES Due to the very nature of agency counseling's espoused goals and mission, a wide range of approaches is employed. The field could be characterized as proactive and relying on approaches that are nontraditional because of its focus on developmental and preventative goals. This dual focus leads directly to a heavy reliance on consultative and educational activities and a corresponding decrease in emphasis on one-to-one counseling activities. The philosophical foundations of community counseling require concentration on environmental modification and alteration, intervention in problem-creating situations, and skill training for members to enable them to cope with and change their community in desirable ways. Knowledge of social systems and skill in problem resolution within the social system, are of paramount importance in community counseling. It should be noted that professional preparation for community counseling does not exclude training in the more traditional counseling approaches. Rather, it builds on traditional preparation and expands into the developmental and preventative areas in those ways viewed as most productive in bringing about change to benefit the individuals who comprise the community.

SETTING Community counseling personnel may be found in educational settings and agency settings. Broadly conceived, these two settings include virtually all types of delivery systems for counseling services such as clinics, community centers, schools, welfare agencies, crisis centers, public offenders services, drug centers, and the like.

NUMBER AND NEED No accurate statement can be made regarding the numbers of personnel involved or the need for personnel in the community counseling field. The wide variety of backgrounds among personnel in the field, the diversity of employment settings available, and the fact that many counselors, regardless of background and place of employment, engage at some time in what could be termed community counseling, prevent the identification of the number of practitioners involved. Added to these complications is the fact that there is heavy reliance on paraprofessional workers. Few would quarrel with the need for community counseling given the many pressing concerns facing society and the individuals who comprise society. However, accurately quantifying this need and the degree to which society will or can organize to respond to it, is virtually impossible. This contributes to the problem of estimating numbers and need in the community counseling field because programs and agencies, along with their services, tend to be unstable, both as regards focus and funding.

PREPARATION AND PROFESSIONAL ORGANIZATIONS Lewis and Lewis stressed a generalist rather than specialist emphasis in training for community counseling and described a training model that allows for educational and experiential breadth as training progresses.[26] These authors include experiences that progress through the following educational and experiential sequence and incorporated training in individual and group helping skills; knowledge of human delivery services; knowledge of social systems and change; ability in program development and administration; skill in education; training and consultation; and strong competency in research and evaluation.

No specific professional organization exists that claims the membership of all those engaged in agency or community counseling. Undoubtedly, this is because of the variety of professional backgrounds represented in the field. Within the American Personnel and Guidance Association one would expect that the American Mental Health Counselor Association and the Public Offender Counselor Association would contain many individuals involved in agency or community counseling. Division 27, the Division of Community Psychology of the American Psychological Association, undoubtedly represents another professional organization available to those in community counseling.

Crisis intervention

The origin of crisis theory has usually been attributed to Lindemann[27] whose pioneering work on bereavement reac-

[25] Gary Seiler and James J. Messina, "Toward Professional Identity: The Dimensions of Mental Health Counseling in Perspective," *AMHCA Journal*, 1 (January 1979), 3–8.

[26] Lewis and Lewis, *Community Counseling*, pp. 311–312.
[27] Erich Lindemann, "Symptomatology and Management of Acute Grief," *American Journal of Psychiatry*, 101 (September 1944), pp. 121–143.

tions was conducted with victims of the Coconut Grove nightclub fire. Caplan extended Lindemann's work and proposed the following widely accepted definition of crisis:

> Crisis is a state provoked when a person faces an obstacle to important life goals that is for a time insurmountable through the utilization of customary methods of problem solving. A period of disorganization ensues; a period of upset during which many abortive attempts at solution are made. Eventually some kind of adaptation is achieved which may or may not be in the best interest of that person and his fellows.[28]

Others have added to this definition of human crisis. There are some common characteristics among these definitions. First, a crisis is of limited duration. Second, a crisis is essentially an interaction between the person and the hazard or the situation, involving such factors as individual strengths, supports, and the intensity or severity of the hazard as experienced by the individual. Third, a crisis produces a deviation from normal behavior patterns. Finally, a crisis is assumed to be reversible and can serve as a vehicle for positive growth.

Floods, airplane crashes, divorce, death of spouse, being fired from a job, accidents, rape, retirement, premature births, getting married, suicide, death—all of these and other crises can trigger feelings of disequilibrium and helplessness in the lives of individuals and families. They call for special skills on the part of helping professionals. Intervention most frequently has to be swift, and the client helped to cope constructively.

Crisis theory translated to crisis intervention practice has the defined goal, according to Schneidman, of restoring individuals to their "pretraumatic level of overt functioning."[29] The focus of crisis intervention is the precipitant of the anxiety rather than the underlying or primary cause. The literature on crisis intervention suggests that counselors could consider the crisis from one or a combination of dimensions: stages of tension, impact-recoil phases, inter-, intra-, or extra-temporal categories, universal or specific crises,

differing etiological processes, levels of frustration. Regardless of orientation or perspective used, most crisis interventions (1) provide for an assessment and utilization of the individual's intellectual and environmental resources, (2) encourage expression of emotions experienced during the crisis, (3) assess the individual's general coping structure and the degree to which it is being employed, and (4) provide opportunities for the individual to re-establish control. A prominent theme is that counselors helping crisis clients need to offer warmth, interest, and concern.

Kennedy has suggested that crisis specialists perform the following functions: (1) help clients identify briefly the precipitating event(s), (2) encourage appropriate release of emotions, (3) help clients identify their past and present coping mechanisms, and (4) discuss alternatives that could lead to adaptive crisis resolution.[30] Rusk mapped out seven steps of crisis intervention. His steps were that (1) counselors present themselves as concerned, effective helpers; (2) counselors focus discussion on client's affect and encourage its expression; (3) counselors explicitly emphasize with the expressed effect; (4) counselors gather information about the crisis-inducing situation; (5) counselors make a comprehensive statement formulating the client's problems(s) with which the client agrees; (6) counselor and client engage in exploration of potential strategies to improve or resolve the crisis-inducing stress; and (7) counselor and client review the mutually determined strategy for the relief of stress and ways of dealing with future stress.[31]

Heppner and Heppner[32] have described the needs of rape victims and suggest that the immediate goals in the initial stages of counseling were to establish a sound working relationship with the client, providing practical information (what happens when the rape is reported, whether to tell parents, where to get V.D. check, and so on), and exploring the need for long-term counseling. Froiland and Hozman[33]

[28] Gerald Caplan, *An Approach to Community Mental Health* (New York: Grune and Stratton, 1961), p. 18.

[29] Edwin Schneidman, "Crisis Intervention: Some Thoughts and Perspectives," in *Crisis Intervention*, ed. Gerald A. Specter and William L. Claiborn (New York: Behavioral Publications, 1973), p. 9.

[30] Judith M. Kennedy, "An Analysis of the Effects of Two Counselor Interview Styles on Client Verbal Behavior and Client Perceptions of the Interview in a Simulated Crisis Situation," *Counselor Education and Supervision*, 18 (June 1979), 303–308.

[31] Thomas N. Rusk, "Opportunity and Technique in Crisis Psychiatry," *Comprehensive Psychiatry*, 12 (May 1971), 249–263.

[32] P. Paul Heppner and Mary Heppner, "Rape: Counseling the Traumatized Victim," *Personnel and Guidance Journal*, 56 (October 1977), 77–80.

[33] Donald J. Froiland and Thomas L. Hozman, "Counseling for Constructive Divorce," *Personnel and Guidance Journal*, 55 (May 1977), 525–529.

conceptualized divorce as the *death* of a relationship and applied the loss model (denial, anger, bargaining, depression, acceptance) presented by Kübler-Ross[34] to counseling individuals who were experiencing the occurrence of divorce. They suggest that the model helps clients re-evaluate their self-worth in a constructive manner.

The decade 1965–1975 was characterized by a proliferation of crisis centers, suicide-prevention clinics, drug-treatment centers, runaway sanctuaries, hotlines for help with child abuse and a variety of crises. Holleg and Abrams cite five characteristics shared by such services: (1) they provided help to youth (aged 14–35), (2) they were staffed primarily by people without professional degrees in psychology or social work, (3) they began and were operated outside traditional service-delivery systems, (4) they provided counseling services, and (5) they remained ideologically committed to providing alternative services.[35]

Particularly important was the emergence of volunteers who staffed these centers. A typical pattern was the employment of a professionally educated counselor as the director of the center who was responsible for training volunteers to be helpful to those who called or walked in. Doyle, Foreman, and Wales investigated the outcomes of three models used to train crisis center volunteers.[36] Training models included preservice training only, preservice training and delayed supervision, and preservice training and immediate supervision. The nonprofessional counselors in each group saw actual walk-in clients and were compared on (1) pattern and timing of interventions, (2) self-evaluations of their interview performance, and (3) client evaluations of treatment received. Analyses of intervention patterns revealed that, except for explicit empathy, the three groups did not differ in frequency of counselor statements. Across time periods, responses by those counselors given immediate supervision began to approximate those of experienced crisis counselors and this group rated their interviews most

positively of the three groups. Clients also reported greatest satisfaction with the treatment extended by nonprofessionals given immediate supervision. These authors concluded that the practice among crisis centers of relying solely on preservice training may promote harmful outcomes for volunteers and might account for the high attrition rates commonly experienced at such centers.

A final note on intervention strategies has been sounded by Warnath.[37] He suggests that the high turnover, transitory nature of the case load of most agencies does not lend itself to the type of client-counselor interactions in which relationships are central to the goals of counseling. Many crisis situations are of a nature that they are not amenable to applying self-exploration and growth experience models with their stress on "here and now" experiences of the client within the counseling room.

Career counseling

Career counseling has evolved with greater clarity, prominence, and vitality during the past few years. More and more schools, community colleges, universities, and community agencies have advertised for and added career counselor positions. The Comprehensive Employment and Training Act of 1973 (PL 93-203) and its extensions—the Career Education Act of 1974 (PL 93-380) and its subsequent extension, and the Career Education Incentive Act of 1977 (PL 95-486) —have been federal legislative initiatives instrumental in focusing attention on and encouraging career development and counseling.

THEORIES OF CAREER DEVELOPMENT Increasing efforts have gone into understanding and explaining vocational choice and career development. Nevertheless, neither *choice* nor *development* is uncomplicated and systematic efforts to explain a particular individual's entry into an occupation and resulting work history are, at best, rudimentary.

[34]Elizabeth Kübler-Ross, *On Death and Dying* (New York: Macmillan, 1969).
[35] Gordon P. Holleg and Walter H. Abrams, *Alternatives in Community Mental Health* (Boston: Beacon Press, 1975), pp. 8–9.
[36] William W. Doyle, Jr., Milton E. Foreman, and Elizabeth Wales, "Effects of Supervision in the Training of Nonprofessional Crisis-Intervention Counselors," *Journal of Counseling Psychology*, 24 (January 1977), 72–78.

[37] Charles F. Warnath, "Relationship and Growth Theories and Agency Counseling," *Counselor Education and Supervision*, 17 (December 1977), 84–91.

Prominent theorists of career development include Eli Ginzberg,[38] Robert Hoppock,[39] Anne Roe,[40] John Holland,[41] Donald Super,[42] David Tiedeman,[43] and Edward S. Bordin.[44] Their theories will not be presented here but the reader is referred to these primary sources and to the secondary source volumes by Osipow[45] and by Pietrofesa and Splete,[46] who have summarized and commented on these and other theories.

Certain career development theories, as well as the set of theories, have been subjected to considerable criticism. For example, Warnath[47] pointed out that an assumption underlying vocational theories is that individuals, given motivation, information, and help, progress through education to satisfying jobs that permit them to express their personalities and implement self-concepts. He asserts that such an assumption, populist in nature, cannot be met unless a prior assumption is held that every job is capable of engaging the human qualities of its holder. And that, of course, is not very likely. Further criticisms by Warnath were that vocational theorists (1) ignored large segments of the labor

force who did not find their work fulfilling, (2) held an outmoded model of the labor market that focused on efficient matching of people to jobs, (3) assumed incorrectly an open job market and that all work had dignity, and (4) operated on the faulty premise that the working world is just and is guided by rational principles.

Baumgardner[48] has argued that current career planning systems should be given up, both as a *descriptor* of how careers are fashioned and as a *prescription* setting forth the ideal process of choosing a career. A theory of nonrationality of career development would serve counselors better, according to Baumgardner, because choice and development involve two dialectical relationships: one with the individual's career goals, experiences, and personal changes and the other between individual career thinking and the social context. Fundamentally, these dialectics originate because the world is not necessarily just; life events disrupt plans, and tradeoffs are the rule of most decisions, whether about careers or other life situations. Osipow responded to Baumgardner's criticisms by stating that they represented a "straw man" because no one had ever proposed that career planning was ". . . entirely rational or that career certainty is necessary (or even desirable)."[49] Osipow suggested that career theories were attempts to identify elements that may be rational and conceivably could come under the control of individuals and be managed by them. Herr[50] also responded to Baumgardner's thesis that career choice involves two dialectical relationships by noting that many theorists had observed that career choice represented a compromise between what one wants to do and what is available to do and that others suggest that it is a continuing synthesis of ideals and realities.

ASSESSING CAREER CORRELATES In career counseling, information about both the individual and the environment is a primary topic to be examined and clarified. Psychological data describing the aptitudes, skills, interests, and personality traits of the client and social data describing the

[38] Eli Ginzberg, "Toward a Theory of Vocational Choice: A Restatement," *Vocational Guidance Quarterly*, 20 (March 1973), 169–176.
[39] Robert Hoppock, *Occupational Information*, 4th ed. (New York: Harper & Row, 1976).
[40] Anne Roe, "Perspectives on Vocational Development," in *Perspectives on Vocational Development*, ed. John M. Whiteley and Arthur Resnikoff (Washington, D.C.: American Personnel and Guidance Association, 1972), pp. 61–82.
[41] John L. Holland, *Making Vocational Choices: A Theory of Careers* (Englewood Cliffs, N.J.: Prentice-Hall, 1973).
[42] Donald E. Super, "Vocational Development Theory: Persons, Positions, and Processes," in *Perspectives on Vocational Development*, ed. John M. Whiteley and Arthur Resnikoff (Washington, D.C.: American Personnel and Guidance Association, 1972), pp. 26–38.
[43] David V. Tiedeman and Robert P. O'Hara, *Career Development: Choice and Adjustment.* (New York: College Entrance Examination Board, 1963).
[44] Edward S. Bordin, *Psychological Counseling*, 2nd ed. (New York: Appleton-Century-Crofts, 1968), pp. 423–444.
[45] Samuel W. Osipow, *Theories of Career Development*, 2nd ed. (Englewood Cliffs, N.J.: Prentice-Hall, 1973).
[46] John J. Pietrofesa and H. Splete. *Career Development: Theory and Research* (New York: Grune and Stratton, 1975).
[47] Charles F. Warnath, "Vocational Theories: Directions to Nowhere," *Personnel and Guidance Journal*, 53 (February 1975), 422–428.
[48] Steve R. Baumgardner, "Vocational Planning: The Great Swindle," *Personnel and Guidance Journal*, 56 (September 1977), 17–22.
[49] Samuel H. Osipow, "The Great Expose Swindle: A Reader's Reaction," *Personnel and Guidance Journal*, 56 (September 1977), 23–24.
[50] Edwin L. Herr, "Vocational Planning: An Alternate View," *Personnel and Guidance Journal*, 56 (September 1977), 25–27.

environment, the influences on the client, and the resources available are needed. Improvements in testing techniques and instrumentation have made it possible to measure an increasing number and variety of important psychological characteristics. Despite this progress, that which can be measured with precision still leaves much to be desired. Considerable advances have been made in vocational interest testing; measures of specific abilities remain crude; those used for assessing personality are still but in their infancy; and methods of testing creativity, persistence, and motivation are largely experimental or nonexistent. Although controversy abounds over testing, when a suitable test is available, its use in career counseling can save time and obtain information in a more objective, valid, and usable form than would otherwise be the case.

Test interpretation has been treated in Chapter 12. Consideration has been given here only to identifying and describing briefly some current career development measures commonly used by counselors.

THE SELF-DIRECTED SEARCH FOR EDUCATIONAL AND VOCATIONAL PLANNING (SDS)   The SDS (originally published in 1970 and revised in 1974) is a product of more than twenty years of research by John Holland.[51] As the title implies, subjects administer the inventory to themselves and tabulate the results. Assistance in interpreting results is provided by a companion booklet, the *Occupations Finder*. Form E of SDS has been designed for students as young as those in fourth grade and for adults with limited reading skills. The SDS takes about forty minutes to complete 228 items related to occupational daydreams, preferences for occupations and activities, competencies, and estimates of abilities in several occupational areas. Each subsection of the inventory presents items related to the six vocational and personality types that form the basis for Holland's theory of vocational choice.

Brown[52] has set forth some difficulties encountered in using the SDS. Among them were, first, that it was too complicated because nearly all users at his institution made a major error, either methodological or conceptual. Second,

Brown stated that it was too smug a package with no caveat that the user should contact a counselor. Third, that the SDS was too experienced based in that students with high aspirations and low occupational and educational histories become discouraged when they obtain realistic and conventional codes and learn that the occupations listed do not require college attendance. In response, Holland[53] agreed that SDS does not always work and that the *Professional Manual* states that in several places that counselors will be needed by some people. Further Holland suggested the SDS is not a test, but more correctly should be viewed as a simulation of a vocational counseling experience.

Cutts,[54] in reviewing the SDS materials, recommended their use with individuals or groups of twenty to thirty students. She also recommended the use of SDS as a teaching instrument that can demonstrate the relationship between occupational activities and personal competencies. Further, the use of SDS in business and industrial settings can be helpful to place employees in their first positions, in transferring employees from one position to another or in assessing those who are having problems in particular jobs. Cutts cautions counselors that (1) the codes obtained by some people are not to be found in the *Occupations Finder*, and (2) some female college students whose clerical competencies have financed their college education may have higher conventional scores even though their interests and plans do not lie in this area.

Dolliver and Hansen,[55] in a second review of the SDS pointed out that because a previous investigation[56] had indicated that over 50 percent of University of Maryland freshman students made errors in developing code summaries, they now introduce the examinees to each SDS section and have counselors talk with examinees about Holland's theory of vocational choice. Also, they have counselors provide assistance to examinees in using the *Occupations Finder*.

[51] John Holland, *Professional Manual, The Self-Directed Search for Educational and Vocational Planning*, Form E (Palo Alto, Calif.: Consulting Psychologists Press, 1974).

[52] Stephen L. Brown, "Career Planning Inventories: 'Do-It Yourself' Won't Do," *Personnel and Guidance Journal*, 53 (March 1975), 512–517.

[53] John L. Holland, "Dilemmas and Remedies," *Personnel and Guidance Journal*, 53 (March 1975), 517–519.

[54] Catherine C. Cutts, "Test Review: The Self-Directed Search," *Measurement and Evaluation in Guidance*, 10 (July 1977), 117–120.

[55] Robert H. Dolliver and Robert N. Hansen, "Second Review, The Self-Directed Search," *Measurement and Evaluation in Guidance*, 10 (July 1977), 120–123.

[56] Kathleen C. Christensen, C. J. Gelso, R. O. Williams, and W. E. Sedlacek, "Variations in the Administration of the Self-Directed Search, Scoring Accuracy and Satisfaction with Results," *Journal of Counseling Psychology*, 22, (January 1975), 12–16.

THE CAREER DEVELOPMENT INVENTORY (CDI) The CDI[57] is an objective, multifactor, self-administered paper-and-pencil inventory for assessing vocational maturity of adolescents. The CDI was designed to assess attitudinal and cognitive development relevant to career choice among high school students. At present, the CDI is composed of three scales. "Scale A, Planning and Orientation" is a self-rated scale that represents the student's attitudes toward and knowledge of career planning. "Scale B, Resources for Exploration" is also a self-rated measure of resources used and those potentially available for career planning. "Scale C, Information and Decision Making" is a cognitive measure of the student's actual occupational knowledge and how well this information has been integrated in order to make educational and vocational decisions. The reading level of the CDI makes it appropriate at or above the sixth-grade level. Administration is easy and self-explanatory. Scoring by hand is difficult but a computer-based format is available.

THE CAREER MATURITY INVENTORY (CMI) The CMI, developed by John Crites,[58] was designed to measure competencies and attitudes of career choice. The CMI is a machine-scored, paper-and-pencil inventory standardized on students, primarily in grades five through twelve but also through the college years. The attitude scale takes about twenty minutes to complete and can be used as a screening device for assessing career maturity. Students below the norm can be encouraged to seek career counseling. The competence scale takes about two and a half hours and can be either hand- or machine-scored. The five subtests of the scale—self-appraisal, occupational information, goal selection, planning, and problem solving—can be used to identify factors that contribute to decisional problems and, therefore, serve as a target for counseling interventions.

WORK VALUES INVENTORY (WVI) The WVI, developed by Donald Super[59] scores fifteen value areas: altruism, esthetics, achievement, independence, prestige, management, economic return, security, surroundings, supervisory relations, associates, way of life, and variety. The WVI is composed of forty-five statements that students can complete in ten to twenty minutes. Percentile norms have been established by sex and grade for grades seven to twelve. The WVI profile can be used in counseling for exploring what clients seek in careers and identifying what is important to them and the lifestyle associated with their values.

Numerous other career development assessment devices have been published in recent years, but have not been identified here. The selections presented are but examples of those available. Other vocational interests measures are not presented here because other sources[60] have treated these in detail.

CAREER DEVELOPMENT INTERVENTIONS Thompson[61] points out that definitions of career counseling frequently use such phrases as "help people make good decisions," "administer and interpret vocational tests," or "help people choose vocations." He suggested that such statements, though accurate, suffered from lack of specificity. Thompson then identified and discussed some misconceptions held by clients about vocational counseling. Among these were (1) that clients come with an erroneous idea that career planning and decision making are highly scientific and that the end product is an exact vocational plan; (2) that vocational decisions made are final; (3) that psychological tests can tell a person what to do; (4) that interests, abilities, and aptitudes are one and the same; (5) that all the steps in a vocational plan should be analyzed (leading to overwhelming oneself with decisions); and (6) that the consequences of vocational aspirations are viewed as either complete success or complete failure.

The traditional pattern pursued by counselors in their interventions with career clients can be described briefly. In the initial interviews clients are encouraged to explore their problems and situations. Following these sessions, clients are administered appropriate tests and these data are interpreted. Attention is given to exploring occupational information. Hypotheses are then formulated by the counselor for the client's consideration relative to the client's functioning in educational preparation required for entry into

[57] Donald E. Super and D. J. Forrest, *Career Development Inventory Form 1, Preliminary Manual for Research and Field Trial*, mimeographed (New York: Teachers College, Columbia University, 1972).
[58] John O. Crites, *Administration and Use Manual for the Career Maturity Inventory* (Monterey, Calif.: CTB/McGraw-Hill, 1973).
[59] Donald Super, *Manual, Work Values Inventory* (Boston: Houghton Mifflin Company, 1970).
[60] See Bruce Shertzer and James D. Linden, *Fundamentals of Individual Appraisal* (Boston: Houghton Mifflin Company, 1979).
[61] Anthony P. Thompson, "Client Misconceptions in Vocational Counseling," *Personnel and Guidance Journal*, 55 (September 1976), 30–33.

the work setting or in work itself. These hypotheses are subjected to verification, reformulation, or rejection as new information about the client and proposed career moves becomes available.

Some time ago, Samler identified and discussed seven procedures for revitalizing career counseling by investing it with its proper psychological meaning and bringing into play a growing understanding of the nature of people at work.[62] His seven proposals required that consideration be given in counseling interventions to the identity, the values, projected roles and self-actualizing needs of the client. But Samler points out that counselors should not expect every client to find identity, fulfillment, or satisfaction in work. His seven proposals, paraphrased here, are that

1. Career exploration is not a separable part of the counseling process.
2. The client's needs should be identified and their strength assessed.
3. The client's potential for commitment to work is assessed.
4. The client is helped to become aware of the nature of career development and progression.
5. The client should be helped to see the working world as a totality and within this totality, the client's view of self is as a psychosocial as well as an economic entity.
6. Exploration of careers by the client is viewed as a psychological process because the client's perceptions are taken into account.
7. Career exploration provides a model for decision making, not necessarily the decision itself.

Finally, Samler noted that these seven proposals represent a model that can either be deduced by the client or it can be taught expressly.

Many programmatic models of career development have emerged within recent years. For example, Gysbers and Moore[63] have broadened career development to make it life-career development. Program elements to facilitate this broadened concept include (1) curriculum-based activities,

(2) individual interventions, and (3) on-call (crisis) interventions. Hansen and Keierleber[64] have described a project, BORN FREE, designed as a collaborative consultation model to create educational environments that encourage students to explore and pursue career and life options available to them. The project uses indirect interventions to communicate that people are born free of stereotypes about what they can do with their lives and that their attitudes about career choices and roles are affected by significant others in their lives.

Counseling: special groups

Among any counselor's clientele are individuals whose special needs must be taken into account. These special needs may have a bearing on the counseling relationship and, even more important, its outcomes for their lives and society.

Obviously these groups have been present in America since its beginning. It is equally obvious that the American ideal of equality within a democratic society has not held true for some groups. Recent social upheavals show that such subgroups are now committed to demanding equality. In some cases their lack of full participation in society stems from outright denial, in others, failure to recognize special problems of subgroups, and, in still others, benign neglect. Recent social history clearly shows that such groups are (1) articulating more urgently than ever before their rights and privileges within a democracy and (2) banding together in more cohesive organizations to achieve their purposes. These two factors have led to a consciousness of how they differ from each other and how they differ from the dominant society. Presumably, stressing such differences focuses attention on needs that have been unmet, characteristics that require specialized consideration, and personal and group goals not necessarily identical to those commonly held by other segments of society or expected of them by society. For the counselor who works with individuals from such subgroups, a thorough understanding of these factors and appreciation of their impact on the individual are essential.

[62] Joseph Samler, "Occupational Exploration in Counseling: A Proposed Reorientation," in *Man in A World at Work*, ed. Henry Borow (Boston: Houghton Mifflin Company, 1964), pp. 411–433.
[63] Norman C. Gysbers and Earl J. Moore, "Beyond Career Development—Life Career Development," *Personnel and Guidance Journal*, 53 (May 1975), 647–652.
[64] L. Sunny Hansen and Dennis L. Keierleber, "BORN FREE: A Collaborative Consultation Model for Career Development and Sex-Role Stereotyping," *Personnel and Guidance Journal*, 56 (March 1978), 395–399.

The reader may remember that Chapter 3 identifies and discusses some of the characteristics of counselees. This chapter presents additional information relevant to the counselor's understanding and work with special subgroups. It must be kept in mind that social forces far beyond the control of individuals in the helping professions have created situations in which a minority group in society may well be the majority group in a specific setting. For example, a counselor may work in an inner-city school that is predominantly black.

Counseling American Indians

The American Indian suffers from much historically based stereotyped thinking. These views derive from diverse sources ranging from television images and Western movies to the paternalistic "great white father" policies practiced by the U.S. government in managing or, as many critics assert, mismanaging Indian affairs. Indian efforts to break out of this situation have been thwarted by racial prejudice, lack of opportunity, poverty, and poor education.

The boarding school system of the Bureau of Indian Affairs has been criticized by child psychologists, educators, family counselors, and Indian activists. Although there is no consensus on what should be done, everyone from outside critics to inside administrators agrees there is room for improvement. The main argument for the boarding school is that there is no alternative to it. The boarding school costs $157 million a year and has 18,562 students aged 6 to 18 nationwide. Of these students, according to the Navajo tribe, 17,262 are in boarding schools on their reservations, which cover some 24,000 square miles in New Mexico, Utah, and Arizona.

The boarding school was born in the days when the Bureau of Indian Affairs was under the Department of the Army; it was part of the forced pacification program for Indians. The charter of the first boarding school on the Navajo reservation in the 1890s stated that the school's purpose was to "remove the Indian child from the influence of savage parents." Accordingly, Indian children often were taken forcibly from their homes, given English names, forced to speak only English and sometimes not allowed to return for years. Such abuses were corrected long ago, but the memory of them fuels the sometimes irrational criticism of the system. And many experts agree that despite the changes, the schools still do a great deal of emotional damage to Indian children and their parents.

Indians under 24 years of age die of alcoholism at a rate twenty-eight times the national average for their age group, according to the Indian Health Service. The Indian suicide rate is twice the national average, according to the National Institutes of Mental Health; on some reservations it is five or six times the national average, with the rates tending to be highest among young people.

The writings of Spang[65] and Bryde[66] demonstrate clearly that counselors have had little contact with Indian youth and all too often they have been ineffective in the contacts that they have had. Too, many who have served as counselors to Indians have not only lacked professional counselor training but also never acquired an understanding of their clients. Both Spang and Bryde highlight the plight of the Indian who is caught between two cultural worlds, one of which lacks any appreciation and understanding of Indian cultural values and tribal diversity.

As is true in dealing with any member of a special subgroup, counselors frequently fail because they do the only thing they know how to do: fit, force, or mold the Indian into white middle-class ways of thinking, feeling, and acting. The counselor's failure, part of the larger failure of the educational enterprise and the society as a whole, undoubtedly contributes to the high school dropout rate, high unemployment, and massive poverty among Indians.

The counselor who seeks to establish a relationship with an Indian is faced with the obligation of understanding that his or her client lives in a world of colliding values, language differences, and highly transient white adult models. Not only are such models transient, particularly in reservation schools, but they often require the child to reject much of his or her early learnings from Indian models.

Observations about counselors and Indian clients have been given by Spang and Bryde and are summarized here. First, both of these authors have stressed the necessity of a counselor's thorough knowledge of Indian ways, including their language. Second, the client's lack of verbal responsiveness is attributed to both an English language deficiency and a value system that prizes contemplation and attentiveness to the wisdom of elders. Third, existing educational

[65] Alonzo T. Spang, Jr., "Understanding the Indian," *Personnel and Guidance Journal*, 50 (October 1971), 97–102.
[66] John F. Bryde, *Indian Students and Guidance*, Guidance Monograph Series (Boston: Houghton Mifflin Company, 1971).

efforts that consist primarily of stressing white middle-class values and knowledge result in a gradual destruction of the mental health of the individual, culminating in feelings of rejection, depression, and anxiety. These find their expression in tendencies toward withdrawal and social alienation, and are often manifested in strikingly high rates of alcoholism and suicide. Bryde cites data that indicate the emergence of these feelings as early as junior high school.[67] Given these three observations about Indian clients, it would seem that the counselor should be able to convey the respect, understanding, and the liking necessary and basic to good counseling relationships.

Sources discussing counselor practices with Indian youth have often suggested a highly directive approach involving advice, suggestion, and persuasion. Presumably, such suggestions are based on the characteristic of Indian cultures that stresses reliance on the wisdom of elders. It may be that such an approach is more functional when clients remain within the Indian culture than when they attempt to cope with white society. The latter situation seemingly would call for a highly sensitive and perceptive counselor, who could extend in full measure those facilitating conditions— empathy, warmth, understanding, genuineness—to Indian clients as they struggle with and examine certain value conflicts or decide on their life or career goals.

Counseling blacks

The last two decades have been a time of increasing social change, upheaval, and searching inquiry in the realm of black-white relationships. A considerable body of literature has accumulated, some of which has only an indirect relevance to counseling but which contributes to an understanding of the existing situation. Other literature has direct relevance to the work of the counselor. It will be assumed that the reader is familiar with recent social history as well as the earlier history of black Americans. Of greater importance here is the literature and experience that applies to the work of the counselor.

Our own limited experience reveals that some black high school and college students too often view their contacts with white counselors as discouraging and unproductive. The charges are repeatedly heard that (1) counselors have discouraged blacks' college aspirations on the grounds that

there was little likelihood of admission or success in college if admitted, (2) little counselor assistance is available to black students for job placement when they leave school, and (3) black students are discouraged from taking those courses that would prepare them for entering post–high school education. Black youth are often confused about the discrepancy between the expressions of these actions and attitudes by counselors and the highly publicized improved educational and employment opportunities available to them in recent years. In particular, some college doors have inched open, not only actively recruiting black students, but also providing financial support and educational remediation for those who need it. To a lesser degree, better occupational opportunities are present, at least for those blacks who have been fortunate enough to secure advanced education or special skills.

Many variables undoubtedly interact to produce negative views of counselors by black counselees. It should not be overlooked that in some cases the black counselee may attribute discouragement to prejudice on the part of the counselor, when in fact that same counselor is equally discouraging to a white client, given similar personal or background data. But it should also be noted that there are very, very few situations in which a counselor can assert that individuals, either black or white, *cannot* pursue their aspirations. The counselor's approach has most often been traditionally and appropriately one of neutrality followed by questioning intended to direct clients toward examining the decision-making process and their strength of commitment to a given objective. Such an approach may be interpreted by the client as disapproving or discouraging, particularly if counselors do not make their purposes clear to the client.

A range of commentary about counseling blacks has been presented by Vontress,[68] Kincaid,[69] Smith,[70] Russell,[71]

[67] Ibid., pp. 40–42.

[68] See, for example, Clemmont E. Vontress, "Counseling Blacks," *Personnel and Guidance Journal*, 48 (May 1970), 713–720; "Racial Differences: Impediments to Rapport," *Journal of Counseling Psychology*, 18 (January 1971), 7–13; and *Counseling Negroes*, Guidance Monograph Series (Boston: Houghton Mifflin Company, 1971), 70 pp.
[69] Marylou Kincaid, "Identity and Therapy in the Black Community," *Personnel and Guidance Journal*, 47 (May 1969), 884–890.
[70] See, for example, Paul M. Smith, Jr., "Black Activists for Liberation, Not Guidance," *Personnel and Guidance Journal*, 49 (May 1971), 721–726; and "Men Who Think Black," *Personnel and Guidance Journal*, 48 (May 1970), 763–766.
[71] R. D. Russell, "Black Perceptions of Guidance," *Personnel and Guidance Journal*, 48 (May 1970), 721–728.

Beck,[72] Johnson[73] and many others. Their observations vary in scope, detail, and degree of optimism held about the value or even the possibility of white counselors providing assistance to blacks.

These sources stress the difficulty of establishing and maintaining a counseling relationship between a white counselor and a black counselee. They have suggested that these difficulties stem from (1) a lack of understanding and appreciation of black cultural values, (2) differences in life experiences, (3) prejudiced attitudes on the part of whites that preclude even the beginnings of the counseling relationship, (4) failure to see blacks as people in viewing all their problems as originating from racial attitudes and conflict, and (5) low expectancies for black performance held by whites. Vontress has identified and discussed how racial differences may influence the relationship between white counselors and black clients.[74] A prominent conclusion in his analysis is that the previous negative experiences between races adversely influence the establishment of the trusting, intimate, self-revealing relationship deemed essential in counseling. According to Vontress the black male client may respond negatively to the white counselor because he transfers to the counselor intense negative emotions stemming from previous experiences with, and feelings toward, whites in general. Similarly, white counselors countertransfer preconceived ideas and attitudes about blacks in general to their black client. Also highlighted in Vontress's analysis of racial differences in counseling is a differential in self-disclosure between white and black clients. The black male client, according to Vontress, is particularly reluctant to disclose his true feelings and situations to a white counselor, for to do so is to reveal his vulnerability. Without doubt, understanding, attentiveness, and sensitivity on the part of the counselor are demanded in such complex situations.

Without denying the relevance of race, it should be noted that socioeconomic factors are inevitably compounded with racial characteristics. Historically, the vast majority of black Americans have been poor. Whether difficulties in establishing and maintaining a relationship occur because of race, poverty, or a combination of both, it is the responsibility of counselors to recognize and cope effectively with their clients as individuals rather than as members of a group with whom they lack experience.

Given these difficulties, many have argued or demanded that black counselors be employed to counsel blacks. Only by doing so, they believe, will black clients ever realize the expectations they have for counseling. Russell has outlined these expectations: (1) that black students will get a fair shake; (2) that they will be accepted rather than rejected; (3) that their dignity will be respected; (4) that their individuality will be recognized; (5) that their right of decision will be respected; (6) that their opportunity to explore, discover, and learn will be upheld; and (7) that their hopes, dreams, and aspirations will be recognized and encouraged.[75] These same expectations are set forth in statements of the principles of counseling. Actual practice should certainly strive to provide no less.

Some final comments are in order here. First, counselors irrespective of their racial or ethnic origins must be alert as to how their own experiences are involved in their responses to their clients. If the prior experiences of counselors have left them with a residue of negative attitudes or feelings toward certain groups, they must become aware of this and attempt to resolve such attitudes and feelings.

Second, much can be done in counselor preparation programs to improve counseling with blacks by (1) exploring means of facilitating black-white relationships; (2) sensitizing counselors to black students' problems, assets, and needs; (3) familiarizing counselors with educational and vocational opportunities available to black students; (4) preparing blacks to be professional counselors; and (5) evaluating the impact of counseling practices and techniques used with black students.

Third, practicing counselors can do much that would be beneficial to all youth in schools, colleges, or agencies by conducting programs that facilitate interracial interpersonal relationships. Beck has described some programs that seek, at a minimum, to prevent the conflict, indeed violence, that marks and scars many integrated schools, and beyond that, to facilitate healthy interpersonal relationships between

---

[72] James D. Beck, *The Counselor and Black-White Relationships,* Guidance Monograph Series (Boston: Houghton Mifflin Company, 1973).

[73] Howard N. Johnson, "A Survey of Students' Attitudes Toward Counseling in a Predominantly Black University," *Journal of Counseling Psychology,* 24 (March 1977), 162–164.

[74] Vontress, "Racial Differences."

[75] Russell, "Black Perceptions of Guidance," pp. 725–726.

blacks and whites, which build toward shared understandings and experiences.[76]

Counseling Spanish-speaking clients

Based on U.S. Bureau of the Census data, Padilla, Ruiz, and Alvarez report that United States residents of Spanish origin number over 9 million. Of this number the Spanish speaking and surnamed can be divided into several subgroups by place of origin: more than 5 million Mexican-Americans, about 1.5 million Puerto Ricans, more than 600,000 Cubans, and 2 million individuals from Central or South America and other localities. These authors characterize the Spanish speaking and surnamed as the second largest minority group in the United States. The foregoing authors discuss this group as homogeneous but also acknowledge identifiable differences among subgroups.[77]

Articles describing the values and needs of Puerto Ricans and Mexican-Americans have been written by Pollack and Menacker,[78] Aragon and Ulibarri,[79] Palomares and Haro,[80] and Christensen.[81] Pollack and Menacker have pointed out that these two groups share some cultural similarities, but also some major differences. They share a similar, though not identical, language and most individuals in each group share severe poverty. Because some differences exist, the largest two groups will be discussed separately.

PUERTO RICANS   Since Puerto Rico became a U.S. territory at the close of the Spanish-American War, many migrants to the mainland (Puerto Ricans are American citizens) have settled in New York City. During the past two decades, they have spread to other major U.S. cities. Even today, Puerto Ricans tend to immigrate for two purposes: to establish permanent residence on the mainland or to seek seasonal employment as farm labor and return to Puerto Rico.

The Puerto Rican value structure differs in important respects from that of the American middle class. Ties to, and a love for, their homeland seem stronger than that of the highly mobile American population. The Puerto Rican family tends to be more patriarchal and protective of female members. Authorities, especially officials, tend to be approached with much more formality. These and other values influence the behavior and personal relationships of those who migrate to this country.

Puerto Rican students often do not complete high school. Many boys leave school to supplement the family income and girls drop out in order to care for younger children while the mother works. Pollack and Menacker describe the recently migrated student as polite, respectful toward teachers who are viewed as high-status individuals, and well behaved in school.[82] In their new culture, Puerto Rican migrant students are confronted with problems of language differences, conflicts with parents over the adoption of new customs and behaviors that clash with their parents' traditions, and a high probability that they will not complete their education because of family economic problems.

MEXICAN-AMERICANS   As an ethnic group, Mexican-Americans are concentrated in the Southwestern United States. Many trace their origins to the early California territory. They automatically became U.S. citizens when that section of the country was ceded to the United States in 1848. Many others have emigrated from Mexico over the years. Across the years this ethnic group has spread nationwide so that they now live in virtually all areas of the country.

Many generalizations are made about Mexican-American culture. Pollack and Menacker in their monograph cite several authorities who support the contention that such generalizations stem from poverty rather than ethnicity.[83] Specific attributes that most accurately characterize many include coming from Mexico, speaking Spanish, being of the Roman Catholic faith, and being dark-skinned. Additionally, most are reputed to lack education and adequate income.

[76] Beck, *The Counselor*.

[77] Amado M. Padilla, Rene A. Ruiz, and Rudolfo Alvarez, "Community Mental Health Services for the Spanish-Speaking/Surnamed Population," *American Psychologist*, 30 (September 1975), 892–905.

[78] Erwin Pollack and Julius Menacker, *Spanish-Speaking Students and Guidance*, Guidance Monograph Series (Boston: Houghton Mifflin Company, 1971).

[79] John A. Aragon and Sabine R. Ulibarri, "Learn, Amigo, Learn," *Personnel and Guidance Journal*, 50 (October 1971), 87–90.

[80] Uvaldo H. Palomares and Juan Haro, "Viva La Paza!" *Personnel and Guidance Journal*, 50 (October 1971), 119–129.

[81] Edward W. Christensen, "When Counseling Puerto Ricans . . ." *Personnel and Guidance Journal*, 55 (March 1977), 412–415.

[82] Pollack and Menacker, *Spanish-Speaking Students*, pp. 27–33.

[83] Ibid., pp. 14–17.

Mexican-American students and their parents commonly place a high value on education as an ideal. However, the reality of the situation is that Mexican-American students leave school early at a high rate (approaching 90 percent in many localities). Undoubtedly, impoverished family situations that demand early employment contribute heavily to this contradiction between aspiration and reality. A serious language problem is another factor since the children often are described as knowing neither Spanish nor English well. Another factor for this minority group that smothers aspirations is pervasive discouragement and pessimism about the chances of breaking the cycle of poverty and prejudice.

To be effective with any group of Spanish-speaking Americans, counselors should know their language and their cultural background. Their attention should focus on the conflict between the culture of the majority and that of their Spanish-speaking clients. This is extremely important for it is here that conflict develops and misunderstanding and failure occur. Counselors may find that extensive counseling and/or consulting with parents of Spanish-speaking youth pays dividends in expediting their children's acculturation.

Counseling Asian Americans

Sue, Sue, and Sue have presented relevant information describing the status of Asian Americans as regards income, education, interracial marriage, and mental health.[84] These authors present data directed toward clarifying the issue of whether Asian Americans as a minority group are successful and well respected or oppressed and neglected. Although the authors find evidence supporting both sides of the issue, their discussion is of value to individuals who work with or wish to understand Asian Americans as a minority group.

Sue[85] has summarized and described some themes often associated with the group of Asian Americans. One theme is that Asian Americans (Chinese, Japanese, Filipinos, Koreans) encounter prejudice and that their psychological, so-

cial, and educational needs have not been met. A second theme is that Asian American ghettoes exist, yet most Asian Americans do not live in ghettos. A third theme is that many live in poverty and drop out of school because of bilingual problems despite considerable evidence that Chinese and Japanese median family incomes in 1970 were far superior to national median incomes. Given that these themes do not portray accurately Asian Americans, Sue then presented some characteristics, based on research, that he believed applied to them. The first was that Chinese and Japanese students have been made to feel less autonomous and more anxious, nervous, lonely, alienated, and rejected than other students. The second was that despite high achievements, many Asian Americans experience feelings of powerlessness and helplessness in their attempts to gain control of their lives. Sue traced this "learned helplessness" to the rapid and unexpected relocations and detentions of Japanese Americans during World War II. He recommended that counselors, in their interventions with Asian Americans, focus on facilitating self-control in life situations. Assertive training, according to Sue, may be valuable.

Counseling women

The literature[86] on women's rights portrays the historic and contemporary stereotyping of women, its causes, and, in particular, its adverse results on both women and men.

The many fictions about women are undoubtedly well known to counselors and need only be mentioned here. Among them are that women are: weak and need to be sheltered; intellectually inferior to men; rightfully belong only in the home; should only work in teaching, nursing, or secretarial jobs; are not good bosses; are absent from work more frequently than men; become emotional in a crisis situation. These and other fictions persist and are used to restrict and limit women's choices and lifestyles.

[84] Stanley Sue, Derald W. Sue, and David W. Sue. "Asian Americans as a Minority Group," *American Psychologist*, 30 (September 1975), 906–910.
[85] Stanley Sue, "Psychological Theory and Implications for Asian Americans," *Personnel and Guidance Journal*, 55 (March 1977), 381–389.
[86] See, for example, Beverly Stone and Barbara Cook, *Women and Guidance*, Guidance Monograph Series (Boston: Houghton Mifflin Company, 1973). The Project on Women in Education, *Taking Sexism Out of Education* (Washington, D.C.: U.S. Government Printing Office, 1978); Karen Keesling, *The Year 2000 and the Prospect for American Women* (Washington, D.C.: Congressional Research Service, Library of Congress, 1977).

FIGURE 14.1 **An average American woman's lifeline**

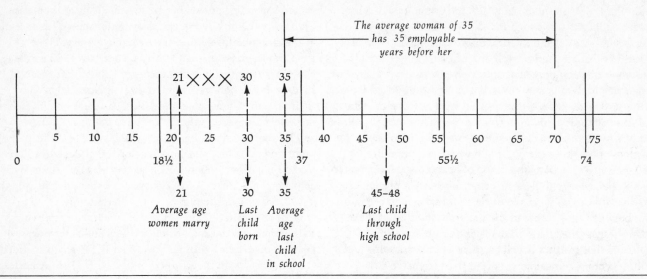

SOURCE: Span Plan, Office of Dean of Students, Purdue University, Lafayette, Indiana. Adapted from U.S. Department of Labor, Women's Bureau, 1979.

Women have engaged in a long struggle to gain equal rights. Many individuals, groups, and organizations have been involved in this pursuit. The capstone of this effort, dating back to the 1800s, is the passage by Congress of the Equal Rights Amendment (ERA). This amendment explicitly forbids discrimination on account of sex in civil rights, employment, and the holding of property. The ERA must be ratified by 38 states and, during 1978, the time for doing so was extended.

Recent literature clearly points out that sexist attitudes and practices are embedded in the very fabric of society. They pervade virtually all institutions including the home, church, school, and employment setting. Until recently, the effects on women of many traditional practices remained unexamined. The chain of events in restrictive practices begins early in the life of females. The family traditionally influences female children toward "acceptable" female roles. The school perpetuates this beginning by encouraging girls to follow certain educational paths viewed as desirable and possible, and employment practices fulfill the prophecy by hiring women only for stereotyped "feminine" positions. Added to this pattern is the tendency of both males and females to view the woman who resists or breaks this cycle as atypical, and threatening to the social system.

The many women's groups have stressed not only the inequities faced by women in a society that operates in the above described manner, but also have clearly pointed out the effects such inequities have on the lives of women. Figure 14.1 depicts key events at various age points during an average woman's life span.

The purpose of presenting this average life span is to call attention to the decisions that confront women at critical stages. Crucial to each stage are the developments of the preceding and subsequent stages. The typical pattern has been completion of school, short-term employment, marriage, and the rearing of children, followed either by re-entry into the labor market or a continuation of their domestic, volunteer, and/or social activities.

The education years are critical, both to initial employment and labor market re-entry after children leave home. It is during those years that skills are developed and knowledge obtained that permit meaningful employment initially and later in life.

The difficulty facing many counselors lies in accommodating the counseling process to the realities of this life pattern when their female clients struggle with choice, decision making, and long-term life plans. Those in the forefront of women's rights emphasize strongly the necessity for a woman to make informed choices among the following: marriage, a career, a career in combination with a marriage, marriage with a re-entry career.

The counseling relationship is often criticized as being vulnerable to unexamined sexist attitudes and beliefs. It should be noted that such attitudes and beliefs affect both client and counselor. The female client who attempts to redefine her situation as a woman often experiences conflict in her struggle against prevailing stereotypes. Too, the male counselor in particular (and the female counselor to some degree) is often caught responding and thinking about a client as female rather than as a person. These and other factors have led many feminists to take a position analogous to that of the black who asserts that no white can effectively work with a black client because he or she cannot fully understand the meaning of blackness. The extreme feminist position is that no male counselor can ever work effectively with a female client because he can never know what it means to be female.

Title IX of the Education Amendments of 1972 prohibits sex discrimination under any education program or activity receiving federal assistance. Verheyden-Hilliard[87] suggests that counselors have the potential to influence not only students and the counseling profession but teachers and administrators to achieve sex-fair education. She points out that the concept of *androgyny* (every individual has both male and female characteristics) provides a way to challenge norms inherent in both personality theories and counseling practices that assume that healthy males and females are those who adhere strictly to masculine or feminine stereotypic behavior.

Counselors, male or female, must be sensitive to and aware of their beliefs about women and their role in contemporary society. Without doubt, these beliefs have an impact on a female client, may well influence the counseling relationship, and may have an affect on the client's future life. The female client must be treated as an individual rather than simply as a member of the female sex. Both participants must consider the future difficulties faced by the liberated female in a society that modifies its expectancies very slowly and grudgingly.

Finally, counselors should note that Division 17 (counseling psychologists) of the American Psychological Associ-ation has endorsed a set of thirteen principles considered essential for counseling women. The principles include statements that counselors (1) are knowledgeable about the biological, psychological, and social issues that affect women; (2) are aware that the assumptions and precepts of counseling theories may apply differently to men and women; (3) are aware of forms of oppression and how these interact with sexism; (4) do not engage in sexual activity with women clients under any circumstance; and (5) support the elimination of sex bias.[88]

Counseling the exceptional

The term *exceptional child* as used in education refers to many kinds of students who differ from the "normal." Any and all physical, mental, and behavioral characteristics may contribute to applying the label *exceptional.* The physically handicapped, the mentally retarded, the emotionally disturbed, learning disabled, and the gifted and talented student are traditional categories of exceptionality. Depending on one's interest, any one of several new subgroupings may be observed within these larger categories.

In 1975, PL 94-142, the Education for All Handicapped Children Act, was passed by Congress. This landmark legislation guarantees free and appropriate public education for all handicapped children. An extremely important aspect of the law is that it goes beyond assuring students' and parents' rights and encourages cooperative efforts by students, parents, school personnel, and specialists to make options available in the areas of education, residential lifestyles, work and careers, and leisure activities.

In addition to direct educational programming, the law includes many other appropriate services among which is counseling. Humes points out the following:

> School counselors may be expected to play key roles in the implementation of PL 94-142, whether they relish the idea or are ready for it. Needless to say, many counselors are not prepared, philosophically or by background for the roles.[89]

[87] Mary Ellen Verheyden-Hilliard, "Counseling: Potential Superbomb Against Sexism," in *Taking Sexism Out of Education* (Washington, D.C.: Superintendent of Documents, 1978), pp. 27–40.

[88] Ad Hoc Committee on Women, "Division 17 Endorses 'Principles Concerning the Counseling/Therapy of Women,' " *The Counseling Psychologist,* 7, No. 4 (1978), 74–76.

[89] Charles W. Humes II, "Implications of PL 94-142 for Training and Supervision," *Counselor Education and Supervision,* 18 (December 1978), 126–129.

Sproles, Panther, and Lanier outline the requirements of PL 94-142 and discuss its challenges and the responses these challenges require.[90] In addition to direct involvement with handicapped students, the authors point out that counselors will undoubtedly become involved in counseling tasks related to attitudinal problems of many others in the school and cite seven possible examples:

The regular teachers' apprehension and resentment at having handicapped children added to their classes;

The special education teacher's input into the regular teacher's operations;

Resentment toward special education teachers' small classes, abundant materials, and seemingly more flexible schedules;

Parents of the handicapped children becoming involved in their children's education (apprehensions for parents, students, and teachers can arise);

Apprehensions and resentments about the material, personnel, and extra time required for exceptional students, their parents, and the community;

Apprehensions of regular students and handicapped students as they integrate; and

Resentment of all adults for the increased paperwork and legal formalities required by PL 94-142.[91]

THE MENTALLY RETARDED   Historically, the majority of counselors have not been involved to any great extent with retarded children in schools. Many factors have contributed to this condition. Not the least is the hard fact that until fairly recently relatively few mentally retarded individuals received much schooling, even in special education programs. The shortage of school-based programs for the mentally retarded was complicated by the fact that most special education programs existed at the elementary school level whereas counseling services have been concentrated in secondary schools. Usually, when retarded individuals reached the age of eligibility (approximately 16) they are referred to services outside the school for rehabilitation counseling. For these and other reasons, school counselors rarely come into contact with retarded youth, and consequently have had little opportunity to acquire knowledge of or provide services to them.

Traditionally, approximately 3 percent of the population could be classified as retarded by conventional individual intelligence measures. Several categories, based on intelligence quotient ranges, are used to identify this population: educable (50–75 IQ), trainable (30–50 IQ), custodial (below 30 IQ). Where special school programs existed, they usually served the educable retarded. The American Association on Mental Deficiency recommends use of a four-category classification system: mild (55–69 IQ), moderate (40–55 IQ), severe (25–39 IQ), and profound (below 25 IQ).

During the 1960s and 1970s increasing attention at national, state, and local levels has been devoted to the mentally retarded. Perhaps more important, material and monetary support has been provided and still more is being actively sought by a number of organizations interested in the retarded. All this with the mandate of PL 94-142 promises improved identification, treatment, and education of this segment of the population.

It has been known for many years that conventional educational procedures are inappropriate and unproductive particularly with the more severely retarded child. Current efforts are being made to conceptualize and actualize programs that more realistically prepare the retarded for as normal a life as possible given the degree of disability. The thrust of these contemporary programs includes incorporating multiple services such as physical therapy, work adjustment training, and vocational education, and de-emphasizing but not excluding repetitive efforts to remedy educational deficiencies. The practice of assigning the child to the regular classroom as much as possible (mainstreaming) and efforts toward placing the handicapped in as normal a social setting as feasible (least-restrictive environment) are rapidly becoming realities. Specialized community agencies have joined public schools in extending services to children well below the conventional age for entering school.

THE LEARNING DISABLED   In about the mid 1960s the label *learning disability* emerged in the literature on exceptional children. Kirk and Gallagher point out the label is applied to a heterogenous group and children who do not fit into the

[90] J. Allen Sproles, Edward E. Panther, and James E. Lanier, "PL 94-142 and Its Impact on the Counselor's Role," *Personnel and Guidance Journal*, 57 (December 1978), 210–212.
[91] Ibid., p. 212.

conventional handicap categories and define these disabilities as follows:

A specific learning disability is a psychological or neurological impediment to spoken or written language or perceptual, cognitive, or motor behavior. The impediment (1) is manifested by discrepancies among specific behaviors and achievements or between evidenced ability and academic achievement, (2) is of such nature and extent that the child does not learn by the instructional methods and materials appropriate for the majority of children and requires specialized procedures for development, and (3) is not primarily due to severe mental retardation, sensory handicaps, emotional problems, or lack of opportunity to learn.[92]

The incidence of learning disabilities in the population is extremely difficult to establish. Estimates in the literature range from 1 to over 20 percent with current best estimates ranging from 1 to 3 percent.[93] Discrepancies in estimates occur because of definitional problems, diagnostic difficulties, the kind and variety of specialized personnel making identifications, and so on.

THE EMOTIONALLY DISTURBED A definition of the emotionally disturbed individual has been presented in Chapter 3. Briefly, the emotionally disturbed individual exhibits an inability to learn that cannot be attributed to intellectual, sensory, or health factors; has difficulty in his or her interpersonal relationships; exhibits inappropriate behavior or feelings; is generally unhappy or depressed; and develops physical symptoms connected with personal or school problems. Estimates of the proportion of emotionally disturbed school-age children vary widely from 4 to 20 percent.

Emotional disturbance in students is often expressed in disruptive behaviors, defiance of authority, truancy, stealing, lying. Withdrawal, pervasive unhappiness, alienation, and marked decline in academic performance are also signs of disturbance. The severely disturbed usually do not remain in the normal classroom but are either institutionalized or attend special schools or programs.

THE GIFTED AND TALENTED Historically, classification of students in this category has varied and was widely based on the use of IQ scores as cutoff points. Some are called *gifted* who score above an IQ of 115. Other classification systems use an IQ score of 140. Using the lower figure, approximately 16 percent of the population would qualify; with the higher figure, less than 1 percent would be included.

A resurgence of interest in the gifted and talented student occurred during the 1970s and has led to a broader definition of the category by Sidney Marland, former U.S. Commissioner of Education.

Gifted and talented children are those identified by professionally qualified persons who by virtue of outstanding abilities are capable of high performance. These children require differentiated educational programs and services beyond those normally provided by the regular program in order to realize their contribution to self and society.

Children capable of high performance include those with demonstrated achievement and/or potential ability in any of the following areas:

1. General intellectual ability
2. Specific academic aptitude
3. Creative or productive thinking
4. Leadership ability
5. Visual and performing arts
6. Psychomotor ability[94]

The last category, psychomotor ability, was dropped by the U.S. Office of Education in 1978.

The gifted and talented student has been characterized as exhibiting a high level of intellectual development at an early age, possessing a wide range of interests, and perhaps exhibiting greater intellectual maturity than social or emotional maturity. Many researchers have cited ways in which superior students differ from others that have implications for counselors. Among them are that they have a greater range of educational and vocational opportunities open to them; that they are able to conceptualize early and at high

[92] Samuel A. Kirk and James J. Gallagher, *Educating Exceptional Children,* 3rd ed. (Boston: Houghton Mifflin Company, 1979), p. 285.
[93] Ibid., pp. 292–294.

[94] Sidney Marland, "Education of the Gifted and Talented," Report to the Subcommittee on Education, Committee on Labor and Public Welfare, U.S. Senate (Washington, D.C., 1972), p. 10.

levels; that they are constantly exposed to parent, teacher, and peer pressures to excel; and that, in general, they frequently lack adult models who are also intellectually superior. Zaffrann[95] has outlined a counseling function, a consultation function, and a research and evaluation function as being interventions conducted by counselors with superior students. He has suggested personal topics—"dominant influences that influence my life," "my responsibilities in my present life," "the future as I see it," and so on—as examples of stimuli that can be used for either structured or unstructured interventions with them.

The counselor's work with the exceptional individual involves several activities. Among these are identification; specialized efforts to design individualized programs for them; consulting with teachers and a wide range of specialized professionals, school administrators, and parents about the exceptionality; and, not least of all, providing counseling that sensitively applies knowledge and understanding of their problems and concerns. Especially in the case of the mentally retarded, learning disabled, and emotionally disturbed, reliance on and work with nonschool community services that provide specialized help and programs are essential. There are probably no other students for whom highly individualized attention is more essential if they are to capitalize on their strengths and realize their potential, whether limited or promising.

Counseling the aged

Selecting an age at which individuals are termed *aged* is risky especially at a time when arbitrarily imposed mandatory retirement is being raised or abolished. However, for discussion and descriptive purposes the arbitrary age of 65 is useful. It is estimated that over 90 percent of an older population of over 20 million live in the community either in their own home or apartment and prefer to do so even if they live alone. With some assistance many who presently live in institutional settings such as nursing homes, hospitals, or homes for the aged could live in their own homes.

Many factors create stress for the aged as a group. Among these are chronic illness, physical and mental impairment,

lowered income, an end to work-related productivity, loss of their marriage partners and friends. The elderly experience a decreased range of personal relationships often resulting in loneliness and a decline in self-esteem. Many older Americans remain active, physically well, continue to hold jobs, have active social lives, and participate in the community. But, for all too many, life is lived in virtual seclusion.

Most experts on the aged agree that successful aging requires remaining active and that continued good health is dependent on remaining in contact with others and functioning as fully as possible physically. Essential to coping with the stress and the physical process of aging is a capacity to adapt to the available social environment and to compensate for changes in it. The availability of supportive interpersonal relationships, health support systems and social support systems is extremely important to the aged.

The Older Americans Act of 1965 provided stimulation for community planning for the elderly and funded the establishment and strengthening of agencies serving the aged. As a direct result of this legislation a wide range of projects was begun in such diverse but necessary fields as homemaker services, legal aid, transportation services, employment counseling, and so on. Since this beginning there has been much improvement, however, services such as day centers for the elderly, meal services, telephone reassurance projects, in-home care service, and services that encourage participation in the opportunity to serve and work are still not present in all communities or can only meet part of the needs.

Counseling within the support system available to the aged is both essential and potentially a powerful force for assisting and encouraging self-reliance in the elderly. Lombana describes several remedial and several preventive ways counseling assistance can benefit the elderly.[96] She cites as remedial measures: (1) personal counseling for serious mental health concerns, (2) supportive counseling for physical health concerns, (3) motivational and adjustment counseling for those residing in or leaving residential institutions, and (4) vocational counseling and retraining. In the prevention area Lombana cites the following as areas needing both public policy and as a source of useful counseling and guid-

[95] Ronald T. Zaffrann, "Counseling the Gifted," *Gifted Child Education*, 1 (December 1978), 9–13.

[96] Judy H. Lombana, "Counseling the Elderly: Remediation Plus Prevention," *Personnel and Guidance Journal*, 55 (November 1976), 143–144.

ance interventions: (1) preretirement counseling, (2) lifelong health education, (3) avocational opportunities and leisure activities, (4) programs of information regarding available services, (5) educational and recreational opportunities, (6) education of the general public, (7) counseling the families of senior citizens, and (8) adequate training and employment of professional and paraprofessional counselors.

Summary

This chapter has sought to draw attention to the emergence and expansion of counseling specialties and extending service to the special subgroups among the counselor's clientele. Counselors who specialize in dealing with certain situations or who practice in certain settings (marriage and family, agency, career development, crisis, and so on) are becoming more numerous.

Special subgroups among most counselors' clientele have special problems caused by society's attitudes and beliefs. Without doubt this complicates their work for there is no easy answer to complex situations. Through this chapter the counselor is urged to work with individuals and to recognize the tremendous impact on an individual that membership in a cultural, social, ethnic, racial, sexual, or exceptional subgroup can have. Despite the many implied shortcomings in counselors' practice and effectiveness with special groups, probably no other personal interaction setting holds greater promise for providing individualized attention to, and appreciation for, the differences between these special individuals. As always a deep social and personal commitment, a broad experience, and continuous updating of knowledge are essential to effective work with any special subgroup among the counselor's clientele.

Issues

Issue 1 Counselor specialization, that is, marriage and family counseling, career counseling, couples counseling, and so forth, is sought most appropriately after initial preparation.

Yes, because
1. The initial graduate year of preparation is best viewed as the time to learn those counseling fundamentals generic to any setting or population.

2. Specialization implies advanced skills and knowledge of setting and clientele that can only be gained after entry-level skills are attained.
3. Most students admitted to graduate counselor preparation programs are unable to specify a specialty.

No, because
1. Sufficient treatment can be given during the initial year of graduate preparation to differential settings and specific clientele to enable individuals to enter and progress in such specialties as marriage and family counseling, career counseling, and the like.
2. Most graduate students have at least a tentative commitment to a counseling specialty.

Discussion Currently, perspectives on specialization in counseling are far from uniform. Examination of views about counselor specialization reveals that a bewildering array of viewpoints is held by counselors and counselor educators across the country. For example, some counselor education institutions have taken the position that individuals who have earned the master's degree in a one-year program are ready for entry-level employment in any setting or with any population. Other institutions take the position that their graduates are ready to enter only those settings in which the program provided specific instruction and information.

Some people use the term *specialty* to refer to certain settings in which counseling is done, whereas others use it to refer to helping people cope with certain life situations. These authors tend to view specialization in counseling as a function of extended preparation and experience. After initial preparation and after experience as an entry-level counselor in a school, college, or community setting, some counselors then begin to specialize in helping people with certain problems or life situations. These specialties are often practiced in specific settings or agencies.

Issue 2 Cross-cultural counseling should not be attempted.

True, because
1. Breakdowns occur frequently in communications between individuals of differing racial, class, ethnic, and sexual backgrounds.
2. Misunderstandings that arise in cross-cultural counseling exacerbate and deepen feelings of aloneness and alienation.

False, because

1. Individuals—regardless of race, class, sex, culture—need and seek help of counselors who can develop relationships with them of sufficient strength to withstand and overcome class, race, language, and other cultural barriers and misunderstandings.

2. Race, class, and cultural factors are better interpreted as calling for counseling interventions that differ in technique and goals from those that work effectively with young, educated, white middle-class Americans.

Discussion Many minority group members have either demanded or recommended that their membership be counseled only by professionals of their membership. That is to say that only blacks should counsel other blacks; only women should counsel women. Behind their statements lie two important considerations. First, minority group members have experienced prejudice and distrust persons from the dominant culture. Second, more minority group members should be encouraged to become counseling professionals.

Admittedly, there are many hazards in and barriers to effective cross-cultural counseling. Although these are becoming better understood, much remains to be done in isolating each variable and determining how it can be overcome. Sue and Sue[97] present a conceptual scheme to compare and contrast how language, culture, and class variables can be used to determine appropriate counseling interventions. They stress that counselors (1) must take into account the interaction of class, cultural variables, and language factors on verbal and nonverbal communications; (2) must avoid misinterpreting client behaviors; (3) must acquire knowledge and understanding of minority group cultures and experiences; and (4) must be more action oriented in initiating, structuring, and helping cross-cultural clients cope with pressing social problems of immediate concern to them.

Annotated references

Ferber, Andrew, Marilyn Mendelsohn, and Augustus Napier, eds. *The Book of Family Therapy.* Boston: Houghton Mifflin Company, 1972. 725 pp.

[97] Derald Wing Sue and David Sue, "Barriers to Effective Cross-Cultural Counseling," *Journal of Counseling Psychology,* 24 (September 1977), 420–429.

A personal account of family therapy written collaboratively by several authors. The four sections of this readable and interesting collection describe what family therapists are, their techniques, their training programs and variations, and the future of family therapy.

Golan, Naomi. *Treatment in Crisis Situations.* New York: The Free Press, 1978. 266 pp.

Presents the theory behind crisis intervention and a model of intervention including stages of crises, goals of treatment at various stages, treatment techniques involved in professional intervention. The latter portion of the book presents case illustrations of typical crisis situations.

Herr, Edwin L. *Research in Career Education: The State of the Art.* Columbus, Ohio: Eric Clearing House on Career Education, 1977. 82 pp.

Herr reviews, analyzes, and synthesizes the research in career education. Emerging trends and program practices are spotlighted by this nationally recognized author.

Kalish, Richard A. *Late Adulthood: Perspectives on Human Development.* Monterey, Calif.: Brooks/Cole Publishing Company, 1975. 133 pp.

A readable and informative monograph covering the basic processes of aging, its effects on the self and personality, relationships with others, and the physical and social environments faced by the aging presented with the goal of making the reader knowledgeable about what it means to grow old.

Kirk, Samuel A. and James J. Gallagher. *Educating Exceptional Children.* 3rd ed. Boston: Houghton Mifflin Company, 1979. 545 pp.

This source is extremely valuable to those wishing up-to-date, reliable, and factual knowledge about the exceptional child. The text is organized around descriptions of the various exceptionalities, curricular and instructional adaptation, and the learning environment. Long a leader in the field, it is a useful basic reference for all counselors and educators.

National Project on Women in Education. *Taking Sexism Out of Education.* Washington, D.C.: U.S. Government Printing Office, 1978. 113 pp.

This monograph reprints a series of articles that treat topics under study by the National Project. The articles were authored by several individuals—Bernice Sandler, Mary Ellen Verheyden-Hilliard, Corinne H. Rieder—recognized nationally in the counseling profession.

Sue, Derald. "Counseling the Culturally Different." *Personnel and Guidance Journal*, 55 (March 1977), 369–432.

This special issue is devoted exclusively to counseling the culturally different. Treatment is given to counseling Asian Americans, blacks, Latinos, Haitians, and Puerto Ricans. A conceptual analysis of many cultural factors is presented by Sue.

Further references

Ad Hoc Committee on Women. "Division 17 Endorses 'Principles Concerning the Counseling/Therapy of Women.' " *The Counseling Psychologist*, 7, No. 4 (1978), 74–76.

Brammer, Lawrence M. "Informal Helping Systems in Selected Subcultures." *Personnel and Guidance Journal*, 56 (April 1978), 471–479.

Dong, Tim, Herbert Wong, Maximo Callao, Aline Nishihara, Robert Chin. "National Asian American Psychology Training Conference." *American Psychologist*, 33 (July 1978), 691–692.

Gordon, Myra and Robert J. Grantham. "Helper Preference is Disadvantaged Students." *Journal of Counseling Psychology*, 26 (July 1979), 337–343.

Harris, John E., and Jack L. Bodden. "An Activity Group Experience for Disengaged Elderly Persons." *Journal of Counseling Psychology*, 25 (July 1978), 325–330.

Grinnell, Richard M., Jr., and Alice Lieberman. "Teaching the Mentally Retarded Job Interviewing Skills." *Journal of Counseling Psychology*, 24 (July 1977), 332–337.

Katz, Judy H., and Allen E. Ivey. "White Awareness: The Frontier of Racism Awareness Training." *Personnel and Guidance Journal*, 55 (April 1977), 485–489.

Lee, Dong Yul. "Evaluation of a Group Counseling Program Designed to Enhance Adjustment of Mentally Retarded Adults." *Journal of Counseling Psychology*, 24 (July 1977), 318–323.

Pedersen, Paul B. "Four Dimensions of Cross-Cultural Skill in Counselor Training." *Personnel and Guidance Journal*, 56 (April 1978), 480–484.

Rappaport, Julian, William S. Davidson, Melvin N. Wilson, and Alonzo Mitchell. "Alternatives to Blaming the Victim or the Environment." *American Psychologist*, 30 (April 1975), 525–528.

Riggar, Theodore F., and Susan W. Riggar. "The Rehabilitation Counselor in an Educational Setting," *Personnel and Guidance Journal*, 57 (September 1978), 60–61.

Shullman, Sandra L., and Nancy E. Betz. "An Investigation of the Effects of Client Sex and Presenting Problem in Referral from Intake." *Journal of Counseling Psychology*, 26 (March 1979), 140–145.

Sue, Derald W. "World Views and Counseling." *Personnel and Guidance Journal*, 56 (April 1978), 458–462.

Webster, Dennis W., and Bruce R. Fretz. "Asian American, Black and White College Students' Preferences for Help-Giving Sources." *Journal of Counseling Psychology*, 25 (March 1978), 124–130.

Westbrook, Franklin D., Javier Miyares, and Joyce H. Roberts. "Perceived Problem Areas of Black and White Students and Hints About Comparative Counseling Needs." *Journal of Counseling Psychology*, 25 (March 1978), 119–123.

up counseling

Group helping processes are being utilized in many forms in diverse settings by many individuals. Attention in this chapter is given to the definition, terminology, and classification employed in group helping relationships, operational practices involved in group counseling, recent research findings, the values and limitations of group counseling, and the similarities and differences between group and individual counseling.

Terminology and classification

Considerable confusion exists over the precise meaning of such words as *groups*, *group dynamics*, *group guidance*, and *group counseling*. This lack of precision is evident in the literature produced by those in the field and contributes markedly to the faulty impressions generated by communications about group work. Some of the terminology and primary concepts that are basic to group work will be presented briefly in this section.

Group defined

In the dictionary the word *group* has many meanings. The least important definition of group for the counselor is the aggregation or collection of objects in close proximity but without any interplay among them. Presumably, an adequate definition would include at least the size, the quality of interaction, and the potential for change within the group. In counseling, a group consists of two or more persons who voluntarily have contact, proximity, and interaction intended to produce change in each member. As a result of participation, members interact with and influence each other. Modification occurs in each member because of participation and experiences shared with other members. Other criteria set forth to characterize a counseling group, rather than merely a collection of individuals, are (1) dynamic interaction between and among members, (2) a

common goal, (3) a relationship between size and function, (4) volition and consent, and (5) a capacity for self-direction.

Classification of groups

Groups have been classified in numerous ways. Size, nature of interaction, goals or purposes, and organization have been used as variables in categorizing them. A common basis of differentiation has been the main function served by the group: educational, religious, recreational, political, and so on. Degree of permanence is another basis for cataloguing. Groups range all the way from the very temporary to the highly stable. But such classifications, though frequently encountered in the literature on groups, are of limited usefulness. Reference here will be to three types of groups.

PRIMARY VERSUS SECONDARY GROUPS Primary groups are those in which the members meet face to face for companionship, mutual aid, and the resolution of questions that confront them. Examples of primary groups include the family, the play group, the partnership, and the study group. Such groups are called primary because they are first in time and importance. They are characterized by (1) small size, (2) similarity of members' background, (3) limited self-interest, and (4) intensity of shared interest. Secondary groups are those in which the members are not as intimate and contact is more casual. Examples include large lecture classes and committees.

INGROUP VERSUS OUTGROUP Groups with which individuals identify, by virtue of their awareness or "consciousness of kind," are their ingroups—their family, sex, club, occupation, religion. An individual's expression of subjective attitudes frequently reveal his or her ingroup memberships that in turn are often related to particular social circumstances.

It follows that the outgroup is defined by the individual with relation to the ingroup, usually by the expression of contrast between *we* and *they*, or *other*. Outgroup attitudes are characterized by expressions of difference and sometimes by varied degrees of antagonism, prejudice, hatred, or apathy.

SOCIO VERSUS PSYCHE GROUPS Coffey differentiates *socio* (school dropout committee) from *psyche* (boys' gang) groups in a number of respects.[1] There is no visualized goal in the psyche group, but goals are an essential characteristic of the socio group. Informal structure, few rules or regulations, voluntary and homogeneous membership characterize the psyche group. Membership in the socio group is often voluntary, but there may be those for whom membership is not by personal inclination but derives from serving as a representative of some organization.

Socio groups are usually more heterogeneous in respect to age, status, and vocation than psyche groups. The purpose of socio groups is to reach some defined goal expressed by the group. The psyche group's purpose—rarely made explicit—is to satisfy the emotional needs of its members. Neither socio nor psyche groups exist in pure form, most groups being a mixture. However, Coffey warns against any deliberate attempt to place simultaneous emphasis on psyche group and socio group processes because the strain frequently leads to dissolution of the group. A therapeutically oriented counseling group would be most like a psyche group.

Goldman differentiates among several types and levels of groups.[2] He has represented the interaction of content and process in group guidance, group counseling, and group therapy and his representation is reproduced here as Table 15.1. Three levels (I, II, and III) of process are presented across the top of the table. Three examples (A, B, C) of content are presented down the left side of the table. Process moves from traditional teacher-directed methods to more member-centered methods. Content moves from traditional academic subject matter to more personal, typically nonschool topics. Cell 1 represents typical interaction between content and process and Cell 9 typifies a group therapy situation. Cell 5 represents group guidance activities. Goldman

points out that group guidance and group counseling have, in many instances, been ineffective because they have been in Cell 2 and 3 kind of operations, rather than Cells 5 or 6. In such situations, the content of group guidance differs from that of traditional school subjects, whereas the process does not. In Goldman's opinion, this has produced ineffective group guidance in the schools.

Group process

Process has been described (see Chapter 1) as continuous, dynamic, and directional movement. Group process refers to the actions and interactions used by a group to develop and maintain its identity and its effects on individuals who compose the group. Process (why and how) is often contrasted to content (what). Process incorporates the sequence by which certain experiences and activities occur, the methods used to provide the experiences, and the approaches to others utilized by group members. In social functioning, the process used is largely from individual to individual, whereas in group functioning there is interdependence of each on the others, operating in three ways: individual to individual, individual to whole, and whole to individual. This quality in the relationship of individuals in the group and the way they work together to produce it is the process.

Group dynamics

Group dynamics is a term used to convey many different aspects of group work. Fundamentally, it refers to the interacting forces within groups as they organize and operate to achieve their objectives. Often, the term *group dynamics* includes group process and group roles. Several techniques have been developed for facilitating group control and group problem solving. One such technique employed by specialists in group dynamics is the utilization of an observer whose task is to keep a running account of the group meeting to discover why things go well or why they bog down. These observations are presented to the group at appropriate intervals. For some types of groups, particularly counseling and therapy groups, the presence of a nonparticipating, judgmental person may limit the security individuals need

[1] Hubert S. Coffey, "Socio and Psyche Group Process: Integrative Concepts," in *Perspectives on the Group Process*, 2nd ed., ed. C. Gratton Kemp (Boston: Houghton Mifflin Company, 1970), p. 50.
[2] Leo Goldman, "Group Guidance: Content and Process," *Personnel and Guidance Journal*, 40 (February 1962), 518–522.

TABLE 15.1 **Interaction of content and process in group guidance, group counseling, and group therapy**

| | | *Process* | | |
		Level I	Level II	Level III
		Leader plans topics; lecture and recitation; facts and skills emphasized; units in regular classes	Leader and group members collaborate in planning topics; discussions, projects, panels, visits; attitudes and opinions emphasized; separate guidance groups meet on schedule	Topics originate with group members; free discussion, role-playing; feelings and needs emphasized; groups organized as needed, meet as needed
	Type A Usual school subject matter (mathematics, English, etc.)	1	4	7
Content	Type B School-related topics (the world of work, choosing a college, how to study, etc.)	2	5	8
	Type C Nonschool topics (dating behavior, parent-child-relations, handling frustrations, etc.)	3	6	9

SOURCE: Leo Goldman, "Group Guidance: Content and Process," *Personnel and Guidance Journal*, 40 (February 1962), 519. Copyright © 1962 American Personnel and Guidance Association. Reprinted with permission.

before they can afford to face the threat within them. Cartwright and Zander define group dynamics as follows:

According to one rather frequent usage, group dynamics refers to a sort of political ideology concerning the ways in which groups should be organized and managed. This ideology emphasizes the importance of democratic leadership, the participation of members in decisions, and the gains both to society and to individuals to be obtained through cooperative activities in groups. The critics of this view have sometimes caricatured it as making "togetherness" the supreme virtue, advocating that everything be done jointly in groups which have and need no leader because everyone participates fully and equally. A second popular usage of the term, group dynamics, has it refer to a set of techniques, such as role playing, buzz-sessions, observation and feedback of group process, and group decision, which have been employed widely during

the past decade or two in training programs designed to improve skill in human relations and in the management of conferences and committees. . . . According to the third usage of the term, group dynamics, it refers to a field of inquiry dedicated to achieving knowledge about the nature of groups, the laws of their development, and their interrelations with individuals, other groups, and larger institutions.[3]

Guidance groups

Group guidance usually refers to any part of a guidance program that is conducted with groups of students rather than one individual. Lifton placed the emphasis in group guid-

[3] Dorwin Cartwright and Alvin Zander, eds., *Group Dynamics*, 3rd ed. (New York: Harper & Row, 1968), p. 4.

ance on the imparting of information,[4] whereas Caldwell stated that "it should also be said at the outset that the common idea of 'group guidance' as an information-giving device is inappropriate to the concept presented here."[5]

Kirby has defined group guidance as follows:

Incremental group guidance refers to a group process whereby the participants (group members) approach the topics or problems presented for group consideration on the here-and-now level, without necessarily having full knowledge nor even seeking full information about the individual or his ultimate goal.[6]

Major reasons for conducting group guidance include (1) providing educational-vocational and personal-social information to students, (2) enabling students to discuss and engage in personal and career planning activities, and (3) giving students opportunities to investigate and discuss common problems, goals, and solutions.

The difference between group guidance and group instruction is not always clear-cut, nor are the terms used with precision. The thread of distinction appears to be related to leadership roles. When the major responsibility for group activities is focused on the adult leader (teacher), the term *group instruction* seems appropriate. When the focus shifts to the members of the group, the term *group guidance* is applicable.

Group counseling

In group counseling one counselor is involved in a relationship with a number of counselees at the same time. Most authorities cite six as the optimum number, with a range from four to twelve. Group counseling is usually concerned with developmental problems and situational concerns of members. Focus is on the attitudes and emotions, the choices and values involved in interpersonal relationships. Members, by interacting with each other, establish helping

relationships that enable them to develop understanding and insight and awareness of self as a first step to effective functioning. The vehicle for accomplishing this goal in a group is that members discuss their personal, emotional concerns and other members provide feedback about their perceptions of these experiences. Group counseling can be conducted for remedial purposes, for developmental purposes, or be preventive in nature, hoping to prevent problems from growing to the point where the individual needs special help to cope with them.

Group counseling has been defined by Gazda as follows:

Group counseling is a dynamic interpersonal process focusing on conscious thought and behavior and involving the therapy functions of permissiveness, orientation to reality, catharsis, and mutual trust, caring, understanding, and support. The therapy functions are created and nurtured in a small group through the sharing of personal concerns with one's peers and the counselor(s). The group counselees are basically normal individuals with various concerns which are not debilitating to the extent requiring extensive personality change. The group counselees may utilize the group interaction to increase understanding and acceptance of values and goals and to learn and/or unlearn certain attitudes and behaviors.[7]

Gazda emphasizes that group counseling is problem centered and feeling oriented. Reflection and clarification of feelings and modification of attitudes are its focal points. Major effort is centered on helping members deal with their problems and experiences, and the emphasis is on growth and adjustment rather than on cure of deficit behavior. Characteristic problems among adolescent groups include conflicts or emotional upheavals such as sibling rivalry, independence-dependence, and the like. Educational-vocational concerns would be dealt with on a feeling level rather than an information-giving or instructional level. Corey and Corey state that "The counseling group *differs* from the therapy group in that it deals with conscious problems, is not aimed at major personality changes, is frequently oriented toward the resolution of specific and short-term is-

---

[4] Walter M. Lifton, *Working with Groups*, 2nd ed. (New York: John Wiley & Sons, 1966), p. 14.
[5] Edson Caldwell, *Group Techniques for the Classroom Teacher* (Chicago: Science Research Associates, 1960), p. 10.
[6] Jonell H. Kirby, "Group Guidance," *Personnel and Guidance Journal*, 49 (April 1971), 596–597.

[7] George M. Gazda, *Group Counseling: A Developmental Approach*, 2nd ed. (Boston: Allyn & Bacon, 1978), p. 8.

sues, and is not concerned with treatment of neurotic or psychotic disorders.''[8]

Some have used the term *multiple counseling* rather than *group counseling*, referring apparently to the fact that participants have a therapeutic effect on one another. However, multiple counseling increasingly is used to mean the presence of two or more counselors with counselees.

T-groups

T-groups were formulated in 1947 by the Basic Skills Training Group of the National Training Laboratory for developing interpersonal skills and sensitivity to communications. The participants in a T-group are involved in an experience in which they learn from their behavior, the T-group being an unstructured group of ten to twelve people in which interpersonal relationships and behavior patterns are stressed. Group members learn to recognize the effect they have on others and how others see them. They probe the strengths and weaknesses of each other's personalities in an unstructured atmosphere but frequently T-groups are task oriented, resolving organization problems. Their objective is to learn by use of group process rather than facilitating personal growth.

Three factors that characterize the T-group have been cited by Golembiewski and Blumberg: (1) it is a learning laboratory, (2) it focuses on learning how to learn, and (3) it places emphasis on immediate ideas, feelings, and reactions.[9]

Personal growth groups

Several names have been used for groups designed to facilitate personal growth: encounter, sensitivity, human awareness, human potential. Such groups are usually composed of eight to twelve members and their focus is on the members' interactions within the group with attention to its implica-

tions for behavior outside the group. Goals of such groups include facilitating personal growth, increased sensitivity to the feelings of the individual and others, and the greater awareness of self and others. Personal growth groups are often led by facilitators who are sometimes trained psychotherapists (some of whom have become highly dissatisfied with dyadic therapy) whereas others are led by individuals who lack professional counseling or clinical preparation. Many groups have two or more leaders or facilitators. An overview of encounter groups and descriptions of behavior change appear in two volumes edited by Arthur Burton.[10]

Family group consultation

A form of group counseling called family group consultation has been developed by the staff of the Division of Continuing Education of the Oregon State System of Higher Education with the assistance and encouragement of the Department of Psychiatry. The term *consultation* rather than *counseling* was used because the staff believed it described more adequately the interfamily communication involved.

In family group consultation three or four families (consisting of up to twenty individuals) meet together weekly with three or four counselors. The typical procedure employed is that, during the first hour, all family members are together with all counselors in one large group. During the second hour, adult family members and children meet with one or more counselors assigned to each of the two groups.

The process, according to Fullmer,[11] was initiated in 1961 to help overcome the poverty of understanding that appeared in families having some degree of disorganization. Among the principles of family group consultation identified by Fullmer were that (1) the individual's personality is formed within the social system of the family; (2) behavior and knowledge (as well as gaps or voids in behavior) are perpetuated on a generation-to-generation basis because of the family social system; (3) each family develops unique characteristics including beliefs, personal mean-

[8] Gerald Corey and Marianne Schneider Corey, *Groups: Process and Practice* (Monterey, Calif.: Brooks/Cole Publishing Company, 1977), p. 8.
[9] Robert T. Golembiewski and Arthur Blumberg, eds., *Sensitivity Training and the Laboratory Approach*, 3rd ed. (Itasca, Ill.: F. E. Peacock Publishers, 1977), pp. 5–8.
[10] Arthur Burton, ed., *Encounter* (San Francisco: Jossey-Bass, 1969) and *What Makes Behavioral Change Possible?* (New York: Brunner/Mazel, 1976).
[11] Daniel W. Fullmer, *Counseling: Group Theory and System*, 2nd ed. (Cranston, R.I.: Carroll Press, 1978), pp. 361–395.

ings, and restricted codes; and (4) the character of a child is formed in the family group by the reinforcement schedules created and maintained by parents, siblings, and significant others. Fullmer stated that counselors assess the involvement of each individual in the family group, learn the patterns of interpersonal loyalties, alliances, and contracts used in the family, point up consistencies and discrepancies so clarification by each person is possible, and teach family members how to assess their input, the input of others and to analyze accurately the relative meaning for each person involved.

CONJOINT FAMILY THERAPY Virginia Satir has formulated and practiced a theory and technique of working with families entitled conjoint family therapy.[12] The theory and technique are based on the premise that successful intervention with individuals is contingent on understanding their role and position within a family. The individual who seeks help is referred to by Satir as the "identified patient," because he or she is the one most obviously affected by a troubled family unit. Individual behavior occurs within a family context consisting of interacting roles, rules, and values. According to Satir, communication between family members occurs at both a "denotative" level, conveying the literal message, and a "metacommunicative" level. Feelings and emotions are conveyed at the latter level. Communications have been classified by Satir into five modes: (1) placating, (2) blaming, (3) super-reasonableness, (4) irrelevant, and (5) congruent.[13] The two messages are contained in each mode.

1. Where the literal message is one of *agreement*.
   Where the affective message is *pleasant and placating*.
2. Where the literal message is *disagreement*.
   Where the affective message is *blaming and attacking*.
3. Where the literal message is *changing the subject*.
   Where the affective message is *being irrelevant or withdrawing*.
4. Where the literal message is *being super-reasonable*.
   Where the affective message is *conniving*.

5. Where the literal message is *reporting oneself*.
   Where the affective message is *making a place for others*.

Communications within the family, according to conjoint therapy, are efforts to influence or ask something of a person to whom they are directed. In short, messages are requests. In this approach, the focus is on developing family members' ability to send and receive clear, functional communications. More attention has been given to this approach in Chapter 14.

Group therapy

Group therapy is usually defined as the application of therapeutic principles to two or more individuals simultaneously to clarify their psychological conflicts so that they may live normally. It is likely to be reserved for the more seriously disturbed and treats disordered personality problems. The term *group therapy* originally was introduced to meet criticisms regarding the use of the term *group psychotherapy* by persons other than psychiatrists or clinical psychologists. Therapy, however, has become practically synonymous with psychotherapy in professional literature.

Corey and Corey say that "many people participate in group therapy to try to alleviate specific symptoms or problems, such as depression, sexual problems, anxiety and psychosomatic disorders."[14]

Group therapy for young married couples, delinquents, executives, and troubled families is increasing rapidly in clinics all over the country. More and more therapists are using video-tape playback as a technique to let members see what, how, and why certain behaviors occurred in the interaction. Group psychotherapy increasingly has made use of certain techniques such as video-tape playback, saturation sessions, physical movement and contact among members during sessions, and the like.

Special therapy groups

In his book, Mowrer refers to special groups and associations that are inspired and operated largely by laymen, and

[12] Virginia Satir, *Conjoint Family Therapy*, rev. ed. (Palo Alto, Calif.: Science and Behavior Books, 1967), 208 pp.
[13] Virginia Satir, "You as a Change Agent," in Virginia Satir, James Stachowiak and Harvey A. Taschman, *Helping Families to Change* (New York: Jason Aronson, 1975), pp. 41–49.
[14] Corey and Corey, *Groups*, p. 7.

designed mainly to provide restorative experiences for their members.[15]

Previously, Mowrer had stated that in private practice

> . . . the patient, in now revealing his long-hidden sins, does so only to one person who, in turn, promises to be as secretive about them as he himself has been. It's as if the patient were suffocating in a closet and the therapist, instead of helping him get out into the fresh air, said to him: "Move over, and I'll get in there with you. This way I can treat you privately, without the necessity of anyone else's knowing what your trouble is."[16]

Alcoholics Anonymous is an example of the approximately 265 such groups in the United States. Mowrer tells why these groups came into existence.

> In short, these groups reflect, first of all, a general loss of confidence in professional "treatment," regardless of whether in an individual or group context. Also they reflect the pervasive failure of existing "natural" groups to perform the ideological and therapeutic functions which they should have been performing. Thus, in "inventing" group therapy for themselves, laymen seem to be creating a new social institution—one might also say a *new culture*—in which a kind of redemptive concern and competence exist which is not otherwise to be found in our time.[17]

Marathon groups

Groups that meet in continuous session longer than the usual one to two hours are often referred to as marathon groups. During such saturation sessions—often lasting fifteen to twenty hours or more—members explore thoroughly their views about themselves and others; their relationships with others; their aspirations and goals; and

typical ways of reacting to threat, disagreement, and prejudice. By confronting and challenging social pretensions, yet accepting each other, members strive to develop open, authentic, self-responsible behavior.

Mintz depicts the nature of a marathon group in these words:

> The group does not deal with anything except its chosen task, which usually is the expression and exploration of immediate feelings. Then conditions create in the marathon, for most participants, a sense of timelessness which makes the present moment very real and intense. And for most participants, the intensity of the marathon experience operates to bring about personality changes, in the direction of self-understanding and self-acceptance, which often endure.[18]

Summary

Table 15.2 presents a classification of several kinds of groups that attempts to differentiate them along ten dimensions. It should be noted that the clear-cut distinctions implied in the classification are difficult to maintain or defend. In reality, a better perspective would be to view the categories as lying on a continuum with overlap occurring to some degree as one moves along the continuum. It should also be noted that little, if any, overlap would occur between categories that are at great distance from each other. Additional commentary on some of the dimensions cited in Table 15.2, as well as other dimensions, is presented later in this chapter.

Operational practices in group counseling

Some of the practices of initiating and working with counseling groups are identified and discussed here. Generally, group counseling principles are similar to those underlying individual counseling.

[15] O. Hobart Mowrer, *The New Group Therapy* (Princeton, N.J.: D. Van Nostrand Co., 1964).
[16] O. Hobart Mowrer, "Payment or Repayment? The Problem of Private Practice," *American Psychologist*, 18 (September 1963), 577–580.
[17] Mowrer, *The New Group Therapy*, p. v.
[18] Elizabeth E. Mintz, *Marathon Groups* (New York: Appleton-Century-Crofts, 1971), p. 1.

Selecting group members

Who should be in group counseling? Frequently the answer given is that members should have similar interests or problems, but this is not a necessity as long as the members can develop and function as a group. A variety of problems often enriches the group's experience. Homogeneous grouping in relation to age and social maturity is usually viewed as desirable, and it is often advantageous to have both sexes in a group.

There are some guidelines useful in selecting individuals who can benefit from group counseling. The counselee must want help, be willing to talk about his or her concerns, and appear to fit into a group. Ethical practice recommends that counselors interview potential members to determine whether they would fit into a group or the kind of group most appropriate for them. If counselors believe the person could benefit from group counseling, they then explain how the group functions and what is expected of its members. Whether to become a group member is left up to the individual. Most individuals who know what is expected of them, if allowed to decide without pressure, will usually be able to determine whether they should join a counseling group. Some enter the group only to find it too threatening and withdraw. Individual counseling should be made available to the person who withdraws.

Not all individuals fit well into certain counseling groups. The very aggressive, the extremely shy, and the seriously maladjusted make poor members of a "normal" group. Previous relationships of members should be considered; close friends or relatives should not be in the same group, so that sharing will be more honest and threat from self-disclosure reduced. Many group specialists believe that it is desirable not to have interaction of members outside the group session. Undoubtedly this restriction would be difficult to maintain in a small school or community.

Size of group

The usual practice is to select six to eight members, but there may be as many as ten or twelve. Most counselors feel more comfortable with five to eight members. As groups increase in size, collateral relationships are often weakened. The tendency is to depend on the counselor rather than to

become involved with other members. The counselor, in turn, is inclined to speak increasingly to the group as a whole rather than to members as individuals.

Length and frequency of sessions

The appropriate length of sessions for group counseling is generally given as an hour for adolescents and thirty to forty-five minutes for elementary school children. Adults usually go for one and a half to two hours. The first hour is usually very active and productive, but accomplishments can dwindle rapidly during the second hour. In school settings the length of session can be regulated by class periods. Many counselors report that the time between sessions should not exceed one week, and two sessions per week are often preferred. Some time lapse between sessions is valuable in that it gives the individual a chance to think over the experience. If counseling groups meet more than two or three hours weekly, productivity of the group may decline.

Closed and continuous groups

The groups may operate as *closed* or *continuous*. The closed group is made up of only those who were present when the group started. No one else joins. This is the most common practice. The continuous group allows others to join at almost any stage. This open policy often creates problems of communication, acceptance, support, and the like, among group members.

Nature of relationship

Opinions differ about the nature of the group counseling relationship. Essentially, the point of contention is whether group members have therapeutic potential by interacting with one another or whether only the counselor is the therapeutic agent. Those who believe that through their interactions members act as counselors conceptualize the relationship as presented in Figure 15.1.

Others believe that gains by members are made primarily through members' interaction with the counselor. In other words, as counselors are involved with one member, in-

TABLE 15.2 **A classification of groups**

Dimensions/categories	Task groups	Guidance groups	Training groups	Counseling groups
1. *Common names*	T-group; planning committee; task force; discussion group	Discussion group; reaction group; planning group; information group; career group	T-group; interpersonal and intrapersonal laboratories	Group counseling
2. *Kind of members*	Self- and other-selected according to potential contribution	Self- or other-selected by need for knowledge in area treated	Self-selection to learn group skills	Self- or other-selected because of perceived need for change
3. *Usual size*	5–15	12–25	8–12	6–12
4. *Focus*	Assigned task independent of member needs	Educational, vocational and personal information and planning	Self-disclosure and feedback; here-and-now interaction patterns; behavioral styles of members	Observable behavior; interaction patterns of members; here-and-now behavior
5. *Typical goals or objectives*	Completion of assigned task	Increased knowledge of environmental and personal influences in planning to aid decision making	Improving the quality of the individual's relationships and skills of interacting with others, primarily in group settings	Provide environment that facilitates self-exploration and allows for alternate behaviors
6. *Usual leadership*	Single elected or appointed chairman	Single counselor or teacher	Often co-led by trainers (educator, psychologist, social worker)	Either singly or co-led by counselors
7. *Usual leadership style*	Ranges from authoritarian or directive to democratic	Leader determines the direction of group and plans content	Leader determines direction of group according to perceived member needs	Ranging from directive to group centered
8. *Duration of group*	Length determined by time necessary to complete task	Length usually predetermined by nature of material to be transmitted	Length predetermined but usually ranges from 1 to 10 days	Length often determined by nature of setting but usually ranges from 5 to 25 meetings
9. *Length of session*	1 to 3 hours	From to 10 to 55 minutes	Usually 8 to 12 hours per day or spread over several days	Usually 1 to 2 hours
10. *Setting*	Varies by nature of task, e.g., community, education, industry. Sometimes held in retreat or workshop	Educational (school, college)	Industrial, religious, educational, medical, and other organizations; sometimes held in retreat or workshop	Educational, religious, and community

TABLE 15.2 *(cont.)*

Personal growth groups	Therapy groups
Sensitivity; encounter; human awareness	Group therapy; group psychotherapy
Self-selection on basis of awareness of personal growth possibilities	Self- or other-selected because of perceived disordered behaviors
8–12	4–10
Quantity and quality of members' interactions within the group and implications for behavior outside the group	Members' behavior in and outside the group; psychological history of members
Personal growth; increased sensitivity to the feelings of others and self; more awareness of others and self	Personal change; modifying disordered behaviors
Often co-led by facilitators (lay and professional)	Therapist (clinical psychologist, psychiatrist, psychiatric social worker); often co-led
Leadership style individualistic depending on facilitators' experience, training, and personal orientation	Leadership style individualistic depending on therapist's experience, training, and personal orientation
Length varies from 1 to 14 days	Length varies from few weeks to several years
Usually 6 to 8 hours per day or spread over several days	Usually 1 to 2 hours
Setting varies but usually removed from member's normal environment; sometimes held in retreat or workshop	Institution, clinic, or private practice

FIGURE 15.1 **Member-based group counseling**

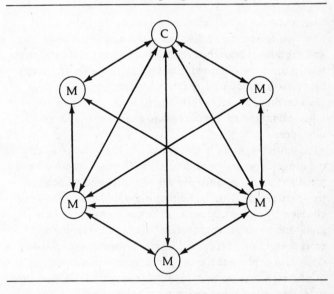

FIGURE 15.2 **Counselor-based group counseling**

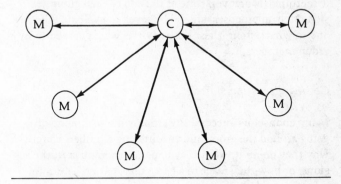

volvement with another is less than meaningful. Basically, group counseling in this situation is viewed as individual counseling conducted in a group setting. Such a relationship is represented by Figure 15.2 (see above), in which the essential focus of the relationship is the counselor and his or her interactions with each member. Interactions between and among members tend not to be considered meaningful or helpful.

Developing the relationship

The counselor is responsible for getting the group organized—quite often, by discussing the role of the counselor and explaining how the group should function if maximum results are to be obtained. The counselor states that members have a responsibility for understanding and helping each member as well as striving to solve their own problems. Members are encouraged to share freely and try out new ideas.

Attention is usually given, early in the process, to time of meeting, place, and confidentiality. Counselors often have members draw up mutually devised rules and guidelines; this participation can be helpful in establishing a working climate. By words and actions the counselor must help group members accept responsibility by developing and maintaining a therapeutic climate. Nelson suggests that the counselor explain at the beginning of group counseling that during each session each member is expected to spend time in (1) deep listening (hearing what is being said), (2) helping another to talk, (3) discussing problems and concerns, (4) discussing feelings, (5) confronting (pointing out when what is said doesn't seem right), and (6) planning (proposing to do something). Moreover, time at the end of each group session, Nelson proposes, should be saved to evaluate whether, and to what extent, these six activities were engaged in by group members.[19]

Getting discussion started

Many counselors successfully employ the technique of going around the group and encouraging members to tell why they are in it, what they hope to accomplish in the sessions, or how they react to a particular matter. The counselor tries to help members learn to interact with one another. Given below are some leads—arranged from least to most structured—typically employed, following introduction of self and group members, by counselors for initiating discussion in the group.

1. Remain silent. Wait for a group member to begin.
2. "Shall we get started?" "Who would like to begin?" "What would you like to talk about?"

[19] Richard C. Nelson, "Organizing for Group Counseling," *Personnel and Guidance Journal*, 50 (September 1971), 25–28.

3. "Perhaps someone will get us started."
4. "You can discuss anything that you wish. This time is yours to use as you see fit."
5. "What is the reason for our being here? Perhaps each of us can discuss what he or she wants to achieve from being here."
6. "Each of you has been selected with the thought that you might gain something from a group experience and that you could help others gain from the experience. Perhaps someone is willing to share some of his or her feelings or concerns."
7. Some groups have found it helpful to have members tell a little about themselves and what they are doing. Would one of you take a few minutes to tell us something about your background and life history?"

If the group does not respond, or if later silence develops, the following leads may be employed:

1. "Everyone is very quiet." "It is difficult to talk, to get started." "It's sometimes hard to speak up, to be the first to talk."
2. "I wonder why the group is silent? What do you think is keeping us from talking?"
3. "Can anyone guess why the group is so silent now? There must be reasons for remaining silent—does someone have an idea?"
4. "Are we trying to figure out what to say? Are we all waiting for the leader to begin? Do we feel that we can't say anything until the leader does?" "Are you waiting for me?" "Are we willing to share feelings?"
5. "Let's start talking about. . . ." "I'd like to raise a question."

Maintaining the relationship

The pace and topics are determined by group members. A general theme may evolve as a focal point for discussion and be used for some time or abandoned early in the counseling session. Group members usually venture into personal problems and return to a central theme. Sharing of personal concerns often builds like a symphony: the theme is the base and as the members recapitulate the whole problem begins to take form and make sense to the individual. Members learn to be themselves, to discuss their concerns, and to identify their real feelings. By trusting, accepting, and trying to understand each other, they provide the mutual encouragement needed to struggle with problems and to try to change. As this becomes evident, members become more ego-involved and participate more meaningfully.

Increasingly, group members learn to play the counselor's role and, if encouraged, develop interpersonal skills and create feelings of mutuality and respect. Brammer and Shostrom suggest that communication within the group will be promoted if the following guidelines are agreed to and observed by the group:

1. The principle of *direct communication* is stated to the group as follows: "We never withhold feelings that we have about another person in the group. When we communicate these feelings we look directly at the person to whom we are talking, and we use his [or her] name or the pronoun *you*."
2. Making statements is preferable to asking questions. The principle of *question analysis* is stated as follows: "Whenever we ask a question, we must state the hypothesis behind our question."
3. The principle of *advice analysis* proceeds as follows: There is a strong tendency to project our needs, wants, perceptions, and meanings to others. "Whenever we give advice we must speculate on what it was in our own life experience which has made us so alert to this particular advice."[20]

The counselor's responsibility

The counselor's skill and confidence are the keys to successful group counseling. Experience in individual counseling often provides a foundation for working with groups. The counselor's responsibilities in group counseling parallel those in the individual situation. Counselors convey feelings of acceptance, warmth, and understanding. They can be aware of their own needs and limitations and try not to let them interfere with the counseling situation. As the group proceeds, they give full attention to the members and their interaction, allowing them to express themselves. Counselors seek to communicate confidence in each member's abil-

ity to solve his or her problems. As counselors work, they help define the working relationship, display consistency, and set an example in accepting and helping others. Unique to group counseling are the crosscurrents that develop among members. The counselor must handle these objectively, being sensitive as to their purpose and usefulness.

The way counselors demonstrate their skills has considerable effect on how the group functions. Research as early as 1953 by Powdermaker and Franks supports some of the following counselor behaviors in working with adolescents in group counseling:

. . . (1) Generalize from one client's remarks in the hope that other clients will see the relevance of the discussion for them; (2) emphasize the similarity between two or more clients' problems and emotions; (3) paraphrase a client's statements to clarify them for other members of the group; (4) encourage mutual respect by referring questions to another client or to the rest of the group; (5) emphasize the continuity of the meetings by reviewing important events at the beginning of the next; (6) apply general statements to immediate situations; and (7) help clients discuss relationships being developed among them.[21]

As in individual counseling, the counselor can capture and reflect the feelings of clients, help them tell their story, and set the stage for desirable learning experiences. Their task is more complicated because they must be aware of group interaction and convey feelings of acceptance and understanding to members.

Ohlsen suggests that counselors can build relationships in group counseling when their clients come to feel that counselors care about them, seem to understand them, believe they can be helped, and are expert in helping people help themselves.[22] Among the skills of group counselors identified by Kottler are those of (1) diagnosis; labeling behavior accurately and identifying areas of feeling, thinking, and behaving; (2) recognizing, explaining, and interpreting meanings behind client behavior; (3) communicating with members by questioning, confronting, disputing, and debat-

[20] Lawrence M. Brammer and Everett L. Shostrom, *Therapeutic Psychology*, 3rd ed. (Englewood Cliffs, N.J.: Prentice-Hall, 1977), pp. 338–339.

[21] Florence B. Powdermaker and J. D. Franks, *Group Psychotherapy* (Cambridge, Mass.: Harvard University Press, 1953), p. 391.
[22] Merle M. Ohlsen, *Group Counseling*, 2nd ed. (New York: Holt, Rinehart and Winston, 1977), p. 39.

ing illogical reasonings; (4) using humor, wit, and innovative strategies to keep sessions interesting; (5) varying methods to fit needs of group members; and (6) countering and confronting group members who enact disruptive roles such as the approval seeker, the hedger, the jester, the martyr, and so on.[23]

Responsibility of group members

Group members have certain responsibilities in group counseling. By choosing to be in a group they agree to share the challenge of helping to build a relationship. Through interaction, each member helps create and maintain a psychological climate that is conducive to sharing experiences and problem solving. This takes time to develop, but it can be done if the counselor's actions and attitudes set a good example. Each member has a responsibility to listen and help others express themselves.

Members usually learn quickly to encourage others to define their thoughts and goals and to think and help others express themselves. Many authorities have recognized the therapeutic potential of the group that evolves from interaction among members. The primary process is not between member and counselor but evolves into member-to-member interactions. Emphasis is on the assistance that is potentially forthcoming from each group member. Commitment to change is enhanced by helping members discover affiliation with other members who work to make similar changes. The counselor acts as a facilitator in this process and plays an ambiguous role, with structure and content evolving from the group itself.

Members of any group enact different roles at different times during group sessions. Benne and Sheets present some of these roles and their work adapted by Lifton appears here.[24]

A. Group Task Roles. Facilitation and coordination of group problem-solving activities.
  1. *Initiator contributor.* Offers new ideas or changed ways of regarding group problem or goal. Suggests

solutions. How to handle group difficulty. New procedure for group. New organization for group.
  2. *Information seeker.* Seeks clarification of suggestions in terms of factual adequacy and/or authoritative information and pertinent facts.
  3. *Opinion seeker.* Seeks clarification of values pertinent to what group is undertaking or values involved in suggestions made.
  4. *Information giver.* Offers facts or generalizations which are "authoritative" or relates own experience *pertinently* to group problem.
  5. *Opinion giver.* States belief or opinion pertinently to suggestions. Emphasis on [own] proposal of what should become group's view of pertinent values.
  6. *Elaborator.* Gives examples or develops meanings, offers rationale for suggestions made before, and tries to deduce how ideas might work out.
  7. *Coordinator.* Clarifies relationships among ideas and suggestions, pulls ideas and suggestions together, or tries to coordinate activities of members of subgroups.
  8. *Orienter.* Defines position of group with respect to goals. Summarizes. Shows departures from agreed directions or goals. Questions direction of discussion.
  9. *Evaluator.* Subjects accomplishment of group to "standards" of group functioning. May evaluate or question "practicability," "logic," "facts," or "procedure" of a suggestion or of some unit of group discussion.
  10. *Energizer.* Prods group to action or decision. Tries to stimulate group to "greater" or "higher quality" activity.
  11. *Procedural technician.* Performs routine tasks (distributes materials, etc.) or manipulates objects for group (rearranging chairs, etc.).
  12. *Recorder.* Writes down suggestions, group decision, or products of discussion. "Group memory."
B. Group Growing and Vitalizing Roles. Building group-centered attitudes and orientation.
  13. *Encourager.* Praises, agrees with, and accepts others' ideas. Indicates warmth and solidarity in his [or her] attitude toward members.

[23] Jeffrey A. Kottler, "How the Effective Counselor Acts," *Journal for Specialists in Group Work*, 3 (Fall 1978), 117–119.
[24] Kenneth Benne and P. Sheets, "Functional Roles of Group Members," in Lifton, *Working with Groups*, 2nd ed., pp. 20–21.

14. *Harmonizer.* Mediates intragroup scraps. Relieves tensions.
15. *Compromiser.* Operates from within a conflict in which [own] idea or position is involved. May yield status, admit error, discipline [one's]self, "come halfway."
16. *Gatekeeper and expediter.* Encourages and facilitates participation of others. Let's hear about . . . Why not limit length of contributions so all can react to problem?
17. *Standard setter or ego ideal.* Expresses standards for group to attempt to achieve in its functioning or applies standards in evaluating the quality of group processes.
18. *Group observer and commentator.* Keeps records of group processes and contributes these data with proposed interpretations into group's evaluation of its own procedures.
19. *Follower.* Goes along somewhat passively. Is friendly audience.

C. Antigroup Roles. Tries to meet felt individual needs at expense of group health rather than through cooperation with group.
20. *Aggressor.* Deflates status of others. Expresses disapproval of values, acts, or feelings of others. Attacks group or problem. Jokes aggressively, shows envy by trying to take credit for other's idea.
21. *Blocker.* Negativistic. Stubbornly and unreasoningly resistant. Tries to bring back issue group intentionally rejected or bypassed.
22. *Recognition seeker.* Tries to call attention to [self]. May boast, report on personal achievements, and in unusual ways struggle to prevent being placed in "inferior" position, etc.
23. *Self-confessor.* Uses group to express personal, nongroup oriented, "feeling," "insight," "ideology," etc.
24. *Playboy.* Displays lack of involvement in group's work. Actions may take form of cynicism, nonchalance, horseplay, or other more or less studied out of "field behavior."
25. *Dominator.* Tries to assert authority in manipulating group or some individuals in group. May be flattery, assertion of superior status or right to at-

tention, giving of directions authoritatively, interrupting contributions of others, etc.
26. *Help seeker.* Tries to get "sympathy" response from others through expressions of insecurity, personal confusion, or depreciation of self beyond "reason."
27. *Special interest pleader.* Verbally for "small business," "grass roots" community, "housewife," "labor," etc. Actually cloaking own prejudices or biases on stereotype which best fits own individual need.

Some group techniques

Various practices have been used in group counseling. Some of the major techniques have been drawn from psychodrama and will be described briefly here.

ROLE PLAYING Numerous group leaders have used role-playing techniques to provide members an opportunity to act as well as talk out problems. It enables group members to gain a better perspective of themselves and others. The utility of role-playing techniques lies in their spontaneity. Because role playing is novel, it may require some preparation of group members before it can be used effectively and without resistance. The counselor who introduces it should know group members well if certain pitfalls are to be avoided. The part of the unpopular character should be played by someone who is well liked or by the counselor. As the group becomes more familiar with role playing, the characters may shift parts, volunteer, and the like.

Unless role playing is used judiciously, it may have some damaging effects. When can role playing be used effectively? Ohlsen suggests that it is applicable:

[to enable clients] to communicate feelings and perceptions concerning problem situations which they have difficulty describing, and perhaps even admitting to themselves. It enables clients to improve communication, to experiment with and practice new ways of behaving, to test their readiness for and performance in new developmental tasks, to solicit feedback on proposed actions, and to see themselves as others see them.[25]

[25] Ohlsen, *Group Counseling*, 2nd ed., p. 133.

Role playing is like other counseling techniques in that basic principles governing human behavior should be observed. Before it is used, the counselor should explain how it works and perhaps give a short demonstration. Its purpose should be understood by the group members. The person who is most closely related to the scene to be acted out should describe the setting and the roles of each of the participants. Individuals who volunteer or are assigned to a particular role should play it as they perceive it; their responses should be spontaneous. As role playing proceeds, the actors should feel free to stop the skit whenever they please. Members of the group may see the roles differently and want to change roles and replay the situation. This can often be profitable for it can convey how others feel in the same situation.

ROLE REVERSAL A procedure that enables two individuals to exchange roles. Situations involving teacher-student, mother-daughter, husband-wife can be enacted and then the participants exchange roles to see the other frame of reference.

DOUBLE TECHNIQUE A second individual assumes the identity of the subject. The double acts as a conscience, verbalizing conflict simultaneously as the subject verbalizes the dilemma.

THE SOLILOQUY This technique is used to bring out hidden thoughts of participants and to clarify and solidify insights. Each participant speaks, the scene is frozen and then each is asked to soliloquize the feelings being experienced but not expressed.

THE MIRROR TECHNIQUE Another person serves as a member's substitute ego and is placed across from the member and mimics his or her behavior. The mirror technique is believed useful when clients wish to observe themselves in action, such as in job interviewing.

HIDDEN THEME This technique is used to bring out the member's ability to identify a behavioral theme in a situation and create an appropriate way of coping with it. The member is sent out of the room but told beforehand that upon return, a social situation will be in progress and that the member is to relate meaningfully to the situation.

MUTE TECHNIQUE A theme is given to members with instructions that they communicate it by gestures and bodily movements. The technique is used to reveal nonverbal resources for communication and expression.

Termination and evaluation

Groups should be terminated when the majority decide to stop or when the situations and concerns that the group wishes to examine are exhausted.

Figure 15.3 presents a process group evaluation scale used in informally studying graduate student process groups at Purdue University. Part I is composed of five behavioral characteristics commonly encountered in group situations. Members rank other members of the group, including themselves, on the basis of behavior observed in the just completed session. Position 1 (under Ranking) on each scale represents the greatest frequency or intensity for each of the dimensions. Four continuums are represented in Part II. Each describes an important aspect of a group situation and can be of value to the counselor or the group as a whole in assessing group progress.

Recent group work research

Mounting involvement in group counseling has led to a sizable crop of research studies. That which is presented here illustrates current direction of such efforts.

Stages of development

Counseling groups, according to Gazda,[26] go through four stages: exploratory, transition, action, and termination. The amount, the kind, and the timing of counselor interventions are related to the stage the group is in.

Lee and Bednar[27] suggest that client risk, personal responsibility, and group structure are factors that influence group

[26] Gazda, *Group Counseling*, p. 45.
[27] Fred Lee and Richard Bednar, "Effects of Group Structure and Risk-Taking Disposition on Group Behavior, Attitudes and Atmosphere," *Journal of Counseling Psychology*, 24 (May 1977), 191–199.

development. Group structure, according to them, regulates client risk taking and responsibility. More specifically, group structure tends to reduce the participant's assumption of personal responsibility for behavior in early group sessions, therefore high risk-taking behaviors increase and lead to the development of group cohesiveness in later group sessions. Self-exploration increases as group cohesion is achieved. Lee and Bednar describe the development of a group as proceeding through the following stages: initial ambiguity, increased structure, increased risk taking, development of group cohesion from shared experiences, increased personal responsibility.

Evensen and Bednar[28] investigated the effects of pregroup information (designated as either behavioral instructions or cognitive descriptions of desired group behaviors) and reported that "high risk" takers given behavioral instructions were more disclosive and engaged in more interpersonal feedback than did those given cognitive descriptions.

Activity of participants

Seligman and Sterne[29] compared the verbal behavior of two groups of male patients in a VA hospital. One group participated in a sequence of five daily therapist-led sessions followed by a five-session sequence in which every other meeting was leaderless. The second group was treated with the sequences reversed. Finally, therapist-led, alternating sequence sessions, and leaderless sessions were compared. Both leaderless and alternating sessions produced more conventional or socially oriented behavior than the therapist-led meetings. However, the therapist-led meetings were considered more pertinent, task oriented, and confrontive than the leaderless sessions. These outcomes were supported in a replicated study by the two investigators.[30]

Conyne compared three facilitator-directed (FD) groups with three self-directed (SD) groups. Each group had eight college students and met for twenty-five hours. Statistically significant differences between the two treatment models were demonstrated. The FD group members, compared to SD group members, perceived more positive understanding in their respective group climate and viewed their groups as being more open, less superficial, and less phony.[31]

Friedman and Ellenhorn sought to determine the best way to facilitate self-disclosure and member involvement when launching encounter groups.[32] They exposed sixteen groups (each composed of three males and three females) to one of four warm-up conditions prior to a forty-five-minute leaderless encounter group: nonverbal exercises, modeling of taped intensive group interaction, exchange of autobiographical information among members, no warm-up. The nonverbal exercises were most effective in promoting increases in self-ratings of extroversion but the modeling condition was most effective in fostering an active group atmosphere and in stimulating intentions to self-disclose among members.

Underachievement and slow learning

Group counseling is often applied as remediation for school underachievement. Presumably, the attempt is made to resolve problems that interfere with educational performance.

Mitchell and Ng investigated the effects of group counseling and behavior therapy on the academic achievement of thirty Australian university students. The students, rated high on test anxiety and low on study-skill competence, were randomly assigned to five experimental conditions and given treatment that involved either single-model procedures (either desensitization or counseling) or multimodel procedures (combinations of both). Significant reductions of test anxiety occurred in groups given desensitization, but both decreased test anxiety and improved study skills occurred in those groups given combinations of desensitiza-

[28] E. Paul Evensen and Richard L. Bednar, "Effects of Specific Cognitive and Behavioral Structure on Early Groups Behavior and Atmosphere," *Journal of Counseling Psychology*, 25 (January 1978), 66–71.
[29] Milton Seligman and David M. Sterne, "Verbal Behavior in Therapist-Led, Leaderless, and Alternating Group Psychotherapy Sessions," *Journal of Counseling Psychology*, 16 (July 1969), 325–328.
[30] David M. Sterne and Milton Seligman, "Further Comparisons of Verbal Behavior in Therapist-Led, Leaderless and Alternating Group Psychotherapy Sessions," *Journal of Counseling Psychology*, 18 (September 1971), 472–477.

[31] Robert K. Conyne, "Effects of Facilitator-Directed and Self-Directed Group Experiences," *Counselor Education and Supervision*, 13 (March 1974), 184–189.
[32] Steven B. Friedman and Lewis J. Ellenhorn, "A Comparison of Four Warm-Up Techniques for Initiating Encounter Groups," *Journal of Counseling Psychology*, 23 (November 1976), 514–519.

FIGURE 15.3 **Process group evaluation scale**

Staff Leader_____

Date_____

In completing the Scale, please consider only the session just ended. In Part I you are asked to rank the members of your group by name, including yourself, with regard to each of the five behavioral characteristics described below. Position 1 represents greatest frequency or intensity and Position 6 refers to least frequency or intensity.

Part I

Ranking		*Behavioral Characteristics*
_____	1.	*Contributing* — Relates experiences pertinently to group discussion, gives information
_____	2.	and/or opinions related to the topic, and, in general, contributes to the discussion.
_____	3.	
_____	4.	
_____	5.	
_____	6.	
_____	1.	*Stimulating* — Encourages the participation of others by introducing topics of mutual
_____	2.	interest; stimulates discussion by soliciting comments from members of the group.
_____	3.	
_____	4.	
_____	5.	
_____	6.	
_____	1.	*Adapting* — Appears willing to adjust attitudes as a result of logical arguments;
_____	2.	remains flexible; open to new ideas and insights.
_____	3.	
_____	4.	
_____	5.	
_____	6.	
_____	1.	*Identifying* — Seems to believe the topics are important; identifies with the group
_____	2.	and appears to be affected by the discussion.
_____	3.	
_____	4.	
_____	5.	
_____	6.	
_____	1.	*Facilitating* — Demonstrates an awareness of process by interpreting and integrating
_____	2.	the reactions of participants; wants the group as a whole to show progress
_____	3.	toward a goal.
_____	4.	
_____	5.	
_____	6.	

FIGURE 15.3 *(cont.)*

Part II

Please indicate your reactions to the session just completed by placing an "X" at what you believe is *the most descriptive* point on each of the following continua:

1. Content (the topics and issues discussed)
   _____ The topics discussed were clearly appropriate for the group's consideration.
   _____ Most of the conversation seemed relevant and productive.
   _____ In spite of much superficial discussion, many topics were worthwhile.
   _____ A few of the topics seemed to be vital but most were unrelated to the group's objectives.
   _____ The topics in this session seemed entirely irrelevant.

2. Process and Climate (interaction among the members; the characteristics and atmosphere in the session)
   _____ The members seemed to be involved and concerned; they reacted to each other.
   _____ Some topics were followed up by the group in a productive way.
   _____ The members used each other for try-out, clarification, interpretation.
   _____ The group indicated more positive than negative feelings, but it wasn't a vital meeting.
   _____ The session lacked cohesiveness; it seemed like we needn't have met today.

3. Leadership (quantitative) — the amount of leader behavior.
   _____ He/she was quite active and spoke very often.
   _____ He/she participated verbally on several occasions.
   _____ There were a few times where he/she had something to say.
   _____ He/she said almost nothing.
   _____ He/she did not speak during this session.

4. Leadership (qualitative) — the nature and effect of leader behavior.
   _____ The leader's comments seemed to elicit insight, to facilitate interaction and mutual understanding.
   _____ The leader functioned primarily as a discussion leader and stimulator.
   _____ His/her comments were received as statements of fact upon which the group could center its discussion.
   _____ He/she participated as a member with no particular leadership influence.
   _____ He/she tended to dominate the discussion with little apparent concern for either group or individual progress.

---

tion and counseling. Multimodel treatment group members, but not single-model treatment group members, improved their academic achievement as measured by course average, passing grades, and change in achievement scores.[33]

Lindquist and Lowe[34] investigated the effects of two preventive interventions designed to reduce stress among first-year college students. A *cohort* program, a written-interaction strategy, was compared to a *peer-led* group program both for their impact on the college freshman population and for their effectiveness as treatments (questionnaire methods). The cohort group attracted more nonusers of traditional services whereas the group program attracted those who typically used campus services. Both programs were viewed as effective by their respective users, but neither

[33] Kenneth R. Mitchell and Kim T. Ng, "Effects of Group Counseling and Behavior Therapy on the Academic Achievement of Test-Anxious Students," *Journal of Counseling Psychology*, 19 (November 1972), 491–497.

[34] Carol V. Lindquist and Steven R. Lowe, "A Community-Oriented Evaluation of Two Prevention Programs for College Freshmen," *Journal of Counseling Psychology*, 25 (January 1978), 53–60.

treatment was effective in reducing dropout rate or improving grade-point average.

Vance and his associates[35] asserted that group counseling with persons who are mentally retarded has been demonstrated to be effective in changing their behaviors and attitudes. The descriptive literature, they report, suggests that group counseling procedures with mentally retarded (1) provide outlets for situational anxiety, (2) are means for them to relieve stress from inadequate social functioning, (3) are opportunities to give and receive support, and (4) are experiences through which they learn they are not alone in their problems. Role playing, according to Vance and his colleagues, is helpful in enabling mentally retarded clients to become more sensitive to their own behaviors and to practice behavioral alternatives.

Block[36] involved forty high school students (nineteen male and twenty-one female black and Hispanic) in groups billed as "intense discussion groups to improve school success" but conducted either as rational-emotive group therapy or human relations. The students, characterized as being high-risk, failure and misconduct prone, were given five weekly sessions over a full semester. Comparisons were made between treatments and a nontreatment control group. Rational-emotive group members showed greatest improvements over the other two groups on such dependent measures as grade-point average, disruptive behaviors, and cutting classes. The investigators described the differences between the rational-emotive approach and the human relations condition as being that the former was active, directive and highly structured whereas the latter was less structured and based on a clarifying, reflective leadership style.

Christen and McKinnon[37] describe use of a group process called the problem-solving circle to help dropouts and truants. The teacher, teacher aide and students sit in a circle to examine the realities of their actions and attitudes and to take responsibility for their own behavior. A typical unit has between twelve and twenty students participating and the group functions as a class throughout the day and maintains its identity in many of the day's activities. Nine rules have been established for circle communications including "talk from your heart—not your head," "speak for yourself," "everything said in the circle stays in it," "no violence or threats," and "talk to the person you address, not about them."

Divorce adjustment

Kessler[38] reports the use of group procedures in helping divorced individuals to develop a sense of belonging and identity during transition periods. Through groups, those involved in uncoupling are able to let go of the past and to learn, by listening to others describe the stresses and strains in their previous marriage, how and why their behavior contributed to the separation. She describes use of structured (brief lecture, tapes, transactional-analysis procedures) and unstructured activities designed to counter members' mood swings, passivity, and vindictiveness.

Adolescent development

Stanley[39] examined the effects of a high school course for ninth and tenth grade students and their parents designed to resolve conflict and advance the moral reasoning of students. Three groups were formed from sixteen couples and their children: parents and their adolescents, parents only, and a control group. Both experimental groups met for ten weekly, two-and-one-half-hour sessions and were given training in conflict resolution and use of family meetings. The *Kohlberg Moral Judgment Interview*, self-report inventories, and an analysis of tape recordings of family meetings served as assessment devices. Results were positive in that parents in both experimental procedures increased in egalitarian attitudes toward family decision making and demonstrated improvement in collective decision making. The

[35] Hubert Vance, Harold J. McGee, and Louis Finkle, "Group Counseling with Mentally Retarded Persons," *Personnel and Guidance Journal*, 56 (November 1977), 148–152.

[36] Joel Block, "Effects of a Rational-Emotive Mental Health Program on Poorly Achieving, Disruptive High School Students," *Journal of Counseling Psychology*, 25 (January 1978), 61–65.

[37] William Christen and Bryon E. McKinnon, "Opportunity Hall: A Place for Dropouts—Truants—Kickouts," *Personnel and Guidance Journal*, 55 (June 1977), 605–607.

[38] Sheila Kessler, "Divorce Adjustment Groups," *Personnel and Guidance Journal*, 54 (January 1975), 251–255.

[39] Sheila F. Stanley, "Family Education to Enhance the Moral Atmosphere of the Family and the Moral Development of Adolescents," *Journal of Counseling Psychology*, 25 (March 1978), 110–117.

family-adolescent group showed greatest improvement of the two groups. Finally, the adolescents who participated in the training improved their scores in moral reasoning and the gain was maintained in a one-year follow-up.

Gatz, Tyler, and Pargament[40] investigated the effects of group counseling on adolescents' goal attainment, locus of control, and coping style. Fifteen high school counselors conducted small group (eight members) counseling sessions with 218 students. Each counselor conducted one group composed of students who were doing well both inside and outside of school and one group composed of students who experienced difficulty either in school or outside. The eight members of each group were equally divided between black and white, male and female students. Nine of the counselors were white females, four were black females, and two were white males.

The investigators reported that students attained both personal and educational goals. Although counselors judged students whose measured locus of control was internal as achieving more goals, moderate internal-external measures generally predicted goal attainment. Black students, according to the investigators, differed from whites, in that those measured as being externals in locus of control gained the most goals. Planning as a coping style was related to goal attainment in that students who attained most goals reported more plans on postcounseling measures of coping style. Gatz and her associates concluded that counseling should include teaching problem solving and should not overemphasize students' internality.

Life planning

Knickerbocker and Davidshofer[41] identify a "Life Planning Workshop" as a developmental outreach program, conducted in a small group setting, and designed to assist individuals with personal, social, and vocational planning. They investigated the impact of a Life Planning Workshop on participants' attitudes toward future planning and the self-

actualizing attitudes of feeling reactivity and self-regard. They hypothesized that the forty-two participants would demonstrate gains in these three areas when compared to controls and that these gains would endure over a three-week follow-up period. A further hypothesis was that members who participated in small groups generating high levels of verbal interaction would demonstrate greater gains than their counterparts in groups producing low levels of verbal interaction. Their findings were that experimental subjects achieved significantly higher means than controls on measured attitudes toward future planning and feeling reactivity and that these gains endured over the three weeks. However, no significant difference in self-regard measures was obtained and there were no significant attitudinal changes associated with differentials of verbal interaction levels.

Assertiveness training

Weiskott and Cleland[42] examined changes in assertiveness, territoriality, and personal space as a function of group assertiveness training. They hypothesized that subjects who participated in the assertiveness training program would increase in assertive behavior, would exhibit reduced personal space zones and would use more space on a drawing task than their control (waiting-list) group counterparts. The first and third hypotheses were supported strongly but the second hypothesis received only partial support. They suggest that if a relationship exists between mental health or self-concept and territoriality or personal space, then it might be possible to change self-concepts of clients by providing them nonverbal as well as verbal skills.

Self-actualization

Foulds and Hannigan[43] replicated an earlier investigation to determine immediate and long-term effects of gestalt

[40] Margaret Gatz, Forrest B. Tyler, and Kenneth I. Pargament, "Goal Attainment, Locus of Control and Coping Style in Adolescent Group Counseling," *Journal of Counseling Psychology*, 25 (July 1978), 310–319.

[41] Barbara Knickerbocker and Charles Davidshofer, "Attitudinal Outcomes of the Life Planning Workshop," *Journal of Counseling Psychology*, 25 (March 1978), 103–109.

[42] Gerald N. Weiskott and Charles C. Cleland, "Assertiveness, Territoriality and Personal Space Behavior as a Function of Group Assertion Training," *Journal of Counseling Psychology*, 24 (March 1977), 111–117.

[43] Melvin L. Foulds and Patricia S. Hannigan, "Effects of Gestalt Marathon Workshops on Measured Self-Actualization: A Replication and Follow-Up Study," *Journal of Counseling Psychology*, 23 (January 1976), 60–65.

marathon workshops on measured self-actualization. Subjects participated in a twenty-four-hour continuous gestalt workshop and completed the *Personal Orientation Inventory* before the workshop, five days later, and six months later. The nontreatment control group completed only pre- and post-test measures and demonstrated no significant change whereas group participants revealed significant positive prepost changes in measured self-actualization and these changes persisted six months later. The investigators concluded that the gestalt marathon workshop is an effective method for fostering psychological development in volunteer growth-seeking college students.

Work adjustment and vocational students

Roessler and his colleagues[44] pointed out that rehabilitation counselors now are encountering more and more clients who, due to psychological deficits, believe themselves no longer capable of productive work. The investigators designed a systematic group counseling approach called Personal Achievement Skills to help clients build psychosocial skills. Through exercises and activities, clients were taught communication, problem solving, and behavioral self-control techniques. Their clients, when compared to a group who had received "work adjustment" services and a placebo treatment (personal hygiene training) reported greater gains on self-ratings of optimism, work-related attitudes, and goal attainment.

Hoffnung and Mills[45] reported that twenty-eight male adolescents in a job training program for culturally disadvantaged young people were provided with fourteen weeks of on-the-job situational group counseling. The purpose of the group counseling was to supplement more conventional casework approaches. Interdisciplinary teams of group leaders (psychologist, caseworker, work trainer) met with work-training crews for discussions of issues relevant to the present life situation of the trainees. The adolescents who met twice weekly showed greater improvement in job performance and in overall adjustment than did those meeting

once a week. Control subjects who did not receive counseling showed less gain than either of the counseled groups.

Prediger and Baumann reported on the outcomes of "developmental group counseling" conducted with thirty groups of randomly selected vocational high school students for a minimum of one academic year. Each group was composed of six to eight members and met for forty minutes each week. Two types of control groups, inactive and placebo, were used for comparative purposes. Outcome was assessed on each of thirty measures, many of which were described as socially valued, external, and objective. No experimental control group difference of practical significance was observed on these measures despite substantial differences between counseling group and placebo control group members in their perceptions of personal benefits.[46]

Leader behavior

The leader is particularly critical in providing group experiences useful to people. Lieberman, Yalom, and Miles,[47] studying the effects of some eighteen encounter groups on members, concluded that the group leader's style (but not the theoretical rationale) was the major cause of "casualties" and "negative changers." Leaders represented an array of the group counseling and therapy theoretical models (personal growth, T-groups, gestalt, TA, and so on) and varied considerably with respect to effectiveness even within a given model. Orientation of the leader did not predict effectiveness. The leaders most destructive to participants were aggressive, authoritarian, and demonstrated little respect (they frequently intruded and challenged group members). They also used confrontations frequently; were impatient with members' progress; and pressed for immediate self-disclosure, emotional expression, and attitude change. Ineffective leaders were described as being highly disclosive (inappropriately so) and rather egocentric.

Leader behaviors were rated and assessed by the participants and external observers on forty-eight scales. Factor analysis reduced the scales to four dimensions: *caring* (of-

[44] Richard Roessler, Daniel Cook, and Delbert Lillard, "Effects of Systematic Group Counseling on Work Adjustment Clients," *Journal of Counseling Psychology*, 24 (July 1977), 313–317.
[45] Robert J. Hoffnung and Robert B. Mills, "Situational Group Counseling with Disadvantaged Youth," *Personnel and Guidance Journal*, 48 (February 1970), 458–464.

[46] Dale J. Prediger and Reemt R. Baumann, "Developmental Group Counseling: An Outcome Study," *Journal of Counseling Psychology*, 17 (November 1970), 527–533.
[47] Reported in Irvin D. Yalom, *The Theory and Practice of Group Psychotherapy*, 2nd ed. (New York: Basic Books, 1975), p. 477.

fering support), *meaning attribution* (explaining, clarifying, interpreting to provide participants ideas about their experiences), *emotional stimulation* (challenging and confronting members), *executive functions* (setting limits, rules, goals, norms). The most successful leaders, based on participant reports, were moderate in the amount of emotional stimulation and executive behaviors they exhibited and high in caring behaviors and meaning attribution. Caring and meaning attribution were strongly and positively associated with positive outcome. Emotional stimulation and executive functions had a curvilinear relationship to outcome—too many or too few of these leader behaviors resulted in lower positive outcome.

Outcomes of group experiences

Most participants in group counseling and other personal growth or encounter groups report satisfaction with the experience. Lieberman, Yalom, and Miles, in the study referred to earlier, were particularly interested in whether the experience in a group affected members.[48] Baseline measures were taken on all participants and controls several weeks before the beginning of the group experience. They were measured again one or two weeks after the groups ended and a third time six to eight months later.

The investigators reported that the members rated their experience as pleasant (65 percent), constructive (78 percent), a good learning experience (50 percent) when asked soon after the groups terminated. However, this enthusiasm and self-reported benefit had diminished six to eight months later. The ratio of persons who rated the experience highly to those who rated it poorly was 4.75 to 1 immediately after the experience, and 2.33 to 1, six months later. Close friends, associates, and relatives reported that specific positive changes had occurred for almost 80 percent of *both* participants and controls. Leaders judged that 90 percent of group members had improved, but members judged that only 37 percent had changed positively.

Lieberman and his colleagues combined questionnaires and test results with information from ratings to compose a *Composite Change Index*. One third of the participants showed positive changes immediately after the experience was over, about one-third showed no change, and the remaining third displayed negative changes. These results held true six months later. "Casualties" of the group experience were reported by Lieberman and his colleagues to be 9 percent of the 179 persons who completed the group experience and assessment procedures. When the "negative changers" were added to the casualties, a bleak picture emerged. The investigators concluded that encounter groups excel at creating instant, brief, and intense interpersonal experiences and that people want and can learn from these experiences. Such experiences are meaningful but not crucial to altering people's behaviors on an enduring basis.

Yalom has identified and described eleven factors that he suggested were "curative" in helping people in groups.[49] These were (1) imparting of information about mental health, (2) installation of hope, (3) universality (participant was not alone in thoughts or unique), (4) altruism (help and support each other), (5) corrective recapitulation of family experiences, (6) development of socialization techniques (learn social skills), (7) imitative behavior (leader as model), (8) interpersonal learning (correct distorted self-perceptions), (9) group cohesion (haven from stress), (10) catharsis, and (11) existential factors (recognizing life is unfair, one is alone and responsible). These eleven factors, according to Yalom, seemed to be present and at work in effective group experiences he led.

Values and limitations

The life of an individual is many sided. Aesthetic, economic, and religious facets are discernible, but blending into them all is a social facet. It is this factor, more than any other, that has led to the use of the group as a means of extending help to individuals. This section attempts to put into perspective other values and the limitations of group counseling.

Values

Group counseling builds on fundamental ways in which people respond to one another and modify one another's behavior. With a predilection for life in groups, a human being

[48] See Yalom, *Theory and Practice*, 2nd ed., pp. 471–476.

[49] Yalom, *Theory and Practice*, 2nd ed., pp. 3–4.

is, as Aristotle said, "a political [social] animal." No evidence exists that any internal drive impels the individual to seek the company of others; sociability is best explained on the basis of need and habit. "People are born into a group, grow as part of a group, develop through a group, create as a member of a group and in death leave the group."[50]

Group counseling appears to develop members' insights into their problems and feelings and helps them to arrive at some understanding of the causes of their concerns. Members talk about themselves, the things that disturb them, and what they can do to improve themselves. Members learn to express themselves in actions, feelings, and attitudes. They learn that they can interact and discuss with one another and that the group will help each person draw out his or her feelings. Alternate ways of behaving and experimenting with different responses may be elicited from and tried out in the group.

Many counselors have reported that individuals respond better in a group of peers than in individual counseling relationships. Adolescent needs for conformity and acceptance by their peer group and for the opportunity to share reactions and ideas, to define meaningful life situations, and to gain independence are all met in part through group counseling. Ohlsen suggests that adolescents benefit particularly from group counseling in that they (1) find it easier to discuss their problems openly in group counseling than in individual counseling, (2) think that their adult leader is more inclined to listen to them and help them discover their own solutions than to manipulate them or even to put pressure on them to do what their parents or teachers would prefer that they do, (3) can observe others discuss their problems openly and sense others' acceptance of those who can talk openly, and (4) value feedback from others.[51]

Three other values may be briefly cited:

1. Participation in group counseling facilitates the development of mutual interaction in realistic and lifelike situations. Members can learn new, more flexible, satisfying ways of relating to each other.
2. Members of counseling groups may accept ideas and suggestions proposed by their peers that they might reject if

proposed by others. Reinforcement provided by members often makes decisions more likely to be viewed as commitments rather than acquiescence to an authority figure.
3. Reference is frequently made to the efficiency of group counseling in terms of time and money. However, a more meaningful criterion would be a measure of the extent to which group counseling achieves its goals.

Limitations

All methods have limitations, and group counseling is no exception. Occasionally, individuals are unable to function as a member of a group. They need to experience a relationship with one individual before they can relate and interact with a group. There are other major limitations:

1. The work of counselors becomes more diffused and difficult. Within the group, their contacts with individuals are diluted and their attempts at being one who is interested, accepting, and understanding are difficult to maintain.
2. The personal problems of certain participants may become secondary to the more general problems of the group.
3. Although the presence of peers undoubtedly has value in many situations, it is sometimes a barrier. For some individuals, revelation of negative feelings or attitudes or unacceptable acts may be too threatening if peers are present.
4. Group members sometimes unquestioningly accept group norms for norms they had unquestioningly acquired previously.
5. Some people become so enamored of group participation they make the group experience the goal itself.

Still an unknown factor is knowledge of what concerns can best be dealt with in groups and what concerns require individual counseling. The potential for harm exists in group counseling just as it does in individual counseling. Many in the counseling field have become deeply concerned about the rush to group activities among those who are ill-prepared and inexperienced for such activities. Many ethical issues are unique to groups and others are compounded within the group setting. Professional organizations have formulated ethical standards for group work.

[50] Cornelius Beukenkamp, *Fortunate Stranger* (New York: Rinehart & Company, 1958), p. 197.
[51] Ohlsen, *Group Counseling*, 2nd ed., p. 2.

Individual and group counseling

Similarities

1. The overall objectives in group and individual counseling frequently are similar. Both seek to help the counselee achieve self-direction, integration, and self-responsibility. In both approaches, counselees are helped toward self-acceptance and understanding of their motivations and behavior.
2. In both individual and group counseling the relationship established is important if the participants' need to maintain their defenses is to be reduced. In both, individuals feel free to examine their feelings and experiences because respect has been accorded them. Both approaches strive to engender confidence in the ability of clients to be responsible for their own choices.
3. In both individual and group counseling the counselor's techniques are important: clarification of feeling, reflection of feeling, restatement of content, structuring, acceptance, and the like. The counselor's skills are used to draw out counselees so that they are aware of their feelings and attitudes and can examine and clarify them.
4. The participants in individual and group counseling are individuals who experience normal developmental problems. Both approaches deal with the common needs, interests, concerns, and experiences of the generality of individuals.
5. For both approaches, individuals need privacy and a confidential relationship in order to develop and to make use of their personal resources.

Differences

1. The group situation provides immediate opportunities to try out ways of relating to individuals and is an excellent way of providing the experience of intimacy with others. The physical proximity to one another can bring emotional satisfaction to members. Members may get their peers' reactions and suggestions concerning alternate ways of behaving with others. An immediate firsthand opportunity is present to test others' perceptions of oneself in relation to others.
2. In group counseling, counselees can receive help and also help others. The more stable and cohesive the group, the more the mutual assistance. The cooperative sharing re-

lationship helps the members feel closer to others, to understand and accept them. The interaction nurtures members, facilitates mutual expression of feelings and interpretation of meanings, and influences behavior.
3. The task of counselors is more complicated in group counseling. They not only have to understand the speaker's feelings and help him or her become aware of them but also must observe how the speaker's comments influence other group members. The counselor must be aware not only of the discussion but of the interplay of relationships among the members.

This discussion has focused on the values and limitations of group counseling and the similarities and differences between individual and group counseling. It should be noted that documentation rests primarily on opinion and belief rather than on experimental findings. Group counseling is not totally new but it is more recent than individual counseling. Therefore its merits and demerits, its use and contraindications, its appropriateness await the test of time. The obvious need is to determine which individuals in what situations are best helped solely by a group approach or in combination with an individual approach. The answer to this question will not be easy to come by, nor, as has been the case of individual counseling, will the evidence satisfy everyone.

Issues

Issue 1 Group guidance and group counseling are two terms that describe an identical construct.

True, because

1. Both terms describe procedures aimed at preventing problems.
2. Both terms denote attempts to provide accurate information that helps individuals develop plans.
3. The content treated in both group guidance and group counseling includes educational, vocational, and personal/social concerns.

False, because

1. Group guidance is recommended for all students on a regularly scheduled basis, whereas group counseling is generally offered only to those who experience stress or anxiety

or exhibit behavioral deficits or excesses in developmental tasks.

2. Group counseling makes a *direct* attempt to modify attitudes and behaviors whereas group guidance represents a more *indirect* attempt to change behavior and attitudes through providing information.

Discussion During the years 1950 to 1965 controversy surrounded the use of the terms *counseling* and *guidance*. Recent years have brought the re-emergence of that controversy, now centered over the terms *group guidance* and *group counseling*. Gazda[52] points out that the setting for group guidance is the classroom; its typical size is twenty to thirty-five people; its leader is a teacher who uses an array of instructional media and group dynamics concepts to motivate students. On the other hand, group counseling can assist with remediation, prevention, or developmental purposes. Its typical size is six to twelve counselees; its setting is an office or conference room; its leader is a counselor or facilitator who has been professionally prepared to do so. These distinctions merit use of each term to convey specific meanings associated with them.

Issue 2 A member's satisfaction with the experience of being in a group is an outcome sufficient to justify offering group experiences.

Yes, because
1. One need not go beyond the immediate reaction to justify providing for or participating in it.
2. Profound, long-term benefits from any type of psychological assistance rarely have been demonstrated.

No, because
1. Arguments for this issue are rationalizations for an inability to demonstrate positive, long-term outcomes of intensive group experiences.
2. Professional justification of these activities must rest on more than spending a few hours in the company of others.

Discussion Presumably, the intensive group experience came into being and attracted the attention of professionals because of its promise as a unique vehicle for helping people

[52] Gazda, *Group Counseling*, pp. 6–7.

and organizations to bring positive change into their lives and ability to function. Somewhat later, the human condition in relation to society—alienation, loneliness, powerlessness, lack of community—supplied a rationale for group experience being sufficient in and of itself. A few hours of intimate, interpersonal relations were highly desired by many. For others, this represented the purchase of friendship, the necessity of which was, indeed, a sad commentary on society. Nevertheless, the group experience creates for some an emotional high and benefits that seem to relate to the experience itself. For such individuals, the opportunity to relate to others and to express themselves may be all that they desire. They may not expect to change their personality or alter other aspects of their life on any enduring basis.

A contrary view and one that relates to the origins of the group movement in group dynamics and group psychotherapy suggests that group experiences were developed because of their inherent potential for attaining specific goals and outcomes. Often these goals are viewed as either unattainable by other means or attainable more efficiently in the context of the group experience. Based on this view, group experiences should lead to desirable and lasting change. The process cannot and should not exist solely for the enjoyment of participants unless the professional declares this as its only purpose.

Annotated references

Benjamin, Alfred. *Behavior in Small Groups*. Boston: Houghton Mifflin Company, 1978. 128 pp.

Benjamin describes his experiences in forming and leading groups. He identifies and discusses skills of both members and leaders and presents a chapter on training group leaders.

Corey, Gerald, and Marianne Schneider Corey. *Groups: Process and Practice*. Monterey, Calif.: Brooks/Cole Publishing Company, 1977. 252 pp.

The authors identify elements of group process and give an overview of eight models of group process. They address how members can get the most out of their experience in groups. Characteristics and skills of group leaders are presented. Ideas about forming, maintaining, and terminating a group are given. Ethical issues are described as well as special groups for children, elderly, couples, and so on.

Gazda, George M. *Group Counseling.* 2nd ed. Boston: Allyn & Bacon, 1978. 425 pp.

The author presents procedures, principles, and practices useful in group counseling as developmental in nature and stresses that it is a preventive-remedial process. In Chapter 9 treatment is given to summarizing group counseling research and, in Chapter 12, to identifying some of the ethical and professional issues involved in group counseling.

Ohlsen, Merle M. *Group Counseling.* 2nd ed. New York: Holt, Rinehart and Winston, 1977. 305 pp.

The author, recognized nationally for his work in group counseling, provides both theoretical ideas and practical suggestions for engaging in group counseling. He draws on the research and literature in the field to highlight the conditions useful in helping individuals in groups.

Further references

Amidon, Edmund, and Raphael R. Kavanaugh. "The Observation of Intimacy in Groups." *Personnel and Guidance Journal*, 57 (May 1979), 464–468.

Bratter, Thomas E. "Classroom Meetings: The Teacher and Group Process." *Journal for Specialists in Group Work*, 3 (Summer 1978), 78–85.

Burress, Carl B. "Group Workshops to Eliminate Self-Defeating Behavior as an Alternative to Suspension in the Secondary School." *Journal for Specialists in Group Work*, 3 (Spring 1978), 32–36.

Cerio, James E. "Structured Experiences with the Educational Growth Group." *Personnel and Guidance Journal*, 57 (April 1979), 398–401.

Gaumer, Jim. "Peer-Facilitator Training and Group Leadership Experiences with Low-Performing Elementary School Students." *Journal for Specialists in Group Work*, 3 (Spring 1978), 4–12.

Huber, Charles H. "Parents of the Handicapped Child: Facilitating Acceptance Through Group Counseling." *Personnel and Guidance Journal*, 57 (January 1979), 267–268.

Kottler, Jeffrey A. "How the Effective Group Counselor Functions." *Journal for Specialists in Group Work*, 3 (Fall 1978), 113–121.

Lee, Dong Yul. "Evaluation of a Group Counseling Program Designed to Enhance Social Adjustment of Mentally Retarded Adults." *Journal of Counseling Psychology*, 24 (July 1977), 318–323.

Robyak, James E., and Michael J. Patton. "The Effectiveness of a Study Skills Course for Students of Different Personality Types." *Journal of Counseling Psychology*, 24 (May 1977), 200–207.

Ross, George R. "Reducing Irrational Personality Traits, Test Anxiety and Intra-Interpersonal Needs in High School Students." *Measurement and Evaluation in Guidance*, 11 (April 1978), 44–49.

Part four
Counseling: a growing profession

Part Four brings together material directly and indirectly pertaining to the rapidly evolving profession of counseling. This part closes with an effort to identify some persistent topics of concern to the profession.

Chapter 16 treats counseling considerations of a legal and ethical nature. Chapter 17 focuses on problems and means involved in the crucial area of evaluating the service provided by counselors. Chapter 18 examines the process of preparing and credentialing counselors. Finally, current trends that, in the authors' judgment, are of importance are identified and discussed in Chapter 19.

16   Counseling: legal and ethical considerations

This chapter treats some of the complex problems of the law and ethics as they bear on the field of counseling. Compared to other professions relatively little direct case material is available, and few legal precedents exist that are specifically applicable to the counseling situation. Comparatively more material related to professional ethics is available.

Legal considerations

There are many disparate meanings attached to the terms *law* and *legality*. Diversity in definitions occurs because writers are generally concerned about different aspects. *Law* is frequently applied to a body of rules recognized by a state or community as binding on its members. It also refers to the condition of society brought about by observance of these rules. *Legal* refers to law or the state of being lawful. Legal considerations that bear on counselors are those that society requires of them in the performance of their profession or imposes to limit their professional activities.

Laws as well as constitutional provisions relating to education should be of concern to all employed in educational settings. Laws express public policy and may be as significant in certain respects as constitutional provisions in determining the scope and adequacy of an educational program.

Any law may be constitutional or unconstitutional. Laws are assumed to be constitutional unless or until they are declared unconstitutional. Courts do not, on their own initiative or volition, rule on the constitutionality of a law. Court rulings occur only when there has been a proper legal action based on a question or a challenge regarding the constitutionality of a particular law or some aspect of it. Some of the aspects of the law as it relates most directly to counselors are described here.

Confidentiality and privileged communication

Those who seek counseling usually reveal intimate, personal, sometimes painful details and experiences. They turn to the professional so that they can disclose their feelings of anxiety, hostility, guilt, indecision, and so on, without being publicly embarrassed, hurt, or punished. Because such highly personal and private revelations may bring embarrassment or ridicule, they do not wish them to be disclosed openly and usually assume that others will not have access to their disclosures without their express consent. When someone enters counseling under this assumption, a confidential relationship exists, and the professional person is obligated to protect the best interests of the client by maintaining it. Confidentiality has both ethical and legal implications.

Legal dimensions of a confidential relationship are as follows: (1) there is no disclosure of information, even though it is accurate, to individuals not entitled to it, and (2) material about the relationship entered in written records is accurate, reliable, and safeguarded. In some confidential relationships, communications between the client and the professional are privileged and *need not be disclosed at judicial proceedings.* In this sense the professional is immune or exempted from testifying to personal and confidential information received in the relationship.

The term *privileged communication* means that a professional, under certain prescribed conditions, is not subject to arrest or prosecution for withholding information needed by the court in its determination of truth. Privileged communications are defined by Black as "any communications made to a counselor, solicitor, or attorney, in professional confidence, and which he is not permitted to divulge; otherwise called a 'confidential communication.' "[1] Black uses *counselor* in the sense of *legal adviser*.

Generally, the disclosure of all facts relevant to a litigated issue takes precedence over any consideration of the inviolability of a communication made in reliance on personal confidence. Consequently, even though a communication is made in confidence, either expressed or implied, it is not

[1] C. Henry Black, *Law Dictionary* (St. Paul, Minn.: West Publishing Co., 1953), p. 29.

privileged per se unless the persons concerned have a relationship that the law specifically recognizes or construes as one that must be retained.

The sanctity of the attorney-client relationship was the first professional one to be widely accepted legally and goes far back in English common law. It evolved from court decisions rather than legislation. Similarly, the clergy-parishioner relationship found protection without legislation. Privileged communication for the clients of both lawyers and clergy was established through court decisions, but it was attained for the patients of doctors through both court action and legislation.

The rationale for granting privileged communication is now and has always been the same: confidentiality promotes full disclosure by the client and better enables the practitioner to provide professional help. The privilege belongs to the client and extends only to the practitioner the client has engaged. It does not apply to a client's relationship with an expert of the court or to the professional person of an opposing side in court to whom he or she may voluntarily submit for examination. It should be noted that the relationship between patient and physician is not completely protected because gunshot wounds, tuberculosis, and venereal disease must be reported to the proper authorities in many, if not most, states. Privileged communication does not accord any direct benefit or immunity to the professional person.

Statutory law grants no privilege to withhold relevant but confidential communications from a court except in a few defined instances. The common law recognizes only one absolute privilege—for communications made for the purpose of avoiding or settling litigation, which means chiefly communications between clients and their legal advisers, unless they be for the furtherance of crime or fraud. The privilege is granted not primarily out of respect for the confidentiality of information, but to secure the efficient administration of justice. It is not difficult to see that this aim would be seriously frustrated if the privilege were not available. The privilege has been extended beyond litigious matters to cover all professional communications between clients and their lawyers, the extension being justified on the ground that anything that calls for legal advice carries some risk, however remote, of future litigation. The extension is capable of abuse. A company, to be on the safe side, might send through its legal department all documents that it would prefer not to be disclosed, and then improperly claim privilege for them. The remedy is for the courts to make better use of their power to inspect documents for which privilege is claimed, and to require more particularity in their description.

A conflict of public interest arises in some cases between the establishment of the truth in the determination of justice and the preservation of confidential relationships, whether personal or professional. General rules are of little assistance in resolving conflicts of this kind, which must be settled in the light of the particular circumstances. The presumption is that the interests of the administration of justice should prevail. But that does not mean that they should invariably prevail.

The common law grants no other absolute privilege to confidential communications. It offers them various degrees of protection, all within the discretion of the judge. Communications between priest and penitent and between doctor and patient are the favorites. The first remains inviolate in practice, not in the least because instances very seldom come up for decision. Concerning doctors, laymen may be surprised to learn how ready the courts are to disregard the Hippocratic oath. Hospital notes apparently are not privileged. About other confidential relationships, involving such people as bankers, accountants, journalists, and counselors, there is little to say except that a duty not to divulge is recognized by the courts and implemented by judges so far as is consistent with the overriding claims of the interests of justice.

Wigmore sets forth four conditions that he believes should be met for granting privileged communication.

1. The communications must arise in a confidence that they will not be disclosed.
2. Confidentiality must be essential to the full and satisfactory maintenance of the relation between parties.
3. The relation must be one that in the opinion of the community ought to be sedulously fostered.
4. The injury that would inure to the relation by the disclosure of the communications must be greater than the benefit thereby gained for the correct disposal of the litigation.[2]

[2] John W. Wigmore, *Evidence*, 3rd ed. (Boston: Little, Brown and Co., 1940), sec. 2285.

As previously stated, the major reason for privileged communication is that it supposedly promoted full disclosure by the client necessary for the professional to be of help. Whereas both lawyers and clergy established privileged communications by withstanding court pressure, physicians, psychologists, counselors, and social workers have sought to do so through both legislation and court procedure. If a counselor was called as a witness and claimed privileged communication immunity—refused to testify—the court might (but probably would not) accede and a common law precedent of considerable value to counselors would be established. Counselors need not feel obligated to give information obtained in counseling to any official unless they are in court under oath. Instances of this nature sometimes occur in connection with suits for divorce and child custody. Counselors may be called by the court because of their knowledge of the children involved, particularly in determination of the fitness or parental competence of the father and mother.

Counselors in many states are working to establish statutes to safeguard the right to confidentiality of the personal information received in counseling. Because of the differences in state laws, it is difficult to determine exactly which states do or do not provide confidentiality and to what degree. An Indiana statute states,

Section 2. Any counselor duly appointed or designated a counselor for the school system by its proper officers and for the purpose of counseling pupils in such school shall be immune from disclosing any privileged or confidential communication made to such counselor by such pupil herein referred to. Such matters so communicated shall be privileged and protected against disclosure.[3]

Gade reports that North Dakota passed a privileged communication law in 1969 for school counselors.[4] It reads as follows:

For the purpose of counseling in a school system, any elementary or secondary school counselor possessing a valid North Dakota Guidance credential from the Department of Public Instruction, and who has been duly appointed a counselor for a school system by its proper authority, shall be legally immune from disclosing any privileged or confidential communication made to such counselor in a counseling interview. Such communication shall be disclosed when requested by the counselee.

While Huckins[5] reported that in 1968 six states had recognized, at least to some degree, privileged communication for counselors, the APGA *Guidepost* (August 31, 1973) reported that confidentiality laws for counselors had been enacted in fifteen states. In 1979, APGA Executive Vice President Charles Lewis estimated that twenty-one states had enacted such legislation.

PRIVILEGE IN GROUP COUNSELING   Counselors have speculated as to whether these privileged communication laws apply to disclosures revealed in group counseling. Burgum and Anderson state that such protection may not exist when others are involved and that ". . . it would seem highly unlikely that the privilege against testifying would be extended to the group session."[6] They point out that some jurisdictions hold that where a third person is present, the privilege is lost to all persons. Meyer and Smith[7] report that recent Congressional rules of evidence make it improbable that federal courts will allow privilege in group therapy.

COUNSELING INTERVIEW INFORMATION AS HEARSAY   Some authorities have speculated that a great deal of the information a school counselor would be called on to reveal in court would be considered hearsay and therefore would not be admissible as evidence. But there are many exceptions to the hearsay rule. Basically, hearsay law prohibits testimony or other proof of statements made out of court by persons not under oath and not presented as witnesses and thus not available for direct and cross-examination. Wrenn, in a widely quoted article, described most of what a counselee tells a counselor as "almost always hearsay evidence and

[3] Indiana, House Enrolled Act No. 1309, sec. 2, 1965.
[4] Eldon M. Gade, "Implications of Privileged Communication Laws for Counselors," *The School Counselor*, 19 (January 1972), 150–152.
[5] Wesley C. Huckins, *Ethical and Legal Considerations in Guidance*, Houghton Mifflin Professional Guidance Monographs (Boston: Houghton Mifflin Company, 1968), p. 37.
[6] Thomas Burgum and Scott Anderson, *The Counselor and the Law*, (Washington, D.C.: APGA Press, 1975), p. 23.
[7] Robert G. Meyer and Steven R. Smith, "A Crisis in Group Therapy," *American Psychologist*, 32 (August 1977), 638–643.

therefore not admissible in court."[8] Counselor recordings of counselee comments might also be considered inadmissible as evidence in the same manner as testimony by counselors concerning a happening or situation described to them by a counselee. However, two considerations should be noted. First, although testimony by counselors regarding something they hear their counselees say might be termed hearsay, the fact that they heard them say it would not be. Second, although witnesses are not expected to testify to knowledge derived from the statements of others, they can testify to knowledge they themselves have acquired in the line of duty or employment.

RECORDS Generally, most authorities believe that counselor-made notes or summaries of the events and/or experiences that occur in counseling can be withheld from subpoena and public inspection because (1) they are not kept by public officers and are not school records, and (2) they are made for the counselor's own convenience. Under common law public records are open to public inspection although in some jurisdictions the right of inspection is limited to those who can demonstrate special interest.

Two federally enacted laws relating to privacy have had great impact in the area of records. The Freedom of Information Act of 1967 has as its purpose permitting public access to all government records when specific government interests would not be harmed, thus assuring the basic principle of freedom of information. In 1974 the Family Educational Rights and Privacy Act, often referred to as the Buckley Amendment, extended access to information in educational records that are "personally identifiable" to parents of students under eighteen and to students themselves if over eighteen. The act states that

. . . the parents of students under eighteen years of age attending any school . . . higher education, community college . . . [have the right] to inspect and review any and all official records, files, and data directly related to their children, including all material that is incorporated into each student's cumulative record folder, and intended for school use or to be available to parties outside the school or school system, and specifically including, but not nec-

essarily limited to, identifying data, academic work completed, level of achievement [grades, standardized achievement test scores], attendance data, scores on standardized intelligence, aptitude, and psychological tests, interest inventory results, health data, family background information, teacher or counselor ratings and observations, and verified reports or serious or recurrent behavior patterns.

Fundamentally, the Family Educational Rights and Privacy Act was written to protect the privacy of individuals. The law indicates that federal funds will not be made available to agencies or institutions that deny parents the right to review records, files, and data related to their children. Further, the act permits withholding federal funds from schools that release records or personal information about students to individuals, agencies, or organizations without written parental consent. The act allows for exceptions where information is released to (1) teachers or other school officials within the local educational system, and (2) officials of other schools to which a student may transfer. In the case of transfer, students or parents may request a copy of the record for their own review and may, if they desire, challenge the contents.

The Family Educational Rights and Privacy Act aroused considerable concern among personnel in educational institutions because it appeared to require disclosure of all personal and confidential information collected within the schools. Interpretation of the act and establishing the internal mechanisms and procedures to comply with its requirements consumed countless hours of staff time and energy. One of the greatest fears evoked by the act and shared by all educational institutions affected was that school personnel would be overwhelmed by hordes of individuals . . . both parents and students over eighteen . . . seeking to exercise their right to examine the contents of their educational records. A second major concern more specific to counseling services, guidance programs, and psychological services, centered on the potential conflict between provisions of the act and (1) special problems inherent in revealing highly sensitive information such personnel are privy to, and (2) problems deriving from the conflict created in complying with regulations that directly violate the ethical code of the professional organizations to which such personnel belong.

[8] C. Gilbert Wrenn, "The Ethics of Counseling," *Educational and Psychological Measurement*, 12 (Summer 1952), 161–177.

Regarding the concern of an influx of persons seeking to examine their records, it appears that the numbers making such requests were not of the magnitude originally feared. As Kadzielski points out in regard to higher education settings, relatively few students demanded access and difficulties of access tended to be handled informally case by case with access under the act ". . . controlled by many pragmatic considerations, viz., the specific nature of the records sought, the specific definition of the parties enabled to see them, the discretionary procedure-making reserved for the educational institution, the encouragement of non-judicial hearings to settle disputes and the ultimate discretionary enforcement problems of the Secretary of Health, Education and Welfare."[9]

For counselors and psychological services personnel in schools, the Buckley Amendment appeared to create a set of circumstances that might foster the disclosure of very sensitive information gained in confidence from school children. Paradoxically, an act that is intended to assure privacy to individuals appeared to assure that information given to counselors by persons under the age of eighteen must be made available for parental inspection. It is now clear that it is mandatory under the act that any material entered into the identifiable educational record is subject to student or parental examination, including sensitive material such as psychological test scores, family background information, ratings, observations, and the like. To further complicate matters, counselors and other psychological services personnel are ethically bound by professional codes that assure confidentiality to individuals. In many states, statutes exist that expressly protect confidences given in the counseling relationship. Rules and regulations published in 1976 by the Department of Health, Education and Welfare offer some relief regarding this dilemma by including the following exception in defining *education records:*

> Records relating to an eligible student which are (i) created or maintained by a physician, psychiatrist, psychologist or other recognized professional or paraprofessional acting in his or her professional or paraprofessional capacity, or assisting in that capacity; (ii) created, maintained, or used only in connection with the provision of

treatment to the student, and (iii) not disclosed to anyone other than individuals providing the treatment; *provided,* that the records can be personally reviewed by a physician or other appropriate professional of the student's choice. For the purpose of this definition, "treatment" does not include remedial educational activities or activities which are a part of the program of instruction at the educational agency or institution.[10]

Although the above exception covers certain specific professionals, for example, psychologists, it is not clear whether school counselors or higher education student development practitioners are included in the phrase "other recognized professional or paraprofessional," but we assume they are.

As of this writing and until additional clarification of the rules and regulations, new laws, or precedent-establishing litigation occurs, the potential conflict between the Buckley Amendment requirements and the legal and ethical canons relating to confidentiality and privileged communication will remain. The current situation is a clear example of Nygaard's view that

> Occasionally the legal way can be unethical. After all, laws are made by man, and man is not perfect. Imperfect laws are present in the statute books today, and probably always will be. In addition, judges make imperfect decisions at times. The most difficult aspect of the relationship between law and ethics is to gain a clear concept of what is both legal and ethical, and to know when a law would be broken in order to pursue the ethical course of action.[11]

Expert witness

Counselors have not, to any appreciable degree, sought recognition as expert witnesses. Psychologists have engaged actively in gaining recognition that their testimony is expert and in establishing a definition of psychology acceptable to

[9] Kadzielski, Mark A., "Privacy in 1977: The Buckley Amendment in Perspective," *NASPA Journal*, 14 (Spring 1977), 18–21.

[10] Presented in Robert B. Callis, ed., *Ethical Standards Casebook*, 2nd ed. (Washington, D.C.: American Personnel and Guidance Association, 1976), p. 104.

[11] Joseph M. Nygaard, *The Counselor and Student's Legal Rights* Houghton Mifflin Professional Guidance Monographs (Boston: Houghton Mifflin Company, 1973), pp. 7–8.

legal authorities. At present whether a psychologist receives professional recognition in a court depends largely on the discretion of the court, except where states have statutes defining a psychologist.

An expert witness is one qualified to give testimony requiring special knowledge, skill, experience, or training. The presiding judge makes the decision as to whether the expert's testimony is admissible. Testimony may be taken in any one of four different ways: by affidavit, by deposition, by interrogatory, or orally from the witness stand. The fundamental qualification governing the competence of a witness to express a professional expert opinion is that he or she have sufficient experience with the subject of the testimony to enable that person to testify with reliability. The expert witness must demonstrate possession of some special and peculiar experience before he or she is permitted to proceed to the substance of the testimony. But there is nothing arcane about this special and peculiar experience. As stated by Wigmore,

> This special and peculiar experience may have been attained, so far as legal rules go, in any way whatever; all the law requires is that it has been attained. Yet it is possible here to group roughly two classes of experience which are usually, though not necessarily, found separately:
> (a) There is, first, an *occupational* experience. . . .
> (b) There is, secondly, a *systematic training.* . . .
> Now, the line, if any can be drawn, between these two had no general legal significance. In truth, no accurate line can be drawn. Each shades into the other imperceptibly. In some instances, the witness will need both; in some instances he may have both, though he does not need both. Neither is generally favored above the other by the Courts. The question in each instance is whether the particular witness is fitted to the matter at hand.[12]

Psychiatrists and clinical psychologists are sometimes called on as expert witnesses to testify as to criminal responsibility. The primary tests of criminal responsibility in the United States are based on two rules, the McNaughten Rule and the Durham Decision. The McNaughten Rule, formulated in England in 1843, essentially states that every person is presumed to be sane and to possess reason so as to be responsible for his or her crimes and that to establish defense on the grounds of insanity it must be clearly proved that at the time of committing the act, the individual did not know that what he or she was doing was wrong. The essence of the Durham Decision (1954) is that an accused criminal will not be held responsible if committing a criminal act was the product of a mental disease or defect, and this is made a matter of fact for the jury to decide.

Leifer provides a penetrating analysis of these two rules and the nature of expert witness by psychiatrists in cases of challenged responsibility.[13] The McNaughten Rule, he points out, asserts that responsibility is a function of the intellect, that reason is aligned with responsibility and defect of reason with nonresponsibility. The key to determination of responsibility is whether the accused *knows* the nature and quality of his or her act and *knows* that what he or she was doing was wrong. Leifer suggests that the applicability of the verb *to know* is based on the evaluation of the behavior of the person in question, but contrary to popular belief, psychiatrists do not infer from behavior what is going on in that private sphere of events, the mind. Rather, evaluation of another person's knowledge is a commentary about his or her behavior. Whether a person "knows" can be told only by applying conventional standards that link behavior and language. Essentially, if the accused replied to questions with irrelevant and disconnected phrases, he or she would be considered not to know the nature and quality of the act in question. On the other hand, if a detailed, coherent account of one's actions could be given, that person would be considered, by convention, to know the nature and quality of his or her acts.

Leifer further points out that the ambiguous terms employed by the McNaughten Rule—right and wrong, nature and quality, and knowing—led to the use of psychiatric experts to aid the court. This has resulted in the impression that determination rests on scientifically determined fact rather than ambiguous semantics. The Durham Decision changes the legal definition of responsibility from imputing it to a competent intellect to imputing it to a well-integrated personality. It acknowledges that the intentionality of human actions is not a function of the intellect alone

[12] Wigmore, *Evidence*, 3rd ed., sec. 556.

[13] Ronald Leifer, "The Psychiatrist and Tests of *Criminal* Responsibility," *American Psychologist*, 19 (November 1964), 825–830.

but results from a complex of cognitive, emotional, and unconscious factors. However, Leifer states that even under the Durham Decision the ascription of responsibility was not made any more scientific because

in psychiatry, the characteristic of behavior which negates its intentional nature and qualifies it for the designation "illness" is precisely that it is unconventional; that is to say, no acceptable conventional explanations can be offered by the actor. It is therefore a history of unconventional behavior of a socially disruptive nature which defeats the ascription of both mental health and intention.[14]

Essentially, Leifer's conclusion is that the primary effect of the Durham Decision was to make psychiatrists more comfortable with their testimony.

Vocational counselors are employed as expert witnesses in processing claims for disability insurance under Section 216 (I) and Section 223 of the Social Security Act. In this capacity, expertness must be demonstrated in the assessment of skills and abilities and in knowledge of jobs and the labor market. Wiener has stated that "the prime difference posed by this experience is that the vocational counselor has no contact with the claimant [client] prior to the hearing and must make his assessment on the basis of official exhibits and the testimony elicited during the hearing."[15]

Counselors in this capacity appear at the request of the government, but they are not to testify on behalf of the government. Rather, their reason for being there is to give expert testimony and they should not go beyond the recognized boundaries of their expertness.

Schofield cites some principles that govern expert testimony. They are summarized here:

1. The expert witness should state the facts as clearly as possible.
2. In addition to a clear statement of their procedures and findings, experts should state their interpretation of those findings, that is, their opinion, in a clear form.

3. Experts should adapt their terminology and grammar to the level of the average lay person.[16]

Libel and slander

Libel and slander are a form of defamation. State statutes vary somewhat in defining defamation. Shrewsbury states that defamation (1) involves exposure to hatred, ridicule, contempt, or pecuniary loss; (2) must affect a living person by blackening the memory of one dead or the reputation of one alive; and (3) must, for purposes of recovery, be revealed to a third party.[17] Defamation is the invasion of people's interest in their reputation and good name, causing others to shun them or to have unpleasant or derogatory feelings about them. If defamation is in written or printed form, it is libel; if in spoken form, slander.

Seitz points out that distinctions between slander and libel have significance and that in civil actions for slander at common law there can be no recovery of damages unless the comment fell within one of four categories or unless special or actual money damages could be demonstrated. The four categories that justify recovery of money for slander are (1) imputation of serious crime; (2) imputation of certain loathsome diseases; (3) imputation of unchastity in a woman; and (4) imputation affecting the plaintiff in conducting business, trade, or profession.[18] Plaintiffs must prove the factors that made the charge defamatory and must prove specific application of the defamation to themselves. Damages can be recovered to the extent that mental suffering and loss of reputation can be proved.

Laws of slander and libel have implications for counselors. First, care must be taken in the preparation, handling, and storage of counseling records and notes. If records containing certain statements about a counselee could be interpreted as damaging or as untrue as revealed to a third

[14] Ibid., p. 830.
[15] Frederick Wiener, "The Role of the Vocational Counselor as an Expert Witness," *Personnel and Guidance Journal*, 43 (December 1964), 348.
[16] William Schofield, "Psychology, Law and Expert Witness," *American Psychologist*, 11, (January 1956), 3.
[17] Thomas B. Shrewsbury, "Legal Implications for Student Personnel Workers," in *Student Personnel Work as Deeper Teaching*, ed. Esther Lloyd-Jones and Margaret R. Smith (New York: Harper & Brothers, 1954), p. 306.
[18] Reynolds C. Seitz, "Law of Slander and Libel," in *Law of Guidance and Counseling,* ed. Martha L. Ware (Cincinnati: N. H. Anderson Co., 1964). p. 22.

person, actions for libel could be initiated. Second, counselors should consider carefully what they say about individuals who have entered into a counseling relationship with them and the situations in which their remarks are made. Truthful and sincere consultations about clients with professional colleagues or administrators would normally not be considered slanderous.

Truth is an absolute defense for charges of slander or libel. Defendants have the burden of convincing the jury that their statements were true. However, some statutes have removed truth as a full defense and require that utterances must be published with good intentions and justifiable ends. At times the law excuses and sanctions dissemination of defamatory material in oral or written form if such statements are of social importance. The law does this under what is known as absolute or qualified privilege. *Absolute privilege* refers to occasions when it is in the public's interest for the utterer to speak his or her mind fully and fearlessly. The privilege is so firmly entrenched that the courts do not permit inquiries into the intentions of the person who makes the statement. Absolute privilege is limited to comments by judges in judicial proceedings, comments by legislators in session, and communications of certain executive officers of the government in the discharge of their duties. *Qualified privilege* recognizes that information must be given whenever it is reasonably necessary for (1) the protection of one's own interest, (2) the interest of third parties, or (3) certain interests of the public. Most jurisdictions afford protection against liability even if, unknowingly, misinformation is given so long as there is an honest and reasonable effort to protect the interest in question.

Qualified privilege differs from privileged communication. Though both terms deal with communication of knowledge about clients, Krauskopf points up the differences.

The former [qualified privilege] is a principle (developed by the courts without the aid of statutes) which protects a defendant from liability if he made a defamatory statement in good faith under justifiable circumstances. The law recognizes that it is sometimes socially desirable for information concerning people to be communicated to others. For example, it is socially desirable for a student's professors to furnish information to prospective employers. A defamatory statement made in good faith and

under these circumstances is said to be qualifiedly privileged. In other words qualified privilege is an expression which connotes only a substantive defense to tort action. . . .

Privileged communication, as used in the law of evidence, is a right of clients of professional persons to prevent the professional person from revealing communications of the client in legal proceedings.[19]

Right of privacy

The right of privacy is a fairly recent rule of law because historically privacy has not been respected or physically possible in the home, place of work, or public accommodation. Although protection long has been given to private property and against defamation of reputation and bodily injury, the law was slow to recognize the primacy of the individual and his or her claim to freedom, dignity, and privacy.

Privacy, in the sense that it indicates the absence of undue interference in the affairs of an individual, is comparable to freedom. The right of privacy is the right to be left alone, to be exempt from the inspection and scrutiny of others. Invasion of privacy is the intrusion into or compulsory exposure of one's private affairs and/or papers. When it causes one emotional distress or damages feelings, it is actionable. The essence of privacy is the freedom to choose the time and place, the circumstances, and the extent to which one's attitudes, beliefs, behavior, and openness are to be shared with or withheld from others. Kelvin[20] argues that the psychological state called *privacy* ultimately is defined subjectively; by how people construe events rather than how the events appear to a third party. Put simply, privacy, according to Kelvin, always is perceived privacy.

Schmidt[21] points out that invasion of privacy differs from libel and slander in that damage under the latter is to the

[19] Charles J. Krauskopf, "Schmidt Is Wrong on Privileged Communications," *Journal of Counseling Psychology*, 9 (May 1966), 425.
[20] Peter Kelvin "A Social-Psychological Examination of Privacy," *British Journal of Social and Clinical Psychology*, 12 (September 1973), 248–261.
[21] Lyle D. Schmidt, "Some Legal Considerations for Counseling and Clinical Psychologists," *Journal of Counseling Psychology*, 9 (Spring 1962), 40.

individual's memory or reputation. Whereas libel and slander involve false or malicious statements, invasion of privacy may result from truthful but damaging publications. Such a claim can be made only by the person whose privacy was thought to be invaded, and a suit for recovery of damages may be brought by that person only. The damages claimed need not be proved special damages and could be sought on the basis of "mental anguish" resulting from the failure of a counseling or clinical psychologist to protect a client's privacy.

Although the mental anguish suffered by a plaintiff in a suit of this nature is not easy to assess in terms of actuality or degree, damages can be recovered. The possibility of feigned injury, analogous to false whiplash claims paid by insurance companies, is always present and does little to increase the emotional serenity of counselors.

Within the past few years, threat to and abrogation of privacy has been charged in three matters of special concern to counselors: use of personality tests, use of human beings as research subjects, and use of large-scale data processing systems. Any test is an invasion of privacy for those individuals who do not wish to reveal themselves, but personality tests are more often regarded as a surreptitious invasion of an individual's rights. Consent of the individual to take such tests is the usual procedure in counselor practice. Cronbach observes that

> The personality test obtains the most significant information by probing deeply into feelings and attitudes which the individual normally conceals. One test purports to assess whether an adolescent boy resents authority. Another tries to determine whether a mother really loves her child. A third has a score indicating the strength of sexual needs. These and virtually all measures of personality seek information in areas which the subject has every reason to regard as private, in normal social intercourse. He is willing to admit the psychologist into these private areas only if he sees the relevance of the questions to the attainment of his goals in working with the psychologist. The psychologist is not "invading privacy" when he is freely admitted and when he has a genuine need of the information obtained.[22]

[22] Lee J. Cronbach, *Essentials of Psychological Testing*, 3rd ed. (New York: Appleton-Century Crofts, 1970), p. 510.

As previously stated, the force of law in most cases protects the confidential nature of communications between lawyer and client, psychiatrist and patient, pastor and penitent. Yet scientists studying antisocial or abnormal human behavior have no such protection, and are open to arrest for participating in illegal activities or concealing information about them. The result, many of these scientists claim, is that little meaningful research is being done in the field of deviant behavior. The perils of this work were exemplified by the dilemma that faced California sociologist Lewis Yablonsky, whose books on teen-age gang life in New York (*The Violent Gang*) and the Synanon cure for drug addiction (*Synanon: The Tunnel Back*) have been widely praised for their realism. *Time* magazine (December 22, 1967, p. 34) reported that Yablonsky lived with the people he studied and was subpoenaed to testify at a marijuana trial. On the stand, Yablonsky pleaded possible self-incrimination and refused to answer nine questions aimed at discovering whether he had observed anyone smoking pot. Yablonsky reported that the possibility of arrest or being forced to reveal sources was a constant state of concern and anxiety to him throughout his research. He argued that to free the social scientist, states should either pass laws granting immunity against prosecution to qualified researchers or allow attorney generals to grant immunity for specific projects. Some sociologists, on the other hand, fear that such laws would bring closer supervision by courts and police and might provide protection for unethical, nonacademic researchers seeking thrills. Three traditional research methods (self-descriptions by interviews, questionnaires, and personality tests; direct observations and recording of individual behavior; descriptions of a person by another serving as an informant) may, on occasion, violate privacy. Each method engages the researcher in one or both of two central issues: the degree of individual consent that exists and the degree of confidentiality that is maintained. Sensitivity on the part of the researcher to maintaining confidentiality of data, provision of civil or criminal remedies for breach of privacy, definition of contexts in which the cost in privacy is marginal or permissible because of positive gains, and preclusion of public officials from disclosure of confidential information acquired during employment would help to secure an accommodation for our society on this issue.

Large-scale data collecting and processing systems raise the specter of a massive invasion of the individual's right to privacy. Lister points out that credit records of more than

100 million people are currently kept in several thousand data bank locations across the United States. Moreover, proposals have been made repeatedly to establish a national data bank that would include several categories of sensitive public records available from schools, colleges, health, welfare, credit, state and federal internal revenue agencies. Lister identifies some of the advances in computerized record keeping that pose dangers to individual privacy. The first is that improved storage and retrieval systems enlarge the sheer quantity of data collected and it becomes less restricted. The second is that data that once might have been immediately discarded because of inconvenience and expense of storage are now more easily retained. The third is that new data systems permit greater use of information collected (correlational analyses can reveal patterns of attitudes and beliefs that previously escaped attention). The fourth is that remote terminals have now made it possible to disseminate information and materials quickly to widely scattered groups of interested but not necessarily authorized recipients. The fifth advance, according to Lister, is that information received through computerized record keeping is usually assumed to have great value or reliability because it comes from a computer.[23]

Although many individuals and groups have advocated the abolition of large-scale personal data systems, few believe that such a measure is wise or realistic. Lister suggests some remedies that, if applied, would do much to reduce many flagrant inequities associated with present data bank systems. Among these are that (1) information about individuals could be collected only when they give prior, informed consent; (2) data could be released or disseminated only when a compelling valid social advantage exists and subjects have given their consent; (3) people have the right to examine their files and challenge the accuracy or completeness of its content, and (4) a legal recourse could be established for those who are injured by neglect or willful misconduct by those responsible for the data system.

Malpractice

Malpractice has been defined as "any professional misconduct or any unreasonable lack of skill or fidelity in the performance of professional or judiciary duties."[24] Review of relevant statutes and court decisions points up the fact that although schools and colleges, or government agencies, are generally shielded by the state's sovereign immunity, the counselor has always been and continues to be liable for negligent acts. Carter Good defines liability in these words: "liability is the legal responsibility of the teacher, school board, or any officer or agent of the school in case of accidents occurring in the school, on school property or in activities under school supervision conducted away from school property."[25] Liability may be of two types: criminal or civil. Criminal liability is the failure to exercise certain responsibilities explicitly demanded by law. Civil liability derives from negligence in carrying out responsibilities. Negligence arises (1) when the school employee fails to exercise the duties, care, or responsibilities expected of reasonably prudent persons in the situation and (2) when injuries are sustained by students to whom the employee owes a duty he or she has not performed. The principle of foreseeability is employed in determining negligence. That is, would a reasonably prudent person have been able to foresee that a certain act would lead to injury or harm?

Malpractice actions differ from other negligence actions in that the defendant purports to be a skilled person. The skill is one that is specially acquired and is not possessed by a lay person. The jury decides the level of this skill and how a reasonable person having the skill would have acted. Juries usually make the decision on the basis of testimony of expert witnesses and the standard employed is not that of the highly skilled or even the average skilled but rather that of persons recognized as competently qualified by the profession. The standard, therefore, is one of minimum competence.

Some years ago (1958), a question of negligence in counseling was raised.[26] The parents of a female student who had committed suicide because of alleged emotional maladjustment brought suit against the college director of student personnel services who had counseled the girl for some five months. The complaint alleged that the defendant negligently and carelessly failed to perform his duties.

---

[23] Charles Lister, "Privacy and Large-Scale Personal Data Systems," *Personnel and Guidance Journal*, 49 (November 1970), 207–211.

[24] *Corpus Juris Secundum*, 54:1111.

[25] Carter V. Good, *Dictionary of Education* (New York: McGraw-Hill 1945).

[26] *Bogust* vs. *Iverson, supra*, n. 4.

Specifically, it was alleged that (1) he failed to secure or attempt to secure emergency psychiatric treatment after he was aware or should have been aware of her inability to care for her own safety; (2) he failed to advise the parents or contact them concerning the true mental and emotional state of their daughter, thus preventing them from securing proper medical care for her; (3) he failed to provide proper student guidance.

Realization of the dangerous precedent that a decision against the defendant would have established for counselors was indicated by the fact that the American Personnel and Guidance Association requested and received permission from the Wisconsin Supreme Court to submit a brief as *amicus curiae* ("friend of court") concerning how it believed the case should be decided. The defense was that the director of student personnel was not trained in medicine or psychiatry and therefore had no legal duty to be aware of the client's suicidal tendencies. The trial court had reasoned that "to hold that a teacher who has had no training, education or experience in medical fields is required to recognize in a student a condition the diagnosis of which is in a specialized and technical field, would require a duty beyond reason." The court ruled in favor of the defendant and the state supreme court upheld the verdict. It should be noted, however, that the court's opinion cannot be construed as being helpful in determining what standards of competence should be applied to counselors or in determining negligence in this and other situations. Future litigation may well decide such standards, and its possibility adds to the necessity for circumspection on the part of counselors.

Beymer has made the following prediction.

Within this decade we are likely to see a charge of malpractice made against a counselor. The lawsuit will not charge that the client was not helped by the treatment, or was worse off after the treatment, or that the counselor made an error in judgment. It will be charged that the counselor behaved in a careless, negligent, or stupid manner; that he could have and should have known better. The client's suit may allege that the procedure followed is not within the realm of presently accepted professional practice, or that a technique was used that the counselor was not trained to use, or that the counselor failed to follow some procedure which might have been more helpful. Or it may charge that the possible consequences of the treatment were not satisfactorily explained to the client and/or his parents.[27]

Criminal liability

Burgum and Anderson[28] suggest that situations arise sometimes that lead counselors to go much further in protecting clients than the law literally allows. In such situations, counselors risk criminal liability of four types: accessory to a crime after the fact; encouraging an illegal abortion; co-conspirator in a civil disobedience; contributing to the delinquency of a minor.

Accessory after the fact generally has been regarded as "one, who, knowing a felony to have been committed, receives, relieves, comforts or assists the felon, or in any manner aids him to escape punishment."[29] Burgum and Anderson point out that knowledge that a crime was committed is necessary to a charge of being an accessory after the fact, but that one cannot escape by merely claiming lack of knowledge. They also suggest that decisions about the assistance rendered, no matter how noble the motivation for them, are made by juries.

Laws governing abortion differ considerably state by state. But the likelihood of a counselor being held criminally liable has been diminished considerably by the Supreme Court decisions in *Roe* vs. *Wade* and *Doe* vs. *Bolton.* However, counselors would be wise to consult with an attorney and the local prosecuting attorney to keep informed and up-to-date about the state statutes and the changes they undergo.

Burgum and Anderson suggest the great majority of prosecutions for contributing to the delinquency of a minor are those in which persons have attempted to subvert the morals of a minor.[30] Further, most states have not prescribed the specific conduct that constitutes such an offense. In many states, guilty intent (*mens rea*) is a necessary element.

[27] Lawrence Beymer, "Who Killed George Washington?" *Personnel and Guidance Journal*, 50 (December 1971), 249–254.
[28] Burgum and Anderson, *The Counselor and the Law*, p. 88.
[29] *Corpus Juris Secundum*, "Criminal Law," 95–97:213.
[30] Ibid., p. 110.

Ethical considerations

Some time ago, Schmidt defined ethical conduct as the standards of right and wrong. He related it to "what the counselor, morally, philosophically, and otherwise, expects from himself as a counselor or limits himself to in his work with clients."[31]

Ethical standards are codified or systematized outlooks that have grown out of humankind's experiences. Therefore, ethical codes define certain ways of behaving that have stood the test of time for a given social group. Both the American Psychological Association[32] and the American Personnel and Guidance Association[33] have developed and revised ethical codes that apply to their membership. Members who were directly involved in formulating or revising the codes reviewed and examined a wide range of ethical behavior and problems of professional practice that were of concern to a broadly based membership. Both codes stress adherence to rigorous professional standards and to exemplary behavior, integrity, and objectivity toward clients. Review and modification of these codes to maintain their salience to evolving professional practice are necessary. The setting down of a code of ethics for its membership was a major achievement for both organizations in providing ethical standards for all counselors, whether members of these organizations or not.

Purposes of ethical codes

McGowan and Schmidt believe that the major purposes of an ethical code are that it:

1. . . . provides a position on standards of practice to assist each member of the profession in deciding what he should do when situations of conflict arise in his work.
2. . . . helps clarify the counselor's responsibilities to the client and protects the client from the counselor's violation of, or his failure to fulfill, these responsibilities.

3. . . . gives the profession some assurance that the practices of members will not be detrimental to its general functions and purposes.
4. . . . gives society some guarantee that the services of the counselor will demonstrate a sensible regard for the social codes and moral expectations of the community in which he works.
5. . . . offers the counselor himself some grounds for safeguarding his own privacy and integrity.[34]

Prior to the development of either the APA or the APGA code of ethics, Wrenn, among others, called attention to the need of an ethical code for the counseling profession.[35] He stated that there were two major reasons for the mounting interest in the ethics of counseling. First, counseling was becoming a profession and consequently was concerned with its dual obligations to society and to the client. A generally accepted characteristic of a profession is that it adopt a code of ethics. Second, the emphasis in counseling was changing. Disclosures of self-information, attitudes, emotions, and self-concepts were increasingly common to counseling, and a greater emphasis was being placed on interview elements outside the client which related to his or her environment. Even back in 1947 Wrenn had suggested a credo for counselors. It still has salience:

I will respect the integrity of each individual with whom I deal. I will accord to him [or her] the same right to self-determination that I want for myself. I will respect as something sacred the personality rights of each person and will not attempt to manipulate him [or her] or meddle in his [or her] life.

I will define my personal and ethical responsibility to my client as well as my legal and vocational responsibility to my organization and to society. I work for both the group to which I am responsible and for each individual that I serve as a client. This dual responsibility must be defined and understood by my employer and by myself.[36]

[31] Lyle D. Schmidt, "Some Ethical, Professional and Legal Considerations for School Counselors," *Personnel and Guidance Journal*, 44 (December 1965), 377.
[32] American Psychological Association, *Ethical Standards of Psychologists*, (Washington, D.C.: The Association, 1973).
[33] American Personnel and Guidance Association, *Ethical Standards*, (Washington, D.C.: The Association, 1974).
[34] John F. McGowan and Lyle D. Schmidt, *Counseling: Readings in Theory and Practice* (New York: Holt, Rinehart and Winston, 1962), pp. 584–586.
[35] Wrenn, "The Ethics of Counseling," 175.
[36] C. Gilbert Wrenn, "Trends and Predictions in Vocational Guidance," *Occupations*, 25 (May 1947), 503–515.

The APGA ethical standards

The code does not contain any classification of misbehavior nor is there any specific penalty prescribed for misconduct. Rather, it focuses on guidelines of professional conduct. The statement of ethics reflects the experiences and judgments of the members; it is not a formulation of arbitrary standards or edicts. The fundamental consideration is that respect and protection must be given to the client, something that can be done only by counselors who manifest honesty, integrity, and objectivity in their behavior toward the recipients of their service. These characteristics apply to both oral and written verbalizations. They apply to every human being with whom the counselor comes in contact professionally and are observed with extreme care in the case of those who are emotionally disturbed, who are in trouble, who are young and immature.

The APGA ethical standards are primarily directed to its membership rather than being addressed to the public served by them. The actions of its members have as their object the human being. The code holds up the dignity and integrity of clients—their rights, interests, and privacy—as the main guide to practitioners.

The standards state that members are obligated to attempt to rectify situations in which they observe or possess information concerning unethical behavior of members. The code suggests that members confer with the individual in question, gather further information about the allegation, confer with local APGA chapter ethics committees, state branch ethics committees, and finally, the national committee. The procedures to do this have been formulated by the APGA so that investigations could be made and penalties assessed that would correspond to the various degrees of misconduct by members.

The APGA's *Ethical Standards* contains a preamble and seven sections: general, counselor-counselee relationship, measurement and evaluation, research and publication, consulting and private practice, personnel administration, and preparation standards. Shertzer and Morris used a critical incident questionnaire to investigate APGA members' ethical discriminatory abilities. Some 729 members were able to discriminate ethically appropriate responses from plausible distractors in twelve critical incidents at a level significantly better than chance. Members tended to be more dis-

criminating in the testing and counseling areas than in general ethical situations.[37]

CONFLICTS IN RESPONSIBILITIES   Considered independently, each statement of an ethical standard seems abundantly clear and simple, yet it often masks ethical conflict. For example, statements in the counselor-counselee section stress the counselor's responsibility to the client: "The member's *primary* obligation is to respect the integrity and promote the welfare of the counselee(s) whether the counselee(s) is (are) assisted individually or in a group relationship." It is further stated that the relationship and information resulting from it is to be kept confidential. But the general section maintains that "the member has a responsibility both to the individual who is served and to the institution within which the service is performed. The acceptance of employment in an institution implies that the member is in substantial agreement with the general policies and principles of the institution." The question often is asked, where is the counselor's first or primary obligation when conflicts develop? And conflicts, though not existing in every activity, are numerous enough to pose dilemmas for the school counselor. Some examples follow:

The unmarried pregnant girl who voluntarily seeks the help of the counselor but is afraid or refuses to inform her parents and/or school administrators of her situation.

The counselee who reveals to the counselor that he had engaged in shoplifting or has committed robbery.

The teacher who refers a student to the counselor and later inquires about the nature of the counselor's interviews with the student so that he can be of help to the individual in the classroom.

The student who informs the counselor that he or she is going to elope.

The individual who, during counseling, reveals that she plans to commit suicide.

The police who request information from the counselor about a counselee who has revealed in counseling his guilt in destroying private property.

[37] Bruce Shertzer and Kenneth Morris, "APGA Members' Ethical Discriminatory Ability," *Counselor Education and Supervision*, 11 (March 1972), 200–206.

The counselee who tells the counselor that she cheated on a test. The counselor keeps it confidential but the student is later caught and tells the principal that she told the counselor all about it.

As previously noted, the values of counselors will enter into their decision as to which ethical standard they will uphold. This, of course, means that counselors should be aware of their personal values and their reasons for adhering to them. *Ethical Standards of Psychologists* places these conflicts in bold relief:

> Very often the resolution of ethical problems requires that the psychologist choose between two or more interests that are in conflict. Are the psychologist's obligations primarily to the social group, or to his individual client, or to his profession, or to himself? There is, of course, no simple answer to this question. Most situations where ethical decisions are necessary involve an implicit hierarchy of values, and this hierarchy has to be redefined for each situation. The equation of ethical responsibility is a complex one: weights for the variables must be computed anew as each new ethical problem is solved.[38]

Because the APGA code of ethics does not, and perhaps could not, offer precise direction in conflicts that arise between clients and institutions, McMillian and Shertzer[39] investigated whether APGA members believed they owed a primary commitment to clients or to the employing institutions. A seven-item critical incident questionnaire was developed to measure members' primary commitment (either responsibility to client or responsibility to employing institution) and an instrument was devised to measure strength of identification with the profession. It consisted of four subscales: client orientation, college orientation, monopoly of knowledge orientation, and decision-making orientation. Some 514 usable critical incident question-

naires were received: 126 from employment counselors, 128 from school counselors, 131 from rehabilitation counselors, and 129 from college student personnel practitioners.

No significant difference was obtained among counselors in the four settings with reference to their measured primary commitment. There was a modest but significant relationship between members' measured professional orientation and primary commitment. An effort was made to determine if there existed an unwritten code, an unarticulated consensus, to which counselors might turn when confronted with the ethical dilemma of conflicting client and institutional commitments. Little hard evidence was uncovered to substantiate such a code, for APGA members seemed to accept their dual professional and institutional responsibilities and adopt a largely middle-of-the-road position. Although members recognized the limitations placed on them by their employing institutions, they were oriented, within these limitations, toward their commitment to the client.

CONFIDENTIALITY It seems clear that maintaining confidentiality of the information received in a counseling interview is one of the most complex and pervasive problems confronting the counselor. As indicated above, confidentiality brings into sharp focus the issue of the responsibilities of counselors to the profession, the institutions that employ them, and, most of all, the individual who seeks their help. These conflicts have been commented on and positions taken by several individuals in the profession.

Warman has recommended that the school or agency establish a written policy about confidentiality.[40] He believes that it helps counselors by (1) presenting them with a ready course of action, (2) providing them with the security that this course of action represents the considered thought of their colleagues, (3) supporting them at those times when they are pressed to do something they feel is not right, and (4) providing them with the knowledge that there is consistency within the agency.

Before passage of the 1974 Family Educational Rights and Privacy Act, Clark surveyed twelve school administrators and eighty school counselors to determine their attitudes about the confidentiality of information received by the

[38] Committee on Ethical Standards for Psychologists, *Ethical Standards of Psychologists* (Washington: American Psychological Association, 1973).
[39] Marvin E. McMillian and Bruce Shertzer, "APGA Members' Measured Client and Organizational Commitments and Professional Orientation," *Personnel and Guidance Journal*, 57 (September 1978), 31–34.

[40] Roy E. Warman, "Confidentiality Interpreted by Established Agency Policy," *Personnel and Guidance Journal*, 42 (November 1963), 257–259.

school counselor.[41] Some 68 percent of the administrators *agreed* and 92 percent of the counselors *disagreed* with the position that a counselor should furnish any information obtained in a counseling situation to parents or the principal on legitimate request. Finally, 52 percent of the administrators *agreed* and 93 percent of the school counselors *disagreed* with the position that a counselor should report to the principal infractions of school rules or civil laws discussed by a client.

The school administrators' position lacks internal consistency, Clark notes, and he interprets the position as one in which the counselor should guard the client's privacy but not to the point of complete confidentiality. He infers that when a client is a minor, counseling information must be shared with parents and school officials in some form or manner. Consequently, the school counselor would give only limited confidentiality to clients. He suggests that the degree of professional authority granted the counselor by the school official determines the amount of confidentiality delegated to the counselor. Further, guidelines in respect to the nature of confidentiality, the form in which pertinent information is to be transmitted, method of transmission, and appropriate receivers should be arrived at by mutual consent of the administrator and the counselor before counseling is undertaken. The counselor, in turn, communicates these conditions or limits to students before a counseling relationship is established. In such a situation, information obtained in a counseling situation will not usually be shared without the previous knowledge and consent of the client.

Phillips and Margoshes disagreed with Clark's contention that when a student is a minor information obtained in counseling must be shared with parents in some manner or form.[42] They also disagree that the amount of confidentiality given to the counselor should be determined by the school or its principal, and that where there is conflict between the school's interests and the student's interests the counselor should give preference to the school. They point out that in counseling, as in other areas, the minor requires more protection than the adult and ought to be able to rely on it from the counselor. They urge that counselors not wait until they

start counseling before discussing these matters with the principal but do so before accepting employment at a school.

Finally, it is counselors who must exercise judgment in these stressful ethical situations. They must be prepared to take personal risks in their protection of confidence for those who make use of their services. Such is the lot of those who claim counseling as their life endeavor. No one can fulfill all these obligations perfectly, but counselors are expected to come closer to the ideal than others. They alone will make the decisions when conflicts arise for it is their obligation and their professional trust.

Causes of unethical practices and behavior

Schwebel sought to identify the causes of unethical behavior and practice.[43] He calls *practice* an act but not the motivation of the practitioner, whereas *behavior* refers to the motivation and the underlying values of the person. Thus, unethical practices are acts not in accord with accepted standards. Unethical behavior occurs when conflicting personal interests lead to unethical practice, and unethical practices result from ignorance and inadequate training and/or supervision. Schwebel cites three hypotheses. In respect to the first—that self-interest causes unethical behavior and unethical practice—he believes that the personal profit motive, need for self-enhancement, and need to maintain security and status are causes. His second hypothesis is that unsound judgment due to inadequate training and/or inadequately supervised experiences leads to unethical behavior. He cites confidences obtained in relationships with staff members and confidences obtained from counselees about antisocial behavior as two examples of where unethical conduct may arise due to lack of training. For his third hypothesis, that ignorance causes unethical practices, Schwebel cites (1) ignorance of technical information and (2) ignorance of the counselor's values.

Summary

The ethical and legal considerations discussed here were presented in the hope that the counselor might attain

[41] Charles M. Clark, "Confidentiality and the School Counselor," *Personnel and Guidance Journal*, 43 (January 1965), 482–484.
[42] John L. Phillips, Jr., and Adam Margoshes, "Confidence and Confidentiality," *The School Counselor*, 13 (May 1966), 235–238.
[43] Milton Schwebel, "Why Unethical Practice?" *Journal of Counseling Psychology*, 2 (Summer 1955), 122–128.

greater objectivity in confronting professional problems. An important lesson to be learned from studying the legal and ethical conditions of counselors is the difficult, yet vital, necessity of maintaining a proper balance between professional privileges and responsibilities. Counselors must beware of using ethical and legal considerations to protect their associates under the guise of safeguarding the interests of their counselees. The traditional reluctance to criticize a professional colleague does not protect the counselee but rather encourages sharp practice and protects the colleague. A related problem that often contributes to shoddy practice stems from situations where counselors who meet state certification requirements receive an unearned increment of status when they are really marginal counselors who barely manage to have the required certificate but are nevertheless protected from justifiable criticism. It is the obligation of these individuals to seek adequate training and the responsibility of the more adequately prepared to encourage those only partially prepared to pursue complete training rather than remain only minimally qualified. Fully prepared counselors are aware of and live within the proper legal and ethical restrictions of their profession.

Although codes of ethics may imply the limits within which counselors can "get away with anything," their intent is to establish positive boundaries of responsible behavior. They also provide a valuable introspective stimulus for practitioners. Thoughtful deliberations lead to a perspective on how to (1) maintain competence over the years, (2) place the counselee's interests ahead of their own, (3) show concern for their colleagues, and (4) reflect standards of good practice. Maturity in one's professional field and being able to work creatively in it come slowly and painfully—and often with anxiety, discouragement, guilt feelings, and despairing inner struggles. Despite this price, maturity can be gained by discussion and reasoning about the challenges faced by the professional.

Issues

Issue 1 When client needs conflict with institutional policies or procedures, the primary responsibility of counselors is to clients, not to the employing institutions.

Yes, because
1. Counselors rightfully are viewed as the advocates of their clients.
2. If counselors don't champion their clients in such conflicts, the institution will be viewed as oppressive, as expecting and exerting conformity at any cost.

No, because
1. Granting exceptions to an institution's policies and procedures produces chaos and anarchy.
2. Belief in and loyalty to an institution, its policies and procedures, are expected of all employees, including counselors.

Discussion This issue emerges frequently in discussions of ethics among individuals preparing to be counselors. Most counselors, within the social systems that employ them, perceive that they have responsibilities to (1) clients, (2) their employers, (3) society, and (4) the counseling profession. Further, most counselors believe their primary responsibility lies with clients and that institutions that employ counselors expect them to champion individuality in order to counter the effects of mass treatment by the organization.

There seems little question but that conflicts between the needs of clients and institutional rules, policies, and procedures sometimes will occur. No magic solution can be given for their management and resolution. Counselors will have to decide, situation by situation, which responsibility has precedence. Human imperfection being what it is, all counselors at times are likely to make decisions that turn out to be less than wise, and conflicts of greater or lesser severity are the inherent lot of all who are alive. In any long-range sense, the relevant questions for counselors involved in such conflicts are those of whether they can struggle with the variables in each situation in ways that are, on balance, productive even when they are immediately unsuccessful; whether they can make decisions with courage and live with those decisions and themselves when they prove over time to have been wrong; whether they can articulate their problems in such situations before they attempt their solution, in ways that give them the greatest cogency for administrators and themselves and permit counselors to attack them in a realistic and intelligent fashion.

Issue 2 Ethical standards of maintaining confidentiality of clients' communications and state statutes that establish privileged communication for counselors have been rendered inoperative by the Family Educational Rights and Privacy Act of 1974.

Yes, because
1. The law states that parents of students and students (18 years of age and over) have the right to review all official educational records, files, and data.
2. The law specifies that the educational records need not be maintained directly by the educational institution, it includes records kept by individuals acting for such an institution.
3. Counseling records, psychological reports, test files, diagnostic and evaluation data are all part of students' records.

No, because
1. Counselor records, case notes, and data collected and disclosed by clients are not part of the official records of an educational agency. They are personal memoranda.
2. The law excludes records relating to students that are maintained by a physician, psychiatrist, psychologist or other recognized professional created in connection with extending treatment to students.

Discussion This issue, raised immediately after the passage of the Buckley Amendment, has yet to be settled. There is little question but that any psychological data that becomes part of the students' cumulative folders are considered educational records and, therefore, potentially are available to students for their own use.

McGuire and Borowy[44] urge that counselors, legislators, and other concerned professional groups distinguish between *counseling-treatment processes* and *academic evaluation* for which personal, psychologically relevant material is obtained and maintained. They conclude that the federal act does not conflict with ethical standards of confidentiality and state statutes of privileged communications particularly if the personal or psychological material is to determine academic or interpersonal competency to receive an academic degree.

[44] John M. McGuire and Thomas D. Borowy, "Confidentiality and the Buckley-Pell Amendment: Ethical and Legal Considerations for Counselors," *Personnel and Guidance Journal*, 56 (May 1978), 554–557.

We believe that such a criterion would be difficult to apply, given the usual way that data are collected from students who become clients of counselors. Although the federal law is well intentioned in seeking to control unlimited data collection and careless use and abuses of access to student data, it appears to require disclosure to parents of all personal and confidential information collected within the school. Special problems have arisen when children reveal things to counselors that their parents consider defamatory. We think either the law or the regulations that interpret it should specify clearly that material supplied by clients to counselors, or by others in behalf of clients, should be excluded from inspection or review.

Annotated references

Ad Hoc Committee on Ethical Standards in Psychological Research. *Ethical Principles in the Conduct of Research with Human Participants*. Washington, D.C.: American Psychological Association, 1973. 104 pp.

Presents and discusses matters pertaining to conducting research with human subjects as regards both scientific and individual responsibility in experimentation. Discusses incidents and principles relevant to issues such as use of research results, informed consent, anonymity, confidentiality, and freedom from coercion.

Burgham, Thomas, and Scott Anderson. *The Counselor and the Law*. Washington, D.C.: American Personnel and Guidance Association, 1975. 116 pp.

Examines the law relating to counseling by treating legal problems arising from possible malpractice related to birth control, abortion, drugs, and illegal search. Written by attorneys knowledgeable about counseling. Issues of confidentiality, civil disobedience, libel, testing, and overt criminality are presented and discussed.

Callis, Robert, ed. *Ethical Standards Casebook*. 2nd ed. Washington, D.C.: American Personnel and Guidance Association, 1976. 116 pp.

Presents specific ethical situations related to statements in the Ethical Standards. *Each incident actually experienced by counselors in a variety of work settings is labeled* plus *or* minus *to denote desirable or undesirable ethical behavior. Pages 7–11 present the APGA Ethical Standards as adopted by the organization's board of directors in 1974. An appendix presents the rules and regulations of HEW Title 45,*

Family Educational Rights and Privacy Act (the Buckley Amendment).

Christiansen, Harley D. *Ethics in Counseling.* Tucson, Ariz.: University of Arizona Press, 1972. 260 pp.

The author presents specific case history examples of ethical conflict situations and then discusses, using a simulated conversational format, the possible applications of an ethical code. The problem situations and the commentary about them were collected from more than sixty counselors and a hundred journal articles.

Committee on Scientific and Professional Ethics and Conduct. *Casebook on Ethical Standards for Psychologists.* Washington, D.C.: American Psychological Association, 1974. 94 pp.

The nineteen principles in the code of ethics for psychologists are presented, each illustrated by several actual cases involving alleged violations and actions taken by the APA's Ethics Committee. Includes the 1972 revision of the code and definitive codes on specific areas of psychological practice.

Hammond, Edward H., and Robert H. Shaffer, eds. *The Legal Foundations of Student Personnel Work in Higher Education.* Washington, D.C.: American Personnel and Guidance Association, 1978. 174 pp.

Informs student personnel professionals of current issues in the field of law relevant to handling student development cases. Court arguments and various viewpoints that relate to implementing student services are presented. A valuable source of citations for those interested in research into legal sources.

Further references

Burcky, William D., and John H. Childers, Jr. "Buckley Amendment: Focus on a Professional Dilemma." *The School Counselor*, 23 (January 1976), 162–164.

Getson, Russell, and Robert Schweid. "School Counselors and the Buckley Amendment—Ethical Standards Squeeze." *The School Counselor*, 24 (September 1976), 56–59.

Kadzielski, Mark A. "Privacy in 1977: The Buckley Amendment in Perspective." *NASPA Journal*, 14, (Spring 1977), 18–21.

Kazalumas, John R. "Conscience, the Law and Practical Requirements of the Buckley Amendment." *The School Counselor*, 24 (March 1977), 243–247.

McGuire, John M., and Thomas D. Borowy. "Confidentiality and the Buckley-Pell Amendment: Ethical and Legal Considerations for Counselors." *Personnel and Guidance Journal*, 56 (May 1978), 554–557.

McMillian, Marvin E., and Bruce Shertzer. "APGA Members' Measured Client and Organizational Commitments and Professional Orientation." *Personnel and Guidance Journal*, 57 (September 1978), 31–34.

Moore, Helen Bowman, and John E. McKee. "Child Abuse and Neglect: The Contemporary Counselor in Conflict." *The School Counselor*, 26 (May 1979), 288–292.

Stude, C. W., and James McKelvey. "Ethics and the Law: Friend or Foe?" *Personnel and Guidance Journal*, 57 (May 1979), 453–456.

Teitlebaum, Vivien Stewart, and David Goslin. "The Russell Sage Guidelines: Reactions from the Field." *Personnel and Guidance Journal*, 50 (December 1971), 311–317.

Wagner, Carol A. "Elementary School Counselors' Perceptions of Confidentiality with Children." *The School Counselor*, 25 (March 1978), 240–249.

17 Evaluation of counseling

Does counseling do any good? How does one know it is effective? How is success determined? These and other questions about the efficacy of counseling are raised with increasing frequency. This chapter discusses (1) research in counseling outcomes, (2) problems of conducting counseling research and accountability, (3) some representative studies of the effectiveness of counseling in educational settings, and (4) the counselor and research and accountability.

Research in counseling outcomes

Evaluation is not intended to be a threatening process; its purpose is to provide insights that will help counselors perform at higher and more efficient levels. Whether in a school, college, or an agency, counseling services are expensive to those who support them. From either a financial or psychological viewpoint, providing such services demands much support from both staff members and the community. Consequently, it is necessary to determine their value by applying standards, and this process is referred to as evaluation. The major aim of evaluation is to ascertain the current status of the counseling service within some frame of reference and, on the basis of this knowledge, to improve its quality and efficacy. Evaluation is the vehicle through which it is learned whether counseling is doing what is expected of it.

Years ago, Edgar described the assumptions underlying counseling research: (1) counseling is lawful and orderly; (2) a cause-and-effect relationship exists within counseling; (3) the counseling relationship is a part of the whole context of the client's life; and (4) predicted outcomes of counseling can be verified by conceivable operations.[1]

Most research in counseling can be classified as either process research or outcome research. *Process research* focuses on what occurs as counseling proceeds; it generally investigates such factors as shifts in content from session to session, the relationship of content to the counselor's remarks, client attention on self versus others, and the like. *Outcome research* is directed toward assessing the final product of counseling and usually focuses on such issues as which techniques work best with which clients, whether counseling was successful, and whether counseling effects were lasting. Frey and his colleagues[2] asserted that evaluating counseling is to ask questions about the qualities inherent in the counseling exchange. Questions directed by process research include: (1) does the counselor accept the client? (2) does the counselor ask critical questions? (3) does the counselor recognize and interpret unconscious material? (4) does the counselor know how to manipulate client anxiety? (5) does the counselor use direct educative methods to teach the client about emotional conflicts? (6) does the counselor support the client's autonomy? On the other hand, outcome questions include (1) was a transfer made from counseling to real life? (2) was there an increased awareness and acceptance of personal conflict? (3) were specific symptoms removed? (4) was ego functioning strengthened? (5) was there an increase in positive inner resources? (6) was there evidence of learning to respond to and control the environment? (7) was there acceptance or negative thoughts and feelings?

During the 1950s and 1960s, disconcerting results of numerous investigations seriously challenged the value of counseling and psychotherapeutic endeavors. A publication on the topic by H. J. Eysenck, of the Institute of Psychiatry, University of London, touched off a frenzy of reactions. Eysenck concluded from his investigation that "roughly two-thirds of a group of neurotic patients will recover or improve to a marked extent within about two years of the onset of their illness, whether they are treated by means of psychotherapy or not."[3] Further, "This figure appears to be

---

[1] Thomas E. Edgar, "Wishful Wish: Evaluation Without Values," *Personnel and Guidance Journal*, 44 (June 1966), 1025–1029.

[2] David H. Frey, Henry D. Raming, and Frances M. Frey, "The Qualitative Description, Interpretation, and Evaluation of Counseling," *Personnel and Guidance Journal*, 56 (June 1978), 621–625.
[3] H. J. Eysenck, "The Effects of Psychotherapy: An Evaluation," *Journal of Consulting Psychology*, 16 (October 1952), 322.

remarkably stable from one investigation to another, regardless of type of patient treated, standard of recovery employed, or method of therapy used." These conclusions were derived from studying the results of nineteen studies reported in the literature, covering 7,293 cases treated by either psychoanalytic or eclectic therapy. Treatment results from these nineteen studies were classified under four headings: cured or much improved; improved; slightly improved; not improved—died, discontinued treatment, and so on. Eysenck was able to place only 4,661 of the 7,293, or 64 percent, in the first two categories. Because approximately one third of the psychoanalytic patients broke off treatment, the percentage of successful treatment of patients who finished their course was placed at 66 percent. Eysenck stated that:

> patients treated by means of psychoanalysis improve to the extent of 44 per cent; patients treated eclectically improve to the extent of 64 per cent; patients treated only custodially or by general practitioners to the extent of 72 per cent. Thus there appears to be an inverse correlation between recovery and psychotherapy; the more psychotherapy, the smaller the recovery rate.[4]

A similar investigation, conducted by Eugene Levitt of the Psychiatric Institute at the Indiana University Medical Center, obtained findings comparable to Eysenck's with respect to results of psychotherapy with children.[5] Of 3,399 cases (age range from preschool to 21 years with the median age estimated at 10 years) surveyed from eighteen reports of evaluation at close of therapy and seventeen at follow-up, two thirds of the evaluations at close and three quarters at follow-up showed improvement. Levitt indicated that time was a factor in improvement in the follow-up studies and the rate of improvement with time was negatively accelerating.

Among others, Rosenzweig criticized the validity of Eysenck's investigation and conclusion.[6] Because the criteria of success varied widely in the studies used by Eysenck, Rosenzweig stated that no valid comparison of rates or percentages of success was possible. Bergin,[7] in a systematic examination of Eysenck's 1952 survey, cited numerous faults in the original report. Among these were the lack of precisely comparable cases across studies, lack of equivalent criteria of outcome, large variations in the amount and quality of therapy received, and imprecision in defining disorders and improvement criteria. He retabulated the data presented in Eysenck's studies and reported different (more beneficial) outcomes than Eysenck.

Bergin[8] concluded from his investigation of 1,000 cases involving delinquent youths, disturbed teenagers, college students, outpatient neurotics, and hospitalized schizophrenics that counseling and psychotherapy produced greater positive outcomes than would occur without treatment. Roughly 65 percent of those counseled got better, but 40 percent of those who never saw a counselor also improved, leaving 25 percent whose improvement could fairly be attributed to the benefits of counseling and therapy. The fact that less than half as many of the therapy cases showed no change in their condition, compared to the untreated controls, demonstrated clear proof of the effectiveness of counseling and therapy. But change was not always beneficial, for in Bergin's outcomes investigation some 10 percent of the treated groups deteriorated compared to 5 percent who deteriorated among the untreated groups. This meant that one of every ten clients ended up in worse condition than when he or she started treatment and in half of those cases the deterioration could be blamed fairly on the therapy itself.

An extensive literature on outcome studies has accumulated since publication of Eysenck's work as researchers sought to determine (1) whether counseling was effective, (2) whether success rates were differential for types of treatment, and (3) the nature of change produced by counselors. Much attention has been given in the literature to the success of achieving behavioral counseling outcomes compared to that obtained by dynamic approaches. Deter-

[4] Ibid.
[5] Eugene E. Levitt, "The Results of Psychotherapy with Children: An Evaluation," *Journal of Consulting Psychology*, 21 (June 1957), 189–196.
[6] Saul Rosenzweig, "A Transvaluation of Psychotherapy: A Reply to Hans Eysenck," *Journal of Abnormal and Social Psychology*, 49 (April 1954), 298–304.
[7] Allen E. Bergin, "The Evaluation of Therapeutic Outcomes," in *Handbook of Psychotherapy and Behavior Change: An Empirical Analysis*, ed. Allen E. Bergin and Sol L. Garfield (New York: John Wiley & Sons, 1971), pp. 217–269.
[8] Ibid.

mining the accuracy of claims for various treatment approaches, assuming an adequate research design is used, is complex and difficult. Certainly, the behavioral approaches have the advantage of being able to clearly specify treatment goals (for example, elimination of a tic, alleviation of sexual impotence) and also to specify more precise treatment procedure. Judgment of cure or much improvement rests on the disappearance of the symptom for which the client seeks treatment. The dynamic therapists are clearly at a disadvantage in any such comparisons because their goals are often vaguely and broadly stated and because their treatment procedures are usually not clearly specified.

Cure, recovery, improvement—regardless of approach—all call for a judgment by the researcher. Here again, the behavioral counselors have an advantage because of their use of observable behaviors as outcomes. Many of the doubts about success rates reported by behavioral counselors focus on the narrowness and superficiality of their criteria. It may be noted that many individuals who see themselves as practicing nonbehavioral counseling also report the disappearance of symptomlike, habitual maladaptive behavior when asked about improvement in their clients.

Conditioning or behavioral counselors have been inclined more than other practitioners to report high success rates produced by their treatment approaches. Not only have data on outcomes been reported but these data indicate a very high rate of recovery, as high as 80 or 90 percent! Wolpe[9] has presented several evaluative reports. The studies he cites include those that rely on clinical experience as well as controlled experimental studies. A few major highlights of his report will be given here.

Wolpe cites recovery rates (patients classified as "apparently cured" or "much improved"), derived from uncontrolled statistical studies, ranging from 78 to 89 percent. He gives comparable rates for psychoanalytic and general hospital therapies as 60 and 53 percent, respectively. Wolpe reports several well-controlled outcome studies in which systematic desensitization techniques were compared to nonbehavioral therapy approaches. Rate of recovery for the desensitization techniques applied in group treatment versus another group in conventional dynamic group treatment favored desensitization by 72 versus 12 percent. Similarly, a study of individual treatment improvement rates using three approaches—insight therapy, suggestion and supportive therapy, and systematic desensitization and a control group—yielded differential success proportions markedly favoring desensitization procedures.

Dua reported that behaviorally oriented group procedures were more effective than psychotherapy re-education group procedures in producing changes in constructs, attitudes, and self-evaluative statements of belief relating to emotionality, extraversion, and externality.[10] Andrews compared behavioral (combination of desensitization and reinforcement) and client-centered counseling to evaluate their effectiveness in reducing anxiety and raising high school students' achievement (grades). Significant anxiety reduction occurred in the behavioral group but not in the client-centered group. However, neither treatment group showed improvement in achievement.[11]

Rachman[12] traced outcome studies derived from psychoanalytic, client-centered and behavioral treatments. He concluded that satisfactory evidence was not available to support the claim that psychotherapy was effective. Also, DiLoreto[13] examined the relative effectiveness of systematic desensitization, client-centered and rational-emotive group counseling in reducing interpersonal and general anxiety among a hundred college students classified as introverts and extroverts. He reported that significant sources of variance were associated with treatment and counselor and client variables as well as their interaction. No significant difference at post-testing was observed between client-centered and rational-emotive approaches. The systematic desensitization treatment was more effective than either client-centered or rational-emotive, demonstrating approximately 30 percent more anxiety reduction on both self-reports and behavior ratings at post-testing. All three forms

[9] Joseph L. Wolpe, *The Practice of Behavior Therapy* (New York: Pergamon Press, 1969), pp. 266–278.

[10] P. S. Dua, "Comparison of the Effects of Behaviorally Oriented Action and Psychotherapy Reeducation on Introversion-Extraversion, Emotionality and Internal-External Control," *Journal of Counseling Psychology*, 17 (November 1970), 567–572.
[11] W. R. Andrews, "Behavioral and Client-Centered Counseling of High School Underachievers," *Journal of Counseling Psychology*, 18 (March 1971), 93–96.
[12] S. Rachman, *The Effects of Psychotherapy* (New York: Pergamon Press, 1971).
[13] Adolph O. DiLoreto, *Comparative Psychotherapy* (Chicago: Aldine-Atherton, 1971).

of group counseling produced significantly greater decrements in interpersonal and general anxiety than either simply the passage of time or the nonspecific benefits that occurred from testing, interviewing, and expectation of treatment.

Sloan and his colleagues[14] reported research designed (1) to compare the effectiveness of behavior therapy, analytically oriented psychotherapy, and a minimal contact treatment; (2) to examine the similarities and differences between behavior therapy and psychotherapy; (3) to investigate the effect on outcome of the therapist's level of experience and certain personality characteristics; and (4) to determine the kind of patients or problems that yield to therapeutic intervention. Measures were taken at the end of a four-month treatment period, one year later, and two years later. At the end of the four-month period, approximately 50 percent of the minimal contact patients and 80 percent of the behavior therapy and psychotherapy patients were considered improved on work, social, sexual, and adjustment scales. There was no difference between the two treatment groups. After all follow-ups, Sloan and his associates concluded that (1) behavior therapy was at least as effective as, if not more so than, psychoanalytically oriented psychotherapy in treating individuals with typically mixed neuroses; (2) behavior therapists were more directive (gave advice, instructions, information) than psychoanalytical therapists (who stressed the relationship); (3) patients who were younger, attractive, verbal, and successful showed more improvement than their less fortunate counterparts.

Fink and his colleagues[15] investigated the effectiveness of a high school peer counseling system. Questionnaires were administered to clients, teachers, students, and peer counselors. Effectiveness was based on global ratings of client improvement and from the client's perspective of the adequacy of the counselor's skills. Both peer counselors and faculty rated most of the students who had received peer counseling services as either "very improved" or "improved." These subjective data have been presented in Table 17.1. Fink and his co-researchers suggested that two distinct

TABLE 17.1 **Percentages of clients in four improvement categories: peer tutor-counselor and faculty ratings**

Rating source	Very improved	Improved	No change	Worse
Peer tutor-counselor				
Academic performance	25%	55%	20%	0%
Personal adjustment	37%	41%	21%	1%
Faculty				
Overall adjustment	25%	39%	36%	0%

SOURCE: Alan M. Fink et al., "Service Delivery and High School Peer Counseling Systems," *Personnel and Guidance Journal*, 57 (October 1978), 81. Copyright © 1978 American Personnel and Guidance Association. Reprinted with permission.

delivery systems existed in peer counseling services. The first was an informal system that served large numbers of self-referred students and dealt primarily with personal-social problems whereas the formal system reached fewer students, relied on faculty referral, and addressed academic difficulties.

Meltzoff and Kornreich[16] evaluated group treatment studies and reported that almost 80 percent of the studies with adequate methodologies produced either major or minor benefits for clients. Comparatively, 70 to 80 percent of those studies with poor methodology produced minor benefits or no effect. Bach,[17] too, in a sophisticated review of group psychotherapy reports, indicates its positive potency.

McCord[18] reported a thirty-year follow-up of a treatment program begun in 1939 when the 500 male clients (both difficult and average boys were recommended for the program by schools, churches, and police) were between 5 and 13 years old. Treatment averaged five years and reducing family related problems was the objective for about one third of the 500 clients. Over half the boys were tutored in academic subjects and over one hundred received medical or psychiatric attention. McCord compared the treated group

[14] R. Bruce Sloan et al., *Psychotherapy Versus Behavior Therapy* (Cambridge, Mass.: Harvard University Press, 1975).
[15] Allen M. Fink et al., "Service Delivery and High School Peer Counseling Systems," *Personnel and Guidance Journal*, 57 (October 1978), 80–83.
[16] J. Meltzoff and M. Kornreich, *Research in Psychotherapy* (New York: Atherton Press, 1970).
[17] K. Bach, "Intervention Techniques: Small Groups," in *Annual Review of Psychology*, ed. M. Rosenzweig and L. Porter (Palo Alto, Calif.: Annual Reviews, 1974).
[18] Joan McCord, "A Thirty-Year Follow-Up of Treatment Effects," *American Psychologist*, 33 (March 1978), 284–289.

and a control group consisting of 253 "matched mates" on a variety of measures for criminal behavior. Approximately equal numbers of both experimental and control subjects had committed crimes as juveniles. As adults, equal numbers had been convicted for some crime. Further, signs of alcoholism, mental illness, stress-related diseases, and early death were used to evaluate the treatment program. It was found that the treatment group members were alcoholic more frequently than the control group and more of the treatment group members had been diagnosed as manic-depressive or schizophrenic. Further, more of the treatment group members had died or exhibited symptoms of stress. In short, none of the comparisons (some seventy-four were made) based on objective measures confirmed hope that treatment had proved beneficial. Among several speculations by McCord to account for this dismal condition were that the treatment program may have generated such high expectations that subsequent experiences tended to produce symptoms of deprivation. She concluded with a clear message: "Intervention programs risk damaging the individuals they are designed to assist."[19]

The results of nearly 400 controlled evaluations of counseling and psychotherapy were coded and integrated by Smith and Glass.[20] A study, to be included by Smith and Glass, had to have at least one therapy group compared to an untreated group or a different therapy group. Rigor of research design was not a selection criterion and drug therapies, hypnotherapy, bibliotherapy, occupational therapy, milieu therapy, and peer counseling were excluded, as were sensitivity training, marathon encounters, consciousness-raising groups, and psychoanalysis.

Smith and Glass analyzed "effect size," or the mean difference between treated and control subjects divided by the standard deviation of the control group. Effect size was calculated on those outcome measures—self-esteem, anxiety, work-school achievement, physiological stress—the original researcher chose to measure. Some 833 effect sizes were computed from 375 studies of various types of counseling or psychotherapy representing 25,000 control and experimental subjects. Clients averaged 22 years of age and were exposed

[19] Ibid., p. 289.
[20] Mary Lee Smith and Gene V. Glass, "Meta-Analysis of Psychotherapy Outcome Studies," *American Psychologist*, 32 (September 1977), 752–760.

FIGURE 17.1 **Effect of therapy on any outcome.***

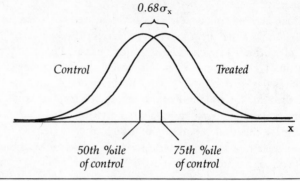

Ave. effect size: $0.68\sigma_x$
Std. dev. of effect size: $0.67\sigma_x$

$0.68\sigma_x$

Control   Treated

x

50th %ile   75th %ile
of control   of control

*(Data based on 375 studies; 833 data points.)

SOURCE: Mary Lee Smith and Gene V. Glass, "Meta-Analysis of Psychotherapy Outcome Studies," *American Psychologist*, 32 (September 1977), 754. Copyright © 1977 by the American Psychological Association. Reprinted by permission.

to seventeen hours of therapy from therapists with about three and one-half years of experience. Measures of outcomes were taken about four months after therapy.

The average study investigated by Smith and Glass showed a .68 standard deviation superiority of the treated group over the control group. These findings at the highest level of aggregation were depicted by Smith and Glass and have been presented here as Figure 17.1. Thus, the average client receiving counseling was better off than 75 percent of the untreated controls. Only 12 percent of the 833 effect-size measures from the 375 studies were negative.

Smith and Glass classified the 833 effect-size measures into ten categories descriptive of the type of outcome being assessed. Four of those categories—fear-anxiety reduction, self-esteem, adjustment, school/work achievement—had effect sizes, respectively, of .97, .90, .56, and .31. Thus, school or work achievement, most frequently, grade-point average, was the smallest of the four outcome classes. Fear and self-esteem changes were more likely to occur in counseling than changes associated with adjustment and achievement.

Smith and Glass presented in tabular form the average effect sizes for ten types of therapy, depicted here as Table 17.2. Examination of Table 17.2 reveals that one hundred

TABLE 17.2 **Effects of ten types of therapy on any outcome measure**

Type of therapy	Average effect size	No. of effect sizes	Standard error of mean effect size	Median treated person's percentile status in control group
Psychodynamic	.59	96	.05	72
Adlerian	.71	16	.19	76
Eclectic	.48	70	.07	68
Transactional analysis	.58	25	.19	72
Rational-emotive	.77	35	.13	78
Gestalt	.26	8	.09	60
Client-centered	.63	94	.08	74
Systematic desensitization	.91	223	.05	82
Implosion	.64	45	.09	74
Behavior modification	.76	132	.06	78

SOURCE: Mary Lee Smith and Gene V. Glass, "Meta-Analysis of Psychotherapy Outcome Studies," *American Psychologist*, 32 (September 1977), 756. Copyright © 1977 by the American Psychological Association. Reprinted by permission.

effect-size measures of psychodynamic therapy (not psychoanalysis) average approximately .6 of a standard deviation similar to that achieved by client-centered counseling (.63) whereas systematic desensitization had an effect size of .9 sigma, the largest average effect size of all therapy types. The investigators point out that the types of therapy presented in Table 17.2 were not equated for duration, severity of problem, or type of outcome.

Smith and Glass concluded that their results demonstrate the beneficial effects of counseling and psychotherapy. Further, they conclude that their results demonstrate negligible differences between and among types of counseling, despite volumes expounding on the theoretical differences of various models of counseling. Finally, they reiterate that unconditional judgments of superiority of one type of psychotherapy over another, and all that these claims imply about treatment and training, are unjustified.

Negative outcomes

The reader will note that some of the outcome studies cited above reported negative outcomes for some individuals. The rate—1 to 5 to 10 percent—varies but nevertheless the fact remains that some individuals are not helped and may, indeed, be harmed by counseling. Bergin[21] proposed that the term *deterioration effect* be used to describe the finding that some individuals were worse after treatment because it implied a reduction in vigor, resilience, or usefulness. Negative outcomes also include sustained dependency on the counselor or counseling and development of unrealistic expectations leading to failure, guilt, or self-contempt. Bergin and Lambert[22] state that their examination of the outcome literature demonstrated that deterioration can and does occur in a wide variety of clients with an equally wide variety of treatment practices, occurring in severely disturbed adults, "normals," delinquents, disturbed adolescents, marriage and family therapy, group and individual counseling. Bergin and Lambert identify some client, counselor, and interactional variables associated with the deterioration effect. Client variables included low levels of self-esteem, great needs for fulfillment, poor social skills, low-level interpersonal relationships, whereas counselor variables included race, gender, socioeconomic level, levels of warmth, empathy and genuineness, and intrusive, aggressive approaches that incorporated premature challenging and confronting, and so forth.

A tripartite conceptual model for evaluation of mental health and psychotherapeutic outcomes has been presented by Strupp and Hadley.[23] The model, presented here as Table 17.3 sets forth the values brought to bear by society, the individual, and mental health professional on evaluations. Strupp and Hadley point out that possible negative effects of psychotherapy is an issue of increasing concern both to the

[21] Allen E. Bergin, "Some Implications of Psychotherapy Research for Therapeutic Practice," *Journal of Abnormal Psychology*, 71 (August 1966), 235–246.
[22] Allen E. Bergin and Michael J. Lambert, "The Evaluation of Therapeutic Outcomes," in *Handbook of Psycho-Therapy and Behavioral Change*, 2nd ed., ed. Sol L. Garfield and Allen E. Bergin (New York: John Wiley & Sons, 1978), pp. 139–189.
[23] Hans H. Strupp and Suzanne W. Hadley, "A Tripartite Model of Mental Health and Therapeutic Outcomes," *American Psychologist*, 32 (March 1977), 187–196.

TABLE 17.3 **Primary perspectives on mental health**

Source	Standards/values	"Measures"
I. Society	Orderly world in which individuals assume responsibility for their assigned social roles (e.g., breadwinner, parent), conform to prevailing mores, and meet situational requirements.	Observations of behavior, extent to which individual fulfills society's expectations and measures up to prevailing standards.
II. Individual	Happiness, gratification of needs.	Subjective perceptions of self-esteem, acceptance, and well-being.
III. Mental health professional	Sound personality structure characterized by growth, development, self-actualization, integration, autonomy, environmental mastery, ability to cope with stress, reality orientation, adaptation.	Clinical judgment, aided by behavioral observations and psychological tests of such variables as self-concept, sense of identity, balance of psychic forces, unified outlook on life, resistance to stress, self-regulation, ability to cope with reality, absence of mental and behavioral symptoms, adequacy in love, work, and play, adequacy in interpersonal relations.

SOURCE: Hans H. Strupp and Suzanne W. Hadley, "A Tripartite Model of Mental Health and Therapeutic Outcomes," *American Psychologist*, 32 (March 1977), 190. Copyright © 1977 by the American Psychological Association. Reprinted by permission.

public and the mental health profession. They believed that the problem of what constitutes a negative effect is inextricably interwoven with a definition of mental health. Further, individuals enter psychotherapy not so much for the cure of traditional symptoms but to try to find meaning in their lives, actualize themselves, or maximize their potential. Their evaluation of counseling follows those lines; mental

health professionals and society evaluate outcomes from different viewpoints (see Table 17.3). Difference in evaluating outcomes arise from the vested interests each party brings to the evaluative task. Strupp and Hadley conclude that because psychotherapy outcomes have been judged by a wide variety of criteria, the research literature as a whole remains in a seriously confused state, precluding comprehensive statements. Further, "a truly adequate, comprehensive picture of an individual's mental health is possible only if the three facets of the tripartite model of functioning—behavior, affect, and inferred psychological structure—are evaluated and integrated."[24] That means that assessments of psychotherapy outcomes should tap all three areas of functioning.

Summary

Outcome studies demonstrate that counseling can help or harm. Examination of the literature on counseling outcomes suggests the following observations:

1. Counseling is generally effective about 75 to 80 percent of the time. Counseling achieves results superior to no treatment or various placebos. Deterioration occurs in 5 to 10 percent of the cases.

2. Different counseling systems are about equally effective with a broad spectrum of clients. The question of what works best for whom and under what circumstances remains unanswered. It could be speculated, and often is, that behavior counseling is best suited to such specific problems as overcoming addiction to smoking or overeating whereas relationship counseling is more useful for treating interpersonal conflict. Moreover, mild depressison may be helped, at the most, by some outpatient psychotherapy whereas schizophrenia may best be treated by drugs and hospitalization.

3. Young people generally benefit from counseling more so than their elders. Moreover, clients who have access to counselors of their own subculture at the very least may find communication easier than those who have to bridge cultural differences, for example, between a middle-class white counselor and a ghetto black.

[24] Ibid., p. 196.

4. The type of outcome that should be produced by counseling is still a question. Should counseling result in clients feeling better or gaining a greater understanding of themselves and others, or achieving specific externally visible outcomes such as holding on to a job or changing failing grades into passing ones? Subjective improvements seem generally more widely achieved than objectively observable ones, except for very specific results such as overcoming the fear of height or flying.

5. The more severe the problem, the less likely that counseling will be effective. It seems strange but the less clients need counseling, the better it appears to work. Outcomes have been better for those with neuroses (anxieties, clashes between desires and duties) than psychopathologies (impulsive lack of self-control, absence of guilt or shame); better results have been obtained for those suffering from depression than with schizophrenia, with certain widespread sexual dysfunctions than with alcoholism or drug addiction, with some psychomatic illnesses than with suicidal tendencies.

Problems involved in conducting counseling research and accountability

Many reasons have been advanced for why school counselors fail to concern themselves with evaluating their services. We previously summarized these reasons as follows:

1. Many counseling practitioners state that they do not have time for evaluation. They claim that the great amount of time and energy demanded for the conduct of programs does not permit them to evaluate, except informally. . . .

2. Many counselors legitimately insist that they do not have the training to conduct either research or evaluative studies. . . .

3. . . . The modification of human behavior is not easily assessed through observation or other tools of measurement. . . .

4. From a pure research point of view, available school data tend to be incomplete and fragmentary. . . .

5. Evaluation costs time and money. . . .

6. Employing a suitable control group . . . is a difficult problem. . . .

7. Obtaining appropriate, assessable criteria is a difficult problem in evaluation and research in guidance.[25]

To Herr these reasons, though plausible and contributory, were not sufficient to explain the lack of evaluative studies:

More important, and perhaps basic, is the need to develop a comprehensive, conceptual theory of guidance based upon a series of postulates derived from (a) observation and study of developmental needs of children variously classified, (b) the continuous examination of the contribution of particular guidance services to the broad or specific socialization of children, (c) an awareness that those concerns and services appropriate to the college-bound, middle-class student may have scant relevance to the larger group which Hoyt has labeled specialty-oriented students.[26]

This lack of a comprehensive framework within which to judge counseling outcomes is a fundamental problem. Some years ago, Pepinsky cited several limitations of research designed to evaluate the effects of counseling, such as

. . . (a) uncontrollable stimuli which impinge upon the client outside the counseling situation, (b) difficulty in establishing controls for the many possible factors in the counseling situation which may be related to changes in client behavior, and which may or may not be responsible for changes attributed to counseling, (c) lack of adequately tested, systematized knowledge requisite to setting up meaningful criteria of change, and (d) lack of adequate criterion measures.[27]

Complicating the problem of defining counselor effectiveness, identifying criteria, and constructing instruments are a host of conflicting observations, hunches, assumptions, and theories. For example, counselors work on differ-

[25] Bruce Shertzer and Shelley C. Stone, *Fundamentals of Guidance*, 3rd ed. (Boston: Houghton Mifflin Company, 1976), pp. 435–436.
[26] Edwin L. Herr, "Basic Issues in Research and Evaluation of Guidance Services," *Counselor Education and Supervision*, 4 (Fall 1964), 9–16.
[27] Harold B. Pepinsky, "Counseling Methods: Therapy," *Annual Review of Psychology*, Vol. 2 (Stanford, Calif.: Annual Reviews, 1951), p. 329.

ent levels with different problems and perform different tasks. Their behavior is viewed by individuals (administrators, counselees, parents, supervisors) with different expectancies. Instruments usually embody limited aspects of counselee change, counselor activity, or segments of existing counseling theory. Finally, there is a growing realization that counseling acts are not inherently good or bad but can be judged only in relation to specific conditions, purposes, counselees, and the particular counseling process dynamics. Clearly, the conceptualization of counseling outcomes and the methods employed to bring counseling under scrutiny must be adequate to handle the complex, many-faceted, dynamic phenomena under study.

Many have identified and discussed the myriad problems that plague those who attempt to assess the outcomes of counseling. Here the major problems will be discussed briefly.

The criterion problem

The major difficulty besetting any evaluator of counseling is often referred to as the criterion problem, and it is crucial, for on it depends the degree of confidence that can be placed in the results. A criterion is some demonstrable characteristic that serves as a standard for making a qualitative or quantitative judgment. The criterion problem has many subissues associated with its attributes that it be definable, stable, and relevant.

TRADITIONAL CRITERIA   In the case of the research on counseling, the judgment usually concerns counseling outcomes or processes considered more efficient or desirable. For example, client self-reports, counselor judgment of improvement, improved grades, change in test scores, and indices of behavioral change, as well as others, have been traditionally used as criteria.

Virtually no criterion is entirely acceptable to all researchers. Too often studies depend on a single criterion when multiple criteria are needed. Some years ago, Rothney and Farwell reported that investigators used some twelve diverse criteria of counseling effectiveness including such things as persistence in school or job performance, grade-point average, satisfaction with job, client self-knowledge,

level of affect, and so on.[28] These writers concluded that the use of varied criteria was a result of the wide assortment of assignments that counselors undertook or were delegated.

Many researchers have indicated that far too many of the criteria employed in counseling research are not appropriate. The criticism is made, for example, that reduction of the problems checked by clients on a problem check list or an inventory immediately after counseling has led to the conclusion that counseling was very effective whereas later information has indicated that changes were of short duration.

One of the frequently used criteria employed in counseling research is the counselee's self-report. Self-reports are highly biased at best because it would be unusual for anyone to request help and invest considerable time and effort in counseling without tending to report that the process was of value. Without other supporting evidence these reports are usually viewed with skepticism. Another commonly used criterion is the counselor's rating of improvement, which needless to say is not independent of the counseling process and has the same shortcomings as the counselee self-report.

Criteria of life adjustment and postcounseling behavioral improvement are difficult to quantify, and sometimes obtaining the information on which to base such judgments presents a difficult problem. Furthermore, each counselee's life situation varies from that of others, and data collected are seldom comparable. Test data used as a criterion frequently are questioned on the grounds that there may be no logical reason for counseling to have impact on traits measured by tests.

PERFORMANCE CRITERIA   The weaknesses of traditional criteria and increasingly urgent demands for accountability both without and within the counseling profession sparked efforts to conceptualize and apply *behavioral* or *performance* criteria. These two terms have become highly fashionable watchwords in recent years. However, it should be remembered that they are a direct outgrowth of efforts beginning as early as the late 1940s to improve the assessment of educational objectives by specifying clearly the actual behaviors that demonstrate the attainment of the objective.

[28] John W. M. Rothney and Gail F. Farwell, "The Evaluation of Guidance and Personnel Services," *Review of Educational Research,* 20 (April 1960), 168–175.

Behind what are currently called performance criteria lie more than twenty years of formulating and classifying educational objectives. Earlier, these efforts focused on the absolute necessity of defining objectives in terms of observable behavior. A description of these efforts may be found in the handbooks of *The Taxonomy of Educational Objectives.* These handbooks reflect years of monumental effort by such individuals as Benjamin S. Bloom, David R. Krathwohl, and many others who contributed through their individual work and a series of conferences that culminated in the publication of the taxonomy.[29]

Mager is frequently cited as one who popularized the specification of criteria in a small book about instructional objectives.[30] Three basic elements considered by Mager as essential to a performance objective are that (1) the terminal behavior expected of the learner or client must be specified, (2) the conditions under which the behavior will be enacted must be stated, and (3) the means used to judge attainment of the criteria must be set forth.[31]

In recent years the rationale involved in the early work in educational objectives has been applied to the field of counseling. Although the terminology varies slightly, the relevance of its fundamental principles to counseling is clearly evident. Those counselors subscribing to learning theory approaches or behavioral counseling models have particularly relied on these principles in their practice and research. This way of thinking about counseling has broader application than modifying client behaviors as is seen in counseling outcome research. It also can be applied as a systematic means of designing and evaluating counselor preparation especially in the skill acquisition area.

The application of performance criteria to counseling, as described by Mager, is considered incomplete by many behavioral counselors. They have added the element of specifying the intermediate or enabling behaviors that led to the terminal behavior. Perhaps an example of the use of performance criteria in counseling is in order. An eleventh-grade girl presents her fear that she is failing English to the school counselor. Clarification of the problem and the client's goals lead to the following sequence of events and activities:

Terminal behavior: Present a suitable, required oral report on Bret Harte (necessary for passing subject).

Conditions: Report will be ten minutes long and will be presented in the presence of twenty-nine other students and the teacher of an eleventh-grade English class.

Techniques or strategies used: (1) Role play with counselor and/or teacher, (2) self-modeling via audio tape, and (3) self-monitoring of activities.

First set of intermediate behaviors: (1) Talk to counselor about giving the report, (2) talk to teacher about giving the report, (3) prepare a report and tape-record in counselee's room, (4) play back report to counselor, (5) play back recorded report to teacher, (6) present an oral report on Bret Harte to counselor, (7) present an oral report to teacher alone.

Second set of related intermediate behaviors: (1) Respond to a teacher's question in class discussion, (2) ask a question in class discussion, (3) serve as a recorder for a committee discussion, (4) read the committee's report to class, (5) serve as a panel member and present a three-minute statement of her views on a topic.

Criteria for judging attainment of intermediate behaviors: Check list of behaviors formulated by counselee and counselor. Counselee checks off behaviors she achieves. Counselor, teacher, and parents check off behaviors that counselee demonstrates in their presence.

Performs terminal behavior: Presents oral report on Bret Harte.

Criteria used to judge attainment of terminal behavior: Timed presentation of ten minutes, duration established by teacher and evaluated by teacher and fellow students.

Numerous examples of performance criteria applied to counseling outcomes have been set forth by Krumboltz and Thoresen. Their volume contains case descriptions that illustrate specification of (1) counseling goals, (2) techniques

---

[29] See Benjamin S. Bloom, ed., *Taxonomy of Educational Objectives,* Handbook I: Cognitive Domain (New York: David McKay, 1956), and David Krathwohl, Benjamin S. Bloom, and Bertram S. Masia, *Taxonomy of Educational Objectives,* Handbook II: Affective Domain (New York: David McKay, 1964).

[30] Robert F. Mager, *Preparing Educational Objectives* (Palo Alto, Calif.: Fearon Publications, 1962).

[31] Ibid., p. 12.

to be utilized to effect modification in behavior, (3) criterion behaviors of the client, (4) the conditions under which these behaviors will be produced, and (5) the means to assess the attainment of goals.[32] A publication by Hackney and Nye provides an excellent example of the application of behavioral methods and performance criteria to the teaching of specific counseling skills.[33]

Bergin and Lambert[34] have recommended (1) that because client change is multidimensional, future research effort should be directed toward carefully delineating the divergent processes of change that take place in counseling; (2) that because changes occur in both behavior and internal states of clients, future studies should include representative measures of both types; (3) that because traditional personality assessment appears to be less promising than "situational" measures, future outcome studies should employ direct behavior observations, either for in vivo or controlled situations such as role playing and self-report measures that are situation specific; (4) that because change criteria should be individualized, *specific* rather than *global* change scales should be utilized wherein consideration can be given to clients moving in different directions for improvement; and (5) a standard assessment procedure, though desirable, does not seem feasible.

The control problem

The use of control groups is mandatory in empirical research. The control group is established in order to judge whether the treatment provided the counseled group is the variable that produced the observed change. Presumably, if change occurs in the group receiving treatment and not in the control group, it is brought about by what was done to the counseled group. Generally, control and experimental groups are selected to be as similar as possible on a large number of variables. Most of the variables do not present major problems—for example, age, sex, social class—but in

counseling research the most relevant characteristics are the hardest to match between counseled and control group subjects. The most obvious of these relevant characteristics is motivation to enter counseling. It is not difficult to come up with two groups that are similar in age, sex, and IQ; however, matching on only these attributes is meaningless if the counseled group actively sought assistance and the control group showed no interest in or need for it. Obviously, the control group must contain individuals who also want and need the counselor's services.

It is at this point in counseling research that a serious ethical issue comes into play. How can individuals who express a need for counseling be relegated to a control group without seriously affecting and possibly harming them? Two compromises are frequently used to cope with this issue: delay of counseling and minimal attention. In the case of limited delay, control group subjects are held on a waiting list while experimental subjects receive counseling. The minimal attention approach to establishing a control group involves very limited noncounseling contact to assure the waiting individuals that they will receive help. It is also used to permit counselor judgment of the counselee's status while waiting.

Selecting control group subjects on the basis of their current comparability with experimental subjects is not easy. The fact that control subjects are similar to experimental subjects at the time the groups are established does not guarantee that their development up to that time has been similar or that it would continue to be so if there had been no special intervention. The point is that differences between groups of subjects are all too often attributed to experimental treatment, when in fact the differences may be related to patterns of development not observed in the original data.

Another important factor involves the counselor rather than the research subject. In good research, control of, or at least information concerning, the counselor is included. Numerous studies have described the importance of the counselor's personal characteristics and the necessary and sufficient conditions that must be created if the counseling relationship is to develop and be effective. Of particular relevance is the extent of the counselor's training and experience so that judgment can be made as to whether the outcome was a function of the counselor rather than the counseling process.

[32] John D. Krumboltz and Carl E. Thoresen, eds., *Behavioral Counseling: Cases and Techniques* (New York: Holt, Rinehart and Winston, 1969), 515 pp.

[33] Harold L. Hackney and Sherilyn Nye, *Counseling Strategies and Objectives*, 2nd ed. (Englewood Cliffs, N.J.: Prentice-Hall, 1979), 167 pp.

[34] Bergin and Lambert, "Evaluation," pp. 172–176.

Placebo effect

A critical issue often raised with respect to adequate research designs is the placebo effect. In medicine a placebo is a substitute for a specific medication that is known to be of no value in the treatment of the disease. For example, some patients are given distilled water injections in lieu of injections of medications or they are administered harmless sugar pills as a substitute for the actual medicine.

Bixler states that

a placebo sets up an expectation of relief. So usually do religious healers, surgeons, charlatans, and counselors. That the beneficial effects of some surgery can be attributed purely to the patient's expectation of help has been clearly demonstrated. The placebo effect is omnipresent. If we are to establish the efficacy of any healing medium we must prove it to be more successful than a placebo-like treatment of the same problem. . . .

I want to be certain that I am understood. If the placebo effect is omnipresent it obviously follows that the therapist must demonstrate that his treatment is better than doing nothing at all.[35]

Patterson points out that there are four aspects of the placebo effect that have apparently been overlooked.

The first concerns the nature of the effect being studied, or the criteria. In any comparison we must specify the criteria, which must be appropriate or pertinent, and the same criteria must be applied in all situations. That is, we cannot accept the removal of symptoms as an adequate or appropriate criterion for the comparison of psychotherapy and the placebo effect, faith healing, or chiropractic. If the latter are as good as therapy in this respect, it does not follow that they are as good in all respects, or that they achieve other results or effects which may occur in psychotherapy. . . .

Second, an adequate comparison must involve more than a comparison limited to one point in time, such as immediately following psychotherapy and the adminis-

tration of the placebo. It is quite possible that the effects of the placebo, even when symptom removal is used as a criterion, dissipate quickly, while the effects of psychotherapy continue or persist.

Third . . . there is no such thing as spontaneous remission. This term only covers our ignorance as to the reasons for the recovery. It is suggested that spontaneous recovery may, in some instances at least, be the result of the inadvertent application of the necessary and sufficient conditions of therapeutic change.

Finally, the nature of the placebo in counseling or psychotherapy must be considered. The placebo effect in medicine is the result of psychological factors. These are usually considered to be suggestion or prestige, but they also include interest, attention and related factors.[36]

Patterson suggested that what is considered a placebo in counseling may actually be the specific remedy. Finally, personal interest and attention, rather than being considered extraneous factors to be excluded or controlled in comparing treatment methods, should be recognized as a powerful, specific remedy, the essence of counseling or psychotherapy.

Bergin[37] credits Landis[38] as the first writer to make a persuasive empirical argument for the notion of a spontaneous recovery rate for mental disturbances. Landis was of the opinion that any therapeutic technique, to be considered efficacious, must exceed the spontaneous recovery base line by some substantial degree. Bergin, examining the evidence on spontaneous recovery, reported that the median rate was 30 percent rather than the 68 to 72 percent previously reported. He stated that to say something was spontaneous was to argue that what happened was unknown and Bergin speculated that those who experience spontaneous recovery from psychological problems (1) probably received help from nonprofessionals, or (2) thought their problems through by themselves. In a later publication, Bergin and Lambert suggest that because people discover potent change agents as they exist naturally in society explains not only spontane-

[35] Bixler, "The Changing World of the Counselor: I—New Approaches Needed," *Counselor Education and Supervision*, 2 (Spring 1963), 102.

[36] C. H. Patterson, "A Note on the Effectiveness of Counseling and Psychotherapy," *Counselor Education and Supervision*, 3 (Spring 1964), 130.

[37] Bergin, "Evaluation," 1971, pp. 239–246.

[38] C. Landis, "A Statistical Evaluation of Psychotherapeutic Methods," in *Concepts and Problems of Psychotherapy*, ed. L. E. Hinsie (New York: Columbia University Press, 1937), pp. 155–165.

ous remission but also accounts for the fact therapy outcome studies sometimes demonstrate no significant difference between experimentals and controls.[39]

Assessment devices

Adequate assessment of changes in the dependent variable as well as assessment of status used for classification purposes is essential if counseling is to be evaluated. Analyses are based on pre- and post-measures. If the assessment devices are insensitive, unreliable, or subject to distortions or contaminating influences, interpretations become difficult if not impossible.

Volsky and his associates have pointed out that certain data usually will be more important than others in evaluating the construct validity of a measure to be used in a treatment evaluation study.

> First, in order for a device to be useful for assessing changes that take place over time, it must reflect a high degree of stability between two administrations in the absence of intervening treatment. Second, an estimate of the internal consistency or homogeneity of the test may be important.[40]

These authors also say that the most casual approaches to the evaluation of treatment outcomes have made use of assessment devices that do not do what they are supposed to do: provide reliable and valid assessments of the outcome variable. Much time, effort, and resources are necessary to assure that assessments, particularly novel ones, mean what they are supposed to mean. Many individuals have observed that an inverse relationship exists between the significance of the variables used in counseling research and their accessibility to measurement.

Longitudinal studies of counseling effectiveness

Two studies of the effectiveness of counseling in educational settings are reviewed here. They describe counseling at the secondary and college levels. These two studies were selected because of the longitudinal quality of their work and the size of the samples involved. Comparable elementary school or agency counseling studies have yet to be published.

Wisconsin secondary school counseling study

John W. M. Rothney, of the University of Wisconsin, has long been engaged in studying the value of counseling.[41] His subjects were selected in 1948 when they were sophomores in four representative Wisconsin high schools. Some 870 students were distributed randomly into control and experimental groups. The latter received counseling throughout grades ten, eleven, and twelve from qualified counselors who were members of the University of Wisconsin staff. Evaluative criteria were (1) measures of satisfaction with and adjustment to post–high school status, (2) measures of optimism in outlook, (3) measures of reflection on post–high school education, and (4) measures of persistence in post–high school endeavors. Follow-up studies of the 690 who graduated were conducted six months, two and one-half years, five, ten, and twenty years after high school graduation.

During the first year all control group subjects were interviewed once and experimental subjects were interviewed twice. Guide sheets were used in the initial interviews and an assortment of information—parents' education and occupations, number of siblings and subjects' relationship with them, parents' vocational expectations for subjects, subjects' vocational and educational aspirations and plans—was discussed with the subjects and collected.

During the second year (subjects' junior year) selected parts of the *Differential Aptitude Test* were administered to all subjects. Rapport was maintained with control group subjects, and individual counseling was extended to experimental subjects. Again, general guide sheets were used in interviewing unless the counselee preferred to discuss other topics. Changes in family situation, present educational and vocational plans, part-time work, school activities, health concerns, and relationships with other pupils, teachers, and parents were topics. In addition, behavioral descriptions, au-

[39] Bergin and Lambert, "Evaluation," 1978, p. 150.
[40] Theodore Volsky, Jr., et al., *The Outcomes of Counseling and Psychotherapy* (Minneapolis: University of Minnesota Press, 1965), p. 60.

[41] John W. M. Rothney, *Guidance Practices and Results* (New York: Harper & Brothers, 1958).

tobiographies, and samples of students' classwork were collected.

Counseling (again, general interview guides were used) was also the major activity of the third year, the last year the subjects were in school. The focus of the interviews was on students' strengths, weaknesses, personal problems, and present and future educational and vocational problems and plans. One month before graduation all subjects indicated their post–high school plans in one of six categories: education, employment, armed forces, work on parents' farm, uncertain, or married within a year (for girls only). Different forms of a senior report questionnaire were then given to each student according to his or her indicated post–high school plan category. Students were asked about their long-term plans, their retrospective feelings about school, and their attitudes toward the future.

SIX-MONTH FOLLOW-UP Six months after high school graduation all 690 subjects who had remained in school to complete their educational programs were contacted by a postcard questionnaire inquiring about their present individual status and degree of satisfaction with this status. The return of questionnaires received in this follow-up, as well as in 1953 (two and one-half years after high school graduation), was 100 percent.

FIVE-YEAR FOLLOW-UP During 1956–1957, after the subjects had been out of high school for five years, a comprehensive three-page questionnaire was sent to the 658 students still alive. Intensive taped interview studies of 50 selected subjects, their employers, and anyone else who had information about their activities were carried out. The four criterion measures of counseling effectiveness (satisfaction and adjustment to school, optimism, reflections on success or failure of high school training, and persistence in post–high school endeavors) were derived from questionnaire data.

Rothney stated that after five years the counseled students, compared with noncounseled students,

1. Achieved slightly higher academic records in high and post–high school education;
2. Indicated more realism about their own strengths and weaknesses at the time they were graduated from high school;
3. Were less dissatisfied with their high school experiences;

4. Had differing vocational aspirations;
5. Were more consistent in expression of, entering into, and remaining in their vocational choices, classified by areas;
6. Made more progress in employment during the five-year period following high school graduation;
7. Were more likely to go on to higher education, to remain to graduate, and to plan for continuation of higher education;
8. Were more satisfied with their post–high school education;
9. Expressed greater satisfaction with their status five years after high school and were more satisfied in retrospect with their high school experiences;
10. Participated in more self-improvement activities after completing high school;
11. Looked back more favorably on the counseling they had obtained.[42]

Merenda and Rothney, in a further report on the results of the five-year study, concluded that desirable outcomes may be enhanced by providing intensive counseling services to high school students.[43] The differences, they noted, were not large between counseled and uncounseled students on criterion variables obtained five years after high school graduation, but they speculated that the "more subtle and lasting effects of counseling require a longer period of time in order to become more clearly apparent." This speculation was based on the likelihood that the early years after high school graduation are given over to exploratory and continued training experiences.

TEN-YEAR FOLLOW-UP In 1961, ten years after high school graduation, all subjects responded to a four-page questionnaire. Although the complete results[44] of this ten-year study have not yet been published in the professional journals, Rothney reported a study of trained and nontrained males

[42] Ibid., pp. 479–480.
[43] Peter F. Merenda and John W. M. Rothney, "Evaluating the Effects of Counseling—Eight Years After," *Journal of Counseling Psychology*, 5 (Fall 1958), 163–168.
[44] John W. M. Rothney, "Educational, Vocational and Social Performances of Counseled and Uncounseled Youth Ten Years After High School." Report submitted to Cooperative Research Program, Department of Health, Education and Welfare, 1963, Project No. SAE 9231.

ten years after high school graduation.[45] The 179 males who constituted the *training* group continued their education after high school either by enrollment in a school or college or by entering a formal apprenticeship. The 142 members of the *no-training* group did not enroll in any educational institution or apprenticeship during the decade after high school graduation. Some members of both groups had attended service schools while in the armed forces.

The most significant differences between the counseled and comparison groups in the follow-up studies were in the number of counseled subjects who began and completed post–high school training. Rothney reports that the training group contained a much higher proportion of counseled students but did not specify the proportion.

Ten years after high school the trained group (and significantly more of them were counseled students) had left their own hometowns, married later, earned more money, were more optimistic, looked back more favorably on their high school experience, reported more educational and vocational plans for the future, and belonged to more organizations and held a few more offices in them. No significant difference existed between the trained and nontrained groups in respect to satisfaction with current status, job satisfaction, satisfaction with what they had done during the past ten years, appraisal of their personal assets, persons to whom they went for advice, confidence in making decisions, numbers of self-improvement activities, and satisfaction with counseling they had received.

In his discussion of the results Rothney asked, "Who can say that the boy who stayed in or near his home town, enjoyed marriage and a family earlier, belonged to fewer organizations (perhaps because fewer were available) and did not burden himself with too many offices was less well off than the boy who went into training?"[46]

Minnesota college student counseling study

Williamson and Bordin sought to determine the effectiveness of counseling provided at the University of Minnesota

Student Counseling Bureau.[47] Their subjects were 384 students who, during 1933–1936, had come to the counseling bureau before November of their freshman year for counseling help with educational, vocational, or personal problems.

The 384 counseled students were designated as the experimental group and selected solely on the basis that complete counseling folders were available. One year later these students were individually paired and matched with other, noncounseled students on college entrance test scores, English proficiency test score, high school rank, age, sex, size and type of high school and college class. The second group was the control group and could have received counseling from other students, administrators, or other staff members. All 768 students were registered in the College of Science, Literature and the Arts (SLA). Half were men; half were women.

Both groups were interviewed roughly one year after counseling (range = 1–4 years; mode = 1 year) and rated on a scale called "Adjustment," which centered mainly on educational-vocational progress. Without benefit of counseling, 68 percent of the control group achieved what was considered by themselves and the evaluating judges to be satisfactory adjustment with respect to their vocational choices and progress in classes. In contrast, 81 percent of the counseled students achieved what was judged to be a correspondingly satisfactory adjustment. Conversely, 27 percent of the noncounseled cases and 15 percent of the counseled students failed to achieve satisfactory adjustment. The two groups were also compared on first-quarter grade-point average (GPA). The results showed that

1. The counseled students rated significantly higher on the Adjustment scale.
2. The counseled students earned significantly better grades than noncounseled students—2.18 to 1.97 respectively (on a four-point scale).

Because criticism was directed at the Williamson-Bordin study on the ground that the two groups were not equated for motivation to seek counseling, Campbell, in a twenty-

[45] John W. M. Rothney, "Trained and Non-trained Males Ten Years After High School Graduation," *Vocational Guidance Quarterly,* 14 (Winter 1966), 247–250.
[46] Ibid., p. 249.

[47] E. G. Williamson and E. S. Bordin, "Evaluating Counseling by Means of a Control-Group Experiment," *School & Society,* 52 (November 1940), 434–440.

five-year follow-up study, identified a third group (N = 62) of former control students who sought counseling after the original study.[48] Both precounseling and postcounseling measures were available for these students. The results showed that before counseling this "better" control group resembled the control students; after counseling, the counseled students.

TWENTY-FIVE-YEAR FOLLOW-UP In 1961–1962 Campbell followed up the individuals in the Williamson-Bordin counseled and noncounseled groups to assess the effects of counseling over a twenty-five-year period.[49] Virtually all "students"—then roughly 45 years old—were located, 761 of the 768. Thirty had died, about 10 percent would not cooperate, and sixty-two had sought help from the counseling bureau during the interval and therefore could no longer be used as controls. Information was collected on their achievements and job and life satisfaction.

Campbell reports that, compared to noncounseled students, counseled students had earned significantly better grades (2.20 versus 2.06 on a 4.00 scale), been graduated in roughly one-fourth greater numbers (59 versus 48 percent), been elected to Phi Beta Kappa (6 versus 2 percent), earned more M.A. degrees (6 versus 2 percent) and more Ph.D. degrees (2 versus 0.3 percent), reported more participation in campus activities, and been elected more often to offices in these activities.

Although more of the counseled group than the noncounseled reported they had published, won athletic awards, been awarded patents, and given invitational addresses, the differences (some statistically significant) were small and discounted by Campbell. The annual family income of counseled males ranged from $1,600 to $150,000 with a median of $14,670 compared to the $4,000 to $70,000 range reported for noncounseled males (their median was $13,500, and the $1,200 difference in median income was not statistically significant). The difference in annual family income between counseled and noncounseled females ($13,300 median versus $13,000) was not statistically significant.

[48] David P. Cambell, "A Counseling Evaluation with a 'Better' Control Group," *Journal of Counseling Psychology*, 10 (Winter 1963), 334–339.
[49] David P. Campbell, "Achievements of Counseled and Non-Counseled Students Twenty-Five Years After Counseling," *Journal of Counseling Psychology*, 12 (Fall 1965), 287–293.

Campbell drew together all achievement data and had each subject rated on a "Contribution to Society" scale by three psychologists working independently (sixteen raters participated). There was perfect agreement among the raters in 299 of the 724 cases, or 41 percent. In the remaining 59 percent, two of the raters agreed, and the third deviated by only one point. The differences between the counseled and noncounseled groups were all in favor of the counseled students but were not statistically significant. However, when the counseled male was compared to his matched noncounseled control (123 pairs of males), differences were significant at the .05 level. This procedure failed to hold for the female matched pairs.

Two conclusions from the follow-up about the effect of counseling on students were drawn by Campbell. First, a very mild difference in achievement existed between counseled and noncounseled students twenty-five years later, especially among men. Second, counseling did exert a beneficial effect on the students' achievement. Although the effect was most visible on immediate criteria such as grades and graduation, and although it declined somewhat, it did not completely disappear over twenty-five years. These conclusions are not too surprising, Campbell points out, since counselors are more effective in dealing with immediate problems and these frequently concern grades and graduation. It is his judgment that counseling is best justified as immediate help to the student bewildered by an increasingly complex range of educational and occupational opportunities.

The school counselor: accountability and research

Sometime ago, Krumboltz pointed out that much counseling research seems designed to determine whether a vaguely defined process (counseling) is a possible panacea for all the problems brought to counselors.[50] All too often, hypotheses state "that juvenile delinquents will become pro-social, that underachievers will become achievers, that vocationally unhappy persons will become satisfied, that complacent persons will become concerned, that shaky marriages will become stable, that fearful persons will become confident—

[50] John D. Krumboltz, "The Agenda for Counseling," *Journal of Counseling Psychology*, 12 (Fall 1965), 226.

all as the result of the same kind of contact with another person called a counselor." Krumboltz believes that, because most evaluations of counseling produce negative findings, the profession ought to abandon the search for some criterion measure that is affected by one process (counseling). Varieties of processes, procedures, and techniques are possible, but they need careful experimental testing. In his words, the agenda for counseling must provide answers to the following question:

For clients desiring help on each type of problem of concern to the counselor
What techniques and procedures,
When used by what kind of counselor,
With which type of clients,
For how long,
and in what sequence,
Will produce which types of behavior change?

Accountability

Observation of the years since that agenda was published leads to the conclusion that its items have not been accorded high priority. But counselors have been subjected to increasing demands to demonstrate the worth of their work.

The demand for accountability contains a strong emphasis on justifying the activities engaged in by counselors to those served and those who finance their work. True professionals have always tried to evaluate their work with an eye toward improvement. They have always needed to know what was productive. Now, more than ever, counseling practitioners are being called on to demonstrate and articulate the outcomes of their work to their employers and the public.

Counselors have been searching for appropriate and sound ways to respond to the demands for accountability. Pulvino and Sanborn[51] present an accountability paradigm based on communication theory. The phases involved in their model include the following:

1. *Dialogue with the public.* Counselors hold meetings with the public so that both they and the public (parents,

teachers, students, administrators) come to understand what needs are to be met, agree on goals to be pursued, and share responsibility based on realistic role expectations for each person involved in the program.
2. *Joint development of measurable objectives.* Faculty, parents, students, and counselors examine and come to some agreement on goals.
3. *Counseling and guidance procedures.* Determination of procedures to be used will become more appropriate if it is based on feedback from those who are the constituents of the services.
4. *Evaluation.* Assessments and judgments must be made on the products of the procedures used as well as the processes employed in reaching stated objectives.
5. *Communication of evaluation results.* Communications here involves determining what others think of the outcomes.

Another commonly used approach to accountability is the planning, programming, budgeting system (PPBS). The PPBS is very similar to management-by-objectives (MBO), long used in business and industry. PPBS is a management technique for allocating resources in a manner that maximizes benefits at a reasonable cost. It provides a structured mechanism of identifying needs, planning programs, choosing among alternative courses of action, allocating and controlling resources and evaluating outcomes.

The heart of the PPBS approach to planning is the program budget, which is formulated on the basis of carefully conceived programs with stated objectives and subobjectives. Another fundamental component of the PPBS approach is systems analysis, or examining the parts of the entire system in order to formulate objectives. Often this starts with identification of needs and priorities. As needs are identified, priorities can be established, and goals and objectives specified. A final component of PPBS is to determine the extent to which program objectives have been accomplished. This evaluation leads to decisions about the allocation of program resources, including personnel.

Thompson and Borsari[52] say that management-by-objectives enables counselors to be accountable and to manage resources properly. They have presented an overview of

[51] Charles J. Pulvino and Marshall P. Sanborn, "Feedback and Accountability," *Personnel and Guidance Journal,* 51 (September 1972), 15–20.

[52] Donald Thompson and Leonard R. Borsari, "An Overview of Management by Objectives for Guidance and Counseling Services," *The School Counselor,* 25 (January 1978), 172–177.

TABLE 17.4 **Excerpts from John Doe's annual accountability record**

Job title—Counselor; Annual salary—$14,000; Contract—40 weeks, 40 hours/week; Overhead factor—50%; Effective rate—$14.00/hour

General Goal A—Adaptive Behavior: Help students develop more adaptive and constructive behavior patterns

| Problem identification | Accomplishment | | Cost | | |
	Method	Outcome	Activity	Hours	Dollars
Olive's mother phoned: Olive depressed, talking vaguely of suicide, no friends	Analysis of social reinforcers for Olive; social skill training; assigned Olive to help new transfer student	Olive increased frequency of initiating social contacts from 0/month to 4/month; reports having 1 good friend vs. 0; mother reports Olive's depression gone—suicide talk from 1/month before referral to 0/month for 3 consecutive months	Conferences with Olive	38	532
			Conferences with mother	3	42
			Conferences with teachers	2	28
					602
Student X came to me worried about his dependence on mood drugs; requested anonymity	Discussions to find other satisfactions, ways of getting his gang to change	Temporary progress in reducing frequency of drug use offset by relapse each time	Conferences with Student X	25	350
			Conferences with physician	0.5	7
					357

SOURCE: John D. Krumboltz, "An Accountability Model for Counselors," *Personnel and Guidance Journal*, 52 (June 1974), 642. Copyright © 1974 American Personnel and Guidance Association. Reprinted with permission.

the process for implementing an MBO system in pupil personnel services. The process they describe includes (1) defining long-range system goals, (2) conducting a needs assessment to focus priorities, (3) establishing pupil personnel objectives, (4) each staff member establishing individual objectives, (5) developing action plans and assessing their feasibility, (6) implementing action plans and monitoring and evaluating operations, (7) reviewing progress toward objectives, and (8) recycling.

A system of accountability for counselors has been proposed by Krumboltz.[53] His system would enable counselors to (1) obtain feedback on the results of their work, (2) select counseling methods based on the demonstrated success, (3) identify students with unmet needs, (4) devise shortcuts for routine operations, (5) support increased staffing to reach attainable goals, and (6) request training for problems requiring new competencies. The accountability system proposed

by Krumboltz is a method of summarizing accomplishments by goal areas, specifying how much each set of accomplishments costs and recommending changes to correct deficiencies. Table 17.4, presented by Krumboltz, portrays excerpts from a counselor's annual record for the general goal of "helping students develop more adaptive and constructive behavior patterns."

The model proposed by Krumboltz, as other models, requires that counselors record their daily activities, collect information about the outcomes of their work, acquire feedback from others on what counselees are doing, and disseminate information to the public. None of these activities is done easily. All take time to develop and continuous experimentation is necessary if the benefits of being accountable are to outweigh the costs.

Knapper[54] stated that the public demand for counselor accountability would persist and that it was in the best inter-

[53] John D. Krumboltz, "An Accountability Model for Counselors," *Personnel and Guidance Journal*, 52 (June 1974), 639–646.

[54] Everette Q. Knapper, "Counselor Accountability," *Personnel and Guidance Journal*, 57 (September 1978), 27–30.

FIGURE 17.2 **Knapper's accountability paradigm**

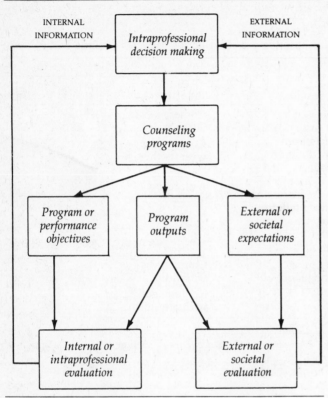

INTERNAL
INFORMATION

EXTERNAL
INFORMATION

Intraprofessional decision making

Counseling programs

Program or performance objectives

Program outputs

External or societal expectations

Internal or intraprofessional evaluation

External or societal evaluation

SOURCE: Everette Q. Knapper, "Counselor Accountability," *Personnel and Guidance Journal*, 57 (September 1978), 29. Copyright © 1978 American Personnel and Guidance Association. Reprinted with permission.

est of the profession to go on the initiative by demonstrating its collective worth. Knapper has suggested a paradigm, reproduced here as Figure 17.2, in which the profession could balance the response to societal expectations and professional goals. The paradigm suggests that professional outputs or accomplishments could be evaluated in terms of both internal and external standards. External evaluations would not imply external monitoring and control.

Properly conducted, accountability would seem to be useful to counselors who for many years have complained about such issues as a lack of a clear role definition, assignment of questionable duties, unavailability of time to

counsel, and the like. Krumboltz[55] pointed out that accountability works best if it focuses on diagnostic and self-improvement functions rather than blame or punishment for poor counselor performance. Moreover, Krumboltz suggested that experimentation should be encouraged and failures should be considered acceptable and inevitable. Pine[56] adds that accountability helps counselors gain insights and improve their counseling skills. By undertaking a program of accountability, Pine believed that counselors would increase their competencies and would obtain evidence to know which counseling techniques produce beneficial outcomes.

Research

Any sophisticated review of the literature on counseling effectiveness will demonstrate that the results have been modest, given that noncounseled individuals change over time. Few if any facts are now deemed established, and many findings have been repudiated. Considering the present state of research on counseling effectiveness, the temptation is great to become a prophet of doom crying out for suspension of further fruitless efforts to determine the outcomes of counseling. However, an alternative action is available to counselors. That is to ask what it is in their modus operandi that consistently leads to conclusions intuitively sensed by every counselor as incomplete. Most practitioners believe that any counselor who chooses to make a difference will do so. Possibly by retracing some of the work in counseling effectiveness and listening with sharpened hearing to the comments of the investigators, often offered parenthetically, fresh approaches may be formulated to investigate unexplored research avenues.

Careful attention needs to be given to the area of counseling theory and how its corresponding implementation in the counseling process produces results. Generally, researchers work with fragmented elements of counseling behavior rather than with a process model. Instruments have often tended to be collections of post hoc memories by counselees and counselors, rather than time samples of behavior in context.

[55] Krumboltz, "Accountability Model."
[56] Gerald J. Pine, "Evaluating School Guidance Programs: Retrospect and Prospect," *Measurement and Evaluation in Guidance*, 8 (October 1975), 136–144.

It is impossible at this stage to speak of trends, but there is certainly within the current Zeitgeist a growing concern for formulating models of the counseling process and a shift to systematic recordings, by either trained recorders or video tape, of total counselor-counselee interactions. Evaluation, in this case, becomes a matter of the degree of correspondence between the behavior observed and that required by the model.

Goldman[57] has questioned the value to counseling practitioners of research that has been conducted. He believes that the current mode for conducting research rarely informs practitioners about the cutting edges of the field or about the major needs of clients. He characterizes the outcomes derived from seventy years of counseling research as trivial and identifies the reasons as being that (1) counseling deals with intangibles (thoughts, feelings, attitudes, goals); (2) the laboratory experiment, borrowed from the physical sciences, has been relied on to the detriment of exploratory studies conducted in natural settings; (3) too many inadequate studies have been published; and (4) important, broad topics are ignored. Goldman recommended that field studies be conducted, that *n* of *1* (or single-case investigations), case study, and systematic observation replace controlled research undertakings, and that investigators turn to practice-oriented studies. A book edited by Goldman[58] is viewed as being particularly helpful in responding to his recommendations.

Frey[59] has advocated *n* of *1* as a mode of research for counselors. Special characteristics of three single case methods have been summarized in tabular form by Frey and Table 17.5 presents those characteristics. Frey suggested that the popularity of one research methodology was seasonal and that attitudes about methods used to establish scientific proof were related to cherished values. He stated that a holistic perspective or a thirst for the "spirit" of things led counseling researchers to use single-case methods rather than group research designs that sum over a client's experience, yielding "on the average" thinking that tells so little about how a particular client reacted to life or to some intervention.

Thoresen,[60] who commented on the work of Frey and others, thought the dichotomy made between single-subject approaches and group approaches was overdrawn because the primary distinction lies in gathering repeated observations over time. Further, he stated that the case study could not be used readily to sort out the effects of multiple causation nor could it be used to evaluate a hypothesis scientifically. However, Thoresen concluded that intensive study of one or a few cases was a research strategy ideally suited for practicing counselors.

Summary

Counseling researchers have been hesitant to formulate counseling models that may be prematurely prescriptive. Yet, even in those situations defined strictly in terms of observables, the observables are themselves abstractions representing judgments to describe some behaviors while ignoring others. Questions of value judgments underlying counseling objectives are inescapable, and perhaps the initial task is to hammer them out anew in public and professional discourse. Given agreement on objectives, systematic study can then be initiated on the conditions and behaviors that maximize the likelihood of their attainment. Certainly, a wider range of psychological and counseling theory is available to draw on than was formerly the case. Technology now permits us to capture and hold for repeated study samples of counseling transactions. Can we use these new tools of theoretical and empirical analysis to replace the search for correlations between counselor traits and observer ratings that have characterized past studies? Can we view counseling behavior as one component in a counseling system performing first one function, then another, as a particular kind of learning sequence unfolds? Can present-day counseling theory eventually culminate in conceptual models useful in evaluating counseling behavior? What institutions, groups, or individuals are committed to these tasks?

No one doubts that conducting counseling research is an extremely complex endeavor. The results of counseling vary

[57] Leo Goldman, "Toward More Meaningful Research," *Personnel and Guidance Journal*, 55 (February 1977), 363–368.
[58] Leo Goldman, ed., *Research and the Counselor* (New York: John Wiley & Sons, 1978).
[59] David Frey, "Science and the Single Case in Counseling Research," *Personnel and Guidance Journal*, 56 (January 1978), 263–268.
[60] Carl Thoresen, "Making Better Science, Intensively," *Personnel and Guidance Journal*, 56 (January 1978), 279–282.

TABLE 17.5 **Three patterns for single case analysis**

Method	Purpose	Research question	Typical methods	Possible outcomes
Psychohistory	Understanding the life patterns of historical figures	How have historical factors influenced an individual's past life?	Historical method Anthropological field study Sociology Psychoanalysis Disciplined subjectivity Literary criticism	The panorama of life Illustration of developmental theory Understanding of different persons, times, and cultures Integration of personal development with cultural development Complexification of the human experience Effect of individuals on historical events Theory building Hypotheses generation Hypotheses validation
Case study	Understanding the life of contemporary clients	How do present and past factors influence an individual's life?	Interviewing Case conference Psychological assessment Clinical synthesis Content analysis	Diagnosis Case examples for instruction Understanding of social factors Illustrate experimental results Illustrate intra-person variation Sort out effects of multiple causation Describe human development Understanding of the culturally different Evaluate clinical intervention Hypotheses generation Hypotheses validation
Intensive design	Analysis of treatment effects for behavior change	How has an intervention influenced an individual's life?	Experimental design Statistical method Behavioral technology Psychological scaling and charting Clinical synthesis	Isolate effects of interventions Evaluate interventions Illustrate development over time Illustrate intra-person variation Simplification of the human experience Hypotheses generation Hypotheses validation

SOURCE: David Frey, "Science and the Single Case in Counseling Research," *Personnel and Guidance Journal*, 56 (January 1978), 264
Copyright © 1978 American Personnel and Guidance Association. Reprinted with permission.

from setting to setting, from counselor to counselor, and from counselee to counselee. The counseling process involves many kinds of counselors attempting to apply many varieties of techniques to a wide range of psychological problems exhibited by many kinds of counselees. Although all these factors are present in questions concerning whether counseling is of value, progress will depend on breaking down the general question into a series of less complicated and more precise questions that lend themselves to systematic investigation.

The aura of desirability surrounding research frequently leaves nonresearchers feeling like second-class citizens because they are not engaged in high-level evaluation of their activities. About counselors in particular, one frequently hears the criticism that they are little inclined to do research because they are service oriented. Counselors themselves are likely to reverse this statement and use it as an apology for not doing research. It is extremely difficult to carry on an active counseling program and conduct research at the same time. Often it is undesirable for researchers to be active participants in their own study lest they bias the results.

A counseling staff should not undertake research because it is the "thing to do" or because someone expects it of them. As can be seen in the foregoing discussion, research into meaningful questions using appropriate criteria and incorporating adequate controls requires a great deal of time and effort and can be disruptive to the counseling service. It should be entered into only when one has a question sufficiently important to justify paying the price attendant upon such disruption. Obviously, good research cannot be conducted without sufficient skills and resources. Many school staffs would be well advised to have it done for them rather than attempting to do it themselves. Although bringing in outsiders may be threatening because it involves exposure of what is done, the school that is seriously inclined toward evaluating its counseling services rarely loses in the process, if the long view is taken.

Issues

Issue 1 Counselors prepared at the master's-degree level ought not to be expected to have research competencies or undertake research on being employed.

True, because
1. There is insufficient time in preparation programs to equip them with the requisite competencies.
2. Few practicing counselors have the time, the inclination, or the encouragement to engage in research.
3. At best, all that can be expected from counselors prepared at the master's-degree level is that they are able to read and understand (consume) the research literature featuring rudimentary statistics and designs.

False, because
1. Such counselors are professionals who should be prepared to be objective and scientific; to use their senses to observe what is happening; to discern the specific features, characteristics, and outcomes of their work; to know what happens in the life and times of their clients and why.
2. Counseling practitioners should possess sufficient research competencies to enable them to assess the outcomes of their practices.
3. Research and practice are tied together.
4. The reason most practicing counselors do not engage in research is because those who prepared them did not emphasize such activities or did not model the behavior needed.

Discussion Many counselor education programs have given short shrift to developing statistical, research design, and measurement competencies among those they prepare and endorse for counseling positions. Many professors in those programs are quick to criticize or to deplore the lack of research among counseling practitioners. Somehow the connections between preparation and practice escaped them. Too often, the fledgling counselor enters practice from a training setting that has been rich with service and experience models but sparsely endowed with research and evaluation models.

It would seem to be legitimate to expect that master's-degree level counselors would have attained fundamental research competencies (descriptive statistics and simple experimental methods) that enable them to inquire into questions and problems associated with their work. Such an expectation is not based on the idea that the best course for counselors to follow is to display the visible attributes of the more prestigious sciences: quantification, precision of measurement, elegance of experimental design, general laws.

Nor is such an expectation based on the belief that even counselor education programs should become knowledge factories, designed to produce rather than organize knowledge. Rather, fundamental research competencies should be attained in preparation to enable counselors, regardless of setting, to make use of systematic observation, analyzing these observations, and confirming hypotheses about how their clients are helped. Equipped with such competencies, counselors could start to ferret out answers to the "agenda for counseling," proposed by John Krumboltz in 1965. If such an expectation were to be met, the beneficiaries would be the clients served by counselors, the practitioners, and the counseling profession.

The contemporary climate in educational institutions clearly stresses accountability. Today, in many communities, counselors find themselves in a position where they must participate actively in evaluation or it will be done for them by others from either outside or inside the system. Most counselors would prefer to become involved in determining their own fate.

Issue 2 Single-subject research methods are particularly appropriate for counseling practitioners.

Yes, because
1. Single-case strategies are designed to focus on an individual's responses; enabling counselors to report the effects of their interventions with particular individuals; thereby illuminating the behavior of the individual rather than having those behaviors obscured in "averages."
2. Experimental research is designed to test cause-and-effect hypotheses and that requires large numbers of subjects; counselors are more interested in changes over time made by an individual and in determining whether a procedure is effective.
3. Single-subject research is particularly applicable to natural settings, such as schools, where practitioners are unable to control all the conditions that obtain in the laboratory. Moreover, it is impossible or unfeasible to arouse in a laboratory situation motives and feelings that equal in intensity some that are common in a natural setting.

No, because
1. Single-case research is difficult, time consuming, expensive, and relatively inelegant; it avoids the big problems and fails to achieve the goal of research, that of establishing general laws of behavior.
2. Overuse of single-subject research methods would get counseling practitioners into trouble because they would lead to too narrow a definition of their problems and cut off inquiry into the more complex, less observable patterns of events that largely may determine their difficulty of the moment.
3. Single-subject research is usually too specific to be generalized to various settings or to illustrate major principles.

Discussion *N* of *1* studies are becoming fashionable again, emphasizing, observing, counting, or monitoring the concrete and the particular. They appear particularly appropriate for the counselor, faced with the task of taking action on short notice and having to deal with what is happening to a certain client in the situation of the moment.

Admittedly, single-subject approaches are a far cry from the characteristic work of a scientist. The counselor, as scientist, must use terms for describing clients that are sufficiently abstract so that one client may be compared to others and to nonclients, the myriad specific acts of clients must be ordered to a conceptual scheme, so that future observations may be systematic, and general relationships among clients' processes may be established. But interest in research for most counseling professionals is usually narrowly focused on a specific problem that seems very pressing. *N* of *1* methodologies may be valuable for studying these practical problems.

Discussion of this issue often is conducted as if it were an either-or situation. Either large group designs or single-case designs should be pursued by counseling practitioners. In truth, research methods are selected best on the basis of the questions, the data, and the situation. Both types are needed if the practice of counseling is to be advanced.

Annotated references

Garfield, Sol L., and Allen E. Bergin, eds. *Handbook of Psychotherapy and Behavior Change: An Empirical Analysis.* 2nd ed. New York: John Wiley & Sons, 1978. 1024 pp.

This doorstop of a book is chock-full of research investigations on psychotherapy synthesized in relation to practice.

Parts II (pp. 217–542) and III (pp. 543–750) are particularly relevant to the evaluation of counseling and counseling outcome research.

Goldman, Leo, ed. *Research and the Counselor.* New York: John Wiley & Sons, 1978. 509 pp.

Several authorities describe approaches to research that appear to have promise for counseling professionals.

Gross, Martin L. *The Psychological Society.* New York: Random House, 1978.

This is an important book that should be read by every counselor. After examining in considerable detail the outcome studies of counseling and psychotherapy, Gross suggests that the personality characteristics of the counselor, the shared world view between counselor and client, and the expectations of the process held by the client are more important than specific techniques. He dissects psychoanalysis, the new therapies (TA, est, primal scream, and the like), behavioral therapies, and cognitive approaches.

Further references

Anton, Jane. "Intensive Experimental Designs: A Model for the Counselor/Researcher." *Personnel and Guidance Journal,* 56 (January 1978), 273–278.

Atkinson, Donald R., Michael J. Furlong, and Dean S. Janoff. "A Four Component Model for Proactive Accountability in School Counseling." *The School Counselor,* 26 (March 1969), 222–228.

Fink, Alan M., Patricia Grandjean, Michael Martin, and Barrett G. Bertolini. "Service Delivery and High School Peer Counseling Systems." *Personnel and Guidance Journal,* 57 (October 1978), 80–83.

Frey, David H. "Science and the Single Case in Counseling Research." *Personnel and Guidance Journal,* 56 (January 1978), 263–268.

Goldman, Leo. "Toward More Meaningful Research," *Personnel and Guidance Journal,* 55 (February 1977), 363–368.

Gladstein, Gerald A. "Integrating Objective and Subjective Methods in Guidance Program Evaluation." *Measurement and Evaluation in Guidance,* 12 (April 1979), 14–18.

Jones, Lawrence J., and Robert M. DeVault. "Evaluation of a Self-Guided Career Exploration System: The Occu-Sort." *The School Counselor,* 26 (May 1979), 334–341.

Knapper, Everette Q. "Counselor Accountability," *Personnel and Guidance Journal,* 57 (September 1978), 27–30.

McCord, Joan. "A Thirty-Year Follow-Up of Treatment Effects." *American Psychologist,* 33 (March 1978), 284–289.

Mehrens, William A. "Rigor and Reality in Counseling Research." *Measurement and Evaluation in Guidance,* 11 (April 1978), 8–13.

Neufeldt, Susan Siegel. "Client Cognitive Characteristics and Preferences for Counseling Approaches." *Journal of Counseling Psychology,* 25 (May 1978), 184–187.

Sarris, Jean. "Vicissitudes of Intensive Life History Research." *Personnel and Guidance Journal,* 56 (January 1978), 269–272.

Smith, Mary Lee, and Gene V. Glass. "Meta-Analysis of Psychotherapy Outcome Studies." *American Psychologist,* 32 (September 1977), 752–760.

Stokes, Joseph, and Gary Lautenschlager. "Development and Validation of the Counselor Response Questionnaire." *Journal of Counseling Psychology,* 25 (March 1978), 157–163.

Thoresen, Carl E. "Making Better Science, Intensively." *Personnel and Guidance Journal,* 56 (January 1978), 279–282.

18   The education and credentialing of counselors

This chapter describes the current status of counselor education programs, the standards used to evaluate counselor education, and the credentialing of counselors. Attaining competence in counselor skills and attitudes is presumably a lifetime commitment. Certainly, four years of college and one or two years of graduate study do not guarantee complete mastery or understanding of all that is involved in becoming a counselor.

The current status of counselor preparation

Hollis and Wantz[1] have charted the expansion of counselor education programs. Institutions that offered counselor preparation numbered 453 in 1976, an increase of about 35 percent from 1964. Expansion took place not only because new programs emerged in colleges and universities that had not previously engaged in such work but because existing programs expanded in numbers of students and staff. In 1979, the 453 programs were estimated to produce some 1,200 counselors prepared at the undergraduate level; some 20,000 counselors at the master's-degree level; 700 sixth-year counselors, and 1,000 at the doctorate level.

This rapid expansion of counselor education programs has aroused concern not only about the quality of counselor education but also about its quantity, the number of programs actually needed to prepare counselors. Needless to say, much diversity exists in both quality and quantity and improvements are being sought actively.

The character of counselor education

There are many who have set down the characteristics of an effective counselor education program. Krumboltz, for

example, proposed four criteria for desired behavior on the part of those who participate in such a program.

1. The counselor should learn for each individual client to specify the objectives of counseling in terms of changes in the client's behavior mutually desired by client and counselor.
2. The counselor should learn to apply facts about the learning process to the modification of client behavior.
3. The counselor should learn that the responses of his client, not the judgment of his practicum supervision, provide the criterion for judging the success of his counseling.
4. The counselor should learn to examine the research literature and to participate in research studies in order to find improved ways of helping clients.[2]

Parker[3] has identified and discussed five issues in counselor education that illustrate much of the present character of such programs. The first is whether counselor preparation should be viewed as training or education. The second is whether the program should focus on personal development of the counselor or on mastering a body of knowledge and skills. The third issue is whether students in such programs should be evaluated. The fourth issue is whether prospective counselors should be taught one systematic approach or exposed to many with encouragement to select and construct an approach that fits them. The fifth issue is whether clients or supervisors are the best source of feedback regarding counseling effectiveness. Parker concluded that:

> The five issues have a seemingly common polarity. Theorists who emphasize empirical approaches to the ac-

[1] Joseph W. Hollis and Richard A. Wantz, *Counselor Education Directory—1977* (Muncie, Ind.: Accelerated Development, 1977).

[2] John D. Krumboltz, "Changing the Behavior of Behavior Changers," *Counselor Education and Supervision*, 6 (Spring 1967, Special Issue), 222–229.

[3] Clyde A. Parker, "Issues, Evidence, and a Beginning," in *Counseling Theories and Counselor Education*, ed., Clyde A. Parker (Boston: Houghton Mifflin Company, 1968), pp. 4–7.

cumulation of knowledge and its dissemination tend to see counselor education as rational rather than experiential, as education rather than training, as requiring carefully evaluated controlled growth rather than allowing self-development, as containing a body of knowledge and techniques universally applicable in counseling rather than depending on individual counselor approaches, and as relying on supervisor knowledge rather than client feedback. Theorists at the other pole emphasize the experiential, self-development, and the importance of individualized approaches or theories of counseling.[4]

The major purpose of any counselor education program is to facilitate an individual's personal and professional development. Most programs are designed to encourage students to develop (1) human relationship skills, (2) technical skills (understanding tests, and so on), and (3) conceptual skills (theorizing and explaining) so they can function as counseling professionals. Blocher[5] reasoned that the counselor in preparation draws on program resources involving certain response modes. He identified three such response modes. The first is the *immediate-intuitive,* or that of doing what feels right is the basis for behavior. The experiential process is emphasized through sensitivity training or variants of small group work. Such modes stress supportive functions, communication and feedback, and awareness of interpersonal behavior. Personal experience, paramount in such programs, constitutes what Hallberg labels the *silent curriculum* in many programs.[6]

The second response mode available to the counselor in preparation, according to Blocher, is the *cognitive-theoretical,* in which some set of cognitive structures is used to assign meanings to the individual's perceptions of the interpersonal situations. Programs characterized by this response mode stress didactic activities such as reading, lectures, discussions, and laboratories.

The third response mode is the *empirical-pragmatic,* or determination of one's behavior by what gives predictable results. Preparation programs characterized by this response mode stress practicum, research, and internship activities so that the counselor can test skills and knowledge. Feedback to the counselor from clients, not just supervisors, is highly important and differentiates this mode from the first two modes. Presumably, the counselor in a preparation program that supplies all three response modes integrated into a cohesive, consistent pattern of behavior would be truly effective.

Jones[7] has reported the results of a 1974 national survey of the program and enrollment characteristics of counselor education. Some three fourths of the counselor education institutions expected to make their programs competency-based within a two-to-five-year period. The universities reported a strong preference for recruiting ethnic minorities and women to fill professional positions and the mean ratio of faculty members to graduate students was 1 to 8. A major finding was that large numbers of counselors have been graduating, too many for the positions available. Given this last finding, Moracco[8] suggested that the Association for Counselor Education and Supervision (ACES) establish a commission to publicize the problem and to censor programs that failed to meet standards for preparing counselors.

Selection of counselors

An urgent problem in counselor education is selecting those who are to become counselors. Practicing counselors should be concerned because professional groups are judged by their members. However, there is no intention here to imply that practicing counselors are responsible for screening out unlikely candidates for admission to counselor education. That duty rightfully belongs to the college or university where preparation is sought.

Few individuals involved in counseling in any capacity disagree with the proposition that selection of prospective

[4] Ibid., p. 7.
[5] Donald H. Blocher, "Counselor Education: Facilitating the Development of a Helping Person," in *Counseling Theories and Counselor Education,* ed. Clyde A. Parker (Boston: Houghton Mifflin Company, 1968), pp. 133–144.
[6] Edmond C. Hallberg, "The Silent Curriculum in Counselor Education," *Personnel and Guidance Journal,* 50 (November 1971), 198–201.
[7] Lawrence K. Jones, "A National Survey of the Program and Enrollment Characteristics of Counselor Education Programs," *Counselor Education and Supervision,* 15 (March 1976), 166–176.
[8] John Moracco, "Another Look at the National Survey: The Problem Won't Go Away," *Counselor Education and Supervision,* 17 (December 1977), 150–153.

counselors is important and should be done rigorously. But no exact criteria for evaluating candidates for admission have yet been established. Some research has focused on predictions of counselor effectiveness, but there appears to be no one yardstick for measuring probable success or failure. Generally, the individual's initial decision to seek admission to counselor education involves self-selection and is purely voluntary. If serious weaknesses become evident, however, somewhere along the line a decision to reject him or her as a counselor candidate must be made by the preparing institution.

Typical criteria for admission to counselor education programs include the candidate's undergraduate grade-point average, a measure of academic ability such as the *Miller Analogies Tests* or the *Graduate Record Examination* (ability section), results of personality inventories such as the *Edwards Personal Preference Schedule* or the *Guilford-Zimmerman Temperament Survey*, and results of interest inventories such as the *Strong-Campbell Interest Inventory* or the *Kuder Occupational Interest Survey*. Several investigators have suggested that present devices are most useful in screening out misfits rather than making fine discriminations regarding degrees of potential effectiveness. An increasing number of institutions request that individuals who express interest in entering counselor education be personally interviewed by staff members before action is taken on their applications.

Currently, most counselor education institutions place substantial reliance on intellective measures in selecting candidates. These estimate whether the individual can succeed in graduate study and usually work best to eliminate those who could not cope intellectually with course work. But study after study suggests that nonintellective variables are of crucial significance to effective counseling. Because of this dilemma, the search for an objective approach to assess nonintellective variables goes on.

Given well-defined selection criteria that are applied stringently, some students are admitted to counselor education programs who do not successfully complete graduate degrees. In some cases they withdraw of their own volition; in others, they are asked to leave as soon as the evidence becomes known. Still another kind of error in selection procedures is the rejection of applications from students who can and do succeed elsewhere, sometimes brilliantly. Errors of this kind are a result of many factors. First, an honest mistake may have been made in estimating the rejected applicant's potential because undue weight was given to one or more of the selection criteria (for example, a recommendation, a test score, marginal grades). Second, the student's application papers may have had such omissions as a missing transcript or a late letter of recommendation. Third, the error may have been made because the application was compared to a set of far superior applications. (This "context effect" can, of course, work in the opposite way; an ordinary application may look very good compared with a set of poor papers.)

Redfering and Biasco,[9] based on data collected from fifty-nine institutions, investigated actual and ideal procedures in the selection and elimination of candidates for counselor preparation program. The rank order of the *most used criteria* in actual selection procedures was (1) grade-point average, (2) interview, (3) test scores, (4) letters of recommendation, (5) personal knowledge of candidate, (6) work experience, (7) undergraduate major, and (8) unstructured tasks. The relationship between actual and ideal criteria yielded a rank-order coefficient of correlation of .66. In eliminating candidates for admission and retention, grade-point average followed by committee action and practicum grades were used most frequently. The investigators concluded that a considerable discrepancy exists between what counselor educators would like to and actually use as criteria for admission and retention.

Selection for counselor training is viewed as a continuous process that takes place not only at the point of admission to the program but throughout as well as at completion of preparation. Selection as a concept, therefore, has continuous applicability to admission, didactic course enrollment, practicum and field practice enrollments, and job placement. After entry, screening should be undertaken in respect to how well students perform in course work, how well they are able to meet the demands of supervised experiences, and how ready they are for an entry-level counseling position. However, dismissal of a student who has gained entry into a program is painful to all concerned. Although it is sometimes done, it is not desirable for those in counselor education to allow "borderline" students to pass through and be

[9] David L. Redfering and Frank Biasco, "Selection and Elimination of Candidates in Counselor Education Programs," *Counselor Education and Supervision*, 15 (June 1976), 298–304.

granted degrees. Presumably, no university program of any kind is free of this kind of problem. In truth, both the discipline and the student suffer from it.

Content in counselor education

Counselor education content varies from state to state and from institution to institution both in quantity of offerings and in quality. Content—courses and experiences provided to students—has long been shaped by state counselor certification programs. Usual offerings include such required courses as the following:

An introductory course (guidance, community or agency counseling, elementary school, college, and so on)
Career theory, development, information
Tests and measurements
Counseling theories and techniques
Developmental psychology (child or adolescent)
Supervised counseling experiences
Guidance program development

Major influences on the selection of content for counselor education programs include (1) Wrenn's *The Counselor in a Changing World*, (2) the National Defense Education Act (NDEA) Counseling and Guidance Institute programs, and (3) the process of developing and adopting counselor preparation standards. Wrenn recommended that a two-year counselor preparation program incorporate a core in psychology, a core in the social sciences (sociology, economics, and so on), a core in counseling and supervised experiences, and a core in educational philosophy, curriculum, and research.[10] The NDEA Counseling and Guidance Institute demonstrated the need and desirability for full-time study and supervised counseling experiences. Development and adoption of the standards dramatized the need for a minimum floor of preparation.

Although little attention in the research literature has been given to content directed to teaching or learning coun-

seling theory, Brammer[11] has suggested that theory should pervade the entire counselor education program. But early in the program, a thorough exposure should be given to various theories of personality with implications for counseling. Following this introduction, both didactic and practicum experiences are needed if the counselor is to make his or her theory explicit. Finally, Brammer recommends a seminar in counseling theory where students can reflect on their practical experiences and personal values and, in effect, engage in personal theory building (see Chapter 11).

More recently, Bergantino[12] has addressed the paradoxical nature involved in teaching counseling theory. Most counseling students are eager to learn *techniques* that work because they believe these techniques will enable them to be good counselors. The paradox, according to Bergantino, is that if students master theory and techniques, they have but tools that distance them from their clients. These tools enable counselors to work *on* clients but not *with* them. Bergantino suggests that what counselors need to do is pay attention to the correctness of their own responses to each client. Presumably "correct" responses come by knowing themselves.

Much more research has gone into the nature of supervised experiences. Some time ago, Johnston and Gysbers, for example, sought to identify the kind of relationship, strategy, and structure employed in supervisory situations.[13] They devised nine situations considered illustrative of typical supervisory contacts with counselor candidates in practicum, and one hundred supervisors indicated their degree of agreement or disagreement with the fifteen alternatives following each situation. Three types of relationships may be identified, Johnston and Gysbers suggest: (1) *paternalistic*, in which counselor candidates are not encouraged to participate in planning supervisory activities; (2) *democratic*, in which candidates participate in supervisory activities; and (3) *laissez faire*, in which supervisors avoid involvement or provide assistance only on request. The

[10] C. Gilbert Wrenn, *The Counselor in a Changing World* (Washington, D.C.: American Personnel and Guidance Association, 1962), pp. 161–168.

[11] Lawrence M. Brammer, "Teaching Counseling Theory: Some Issues and Points of View," *Counselor Education and Supervision*, 5 (Spring 1966), 120–130.
[12] Len Bergantino, "A Theory of Imperfection," *Counselor Education and Supervision*, 17 (June 1978), 286–292.
[13] Joseph A. Johnston and Norman C. Gysbers, "Practicum Supervisory Relationships: A Majority Report," *Counselor Education and Supervision*, 6 (Fall 1966), 3–10.

practicum supervisors expressed preference for democratic relationships. In respect to the strategies employed by supervisors in handling situations, the respondents chose alternatives in which they remained personally involved (demonstration, intervention, evaluation, or discussion). As far as structure went, the respondents expressed preference for alternatives classified as minimal.

More recently, Karr and Geist[14] divided the supervisory approach into either a didactic or an experiential approach. The didactic approach, according to them, involves direct teaching of theory and techniques with emphasis on client behavior and counseling practices. The experiential approach treats trainees' personal feelings and their functioning as counselors. These two investigators studied actual supervision sessions and their relationship to trainee functioning. Nineteen supervision dyads were used and tapes of both the supervision sessions and trainee counseling sessions were collected at three time intervals and rated by two independent judges using the scales by Carkhuff and Berenson to assess empathy, genuineness, specificity, and respect. Supervisor dimensions of genuineness, respect, and specificity were related significantly to trainee level of functioning on these same dimensions for all time intervals, except for respect at the first assessment time and specificity at the second assessment time. However, there was no significant relationship between these qualities and supervisors' empathy level in counseling. Further, trainee perceptions of supervisor offered facilitative conditions as assessed by the *Barrett-Leonard Relationship Inventory*, were not related significantly to their own level of functioning in therapy. Finally, the type of supervision (didactic or experiential) extended to the trainees was not related significantly to higher levels of trainee genuineness and empathy at the third assessment period. The investigators concluded that their investigation offered little support that one type of supervision was superior to the other. The presence of facilitative conditions rather than the supervisory mode, was the more relevant change factor.

Counselor educators who seek to change the curriculum are confronted with a number of issues that must be re-solved. One is selecting content from the many disciplines related to counseling. It is generally insisted that contributions from related disciplines are essential; the problem lies in deciding just what content truly enhances counselor functioning and understanding.

A second major tactical decision is where and how counseling theory is to be presented to students: in a separate course or combined with techniques and practices? Many have expressed dissatisfaction with current modes of exposing students to counseling theories. Presentation of theory is generally characterized as consisting of a motley set of views, some current and some outdated, taught without connecting ties to information obtained in other prior content areas. A middle-ground approach may be the only realistic or practical resolution.

A third issue is whether counseling practicum is to be offered at the beginning and continue throughout preparation or only during the terminal portion. Those who advocate that it be introduced early view it as an opportunity for testing out theory. Those who advocate that it constitutes a terminal experience argue that a foundation of theory, understandings, and skills must be developed before counselors can help counselees professionally and ethically.

Finally, a persisting issue is how much content should be devoted to statistics, testing, and research. Many have been critical about the lack of test and research sophistication among counselors. How can counselor education programs provide carefully selected experiences so that the student acquires more competent skills and understanding of what psychological data and research procedures mean?

Policy decisions in these matters do not come easily. They require continuing reasoning to search out and deal forthrightly with persisting problems. Implementation of change depends on program objectives, local circumstances, staff available, and, last but not least, the degree of compromise that can be struck.

Current developments

An analysis of counselor education since its inception at Harvard in 1911 reveals modification of many kinds, interrelated or interdependent, and to a great extent reflects changes in concepts of counseling as well as change in our society.

[14] Jeffrey T. Karr and Glen O. Geist, "Facilitation in Supervision as Related to Facilitation in Therapy," *Counselor Education and Supervision*, 16 (June 1977), 263–268.

MORE SPECIFIC AND DEFINITIVE IMAGE OF THE COUNSELOR
In many respects the model of the counselor exhibited in counselor education in this country until 1958 was general in character—general in the sense that it was of a professional whose role and functions were diverse and often conflicting. A large number of those who entered counselor education became deans, assistant principals, directors of student activities, or curriculum coordinators. Little attention, time, or effort was devoted to the counseling relationship.

Current counselor education is more restricted in scope in the sense that the model on which it is based is that of establishing and maintaining the counseling relationship. With the emergence of counseling as the primary function of those employed as counselors in diverse settings, modifications have been incorporated in counselor education which in effect limit preparation to that considered appropriate to the counselor (that is, to the demands of counseling). Standards of training and practice have been stepped up and correspondingly, in many programs, fewer electives permitted. Course work in individual and group counseling is being stressed. Appropriate consideration of various theories is included. Study based on case conferences, recordings, role playing, and laboratory experiences is receiving greater attention than ever before.

MORE CONTENT AND EMPHASIS DRAWN FROM THE BEHAVIORAL AND SOCIAL SCIENCES Because it is essential that the counselor understand the dynamics of human behavior and of the individual in his or her culture, programs now require more study in psychology, sociology, and the humanities. Certainly, more programs require candidates to develop greater understanding in child and adolescent psychology, personality theory, and learning theory. The fields of sociology, anthropology, and economics—becoming more evident in counselor education—are viewed as vehicles for providing candidates with a heightened awareness of social forces and cultural changes that impinge on individuals.

MOVE AWAY FROM TRADITIONAL EMPHASIS ON METHODS, MATERIALS, AND TECHNIQUES Integration of theory and practice is sought through a planned sequence of educational experiences that spiral toward more advanced concepts. Counselors are no longer regarded as technicians but are considered to be professionals able to utilize relevant techniques

because they understand human behavior, the community, and complex social forces.

More emphasis is being given to the philosophy and principles of counseling, the nature and range of human characteristics, professional relationships, and ethics governing the counselor's behavior. The "why" of certain factors influencing humankind is examined to enhance skill in analysis and to increase the counselor's capacity for dispassionate judgment, which typifies the professional rather than the technician. Counselor education seeks to make it possible for candidates to pursue knowledge and to master information and attitudes of many kinds so that the professional's grasp of reality is broadened and the deadening hand of traditionalism is reduced.

OPPORTUNITIES TO ACHIEVE SELF-AWARENESS AND SELF-UNDERSTANDING It is essential for counselors to examine their own values and those of society, the sources of their motivation, and their relationships with others. Opportunities are now provided through workshops and T-groups, through individual and group counseling for trainees, and through seminars for thorough examination of the self. Candidates in counselor education extend their personal philosophy and become sensitive to their own outlook and style of dealing with the world. Self-understanding contributes to personal and professional maturity as well as to the capacity for good judgment.

PREPARATION FOR DIVERSE SETTINGS A prominent current development in most counselor education programs has been that increasing numbers of students prepare to serve as counselors in other than educational settings. Counselor preparation programs have been modified so as to equip individuals to serve as counselors in mental health agencies, rehabilitation centers, employment offices, career development programs, centers that served the aged, and so forth. Courses that treat the important elements of these diverse settings have become part of the preparation program.

CAREER COUNSELING BEING STRESSED More and more programs have modified the experiences they provide students to equip them in career development skills. Hansen[15] has

[15] L. Sunny Hansen (chairperson), "ACES Position Paper: Counselor Preparation for Career Development and Career Education," *Counselor Education and Supervision*, 17 (March 1978), 168–179.

presented a position paper addressing counselor preparation on that topic. The paper was developed by a commission from the Association for Counselor Education and Supervision (ACES) and called for changes to be made that would enable counselors to provide leadership and participatory functions in career development programs. Some fifteen areas of career counseling competencies were identified including career assessment, facilitating career decision making, reducing institutional discrimination, sexism and racism, consultation strategies, and so on.

COMPETENCY-BASED PROGRAMS Counselor education programs increasingly have become based on performance objectives that enable assessments to be made of the outcomes of a student's experience. The state of Washington has been a leader in designing and implementing competency-based programs of counselor preparation and state certification. Individuals to be certified as counselors are assessed against behavior objectives. Figure 18.1 depicts the system used by the state of Washington.

Noble[16] has presented ninety counselor competencies judged by fifty counselor educators to be critical or important. Among the critical competencies were (1) adhering to ethical standards; (2) being aware of and not going beyond counseling abilities; (3) attending to client's cognitions, behaviors, and feelings; (4) maintaining confidentiality; (5) accurately describing the client's affective state from nonverbal cues, and the like. Noble states that his study demonstrated that considerable agreement exists among counselor educators that certain competencies should be common to all counselors. However, the movement toward implementing a set of generic counselor competencies will not be easy to complete. Evaluating the appropriate use of these counselor competencies in a preparation program as well as their effectiveness still remains highly subjective.

SUPERVISED COUNSELING EXPERIENCES HAVE BEEN EXTENDED Experiences are provided those in counselor education through laboratories, counseling practicums, and internship. Laboratory experiences are either self-contained or integrated with classroom instruction. They deal with testing, study, and development of case records, observation of ac-

[16] Frank Noble, "Ratings on a Comprehensive Set of Counselor Competencies" (Unpublished paper, 1979).

FIGURE 18.1 **A system for counselor development and certification**

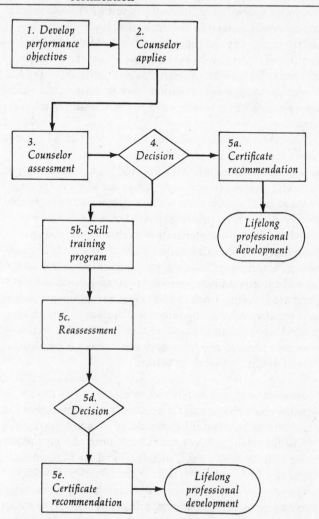

SOURCE: Lawrence M. Brammer and Harry C. Springer, "A Radical Change in Counselor Education and Certification," *Personnel and Guidance Journal*, 49 (June 1971), 806. Copyright © 1971 American Personnel and Guidance Association. Reprinted with permission.

tual counseling, role playing, and the like. Counseling practicum provides experiences in actual individual and group counseling either on or off campus. Internship supplies on-the-job counselor activities under the joint supervision of the local school, clinic, or agency counselor and a university supervisor. The purpose of these supervised experiences is to transform the student counselor into an independently functioning counselor. Supervised experience is seen as the most critical and necessary component of a counselor education program.

Standards for preparing counselors

Serious concerns about the quality of counselor education have led to the development of preparation standards. The major purpose of preparation standards is to improve program quality and effectiveness by identifying the minimal acceptable levels and types of training experiences judged consistent with and appropriate to functions performed by counselors. Another purpose is to provide a degree of uniformity in preparation quality and quantity, therefore giving some assurance of acceptability of counselors to those institutions and agencies that employ them. Still another purpose is that standards give specific content to the profession's concept of ethical practice, so that those who use counseling services can have some confidence in the competence of counselors. Finally, standards provide a foundation on which the credentialing of counselors can be built.

History of standards

The American Personnel and Guidance Association (APGA) became actively involved in developing preparation standards in 1959. For it was then that a five-year grass-roots study of counselor education was started, involving, according to Stripling,[17] over 700 counselor educators, supervisors, and practicing counselors in 50 states working on 150 local committees. That effort was capped in 1964 by the approval of the Association for Counselor Education and

Supervision (ACES) and APGA of "Standards for Counselor Education in the Preparation of Secondary School Counselors." Stripling has been the professional most consistently associated with APGA preparation standards. The major milestones drawn from Stripling's account of the development of preparation standards are outlined here.

1. In 1968, "Standards for the Preparation of Elementary School Counselors" were approved by APGA.
2. In that same year, 1968, an APGA interdivisional committee, composed of members from ACES, the American College Personnel Association and the Student Personnel Association for Teacher Education formulated and published a statement of the role and preparation of the college counselor and other student personnel specialists in junior colleges, colleges and universities.
3. In 1972, an ACES commission was formed that revised and combined the three sets of standards into one document. That document was submitted to ACES membership and adopted overwhelmingly in 1973. In turn, the combined set of standards was approved by the governing boards of both ACES and APGA.
4. In 1978, ACES membership approved "Guidelines for Doctoral Preparation in Counselor Education." Stripling states that these guidelines were to be viewed as an extension upward of the 1973 standards for entry programs of preparation.
5. Associated with these key developments noted by Stripling should be added at least one other. It was that a document entitled "Standards and Criteria for Rehabilitation Counselor Certification" was approved, in 1970, by the American Rehabilitation Counselors Association.

Four major sections compose the 1973 composite standards statement.[18] The first section requires that the institution develop a stated philosophy of education and a set of objectives for counselor education that is consistent with that philosophy. No single philosophy is expressed or implied in the standards. Rather, it is recommended that the philosophy and counselor education objectives be developed

[17] Robert Stripling, "Standards and Accreditation in Counselor Education: A Proposal," *Personnel and Guidance Journal*, 56 (June 1978), 608–611.

[18] American Personnel and Guidance Association, "Standards for the Preparation of Counselors and Other Personnel Services Specialists," *Personnel and Guidance Journal*, 55 (June 1977), 596–601.

cooperatively by staff members and state and local counseling personnel and representatives from related disciplines.

The second section outlines the program of studies and
supervised experiences in counselor education. Full-time
study is recommended. A planned sequence of educational
experiences is to be defined and prerequisites must be identified.

The third section sets forth standards for selection, retention, endorsement, and placement of students.

The fourth section outlines the support, administrative
relations, and institutional resources required for a program
of counselor education. Three full-time qualified staff members are viewed as the minimum in a program. Budgets,
physical facilities, library resources, and student financial
aid are established as essential.

The doctoral guidelines[19] document, now entitled "Standards for Advanced Preparation (Doctoral) in Counselor
Education," has four sections. Section one sets forth the
objectives of doctoral programs in counselor education,
namely, to prepare leaders for counseling, guidance, and
student services. Section two addresses the program of
studies and supervised experiences needed by those at the
doctoral level. Section three outlines the responsibilities
owed by professors to students, including selection, retention, endorsement, and placement. The final part, section
four, identifies the kind and type of institutional support,
administrative relationships, faculty loads, and institutional
resources required to offer advanced graduate preparation in
counselor education.

Current and future developments

An old issue of whether standards are necessary has been
settled. Most counseling professionals believe that the standards represent minimum characteristics that should be
present in any program that prepares counselors. An issue,
present since the origin of the standards, is how and by
whom the standards will be used to accredit counselor education programs. The standards represent criteria by which

programs may be accredited or approved rather than certification of individuals graduating from such programs. The
major problem in program accreditation is the tremendous
expense incurred in conducting such an operation. Additionally, university and college presidents long have sought
to reduce the number of accrediting bodies that visit their
institutions to conduct either *program* or *institutional* accreditation.

These problems were so formidable that during the late
1960s and early 1970s, little progress was made in solving
them. The most substantial achievement during that period was that the ACES Commission on Standards and Accreditation worked with the executive officer of the National Council for the Accreditation of Teacher Education
(NCATE) to establish that (1) the team of educators that
visits institutions that are applicants or renewal applicants
for NCATE membership contain at least one counselor
educator (counselor educator team members are recommended to NCATE by the ACES commission) and (2) those
counselor education programs that meet NCATE approval
be publicized by both NCATE and APGA. The most trou-
bling aspect of that arrangement was that NCATE confined
its review and endorsement to teacher education programs.
Nonschool areas in counselor education, such as rehabilitation counseling, employment counseling, and community agency counseling were not included.

During the 1970s, various proposals were advanced for
accrediting counselor education programs. The first was
that the national organization, the American Personnel and
Guidance Association, be the organization that uses the
standards to approve counselor preparation programs. The
second proposal was that Division 2, ACES, would do so.
Others have proposed that a voluntary association be formed
of institutions that have applied, through self-study, the
counselor education standards and then been visited by an
external evaluation committee.

The ACES Committee for Professional Preparation and
Standards promoted self-study by counselor education institutions. It published a document entitled *Manual for
Self-Study by a Counselor Education Staff*. During 1977, a
nationwide effort was made to have institutions try out a
questionnaire that reported institutions' responses to the
application of the standards to their programs. Simultaneously, Norman Gysbers, then APGA president, appointed a
national committee to examine the host of credentialing

[19] Association for Counselor Education and Supervision, "Guidelines for Doctoral Preparation in Counselor Education," *Counselor
Education and Supervision*, 17 (March 1978), 163–167.

problems confronting the counseling professions and to make recommendations deemed necessary to reduce the problems and advance the profession. The committee, reporting to the APGA board of directors in December 1978, recommended that the APGA: (1) conduct counselor preparation program accreditation, (2) establish a registry of professional counselors, and (3) intensify its leadership efforts in securing counselor licensure laws in the fifty states.[20] The governing board approved the recommendations of this committee. Despite this approval, the future of the standards and their use are far from clear. Nevertheless, it appears more likely than ever before that gains can be made in improving the quality of counselor preparation.

Credentialing counselors

The credentialing of counseling professionals has been a problem for many years but recently it has emerged with considerable force because counselors outside the public school setting have lacked the means of establishing public recognition of what it is they are and do. Forster defines a credential as "anything that provides the basis for confidence, belief, credit, etc.," and "contributes to a sense of confidence in the counselor."[21] In short, a credential is the authority to practice an occupation. The common methods used to credential practitioners of a profession such as counseling were set out by Forster and are summarized here:

1. *Certification.* This process recognizes the competence of practitioners by authorizing them to use the title adopted by the profession. Certification can be awarded by voluntary associations, by governmental bodies, some of which are recognized by state laws. Public school counseling certification, for example, usually has been established by state laws and conducted by state education agencies.
2. *Licensure.* This process, authorized by state legislation, regulates the *practice* and/or the *title* of the profession. Licensure, because of its regulation of *practice,* subjects

[20] Special APGA Committee for Counselor Credentialing, "Final Report," mimeographed (Washington, D.C.: American Personnel and Guidance Association, 1977).
[21] Jerald R. Forster, "What Shall We Do About Credentialing," *Personnel and Guidance Journal,* 55 (June 1977), 573.

violators to greater legal sanctions than certification that grants use of the *title.*
3. *Accreditation.* This process grants public recognition to a school, college, university or one of its programs that meets established criteria as determined by initial and periodic evaluations. Accreditation can be either *institutional* or *program* or both. Regional educational accrediting agencies (such as the North Central Association of Colleges and Secondary Schools) provide institutional approval whereas professional organizations (such as the American Psychological Association) give program approval.

Forster's article is an excellent account of the history associated with credentialing the counseling professions and the issues that have emerged within the last few years. These major historical factors and issues are outlined briefly here.

1. Until recently, few problems of credentialing counselors existed because almost all who were prepared entered educational settings. Those who entered public school settings were credentialed by obtaining counselor certificates from state educational agencies. Their preparation program usually was structured to enable them to meet state certification requirements. Further, most institutions that offered graduate preparation in counselor education had been granted approval by the state educational agency to do so. Individuals who sought employment as counselors in colleges and universities did not have to meet any state certification requirements, except in a few states where community colleges were administered by state educational agencies.
2. Beginning in the early 1970s, more and more individuals were admitted to counselor preparation who sought to practice outside the educational setting. The major factors that accounted, at least in part, for more graduates seeking employment in agencies supported by community or governmental funds were (a) declining enrollments diminished the number of counselor openings in educational settings (see Chapter 2) and (b) increases occurred in the number of agencies that sought to provide counseling.
3. During the 1960s and early 1970s, psychologists sought and obtained state legislation that licensed the *practice* (not just the title) of psychology. These laws, in many states, identified *counseling* among the functions performed by

psychologists who sought licensure to engage in private practice. This tightening of control by psychologists came simultaneously as more and more graduates of counselor education programs sought employment in a broader array of settings.

4. Private and public counseling agencies depend at least in part on revenue generated from "third-party payments" or insurance payments for treating mental health problems. If a comprehensive national health insurance law were passed, those professionals who are licensed will be in a position to provide counseling and other mental health services in any expanded mental health coverage brought about by this national health legislation.

5. Counselors who have sought to engage in the practice of counseling, either for fees or "third party payments," have had to apply and meet licensure as psychologists. Until recently, no state had created a counselor license. Those who sought licensure as psychologists, even those who held doctorates granted by counselor education programs located in schools or departments of education, have had to demonstrate to psychology examining boards that their degree was "primarily psychological in nature."

Sweeney and Witmer[22] present briefly four court cases that have implications for licensure of counselors. These cases include a district judge who ruled that counseling and guidance was a separate profession from psychology (*Weldon* vs. *Virginia State Board of Psychologists' Examiners*) and therefore required regulation separate from psychology; a judge reaffirmed the rights of competent counselors when he dismissed the charges of a psychology board brought against a trained person who was not a licensed psychologist (*Ohio State Board of Psychology* vs. *Cook*); a court in Mississippi directed that state's board of examiners in psychology to license a doctoral-trained person in counseling without examination because of inconsistencies in the board's practices (the board had denied the person the right to take the state examination); a District of Columbia court directed a board to grandfather license a person who was denied by the board. Sweeney and Witmer concluded from these cases and other situations that counselors, under

existing conditions, were being discriminated against in a manner that deprived the public of services it needs and that unjust or indiscriminate enforcement of current licensure laws can be corrected.

The American Personnel and Guidance Association has sought to encourage its members to seek state legislation to license counselors. At this time, only three states, Virginia (in 1976) and Alabama and Arkansas (in 1979) have done so. Cottingham and Warner have identified Ohio and Texas as states where strong efforts have been mounted to secure counselor licensure laws. They also identify Utah and Idaho as starting to do so.[23]

Not all counselors, let alone APGA members, have been enthusiastic about the movement to gain counselor licensure. Some school counselors have been opposed because they had the erroneous idea that as school counselors they would have to meet licensure requirements (licensure would not be required of counselors who confine their practice to public institutions; it regulates those who receive fees for their services). Still other counselors are against licensure for philosophical and practical reasons.

Gross,[24] charges that licensing is misleading in that it promises to, but does not, work in the public interest. Rather, it protects the vested interests of professionals and produces an insidious effect by creating a dependency on professionals, thus reducing the ability of people to care for themselves. An alternative to licensure, according to Gross,[25] would be professional disclosure. Although professional disclosure would not regulate who can or cannot counsel, the disclosure advocated by Gross would include name, business address, telephone number, philosophy of counseling, specifics of formal education, particulars of informal education, association memberships, and fee schedule. The methods of implementing professional disclosure established by state statute would include (1) that disclosure be made to prospective clients (by written statements) before any counseling for which a fee is charged takes place,

[22] Thomas J. Sweeney and J. Melvin Wittmer, "Who Says You're a Counselor?" *Personnel and Guidance Journal*, 55 (June 1977), 589–594.

[23] Harold F. Cottingham and Richard W. Warner, Jr., "APGA and Counselor Licensure: A Status Report," *Personnel and Guidance Journal*, 56 (June 1978), 604–607.
[24] Stanley J. Gross, "The Myth of Professional Licensing," *American Psychologist*, 33 (November 1978), 1009–1016.
[25] Stanley J. Gross, "Professional Disclosure: An Alternative to Licensing," *Personnel and Guidance Journal*, 55 (June 1977), 586–588.

and (2) that a notarized form is filed annually or whenever a change is made in the statement.

The establishment of state counselor licensing laws will not come easily or quickly. Although model legislation to do so has been formulated and presented by the APGA Licensure Commission,[26] getting a law enacted, difficult in itself, is made even more demanding because of the opposition of psychologists and others with vested interests who stand to lose if such a law is passed. Other difficulties include the need to clarify the identity of counselors (see Chapter 6); the definition associated with the word *counseling*; the functions incorporated in counseling. Still another problem is to specify the level of training expected of those who counsel. Despite this complex array of problems associated with counselor licensure, the counseling profession and the public it strives to serve will gain by licensure.

Summary

Counselor education in America is in a process of profound change. A balance is being struck with philosophy, theory, practice, self-exploration, and the like, which seems almost inevitable, because method cannot be taught in the abstract. Content is being ordered more into sequential arrangements. The educational process is coming under scrutiny, and present-day counselor education is stressing mastery of certain competencies. Increasingly, those institutions that prepare counselors will have to meet the standards created by the profession. These standards will become more and more important because the key to becoming credentialed as a helping professional lies in the education one has received. Graduation from an approved counselor education program will enable the graduate to be certified, licensed, or registered as a professional counselor.

Issues

Issue 1 Are two years of full-time, as opposed to one year or part-time graduate study needed to prepare counselors?

[26] APGA Licensure Commission, "Licensure Commission Action Packet," mimeographed (Washington, D.C.: American Personnel and Guidance Association, 1977), 91 pp.

Yes, because
1. The complexity of the counselor's job demands better preparation for effective discharge of his or her obligations.
2. Counselors themselves report that they are inadequately prepared after only a single year of training.
3. Extended periods of practicum and internship experience are needed if counselors are to be adequately prepared. The didactic background courses plus practicum and internship cannot be completed properly in a single year or by part-time study.
4. Part-time study leads to partial and fractionated knowledge and fails to produce an occupational identity as a counselor.

No, because
1. Existing counselor-client ratios demand that counselor supply be increased. The addition of a second year of preparation will curtail the number of counselors available.
2. Requiring two years merely represents empire building by counselor educators, who strive to hold on to students and secure physical facilities simply to increase their own stature in universities.
3. The nature of the counselors' present assignment does not require an additional year of preparation. A second year will isolate them from other personnel, who will view them with suspicion because they have more education.
4. Part-time study is a practical necessity for most since sufficient financial support is unavailable for counselor trainees.

Discussion Basically, this issue turns on the matter of quality versus quantity. There seems to be little to counter the argument that more extensive training, well organized and purposefully directed, will produce a better counselor. Few counselor educators would dispute the fact that continuous full-time study is far superior to disjointed, piecemeal preparation over several years.

Many factors could be cited that inhibit the quick acceptance of two years of full-time study. Not the least is the discontinuance of counselor education programs that lack the staff and resources necessary to provide more than occasional courses on a part-time basis.

Issue 2 How can existing professional standards for preparing counselors be implemented?

Implementation should be left to the judgment of each educational institution, because
1. Application of standards fosters inflexibility and tends to stifle innovation.
2. Application of externally derived standards impinges upon institutional and academic freedom.

Implementation should be administered through an agency independent from counselor education institutions, because
1. Professionalization will be attained only when members of the profession assume responsibility for the quality preparation of those who enter its ranks.
2. Institutional self-evaluation would be ineffective because vested interests have to be protected and many programs would constantly be moving toward meeting standards.
3. Implementation of standards is a pressing responsibility because its ultimate aim is to protect the consumer of counseling service by assuring at least minimal quality of practitioners.

Discussion This is a salient issue in contemporary counselor education. Beginning in 1960 and up to the present time professional groups such as ACES and the American School Counselor Association (ASCA) have made a tremendous effort to formulate standards for counselor education. During the past decade the standards have been developed, published, tried, and refined. The profession is now confronted with taking the extremely difficult step of implementing them.

The issue resolves itself into the fundamental question: how should the standards be enforced? One alternative is independent, voluntary institutional application through self-study followed by responsible action to improve in areas the institution finds itself lacking. Presumably, subtle forces such as program reputation, the persuasive efforts of professional groups, public opinion, and awareness of shortcomings would gradually bring compliance with the standards. A second alternative would be a step short of formal accreditation but would involve fairly formalized procedures designating approved preparation programs by a committee of a professional association. The committee would study, evaluate, and publish listings of approved programs after making judgments based on the standards. The most rigorous form of application would be the enforcement of the standards by a formal accrediting association. Without doubt the latter

step would accomplish the quickest compliance. Undoubtedly it would also reduce the number of institutions that purport to prepare counselors.

Issue 3 Should counselor preparation be conducted at the undergraduate level?

Yes, because
1. Existing graduate-level education requires too much time in preparation.
2. The vagueness and level of generality that characterizes the content of counselor preparation do not warrant graduate status.
3. Considerable financial savings could accrue to both the individual and the employing institution if counselors could enter the profession on completion of undergraduate degrees.

No, because
1. The counselor's work requires a mature and widely experienced individual.
2. Counselor preparation consists of specialized graduate-level content built on broad undergraduate preparation in the social and behavioral sciences.
3. Within the traditional status hierarchy of schools and other institutions, undergraduate-trained counselors would be at a disadvantage in comparison with professionals with advanced degrees.

Discussion This issue surfaced during the early 1970s and has become the focal point of much heated discussion at professional meetings, particularly when training standards and certification requirements are under discussion. To many, adoption of undergraduate preparation represents a step backward and undercuts efforts invested in developing standards and upgrading the profession. Others view it as an innovation long needed to infuse life into a field weighed down by the past.

At least two states, Texas and South Carolina, have adopted certification regulations that permit counselors with only undergraduate training to be employed in public schools. However, it should be noted that in Texas certification as a professional school counselor requires a year of graduate preparation. This underscores the fact that some who advocate undergraduate preparation of counselors view it as a subprofessional entry point or as incomplete education for the professional counselor.

We believe that preparation of professional counselors should remain in graduate programs. The effectiveness of the counselor depends on a broad understanding of the individuals with whom he or she works and the complex, varied factors that influence individuals. This understanding requires extensive, in-depth study in those fields that can contribute necessary understanding and knowledge. To eliminate the breadth obtained in undergraduate work and substitute premature specialization would only serve to substantiate the claims of many critics that counselors are ill-prepared to deal with the concerns of their clients. Moreover, premature specialization at the undergraduate level requires a vocational commitment that few are prepared to make.

Issue 4 At what point should supervised experiences be introduced in the preparation of counselors?

At entry, because
1. Such experiences facilitate the early development of an occupational identity.
2. These experiences represent an ideal example of learning by doing and enable the enrollee to test out theory.

After familiarization with basic skills, because
1. A minimal professional competence is required to maximize counselor learning as well as to ensure gainful client experience.
2. Ethics demand that some minimal screening of counselors in the areas of skills and personal characteristics precede contact with clients.

Discussion Supervised experience is viewed as the focal point for the integration and synthesis of prior didactic and laboratory work in counselor training. Didactic preparation and laboratory experience lead directly to application in actual counseling activity in practicum and internship under supervision. Sequential programs result in preparation that progresses logically toward increased responsibility for real counseling activities. It is the consensus of most counselor educators that preparatory work, particularly in the areas of educational and occupational information, testing and appraisal techniques, and counseling theory and technique, is

requisite to adequate performance when the candidate assumes individual responsibility for clients. Besides, synthesis of prior learnings and new learning increments appears to occur best when adequate preparation in these content areas precedes application in the actual counseling setting.

Usually laboratory experiences are integrated with course work. Courses taken during the first year of the two-year program have laboratory sessions devoted to application of statistical procedures, familiarization with tests, observation of interviews, familiarization and analysis of occupational materials, role playing, use of case records, and the like. These are a continuing part of counselor education.

Usually, practicum activities consist of direct counseling experience with elementary, high school, college students, and/or other clients drawn from the community. Close supervision is given to candidates engaged in individual counseling of clients. Ideally, supervision employs direct observation, tape recordings, and video tapes.

Most counselor educators believe that the nature of the supervisory process determines in large measure the success with which counselors begin to function independently. Careful attention is given at all times to observing trainees as they work with clients; the supervisor normally evaluates the counselor's progress in such aspects as rapport, structure, empathy, content variables, and process variables Practicum supervisors are available for immediate consultations with counselors as well as for scheduled case conference discussions. In all supervised contacts precautions are taken to protect counselees in accordance with the ethical principles of the profession.

After the student counselor has completed contact with the counselee, conferences between the counselor and the supervisor clarify counselor-counselee interaction or deal with specifics needing attention. Counselor and supervisor review the many aspects of the interview. They tend to move from an instructor-student relationship to a more process-oriented relationship. The chief focus of these conferences is the progress and professional development of counselors. They discuss their actions, feelings, and attitudes, their perceptions of the client, and the client's needs and resources. In case conferences conducted with small groups of student counselors other trainees attending the conference relate their perceptions of the case, question the counselor and supervisor about any variable, and make suggestions for the participant.

Annotated references

APGA Licensure Commission. "Licensure Commission Action Packet." Mimeographed. Washington, D.C.: American Personnel and Guidance Association, 1977. 91 pp.

Presents the case for counselor licensure, the legislative steps to be taken to secure such legislation, and sample or model bills.

Koocher, Gerald P. "Credentialing in Psychology." *American Psychologist*, 34 (August 1979), 696–702.

Reviews existing credentialing systems in relation to competence. The author classifies credentialing by types and concludes that no existing type provides assurance of competence.

Parker, Clyde A., ed. *Counseling Theories and Counselor Education*. Boston: Houghton Mifflin Company, 1968. 166 pp.

Papers are presented that were prepared for an invited seminar on counselor education. Authors include Clyde A. Parker, Jack R. Gibb, Harold B. Pepinsky, C. H. Patterson, Forrest L. Vance, Edward S. Bordin, Donald H. Clocker, and Charles B. Truax. Excerpts from the discussions are also given.

Further references

Atkinson, Donald R., and Jules M. Zimmer. "The Counselor Trainee Portfolio," *Counselor Education and Supervision*, 16 (June 1977), 257–262.

Carrol, Marguerite R., Fredrica G. Halligan, and Shirley A. Griggs. "The Licensure Issue: How Real Is It?" *Personnel and Guidance Journal*, 55 (June 1977), 577–580.

Cottingham, Harold F., and Richard Warner. "APGA and Counselor Licensure: A Status Report." *Personnel and Guidance Journal*, 56 (June 1978), 604–607.

Davis, Kathleen L., and H. Arvey. "Dual Supervision: A Model for Counseling and Supervision." *Counselor Education and Supervision*, 17 (June 1978), 293–299.

Ford, Julian D. "Research on Training Counselors and Clinicians." *Review of Educational Research*, 39 (Winter 1979), 87–130.

Forster, Jerald R. "Counselor Credentialing Revisited." *Personnel and Guidance Journal*, 56 (June 1978), 593–598.

Forster, Jerald S. "What Shall We Do About Credentialing?" *Personnel and Guidance Journal*, 55 (June 1977), 573–576.

Gross, Stanley J. "The Myth of Professional Licensing," *American Psychologist*, 33 (November 1978), 1009–1016.

Gurk, Mitchell D., and Edward A. Wicas. "Generic Models of Counseling Supervision: Counseling/Instruction Dichotomy and Consultation Metamodel." *Personnel and Guidance Journal*, 57 (April 1979), 402–407.

Mahon, Bruce R., and Hal A. Altmann. "Skill Training: Cautions and Recommendations," *Counselor Education and Supervision*, 17 (September 1977), 42–50.

McGreevy, C. Patrick. "Training Consultants: Issues and Approaches." *Personnel and Guidance Journal*, 56 (March 1978), 432–435.

Messina, James J. "Why Establish a Certification System for Professional Counselors?" *American Mental Health Counselors Association Journal*, 1 (January 1979), 9–22.

Stahl, Earl, and Robert I. Havens. "The Case for ACES Program Accreditation." *Counselor Education and Supervision*, 17 (March 1978), 180–187.

Stripling, Robert O. "Standards and Accreditation in Counselor Education: A Proposal." *Personnel and Guidance Journal*, 56 (June 1978), 608–611.

19 Trends in counseling

Counseling, as it is known today, did not, like Minerva, spring fully grown from the head of Jupiter. Rather, it is the logical outgrowth of historical forces and factors (see Chapter 2) that produced persistence of some features and change in others. To suggest that the current status of counseling was arrived at in that manner is to ascribe to a viewpoint of change classified by Hays[1] as being *extrapolation*. He explains that extrapolators project the future from current and past developments. Two other types of futurists were noted by Hays: one was the *romantic* who believes that changes take place because individuals create new lifestyles that change the system; the other was the *system thinkers* who believe that transformations come because they were managed by humans who create the methods to move from the present into a projected future.

Setting forth the trends in counseling is similar in nature to describing change in counseling. For counseling itself is sought not primarily for enlightenment about the unchangeable past but because of dissatisfaction with the present and a desire to better the future. Neither the precise directions nor the degree of change is known beforehand by either the counselee or the counselor. But a change in the current situation is required, and once begun, however small, necessitates other minor changes, and a snowballing effect of these minor changes leads to more significant changes in accord with the client's potentials. Whether the changes in the counseling profession are evanescent, permanent, or evolve into other changes is of vital importance in gaining a grasp of where counseling has been and where it is likely to go.

Watzlawick and his associates have noted that "The French proverb according to which the more something changes the more it remains the same is more than a witticism. It is a wonderfully concise expression of the puzzling and paradoxical relationship between persistence and change."[2] As counselors reflect on current conditions, they can see the truth of the proverb: social crises all around, intense and agonizing questioning of counselor practices, new theories of counseling, the emergence of new generalizations about counseling outcomes. Which will fade or endure? Which will prove harmful or helpful? Important as these questions may be, counselors must wait for answers, even though waiting is a luxury they cannot afford.

This chapter identifies and describes some trends that are taking place in counseling. Some counseling innovations come and go, but their effects, like radiation, accumulate in the practices and ideas from which they emerged and they have residual effects. Trends in counseling must be viewed, at least in part, as a function of a larger society going through one of the most difficult periods of its history. Time is rapidly closing in on George Orwell's biting, prophetic novel *1984*, which postulated a world inimical to human freedom, beset by totalitarianism and dehumanization. More recent predictions about 1984 by Richard A. Easterlin are far more optimistic about life. Collins[3] reports that Easterlin's predictions have been based on a previously unknown demographic structure: the relationship between the number of younger workers and the total population that affects fertility, future census patterns, and everything from unemployment to the divorce rate and the women's movement. Among his predictions were that the 1980s would be a time in which (1) crime rates will lower, (2) rising divorce rates will slow down, (3) fertility will increase, (4) political alienation among the young will lessen, (5) rising unemployment and accelerating inflation will moderate, (6) suicide rates among young men will decline, (7) the relative income of young men will improve, (8) more older women will be employed in the labor market, (9) college enroll-

[1] Donald G. Hays, "2001: A Counseling Odyssey," *Personnel and Guidance Journal*, 57 (September 1978), 17–21.

[2] Paul Watzlawick, John H. Weakland, and Richard Fisch, *Change* (New York: W. W. Norton & Company, 1974), p. 1.

[3] Glenn Collins, "The Good News About 1984," *Psychology Today* (January 1979), 34–48.

ments will rise, and (10) the level of *Scholastic Aptitude Test* scores will rise.

These extrapolations have implications for education, politics, and the overall quality of life in the 1980s. But changes do not affect all counselors simultaneously or equally. Some bitterly resent them; others stubbornly resist them. Some become confused, fearful, and uncertain and, because of this, attempt to ignore change. For others, counseling is sometimes viewed as being a move from one contretemps to another. But most counselors are pragmatic professionals who are concerned about the usefulness of their practices, reflective about their goals, and quick to question established policy and practice. The trends in counseling set forth here have been organized into three categories. Of course, overlap among categories cannot be totally avoided.

General trends

Trend 1

New systems of counseling and psychotherapy will continue to emerge and flourish. Examination of the present counseling scene reveals a proliferation of counseling theories or therapies that range from respectable to far out, emphasizing everything from self-understanding to insight into one's unconscious to body awareness. New counseling systems rise and fall like pop songs, and popular psychology magazines feature their emergence, but not their decline. An element common to both the new and the old systems is that they hold forth the promise of learning about oneself and others, about feelings and about behavior. They suggest hypotheses and techniques directed toward explaining how people acquire knowledge, attitudes, and skills: knowledge such as why people react as they do toward certain people; attitudes such as the expectation of success rather than failure; and skills such as handling interpersonal relationships. Essentially, these systems represent attempts to describe how people learn and how they cope.

New models that challenge the status quo will continue to be conceptualized. Those who formulate them will claim their system is the best one for helping people assess and understand their behavior, of knowing how they have learned to behave, of coping with the human paradoxes and dilemmas.

Trend 2

Career counseling increasingly will become a dominant force in counselor practice, theory, and research. Counseling directed toward making or narrowing down career choices always has been a prominent theme in the work of counselors. Beyond the narrow fact of choice, broadened views of what is involved—life roles and lifestyles; special needs of women, minorities, and the handicapped; and use of computer technology, to cite but a few—have brought forth models, strategies, and competencies that enable counselors to help individuals manage their career development. More and more agencies, schools, and universities are specifying *career* counselor when they publicize staff openings. Career counseling will intensify in future years because it is viewed as being integral both to the continuing development of the individual and as a crucial vehicle for reforming social programs. Career counselors are viewed as capable of helping many individuals—bilingual persons, correctional populations, disadvantaged persons, out-of-school adults, and individuals living in rural and inner cities—locate and enter appropriate educational opportunities, find and hold jobs, and progress through their career. Moreover, career counselors are expected to give special attention to the problems of sex bias and sex stereotyping in education and careers. Career counseling will be at the focal point of even more future federal legislation that will augment and strengthen this trend.

Trend 3

Increasing numbers of counselors will be employed in a great variety of settings. This projection is easily documented by reference to the increased numbers of counselors employed from year to year and by the amounts of money spent for salaries and on preparation programs. During the 1960s the annual growth rate for counselor employment was approximately 6 percent. Projections for the 1980s indicate that the annual growth rate will be approximately 3 percent. Counseling services have been extended downward into elementary schools and upward into higher education. Nonschool demands for counselors have increased in community action programs, the CETA program, and the like. There is every indication that such demands will continue but at a rate somewhat below that of the 1960s and 1970s.

Obviously, well-trained counselors have the advantage in competing for employment. This enables them not only to choose their work setting discriminatingly but to be influential in determining its work demands and defining the services offered.

Trend 4

Professionalization in counseling will intensify. Professional organizations will become more and more influential in interpreting counselor role and functions. A greater proportion of counselors will participate actively in professional organizations that work to determine the direction, influence, and growth of the work of the counselor. Increased professionalization among school counselors parallels longer and better training programs. It will continue to facilitate the development of the image counselors desire and make it easier for them to extend to clients the kind of helping relationship that they deem appropriate to the work setting.

Trend 5

Accountability in counselor education and counseling practice will continue to exert influence. Recent emphasis on accountability applies to all settings, including the preparation of counselors and the services they provide after they are employed. Undoubtedly, advances in greater specification of objectives, more clearly defined functions, and improved evaluation procedures will benefit both the profession and the public it serves.

Trend 6

Licensure of counselors for practice in noneducational settings, independent of psychology licensing laws, will become a reality in state after state. Currently, counselor licensing laws have been enacted only in three states, but counselors are actively pursuing such legislation in many states. Cottingham[4] has identified some of the gov-

ernmental, political, legal, economic, and professional forces that serve to accelerate or to inhibit the movement to establish counselor licensure. He points out, among other things, that counselors have little national visibility or creditability as professionals and this hinders the development of a common image among the public, government, and industry. But he suggests that as a professional group, counselors can work toward identification of counseling functions legally distinct from those included in psychology licensure.

Trends in counselor education and supervision

Trend 7

Modifications in counselor education programs will continue but at a slower rate than in the past decade. Massive changes have occurred, particularly if one compares counselor education of the 1950s to that of the 1970s. Improvement in quality stemmed from intensification of two areas present in high-quality programs: an interdisciplinary core of course work and extended supervised counseling experiences (practicum, field practice, and/or internship).

Much study has been devoted to the contributions that related disciplines can make to the preparation of counselors. Without doubt, the most directly contributory will be the disciplines of psychology and sociology. They are most closely related to, and indeed frequently undergird, the work of the counselor. It is highly probable that extended core programs will continue to rely more heavily on knowledge from these fields than in the past.

Laboratory work and direct experience with real clients currently enjoy a favored position in quality preparation programs. Probably they will be emphasized to a greater degree both by spreading them throughout the training period and by intensifying the amount and diversifying the kind of experiences provided, particularly in the later stage of training. As the demand for counselors for nonschool agencies increases, supervised practicum and internship experiences in a wider variety of settings will become available. In all probability counselor education programs will attempt to integrate the advantages of nonschool settings with school-related experiences. The focus will be on breadth and variety of experience rather than preparation for work within a specific setting.

[4] Harold F. Cottingham, "Impelling Forces for Counselor Licensure: A Capsule Summary," *The School Counselor*, 25 (May 1978), 330–334.

Supervisory practices will be refined and will make better use of the mechanical paraphernalia facilitating the supervision process. Most notable so far is video-taping of interview sessions, which is far superior to sound recordings and frequently has the advantage of being less disruptive than direct observation. A benefit not to be overlooked in the use of video tape is the flexibility provided in scheduling supervisory activities. Most high-quality counselor education programs are attentive to student input and will continue to incorporate their contributions. Undoubtedly caution will be exercised in this area as it is in the inclusion of all new modifications.

Trend 8

Supervision and education will continue after initial entry into the counseling field. Improved and extended training as well as the movement toward professionalization will combine to force continued study and upgrading among counseling practitioners. The arrival of better qualified personnel will result in extended on-the-job supervision of novice counselors. As the number of agencies employing several counselors increases, it will be essential that their activities be coordinated and supervised. This activity will go beyond mere administrative overseeing. It will be similar to the supervision received in counseling practicum and internship experiences.

If counselors are to become true professionals, they are obligated to upgrade their skills continuously, both by formal education and by additional in-service training. Used in this context, in-service education involves professional upgrading of counseling skills and personal development.

Trend 9

Counselor education programs increasingly will become competency based. The key idea in formulating competencies or performance objectives is that students develop and demonstrate the actual skills deemed useful in performing as counselors in given settings. Traditionally, graduate counselor education programs have concentrated on the courses taken, credits earned, and the cognitive outcomes of the experience rather than actual performance, either in

simulated or real-life situations, of the counseling skills. While competency-based preparation of counselors is in its infant stage, it seems likely that it will intensify, although its development will be slower than many have speculated. A major criticism of competency-based counselor preparation is that focusing on skills is insufficient because the counseling relationship is a process in which being helpful depends on how counselors use their personal qualities, the "self." It should be noted that few experimental studies have been undertaken as to the comparative effects of competency-based and conventional counselor preparation programs. However, as the research on the matter is now underway, and as the primitive models of counselor competencies are refined, sizable changes will take place in the preparation of counselors. Further, these changes will mean that the mechanics of instruction will evolve. Teaching methods, materials, and sequences, for all practical purposes, are inseparable from educational processes and goals. It will be necessary to deploy old instructional mechanics in different ways and invent new techniques and materials to enable students to learn predetermined counseling competencies.

Trend 10

The American Personnel and Guidance Association will undertake accreditation of counselor education programs. Success of the licensure movement (see *Trend 5*) is dependent, in large measure, on implementing quality control measures in the preparation of counselors to equip them to perform the functions for which they are licensed. At the present time, the counseling profession has made substantial progress toward program accreditation by adopting the "Standards for the Preparation of Counselors and Other Personnel Services Specialists" and the "Guidelines for Doctoral Preparation in Counselor Education" (see Chapter 18). The value and acceptability of these documents have been enhanced by the imperative represented by counselor licensure.

The national organization, APGA, is the association that can provide the leadership for implementing accreditation of counselor preparation programs. The APGA, given its national office, divisional representation, and state branches, appears to be equipped with the human and financial resources necessary to develop and establish the procedures for program approval likely to be acceptable to the Council on Post-Secondary Accreditation, the association representing national accrediting bodies.

Trends in counselor role and function

Trend 11

Increasingly counseling will become a lifetime career commitment. Several factors are instrumental in making counseling attractive as a lifetime career commitment. Nationwide, the salaries of counselors have increased, and consequently institutions have more holding power than ever before. With less discrepancy between administrative salaries and those of personnel in other echelons, the lure of administrative positions is lessened. Furthermore, specialized preparation programs in administration and counseling mitigate against shifting fields of professional endeavor. Paralleling distinctions of training programs is the increasing emphasis on an extended educational experience so that the individual's original choice is one field and his or her investment in securing specialized training operates to produce greater loyalty and commitment to that field.

In addition, the efforts toward professionalization presumably will create a climate in which counselors can strongly identify with a professional group. They will no longer have to move outside their profession to secure the status and recognition that they deserve.

Trend 12

Specialization in counseling will continue and intensify. As public receptivity of counseling services expands, utilization of and expectations for the counselor will become increasingly sophisticated. Knowledge that certain kinds of people can best provide assistance with specific kinds of problems will facilitate choice among the various services. Many agencies and schools now employing several counselors already make work assignments in accordance with the strengths, interests, and skills of their personnel as well as the particular needs of the clientele they serve. Thus, for

example, heavy reliance is placed on one counselor who is an expert in career planning and placement.

Contributing to this trend, as well as those already discussed, is the factor of extended training that will permit the counselor to implement preferences and competencies for certain kinds of counseling activities. Thoroughly trained individuals are more likely to be aware of the fact that they enjoy and do their best work with, for example, clients with educational and vocational problems, whereas others may realistically see their strengths in working with clients with personal-social problems.

Trend 13

Increasingly the counselor will become a consultant. Counselors' skills will be utilized to serve the population indirectly by working directly with those who interact daily with the client. Increasing focus of the recent literature is on the counselor's consultant role and on viewing the counselor as an agent of environmental change.

The key to how much of a consultant the counselor becomes lies with the counselor education institutions, which are emphasizing the need for such activities and providing experiences in conducting them. Presumably, preparation stimulates practice, and unless the experiences are provided in training there seems little likelihood that more than an occasional counselor will make consultative efforts that often require particular skills, knowledge, and temperament. During the past five years many counselors have reported increasing their consultative activities. Undoubtedly, these contacts will continue and increase because they result in valuable gains for their clientele.

Trend 14

Small group counseling will be used increasingly. The advantages cited for small group counseling in Chapter 15 will become increasingly attractive. Moreover, a greater number of preparation programs will incorporate training in group procedures. As group procedures are employed more frequently, more will be learned of their utility and appropriateness for certain clients and problem situations.

Trend 15

Subprofessionals or support personnel will be utilized by counseling professionals. The advent of preparation for sub-professionals in 1964 (for example, the CAUSE program) stimulated much controversy over the use and qualifications of such personnel. For many, the threat stemmed from the fact that little was known about the proposed role and function of subprofessionals. The initial statements were ambiguous, and misunderstandings arose. This controversy led to a policy statement formulated by a subcommittee on support personnel of the Professional Preparation and Standards Committee.[5] Adopted by the APGA executive council in November 1966, the statement provided guidelines for the development of job descriptions for support personnel. Support personnel will be involved in both direct and indirect helping relationships, and appropriate use of them will facilitate and extend the work of counselors and make their total endeavor more effective.

Trend 16

The work of counselors will no longer be confined to that which takes place in their offices. The concept of the counselor as one who sits in his or her office and waits for self-referred clients is gradually being replaced by one involving more active outreach activities. Such activities range from teaching minicourses to being available to clients in informal settings. Several advantages accrue from abandonment of the more traditional role. One is that a much wider segment of the clientele will come in contact with counselors. Another advantage is that counselors are directly exposed to the realities in which their clients live and struggle. They no longer hear secondhand descriptions or have to react out of an assumed set of beliefs on what the agency or school hopes to do as opposed to what is actually going on. An additional advantage is that their scope of contacts is broadened to include parents, client peers, personnel in other agencies, and a wider range of staff. It is important to note that the fundamental purpose of this type of activity is

to increase the counselor's effectiveness and availability. There is no doubt, however, that the bulk of their time will be spent privately with individuals because of the very nature of counseling.

Trend 17

Counselors increasingly will become involved in providing services to handicapped individuals. Counselors in all settings, but particularly those in educational institutions, must contribute their skills and understanding if the human development goals envisioned in PL 94-142 are to become a reality. The counselor's skills in assessment and consultation can be brought to bear on identifying handicapped individuals, planning individual educational programs and providing due-process procedures for them. Counselors will respond positively to the challenges and opportunities presented by these endeavors.

Trend 18

Conflict, dissension, and professional differences will continue to characterize the field of counseling. Although some consensus exists and will persist, no truly vital field should be devoid of controversy, discussion, and debate, from which emerge change and improvement. For the individual who is committed to the field this factor represents stimulation rather than discouragement.

Issues associated with the content of the chapter have been presented at this point in previous chapters. Given the content of this chapter, that will not be done here.

And so this volume is closed with the belief that those who fully commit themselves to providing the helping relationship will welcome the challenge found in a fluid and evolving field of human endeavor. Because of their commitment, the challenge gives their activities meaning. Both the commitment and the challenge become a trust.

Annotated references

American Personnel and Guidance Association. *The Status of Guidance and Counseling in the Nation's Schools.*

[5] "Support Personnel for the Counselor: Their Technical and Non-Technical Roles and Preparation," *Personnel and Guidance Journal*, 45 (April 1967), 857–861.

Mimeographed. Washington, D.C.: The Association, 1978. 251 pp.

Some eighteen papers have been prepared by various professionals designed to stimulate professional and public discussion regarding the current status of the counseling profession. A major objective is that their content will lead to a sense of future direction.

Herr, Edwin L. *Guidance and Counseling in the Schools.* Washington, D.C.: American Personnel and Guidance Association, 1979. 242 pp.

Herr presents perspectives on the past, present, and future of guidance. Part V (pp. 139–174) gives unresolved problems and recommended actions.

Wrenn, C. Gilbert. *The World of the Contemporary Counselor.* Boston: Houghton Mifflin Company, 1973. 294 pp.

Change—its form, meaning, and implications—is the focus of Wrenn's work. His grasp of what is taking place in many sectors of life is comprehensive and sure. Recommendations, based on his analysis of change, are made that will be helpful not only to counselors but also those they serve.

Further references

Beale, Andrew V., and William A. Bost. "Selecting School Counselors: The Guidance Supervisor's Perspective." *The School Counselor*, 26 (May 1979), 307–310.

Bishop, John B. "Combining Counseling and Career Services: Conflicts and Choices." *Personnel and Guidance Journal*, 57 (June 1979), 550–552.

Bradley, Marjorie K. "Counseling Past and Present: Is There a Future?" *Personnel and Guidance Journal*, 57 (September 1978), 42–45.

Brammer, Lawrence M. "Who Can Be a Helper?" *Personnel and Guidance Journal*, 55 (February 1977), 303–308.

Goldman, Leo, et al. "How Are We Doing in School Guidance?" *The School Counselor*, 25 (May 1978), 307–325.

Hays, Donald G. "2001: A Counseling Odyssey." *Personnel and Guidance Journal*, 57 (September 1978), 17–21.

Kurpius, DeWayne, and Sharon E. Robinson. "An Overview of Consultation." *Personnel and Guidance Journal*, 56 (February 1978), 321–323.

Loughary, John W. "Technology and Counseling." *Personnel and Guidance Journal*, 55 (February 1977), 346–351.

McIlroy, Joan H. "Career as Life-Style: An Existential View." *Personnel and Guidance Journal*, 57 (March 1979), 351–355.

Noble, Vicente N., and Thomas J. Kampwirth. "PL 94-142 and Counselor Activities." *Elementary School Guidance and Counseling*, 13 (February 1979), 164–170.

Ritter, Kathleen Y. "The Present and Future of the Profession: View from a Counselor Education Program." *Personnel and Guidance Journal*, 57 (February 1979), 279–284.

Ryan, Charles W., and John M. Sutton, Jr. "Perceptions of Career Education: Implications for School Counselors." *The School Counselor*, 25 (March 1978), 265–270.

Wertheimer, Michael, et al. "Psychology and the Future." *American Psychologist*, 33 (July 1978), 631–647.

Index of names

Abbott, Anne H., 74, 231
Abeles, Norman, 111, 114
Abrams, Walter H., 22, 340
Adler, Alfred, 202–203, 204–205, 234
Alexander, Franz, 167, 196, 230
Allen, Frederick, 212
Allen, Frederick J., 24
Allport, Gordon W., 57, 244, 324
Alschuler, Alfred S., 134
Altekruse, Michael K., 270, 332
Altmann, Hal A., 442
Alvarez, Rudolfo, 348
Amidon, Edmund, 269, 383
Anderson, Jacquelyn, 64
Anderson, Scott, 388, 396, 402
Anderson, Wayne, 112
Andrews, W. R., 406
Angel, Ernest, 220
Annis, Arthur P., 322
Ansbacher, Heinz L., 202, 204
Ansbacher, Rowena R., 202, 204
Anton, Jane, 427
Aplin, John C., 332
Apostal, R. A., 308
Aragon, John A., 348
Arbuckle, Dugald S., 86, 90, 102, 126, 134, 144, 220, 222n, 254, 255, 257, 258, 263, 288n, 296
Archer, James, Jr., 74
Ardrey, Robert, 154n
Aristotle, 23
Arlow, Jacob A., 196, 197
Aronson, H., 79
Arvey, H., 442
Arvey, Richard D., 41
Atkinson, Donald R., 97, 100, 137, 144, 427, 442
Aubrey, Roger, 40, 117, 143
Austin, Brian, 91
Avery, Arthur W., 264
Avila, Donald L., 269
Ayer, A. J., 241

Baccus, Grady K., 117, 248
Bach, K., 407
Bachman, Randall W., 76
Baird, C. R., 324
Baker, Sherry, 87
Baker, Stanley B., 133

Baldwin, A. L., 323
Balogh, Sara Carter, 273, 295
Bandler, Richard, 289, 290, 297
Bandura, Albert, 25, 93
Banks, William, 22
Barak, Azy, 96, 116
Barcikowski, Robert S., 97
Bardo, H., 78
Bartlett, Jane C., 144
Bath, Kent E., 269
Bauer, David, 332
Baumann, Reemt R., 378
Baumgardner, Steve R., 341
Bayles, Ernest E., 167
Beale, Andrew V., 449
Beals, Ralph L., 167
Beck, Carlton E., 196, 220, 221, 222, 230, 241, 243, 244, 245
Beck, James D., 347
Bedell, Ralph, 25
Bednar, Richard, 109, 372, 373
Beers, Clifford, 24, 28
Bellet, William, 117, 332
Benjamin, Alfred, 5, 22, 105, 269, 382
Benjamin, Libby, 41
Benjamin, Lorna S., 332
Benne, Kenneth, 370
Benning, James J., 325n
Bentley, Joseph C., 119
Benton, Barbara L., 79
Berdie, Ralph F., 134–135
Berenson, B. G., 98, 265, 281n, 282n
Berezin, Annabel G., 308
Bergantino, Len, 431
Bergin, Allen E., 405, 409, 414, 415, 416, 426
Berkeley, George, 23
Berman, Judith, 297
Bernard, Harold W., 104
Berne, Eric, 164, 167, 206, 207, 208, 209, 210
Berry, Elizabeth, 144
Bertolini, Barrett G., 427
Betz, B., 111, 112
Betz, Nancy E., 357
Betz, Robert L., 95
Beukenkamp, Cornelius, 380n
Beymer, Lawrence, 396
Biasco, Frank, 430
Bickel, Frank, 74

Index of subjects

Abnormality, 55–56
Abortions, 68
Absolute privilege, 393
Academic aptitude, counselor effectiveness and, 93
Acceptance, 259, 279
  characteristics of, 260
  defined, 259–260
Accountability, 445
  paradigm for, 421–422, 422(fig.)
  record for, 421(table)
  school counselor and, 419–422
Accreditation
  of counselor education programs, 436–437
  of counselors, 437
Achieved positions, 118
Action limits, 272
Adapters, nonverbal behaviors as, 300
Adjustment, marital, 333–334
Adjustment model, 109
Administrators
  counselors as, 131
  power of, 158
Adolescents
  alcohol and drugs and, 70–71, 72(table)
  causes of problems among, 57–58
  concerns of, 61–64, 62(table), 63(table), 64(table), 65(table), 66(table)
  crime and delinquency among, 69–70
  expectancies for counseling, 77
  group counseling and, 376–377
  helping services chosen by, 77(table)
  pregnancies, marriages, and divorce among, 68–69
  school and college dropouts among, 67–68
  unemployment among, 70
  venereal disease among, 71–72
  views on parents, 64
Adoption, teenage pregnancy and, 69
Adult(s)
  developmental tasks of, 47, 49–50, 49(fig.)
  expectancies for counseling, 79–80
Adult state, 207–208
  emergence of, 208(fig.)
Advice
  analysis of, 369
  facilitative, 280
  in trait and factor approach, 173

Affect
  in helping relationship, 8
  nonverbal communication of, 305
Affect displays, nonverbal behaviors as, 300
Affective responses, 292–293
Age
  of counselor, 99
  developmental tasks and, 43
  See also Elderly persons
Agency counseling, 337–338
  approaches to, 338
  availability and need, 338
  preparation and professional organizations for, 338
  setting for, 338
Alcohol use, among youth, 70–71
Alienation, in gestalt therapy, 225
Ambiguity, counselors' tolerance for, 101
American Association of Marriage and Family Counselors (AAMFC), 337
American Board of Psychiatry and Neurology, 12
American Indians, 345–346
American Personnel and Guidance Association (APGA), 16, 29, 338, 396, 437, 446–447
  counselor education standards of, 435–436
  divisions of, 32
  ethical standards of, 398–400
  governmental structure and services of, 32
  publications of, 33
  purposes of, 31–32
American Psychiatric Association, 12–13
American Psychological Association (APA), 14, 16, 338, 351
  Division of Counseling Psychology of, 32–33
American School Counselor Association (ASCA), 32
Anal phase, 198
Androgyny, 351
Anomie, 7
Anthropology, 153
Antirationalism, 197
Anxiety
  in client-centered viewpoint, 214–215
  comparison of viewpoints of, 235, 238
  concerning choices, 307
  counselor competence and, 93–94
  in existential viewpoint, 221
  in gestalt viewpoint, 227
  moral, 199

To students

We would like to find out your reactions to this third edition of *Fundamentals of Counseling*. Your evaluation of the book will help us respond to both the interest and the needs of the readers of future editions. Please fill out the form and return it to: College Marketing, Houghton Mifflin Company, One Beacon Street, Boston, MA 02107.

1. Do you think the style
   of the book is clear? Yes _____   readable? Yes _____   understandable? Yes _____

                         No _____   No _____   No _____

   Please comment.

   _____

   _____

   _____

2. Are *all* terms and concepts defined adequately when they are first introduced?

   _____

   _____

   _____

3. Which chapters or features did you particularly like *or* dislike?

   _____

   _____

   _____

4. Which chapters were required reading?

   _____

   _____

   _____

5. For each chapter that you have read, please mark a check on the corresponding line to indicate your evaluation of the material presented.

	Informational value			Interest		
	High	Avg.	Low	High	Avg.	Low
1 The helping relationship	____	____	____	____	____	____
2 Counseling: origin and development	____	____	____	____	____	____
3 The counselee: developmental characteristics and concerns	____	____	____	____	____	____
4 Counseling: expectations and goals	____	____	____	____	____	____
5 Counselor and counselee characteristics	____	____	____	____	____	____
6 Counselor role and function	____	____	____	____	____	____
7 Counseling and the social sciences	____	____	____	____	____	____
8 Cognitively oriented counseling approaches	____	____	____	____	____	____
9 Affectively oriented counseling approaches	____	____	____	____	____	____
10 Building a personal theory of counseling	____	____	____	____	____	____
11 Core elements that facilitate counseling	____	____	____	____	____	____
12 Counseling techniques and practices: I	____	____	____	____	____	____
13 Counseling techniques and practices: II	____	____	____	____	____	____
14 Counseling: special areas and populations	____	____	____	____	____	____
15 Group counseling	____	____	____	____	____	____
16 Counseling: legal and ethical considerations	____	____	____	____	____	____
17 Evaluation of counseling	____	____	____	____	____	____
18 The education and credentialing of counselors	____	____	____	____	____	____
19 Trends in counseling	____	____	____	____	____	____